T0340113

THE ANALYTICS OF UNCERTAINTY
AND INFORMATION
SECOND EDITION

There has been explosive progress in the economic theory of uncertainty and information in the past few decades. This subject is now taught not only in departments of economics but also in professional schools and programs oriented toward business, government and administration, and public policy. This book attempts to unify the subject matter in a simple, accessible manner. Part I of the book focuses on the economics of uncertainty; Part II examines the economics of information.

This revised and updated second edition places a greater focus on game theory. New topics include posted-price markets, mechanism design, common-value auctions, and the one-shot deviation principle for repeated games.

Sushil Bikhchandani is a professor in the Anderson School of Management at the University of California, Los Angeles. His interests include auctions, market institutions, herd behavior, and information economics. Professor Bikhchandani has published in numerous academic journals, including *Theoretical Economics, Operations Research, Journal of Economic Theory, Journal of Political Economy,* and *Econometrica.*

Jack Hirshleifer (August 26, 1925–July 26, 2005) was an American economist and long time professor at the University of California, Los Angeles. He taught at the University of Chicago from 1955 to 1960, and thereafter at UCLA until 2001. Professor Hirshleifer was well known for his work on uncertainty and information in economics, the economic analysis of conflict, and bioeconomics. His undergraduate textbook, *Price Theory and Applications,* went into seven editions. A 1958 article by Hirshleifer began the triumphant comeback of Irving Fisher's theory of capital and interest, now deemed canonical.

John G. Riley is Distinguished Professor of Economics at the University of California, Los Angeles. A Fellow of the Econometric Society, his research has appeared in eminent journals such as the *American Economic Review, Econometrica, Journal of Political Economy, Quarterly Journal of Economics, Review of Economic Studies, Journal of Economic Theory,* and the *RAND Journal of Economics.* Professor Riley is the author of *Essential Microeconomics* (Cambridge University Press, 2012) and co-author, with the late Jack Hirshleifer, of the first edition of *The Analytics of Uncertainty and Information* (Cambridge University Press, 1992).

CAMBRIDGE SURVEYS OF ECONOMIC LITERATURE

Series Editor
Professor Frank Wolak, *Stanford University*

Series Advisor
Professor John Pencavel, *Stanford University*

The literature of economics is rapidly expanding, and within just a few years, many subjects have changed in recognition. Perceiving the state of knowledge in fast-developing subjects is difficult for students and time consuming for professional economists. This series of books is intended to help with this problem. Each book gives a clear structure to and balanced overview of the topic and is written at an intelligible level for the senior undergraduate. They will be useful for teaching as well as provide a mature, yet compact, presentation of the subject for economists wishing to update their knowledge outside their own specialties.

Other Titles in the Series

Sanford V. Berg and John Tschirhart, *Natural Monopoly Regulation:*
Principles and Practice
Mark Blaug, *The Methodology of Economics: Or How Economists Explain*
(Second Edition)
Edwin Burmeister, *Capital Theory and Dynamics*
Richard E. Caves, *Multinational Enterprise and Economic Analysis*
(Third Edition)
Robert Clark and Joseph Spengler, *The Economics of Individual and Population Aging*
Thrainn Eggertsson, *Economic Behavior and Institutions*
Robert Ferber and Werner Z. Hirsch, *Social Experimentation and Economic Policy*
Anthony C. Fisher, *Resource and Environmental Economics*
James W. Friedman, *Oligopoly Theory*
Helmut Frisch, *Theories of Inflation*
Peter Isard, *Exchange Rate Economics*
Morton I. Kamien and Nancy L. Schwartz, *Market Structure and Innovation*
Mark Kilingsworth, *Labor Supply*
Anne O. Krueger, *Exchange Rate Determination*
Dennis C. Mueller, *Public Choice*
Todd Sandler and Keith Hartley, *The Economics of Defense*
Steven M. Sheffrin, *Rational Expectations* (Second Edition)
John B. Shoven and John Whalley, *Applying General Equilibrium*
E. Roy Weintraub, *Microfoundations: The Compatibility of Microeconomics*
and Macroeconomics

The Analytics of Uncertainty and Information
Second Edition

SUSHIL BIKHCHANDANI

University of California, Los Angeles

JACK HIRSHLEIFER

JOHN G. RILEY

University of California, Los Angeles

CAMBRIDGE
UNIVERSITY PRESS

CAMBRIDGE
UNIVERSITY PRESS

University Printing House, Cambridge CB2 8BS, United Kingdom

One Liberty Plaza, 20th Floor, New York, NY 10006, USA

477 Williamstown Road, Port Melbourne, VIC 3207, Australia

4843/24, 2nd Floor, Ansari Road, Daryaganj, Delhi - 110002, India

79 Anson Road, #06-04/06, Singapore 079906

Cambridge University Press is part of the University of Cambridge.

It furthers the University's mission by disseminating knowledge in the pursuit of education, learning and research at the highest international levels of excellence.

www.cambridge.org
Information on this title: www.cambridge.org/9780521541961

First published 1992
Second Edition 2013
Reprinted 2014

A catalogue record for this publication is available from the British Library

Library of Congress Cataloging in Publication data
Bikhchandani, Sushil.
The analytics of uncertainty and information / Sushil Bikhchandani, University of California – Los Angeles, Jack Hirshleifer, John G. Riley, University of California, Los Angeles. – Second Edition.
  pages cm
Includes bibliographical references and index.
ISBN 978-0-521-83408-7 (hard covers) – ISBN 978-0-521-54196-1 (pbk.)
1. Uncertainty. 2. Equilibrium (Economics) 3. Decision making. 4. Information theory in economics. I. Hirshleifer, Jack. II. Riley, John G. III. Title.
HB615.H568 2013
339.5–dc23   2013005525

ISBN 978-0-521-83408-7 Hardback
ISBN 978-0-521-54196-1 Paperback

Contents

---

* Starred sections represent more difficult or specialized materials that can be omitted
without significant loss of continuity.

* Starred sections represent more difficult or specialized materials that can be omitted without significant loss of continuity.

* Starred sections represent more difficult or specialized materials that can be omitted without significant loss of continuity.

Acknowledgments

The number of people who have made helpful contributions is very great indeed. In particular, we are indebted to the following current or former UCLA graduate students for their assistance: Svend Albaek, Nigel Chalk, Jen-Wen Chang, Alex David, Maxim Engers, Deborah Frohman, Gerry Garvey, Geoffrey Hosta, Kwanho Kim, Son Ku Kim, Fernando Losada, Wai-Nang Po, and Eduardo Siandra. Jen-Wen Chang wrote solutions to the Exercises and Excursions at the end of each chapter. Special thanks to Daniel A. Graham for informing us of errors he discovered in using the book as a course text.

In Memoriam: Jack Hirshleifer

The origins of this book go back to the mid-1970s at UCLA, when Jack and I decided to team teach a course on uncertainty and information. The first year we sat in on each other's lectures, and I certainly learned a lot, not just about how to extract insights from formal economics models, but also how to teach the material. After some years we were invited to write on these topics for the *Journal of Economic Literature*, and the first edition grew out of this effort. We both worked hard on the project, but even when I was satisfied, Jack demanded more. If an argument was not immediately transparent, it was sent back to the drawing board.

As a result of our joint project we became friends, and it was always a pleasure to join Jack for lunch at UCLA or in one of our homes. Even at the end of his life, when his body was ravaged by sickness, Jack's mind was as curious as ever. His range of interests stretched to the boundaries of economics and beyond. I never fully lost my sense of awe.

Originally, we were going to work on the second edition together with our colleague and friend "Bikh." Our goal was to add new applications and insights. Alas, Jack left us too soon. Given the clarity of much of the first edition, many of the original chapters have been only lightly edited. Therefore Jack's words and wisdom continue to resonate. It will be up to the reader to decide if we have retained the level of clarity demanded by Jack. Certainly, this was our aspiration.

John G. Riley

Introduction

The Economics of Uncertainty and Information

All human endeavors are constrained by our limited and uncertain knowledge – about external events past, present, and future; about the laws of nature, God, and man; about our own productive and exchange opportunities; about how other people and even we ourselves are likely to behave. Economists have, of course, always recognized the all-pervasive influence of inadequate information, and its correlate of risk, on human affairs. But only in the period after the Second World War did an accepted *theory of uncertainty and information* begin to evolve. This theory provides a rigorous foundation for the analysis of individual decision making and of market equilibrium, under conditions where economic agents are unsure about their own situations and/or about the opportunities offered them by market dealings.

With recent explosive progress in the analysis of uncertainty, the topic can no longer be described as neglected. Nor have the advances been "merely academic." The economic theory of uncertainty and information now flourishes not only in departments of economics but also in professional schools and programs oriented toward business, government and administration, and public policy. In the world of commerce, stock market analysts now regularly report measures of share-price uncertainty devised by economic theorists. Even in government and the law, formal analysis of uncertainty plays a role in dealing with issues like safety and health, allowable return on investment, and income distribution.

Unfortunately, these new advances have not always taken a form comprehensible to the general economic reader. Brilliant intellectual progress often appears in erratic and idiosyncratic guise; novel terminologies, approaches, and modes of thought can easily hamper understanding. That has certainly been the case here. Even specialists in some areas of the economics of uncertainty and information often find it hard to grasp the import of closely related research originating from a slightly different angle. As a related point, early explorers may have mistaken the part for the whole – a foothill for the mountain, an outlying peninsula for the mainland. Specifically, some scientific contributions that have appeared under ambitious titles like "the economics of information" or the "economics of uncertainty" actually deal only with tiny portions of those large subjects.

We view our task mainly as one of integration: unifying these important though partial new results and concepts into a satisfying single picture. We would not want to claim that our own view of the whole is the only one logically possible or useful. But we believe that it is an outlook with many appealing and satisfying features: (1) it goes far in de-mystifying the topic; (2) with certain significant exceptions, it provides a natural taxonomy for most of the major problems that have been studied; and (3) most important of all, our approach makes it clear that the economics of uncertainty and information is not a totally new field utterly disconnected from previous economic reasoning, but is rather a natural generalization and extension of standard economic analysis.

A fundamental distinction is between the *economics of uncertainty* and the *economics of information*. In the economics of uncertainty, each person adapts to his or her given state of limited information by choosing the best "terminal" action available. In the economics of information, in contrast, individuals can attempt to *overcome* their ignorance by "informational" actions designed to generate or otherwise acquire new knowledge before a final decision is made. Put another way, in the economics of uncertainty the individual is presumed to act on the basis of *current fixed beliefs* (e.g., deciding whether or not to carry an umbrella in accordance with one's present estimate of the chance of rain). In the economics of information, a person typically is trying to arrive at improved beliefs – for example, by studying a weather report or by looking at a barometer before deciding to take the umbrella.

Another crucial element is *strategic uncertainty*. If there are a large number of individuals, then each acts as price-taker. In contrast, in economic interactions between only a few individuals, each individual may have an appreciable impact on the terms of trade through his or her actions. There are gains from behaving strategically. Consequently, in addition to possibly limited knowledge about preferences and endowments of others, each individual cares about, and is uncertain about, actions other individuals may take. There is strategic uncertainty. The best course of action available to individual A depends on what individual B might do, and vice versa. Game-theoretic reasoning cuts through this morass.

The sequence of topics in this book is guided by the pedagogical principle of advancing from the easy to the difficult, from the familiar to the more strange and exotic. Part I deals with terminal actions only – the economics of uncertainty. The first three chapters analyze the optimal risk-involved decisions of the individual. Chapter 4 moves on to the market as a whole, showing how the overall equilibrium that determines the prices of risky assets also distributes social risks among all individuals in the economy.

Part II turns to the economics of information and to strategic uncertainty. Starting with a discussion of the value of better information in Chapter 5, we then explore the effect of autonomously *emergent* information upon the market equilibrium solution (Chapter 6). The issue of information leakage via changes in asset prices is also considered.

In preparation for analyzing strategic uncertainty, Chapter 7 provides an introduction to game theory. The standard Nash equilibrium concept often produces multiple equilibria, some of which seem intuitively implausible. Chapter 7 reviews various efforts to refine the notion of equilibrium. Chapter 8 then analyzes contracting between two agents, one of whom has only imperfect information about the other's preferences (hidden knowledge) or is unable to observe the other's behavior (hidden actions). The former condition leads to *adverse selection* in markets while the latter results in *moral hazard*. Chapter 9 examines market equilibrium under adverse selection.

In Chapter 10 we analyze auctions and other market mechanisms. Issues that arise when interactions among agents are repeated over long or indefinite time periods are considered in Chapter 11. We end with an analysis of information transmission, acquisition, and aggregation in Chapter 12.

Our mode of exposition is highly eclectic. "Literary" reasoning, geometrical demonstration, and analytical proofs are all employed from time to time – as called for by the nature of the topic, by the psychological need for variety, and by our desire to illustrate all the major forms of economic argument arising in these contexts. In addition, certain more advanced topics are separated from the main text in specially marked starred sections that can be omitted with minimal loss of continuity. Finally, mixed with the more purely formal portions of our analysis will be applications to important real-world phenomena such as insurance, securities markets, corporate financial structures, the use of experts and agents, group decisions where returns and risks are shared, and the value of education.

Over the last 20 years, game-theoretic reasoning has become widespread in economics. Therefore, in this second edition, we have placed greater emphasis on game theory. Consequently, most of the changes are in part II of the book (although every chapter has at least some modifications to improve the logical flow of material). The chapter on game theory (Chapter 7) has been rewritten and appears earlier. New topics in Part II include posted-price markets, mechanism design, common-value auctions, and the one-shot deviation principle for repeated games. Chapter 12 is entirely new; the results on information aggregation and acquisition that are described here were published after the first edition.

PART I

Elements of Decision under Uncertainty

We introduce a model for decision making under uncertainty that will be our workhorse throughout the book. Uncertainty is modeled with a set of states of nature, one of which will occur. The decision maker or individual has a probability distribution over the states of nature that represents his (or her) subjective beliefs about the likelihood of different states of nature. This individual chooses actions and actions have consequences. The consequence for the individual depends on the state of nature and his choice of action. The states of nature are represented in a way that the probabilities of states are unaffected by the individual's actions. The individual's preferences over consequences are captured by a utility function. The probability distribution over states of nature and the utility function over consequences, both of which are subjective,[1] are combined by the expected-utility rule to induce an expected utility over actions.

An individual must choose among *acts* – or synonymously, he or she must make *decisions*, or select among *actions, options*, or *moves*. And, where there is uncertainty, nature may be said to "choose" the *state of the world* (or *state*, for short). You decide whether or not to carry an umbrella; nature "decides" on rain or sunshine. Table 1.1 pictures an especially simple 2×2 situation. Your alternative acts $x = (1, 2)$ are shown along the left margin, and nature's alternative states $s = (1, 2)$ across the top. The body of the table shows the *consequences* c_{xs} resulting from your choice of act x and nature's choice of state s.

---

[1] Subjective in the sense that another individual, faced with the same decision problem, may have a different probability distribution and a different utility function: beliefs and tastes may differ from person to person.

Table 1.1. *Consequences of alternative acts and states*

		States	
		$s = 1$	$s = 2$
Acts	$x = 1$	c_{11}	c_{12}
	$x = 2$	c_{21}	c_{22}

More generally, the individual under uncertainty will, according to this analysis, specify the following elements of his decision problem:

(1) a *set of acts* $(1, \ldots, x, \ldots, X)$ available to him;
(2) a *set of states* $(1, \ldots, s, \ldots, S)$ available to nature;
(3) a *consequence function* c_{xs} showing outcomes under all combinations of acts and states.

And, in addition:

(4) a *probability function* $\pi(s)$ expressing his beliefs (as to the likelihood of nature choosing each and every state);
(5) an *elementary-utility function* $v(c)$ measuring the desirability of the different possible consequences to him.

We will explain below how the "expected-utility rule" integrates all these elements so as to enable the individual to decide upon the most advantageous action. Put another way, we will show how the economic agent can derive a personal preference ordering of his possible *acts* from his given preference scaling over *consequences*.

COMMENT: The approach here does not allow for the psychological sensations of vagueness or confusion that people often suffer in facing situations with uncertain (risky) outcomes. In our model, the individual is neither vague nor confused. While recognizing that his knowledge is imperfect, so that he cannot be sure which state of the world will occur, he nevertheless can assign exact numerical probabilities representing his degree of belief as to the likelihood of each possible state. Our excuse for not picturing vagueness or confusion is that we are trying to model economics, not psychology. Even the very simplest models in economic textbooks, for example, indifference-curve diagrams, implicitly postulate a degree of precise self-knowledge that is descriptively unrealistic. The ultimate justification, for indifference-curve diagrams or for theories of decision under uncertainty, is the ability of such models to help us understand and predict behavior.

1.1 The Menu of Acts

There are two main classes of individual actions: *terminal* moves versus *informational* moves. Here, in Part I of the book, we consider a simplified world where only terminal acts are available, so that the individual is limited to making the best of his or her existing combination of knowledge and ignorance. An example of terminal action under uncertainty is the statistical problem of coming to a decision on the basis of sample evidence now in hand: for instance, when a regulatory agency has to decide whether or not to approve a new drug on the basis of experimental test results. We will be considering terminal actions of this type, and especially the risk-involved decisions of *individuals in markets*: whether or not to purchase insurance, to buy or sell stocks and bonds, to participate in a partnership, etc. Anticipating a bit, a key theme of our analysis will be that markets allow decision makers to share risks and returns in ways that accord with the particular preferences and opportunities of the different transactors.

Part II of the book will be covering *informational* actions – decisions concerning whether and how to improve upon one's state of knowledge before making a terminal move. In the class of informational actions would fall statistical choices such as how much additional evidence to collect before coming to a terminal decision, what sampling technique to employ, etc. Once again, our emphasis will be on ways of acquiring new information *through markets*. Knowledge can be acquired by direct market purchase – by buying newspapers for weather and stock market reports, by undergoing a course of training to gain "know how" in a trade, or by employing an expert for private advice. Rather less obviously, markets open up an indirect means of acquiring information: for example, a person can observe the market choices of better-informed traders, or might draw inferences from people's reputations acquired in the course of their previous market dealings. Or, a producing firm might imitate other commercially successful firms. But these interesting phenomena involving information-involved actions will have to be set aside until Part II.

1.2 The Probability Distribution

We assume that each person is able to represent his beliefs as to the likelihood of the different states of the world (e.g., as to whether nature will choose rain or shine) by a "subjective" probability distribution (Savage, 1954). Assuming discrete states of the world, the individual is supposed to be able to assign to each state s a degree of belief, in the form of numerical weights

π_s lying between zero and one inclusive, and summing to unity: $\Sigma_s \pi_s = 1$. In the extreme case, if the person were certain that some particular state s would be occurring, the full probabilistic weight of unity would be assigned to that state. Then $\pi_s = 1$, so that zero probability is attached to every other state in the set $1, \ldots, s, \ldots, S$. More generally, a high degree of subjective assurance will be reflected by a relatively "tight" probability distribution over the range of possible states; a high degree of doubt would be reflected by a wide dispersion.

At times, we shall find it will be more convenient to assume that the variable or variables defining the state of the world vary continuously (rather than discretely) so that the number of distinct states is uncountably infinite. Here the probability of any exact single state coming about is regarded as zero ("infinitesimal"), although the event is not *impossible*. Making use of a continuous state-defining variable s, where s can be any real number between 0 and S, the individual's subjective probability beliefs would be represented by a probability density function $\pi(s)$ such that $\int_0^S \pi(s)\ ds = 1$.

1.2.1 Risk versus Uncertainty

A number of economists have attempted to distinguish between risk and uncertainty, as originally proposed by Frank H. Knight (1921, pp. 20, 226). (1) "Risk," Knight said, refers to situations where an individual is able to calculate probabilities on the basis of an *objective* classification of instances. For example, in tossing a fair die the chance of any single one of the six faces showing is exactly one-sixth. (2) "Uncertainty," he contended, refers to situations where no objective classification is possible, for example, in estimating whether or not a cure for cancer will be discovered in the next decade.

In this book, we disregard Knight's distinction. For our purposes, risk and uncertainty mean the same thing. It does not matter, we contend, whether an "objective" classification is or is not possible. For we will be dealing throughout with a "subjective" probability concept (as developed especially by Savage, 1954): probability is simply *degree of belief*. In fact, even in cases like the toss of a die where assigning "objective" probabilities appears possible, such an appearance is really illusory. That the chance of any single face turning up is one-sixth is a valid inference *only if the die is a fair one* – a condition about which no one could ever be "objectively" certain. Decision makers are therefore never in Knight's world of risk but instead always in his world of uncertainty. That this approach, assigning probabilities on the basis of subjective degree of belief, is a workable and fruitful procedure will be shown constructively throughout the book.[2]

1.2.2 "Hard" versus "Soft" Probabilities

While we do not distinguish between what Knight called risk and uncertainty, he was getting at – though imperfectly expressing – an important and valid point. In his discussion, Knight suggested that a person's actions may well depend upon his "estimate of the chance that his estimates are correct," or, we shall say, upon his *confidence in his beliefs*. This brings us to a distinction between "hard" versus "soft" probability estimates.

Suppose that for purposes of an immediate bet you had to estimate the probability of heads coming up on the next toss of coin A – the coin having been previously tested many times by you and found to have historically come up heads and tails with just about equal frequency. If you are a reasonable person, you would assign a degree of belief (subjective probability) of about 0.5 to heads, and you would be rather confident about that number. In contrast, imagine instead that you are dealing with coin B, about which you know absolutely nothing. You have not even been able to inspect it to verify whether it is possibly two tailed or two headed. Nevertheless, if you *had* to pick some single number you would be compelled again to assign 0.5 probability to heads coming up on the next toss, since as a reasonable person you lack any basis for a greater or lesser degree of belief in heads than tails. But, your *confidence* in the 0.5 figure for coin B would surely be much less.

It is not the psychological sensation of confidence or doubt that interests us, but the possible implications for decisions. If the same probability assignment of 0.5 will be made either way, as has just been argued, is there any action-relevant difference between the two cases? For our purpose, the answer is NO, if you are committed to *terminal* action.[3] If you must bet now on the basis of your current information, 0.5 is the relevant probability for guiding your choice of heads or tails. In either situation, you have no grounds for thinking heads more likely or tails more likely. But the answer is YES, there is indeed a difference between the two situations if you have the

---

[2] See Schmeidler (1989) for the foundations of an alternative approach that explicitly models Knightian uncertainty and individuals' attitudes to it.

[3] Later in this chapter, we describe the Ellsberg paradox, which is an experiment indicating that individuals may react differently to hard and soft probabilities in a setting with terminal actions.

option of *informational* action. When this option is available, you should be more willing to invest money or effort to obtain additional information about coin B than about coin A. In short, greater prior doubt (lesser degree of confidence) makes it more important to acquire additional evidence before making a terminal move. So, we see that a person's *informational* actions, though not his *terminal* actions, do depend upon his confidence in his beliefs – in Knight's language, upon his "estimate of the chance that his estimates are correct." Confidence will be an important topic in Part II of the book, where we cover the economics of information, but will not be involved in our more elementary treatment of the economics of uncertainty in Part I.

Exercises and Excursions 1.2

1 Consistency of Probability Beliefs

An individual believes that credible information will soon arrive in the form of news about the probability of rain. He believes there is a 50% chance that the news will be "rain certain," a 30% chance that the news will be "no rain," and a 20% chance that the news will be "rain with probability 0.5." Is this consistent with his currently believing that the odds in favor of rain are 2:1?

2 Information and Confidence

In terms of the chances of a coin coming up heads, suppose there are three states of the world regarded as possible:

State 1: chance of heads is 100% [coin is two headed]
State 2: chance of heads is 50% [coin is fair]
State 3: chance of heads is 0% [coin is two tailed].

An individual initially assigns equal probabilities $(\pi_1, \pi_2, \pi_3) = (\frac{1}{3}, \frac{1}{3}, \frac{1}{3})$ to all three states.

(A) For an immediate bet (terminal action), what is his best estimate for the probability p of heads on the next toss?
(B) Suppose new information were now to change his probability vector to $(\pi_1, \pi_2, \pi_3) = (0, 1, 0)$. What can you now say about his best estimate for p? What has happened to his *confidence* in that estimate?
(C) Same question if, instead, the new information changed his probability vector to $(\frac{1}{2}, 0, \frac{1}{2})$.

1.3 The Utility Function

As shown in Table 1.1, each *consequence* is the outcome of an economic agent's choice of action combined with nature's "choice" of the state of the world. In principle, the consequence is a full description of all aspects of the individual's environment resulting from such an interaction. For example, if someone decides not to carry an umbrella and nature chooses rain, the consequences might include getting wet, being late for work, and a variety of other discomforts. But we shall mainly be concerned with consequences describable in terms of alternative *baskets of consumption goods* that enter into individuals' utility functions. Very frequently we shall deal with an even simpler picture in which consequences take the form of entitlements to a single summary variable like monetary *income*.

Consequences might be quantities that are certain, or might themselves be probabilistic – depending upon how states of the world are described. If the states are defined deterministically, as in "Coin shows heads," and supposing the action chosen was "Bet $1 at even money on heads," then the consequence would be "Win one dollar." But states of the world can sometimes be defined as probabilistic processes. The relevant states might be "Coin has 50% chance of coming up heads" versus "Coin is biased to have 75% chance of coming up heads." Here the act "Bet on heads" will be reflected, in either state of the world, by an uncertain consequence taking the form of a specified chance of winning the dollar.

We shall use the notation $v(c)$ to represent a person's *utility function* (or *elementary-utility function*) over the consequences c.

1.4 The Expected-Utility Rule

Utility attaches directly to consequences, and only derivatively to actions. To emphasize this distinction, we shall use the notation $U(x)$ for a person's derived preference ordering over actions x. The expected-utility rule is used to derive $U(x)$ from the utility function $v(c)$, as explained below.

A CRUCIAL DISTINCTION
$v(c)$ is a utility function defined over consequences
$U(x)$ is the expected-utility function defined over actions

The analytical problem is to explain and justify this derivation, that is, to show how, given his direct preferences over *consequences*, the individual can order the desirability of the *actions* available to him.

To choose an act is to choose one of the rows of a consequence matrix like Table 1.1. As the individual is also supposed to have attached a probability (degree of belief) to the occurrence of every state, each such row can be regarded as a probability distribution. We may therefore think of a person as choosing among probability distributions or "prospects." A convenient notation for the "prospect" associated with an act x, whose uncertain consequences $c_x = (c_{x1}, c_{x2}, \ldots, c_{xS})$ are to be received with respective state probabilities $\pi = (\pi_1, \pi_2, \ldots, \pi_S)$ – the probabilities summing, of course, to unity – is:

$$X \equiv (c_{x1}, c_{x2}, \ldots, c_{xS}; \pi_1, \pi_2, \ldots, \pi_S)$$

The crucial step is to connect the $v(c)$ function for consequences with the utility ordering $U(x)$ of acts. We can take this step using the famous "expected-utility rule" of John von Neumann and Oskar Morgenstern (1944, pp. 15–31):

EXPECTED-UTILITY RULE

$$U(x) \equiv \pi_1 v(c_{x1}) + \pi_2 v(c_{x2}) + \cdots + \pi_S v(c_{xS})$$
$$\equiv \sum_{s=1}^{S} \pi_s v(c_{xs}) \tag{1.4.1}$$

This says that the expected utility $U(x)$ of act x is calculable in an especially simple way: to wit, as the mathematical expectation (the probability-weighted average) of the elementary utilities $v(c_{xs})$ of the associated consequences. Note that Equation (1.4.1) is simply additive over states of the world, which means that the consequence c_{xs} realized in any state s in no way affects the preference scaling $v(c_{xs^0})$ of consequences in any other state s^0. Equation (1.4.1) is also linear in the probabilities, another very specific and special functional form. As the von Neumann–Morgenstern expected-utility rule is absolutely crucial for our theory of decision under uncertainty, we shall be devoting considerable space to it.

It turns out that the expected-utility rule is applicable *if and only if the $v(c)$ function has been determined in a particular way that has been termed the assignment of "cardinal" utilities to consequences.* More specifically, the proposition that we will attempt to explain and justify (though not rigorously prove) can be stated as follows:

Given certain "postulates of rational choice," there is a way of assigning a cardinal utility function $v(c)$ *over consequences* such that the expected-utility rule determines the individual's preference ranking $U(x)$ *over actions.*

A "cardinal" variable is one that can be measured quantitatively, like altitude, time, or temperature. While different measuring scales might be employed, such scales can diverge only in zero-point and unit-interval. Temperature, for example, can be measured according to the Celsius or the Fahrenheit scales; 32° Fahrenheit is 0° Celsius, and each degree up or down of Celsius is 1.8° up or down of Fahrenheit. Similarly, altitude could be measured from sea level or from the center of the Earth (shift of zero-point) and in feet or meters (shift of unit-interval). Cardinal variables have the following property: regardless of shift of zero-point and unit-interval, the relative magnitudes of *differences* remains unchanged. The altitude difference between the base and crest of Mount Everest exceeds the difference between the foundation and roof of even the tallest man-made building – whether we measure in feet above sea level or in meters from the center of the Earth.

In dealing with certainty choices, standard economic theory treats utility (intensity of preference) as an *ordinal* rather than a cardinal variable. The individual, it is postulated, can say "I prefer basket A to basket B." He is not required to quantify *how much* he prefers A to B. Put another way, if any given utility function in the form of an assignment of cardinal numbers to consequences (consumption baskets) correctly describes choices under certainty, so will any ordinal (positive monotonic) transformation of that function. Suppose that, for choices not involving risks, some scale u of cardinal numbers was attached as preference labels to consequences – where, of course, higher u indicates greater level of satisfaction. Then any positive monotonic transformation of those numbers would lead to the same decisions. For example, suppose an individual always prefers more consumption income c to less. Then we might say, "He is trying to maximize the function $u = c$." But the income level that maximizes u also maximizes log u or e^u, both of which are positive monotonic transformations of u. So $u = e^c$ or $u = \log c$ could equally well have served to indicate the preference scaling. More formally, if u is a satisfactory function for choices under certainty, then so is $\hat{u} \equiv F(u)$, provided only that the first derivative is positive: $F'(u) > 0$.

In contrast, when it comes to choices under *uncertainty*, the expected-utility rule is applicable only if the utility function $v(c)$ has been constructed in a particular way that provides fewer degrees of freedom. In fact, as will shortly be seen, given any initially satisfactory $v(c)$ function, only the *cardinal* (positive linear, rather than positive monotonic) transformations of $v(c)$ will leave preference rankings unchanged. Formally, if $v(c)$ satisfactorily describes the individual's choices under uncertainty, then so does $\hat{v} = \alpha + \beta v$, where α is any constant and β is any positive constant.

Why are all the positive monotonic transformations of the utility function permissible in the riskless case, while only the positive *linear* transformations are allowed when it comes to risky choices? In the absence of uncertainty, deciding upon an action is immediately equivalent to selecting a single definite consequence. It follows that if someone can rank *consequences* in terms of preferences he has already determined the preference ordering of his *actions* – which is all that is needed for purposes of decision. But in dealing with risky choices it is not immediately evident how a ranking of consequences leads to an ordering of actions, since each action will in general imply a probabilistic mix of possible consequences. The great contribution of von Neumann and Morgenstern was to show that, given plausible assumptions about individual preferences, it is possible to construct a $v(c)$ function – "cardinal" in that only positive linear transformations thereof are permissible – whose *joint* use with the expected-utility rule (1.4.1) will lead to the correct ordering of actions.

1.4.1 An Informal Presentation

To formally justify the joint use of a cardinal utility function and the expected-utility rule, for dealing with choices among risky prospects, involves a somewhat higher order of technical difficulty. What follows here is an informal presentation (based mainly upon Schlaifer, 1959) illustrating, by direct construction, how the required type of utility function can be developed.

For the purpose of this discussion, assume that the consequences c are simply amounts of income a person might receive. Let m represent the worst possible consequence (the smallest amount of income) that can occur with positive probability, and M the best possible consequence (the largest amount of income). More income is preferred to less – so the individual already has, to begin with, an *ordinal* utility scale. The problem is to "cardinalize" this scale, that is, to show that there is a way of assigning numerical values (arbitrary only with respect to zero-point and unit-interval) to the degrees of preference associated with all levels of income. These values must be rising with income, else they would not be consistent with the given ordinal preference ("more is preferred to less"). But the chosen scale must also lead to correct answers when used in conjunction with the expected-utility rule. The method we shall employ to establish such a cardinal scale is called "the reference-lottery technique."

Consider any level of income c^* between m and M. Imagine that the individual is faced with the choice between c^* and some "reference lottery" having the form $(M, m; \pi, 1 - \pi)$ in prospect notation. That is, he has a choice between c^* for certain versus a gamble yielding the best possible outcome M with probability π and the worst possible outcome m with probability $1 - \pi$. We shall suppose that the individual can say to himself: "When π becomes very close to unity, I surely will prefer the gamble; for lotteries with π very close to zero, I surely prefer the certainty of c^*. Consequently, in between there must be some intermediate probability π^* of success in the reference lottery, such that I am exactly indifferent between the certain income c^* and the prospect $(M, m; \pi^*, 1 - \pi^*)$." After due introspection, we assume, the individual can in fact specify this π^*. We may set $v(m) = 0$ and $v(M) = 1$. Then the π^* so derived is a cardinal measure of the utility of income level c^* for him. That is: $v(c^*) = \pi^*$.[4] Or, more elaborately:

$$v(c^*) \equiv U(M, m; \pi^*, 1 - \pi^*) \equiv \pi^* \tag{1.4.2}$$

An individual proceeding to assign cardinal preference values to income in this way will generate a $v(c)$ function over the range $m \leq c \leq M$, which can be employed with the expected-utility rule (1.4.1) to order his choices among actions.

Figure 1.1 illustrates a hypothetical individual situation. Let $m = 0$ and $M = 1,000$ (in dollars, we can suppose) be the extremes of income that need be considered. For the specific income $c^* = 250$, the person's success-in-equivalent-reference-lottery probability is assumed to be $\pi^* = 0.5$ – meaning that he finds himself indifferent between a sure income of $250 and a 50% chance of winning in an income lottery whose alternative outcomes are $1,000 or nothing. Then the utility assigned to the sure consequence $250 is just $\frac{1}{2}$ – that is, $v(250) = 0.5$, determining the location of point Q on the $v(c)$ curve. Repeating this process, the reference-lottery technique generates the entire $v(c)$ curve between $m = 0$ and $M = 1,000$.

A full justification, showing why this particular procedure works to derive a suitable cardinal scale, requires a more formal analysis (to be touched on in Section 1.4.2). But we can give a geometric intuition here. The essential point is that the $v(c)$ measure obtained via the reference-lottery technique is in the form of a *probability*, so that the expected-utility rule (1.4.1) becomes equivalent to the standard formula for compounding probabilities.

---

[4] Because shifts of zero-point and unit-interval are permissible for cardinal scaling, more generally we can write $v(c^*) = \alpha + \beta\pi^*$, for arbitrary α and $\beta > 0$. This is equivalent to assuming $v(m) = \alpha$ and $v(M) = \alpha + \beta$. We will henceforth ignore this uninteresting generalization.

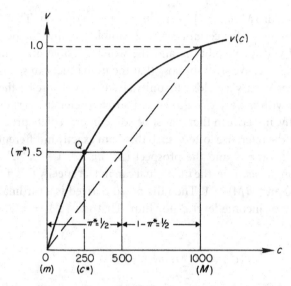

Figure 1.1. Utility function.

A Geometric Interpretation

The expected-utility rule is equivalent to the assumption that indifference curves over lotteries are parallel straight lines. To see this, consider lotteries over three possible consequences m, c^*, and M. Any lottery

$$x = (m, c^*, M; \hat{\pi}_1, \hat{\pi}_2, \hat{\pi}_3) = (m, c^*, M; \hat{\pi}_1, 1 - \hat{\pi}_1 - \hat{\pi}_3, \hat{\pi}_3)$$

may be represented as a point in (π_1, π_3) space; see Figure 1.2. The triangle ABC is the set of all possible lotteries with outcomes m, c^*, and M. Point A corresponds to getting c^* for sure, point B is M for sure, and point C is m for sure. In the lottery x, the probabilities $\hat{\pi}_1$ and $\hat{\pi}_3$ (of outcomes m and M, respectively) are the coordinates of the point x. The probability of outcome c^* in this lottery, $\hat{\pi}_2$, is the horizontal (or equivalently vertical) distance from point x in Figure 1.2 to the hypotenuse BC of the triangle. The expected utility of x is:

$$U(x) = \hat{\pi}_1 v(m) + (1 - \hat{\pi}_1 - \hat{\pi}_3)v(c^*) + \hat{\pi}_3 v(M)$$
$$= v(c^*) - \hat{\pi}_1 v(c^*) + \hat{\pi}_3(1 - v(c^*))$$

where we substitute $v(m) = 0$ and $v(M) = 1$.

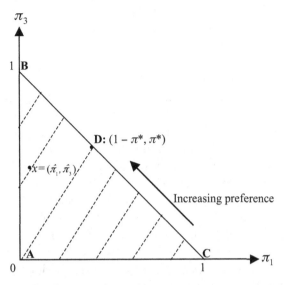

Figure 1.2. Indifference curves under expected-utility rule.

Let $y = (m, c^*, M; \pi_1, 1 - \pi_1 - \pi_3, \pi_3)$ be any other lottery. A similar calculation shows that $U(y) = v(c^*) - \pi_1 v(c^*) - \pi_3(1 - v(c^*))$. If lottery y yields the same expected utility as lottery x, then:

$$U(y) = v(c^*) - \pi_1 v(c^*) + \pi_3(1 - v(c^*))$$
$$= v(c^*) - \hat{\pi}_1 v(c^*) + \hat{\pi}_3(1 - v(c^*)) = U(x)$$

Re-arranging this we have:

$$\pi_3 = \frac{U(x) - v(c^*)}{1 - v(c^*)} + \frac{v(c^*)}{1 - v(c^*)}\pi_1$$

This is the equation of the (straight line) indifference curve through x. Observe that the slope of the indifference curve, $v(c^*)/(1 - v(c^*))$, does not depend on the lottery x. Thus, all indifference curves are parallel straight lines (shown as broken lines in the Figure 1.2). The indifference lines have positive slope because (i) any rightward movement from x leads to a *less* desirable lottery as it corresponds to increasing π_1 at the expense π_2 and (ii) any upward movement from x leads to a *more* desirable lottery as it corresponds to increasing π_3 at the expense π_2. The direction of increasing preference is northwest, as indicated by the arrow in Figure 1.2.

Point D on the line segment BC in Figure 1.2 corresponds to the lottery $(m, c^*, M; 1 - \pi^*, 0, \pi^*)$. This lottery has expected utility π^*. As $v(c^*) = \pi^*$, point D is on the same indifference line as point A.

Example 1.1: Imagine that an individual finds that his reference-lottery utilities over the range $0 \le c \le 1{,}000$ satisfy the specific utility function $v(c) = (c/1{,}000)^{1/2}$. (This formula is consistent with the previously obtained point $v(250) = 0.5$ in Figure 1.1.) Suppose he is now offered a choice between option A, representing \$250 for certain once again, and option E taking the form of a three-way prospect: E = (810, 360, 160; 0.1, 0.5, 0.4). Which should he choose?[5]

We already know that $v(250) = 0.5$: option A is equivalent to a reference lottery with 50% chance of success. For the elements of option E, we can readily compute: $v(810) = 0.9$, $v(360) = 0.6$, and $v(160) = 0.4$. That is, in option E the high possible payoff of \$810 is equivalent in preference to a reference lottery with 90% chance of success, the middling payoff \$360 is equivalent to a 60% chance of success, and the poor payoff \$160 to a 40% chance of success. Now we ask ourselves: What is the *overall* equivalent probability of success associated with option E? We can simply compute it by using the rule for compounding probabilities:

$$0.1(0.9) + 0.5(0.6) + 0.4(0.4) = 0.55$$

So prospect E offers, overall, the equivalent of a 0.55 chance of success in the reference lottery whereas option A was equivalent only to a 0.5 chance of success. Evidently, option E is better. The key point is that the equation leading to the 0.55 number, which we presented as the familiar formula for compounding probabilities, is also an instance of applying the expected-utility rule (1.4.1).   □

In short, the prescribed way of determining a cardinal $v(c)$ function for use with the expected-utility rule *makes it possible to interpret each $v(c)$ value as a probability* – to wit, the equivalent chance of success in a standardized reference lottery – and therefore to use the laws of compounding probabilities for determining the desirability of more complicated prospects.

A few additional comments:

1. We have been assuming here that consequences take the form of simple quantities of income. More generally, each consequence c might be a

---

[5] The prospect E cannot be represented in Figure 1.2. Only prospects that yield \$0, \$250, or \$1000 are depicted in Figure 1.2.

basket (vector) of consumption goods. The same technique can be employed so long as the individual has an *ordinal* preference scaling of baskets (an indifference map) to begin with.

2. We have also assumed that the same $v(c)$ scale is applicable in each and every state of the world. But, if the states are defined as "rain versus shine," or "healthy versus sick," it might appear that attitudes toward income and income risks, as reflected in the $v(c)$ function, could differ from state to state. We shall see in Chapter 2, under the heading of "state-dependent utilities," how this difficulty can be handled.

3. Some people find it disturbing that the additive form of the expected-utility rule (1.4.1) excludes any "complementarities," positive or negative, between consequences in different states. For example, if consequences are simple incomes, a higher or lower income in any state s^o is supposed in no way to affect the $v(c)$ number assigned to income received in any other state s^*. The reason is simple: incomes in the distinct states s^o and s^* can never be received *in combination* but only as *mutually exclusive alternatives*. There can be no complementarity where no possibility of jointness exists.

4. There can be confusion over whether or not the von Neumann–Morgenstern analysis proves that utility is "really" cardinal rather than ordinal. Some of the difficulty stems from a mix-up between the $v(c)$ and the $U(x)$ functions. The cardinality restriction applies to the $v(c)$ function – the preference scaling over *consequences*. But we are ultimately interested in the utility rankings of alternative *actions*, and when it comes to actions any ordinal transformation of an acceptable utility measure will always serve equally well. Suppose, for example, that use of the reference-lottery technique provides the needed utility function $v(c)$ such that an individual's *actions* (prospects) are correctly ordered by the expected-utility formula $U(x) = \Sigma_S \pi_S v(c_S)$. Then any positive monotonic transformation of $U(x)$, such as $\hat{U}(x) = e^{U(x)}$, would provide an equally correct ordering of the *actions*. Observe that if $U(x) > U(y)$ then $\hat{U}(x) = e^{U(x)} > e^{U(y)} = \hat{U}(y)$.

5. We have emphasized that the von Neumann–Morgenstern analysis justifies this particular method of constructing a cardinal $v(c)$ scale only when jointly used with the expected-utility rule. Correspondingly, the expected-utility rule has not been "proved" to be true. All that has been shown is that there exists a way of constructing a $v(c)$ function that *makes* the expected-utility rule valid as a way of deriving preferences as to actions from given preferences as to consequences.

1.4.2 The Independence Axiom

We are not providing here a formal proof of the expected-utility rule. Instead, our objective is to clarify the crucial element in the proof, the principle of *non-complementarity of incomes in different states* (see Comment 3 above). The formal postulate expressing this principle, the Independence Axiom, is also known as the substitution axiom or the axiom of complex gambles.

Independence Axiom: Suppose an individual is indifferent between two actions or prospects x and y. Then, for any other prospect z and any fixed probability p, he will be indifferent between a first complex lottery in which he receives x with probability p and z otherwise, versus a second complex lottery yielding y with probability p and z otherwise. Moreover, if he strictly prefers x over y, he will strictly prefer the first complex lottery. Thus, using the symbol $\sim$ to indicate indifference and the symbol $\succ$ for strict preference:

$$\text{If } x \sim y, \text{ then } (x, z; p, 1 - p) \sim (y, z; p, 1 - p)$$
$$\text{If } x \succ y, \text{ then } (x, z; p, 1 - p) \succ (y, z; p, 1 - p)$$

This axiom would be violated if, in a complex prospect, the presence of z differentially affected the attractiveness of x relative to y – i.e., if there were any complementarity effect. It might seem this could happen if, say, x and y were amounts of ordinary commodities like bread and margarine and z were a commodity like butter (since butter is a consumption complement for bread but a substitute for margarine). However, in the complex prospects or lotteries dealt with here, positive or negative complementarity has no role. The rationale behind this is that the occurrence of x in the one case or of y in the other rules out z. An individual can never simultaneously enjoy both *x and z* together, or both *y and z*.

An immediate implication of this axiom is that, for two lotteries x and y such that $x \sim y$, we can *substitute* one for the other in any prospect in which either appears, without changing the relative preference ordering of prospects.

In the reference-lottery process, the $v(c)$ associated with any income level c was determined by finding the probability of success in the reference lottery equally preferred to that income, i.e.:

$$\text{If } c \sim (M, m; \pi, 1 - \pi), \text{ then, because } v(m) = 0 \text{ and } v(M) = 1, \text{ we have}$$
$$v(c) = \pi$$

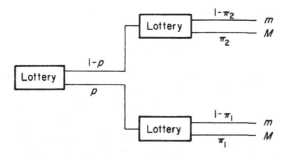

Figure 1.3. Tree diagram of compound lottery.

In what follows, it will be helpful to introduce the notation $l^*(\pi)$ to represent a reference lottery in which M is the outcome with probability π and m is the outcome with probability $1 - \pi$:

$$l^*(\pi) = (M, m; \pi, 1 - \pi)$$

Thus, if $c \sim l^*(\pi)$ then $v(c) = \pi$.

Consider now two levels of income c_1 and c_2 and their equivalent reference lotteries $l^*(\pi_1)$ and $l^*(\pi_2)$. Then $v(c_1) = \pi_1$ and $v(c_2) = \pi_2$. Suppose we wanted to find the preference equivalent of a lottery $(c_1, c_2; p, 1 - p)$ involving consequences c_1 and c_2 with respective probabilities p and $1 - p$. Using the ability to *substitute* preference-equivalent prospects:

$$c_1 \sim l^*(\pi_1) \Rightarrow (c_1, c_2; p, 1 - p) \sim (l^*(\pi_1), c_2; p, 1 - p)$$

Moreover:

$$c_2 \sim l^*(\pi_2) \Rightarrow (l^*(\pi_1), c_2; p, 1 - p) \sim (l^*(\pi_1), l^*(\pi_2); p, 1 - p)$$

Combining these implications:

$$(c_1, c_2; p, 1 - p) \sim (l^*(\pi_1), l^*(\pi_2); p, 1 - p) \qquad (1.4.3)$$

The lottery on the right-hand side of (1.4.3) is depicted as a "tree diagram" in Figure 1.3. Each box or "node" represents a point at which nature makes a move. Outcomes are indicated at the end of each branch of the tree.

At the initial node, nature "chooses" probabilistically between the two reference lotteries. Then, depending on this choice, one of the reference lotteries is played. Note that there are only two outcomes of this compound lottery, M and m. Adding probabilities, outcome M is reached with probability $p\pi_1 + (1 - p)\pi_2$. Then the compound lottery is itself equivalent to a reference lottery:

$$(l^*(\pi_1), l^*(\pi_2); p, 1 - p) = l^*(p\pi_1 + (1 - p)\pi_2) \qquad (1.4.4)$$

Combining (1.4.3) and (1.4.4) it follows that the individual is indifferent between $(c_1, c_2; p, 1 - p)$ and a reference lottery in which the probability of success is $p\pi_1 + (1 - p)\pi_2$. As $\pi_1 \equiv v(c_1)$ and $\pi_2 \equiv v(c_2)$, it follows that:

$$U(c_1, c_2; p, 1 - p) = p\pi_1 + (1 - p)\pi_2$$
$$= pv(c_1) + (1 - p)v(c_2)$$

Thus, the independence axiom, which formalizes the principle of non-complementarity of income over states of the world, leads directly to the von Neumann–Morgenstern expected-utility rule.

Exercises and Excursions 1.4

1　Transformation of Preferences
An individual claims to be maximizing:

$$U = (1 + c_1)^{\pi_1}(1 + c_2)^{\pi_2}$$

where $(c_1, c_2; \pi_1, \pi_2)$ is a two-state prospect (which means that $\pi_1 + \pi_2 = 1$). Is he a von Neumann–Morgenstern expected-utility (EU) maximizer? Would all his decisions be consistent with those of an EU maximizer?

2　Indifference Curves in Consequence Space
(A) If the utility function is $v(c) = c^{\frac{1}{2}}$, where c is income, suppose a person's preference ordering over actions or prospects in a two-state world is given by:

$$U(c_1, c_2; \pi_1, \pi_2) = \pi_1(c_1)^{\frac{1}{2}} + \pi_2(c_2)^{\frac{1}{2}}$$

Depict the indifference curves in a diagram with c_1 on the horizontal axis and c_2 on the vertical axis (probabilities held constant). Show that each indifference curve touches the axes and is everywhere bowed toward the origin.

(B) If $U = \sum_1^2 \pi_s v(c_s)$ and $v(.)$ is a strictly concave function, show that if the individual is indifferent between (c_1, c_2) and (c_1', c_2') he will strictly prefer the convex combination $(\lambda c_1 + (1 - \lambda)c_1', \lambda c_2 + (1 - \lambda)c_2')$. Hence draw a conclusion about the shape of the indifference curves in the (c_1, c_2) plane.

3 *The Expected-Utility Rule*

Let $v(c)$ be the utility functions for certain outcomes. Then, for lotteries of the form $(c_1, c_2; \pi_1, \pi_2)$, we have seen that:

$$U(c_1, c_2; \pi_1, \pi_2) = \sum_{s=1}^{2} \pi_s v(c_s)$$

In this exercise, you are asked to generalize this result to lotteries with three outcomes. An inductive argument can then be used to show that for any lottery $(c_1, c_2, \ldots, c_s; \pi_1, \pi_2, \ldots, \pi_s)$:

$$U(c_1, \ldots, c_s; \pi_1, \ldots, \pi_s) = \sum_{s=1}^{S} \pi_s v(c_s)$$

(A) Consider the lottery:

$$\hat{l} \equiv \left(c_1, c_2; \frac{\pi_1}{\pi_1 + \pi_2}, \frac{\pi_2}{\pi_1 + \pi_2} \right)$$

Explain why $\hat{l} \sim l^*(\bar{v})$ where:

$$\bar{v} \equiv \frac{\pi_1}{\pi_1 + \pi_2} v(c_1) + \frac{\pi_2}{\pi_1 + \pi_2} v(c_2)$$

(B) Appeal to the independence axiom to establish that:

$$(\hat{l}, c_3; 1 - \pi_3, \pi_3) \sim (l^*(\bar{v}), c_3; 1 - \pi_3, \pi_3)$$

and

$$(l^*(\bar{v}), c_3; 1 - \pi_3, \pi_3) \sim (l^*(\bar{v}), l^*(c_3); 1 - \pi_3, \pi_3)$$

(C) Depict the two lotteries $(\hat{l}, c_3; 1 - \pi_3, \pi_3)$ and $(l^*(\bar{v}), l^*(v(c_3)); 1 - \pi_3, \pi_3)$ in tree diagrams.

(D) Confirm that the first is equivalent to the lottery $(c_1, c_2, c_3; \pi_1, \pi_2, \pi_3)$. Confirm that the second is equivalent to the reference lottery with success probability $\sum_{s=1}^{3} \pi_s v(c_s)$.

(E) Suppose the expected-utility rule is true for prospects with S outcomes. (We have seen that it is true for $S = 2$ and 3.) Show that the above argument can, with only slight modifications, be used to establish that the expected-utility rule must be true for prospects with $S + 1$ outcomes.

1.5 Risk Aversion

In Figure 1.1 the individual pictured was indifferent between a certainty income of \$250 and a prospect yielding equal chances of \$1,000 or nothing. Such a person is termed *risk averse*. More generally:

DEFINITION: A person is *risk averse* (displays *risk aversion*) if he strictly prefers a certainty consequence to any risky prospect whose mathematical expectation of consequences equals that certainty. If his preferences go the other way he is a *risk preferrer or loving* (displays *risk preference*); if he is indifferent between the certainty consequence and such a risky prospect he is *risk neutral* (displays *risk neutrality*).

The risky prospect described above, equal chances of \$1,000 or nothing, has a mathematical expectation of \$500 of income. Since our individual was indifferent between the prospect and a mere \$250 certain, for him \$500 certain is surely preferable to the risky prospect, which verifies that he is indeed risk averse.

The term "fair gamble" is used to describe an uncertain prospect whose mathematical expectation is zero. (A gamble with negative expectation is called "unfavorable"; one with positive expectation is called "favorable.") For example, odds of 5:1 on a roll of a fair die represent a fair gamble: since you lose (say) a dollar if the face you name does not come up, and win five dollars if it does come up, the expectation of gain is $(-1)\frac{5}{6} + 5\left(\frac{1}{6}\right) = 0$. Then a risk-averse person would refuse a fair gamble; a risk preferrer would accept a fair gamble; and a risk-neutral person would be indifferent.[6]

Figure 1.4 displays three possible utility functions: $v_1(c)$ would apply to a risk-averse individual, $v_2(c)$ to someone who is risk neutral, and $v_3(c)$ to a risk preferrer. Consider the fair prospect or gamble $G = (750, 250; \frac{1}{2}, \frac{1}{2})$ whose mathematical expectation is \$500. For the first or risk-averse individual the utility of \$500 certain, $v_1(500)$, is indicated by the height of point T along the $v_1(c)$ curve. The utility he attaches to the risky prospect, choosing the gamble G, is indicated by point L – whose height is the probability-weighted average of the heights of points J and K. This is, of course, the geometrical equivalent of the expected-utility rule, which tells us that $U_1(G) = \frac{1}{2} v_1(750) + \frac{1}{2} v_1(250)$. Evidently, whenever the utility function has the "concave" shape of $v_1(c)$, points associated with a certainty income (like T in the diagram) will be higher than points (like L) representing a fair gamble with the same expectation of income. By an analogous argument,

---

[6] However, as we shall see below, a risk-averse individual would accept a fair gamble if it offset *other* risks to which he was exposed. To purchase insurance, for example, is to accept an offsetting (risk-reducing) gamble.

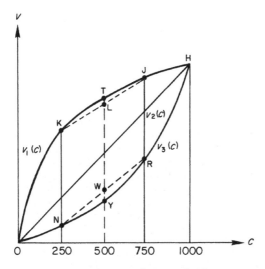

Figure 1.4. Attitudes toward risk.

for the risk-preferring individual, $v_3(500)$ at point Y will be less than at point W; such a person would choose the gamble G rather than receive its mathematical expectation of income, \$500, as a certainty. Finally, the $v_2(c)$ curve indicates that the risk-neutral person would be indifferent between the gamble G and the certainty of \$500.

We will often have occasion to make use of *Jensen's inequality*: If $\tilde{c}$ is a random variable (taking on at least two values with non-zero probability) and $v(c)$ is a twice-differentiable function:

If $v''(c) < 0$, then $E[v(c)] < v[E(c)]$
If $v''(c) = 0$, then $E[v(c)] = v[E(c)]$
If $v''(c) > 0$, then $E[v(c)] > v[E(c)]$

Evidently, these conditions correspond immediately to the risk-averse, risk-neutral, and risk-preferring cases of Figure 1.4.

It is useful to consider how attitude toward risk is reflected in the triangle diagram introduced in Section 1.4.1. Figure 1.5 below shows the set of lotteries over three income levels, \$0, \$500, \$1,000. Thus, π_1 is the probability of getting \$0 and π_3 is the probability of \$1,000. The origin corresponds to getting \$500 for sure.

Point L in Figure 1.5 is the lottery that gives either \$1,000 or nothing with equal probability. A risk-neutral individual is indifferent between this prospect and \$500 for sure. Hence, the solid line joining L to the origin is the indifference line through L for a risk-neutral person. As indifference

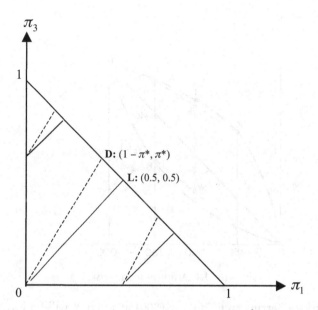

Figure 1.5. Risk-averse and risk-neutral indifference lines.

lines under the expected-utility rule are parallel straight lines, the solid lines inside the triangle are indifference lines under risk neutrality. That is, all lotteries on a solid line have the same expected value *and* the same expected utility for a risk-neutral person.

Any risk-averse individual strictly prefers \$500 for sure to the prospect L. Thus, since the direction of increasing preference is to the northwest, any risk-averse indifference line through the origin must intersect the hypotenuse of the triangle at a point D to the northwest of L ($\pi^* > 0.5$). Hence, indifference lines for a risk-averse person (the broken lines in the triangle) are steeper than the indifference lines for a risk-neutral person (the solid lines in the triangle). Similarly, the indifference lines for a risk-neutral person are steeper than indifference lines for a risk-preferring person.

We now consider what observation of the world tells us about the actual $v(c)$ curves entering into people's decisions. First of all, we have already postulated that *more income is preferred to less,* justified by the observation that only rarely do people throw away income. This implies a rising $v(c)$ function, with positive first derivative $v'(c)$, that is, positive marginal utility of income. The question of risk aversion versus risk preference concerns the second derivative $v''(c)$ – whether marginal utility of income falls or rises with income.

Risk aversion – "concave" curves like $v_1(c)$ displaying diminishing marginal utility – is considered to be the normal case, based upon the observation that individuals typically hold *diversified portfolios*. Suppose someone were merely risk neutral, so that for him $v''(c) = 0$. Then he would ignore the riskiness or variance of different investment options or assets (gambles), and take account only of the mathematical expectation of income associated with each. Such a person would plunge all his wealth into that single asset that, regardless of its riskiness, offered the highest mathematical expectation of income. But we scarcely ever see this behavior pattern, and more commonly observe individuals holding a variety of assets. Since the risks associated with different assets are generally partially offsetting, diversification reduces the chance of ending up with an extremely low level of income. This safety feature is achieved, however, only by accepting a lower overall mathematical expectation of income; some expected income has been sacrificed in order to reduce risk.[7]

What of the seemingly contrary evidence that "unfavorable" (negative mathematical expectation) gambles are cheerfully accepted by bettors at Las Vegas and elsewhere? Even more puzzling, why is it that the same person might behave quite conservatively (insure his house, diversify his asset holdings) in some circumstances, and in other circumstances accept fair or even unfavorable gambles? There have been attempts to construct utility functions $v(c)$ that would be consistent with avoiding gambles (insuring) over certain ranges of income *and* with seeking gambles over other ranges (Friedman and Savage, 1948; Markowitz, 1952). We will briefly discuss the Friedman-Savage version.

Consider the doubly inflected utility function in Figure 1.6. The $v(c)$ curve is concave, reflecting normal risk aversion, in the region OK and once again in the region LN. But it is convex, reflecting risk preference, in the middle region KL. With this sort of $v(c)$ function, risk-taking behavior will vary with wealth. For those whose endowments fall in the first concave segment, the tendency is to insure against relatively small risks but to accept fair (or even mildly adverse) long-shot big-payoff gambles, offering a chance of landing somewhere toward the upper end of the curve. It can be verified that this pattern will particularly apply for those with incomes toward the upper edge of the bottom segment – the less indigent poor, and perhaps the lower-middle class. The *very* poor, in contrast, would be much less inclined to gamble. Looking now toward the top of the scale, those with incomes near the lower edge of the upper concave segment – the rich but not super-rich,

---

[7] An individual characterized by *risk-preference* might also plunge all of his wealth into a single asset, but this need not be the asset with the highest mathematical expectation of income. He might choose an asset with greater riskiness over the asset with highest income yield (that is, he would sacrifice some expected income in order to *enlarge* his risk).

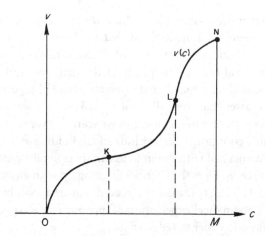

Figure 1.6. Gambling and insuring – doubly inflected utility function.

and perhaps the upper middle class – would seem to have a taste for risks likely to have a favorable payoff but offering a long-shot chance of a really large loss. (But the super-rich, like the super-poor, are very disinclined to gamble at all.) The central group, finally, would be happy to accept almost any fair or not-too-unfavorable gamble.

The doubly inflected utility function of Figure 1.6 does then explain why a person might gamble in some circumstances and insure in others, or accept some fair gambles while rejecting other ones. But it also implies other behavior that is quite inconsistent with common observation. It is hard to believe that people of middling incomes are always great gamblers. If the picture in Figure 1.6 were correct, the middle group in the convex KL segment would be so anxious to gamble as to seek out enormous riches-or-ruin bets. These middle ranges of income would then rapidly be depopulated, which is surely not what is observed. And that the really solid risk avoiders in our society are only the very poor and the super-rich is equally difficult to credit.

A more acceptable explanation, of why people simultaneously gamble and insure, is that most of us engage in gambling as a recreational rather than an income-determining activity. Put another way, gambling is normally more like a consumption good than an investment good. As it happens, it is quite possible operationally to distinguish recreational or pleasure-oriented from serious wealth-oriented gambling. The latter, if efficiently conducted, would take the form of once-and-for-all wagers at enormous stakes. Pleasure-oriented gambling, in contrast, being designed to yield enjoyment over some period of time, will be characterized by repetitive minuscule bets practically guaranteed *not* to change one's wealth status in any drastic way. What is observed at Las Vegas is very much more the repetitive small-stake than the riches-or-ruin huge-stake betting pattern.

Nevertheless, in exceptional situations, risk-preferring behavior does indeed surely occur. Consider the following. As bank cashier you have dipped into the till to the extent of $30,000. The bank examiners are arriving tomorrow, so you have time to replace the missing funds, but you have only $10,000 left on hand. Suppose you value the consumption benefit of spending the remaining $10,000 today far less than you value avoiding the shame and pain of exposure as an embezzler. Then you surely would be willing to risk the $10,000 on a fair gamble today – say, with a $\frac{1}{3}$ chance of winning $20,000. You would probably even take quite an adverse bet if necessary, so long as the possible payoff sufficed to cover the $20,000 of additional funds you need.

What is involved here is a "threshold" phenomenon, a critical level of income where a little bit more can make a big difference. Put another way, there is a range of *increasing* marginal utility – in the extreme, a single discrete step to a higher utility level. Threshold phenomena are quite common in nature. In many species, animals must take risks in accumulating resources or engaging in combat in order to achieve nutritional viability or win the privilege of mating. These phenomena have evident analogs for humans living in primitive societies. To what extent they may explain risk-taking behavior under modern conditions may be left an open question.[8]

This discussion may possibly suggest, contrary to a point made earlier, that it is after all true that utility must "really" be cardinal. A viability threshold, for example, might seem to be a cardinal feature of preference that would apply to riskless as well as to risky decision making. Nevertheless, our original point remains valid. For certainty choices, only ordinal comparisons of consequences are needed. For decisions under uncertainty we can derive, by the reference-lottery technique, a $v(c)$ function that may have convex or concave or mixed curvature, as the case may be. But the shape of this function for any individual is an inseparable blend of two elements: (i) the individual's valuations of the consequences, and (ii) his attitudes toward

---

[8] See Rubin and Paul (1979). These authors suggest that the propensity of young males to engage in highly risky activities – as evidenced, for example, by their high automobile accident rates – may be the result of natural selection for risk-taking. The evolutionary history of the human species may have instilled risk-preferring attitudes among individuals in age and sex groups liable to encounter viability or mating thresholds. (Note that the threshold argument is also consistent with the observation that risk-taking behavior will be observed predominantly *among the poor*.)

risk. We may therefore interpret a concave $v(c)$ function as reflecting *either* risk aversion (attitude toward risk) or diminishing marginal utility (attitude toward income); similarly, a convex $v(c)$ function can be said to reflect *either* risk preference or increasing marginal utility. Both terminologies are somewhat misleading, since what the curvature of $v(c)$ really represents is the *interaction* of the two factors working together.

Finally, another category of seeming risk-taking behavior may be explainable in terms of *state-dependent utility functions*. An example: Suppose it is very important to me, as the psychological equivalent of having a large sum of money, that the home team wins the big game. Then I might plausibly bet *against* the home team, at fair or even adverse odds! (How this works out in detail will be left for the chapter following.)

Exercises and Excursions 1.5

1 Risk Aversion, Risk Preference, Risk Neutrality
  (A) Identify each of the following "cardinal" utility functions with risk-averse, risk-preferring, or risk-neutral behavior:

  (i) $v = \ln c$ (ii) $v = ac - bc^2$ (a, b positive constants)
  (iii) $v = c^2$ (iv) $v = c^{\frac{1}{2}}$
  (v) $v = 100 + 6c$ (vi) $v = 1 - e^{-c}$

  (B) The quadratic form (ii) above has an unsatisfactory feature for $c > a/2b$. Explain.

2 Diversification
Three individuals have respective utility functions $v_1 = c$ (risk neutral), $v_2 = c^{0.5}$ (risk averse), and $v_3 = c^2$ (risk preferrer). They each have the option of investing in *any one* of the three following prospects or gambles, with mathematical expectations of income as shown:

  G1 = (480, 480; 0.5, 0.5)   E[G1] = 480
  G2 = (850, 200; 0.5, 0.5)   E[G2] = 525
  G3 = (1,000, 0; 0.5, 0.5)   E[G3] = 500

Notice that, comparing the first two gambles, higher risk is associated with greater mathematical expectation of income. The third gamble has highest risk of all, but intermediate mathematical expectation.

  (A) Show that risk-neutral individual 1 will prefer gamble G2 with the highest expectation, while risk-averse individual 2 will prefer gamble

G1 with the lowest risk. Show that the risk-preferring individual 3 is willing to sacrifice some expectation to *increase* his risk, by choosing G3.

(B) If the individuals could "diversify" by choosing any desired mixture of these gambles, which of them would diversify? (Assume that the payoffs of gambles G2 and G3 are perfectly correlated.)

3 Doubly Inflected Utility Function

In the doubly inflected $v(c)$ curve shown in Figure 1.6, suppose that the borders of the segments (inflection points) occur at $c = 250$ and at $c = 750$.

(A) Illustrate geometrically that an individual with initial income of $240 would be likely to accept a (fair) gamble offering a one-sixth chance of a $600 gain and a five-sixth chance of a $120 loss. Show that someone with initial income of $120 would be much less likely to accept the same gamble.

(B) Show that someone with initial endowed income of $760 would be likely to accept a fair gamble which is the reverse of the above: a five-sixth chance of a $120 gain and a one-sixth chance of a $600 loss. What about a person with initial wealth of $880?

(C) Show that someone with endowed wealth of exactly $500 would surely accept *any* fair gamble with 50 : 50 odds – at least up to a scale of $250 gain and $250 loss. He might even accept much larger fair gambles of this type; indicate geometrically the limits of what he would accept.

4 Linear Risk Tolerance

Risk aversion is characterized by the condition $v''(c) < 0$. For some purposes, as we shall see below, the ratio $-v''/v'$ is a useful measure of risk aversion. The reciprocal of this ratio, $-v'/v''$, is known as the *risk tolerance*. An interesting class of $v(c)$ functions is defined by the condition of *linear risk tolerance*: $-v'/v'' = \alpha + \beta c$.

(A) Show that, for arbitrary constants M, N with $N > 0$:
   (i) $\beta = 0$ implies $v = M - Ne^{-c/\alpha}$
   (ii) $\alpha = 0, \beta \neq 1$ implies $v = M + Nc^{1-\gamma/(1-\gamma))}$ where $\gamma = 1/\beta$
   (iii) $\alpha = 0, \beta = 1$ implies $v = M + N \ln c$
   (iv) $\alpha > 0, \beta = -1$ implies $v = M - N(\alpha - c)^2$

(B) Some of the above functions are valid only in restricted ranges of c. Indicate the restrictions, if any, that apply in each case. Also explain why N must be positive if v is to be a well-behaved utility function.

5 The Bank Examiner Is Coming

You have stolen $30,000 from the bank but have the opportunity to replace it by winning a fair gamble. You have at your disposal just $10,000. Your utility function is such that $v(c) = -B$, where B is a very big number, when $c < 0$ (i.e., should you not replace *all* the missing funds), and otherwise $v(c) = c^{\frac{1}{2}}$. Assuming fair gambles are available at any terms you desire, solve *geometrically* for your optimal fair gamble. Will you surely stake all your $10,000? Will you look only for a $20,000 payoff, or would you prefer a bet with a smaller chance of a bigger payoff?

6 Utility Functions with Multiple Goods

The argument in the text above, developing a cardinal utility function $v(c)$ for use with the expected-utility rule, ran in terms of a single desired good or commodity c. Extend the argument to cardinal utility functions of two goods, in the form $v(a, b)$. Show that, starting with an *ordinal* preference function defined over combinations of a and b (that is, starting with an ordinary indifference map on a, b axes), the reference-lottery technique can be used to generate a cardinal scaling that amounts to giving a numerical utility value to each indifference curve.

7 Risk Aversion with Multiple Goods

An individual has a utility function $v(a, b) = a^{\frac{1}{2}} b^{\frac{1}{4}}$. He has income I available for spending on a and b, and faces fixed prices $P_a = P_b = 1$.

(A) Show that he would strictly prefer the certain income of 50 to an equal chance of his income rising or falling by 49 before he makes his consumption choices.

(B) Obtain an expression for the individual's "indirect" utility function. (That is, the maximized level of v given income I and prices P_a and P_b.) Hence show that this individual exhibits aversion to income risks.

(C) Suppose $I = 50$ and $P_b = 16$. Would the individual prefer to face a certain $P_a = 64$ or a stochastically varying P_a that might equal 1 or 81 with equal chances? Does your answer cast doubt upon whether the individual is really risk averse? Explain.

8 Jensen's Inequality (I)

(A) If the utility function $v(c)$ is twice continuously differentiable with $v''(c) \leq 0$, show that for any random variable $\tilde{c}$:

$$E[v(\tilde{c})] \leq v(E[\tilde{c}])$$

(B) If $v''(c) < 0$ and $\Pr[\tilde{c} \neq \mathrm{E}[\tilde{c}]] > 0$ show that:

$$\mathrm{E}[v(\tilde{c})] < v(\mathrm{E}[\tilde{c}])$$

9 Jensen's Inequality (II)
Suppose $v(c)$ is a concave function (not necessarily differentiable), that is, for any c_1, c_2:

$$v((1 - \lambda)c_1 + \lambda c_2) \geq (1 - \lambda)v(c_1) + \lambda v(c_2), 0 \leq \lambda \leq 1$$

(A) Prove by induction that, for any $c_1, \ldots, c_n$:

$$v\left(\sum_{i=1}^{n} \mu_i c_i\right) \geq \sum_{i=1}^{n} \mu_i v(c_i), \quad \text{for } \mu_i \geq 0, \sum_{i=1}^{n} \mu_i = 1$$

(B) Hence derive Jensen's inequality once again.

1.6 Utility Paradoxes and Rationality

A very considerable literature arguing against expected utility as a good descriptive theory has appeared in the last 30 years. Its main thrust has been that actual decision makers do not behave rationally in the face of uncertainty, or at any rate do not consistently follow the expected-utility rule.[9] To some extent, these complaints have been supported by experimental evidence.[10] We provide four illustrations of which the first two are the following.

1.6.1 Probability Matching

You are paid $1 each time you guess correctly whether a red or a white light will flash. The lights flash randomly, but the red is set to turn on twice as often as the white.

It has been found that subjects tend to guess red about two-thirds of the time and white one-third. Yet, obviously, it would be more profitable always to guess red.

[9] Machina (1987) provides a very helpful and clear survey to this literature. A more recent survey is Starmer (2000).
[10] See, for example, Slovic and Lichtenstein (1983), Tversky and Kahneman (1981), and Schoemaker (1982).

1.6.2 Framing the Question

Imagine that you have been given $200 and are asked to choose between (i) $50 additional or (ii) a 25% chance of winning $200 additional (or else, gaining nothing). Alternatively, imagine that you have been given $400, but you must now choose between (i) giving up $150 or (ii) a 75% chance of losing $200 (or else, losing nothing).

Most experimental subjects choose option (i) in the first version of the question, but option (ii) in the second. Yet, obviously, option (i) generates the same income prospect whichever way the question is framed, and similarly for option (ii).

This literature on non-expected utility theory claims that the discrepancies revealed by these results refute the economist's standard assumption of rationality, or at least the expected-utility rule as a specific implication of that assumption. We do not accept this interpretation. A much more parsimonious explanation, in our opinion, is that this evidence merely illustrates certain limitations of the human mind as a computer. It is possible to fool the brain by the way a question is posed, just as optical illusions may be arranged to fool the eye. Discovering and classifying such mental illusions are fruitful activities for psychologists, but these paradoxes have less significance for economics.

We would not go so far as to insist that rationality failures have *no* economic implications. If these shortcomings do indeed represent ways in which people could systematically be fooled, economists would predict that tricksters, confidence men, and assorted rogues would enter the "industry" offering such gambles to naive subjects. For example:

PROBABILITY MATCHING: The trickster could challenge the subject along the following line: "I have a secret method of guessing which light will flash. (His secret method, of course, is always to bet on red.) I will write my guess down on paper each time, and you will write yours down. At the end we will total up our successes. For each time I am right and you are wrong, you will pay me $1; in the reverse case, I will pay you $1.50."[11] If the subject really believes that his is the right method, he should surely accept so generous an offer.

And similarly, clever tricksters could win sure-thing income from the inconsistent answers offered by naive individuals in our other illustration. The confidence-man profession does obviously exist, and is unlikely (given the

---

[11] The maximum or breakeven payment that the trickster could offer is $2 exactly. Clearly, there will be no payment either way in the two-thirds of the cases where the naive subject bets on red. And when he bets on white, he will be wrong twice as often as he is right.

limitations of the human mind) ever to disappear.[12] But the more important the decision, the more it is worth people's while to learn how not to be fooled.

It will be of interest to analyze some of the parallels and differences among these various rationality failures, and in particular to attempt to identify more precisely the source of the slippage in each case.

If the subjects in PROBABILITY MATCHING did mentally compare the matching rule with "Always bet on red" and chose the former, they committed a straightforward logical error.[13] We know that people do often commit such errors, even in contexts where no uncertainty is involved. Consider the following example from a psychological experiment (adapted from Cosmides, 1989):

> You are faced with a card-sorting task, in which each card has a number on one side and a letter on the other. There is only one rule: "Every card marked with an 'X' on one side should have a '1' on the other." Indicate whether you need to inspect the reverse side of the following cards to detect violation of the rule: (a) a card showing an 'X'; (b) a card showing a 'Y'; (c) a card showing a '1'; (d) a card showing a '2'.

In a large preponderance of cases, while the subjects correctly realized the need to inspect the reverse of card (a), they failed to notice that they should do the same for card (d).

What is instructive for our purposes, however, is that the experimenter went on to investigate a logically identical choice, presented to the subjects more or less as follows:

> You are the bouncer in a Boston bar, assigned to enforce the following rule: "Anyone who consumes alcohol on the premises must be at least twenty years old." To detect violation of the rule, indicate whether you need more information about any of the following individuals: (a) someone drinking whisky; (b) someone drinking soda; (c) an individual aged twenty-five; (d) an individual aged sixteen.

Here almost everyone perceived the need for more information about individual (d) as well as individual (a). Evidently, humans have trouble with purely abstract problems, but do a lot better when the logically equivalent choices are offered in a realistic context – particularly where possible cheating or violations of social norms may be involved. Returning to

---

[12] An analogous example is the racetrack tout who offers to predict the winning horse for $20, telling you that he will refund your money unless his prediction is correct. His intention, of course, is to tout customers onto all the horses in the race.

[13] Another possibility is that the correct rule never came to mind at all – in effect, the subjects did not think very hard about what was going on. This would not be too surprising if the stakes were trivial in magnitude.

PROBABILITY MATCHING, in our opinion few individuals would be more than momentarily fooled by the trickster described above if some serious issue or some substantial amount of money were at stake.

The second example, FRAMING THE QUESTION, is rather like an optical illusion involving perspective, a nearby small object being made to seem larger than a far-off large object. In the first choice offered the subjects, the risk – the chance of losing $50 – is placed in the foreground, so to speak. From this viewpoint, the 25% chance of gaining an extra $200 does not seem enough recompense. In the second version what is placed in the foreground is the unpleasant option of a $150 loss. Here the risk of losing an additional $50 fades into comparative insignificance, as compared with the 25% hope of recouping the $150 and suffering no loss at all. Notice that these experimental subjects proved to be highly risk averse; they were fooled by a shift in the setting, the same risk being highlighted in the one choice and left in the shadows in the other case.

1.6.3 Allais Paradox

We will provide a more extended discussion of a third example, the ALLAIS PARADOX, which illustrates the powerful effect of just how the choices are framed (Allais (1953)):

You are offered the choice between prospects A and B:

> A: with certainty, receive $1,000,000
> B: with probability 0.10, receive $5,000,000
>   with probability 0.89, receive $1,000,000
>   with probability 0.01, receive zero.

Alternatively, you are offered the choice between C and D:

> C: with probability 0.11, receive $1,000,000
>   with probability 0.89, receive zero
> D: with probability 0.10, receive $5,000,000
>   with probability 0.90, receive zero.

It has been found that most people prefer A to B, but D to C. But it is easy to show that choosing A over B but D over C is inconsistent with the expected-utility rule. According to that theorem:

If $A \succ B$, then $v(\$1,000,000) > 0.10\, v(\$5,000,000) + 0.89\, v(\$1,000,000)$
$$+ 0.01\, v(\$0)$$

Then, by elementary algebra:

$$0.11\,v(\$1,000,000) + 0.89\,v(\$0) > 0.10\,v(\$5,000,000) + 0.90\,v(\$0)$$

But the latter inequality is equivalent, according to the expected-utility rule, to $C \succ D$.

The explanation, in perceptual terms, appears to be that the A versus B framing makes the 0.01 chance of receiving zero stand out as a very adverse feature in making option B undesired – but exactly the same chance fades into comparative insignificance, psychologically speaking, as an adverse feature of D in comparison with C.

The question is, does the observed failure of subjects to follow the dictates of the expected-utility rule represent only a logical lapse, akin to an optical illusion? Or is it perhaps that the rule is an incorrect, or at least an excessively narrow, specification of rational behavior? The latter was the position taken by Allais.

Individuals who choose in accordance with the Allais Paradox example are violating the independence axiom: that any complex lottery can be reduced to its elements. The following thought experiment reveals how the choices described by Allais violate this axiom. Consider the prospect X and sure thing Y:

> X: with probability 10/11, receive $5,000,000
> with probability 1/11, receive zero.
> Y: receive $1,000,000 with probability 1.

Then, the prospects A, B, C, and D may be written as the following complex gambles:

Thus, A is decomposed into a gamble which yields Y with probability 0.11 and $1,000,000 with probability 0.89, B is the complex gamble which leads to X with probability 0.11 and $1,000,000 with probability 0.89, and so on.

According to the independence axiom, the choice between A and B, and between C and D should be determined by choice between Y and X. Thus:

If $Y \succ X$ then $A \succ B$ and $C \succ D$
If $Y \prec X$ then $A \prec B$ and $C \prec D$.

However, as noted above, for most subjects $A \succ B$ and $C \prec D$. Thus, the attractiveness of Y relative to X depends on the lower branches of the complex gambles A, B, C, and D in Figure 1.7, i.e., on what might happen in the

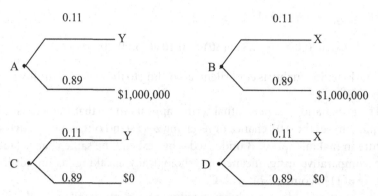

Figure 1.7. Allais Paradox lotteries.

event one does not have to make a choice between Y and X. This complementarity between the lower and upper branches of the complex gambles depicted in Figure 1.7 represents a violation of the independence axiom. As Machina (1987) points out, in comparing A and B, subjects judge the relative attractiveness of Y and X in the event of an opportunity loss of $1,000,000 (i.e., in the event that a 0.89 chance of winning $1,000,000 does not occur); this opportunity loss makes them very risk averse and they prefer $Y \succ X$. In comparing C and D, on the other hand, there is no opportunity loss when faced with a choice between Y and X; subjects are less risk averse and prefer $X \succ Y$. This in turn implies that the indifference curves for Allais Paradox preferences, when depicted as solid straight lines in Figure 1.8, cannot be parallel straight lines. The indifference curves, instead of being parallel, fan out as shown in Figure 1.8.

The triangle diagram represents prospects with outcomes $0, $1,000,000, and $5,000,000. The origin represents getting $1,000,000 with certainty. The right-hand corner $(\pi_1 = 1, \pi_3 = 0)$ represents $0 for sure and the third corner of the triangle, $(\pi_1 = 0, \pi_3 = 1)$, is $5,000,000 for sure. Thus, the gamble X is on the hypotenuse of the triangle, as shown, and the sure thing Y is at the origin.

Complex gambles A and C are obtained by combining (in proportion 0.11 to 0.89) Y with the origin and with the right-hand corner, respectively. Similarly, B and D are obtained by combining X with the origin and with the right-hand corner, respectively. The solid lines in the triangle are indifference lines consistent with Allais Paradox preferences. The prospect C lies below the indifference line through D and A lies above the indifference line through B. By simple geometry, the line segments AB and CD are parallel. Thus, indifference lines must fan out as shown. At the lower right-hand side

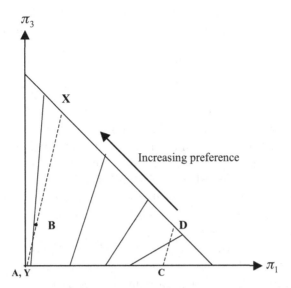

Figure 1.8. Allais Paradox indifference lines.

of the triangle, indifference lines are less steep (less risk averse), and to the upper left-hand side they are steeper (more risk averse).

In order to explain the Allais Paradox and other experimental evidence, various generalizations of the expected-utility rule have been proposed. One generalization, due to Machina (1982), is to allow the utility function for consequences to depend on the prospect being evaluated. Thus, the "expected utility" of x is

$$U(x) = E[v(c_{xs}, x)] \tag{1.6.1}$$

The preceding discussion implies that $v(c_{xs}, x)$ is less risk averse for x in the lower right-hand side of the triangle and more risk averse for x in the upper left-hand side of the triangle.

However, even this generalization of the expected-utility rule cannot explain the next example.

1.6.4 Ellsberg Paradox

Urn I has 50 red balls and 50 black balls. Urn II also has 100 red and black balls, but in unknown proportions. You are invited to bet on the color of a ball that will be drawn randomly from one of the two urns. You will win $100 in the event of a correct choice.

(A) Of the two red bets R_I or R_{II} (a bet on red if the drawing is made from the first, or alternatively from the second urn), which do you prefer?

(B) Same question, for the two black bets B_I and B_{II}.

It has been found that most subjects prefer R_I over R_{II}, and also prefer B_I over B_{II}. To say that you prefer R_I over R_{II} is to say that you believe that the probability of a red ball from urn II is less than 0.5. But this implies that the probability of a black ball from urn II is more than 0.5 and hence subjects should prefer B_{II} over B_I. Thus, preferences reported by most subjects are inconsistent with the idea that subjects' beliefs about uncertainty can be expressed as probabilities. In particular, the expected-utility rule or even a generalization such as the formula (1.6.1) cannot be used to express these preferences (see Ellsberg 1961).

The ELLSBERG PARADOX plays on the subjects' aversion to ambiguity and vagueness. Recalling the discussion of "hard" versus "soft" probability estimates earlier in the chapter, the subjects have a preference for acting on the basis of a hard probability (the urn known to have 50 black and 50 red balls) than acting on the basis of a soft probability (the urn with an unknown mixture). But if only an immediate *terminal* action is called for, as postulated here, it makes no difference whether the probability is hard or soft. In the absence of any basis for one color being more likely than the other, the subjective probability of success has to be the same for the second as for the first urn – whether betting on black or on red. The subjects seem to associate *higher confidence* (which indeed holds with regard to the probability of success using the first urn) with *lesser risk*. A generalization of the expected-utility rule that is consistent with the Ellsberg Paradox has been proposed by Schmeidler (1989).[14] Soft and hard probabilities are processed differently in this generalization so as to allow for aversion to ambiguity.

We do not want to be dismissive of what is, on a number of grounds, an intellectually significant literature. But we do note that most of the evidence of violations to the expected-utility rule has been experimental evidence gathered in an economics laboratory. Subjects are asked to make certain

---

[14] There is also an alternative explanation, entirely consistent with expected-utility behavior. In an actual experiment the first urn would presumably be transparent, to allow everyone to see that half the balls are red and half black. But, of course, the second urn could not be transparent, which makes trickery more possible. A subject attaching even a small likelihood to being cheated (by the experimenter shifting the proportions in the second urn after the bet is down) would definitely and quite rationally prefer drawing from the first urn.

choices. In a real setting where individuals make choices repeatedly, there is a greater opportunity and incentive to learn and reconsider the kinds of choices made by subjects in the four examples presented here.

As an empirical matter, such important phenomena as advertising and political persuasion depend very importantly upon clever use of fallacious analogy, irrelevant associations, and other confidence-man tricks. But the analysis of error is only a footnote to the analysis of valid inference. It is only because people have a well-justified confidence in reason that deception, whether artful or unintended, can sometimes occur. Especially when it comes to subtle matters and small differences, it is easy for people to fool themselves, or to be fooled. But less so when the issues are really important, for the economically sound reason that correct analysis is more profitable than error.

Exercises and Excursions 1.6

1 Framing the Question
Could a confidence-man or trickster exploit individuals whose choices are as described in the *framing the question* example above?

2 A Second Ellsberg Paradox
An urn contains 30 red balls and 60 other balls, some yellow and some black. One ball is to be drawn at random from the urn.

(A) You are offered the opportunity to choose either red or black. If you pick the color of the ball drawn, you win $100. Which color do you choose?

(B) Alternatively, suppose you are offered once again the opportunity to choose either red or black. However, now you win $100 as long as the ball drawn is *not* the color picked. Which color do you choose?

(C) Show that only two of the four possible combinations of choices (for questions A and B, respectively) – red-red, red-black, black-red, and black-black – are consistent with the independence axiom.

(D) If your choices were inconsistent with the axiom, do you wish to change either of them?

3 The Allais Paradox
(A) Does Allais Paradox violate the independence axiom? If so, how?

(B) As a confidence-man, how would you exploit an individual whose choices were consistent with Allais Paradox?

4   Risk Aversion – Price or Quantity?

This exercise illustrates a different kind of utility "paradox." Suppose an individual with given wealth W can purchase commodities x and y. Let his utility function be:

$$v(x, y) = x + \alpha \ln y$$

Note that, in terms of our definitions above, for variations in x alone the individual is risk neutral ($\partial^2 v/\partial x^2 = 0$), while for variations in y alone he is risk averse ($\partial^2 v/\partial y^2 < 0$).

(A) Let the price of x be fixed at unity, and let p be the price of y. Show that his "indirect" utility, that is, elementary utility as a function of p, is given by:

$$\hat{v}(p) = \operatorname*{Max}_{x,y} \left\{ v(x, y) | x + py = W \right\} = \operatorname*{Max}_{y}(W + \alpha \ln y - py)$$

(B) Letting y^* denote his optimal consumption of good y, show that:

$$y^*(p) = \alpha/p$$
$$\hat{v}(p) = W - \alpha + \alpha \ln \alpha - \alpha \ln p$$

(C) Show that $\hat{v}(p)$ is a *convex* function of p, that is, $d^2\hat{v}/dp^2 > 0$.

(D) Explain the paradox that, while the $v(x, y)$ function displays risk aversion with respect to quantities of y, the $\hat{v}(p)$ function seems to display risk preference with respect to the price of y.

SUGGESTIONS FOR FURTHER READING: The expected-utility rule for objective probabilities was derived from a set of axioms on individual behavior by von Neumann and Morgenstern (1944). For a proof of the expected-utility rule, see Kreps (1988). Savage (1954) increased the domain of applicability of the expected-utility rule by allowing probabilities to be subjective. In Savage's world, both the utility over consequences *and* probabilities over uncertain events are personalized and may differ among individuals; in this setting Savage derives the expected-utility rule from a set of axioms. Kreps (1988) provides a relatively reader-friendly development of Savage's theory of expected utility with subjective probability. The literature on non-expected utility theory has burgeoned over the last twenty years. In addition to surveys by Machina (1987) and Starmer (2000) mentioned in the chapter, see the books by Schmidt (1998) and Gilboa (2009) for more on this subject.

References

Allais, Maurice, "Le Comportement de l'homme rationnel devant le risque," *Econometrica*, 21 (1953), 505–546.

Cosmides, Leda, "The Logic of Social Exchange: Has Natural Selection Shaped How Humans Reason? Studies with the Wason Selection Task," *Cognition*, 31 (1989), 187–276.

Ellsberg, Daniel, "Risk, Ambiguity, and the Savage Axioms," *Quarterly Journal of Economics*, 75 (1961), 643–669.

Friedman, Milton and Savage, Leonard J., "The Utility Analysis of Choices Involving Risks," *Journal of Political Economy*, 56 (1948), 279–304.

Gilboa, Itzhak, *Theory of Decision under Uncertainty*, Econometric Society Monographs, Cambridge: Cambridge University Press, 2009.

Knight, Frank H., *Risk, Uncertainty and Profit*, New York: Houghton Mifflin, 1921.

Kreps, David, *Notes on the Theory of Choice*, Boulder: Westview Press, 1988.

Machina, Mark J., "'Expected Utility' Analysis without the Independence Axiom," *Econometrica*, 50 (1982), 277–323.

———, "Choice under Uncertainty: Problems Solved and Unsolved," *Journal of Economic Perspectives*, 1 (1987), 121–154.

Markowitz, Harry, "The Utility of Wealth," *Journal of Political Economy*, 60 (1952), 151–158.

Neumann, John von and Morgenstern, Oskar, *Theory of Games and Economic Behavior*, Princeton: Princeton University Press, 1944.

Rubin, Paul H., and Paul, Chris W., "An Evolutionary Model of the Taste for Risk," *Economic Inquiry*, 17 (1979), 585–596.

Savage, Leonard J., *The Foundations of Statistics*, New York: Wiley, 1954.

Schlaifer, Robert, *Probability and Statistics for Business Decisions*, New York: McGraw-Hill, 1959.

Schmeidler, David, "Subjective Probability and Expected Utility without Additivity," *Econometrica*, 57 (1989), 571–587.

Schmidt, Ulrich, *Axiomatic Utility Theory under Risk: Non-Archimedean Representations and Application to Insurance Economics*, Berlin: Springer-Verlag, 1998.

Schoemaker, Paul J. H., "The Expected Utility Model: Its Variants, Purposes, Evidence and Limitations," *Journal of Economic Literature*, 20 (1982), 529–563.

Slovic, Paul and Lichtenstein, Sarah, "Preference Reversals: A Broader Perspective," *American Economic Review*, 83 (1983), 596–605.

Starmer, Chris, "Developments in Non-expected Utility Theory: The Hunt for a Descriptive Theory of Choice under Risk," *Journal of Economic Literature*, 38 (2000), 332–382.

Tversky, Amos and Kahneman, Daniel, "The Framing of Decisions and the Psychology of Choice," *Science*, 211 (1981), 453–458.

2

Risk Bearing

The Optimum of the Individual

In this chapter, we address a basic problem in decision making under uncertainty: how should an individual select consumption across different states of nature so as to maximize his expected utility? The trick is to view consumption in one state of nature as a separate good from consumption in another state of nature. We then apply an indispensable technique in microeconomics – indifference curve analysis – to the problem to obtain the Fundamental Theorem of Risk Bearing. This theorem is directly applicable only when all state claims are available, i.e., for each state there is a good that pays if and only if that state obtains. However, trading in state claims is usually not a feasible option. Therefore, we generalize to a model with assets, where each asset is viewed as a vector of payoffs, one for each state of nature. This leads to the Risk-Bearing Theorem for Assets Markets. Next, we investigate risky choices made by an individual who cares only about the mean and standard deviation of his consumption. We end the chapter with a model of state-dependent utility.

The individual's best action under uncertainty – the "risk-bearing optimum" – involves choosing among prospects $x \equiv (c; \pi) \equiv (c_1, \ldots, c_S; \pi_1, \ldots, \pi_S)$ where the c_s are the state-distributed consequences and π_s are the state probabilities. In the realm of the economics of *uncertainty* proper, before turning to the economics of *information*, the individual's probability beliefs π remain constant and so $c_1, \ldots, c_S$ are the only decision variables. In general, each c_S represents the multi-good basket that the individual is entitled to consume if state s occurs. For simplicity, however, we will often think in terms of a single generalized consumption good ("corn"). Then c_s would simply be the individual's state-s entitlement to corn if state s occurs, and the risk-bearing problem is how to choose among alternative vectors $(c_1, \ldots, c_s)$ of "corn incomes" distributed over states of the world. Unless otherwise indicated, when the symbol c_s is described as representing

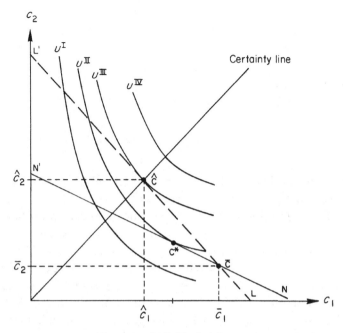

Figure 2.1. Individual optimum.

"income" the implication is that we are using the simplified model of a single consumption good.[1]

2.1 The Risk-Bearing Optimum: Basic Analysis

Suppose there are only two states of the world $s = 1, 2$. The two states might represent war versus peace, or prosperity versus depression. In the state-claim space of Figure 2.1 the axes indicate amounts of the contingent income claims c_1 and c_2.

To represent preferences in this space, we can start with Equation (1.4.1), the expected-utility rule. In a simplified two-state world, this reduces to:

$$U \equiv \pi_1 v(c_1) + \pi_2 v(c_2), \text{ where } \pi_1 + \pi_2 = 1 \qquad (2.1.1)$$

For a given level of U, Equation (2.1.1) describes an entire set of c_1, c_2 combinations that are equally preferred, so this is the equation of an indifference

---

[1] With multiple consumption goods, only if the price ratios among them were *independent of state* could there be an unambiguous interpretation of "income." Consider an individual whose multi-commodity physical endowment is distributed over two states s^o and s^*. When price ratios vary over states it might be that, valued in terms of good g as numeraire, his endowed "income" is higher in state s^o – while in terms of good h as numeraire instead, the value of endowed "income" in state s^* is higher.

curve. As U varies, the whole family of indifference curves implied by the individual's utility function $v(c)$ and probability beliefs π_1, π_2 is traced out – as indicated by the various curves U^I, U^{II}, ..., shown in the diagram.

It is elementary to verify that the absolute indifference-curve slope $M(c_1, c_2)$ in Figure 2.1, the Marginal Rate of Substitution in Consumption, is related to the marginal utilities $v'(c_1)$ and $v'(c_2)$ via:[2]

$$M(c_1, c_2) \equiv -\frac{dc_2}{dc_1}\bigg|_{U=\text{constant}} \equiv \frac{\pi_1 v'(c_1)}{\pi_2 v'(c_2)} \tag{2.1.2}$$

The 45° "certainty line" in the diagram connects all the points such that $c_1 = c_2$. Note that any indifference curve, as it crosses the certainty line, has absolute slope equal simply to π_1/π_2 – the ratio of the state probabilities.

Intuitively, risk aversion in state-claim space corresponds to convex ("bowed toward the origin") indifference curves as shown in Figure 2.1. Risk aversion, we know, leads to diversification. Non-convex indifference curves, when juxtaposed against the individual's opportunity set, would lead to a corner optimum – to choice of an all c_1 or an all c_2 state-claim holding, a non-diversified portfolio. More specifically, a risk-averse utility function $v(c)$, one with positive first derivative $v'(c)$ and negative second derivative $v''(c)$, does indeed imply that indifference curves in state-claim space will be bowed toward the origin. That is, $v'(c) > 0$, $v''(c) < 0$ imply that along any indifference curve, the absolute indifference curve slope diminishes moving to the right: $dM(c_1, c_2)/dc_1$ will be *negative*.[3]

It will also be of interest to translate into state-claim space the proposition that a risk-averse individual would never accept a fair gamble in "corn" income (would always prefer a sure consequence to any probabilistic mixture of consequences having the same mathematical expectation). In Figure 2.1, the dashed line LL′ through the point $\bar{C} \equiv (\bar{c}_1, \bar{c}_2)$ shows all the c_1, c_2

---

[2] Along an iso-utility curve, $0 = dU \equiv \pi_1 v'(c_1) \, dc_1 + \pi_2 v'(c_2) \, dc_2$. Then, $-dc_2/dc_1 = [\pi_1 v'(c_1)]/[\pi_2 v'(c_2)]$.

[3] The sign of $dM(c_1, c_2)/dc_1$ will be the same as that of $d \ln M(c_1, c_2)/dc_1$ where:

$$\frac{d}{dc_1} \ln M(c_1, c_2) = \frac{d}{dc_1} [\ln \pi_1 + \ln v'(c_1) - \ln \pi_2 - \ln v'(c_2)]$$

$$= \frac{v''(c_1)}{v'(c_1)} - \frac{v''(c_2)}{v'(c_2)} \frac{dc_2}{dc_1}$$

$$= \frac{v''(c_1)}{v'(c_1)} + \frac{v''(c_2)}{v'(c_2)} \frac{\pi_1}{\pi_2} \frac{v'(c_1)}{v'(c_2)}$$

Since the first derivatives are both positive, $v''(c_1)$ and $v''(c_2)$ both negative imply a diminishing Marginal Rate of Substitution.

combinations having the same mathematical expectation of income $E[c] = \hat{c}$ as the combination $(\bar{c}_1, \bar{c}_2)$. The equation for LL′ is:

$$\pi_1 c_1 + \pi_2 c_2 = \pi_1 \bar{c}_1 + \pi_2 \bar{c}_2 = \hat{c} \qquad (2.1.3)$$

Along LL′ the most preferred point must be where the line is just tangent to an indifference curve of expected utility. The slope of LL′ is $dc_2/dc_1 = -\pi_1/\pi_2$, which (we know from 2.1.2) is the same as the slope along any indifference curve where it crosses the 45° line. Hence the tangency must be on the 45° line, to wit, at point $\hat{C}$ where $c_1 = c_2 = \hat{c}$. Thus, the certainty of having income $\hat{c}$ is preferred to any other c_1, c_2 combination whose mathematical expectation is $\hat{c}$.

2.1.1 Contingent-Claims Markets

As discussed in Chapter 1, Section 1.1, we are particularly interested in the risk-involved actions that economic agents can take through *market* dealings. Suppose the individual is a price taker in a market where contingent income claims c_1 and c_2 – each of which offers a unit of "corn income" if and only if the corresponding state obtains – can be exchanged in accordance with the price ratio P_1/P_2. This is indicated in Figure 2.1 by the budget line NN′ through the point $\bar{C} \equiv (\bar{c}_1, \bar{c}_2)$, now interpreted as the individual's endowment position. (The overbar will be used henceforth to represent endowed quantities.) The equation for the budget line NN′ is:

$$P_1 c_1 + P_2 c_2 = P_1 \bar{c}_1 + P_2 \bar{c}_2 \qquad (2.1.4)$$

Maximizing expected utility from (2.1.1), subject to the budget constraint (2.1.4), leads (assuming an interior solution) to the indifference-curve tangency[4] condition:

$$\frac{\pi_1 v'(c_1)}{\pi_2 v'(c_2)} = \frac{P_1}{P_2} \qquad (2.1.5)$$

---

[4] The necessary conditions for maximizing expected utility are obtained from the usual Lagrangian expression:

$$L(c_1, c_2, \lambda) = U(c_1, c_2) - \lambda(P_1 c_1 + P_2 c_2 - P_1 \bar{c}_1 - P_2 \bar{c}_2)$$

Using the expected-utility formula (2.1.1), setting the partial derivatives equal to zero implies:

$$\pi_1 v'(c_1) = \lambda P_1 \text{ and } \pi_2 v'(c_2) = \lambda P_2$$

Dividing the first equality by the second, we obtain (2.1.5). Conceivably, however, the tangency conditions cannot be met in the interior (i.e., for non-negative c_1, c_2) in which

Thus, at the individual's risk-bearing optimum, shown as point C^* in Figure 2.1 along indifference curve U^{II}, the quantities of state claims held are such that the ratio of the probability-weighted marginal utilities equals the ratio of the state-claim prices.

Making the obvious generalization to S states, we arrive at an equation that will be used repeatedly throughout the book:

FUNDAMENTAL THEOREM OF RISK BEARING

$$\frac{\pi_1 v'(c_1)}{P_1} = \frac{\pi_2 v'(c_2)}{P_2} = \cdots = \frac{\pi_s v'(c_s)}{P_s} \qquad (2.1.6)$$

In words: Assuming an interior solution, at the individual's risk-bearing optimum the expected (probability-weighted) marginal utility per dollar of income will be equal in each and every state. (The interior-solution condition will henceforth be implicitly assumed, except where the contrary is indicated.)

In terms of the simplified two-state optimum condition (2.1.5), we can reconsider once again the acceptance or rejection of fair gambles. If a gamble is fair, then $\pi_1 \Delta c_1 + \pi_2 \Delta c_2 = 0$ – the mathematical expectation of the contingent net gains must be zero. But in market transactions $P_1 \Delta c_1 + P_2 \Delta c_2 = 0$ – the exchange value of what you give up equals the value of what you receive. So if the price ratio P_1/P_2 equals the probability ratio π_1/π_2, the market is offering an opportunity to transact fair gambles. Geometrically, the line NN′ would coincide with LL′ in Figure 2.1. It follows immediately from Equation (2.1.5) that the tangency optimum would be the certainty combination where $c_1 = c_2 = \hat{c}$.

Thus, confirming our earlier result, *starting from a certainty position* a risk-averse individual would never accept any gamble at fair odds. But, if his initial endowment were not a certainty position (if $\bar{c}_1 \neq \bar{c}_2$), when offered the opportunity to transact at a price ratio corresponding to fair odds he would want to "insure" by moving to a certainty position – as indicated by the solution $\hat{C}$ along the fair market line LL′. Thus, an individual with an uncertain endowment might accept a "gamble" in the form of a risky contract offering contingent income in one state in exchange for income in another. But he would accept only very particular risky contracts, those that offset the riskiness of his endowed gamble. (Notice that mere acceptance

---

case the optimum would be at an intersection of the budget line with one of the axes. If such holds at the c_1-axis, (2.1.5) would be translated to an inequality:

$$\frac{\pi_1 v'(c_1)}{\pi_2 v'(c_2)} > \frac{P_1}{P_2}$$

where $c_2 = 0$, $c_1 = (P_1 \bar{c}_1 + P_2 \bar{c}_2)/P_1$.

of a risky contract therefore does not tell us whether the individual is augmenting or offsetting his endowed risk.) Finally, if the market price ratio did not represent fair odds, as in the case of market line NN' in Figure 2.1, whether or not he starts from a certainty endowment the individual *would* accept some risk; his tangency optimum would lie off the 45° line at a point like C* in the direction of the favorable odds.

2.1.2 Regimes of Asset Markets – Complete and Incomplete

In their risk-bearing decisions, individuals do not typically deal directly with elementary state claims – entitlements to consumption income under different states of the world like war versus peace, prosperity versus depression, etc. Rather, a person is generally endowed with, and may be in a position to trade, *assets* like stocks, bonds, and real estate. An asset is a more or less complicated bundle of underlying pure state claims. A share of stock in some corporation is desired by an individual because it promises to yield him a particular amount of income if state 1 occurs, perhaps a different amount under state 2, and so on through the entire list of states of the world that he perceives. There must then be a relationship between the price of any such marketable asset and the underlying values that individuals place upon the contingent-claim elements of the bundle. This is the relationship we now proceed to analyze.

The income yielded by asset a in state s will be denoted z_{as}. Suppose there are only two states of the world $s = 1, 2$ and just two assets $a = 1, 2$ with prices P_1^A and P_2^A.[5] Then the budget constraint can be written:

$$P_1^A q_1 + P_2^A q_2 = P_1^A \bar{q}_1 + P_2^A \bar{q}_2 \equiv \bar{W} \qquad (2.1.7)$$

Here, q_1 and q_2 represent the numbers of units held of each asset, and as usual the overbar indicates endowed quantities. The individual's endowed wealth, $\bar{W}$, is defined as the market value of his asset endowment.

Someone might possibly hold an asset as a "non-diversified" (single-asset) portfolio, in which case $q_a = \bar{W}/P_a^A$ for the single asset held (while $q_{a^o} = 0$ for any other asset $a^o \neq a$). The vector of state-contingent incomes generated by such a single-asset portfolio would be:

$$\begin{pmatrix} c_1 \\ c_2 \end{pmatrix} = \begin{pmatrix} z_{a1} \\ z_{a2} \end{pmatrix} \bar{W}/P_a^A \qquad (2.1.8)$$

More generally, a person in a two-asset world will hold some fraction K_1 of his wealth in asset 1 and $K_2 \equiv 1 - K_1$ in asset 2, so that

---

[5] *Asset* prices will be written P_1^A, P_2^A, etc. to distinguish them from *state-claim* prices which have numerical subscripts only (P_1, P_2, etc.) Throughout this discussion we continue to assume that individuals are price-takers in all markets.

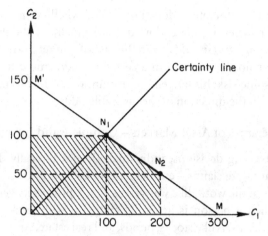

Figure 2.2. Trading in asset markets.

$q_1 = K_1 \, \bar{W}/P_1^A$ and $q_2 = K_2 \, \bar{W}/P_2^A$. Then the contingent incomes from the portfolio will be:

$$\begin{pmatrix} c_1 \\ c_2 \end{pmatrix} \equiv q_1 \begin{pmatrix} z_{11} \\ z_{12} \end{pmatrix} + q_2 \begin{pmatrix} z_{21} \\ z_{22} \end{pmatrix} = K_1 \, (\bar{W}/P_1^A) \begin{pmatrix} z_{11} \\ z_{12} \end{pmatrix} + K_2 \, (\bar{W}/P_2^A) \begin{pmatrix} z_{21} \\ z_{22} \end{pmatrix}$$

(2.1.9)

Equation (2.1.9) expresses the vector of state-contingent portfolio incomes as the share-weighted average of the incomes generated by the two single-asset portfolios.

For concreteness, define a unit of a *certainty asset* (asset 1) so that the contingent returns are unity for each state: $(z_{11}, z_{12}) = (1, 1)$. Let its price be $P_1^A = 1$. Suppose there is also an asset 2 that pays off relatively more heavily in state 1 than in state 2 – specifically, $(z_{21}, z_{22}) = (4, 1)$ – and that its price is $P_2^A = 2$. But imagine that the individual is initially endowed with nothing but 100 units of asset 1 ($\bar{q}_1 = 100$, $\bar{q}_2 = 0$). Then point N_1 in Figure 2.2 pictures the implied endowed contingent incomes $(\bar{c}_1, \bar{c}_2) = (100, 100)$. Since the value of the individual's endowment is $\bar{W} = 100$, he could trade away his entire endowment of asset 1 for 50 units of asset 2 and attain the final consumptions $(c_1, c_2) = (200, 50)$ – point N_2 in the diagram. More generally, from Equation (2.1.9) we see that the final consumption vector (c_1, c_2) will lie along the line joining N_1 and N_2, at distances toward N_1 and N_2 in proportion to the relative wealth shares K_1 and K_2.

If the individual were constrained to hold non-negative amounts of assets, the opportunity boundary would be only the line segment between N_1 and N_2 in the diagram. However, it is entirely permissible to let either q_1 or q_2 go negative. A negative q_1 (which implies, of course, a negative $K_1 \equiv P_1^A q_1 / \bar{W}$) means that the individual holds *liabilities* rather than assets of type 1; he is, in effect, committed to *deliver* the amount $|q_1 z_{11}|$ if state 1 occurs and the amount $|q_1 z_{12}|$ if state 2 occurs. (This is sometimes described as being in a "short" position with regard to asset 1.) We will, however, be imposing a *non-negativity constraint upon the ultimate* c_1, c_2 combinations *arrived* at; the individual cannot end up consuming negative income in either state of the world. He cannot therefore go short on any asset to the extent of violating any of his delivery commitments – in effect, he is not permitted to "go bankrupt" in any state of the world. (And, *a fortiori*, he cannot go short on *all* assets simultaneously!) This means that, while the trading possible along the line MM′ in Figure 2.2 may extend beyond points N_1 and N_2, the attainable combinations remain bounded by the vertical and horizontal axes.

Having described the feasible alternatives, we now consider the individual's actual portfolio-choice decision. Since the consumption vector (c_1, c_2) is generated by his asset holdings as shown in (2.1.9), the individual can be regarded as choosing his portfolio asset shares $(K_1, K_2) \equiv (q_1 P_1^A / \bar{W}, q_2 P_2^A / \bar{W})$ so as to maximize expected utility subject to his asset-holding constraint, that is:

$$\underset{(K_1, K_2)}{\text{Max }} U = \pi_1 v(c_1) + \pi_2 v(c_2) \text{ subject to } K_1 + K_2 = 1$$

From (2.1.9) we know that:

$$\frac{\partial c_s}{\partial K_1} = \frac{\bar{W}}{P_1^A} z_{1s} \quad \text{and} \quad \frac{\partial c_s}{\partial K_2} = \frac{\bar{W}}{P_2^A} z_{2s}$$

Then the endowed wealth cancels out of the first-order condition for an interior optimum, which can be written:[6]

$$\frac{\sum_{s=1}^{2} \pi_s v'(c_s) z_{1s}}{P_1^A} = \frac{\sum_{s=1}^{2} \pi_s v'(c_s) z_{2s}}{P_2^A}$$

[6] The Lagrangian expression is:

$$L(K_1, K_2, \lambda) = \pi_1 v(c_1) + \pi_2 v(c_2) - \lambda(K_1 + K_2 - 1)$$

Setting the partial derivatives equal to zero leads to:

$$\pi_1 v'(c_1) \left(\bar{W}/P_1^A\right) z_{11} + \pi_2 v'(c_2) \left(\bar{W}/P_1^A\right) z_{12} = \lambda$$

$$\pi_1 v'(c_1) \left(\bar{W}/P_2^A\right) z_{21} + \pi_2 v'(c_2) \left(\bar{W}/P_2^A\right) z_{22} = \lambda$$

(Henceforth, the maximization calculus will not be spelled out in detail except where points of special interest or difficulty arise.)

This says that, at his risk-bearing optimum, the individual will have adjusted his holdings of the two assets until their given prices become proportional to the expected marginal utilities he derives from the contingent consumptions they generate. Or, we can say: at the optimum, he will derive the same *expected marginal utility per dollar* held in each asset.

An obvious generalization to any number A of assets and S of states leads to an adaptation of (2.1.6), The Fundamental Theorem of Risk Bearing, for a regime of asset markets:

RISK-BEARING THEOREM FOR ASSET MARKETS

$$\frac{\sum_s \pi_s v'(c_s) z_{1s}}{P_1^A} = \frac{\sum_s \pi_s v'(c_s) z_{2s}}{P_2^A} = \cdots = \frac{\sum_s \pi_s v'(c_s) z_{As}}{P_A^A} \quad (2.1.10)$$

We have now described the individual's optimal risk-bearing decision (i) in a market of elementary state claims and (ii) in a market of more generally defined assets. It is natural to ask if trading in asset markets can replicate the results of a regime in which all state claims are explicitly traded. The answer turns out to depend upon whether the set of tradable assets constitutes a regime of *complete* or *incomplete* markets. Intuitively, markets are complete if a rich enough class of assets is traded so that the equilibrium consumption of the state-claim regime is attained. That is, the consumption vector $c_1, c_2, \ldots, c_S$ that satisfies equilibrium condition (2.1.10) also satisfies the equilibrium condition (2.1.6).

Complete Markets
Returning to the numerical example depicted in Figure 2.2, where A (the number of distinct assets) and S (the number of states) both equal 2, if the individual has endowment N_1 and can trade elementary state claims at prices P_1 and P_2 his budget constraint (line MM' in the diagram) would be:

$$P_1 c_1 + P_2 c_2 = P_1(100) + P_2(100) = \bar{W}$$

A market regime allowing trading in all the elementary state claims is obviously complete. We will call it a regime of Complete Contingent Markets (CCM). The CCM regime provides a benchmark for measuring the completeness of alternative asset-market regimes.

In any asset-trading regime, the prices of assets can be directly computed if the state-claim prices are known. Specifically in our example, since any asset a has state-contingent yields z_{a1}, z_{a2}, the market values of assets 1 and 2 are:

$$P_1^A = z_{11}P_1 + z_{12}P_2 = P_1 + P_2$$

$$P_2^A = z_{21}P_1 + z_{22}P_2 = 4P_1 + P_2$$

In order to establish whether an asset-market regime is or is not complete, we must invert this analysis. That is, for given asset prices P_a^A ($a = 1, \ldots, A$), the question is whether or not it is possible to extract the implicit state-claim prices. In our example, knowing that $(z_{11}, z_{12}) = (1, 1)$ and $(z_{21}, z_{22}) = (4, 1)$, we can rewrite the above equations in matrix form:

$$\begin{bmatrix} P_1^A \\ P_2^A \end{bmatrix} = \begin{bmatrix} 1 & 1 \\ 4 & 1 \end{bmatrix} \begin{bmatrix} P_1 \\ P_2 \end{bmatrix}$$

As the two rows are not proportional, we can invert the matrix and obtain:

$$\begin{bmatrix} P_1 \\ P_2 \end{bmatrix} = \begin{bmatrix} 1 & 1 \\ 4 & 1 \end{bmatrix}^{-1} \begin{bmatrix} P_1^A \\ P_2^A \end{bmatrix} = \begin{bmatrix} -\frac{1}{3} & \frac{1}{3} \\ \frac{4}{3} & -\frac{1}{3} \end{bmatrix} \begin{bmatrix} P_1^A \\ P_2^A \end{bmatrix}$$

So in this case it *is* possible to compute "implicit" state-claim prices from given asset prices. In our example, if (say) $P_1^A = 1$ and $P_2^A = 2$, then $P_1 = 1/3$ and $P_2 = 2/3$. So the implicit budget constraint in state-claim units would be:

$$\frac{1}{3}c_1 + \frac{2}{3}c_2 = \frac{1}{3}(100) + \frac{2}{3}(100) = 100$$

Thus, on the assumption (as already discussed) that traders are allowed to "go short" on either asset so long as they can guarantee delivery, the asset-market equilibrium is the same as would be attained under CCM. We will call a set of asset markets meeting this condition a regime of Complete Asset Markets (CAM).

Generalizing this example, suppose there are S states and A assets, and exactly S of the assets have *linearly independent* yield vectors. That is, suppose it is impossible to express any one of these S yield vectors as a linear sum of the other $S - 1$ asset yields. In economic terms this means that it is not possible to duplicate any of these S assets by buying a combination of the other $S - 1$ assets – i.e., all of the S assets are economically distinct.[7] (Of

---

[7] In our simple example with $A = S = 2$, the two yield vectors (z_{11}, z_{12}) and (z_{21}, z_{22}) were linearly independent since otherwise one vector would have been a scalar multiple of the other. That is, the two rows of the z-matrix were not proportional, which is what permitted inverting the matrix.

course, this case can only come about if $A \geq S$, although A greater than or equal to S does not *guarantee* the existence of S linearly independent assets.) So, a CAM regime exists, in a world of S states, if among the A assets there are S with linearly independent yield vectors.

Summarizing in compact and general form, given a state-claim price vector $(P_1, \ldots, P_s)$ the market value of asset a is:

$$P_a^A = \sum_s z_{as} P_s \qquad (2.1.11)$$

Or, in matrix notation for the entire set of assets:

$$P^A = P[z_{as}] \equiv PZ \qquad (2.1.12)$$

This permits us always to generate asset prices from a known state-claim price vector. But the reverse can be done only under linear independence (so that the matrix $Z \equiv [z_{as}]$ can be inverted). If so, the asset-market regime is complete (CAM holds): for any prices $P_1^A, \ldots, P_A^A$ of the A assets there will be a unique implicit state-claim price vector $(P_1, \ldots, P_s)$. It follows that under CAM, the Fundamental Theorem of Risk Bearing (2.1.6) also holds, in addition to the weaker Risk-Bearing Theorem for Asset Markets (2.1.10).

Incomplete Markets

Consider now a three-state world with asset trading. For this trading regime to be complete, there would have to be three assets with linearly independent return vectors. In Figure 2.3 the points N_1, N_2, N_3 represent an individual's three attainable single-asset portfolios, for assets 1, 2, 3, respectively, while E indicates his endowed mixed portfolio of these three assets. The interior of the shaded triangle $N_1 N_2 N_3$ represents the state-contingent consumption combinations attainable by holding non-negative amounts of all three assets. As in the previous two-asset case, however, there is no reason to exclude "going short" on any asset − so long as the individual ends up with non-negative *consumption* entitlements in all three states, i.e., in the positive orthant. If going short to this extent is allowed, any point in the larger triangle MM′M″ is an income combination attainable by holding some diversified portfolio. The equation of the "budget plane" through MM′M″ is:

$$P_1 c_1 + P_2 c_2 + P_3 c_3 = \bar{W} = P_1^A q_1 + P_2^A q_2 + P_3^A q_3$$

It will be evident that, if the asset-market budget constraint corresponds to the full triangle MM′M″, we have a CAM regime: the choice of an optimal asset portfolio at given asset prices (P_1^A, P_2^A, P_3^A) is equivalent to choosing

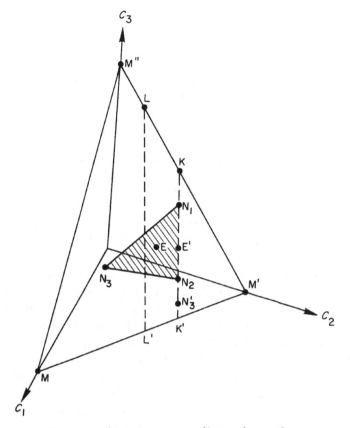

Figure 2.3. Alternative patterns of incomplete markets.

an optimal state-claim consumption vector given some endowment point and a full set of implicit state-claim prices (P_1, P_2, P_3).

Markets in such a three-state world can be *incomplete* in several distinct ways. First, there might simply be fewer than three assets available. In Figure 2.3, if only assets 1 and 2 exist the individual's market opportunities consist only of the state-claim combinations shown by a "degenerate" budget constraint – the market line KK' through points N_1 and N_2. In this case, the endowment E' is a mixed portfolio of the two assets. Second, it might be that there is a third asset, in addition to asset 1 and 2, but this third asset is linearly dependent[8] upon 1 and 2 – indicated geometrically by the collinearity of points N_1, N_2, and N_3'. The line KK' through these three points remains degenerate; once again, not all the c_1, c_2, c_3 state-claim

[8] That is, it is possible to find an α and β such that $(z_{31}, z_{32}, z_{33}) = \alpha(z_{11}, z_{12}, z_{13}) + \beta (z_{21}, z_{22}, z_{23})$.

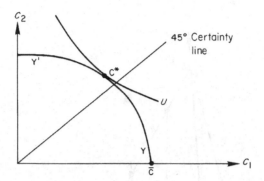

Figure 2.4. Risk-bearing with production.

combinations are attainable by market trading. Third, it might be that the third asset, while present in an individual's endowment and linearly independent of the other two, is *non-tradable*. (An example of such a non-tradable asset might be one's "human capital.") Suppose now that point E in Figure 2.3 represents an endowment containing positive amounts of a non-tradable asset 3 as well as of marketable assets 1 and 2. Here the dotted line LL' is the "degenerate" budget constraint for the individual. Note that LL' is parallel to the KK' line that applied when there was no third asset at all.

In each of these cases there is no longer equivalence between trading in asset markets and trading in CCM. It follows, and this is the crucial point, that, while the Risk-Bearing Theorem for Asset Markets (2.1.10) will always hold, the Fundamental Theorem of Risk Bearing (2.1.6) does not.

When and why it is that *incomplete* trading regimes exist, despite the disadvantages just described, is a question we must leave to Chapter 4.

2.1.3 Productive Opportunities

So far in this section we have considered only the risk-bearing decisions of individuals in markets. But it is also possible to respond to risk by *productive* adjustments.

A Robinson Crusoe isolated from trading can adapt to risk solely by productive transformation. Before he takes productive action, suppose Robinson's corn crop is sure to be good if the weather is moist (state 1) but will fail entirely if the weather is dry (state 2). Thus, Robinson's endowment position $\bar{C}$ is along the c_1-axis of Figure 2.4. However, by installing irrigation systems of greater or lesser extent, Robinson can improve his state-2 crop y_2. On the other hand, the effort required to do so will divert him from ordinary cultivation, and hence reduce his state-1 crop y_1. Then Robinson's feasible

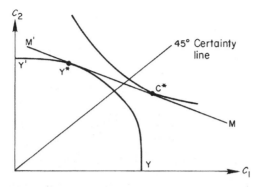

Figure 2.5. Productive and consumptive risk bearing.

state-contingent outputs (y_1, y_2) might lie in the convex set bounded by the axes and the curve YY'. This curve is "bowed away from the origin" reflecting the operation of diminishing returns. Robinson's productive-consumptive risk-bearing optimum will evidently be at point C* (*not* in general on the 45° certainty line) where the production frontier YY' is tangent to his highest attainable indifference curve.

Writing Robinson's productive opportunity constraint as $F(y_1, y_2) = 0$, his optimum (tangency) condition can be expressed as:

$$\frac{\partial F/\partial y_1}{\partial F/\partial y_2} \equiv -\frac{dy_2}{dy_1}\bigg|_F = -\frac{dc_2}{dc_1}\bigg|_U \equiv \frac{\pi_1 v'(c_1)}{\pi_2 v'(c_2)} \qquad (2.1.13)$$

By an obvious modification of our earlier argument, Robinson's optimum will lie on the 45° line only in the exceptional case where his Marginal Rate of Technical Substitution (the absolute slope $- dy_2/dy_1$ along YY') happens to be exactly equal to the probability ratio π_1/π_2 at the point where YY' cuts the certainty line. So, in his productive decisions, Robinson will not in general want to avoid all risk, even though it may be possible for him to do so. Some risks are profitable enough to be worth taking, i.e., they may represent sufficiently favorable productive gambles.

Now consider individuals who can combine both market opportunities and physical productive opportunities. In general, any such individual will have a productive optimum (indicated by Y* in Figure 2.5) distinct from his consumptive optimum (indicated by C*). The availability of markets for trading contingent claims makes it possible to separate *productive* risk bearing from *consumptive* risk bearing. An example in everyday terms: a corporation may engage in risky productive activities, yet the shareholders may be able to largely eliminate personal risks by diversifying their individual portfolios.

Without going through the straightforward derivation, we will state the conditions for the individual's productive and consumptive optimum positions – assuming a regime of CCM with explicit state-claim prices P_1 and P_2 (or an equivalent CAM regime for which the corresponding prices are implicitly calculable):

$$-\frac{dy_2}{dy_1}\bigg|_F \overset{\substack{\text{PRODUCTIVE} \\ \text{OPTIMUM} \\ \text{CONDITION}}}{=} \frac{P_1}{P_2} \overset{\substack{\text{CONSUMPTIVE} \\ \text{OPTIMUM} \\ \text{CONDITION}}}{=} -\frac{dc_2}{dc_1}\bigg|_U \qquad (2.1.14)$$

The price ratio here may be said to *mediate* between the individual's productive optimum and consumptive optimum. Whereas the Crusoe condition (2.1.13) required a direct equality of the YY' slope with an indifference curve at a single common productive-consumptive optimum, the availability of markets makes it possible for a person to separate his Y* and C* positions and thereby attain improved combinations of contingent consumptions.

As no essentially new ideas depend thereon, the generalized productive solutions for any number S of states of the world and the complexities introduced by regimes of incomplete markets will not be detailed here.

Exercises and Excursions 2.1

1 *Linear Independence*
   (A) With state yields expressed in the form (z_{a1}, z_{a2}, z_{a3}), the rows below indicate four different three-asset combinations, labeled (i) through (iv). Verify that only asset combinations (i) and (ii) are linearly independent.

	$a = 1$	$a = 2$	$a = 3$
(i)	(1,0,0)	(0,1,0)	(0,0,1)
(ii)	(1,1,1)	(1,4,0)	(0,7,1)
(iii)	(0,2,3)	(1,0,1)	(0,4,6)
(iv)	(1,3,2)	(4,0,5)	(2,2,3)

   (B) For each of the combinations above, *if* it is possible to have $P_1^A = P_2^A = P_3^A = 1$ what can you say about the implied state-claim prices P_1, P_2, P_3? For given asset endowment holdings $\bar{q}_1 = \bar{q}_2 = \bar{q}_3 = 1$ solve for and picture the market plane MM'M'' in state-claim space, wherever it is possible to do so. (Where it is not possible to do so, picture the relevant trading opportunity constraint.)

(C) For cases (i) and (ii) only of (A) above, assume instead that the endowment is given in state-claim units as $(\bar{c}_1, \bar{c}_2, \bar{c}_3) = (1, 1, 1)$, and that $P_2^A = P_3^A = 1$ while no trading is possible in asset 1. Picture the trading opportunity constraint in state-claim space.

2 Non-negativity

(A) For each of the combinations in 1(A) above, would the asset-holding portfolio $q_1 = -1, q_2 = q_3 = 1$ violate the non-negativity constraint on state incomes?

(B) Suppose case (i) above were modified by replacing $a = 1$ with a new $a = 1'$ whose returns are $(-1, 2, 3)$. Would the combination $q_1 = q_2 = q_3 = 1$ be feasible? What if this new asset were instead to replace the first asset in case (ii) above?

3 Risk-Bearing Optimum

(A) In cases (i) and (ii) under 1(A), if explicit trading in state claims is ruled out, find the individual's risk-bearing optimum expressed as (q_1^*, q_2^*, q_3^*) in asset units and as (c_1^*, c_2^*, c_3^*) in state-claim units – if: $\pi_1 = \pi_2 = \pi_3 = 1/3$, $P_1^A = P_2^A = P_3^A = 1$, $\bar{q}_1 = \bar{q}_2 = \bar{q}_3 = 1$, and $v(c) = \ln c$.

(B) What can you say about cases (iii) and (iv)?

4 Consumer Choice

An individual with utility function $v(c) = \ln c$ must choose a state-contingent consumption bundle $(c_1, \ldots, c_S)$. The price of a state-s claim is P_s and the consumer's initial endowment has a value of $\bar{W}$.

(A) Solve for the individual's optimum in each state.

(B) Hence show that for any pair of states s and s':

$$\frac{c_s}{c_{s'}} = \frac{\pi_s}{\pi_{s'}} \frac{P_{s'}}{P_s}$$

(C) What condition defines the state in which consumption is greatest? Least?

(D) Is the rule derived in (C) true for any concave utility function $v(c)$?

5 Portfolio Choice

Asset 1 and asset 2 both cost \$150. Yields on asset 1 in states 1 and 2 are $(z_{11}, z_{12}) = (100, 200)$ and on asset 2 are $(z_{21}, z_{22}) = (200, 100)$. An individual with an initial wealth of \$150 has a utility function:

$$v(c) = -e^{-c}$$

(A) Show that the state-contingent budget constraint can be expressed as:

$$c_1 + c_2 = 300$$

(B) If the individual believes that state 1 will occur with probability π, show that his optimal consumption in state 1 is:

$$c_1^* = 150 + \frac{1}{2} \ln(\pi/(1 - \pi))$$

(C) If q_1 is the number of units of asset 1 purchased show that:

$$c_1^* = 200 - 100 q_1^*$$

and hence obtain an expression for q_1^* in terms of π, the probability of state 1.

(D) What values do c_1^* and q_1^* approach as the probability of state 1 becomes very small?

2.2 Choosing Combinations of Mean and Standard Deviation of Income

2.2.1 μ, σ, Preferences

We have described decision making under uncertainty as choice among actions or prospects $x = (c_1, \ldots, c_S; \pi_1, \ldots, \pi_S)$ – probability distributions that associate an amount of contingent consumption in each state of the world with the degree of belief attaching to that state. There is another approach to the risk-bearing decision that has proved to be very useful in modern finance theory and its applications. This alternative approach postulates that, for any individual, the probability distribution associated with any prospect is effectively represented by just two summary statistical measures: the *mean* and the *standard deviation* of income. Specifically, the

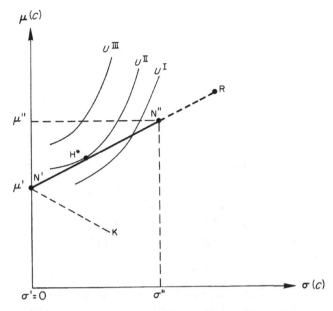

Figure 2.6. Portfolio choice with one riskless and one risky asset.

individual is supposed always to prefer higher average income (measured by the expectation or mean $\mu(c)$ of the probability distribution achieved by holding any particular portfolio of assets) and lower variability of income (measured by the standard deviation $\sigma(c)$).[9] His preferences can therefore be represented by the indifference curves pictured on $\mu(c)$ and $\sigma(c)$ axes as in Figure 2.6.

The approach in terms of preference for high $\mu(c)$ and low $\sigma(c)$ is broadly consistent with the previous analysis. In maximizing expected utility $E[v(c)]$ under uncertainty, other things equal, a higher average level of income is surely to be preferred. And, given risk aversion, the theorem that fair gambles would not be accepted implies that distributions with low $\sigma(c)$ tend to be more desirable. Nevertheless, in moving from a probability distribution that was fully defined in terms of consequences in each and every state of the world to a mere statistical summary of that distribution – one that makes use only of the two parameters $\mu(c)$ and $\sigma(c)$ – some information has been lost. The question addressed here is: when, if ever, is such a reduction valid,

---

[9] Some analysts prefer to think in terms of the variance of income $\sigma^2(c)$. But for purposes of economic interpretation the standard deviation is more convenient, since $\sigma(c)$ has the same dimensionality as $\mu(c)$ and c itself.

exactly or at least approximately? That is, when can we justifiably convert $U = E[v(c)]$ into a function only of $\mu(c)$ and $\sigma(c)$?

To indicate the nature of the approximation involved, $v(c)$ can be expanded in a Taylor's series about its expected value $E[\tilde{c}] = \mu$:[10]

$$v(\tilde{c}) = v(\mu) + \frac{v'(\mu)}{1!}(\tilde{c} - \mu) + \frac{v''(\mu)}{2!}(\tilde{c} - \mu)^2 + \frac{v'''(\mu)}{3!}(\tilde{c} - \mu)^3 + \cdots$$

Taking expectations, remembering that $U = E[v(\tilde{c})]$ while noticing that the expectation of $(\tilde{c} - \mu)$ is zero and that the expectation of $(\tilde{c} - \mu)^2$ is the variance $\sigma^2(\tilde{c})$, we have:

$$U = v(\mu) + \frac{v''(\mu)}{2!}\sigma^2 + \frac{v'''(\mu)}{3!}E[(c - \mu)^3] + \cdots \qquad (2.2.1)$$

The omitted terms suggested by the dots are functions of the fourth or higher powers of $(\tilde{c} - \mu)$ – higher moments about the mean, in statistical terminology.

Possible justifications for treating U as a function only of the mean and standard deviation of income may be found (i) in the properties we are willing to assume for the utility function $v(c)$ or (ii) in the properties of the probability distribution of $\tilde{c}$.

(i) First of all, suppose that the $v(c)$ function is quadratic, so that it can be written (with K_0, K_1, and K_2 as constants):

$$v(c) = K_0 + K_1 c - \frac{1}{2}K_2 c^2 \qquad (2.2.2)$$

where $K_1, K_2 > 0$. Then the third derivative $v'''(c)$ is always zero, as are all higher derivatives. So (2.2.1) can be expressed more specifically as:

$$U = K_0 + K_1\mu - \frac{1}{2}K_2(\mu^2 + \sigma^2)$$

With U as parameter, this equation represents a family of indifference curves on μ, σ, axes in Figure 2.6. By completing the square it may be verified that the curves constitute a set of concentric circles, the center being $\mu = K_1/K_2$, $\sigma = 0$.

However, the utility function $v(c)$ given by (2.2.2) has an economically unacceptable implication – that the marginal utility of income, $v'(c) = K_1 - K_2 c$, eventually becomes negative. A quadratic $v(c)$ function thus leads to a highly special indifference-curve map, with acceptable properties only over a limited range.

---

[10] A tilde overlying any symbol indicates a random variable. We will use this notation only when it is desired to emphasize that feature.

(ii) Turning now to possible justifications that run in terms of probability distributions for $\tilde{c}$, the Central Limit Theorem of probability theory offers a lead. While a full discussion would be out of place here, the Central Limit Theorem essentially says that the distribution of the sum of any large number N of random variables approaches the *normal distribution* as N increases – provided only that the variables are not too correlated. The point is that the overall or portfolio income $\tilde{c}$ yielded by an individual's holdings of assets can be regarded as the sum of underlying random variables, each summand representing the income generated by one of the assets entering into his portfolio. The normal distribution is fully specified by just two parameters, its mean and standard deviation. Then, in Equation (2.2.1), while the terms involving higher moments do not all disappear,[11] the higher moments remaining are functions of the mean and standard deviation.[12] It therefore follows that indifference curves for alternative normal distributions of consumption income $\tilde{c}$ can be drawn on $\mu(c)$, $\sigma(c)$ axes.[13]

The tendency toward normality under the Central Limit Theorem is the stronger, roughly speaking, the closer to normal are the underlying random variables, the more equal are their weights in the summation, and the less correlated they are with one another. Looking at portfolio income as the summation variable, income yields of the assets that comprise portfolios will rarely if ever have normal distributions themselves. In particular, the normal distribution extends out to negative infinity, whereas any "limited liability" asset cannot generate unlimited negative income. (And even without limited liability, personal bankruptcy establishes a lower limit on how large a negative yield the individual need consider.) Furthermore, asset weights in portfolios tend to be highly unequal: a person will likely have more than half his income associated with his wage earnings – the income generated by his single "human capital" asset. And, finally, there typically is

---

[11] Since the normal distribution is symmetrical about its mean, all the higher *odd* moments are zero, but the even moments do not disappear.

[12] There are other families of statistical distributions, besides the normal, that are fully specified by the mean and standard deviation. However, as we have seen, the Central Limit Theorem leads specifically to the normal as the approximating distribution of portfolio income.

[13] We have not, however, justified the standard shape of the preference map pictured in Figure 2.9. A proof that normally distributed returns imply positive indifference-curve slope and curvature, as shown in the diagram, is provided in Copeland, Weston, and Shastri (2004).

considerable correlation among returns on the different assets making up any portfolio. Portfolios for which the Central Limit Theorem justifies use of the normal distribution as approximation are called "well-diversified"; unfortunately, we have no handy rule for deciding when a portfolio may be considered well-diversified. For all the reasons given above, use of the normal distribution as approximation remains subject to considerable questions.

It is of interest to consider the effect upon utility of the third moment $E[(\tilde{c} - \mu)^3] -$ entering into the leading term dropped from (2.2.1) if the normal approximation is adopted. The third moment is a measure of *skewness*: skewness is zero if the two tails of a distribution are symmetrical, positive if the probability mass humps toward the left (so that the right tail is long and thin), and negative in the opposite case. To see the effect of skewness, consider an investor choosing between two gambles with the same means and standard deviations. Specifically, suppose gamble J offers 0.999 probability of losing \$1 and 0.001 probability of gaining \$999, while gamble K offers 0.999 probability of gaining \$1 and 0.001 probability of losing \$999. J and K have the same mean (zero) and the same standard deviation, but J is positively skewed while K is negatively skewed. Almost all commercial lotteries and games of chance are of form J, thus suggesting that individuals tend to prefer positive skewness. While the primary purpose of diversification is to reduce the standard deviation of income, diversification also tends to eliminate skewness – since the normal distribution that is approached has zero skewness. We would expect to see, therefore, lesser desire to diversify where skewness of the portfolio held is positive, greater desire to diversify where skewness is negative. But the main point is that the survival of preference for positive skewness suggests that individual real-world portfolios are typically not so well-diversified.

The upshot, then, is that the attempt to reduce preferences for income prospects to preferences in terms of $\mu(c)$ and $\sigma(c)$ falls short of being fully satisfying. But the approach remains an eminently manageable approximation, expressed as it is in terms of potentially measurable characteristics of individual portfolios and (as we shall see shortly) of the assets that comprise portfolios. The ultimate test of any such approximation is, of course, its value as a guide to understanding and prediction.

2.2.2 Opportunity Set and Risk-Bearing Optimum

In examining the individual's opportunities for achieving combinations of mean and standard deviation of portfolio income – $\mu(c)$ and $\sigma(c)$ – in his risk-bearing decisions, we need to show how these statistical properties of consumption income emerge from the yields generated by the separate assets held.

For any asset a, let μ_a represent the mean of the income yield $\tilde{z}_a$ per unit of a held. Let σ_a represent the standard deviation of $\tilde{z}_a$, and σ_{ab} the covariance of $\tilde{z}_a$ and $\tilde{z}_b$. Then, following the usual statistical definitions:

$$\mu_a \equiv E(\tilde{z}_a)$$
$$\sigma_a \equiv [E(\tilde{z}_a - \mu_a)^2]^{\frac{1}{2}}$$
$$\sigma_{ab} \equiv E[(\tilde{z}_a - \mu_a)(\tilde{z}_b - \mu_b)]$$

And, of course, $\sigma_a \equiv (\sigma_{aa})^{\frac{1}{2}}$.

If the individual holds a portfolio consisting of q_a units each of assets $a = 1, \ldots, A$ his portfolio income statistics are related to the asset return parameters above via:

$$\mu(c) \equiv \mu \equiv \sum_a q_a \mu_a$$

$$\sigma(c) \equiv \sigma \equiv \left(\sum_a \sum_b q_a \sigma_{ab} q_b \right)^{\frac{1}{2}} \equiv \left(\sum_a \sum_b \sigma_a q_a \rho_{ab} q_b \sigma_b \right)^{\frac{1}{2}}$$

Here ρ_{ab} is the simple correlation coefficient between the distributions of $\tilde{z}_a$ and $\tilde{z}_b$, using the identity $\sigma_{ab} \equiv \sigma_a \rho_{ab} \sigma_b$ that relates covariance and the correlation coefficient.

The individual's budget constraint can be written in terms of his asset holdings (compare Equation (2.1.7)) as:

$$\sum_a P_a^A q_a = \sum_a P_a^A \bar{q}_a \equiv \bar{W}$$

Drawn on $\mu(c), \sigma(c)$ axes, this budget constraint bounds an opportunity set of feasible combinations of mean and standard deviation of portfolio income. We now need to determine the characteristic shape of this opportunity set. (But notice that, since the individual desires high μ and low σ, he will be interested only in the northwest boundary.)

To start with the simplest case, suppose there are just two assets, and that asset 1 is riskless ($\sigma_1 = 0$) while asset 2 is risky ($\sigma_2 > 0$). For this to be at all an interesting situation, it must, of course, also be true that $\mu_2/P_2^A > \mu_1/P_1^A$ — i.e., the risky asset has a higher mean yield per dollar. The portfolio income yield is a random variable given by:

$$\tilde{c} \equiv q_1 z_1 + q_2 \tilde{z}_2 \qquad (2.2.3)$$

In this simplest case, with q_2 units of asset 2 purchased at a cost of $P_2^A q_2$, the individual has $\bar{W} - P_2^A q_2$ dollars to invest in the riskless asset 1. For any security a, we can define its rate of return R_a in:

$$\frac{z_a}{P_a^A} \equiv 1 + R_a$$

Then $R_1 \equiv z_1/P_1^A - 1$ is the rate of return on the riskless asset.[14] Expression (2.2.3) can then be rewritten as:

$$\tilde{c} = \left(\bar{W} - P_2^A q_2\right)(1 + R_1) + q_2 \tilde{z}_2$$

And the parameters of the income distribution become:

$$\mu(c) = \bar{W}(1 + R_1) + \left[\mu_2 - (1 + R_1)P_2^A\right]q_2$$
$$\sigma(c) = \sigma_2 q_2$$

It then follows that the budget constraint on μ, σ, axes is a straight line, shown as N'N'' in Figure 2.6. (The opportunity set consists of the line and the area lying below it in the diagram.) Point N' is the μ, σ, combination μ', σ' attainable by holding a single-asset portfolio consisting of the riskless asset (asset 1) exclusively. For this portfolio, $\mu'(\tilde{c}) = (\bar{W}/P_1^A)z_1 = \bar{W}(1 + R_1)$ while $\sigma'(\tilde{c}) = 0$. Point N'' is the μ, σ, combination μ'', σ'', generated by the single-asset portfolio consisting of the risky asset (asset 2). Here $\mu''(\tilde{c}) = (\bar{W}/P_2^A)\mu_2$ while $\sigma''(\tilde{c}) = (\bar{W}/P_2^A)\sigma_2$.

What about portfolios containing mixtures of the two assets? If the fractional shares of wealth devoted to the riskless and the risky assets are $\alpha = q_1 P_1^A/\bar{W}$ and $\kappa = q_2 P_2^A/\bar{W}$, respectively, where $\alpha + \kappa = 1$, the portfolio statistics μ and σ can each be written in two useful ways:

$$\mu = \alpha\mu' + \kappa\mu'' = \bar{W}(1 + R_1) + \left[\mu_2 - (1 + R_1)P_2^A\right]q_2$$
$$\sigma = \kappa\sigma'' = \sigma_2 q_2$$

---

[14] This terminology would be appropriate if, as is usually assumed in the finance literature, the assets are purchased (the prices P_a^A are paid out) one time period earlier than the date of the income yields $\tilde{z}_a$. Strictly speaking, such a convention implies an *intertemporal* choice situation, where earlier consumption should be balanced against later consumption, over and above the atemporal risk-bearing choices we have dealt with so far. However, we will follow the finance tradition in using "rate of interest" terminology without necessarily addressing the problem of intertemporal choice.

It follows that the budget constraint can also be written in two ways:

$$\mu = \frac{\mu'' - \mu'}{\sigma''}\sigma + \mu'$$

$$\mu = \bar{W}(1 + R_1) + \left[\mu_2 - (1 + R_1)P_2^A\right]\sigma/\sigma_2$$

It is evident that all the μ, σ combinations satisfying these conditions (meeting the budget constraint) fall along the straight line N'N'' in the diagram. The constant slope $d\mu/d\sigma$ of this budget constraint line is known as the *price of risk reduction*, also known as the *Sharpe ratio*, which we will symbolize as Θ:

THE PRICE OF RISK REDUCTION OR THE SHARPE RATIO

$$\Theta \equiv \frac{d\mu}{d\sigma} = \frac{\mu'' - \mu'}{\sigma''} = \frac{\mu_2 - (1 + R_1)P_2^A}{\sigma_2} \quad (2.2.4)$$

Note that the steepness of the opportunity line reflects only the market or "objective" data.[15]

To find the individual optimum, the budget constraint must be juxtaposed against the "subjective" data of the individual's preference function. This solution is, of course, a familiar type of tangency: in Figure 2.6, the point H* is the individual's risk-bearing optimum on μ, σ axes.

Could a portfolio be represented by a μ, σ combination along the (dashed) extension of N'N'' lying to the northeast of point N'', which would correspond to holding *negative amounts* of the riskless security? This is sometimes referred to as "selling short" the riskless security, which means incurring a liability requiring *delivery* of the promised amount of income certain. Incurring such a debt can also be thought of as "issuing" units of the riskless security. As explained earlier, doing so would be perfectly reasonable provided that the issuer can really satisfy such an obligation with certainty. Clearly, the opportunity line N'N'' cannot be extended to the northeast without limit: someone with risky assets and riskless liabilities faces some likelihood of bankruptcy, owing to states of the world in which

---

[15] The parameters involved in the expression for $d\mu/d\sigma$ are "objective" in that they reflect the individual's market opportunities independent of what his personal *preferences* might be. However, a "subjective" element may still enter if *beliefs* about market parameters vary from person to person. While asset prices P_a^A can usually be taken as interpersonally agreed data, there might well be disagreement about some or all of the security yield parameters μ_a, σ_a. If there were such disagreement, the implicit "price of risk reduction" would vary from person to person.

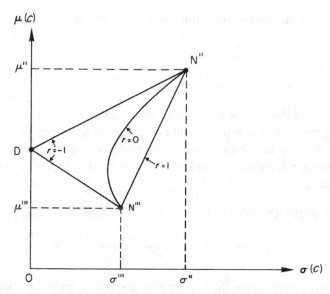

Figure 2.7. Portfolio choice with two risky assets.

the risky earnings fail to cover the fixed obligation of repaying the debt.[16] In the literature of finance theory it is usually assumed that tangencies in the "short sales" region are possible, at least within the range of practical interest. In our diagram, the termination of the dashed extension of N′N″ at point R indicates the limit to which riskless debt can be issued by the investor in order to achieve a larger holding of risky assets.

What about "selling short" the *risky* security instead – i.e., incurring an obligation to meet varying payments over states of the world, while enlarging one's holding of riskless claims? By an analogous argument, this may also be feasible up to a point. It is not difficult to show that such portfolios lead to μ, σ combinations along a line like N′K in Figure 2.6, which clearly cannot be a portion of the efficient opportunity boundary.

Figure 2.7 illustrates the efficient boundary for proper portfolio combinations of two *risky* securities. (We will not consider "short selling" in this discussion.) If asset 2, let us say, has a higher mean return per dollar than asset 3 ($\mu_2/P_2^A > \mu_3/P_3^A$), then for the situation to be interesting once again it must also be that asset 2 involves a greater risk per dollar as well ($\sigma_2/P_2^A > \sigma_3/P_3^A$) In the diagram, points N″ and N‴ represent the

---

[16] If risky portfolio income were normally distributed, there would always be some non-zero probability of negative returns exceeding *any* preassigned limit. No holder of such a risky distribution could ever issue even the tiniest riskless security obligation, since he could not guarantee to repay a debt with certainty.

single-asset portfolios for securities 2 and 3, respectively, where $\mu'' > \mu'''$ and $\sigma'' > \sigma'''$.

The diagram illustrates how *diversification*, holding a mixture of assets, tends to reduce portfolio standard deviation σ. The power of diversification is a function of the size and sign of the correlation coefficient $\rho_{23} \equiv \sigma_{23}/\sigma_2\sigma_3$ (henceforth, ρ for short) between the asset return distributions $\tilde{z}_2$ and $\tilde{z}_3$.

Consider first the limiting case of *perfect positive correlation* ($\rho = 1$). Here the μ, σ combinations associated with mixtures of assets 2 and 3 would lie along the straight line N′N″ in Figure 2.7, at distances proportionate to the relative budget shares.[17] If instead the yields on the two assets were *uncorrelated* ($\rho = 0$), the attainable μ, σ combinations would fall on a boundary represented by the middle curve connecting N″ and N‴ in the diagram. It is important to notice that in the region of point N‴ the slope $d\mu/d\sigma$ of this curve becomes actually negative, the implication being that the efficient opportunity boundary no longer includes point N‴ itself.[18] Thus, for any portfolio of two uncorrelated risky assets, the single-asset portfolio consisting of the lower-μ, lower-σ (per dollar of cost) security is driven out of the efficient set. More generally, the slope $d\mu/d\sigma$ will be negative if $\sigma''' > \rho\sigma''$.[19] So, for any number of risky assets, if all yields are uncorrelated then only one single-asset portfolio would be located on the efficient boundary, to wit, the portfolio consisting of that asset a^* that offers highest yield per dollar ($\mu_{a^*}/P_{a^*}^A > \mu_a/P_a^A$ for any $a \neq a^*$). But, if asset yields are correlated, any asset with sufficiently high positive correlation with a^* might also be an efficient single-asset portfolio.

Finally, in the limiting case of *perfect negative correlation* ($\rho = -1$), the σ-reducing effect of diversification is so great that the curve N″N‴ breaks

---

[17] If the budget shares are $\kappa = q_2 P_2^A/\bar{W}$ and $1 - \kappa = q_3 P_3^A/\bar{W}$ then $\mu = \kappa\mu'' + (1 - \kappa)\mu'''$, where $\mu'' = \bar{W}\mu_2/P_2^A$ and $\mu''' = \bar{W}\mu_3/P_3^A$ are the mean yields on the respective single-asset portfolios. And σ is:

$$\sigma = [(\kappa\sigma'')^2 + 2\rho\kappa(1 - \kappa)\sigma''\sigma''' + ((1 - \kappa)\sigma''')^2]^{\frac{1}{2}}$$

If $\rho = 1$, then $\sigma = \kappa\sigma'' + (1 - \kappa)\sigma'''$. So μ and σ both increase linearly with K, proving the assertion in the text.

[18] As κ increases, the slope along any of the curves connecting N″ and N‴ can be written:

$$\frac{d\mu}{d\sigma} = \frac{d\mu/d\kappa}{d\sigma/d\kappa} = \frac{\mu'' - \mu'''}{[\kappa(\sigma'')^2 + (1 - 2\kappa)\sigma''\rho\sigma''' - (1 - \kappa)(\sigma''')^2]/\sigma}$$

If $p \leq 0$, at point N‴ where $\kappa = 0$ the denominator will be negative, hence $d\mu/d\sigma$ will be negative. So there will exist a portfolio with $\kappa > 0$ having lower σ and higher μ than the asset-3 single-asset portfolio.

[19] From the preceding footnote, the sign of $d\mu/d\sigma$ when $\kappa = 0$ will be the same as the sign of $\rho\sigma''\sigma''' - (\sigma''')^2$ or $\rho\sigma'' - \sigma'''$.

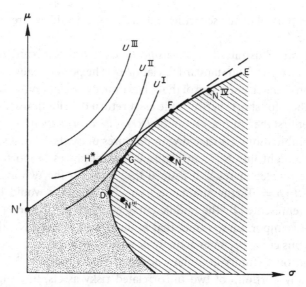

Figure 2.8. Mutual-Fund Theorem.

into two lines meeting at the vertical axis (at point D). Thus, with $\rho = -1$, it is possible to achieve a riskless combination of two risky assets.[20] Of course, here again point N''' can no longer be in the efficient set.

Generalizing the previous diagram to any number of assets, Figure 2.8 is intended to suggest the nature of the opportunity set and efficient (northwest) boundary. If there are only risky securities available, the opportunity set will be the shaded area whose northwest (efficient) boundary is the curve DE. Here points N'' and N''' represent single-asset portfolios that are not efficient, whereas point N^{IV} represents an efficient single-asset portfolio. Owing to the power of diversification, almost all of the boundary DE would likely represent multiasset portfolio mixtures.

The introduction of a *riskless* asset, whose single-asset portfolio is represented by point N', enlarges the opportunity set by the dotted area in the diagram. The efficient boundary now becomes the line from N' drawn tangent to the DE curve (at point F). In general, as just argued, F would represent a particular mixed portfolio of assets.

In the absence of the riskless asset, the individual's risk-bearing optimum (indifference-curve tangency) would be at point G along the curve DE. But for the opportunity set enlarged by the presence of the riskless asset, the

[20] If $\rho = -1$, then $\sigma = \kappa\sigma'' - (1-\kappa)\sigma'''$. Setting $\kappa = \sigma''/(\sigma'' + \sigma''')$, we have $\sigma = 0$.

optimum is at point H* along the line N'F. As discussed earlier, we also admit the possibility that H* might fall in the dashed extension to the northeast of F along this line, representing an individual who issues riskless obligations in order to hold more than 100% of his endowed wealth in the form of the risky combination F.

The Mutual-Fund Theorem

An important result follows from our previous discussion:

If individuals' preferences are summarized by desire for large μ and small σ, and if there exists a single riskless asset and a number of risky assets, in equilibrium the asset prices will be such that everyone will wish to purchase the *risky* assets in the same proportions.

Thus, if one individual holds risky assets 2 and 3 in the quantities $q_2 = 10$ and $q_3 = 9$, someone who is richer (or less risk averse) might hold larger amounts of each risky asset – but still in the ratio 10:9! This remarkable "Mutual-Fund Theorem" underlies all the main properties of the Capital Asset Pricing Model (CAPM), which constitutes the centerpiece of modern finance theory. (CAPM will be discussed further in Chapter 4.)

Justification of the theorem requires no complicated analytical apparatus. All we need do is to re-interpret the opportunity set of Figure 2.8 in per-dollar-of-wealth terms. Thus, for any individual the vertical axis would now be scaled in units of $\mu/\bar{W}$ and the horizontal axis in units of $\sigma/\bar{W}$ Since both axes are being divided by the same constant, the opportunity set would change only by a scale factor. For example, the single-asset portfolio corresponding to any asset a that formerly was represented by the vector (μ^a, σ^a), where $\mu^a = (\bar{W}/P_a^A)\mu_a$ and $\sigma^a = (\bar{W}/P_a^A)\sigma_a$, would now have the coordinates $\mu^a/\bar{W} = \mu_a/P_a^A$ and $\sigma^a/\bar{W} = \sigma_a/P_a^A$. And, in particular, points N' and F would similarly maintain their positions, so that the efficient boundary N'F would have the same slope as before.

The significance of this conversion to per-dollar dimensions is that, in these per-dollar units, *every individual in the economy, regardless of wealth, faces exactly the same opportunities!* If asset a offers a mean yield per dollar μ_a/P_a^A to one individual, it offers the same per-dollar mean yield to everyone. And similarly for the standard deviation per dollar σ_a/P_a^A of asset a, and for all combinations of assets as well. Thus, every individual will hold, in whatever fraction of his wealth is devoted to risky securities, the same proportionate mixture of assets represented by point F in the diagram. So, we can say, a "mutual fund" of risky securities set up to meet the needs of any single investor will meet the needs of all.[21] What still does vary among individuals is the *fraction of wealth held in riskless versus risky form*, a decision that will depend upon individuals' varying personal preferences as to risk bearing (the shapes of their indifference curves in the original diagram of Figure 2.8).

In the economy as a whole, there is exactly one unit of this mutual fund F, corresponding to the economy-wide amounts $q_2^F, \ldots, q_A^F$ of the risky assets $a = 2, \ldots, A$. (So the typical individual will be holding a fractional unit of F.) Then the price P_F^A of a unit of the fund is:

$$P_F^A = \sum_{a=2}^{A} q_a^F P_a^A$$

Writing the mean return and standard deviation of return for a unit of portfolio F as μ_F and σ_F, we can obtain an expression for $\Theta \equiv d\mu/d\sigma$ – the price of risk reduction – in terms of the slope of the line N'F in Figure 2.8. For any individual, point N' (the riskless single-asset portfolio) has μ-coordinate $\mu' = (\bar{W}/P_1^A)\mu_1 = \bar{W}(1 + R_1)$ and μ-coordinate $\sigma' = 0$. Point F (the portfolio held entirely in the mutual fund) has μ-coordinate $\mu^F = (\bar{W}/P_F^A)\mu_F$ and σ-coordinate $\sigma^F = (\bar{W}/P_F^A)\sigma_F$. So the steepness of the line is:

$$\frac{d\mu}{d\sigma} = \frac{\mu^F - \mu'}{\sigma^F - \sigma'} = \frac{(\bar{W}/P_F^A)\,\mu_F - \bar{W}(1 + R_1)}{(\bar{W}/P_F^A)\,\sigma_F} = \frac{\mu_F/P_F^A - (1 + R_1)}{\sigma_F/P_F^A}$$

Note that, consistent with our previous discussion, the individual wealth parameter $\bar{W}$ has cancelled out. Thus, a corollary of the Mutual-Fund Theorem is that *the price of risk reduction is the same for every individual*.

Exercises and Excursions 2.2

1 Ranking of Alternative Wealth Prospects
An individual with utility function $v(c) = c^{0.5}$ has an initial wealth of zero. He must choose one of two jobs. In the first there is an equal probability of earning 1 or 3. In the second there is a probability of 1/9 that he will earn zero, a probability of 7/9 that he will earn 2, and a probability of 1/9 that he will earn 4.

---

[21] If, however, individuals differed in their personal estimates of the asset characteristics μ_a and σ_a, their perceived opportunity sets would not be identical in per-dollar units and the Mutual-Fund Theorem would not be valid.

(A) Show that both jobs have the same mean income μ, that the standard deviation of income σ is lower in the second job, and that despite this the individual will choose the first job.

(B) Can you explain this result in terms of preferences for skewness? If not, what is the explanation?

2 Constant Absolute Risk Aversion and Normally Distributed Asset Returns

(A) Show that:

$$Ac + \frac{1}{2}\left(\frac{c - \mu}{\sigma}\right)^2 = \frac{1}{2}\left(\frac{c - (\mu - A\sigma^2)}{\sigma}\right)^2 + A\left(\mu - \frac{1}{2}A\sigma^2\right)$$

where $A \equiv -v''(c)/v'(c)$ is known as the measure of "absolute risk aversion." Hence, or otherwise, show that if c is distributed normally with mean μ and variance σ^2 and if $v(c) = -e^{-Ac}$ then:

$$E[v(c)] = -\int_{-\infty}^{\infty} e^{-Ac}\frac{1}{(2\pi)^{\frac{1}{2}}}\exp\left\{-\frac{1}{2}\left(\frac{c - \mu}{\sigma}\right)^2\right\}dc = -e^{-A(\mu - \frac{1}{2}A\sigma^2)}$$

(B) Under the above assumption, it follows that preference can be represented by the indirect utility function:

$$U(\mu, \sigma) = \mu - \frac{1}{2}A\sigma^2$$

Suppose an individual with such preferences must choose between a riskless asset and a normally distributed risky asset. Show that the amount of the risky asset purchased is independent of initial wealth and decreasing in the degree of absolute risk aversion A. What happens if the indicated expenditure on the risky asset exceeds the individual's endowed wealth $\bar{W}$?

3 The μ, σ Opportunity Locus

An individual spends a fraction κ of his wealth $\bar{W}$ on asset a and the remainder on asset b. Each asset has a price of unity and the yields $(\tilde{z}_a, \tilde{z}_b)$ have means μ_a and μ_b and covariance matrix $[\sigma_{ab}]$.

(A) Obtain expressions for the mean μ and standard deviation σ of the portfolio as functions of κ.

(B) Hence show that the standard deviation can be expressed as:

$$\sigma = \{[(\mu - \bar{W}\mu_a)^2\sigma_{aa} - 2(\mu - \bar{W}\mu_a)(\mu - \bar{W}\mu_b)\sigma_{ab} + (\mu - \bar{W}\mu_b)^2\sigma_{bb}]/(\mu_a - \mu_b)^2\}^{\frac{1}{2}}$$

(C) Suppose $\mu_a > \mu_b$ and $\sigma_{aa} > \sigma_{bb} > 0 \geq \sigma_{ab}$. Obtain an expression for the rate of change of σ with respect to μ. Hence establish that if the individual begins with all his wealth in asset b, he can increase the mean yield and simultaneously reduce the standard deviation by trading some of asset b for asset a. Illustrate the locus of feasible μ, σ combinations in a diagram.

(D) Assuming the individual's utility is a function only of the mean and standard deviation, can you draw any conclusions as to the composition of his optimal portfolio?

4 Investor's Portfolio Optimum in a μ, σ Model

In a competitive economy there are I investors, all having the same utility function $U = \mu^{10}e^{-\sigma}$. Each individual is endowed with exactly one unit each of assets 1, 2, and 3 with payoff statistics as shown in the table below, all the payoff distributions being uncorrelated ($\sigma_{ab} = 0$, for all $a \neq b$). Given asset prices are also shown:

	μ_a	σ_a	P_a^A
Asset 1	1	0	1.0
Asset 2	1	3	0.46
Asset 3	1	4	0.04

(A) Sketch the indifference curves on $\mu(c)$, $\sigma(c)$ axes. Locate, for any single individual, the three single-asset portfolios he might hold.

(B) Under the assumptions here, each individual's optimum portfolio H^* must evidently be the same as his endowed portfolio. Locate this portfolio, and also the mutual fund portfolio F. What fraction of his wealth does the individual hold in the mutual fund?

(C) Verify that the price of risk reduction is $\Theta = \frac{3}{10}$. What is the equation of the individual's budget line? What is his Marginal Rate of Substitution (the slope of the indifference curve) at H^*?

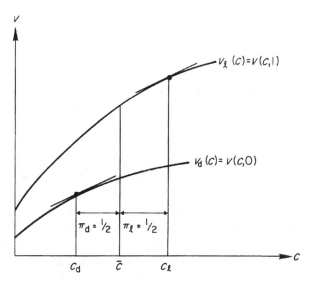

Figure 2.9. State-dependent utility – complementary preferences.

2.3 State-Dependent Utility

In risk-bearing decisions it sometimes appears that the individual's utility function $v(c)$ might itself depend upon the state of the world, contrary to our assumption in Section 1.4 in Chapter 1. To take an extreme case, if the states under consideration were "being alive" versus "being dead", a typical individual would likely value rights to income in the former state more heavily! (Yet he might attach *some* "bequest utility" to income contingent upon his own death.) Similar considerations could apply if states of the world were defined in terms of one's sickness versus health, or life versus death of one's child, or success versus failure at love, or retention versus loss of a unique heirloom.[22]

For concreteness, think in terms of two states $s = \ell$, d corresponding to life versus death of one's child. Then we can imagine a *pair* of utility functions for consumption income, $v_\ell(c)$ and $v_d(c)$ as in Figure 2.9. For any given amount of income c, the former curve would definitely be the higher (an *ordinal* comparison). But the question is whether our analysis in Section 1.4 can be extended so that, despite what appear to be two distinct $v(c)$ functions, a single cardinal scaling can be arrived at permitting use of the expected-utility rule.

---

[22] Our discussion here follows Cook and Graham (1977) and Marshall (1984).

This seemingly difficult problem resolves itself immediately, once it is realized that we are still really dealing with a *single* underlying utility function v. The only change is that v is now to be regarded as a function of two "goods": $v \equiv v(c, h)$. The first argument c still represents amounts of the consumption commodity, just as before. The second argument h represents the amount of the state-determining or "heirloom" good; in our example, if the child lives (state ℓ) then $h = 1$, if she dies (state d) then $h = 0$. The curves $v_l(c)$ and $v_d(c)$ can therefore be more explicitly labeled $v(c, 1)$ and $v(c, 0)$; these two curves are not two separate utility functions for the parent, but two sections of his single overall $v(c, h)$ function. We already know, of course, that there is no difficulty deriving a cardinal utility function, where v is a function of two or more goods (see Exercises and Excursions 1.5.6).

We now turn to the risk-bearing decision under state-dependent utility. Suppose a risk-averse person is endowed with a given quantity $\bar{c}$ of income certain, but faces a gamble involving the heirloom commodity – his child might live or might die. Is it rational to insure one's child's life, at actuarial ("fair") odds? (Doing so means that the parent will end up with higher income if the child dies.) Or, should the parent do the opposite and buy an annuity upon his child's life, a contractual arrangement that provides more income so long as the child lives, but less if the child dies? Here is a less agitating example: if our college team is playing its traditional rivals in a crucial match, is it rational for us as loyal yet risk-averse fans to bet at fair odds *against* our team (equivalent to insuring our child's life), or to bet the other way (buy the annuity instead)?

Since, as argued above, there is no difficulty in developing a cardinal $v(c, h)$ scale for use with the expected-utility rule, then (given Complete Contingent Markets [CCM]) the Fundamental Theorem of Risk Bearing continues to apply. In terms of the states $s = \ell$ and $s = $ d, we can rewrite (2.1.6) in the form:

$$\frac{\pi_\ell v_\ell'(c_\ell)}{P_\ell} = \frac{\pi_d v_d'(c_d)}{P_d} \tag{2.3.1}$$

Here $v_\ell'(c_\ell)$, the state-ℓ marginal utility – which could also be written $\partial v(c, 1)/\partial c-$ corresponds to the slope along the upper $v(c)$ curve in Figure 2.9 and is a *partial* derivative of the underlying $v(c, h)$ function. Similarly, $v_d'(c_d) \equiv \partial v(c, 0)/\partial c$ corresponds to the slope along the lower $v(c)$ curve in the diagram.

Suppose that the parent is offered a contract of insurance or annuity on his child's life, at fair odds in either case. Imagine that his optimizing choice is to accept neither, but remain at his endowed certainty-income position.

Then, in Equation (2.3.1) it must be that $v'_\ell(c_\ell) = v'_d(c_d)$ when $\bar{c}_\ell = \bar{c}_d = \bar{c}$. Geometrically, for this to occur the two curves in Figure 2.9 would have to be vertically parallel at the endowment level of income. In economic terms we would say that the two goods are "independent in preference": varying the amount of h by having the child live or die does not affect the *marginal* utility of the c commodity (although it certainly affects the parent's *total* utility).

Suppose instead that the two goods are "complements in preference": an increase in h raises $v'(c)$. Then at the endowment level of income the upper curve has steeper slope: $v'_\ell(\bar{c}) > v'_d(\bar{c})$; this is the situation pictured in Figure 2.9. Because the slope along either curve diminishes as income increases (diminishing marginal utility, reflecting the risk-aversion property), it follows that the optimality Equation (2.3.1) can be satisfied only by having $c_\ell > c_d$. (And specifically, if the probabilities are $\pi_\ell = \pi_d = \frac{1}{2}$, as in the diagram, then $c_\ell - \bar{c} = \bar{c} - c_d$.) To achieve this position, the parent would purchase an annuity on his child's life. The economic interpretation is this: if having your child alive raises the marginal utility of income to you (perhaps because you mainly desire income only in order to meet her needs), then at fair odds you would not insure your child's life but would buy the annuity to generate more income while she lives.

Finally, if c and h are "substitutes in preference," i.e., if $v'_\ell(c) < v'_d(c)$, you would insure your child's life. This might correspond to a situation where your child, if she lives, would support you in your old age; not having that source of future support raises your marginal utility of income, since should the child die you will have to provide for your declining years yourself.

What about a parent insuring his *own* life on behalf of a child? Here the child's survival is not in question, so now we must let the states $s = \ell$ versus $s = d$ refer to the *parent's* life as the "heirloom" commodity. In such a situation the upper curve $v_\ell(c) \equiv v(c, 1)$ in Figure 2.9 pictures the parent's "living utility" of consumption income while the lower curve $v_d(c) \equiv v(c, 0)$ shows the "bequest utility" he attaches to the child's income after his own death. There appears to be a puzzle here. It is reasonable to assume that h and c are complements in preference – in state ℓ there are two persons, parent and child, who need income for purpose of consumption while in state d only the latter requires income. But whereas in our previous discussion complementary preferences led to purchase of an annuity rather than insuring, we know that parents do typically insure their lives on behalf of their children.

The puzzle is resolved when we realize that death of a parent will typically mean not only loss of the heirloom commodity (life), but *also* loss of

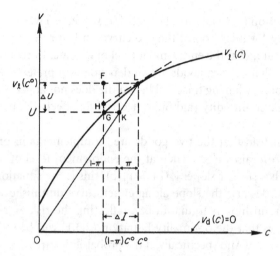

Figure 2.10. Value of a life.

income earnings that the parent would have generated. Consequently, the typical endowment position is not a life risk plus a quantity of income certain ($\bar{c}_\ell = \bar{c}_d$), but rather involves a life risk plus a correlated income risk ($\bar{c}_\ell > \bar{c}_d$). In buying life insurance a risk-averse parent is purchasing an *offsetting gamble*, tending to reduce the overall riskiness of a situation in which both c and h take on low values should the state d occur.

2.3.1 An Application: The "Value of Life"

Figure 2.10 illustrates the situation of an individual choosing between higher income and higher survival probability, for example, working at a risky high-income profession versus a lower-paying but safer occupation.

As an analytical simplification, suppose that the individual has no dependents, so that his "bequest utility" function $v_d(c)$ can be assumed to be everywhere zero. Thus, the lower curve of our previous diagram now runs along the horizontal axis.[23] Let us suppose that he finds himself initially in the risky situation, with income c^o if he survives. (His non-survival income, if any, is irrelevant since $v_d(c) = 0$ everywhere.) Denote the death probability

---

[23] The $v_\ell(c)$ curve is shown as intersecting the vertical axis, which represents an arguable assumption that life (even at zero income) is preferable to death. However, only the local shape of $v_\ell(c)$ in the neighborhood of the endowment income plays any role in the analysis, so there is no need to insist upon this assumption.

as π, so the probability of survival is $1 - \pi$. Then the expected utility U of this risky prospect is:

$$U = (1 - \pi)v_\ell(c^\circ)$$

The expected utility of the endowed gamble is indicated in the diagram by the vertical height of point K, which is the probability-weighted average of point L where $(c, h) = (c^\circ, 1)$ and the origin 0 where $(c, h) = (0, 0)$. (Here as before, life is the "heirloom" commodity h.)

The *utility loss* due to the existence of the hazard (that is, in comparison with a situation with the same c° but where the death probability is $\pi = 0$) can be expressed as:

$$\Delta U = v_\ell(c^\circ) - U = \pi v_\ell(c^\circ)$$

This corresponds to the vertical distance between $v_\ell(c^\circ)$ and U as marked off on the vertical axis of the diagram – the vertical distance between points F and G. Along the v_ℓ function, point G has the same utility as the endowed gamble (point K). So ΔI, the income equivalent of the utility loss, is the horizontal difference between points G and L. ΔI may be termed the income-compensation differential: the remuneration reduction (viewed from point L) that this individual would be just willing to accept to be free of his endowed death risk.

We now seek a more general analytical expression for ΔI. The line tangent to the $v_\ell(c)$ curve at L has slope $v_\ell'(c^\circ)$. Then the vertical distance between points F and H equals $\Delta I v_\ell'(c^\circ)$. As long as the death probability is fairly small, this distance is approximately equal to the vertical distance between the points F and G, which we have already seen is the utility loss $\pi v_\ell(c^\circ)$. So, to a first approximation:

$$\Delta I v_\ell'(c^\circ) = \pi v_\ell(c^\circ)$$

or:

$$\Delta I = \frac{\pi v_\ell(c^\circ)}{v_\ell'(c^\circ)} = \frac{\pi c^\circ}{e}$$

where:

$$e = \frac{dU/dI}{U/I} = \frac{v_\ell'(c^\circ)}{v_\ell(c^\circ)/c^\circ}$$

Here e signifies the income elasticity of utility, evaluated at the income level c°. Since π is the probability of loss, the other factor $v_\ell(c^\circ)/v_\ell'(c^\circ) = c^\circ/e$ then represents the *value of life*[24] implied by this analysis.

We must be careful not to misinterpret this value, however. It does not represent the amount that an individual would pay to "buy his life," for example, if he were being held for ransom. It represents the exchange rate at which he would be willing to give up a *small* amount of income for a *small* reduction in the probability of death π (when π is close to zero). This can be shown more explicitly as follows. Since $U = (1 - \pi)v_l(c^\circ)$, the Marginal Rate of Substitution $M(c, \pi)$ between income c and death probability π is:

$$M(c, \pi) \equiv \left.\frac{dc}{d\pi}\right|_U \equiv \frac{-\partial U/\partial \pi}{\partial U/\partial c} = \frac{v_\ell(c^\circ)}{(1 - \pi)\,v_\ell'(c^\circ)}$$

For π close to zero the denominator is approximately $v_\ell'(c^\circ)$. Thus $v_\ell(c^\circ)/v_\ell'(c^\circ) = c^\circ/e$ does not represent the purchase price of a whole life, but the *Marginal Rate of Substitution* between small increments of income and survival probability.

Nevertheless, the interpretation in terms of "value of life" is not wholly unwarranted when we think in terms of society as a whole. Suppose that each member of a large population voluntarily accepts a 0.001 decrease in survival probability in order to earn \$500 more income, implying a figure of \$500,000 for the "value of life." Again, this does not mean that any single individual would trade his whole life for \$500,000; indeed, there might be no one willing to make such a trade, for any amount of income whatsoever. But if everyone in a population of 1,000,000 accepts such a small per-capita hazard, there will be about \$500,000,000 more of income and about 1,000 additional deaths. So, in a sense, \$500,000 is indeed the "value of a life"!

Exercises and Excursions 2.3

1 *Betting for or against the Home Team?*

Your endowed income is $\bar{c} = 100$. There is a 50:50 chance that the home team will win the big game. You can bet at fair odds, picking either side to win and for any amount of money. Each of the utility functions (i) through

---

[24] Of course, since death is ultimately certain, any increased chance of life can only be temporary. If we are dealing with *annual* death probability, we should really speak of the value of an *incremental year of life expectation*. But the dramatic, if misleading, term "value of life" is too firmly established to be displaced.

(iv) below consists of a *pair* of utility functions, which differ depending upon whether the home team wins (W) or loses (L):

(i) $v_W(c) = 2c^{0.5}$ and $v_L(c) = c^{0.5}$

(ii) $v_W(c) = 2 - \exp(-c)$ and $v_L(c) = 1 - \exp(-c)$

(iii) $v_W(c) = 1 - \exp(-2c)$ and $v_L(c) = 1 - \exp(-c)$

(iv) $v_W(c) = \ln(50 + c)$ and $v_L(c) = \ln(c)$

For each utility function:

(A) Verify that, at any level of income c, you prefer the home team to win.

(B) Find the optimal b, the amount of money bet on the home team (so that b is negative if you bet *against* the home team).

(C) Having made the optimal bet, do you still want the home team to win? Explain the differences among the four cases.

2   Risk Preference under State-Dependent Utility?

An individual can choose between two suburbs in which to live. The homes in the first suburb are small, while in the second they are large. Utility in the first suburb is:

$$v(c, h_1) = 8c^{\frac{1}{2}}$$

where c is spending on goods other than housing (i.e., on "corn," whose price is unity). Utility in the second suburb is:

$$v(c, h_2) = 5c^{\frac{2}{3}}$$

Housing in the first suburb costs $20 per year and in the second costs $56.

(A) Sketch the two utility functions. Verify that the utility functions cross at $\bar{c} = 120$, and explain what this signifies.

(B) Suppose that before having invested in housing, the individual's endowed income was $120. Consider the gamble corresponding to the prospect $(181, 56; 0.5, 0.5)$. Note that this is an adverse gamble; in comparison with the endowment income, the payoff is $61 and the possible loss is $64. Compute the individual's utility for each outcome and hence confirm that taking the gamble does raise expected utility.

(C) Indicate, geometrically, the optimal gamble for this individual. Explain why the individual wants to undertake such a gamble.

[HINT: Are c and h complements here?]

(D) Can this kind of argument explain why some people gamble regularly?

3 *"Superstars" and the Value of Life*

An individual with endowed income $\bar{c}$ has a concave utility function $v(c)$. He has contracted a disease which, if not treated, will be fatal with probability $1 - p_o$ and will spontaneously cure itself with probability p_o. His "bequest utility" in the event of death is zero everywhere.

(A) Suppose that, when treated by a physician who charges z, his probability of survival rises to p. If z is his maximum willingness to pay for that treatment, show that:

$$pv(\bar{c} - z) = p_o v(\bar{c})$$

(B) Hence show that:

$$\frac{dp}{dz} = \frac{p_o v(\bar{c}) v'(\bar{c} - z)}{v(\bar{c} - z)^2}$$

Depict the relationship between p and z in a figure. Interpret its shape.

(C) Suppose a "superstar" physician can increase the individual's probability of survival by $1 - p_o$, so that he is sure to live, while another physician can increase this probability by only $(1 - p_o)/2$. Indicate in the figure the maximum amounts X and Y that the two physicians could charge.

(D) It has been asserted that "superstars" tend to receive disproportionally high incomes. In this context, this means that the ratio of physicians' fees would exceed the ratio of the survival rate increments that they provide. Assuming that both physicians can charge the maximum, is the assertion $X/Y > 2$ valid here?

(E) The maximum that the individual would be willing to pay a physician, who (in effect) provides him with "a fraction $p - p_o$ of his life," is $z(p)$ where this function is defined implicitly in part (A). Then it can be argued that his implied valuation of his own life is $z(p)/(p - p_o)$. For example, if $p_o = p - p_o = 0.5$ and X $= \$100,000$, the value of his life would be $\$200,000$. Carry this argument to the limit in which p is small and show that, at this limit, the value he places upon his life is $v(\bar{c})/p^o v'(\bar{c})$. Compare this conclusion with that reached at the end of the discussion in the text.

SUGGESTIONS FOR FURTHER READING: The state-contingent claims model was introduced by Arrow (1953, reprinted 1964). See also Debreu (1959). A classical treatment of asset-pricing and the CAPM model is provided in Ingersoll (1987). Some recent work in finance extends beyond the traditional μ, σ preferences of Section 2.2; see Leland (1999). An important issue in state-dependent utility is that the subjective probability distribution over states is not unique. For more on this, see Karni (1993).

References

Arrow, Kenneth J., "The Role of Securities in the Optimal Allocation of Risk Bearing," *Econometrie* (1953), as translated and reprinted in 1964, *Review of Economic Studies*, 31 (1964), 91–96.

Cook, Philip J. and Graham, Daniel A., "The Demand for Insurance and Protection: The Case of Irreplaceable Commodities," *Quarterly Journal of Economics*, 91 (1977), 143–156.

Copeland, Thomas E., Weston, J. Fred, and Shastri, Kuldeep, *Financial Theory and Corporate Policy*, 4th edition, Reading, MA: Addison-Wesley, 2004.

Debreu, Gerard, *Theory of Value: An Axiomatic Analysis of Economic Equilibrium*, New Haven: Yale University Press, 1959.

Ingersoll, Jonathan E., *The Theory of Financial Decision Making*, New York: Rowman and Littlefield, 1987.

Karni, Edi, "Subjective Expected Utility Theory with State-Dependent Preferences," *Journal of Economic Theory*, 60 (1993), 428–438.

Leland, Hayne E., "Beyond Mean-Variance: Performance Measurement in a Nonsymmetrical World," *Financial Analysts Journal*, 55 (1999), 27–36.

Marshall, John M., "Gambles and the Shadow Price of Death," *American Economic Review*, 74 (1984), 73–86.

Comparative Statics of the Risk-Bearing Optimum

The elements of the decision problem under uncertainty – the individual's preferences, opportunities, and beliefs – were surveyed in Chapter 1. We distinguished between *terminal* choices, actions undertaken on the basis of given probability beliefs (covered in Part I of this volume), and *informational* choices, actions designed to improve one's knowledge of the world before a terminal decision has to be made (to be covered in Part II). Chapter 2 analyzed the individual's *risk-bearing optimum*, the best terminal action to take in the face of uncertainty.

We now want to explore how these optimizing decisions change in response to variations in the person's character or situation (his or her wealth, tastes for risk, the endowment of goods, the market prices faced, and so forth). Modeling the before-and-after effects of such "parametric" changes, without attending to the dynamics of the actual transition path from one solution to another, is called the *method of comparative statics*. This chapter is devoted to the comparative statics of the individual's risk-bearing optimum.

3.1 Measures of Risk Aversion

The individual's risk-bearing optimum depends critically upon his attitudes toward risk. And, since parametric changes generally involve positive or negative wealth effects, it will often be crucial to take into account how attitudes toward risk vary as a function of wealth.

As discussed in Chapter 2, in a regime of Complete Contingent Markets with two states of the world, the individual's wealth constraint is:

$$P_1 c_1 + P_2 c_2 = P_1 \bar{c}_1 + P_2 \bar{c}_2 \equiv \bar{W} \qquad (3.1.1)$$

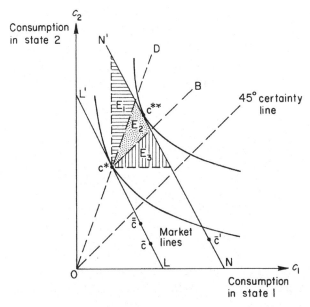

Figure 3.1. Wealth effects.

Endowed wealth, $\bar{W}$, represents the market value of the endowment vector $\bar{C} = (\bar{c}_1, \bar{c}_2)$. As shown in Figure 3.1, expected utility is maximized at the indifference-curve tangency C^* along the original budget line LL' (assuming an interior solution). As endowed wealth increases, the optimum position moves outward from C^* along some *wealth expansion path* like C^*B or C^*D in the diagram.

Suppose that, after an increase in endowed wealth, the individual's new optimum lies northeast of the old optimum C^* but below the line C^*B (i.e., in region E_3). Since C^*B is drawn parallel to the 45° line, all the points in E_3 lie closer to the 45° line than does C^*. Thus, an individual whose wealth expansion path lies in this region reduces his *absolute consumption risk* (gap between c_1 and c_2) as his wealth increases. If instead (as shown in the diagram) his new optimum lies above the line C^*B (in regions E_1 or E_2) his "tolerance" for absolute risk must be increasing with wealth. A solution along the dividing line C^*B would represent constant tolerance for absolute risk. Or, putting it the other way, we can speak of increasing, decreasing, or constant *absolute risk aversion* as wealth increases.

These alternative responses to changes in wealth imply restrictions upon the shape of the individual's utility function $v(c)$. We can use these restrictions to construct a measure of the individual's absolute risk aversion. Consider a change in the absolute steepness of the indifference curve – the Marginal Rate of Substitution $M(c_1, c_2)$ – in moving from some arbitrary point (c_1, c_2) to a nearby point $(c_1 + dc_1, c_2 + dc_2)$. From Equation (2.1.2) the Marginal Rate of Substitution can be expressed as:

$$M(c_1, c_2) = \frac{\pi_1 v'(c_1)}{\pi_2 v'(c_2)} \qquad (3.1.2)$$

Taking the logarithm of both sides:

$$\ln M = \ln \pi_1 + \ln v'(c_1) - \ln \pi_2 - \ln v'(c_2)$$

The total differential of the expression is then:

$$d \ln M = \frac{dM}{M} = \frac{v''(c_1)}{v'(c_1)} dc_1 - \frac{v''(c_2)}{v'(c_2)} dc_2 \qquad (3.1.3)$$

If c_1 and c_2 increase by the same absolute amount $(dc_1 = dc_2 = dx)$, the (c_1, c_2) vector moves outward parallel to the 45° line. Then the proportionate change in $M(c_1, c_2)$ is:

$$\frac{dM}{M} = \left[\frac{v''(c_1)}{v'(c_1)} - \frac{v''(c_2)}{v'(c_2)} \right] dx \qquad (3.1.4)$$

Suppose that, as depicted in Figure 3.1, an increase in wealth leads to a new optimum C** that lies in region E$_2$ and therefore is further from the 45° line. Since the Marginal Rate of Substitution is the same at C* and C**, it follows that $M(c_1, c_2)$ is necessarily lower where the new budget line NN' intersects the line C*B parallel to the 45° line. If this holds everywhere, then, from (3.1.4):

$$c_1 < c_2 \Rightarrow \frac{dM}{M} = \left[\frac{v''(c_1)}{v'(c_1)} - \frac{v''(c_2)}{v'(c_2)} \right] dx < 0$$

Rearranging we obtain:

$$c_1 < c_2 \Rightarrow \frac{-v''(c_1)}{v'(c_1)} > \frac{-v''(c_2)}{v'(c_2)}$$

Of course, the condition is reversed below the 45° line where $c_1 > c_2$.

Thus, an individual displays decreasing aversion to absolute wealth risks if and only if $A(c)$ is a decreasing function, where:

$$A(c) \equiv \frac{-v''(c)}{v'(c)} \qquad (3.1.5)$$

The function $A(c)$, which is evidently a property of the individual's utility function $v(c)$, measures the individual's *absolute risk aversion*.

Since the individual depicted in Figure 3.1 moves farther from the 45° line as his wealth grows, he exhibits Decreasing Absolute Risk Aversion (DARA). If instead he had Constant Absolute Risk Aversion (CARA), $A(c)$ would remain unchanged as wealth rises. In that case the wealth expansion path would be parallel to the 45° line (line C^*B). Finally, if $A(c)$ rises with wealth, the individual exhibits Increasing Absolute Risk Aversion (IARA); the wealth expansion path would then converge toward the 45° line, and the new optimum would lie in region E_3.

A second useful measure of attitude toward risk is obtained by considering *proportional* rather than absolute changes in an individual's consumption levels. If c_1 and c_2 increase proportionately, the consumption vector moves outward along a ray out of the origin. Along such a ray:

$$c_2 = kc_1 \quad \text{and} \quad dc_2 = kdc_1$$

Eliminating k we obtain:

$$\frac{dc_2}{c_2} = \frac{dc_1}{c_1}$$

Rearranging terms in (3.1.3) and substituting, we can see that along the ray C^*D in Figure 3.1 the Marginal Rate of Substitution changes in accordance with:

$$\frac{dM}{M} = \left[\frac{c_1 v''(c_1)}{v'(c_1)} - \frac{c_2 v''(c_2)}{v'(c_2)} \right] \frac{dc_1}{c_1} \tag{3.1.6}$$

As depicted, C^{**}, the optimum at the higher wealth level, lies in region E_2 and so is closer to the 45° line than the ray C^*D. To be the same at C^* and C^{**}, the absolute indifference-curve slope $M(c_1, c_2)$ must be increasing along the ray C^*D. That is, from (3.1.6):

$$c_1 < c_2 \Rightarrow \frac{dM}{M} = \left[\frac{c_1 v''(c_1)}{v'(c_1)} - \frac{c_2 v''(c_2)}{v'(c_2)} \right] \frac{dc_1}{c_1} > 0$$

Rearranging, we obtain:

$$c_1 < c_2 \Rightarrow \frac{-c_1 v''(c_1)}{v'(c_1)} < \frac{-c_2 v''(c_2)}{v'(c_2)}$$

Let us define as measure of *relative risk aversion*:

$$R(c) \equiv \frac{-cv''(c)}{v'(c)} \qquad (3.1.7)$$

Then an individual like the one depicted, who displays *increasing* aversion to proportional (or relative) risk as wealth grows, must be characterized by an $R(c)$ that is an increasing function. We say he displays Increasing Relative Risk Aversion (IRRA).

If the wealth expansion path is a ray out of the origin, so that the individual prefers to accept risks that are exactly proportionally larger as his wealth rises, his $R(c)$ is constant – he displays Constant Relative Risk Aversion (CRRA). Finally, if his tolerance for risk rises more than proportionally with wealth, then $R(c)$ declines with c and the individual is said to exhibit decreasing relative risk aversion (DRRA).

Both $A(c)$ and $R(c)$ are *local* measures. That is, they are defined in terms of small changes in wealth and consumption. In general, there is no reason why an individual should not exhibit increasing absolute or relative risk aversion over some consumption levels and decreasing risk aversion over others. However, in theoretical investigations it is common to make *global* assumptions about both measures of risk aversion.

Pratt (1964) has argued, as an empirical generalization, that individuals will be willing to bear greater *absolute* risk as wealth rises. This is very plausible. Every unit purchased of a risky asset buys a given absolute risk. Assuming that the state-1 yield of asset a is greater than its state-2 yield, the absolute risk per unit of a held is $Z_{a1} - Z_{a2}$. A rich individual, other things equal, should be willing to hold more of every kind of asset; acquiring more units of risky assets, he would inevitably accumulate a larger absolute consumption risk. Empirically less obvious is the contention by Arrow (1965) that individuals, as they become richer, will buy relatively more safety so as to reduce their *proportionate* risk. If both arguments are accepted, the typical wealth expansion path will lie in the region E_2 as depicted in Figure 3.1, rather than in E_1 or E_3. Individuals will be characterized by DARA and IRRA.

We now compare the preference maps of two individuals, one of whom is everywhere more risk averse. In Figure 3.2 the solid curve is an indifference curve for individual K. As depicted, this individual is indifferent between a certainty endowment point $\bar{C} = (\bar{c}, \ \bar{c})$ along the 45° line and the gamble B. Moving away from the certainty line to the northwest, i.e., to consumption vectors with $c_2 > c_1$, his Marginal Rate of Substitution (steepness of the indifference curve) must evidently increase. Since the Marginal Rate of

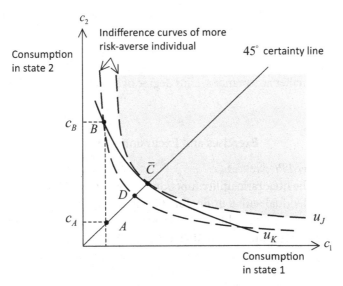

Figure 3.2. Acceptable gambles.

Substitution $M(c_1, c_2)$ is the same everywhere along the certainty line, the change $M(c_1, c_2)$ in moving from $\bar{C}$ to B can be expressed logarithmically as:

$$\ln M_B - \ln M_{\bar{C}} = \ln M_B - \ln M_D$$
$$= \int_{c_D}^{c_B} -\frac{v''(c_2)}{v'(c_2)} dc_2$$
$$= \int_{c_D}^{c_B} A_K(c_2) dc_2$$

The proportional decline in $M(c_1, c_2)$ around the indifference curve therefore varies with the degree of absolute risk aversion. It follows immediately that if individual J has an everywhere greater degree of absolute risk aversion than individual K, so that $A_J(c) > A_K(c)$, the proportional decline in J's $M(c_1, c_2)$ is greater. Yet, if both have the same beliefs, we know from Section 2.1 and Equation (2.1.2) that along the 45° line the Marginal Rates of Substitution are equal to one another. Therefore, at any point B above the 45° line, the more risk-averse individual has a steeper indifference curve. Exactly the same logic reveals that below the 45° line the more risk-averse individual has a flatter indifference curve.

It follows that individual J's indifference curves must be "curvier" than K's (compare the dotted and the solid indifference curves in Figure 3.2).

So, starting from the same endowment, the set of gambles acceptable to J is strictly smaller than the acceptable set for K.

We have shown that greater $A(c)$ implies a smaller set of acceptable gambles. It is easy to verify that the converse is also true. That is, if J has an everywhere smaller acceptance set, his degree of absolute risk aversion $A_J(c)$ is greater.

Exercises and Excursions 3.1

1   *Well-Behaved Preferences*
   (A) Does the quadratic utility function exhibit either DARA or IRRA?
   (B) An individual with a utility function $v(c)$ such that $-v'(c)/v''(c) = \alpha + \beta c$ is said to exhibit linear risk tolerance. For what parameter values does such an individual exhibit DARA and IRRA?

2   *CARA and CRRA Preferences*
   (A) Show that the utility function $v(c) = -e^{-Ac}$ exhibits CARA with coefficient of absolute risk aversion A. Show that it is the unique such function. That is, any other CARA utility function with constant coefficient of absolute risk aversion equal to A must be of the form $v(c) = -ae^{-Ac} + b$ where $a > 0$ and b are constants.

   [HINT: To show uniqueness, integrate the function $-\frac{v''(c)}{v'(c)} = A$.]

   (B) Show that the utility function (i) $v(c) = c^{1-R}$, $0 < R < 1$ exhibits CRRA with coefficient of relative risk aversion equal to R and (ii) $v(c) = \ln c$ exhibits CRRA with coefficient of relative risk aversion equal to 1.

3   *Preference for Positive Skewness*
Suppose two prospects $\tilde{c}_1$ and $\tilde{c}_2$ have the same mean and variance but $\tilde{c}_1$ has negative and $\tilde{c}_2$ positive skewness, that is:

$$E[(\tilde{c}_1 - \mu)^3] < 0 < E[(\tilde{c}_2 - \mu)^3]$$

   (A) Does the typical lottery, offering just a few large prizes with a high probability of a small loss, exhibit positive skewness? Demonstrate.
   (B) Ignoring moments higher than the third, use Taylor's expansion to show that, if $v'''(c)$ is positive, then positive skewness is indeed preferred.

(C) Show that decreasing absolute risk aversion is a sufficient condition for $v'''(c)$ to be positive.

4 Absolute Risk Aversion and Concavity of the Utility Function

Let $A_i(c)$ be the degree of absolute risk aversion corresponding to the twice-differentiable increasing functions $v_i(c)$, $i = J, K$.

(A) If individual J's utility function $v_J(c)$ can be written as an increasing twice-differentiable concave function of individual K's $v_K(c)$, that is:

$$v_J(c) = f(v_K(c)), \quad f'(\cdot) > 0, \; f''(\cdot) < 0$$

show that $A_J(c) > A_K(c)$.

(B) Since $v_J(c)$ is an increasing function, there is a one-to-one mapping $g: v \to v$ such that $g(v_K(c)) = v_J(c)$. Differentiate twice and rearrange to establish that:

$$g'(v_K(c)) = \frac{v_J'(c)}{v_K'(c)} \quad \text{and} \quad g''(v_K(c)) = \frac{-v_J'(c)}{v_K'(c)^2}[A_J(c) - A_K(c)]$$

Hence, establish the converse of (A).

5 Small and Large Gambles

An individual exhibits constant absolute risk aversion of degree A. This individual will *not* take the 50–50 gamble that gives a gain of $110 and loss of $100 (with equal probability).

(A) What is smallest value of A (to three decimal places) that is consistent with this behavior?

Now suppose that this individual is offered another 50–50 gamble with a gain of G (greater than $1,100) and a loss of $1,000.

(B) Is there any value G that would make this individual accept this second gamble?

6 The Risk Premium

Formally, the "risk premium" associated with a risky prospect $\tilde{c}$ is the amount of income b that an individual is willing to give up in order to receive the expected value of $\tilde{c}$ with certainty. That is:

$$E[v(\tilde{c})] = v(\bar{c} - b), \quad \text{where } \bar{c} = E[\tilde{c}]$$

(A) If the risk is small so that third and higher-order terms can be neglected, apply Taylor's expansion to show that the risk premium is proportional to the degree of absolute risk aversion.

(B) Let b_0 be the initial risk premium and let b_1 be the risk premium when the individual's wealth rises by w. That is:

(i) $E[v(\tilde{c})] = v(\bar{c} - b_0)$

(ii) $E[v(w + \tilde{c})] = v(w + \bar{c} - b_1)$

If the risk is small, appeal to (A) to establish that, if absolute risk aversion is decreasing with wealth, then $b_0 > b_1$.

(C) *Show that this result holds for all risks as long as the degree of absolute risk aversion is decreasing with wealth.

[HINT: Define the new utility function $\bar{v}(c) = v(w + c)$. That is, we can think of the wealth effect as changing the utility function. Given the assumptions, explain why the utility function $\bar{v}(c)$ exhibits a lower degree of risk aversion than $v(c)$. Then appeal to Exercise 4 to establish that $v(w + \tilde{c}) = f(v(\tilde{c}))$, where f is a convex function.]

7 *Effect of an Uncertain Increase in Wealth on the Risk Premium*

Extending the analysis of Exercise 6, suppose two individuals face the same income risk $\tilde{c}$ but one has an additional uncertain endowment $\tilde{w}$. Let b_0 be the amount the first individual is willing to pay to replace the income risk with its expected value $\bar{c}$. Then b_0 satisfies (i) above. Similarly, let b_2 be the amount the second individual is willing to pay to replace the income risk with its expected value. That is:

(iii) $E[v(\tilde{w} + \tilde{c})] = E[v(\tilde{w} + \bar{c} - b_2)]$

Arguing by analogy with Exercise 6, it is tempting to think that, with decreasing absolute risk aversion, $b_0 > b_2$. However, consider the following example. There are three states and each is equally likely. The two risky prospects are:

$$\tilde{w} = (w, 0, 0) \quad \text{and} \quad \tilde{c} = (\bar{c}, \bar{c} + e, \bar{c} - e)$$

where $w > 0$ and $\bar{c} > e$.

(A) Write out Equations (i) and (iii) for this example and hence show that b_2 must satisfy:

$$[v(\bar{c} + w) - v(\bar{c} + w - b_2)] - [v(\bar{c}) - v(\bar{c} - b_2)]$$
$$= 3[v(\bar{c} - b_2)] - v(\bar{c} - b_0)]$$

---

* Starred questions or portions of questions may be somewhat more difficult.

(B) Explain why the left-hand side of this expression is negative and hence why $b_2 > b_0$. That is, the risk premium may *rise* as wealth increases stochastically regardless of whether or not absolute risk aversion is decreasing (see Machina, 1982).

(C) What is the intuition behind this result?

[HINT: You can also show that b_2 is a strictly increasing function of w. Then compare the effect of paying a risk premium on state-1 utility (i) when $w = 0$ and (ii) when w is large.]

3.2 Endowment and Price Effects

This section analyzes the effects of parametric changes in endowments and in prices upon the individual's risk-bearing optimum. We first take up the case where Complete Contingent Markets (CCM) are provided by a full set of tradable state claims (Section 3.2.1). Equivalent results can, of course, be obtained under Complete Asset Markets (CAM) – i.e., where the number of tradable assets with linearly independent return vectors equals the number of states. Section 3.2.2 then covers *incomplete* market regimes.

3.2.1 Complete Markets

In accordance with the analysis in Chapter 2, Section 1, under Complete Contingent Markets the individual chooses among state-claim bundles $(c_1, \ldots, c_S)$ so as to maximize expected utility $U = \sum_s \pi_s v(c_s)$ subject to the budget constraint:

$$\sum_{s=1}^{S} P_s c_s = \sum_{s=1}^{S} P_s \bar{c}_s \equiv \bar{W} \tag{3.2.1}$$

Ignoring for expositional ease the possibility of a corner solution, the preferred position C^* is the one satisfying the budget constraint and the Fundamental Theorem of Risk Bearing:

$$\frac{\pi_1 v'(c_1)}{P_1} = \frac{\pi_2 v'(c_2)}{P_2} = \cdots = \frac{\pi_s v'(c_s)}{P_s} = \lambda \tag{3.2.2}$$

where λ can be interpreted as the expected marginal utility of income. This condition can only be an optimum, of course, if risk aversion ($v''(c) < 0$) is postulated – else a corner solution would always be preferred.

In the two-state diagram of Figure 3.1, consider exogenous shifts in the individual's endowment vector, state-claim prices being held constant. The effect upon the risk-bearing optimum depends only upon whether or not the change in endowment alters endowed wealth $\bar{W}$ in (3.2.1). An endowment variation leaving $\bar{W}$ unchanged is illustrated in Figure 3.1 by a shift from $\bar{C}$ to $\bar{\bar{C}}$ along the same market line LL′. Such a change in the composition of the endowment does not in any way affect the position of the optimum vector C*. (On the other hand, this change will of necessity affect the scope of the *transactions* undertaken by the individual in order to attain the C* optimum.) The more interesting class of endowment shifts will be those in which $\bar{W}$ does change, so that the individual's optimum position must also be revised. (But, it is at least possible that the *transactions* he must undertake to attain his new optimum from his new endowment might remain unchanged.) For concreteness, we will speak in terms of *increases* in $\bar{W}$.

An increase in wealth at given prices must raise the optimum amount of contingent consumption claims held in at least one state t. Assuming risk aversion, λ must fall in (3.2.2). And, given the separable form of the expected-utility function, as in Equation (1.4.1), when any c_t rises in (3.2.2) then c_s must increase in each and every other state as well. Thus, in risk-bearing theory under the von Neumann–Morgenstern postulates, there are no "inferior-good" state claims; all wealth effects are necessarily "normal." Then the analysis of wealth expansion paths in the previous section can be applied directly. For any pair of states s and t the impact of an increase in wealth can be depicted essentially as in Figure 3.1. We need only let the axes be c_s and c_t, and interpret the budget lines LL′ and NN′ as indicating those combinations of state claims costing the same as the *optimal* purchase of state claims at the two wealth levels. It follows directly that under the assumption of decreasing (increasing) *absolute* risk aversion, the absolute difference between any pair of state claim holdings, $|c_t^* - c_s^*|$, rises (falls) with wealth. Similarly, under the assumption of decreasing (increasing) *relative* risk aversion, if $c_t > c_s$ then the ratio of expenditures $P_t c_t / P_s c_s$ rises (falls) with wealth.

We next consider the "pure substitution effect," the impact upon c_s of a *compensated* increase in the price P_s of one of the state claims. That is, we postulate an exogenous increase in P_s together with a simultaneous change in endowment such that expected utility (after the individual revises his state-claim holdings in accordance with the new price vector) is the same as before.

Suppose for concreteness that it is P_1, the price of claims to consumption in state 1, that rises. Under our standard assumption of state independence (so that $v'(c_s)$ is independent of consumption in any state $t \neq s$), and, since $P_2, \ldots, P_s$ are all unchanged, the Fundamental Theorem of Risk Bearing indicates that if λ rises $c_2, \ldots, c_s$ must fall and vice versa. That is, claims in all states other than state 1 move together. Since expected utility is required to remain constant, either c_1 falls and $c_2, \ldots, c_s$ all rise or the reverse. But, if c_1 and P_1 both were to rise, the marginal utility of income λ in Equation (3.2.3) would fall. Then, to maintain the equality, holdings of all other state claims would also rise. But this is inconsistent with constant utility. We have therefore established that the "pure substitution effect" of a price increase is negative and that all cross-effects are positive. In the language of traditional theory, state claims must be *net substitutes* in demand.

To determine the *uncompensated* effect of an increase in P_s on demand, note that, if $\bar{c}_s$ is the individual's state-s endowment, the Slutsky equation is:

$$\frac{\partial c_s}{\partial P_s} = \frac{\partial c_s}{\partial P_s}\bigg|_{\text{comp}} - (c_s - \bar{c}_s)\frac{\partial c_s}{\partial W}$$

Since it has been shown that all wealth effects are normal, the two terms on the right-hand side of this expression are reinforcing as long as the individual is a net buyer of state-s claims. Informally, the increase in P_s makes a net buyer poorer, and so the income effect is negative. However, when we consider the effect of a rise in P_t upon the demand for state-s claims c_s, the substitution effect tending to increase c_s must be weighed against the income effect that tends to reduce c_s. So, state claims may be either *gross substitutes* or *gross complements* in demand.

Exercises and Excursions 3.2.1

1 The Law of Demand for State Claims

(A) Suppose an individual is a net buyer of consumption claims in state 1, i.e., $c_1^* > \bar{c}_1$. If the price of state-1 claims rises, show directly that the quantity of state-1 claims demanded must fall.

[HINT: Suppose the proposition is false. Then c_1^* does not fall and spending on state-1 claims must rise. Apply the Fundamental Theorem of Risk Bearing to show that $c_2^*, \ldots, c_s^*$ must also rise. Hence obtain a contradiction.]

(B) What if the individual is a net *seller* of state-1 claims?

2 Elastic Own-Demand Curves and Gross Substitutes in Demand
An individual begins with a fixed nominal wealth $\bar{W}$.

(A) Show that if, for each state s, the own-price elasticity of demand exceeds unity so that total spending on state-s claims falls with a rise in P_s, then all state claims are gross substitutes in demand.

[HINT: Use the Fundamental Theorem of Risk Bearing, and the fact that $P_s c_s$ declines as P_s rises, to establish that λ must decline.]

(B) If an individual is highly risk averse (so that indifference curves are essentially L-shaped) explain graphically why consumption in each state declines as P_s rises. In this case, does the own-price elasticity of demand exceed unity?

(C) Show that the own-price elasticity of demand exceeds unity if and only if relative risk aversion is less than unity.

[HINT: Show that consumption in state s and state 1 must satisfy:

$$\pi_s c_s v'(c_s) = (P_s c_s) \pi_1 v'(c_1)/P_1$$

Use (A) to establish that, as P_s rises, the right-hand side of this equation declines if and only if own-price elasticity exceeds unity. What happens to the left-hand side as c_s declines?]

3.2.2 Incomplete Markets

To illustrate trading in a regime of incomplete markets, in a world of $S > 2$ states consider an individual who must balance his portfolio between a riskless asset and a single risky asset. As before, we want to examine the effect of changes in endowments or in prices upon the individual's risk-bearing optimum.

Let the first asset, with price P_1^A, have the certain return z_1 while the second asset, with price P_2^A, pays off z_{2s} dollars in state s ($s = 1, 2, \ldots, S$). Equivalently, the return on asset 2 is a random variable $\tilde{z}_2$ with realizations $z_{21}, \ldots, z_{2S}$. Then, if an individual with utility function $v(\cdot)$ holds q_1 units of asset 1 and q_2 units of asset 2, and if he has no source of income in any state other than returns from asset holdings, his expected utility is:

$$U(q_1, q_2) = E_s[v(q_1 z_1 + q_2 \tilde{z}_2)] = \sum_s \pi_s v(q_1 z_1 + q_2 z_{2s}) \quad (3.2.3)$$

As long as the individual is risk averse so that $v(c)$ is a concave function, it can be shown that his derived preferences *over assets* must be convex ("bowed toward the origin") as depicted in Figure 3.3.[1]

Asset demands must satisfy the budget constraint:

$$P_1^A q_1 + P_2^A q_2 = P_1^A \bar{q}_1 + P_2^A \bar{q}_2 \equiv \bar{W} \quad (3.2.4)$$

---

[1] See the first exercise at the end of this section.

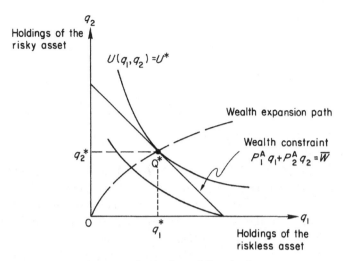

Figure 3.3. Optimal portfolio selection.

Using the budget constraint, we can substitute for q_1 in (3.2.3) so as to express expected utility as a function $\bar{U}(q_2)$ of q_2 only:

$$
\begin{aligned}
\bar{U}(q_2) &= E\left[v\left(\left(\frac{\bar{W}}{P_1^A} - \frac{P_2^A}{P_1^A}q_2\right)z_1 + q_2\tilde{z}_2\right)\right] \\
&= E\left[v\left(\frac{\bar{W}z_1}{P_1^A} - P_2^A q_2\left(\frac{\tilde{z}_2}{P_2^A} - \frac{z_1}{P_1^A}\right)\right)\right]
\end{aligned}
\tag{3.2.5}
$$

For the analysis that follows, it is more convenient to work with net asset yields per dollar invested (or, for short, simply the *yields*) rather than with the asset payoffs or returns.

For any asset a, the yield distribution is definitionally related to the payoff distribution by:

$$
1 + \tilde{R}_a \equiv \frac{\tilde{z}_a}{P_a^A}
\tag{3.2.6}
$$

Substituting into (3.2.5) we obtain:

$$
\bar{U}(q_2) = E\left[v((1 + R_1)\bar{W} + (\tilde{R}_2 - R_1)P_2^A q_2)\right]
$$

where R_1 (like z_1) is non-stochastic. The marginal increase in expected utility associated with an increased demand for the risky asset is then:

$$
\bar{U}'(q_2) = P_2^A E[(\tilde{R}_2 - R_1)v'(\tilde{c})]
\tag{3.2.7}
$$

The random variable $\tilde{c}$ represents contingent consumption over states:

$$\tilde{c} \equiv (1 + R_1)\bar{W} + (\tilde{R}_2 - R_1)P_2^A q_2 \qquad (3.2.8)$$

In particular, at $q_2 = 0$ we have:

$$\bar{U}'(0) = P_2^A v'((1 + R_1)\bar{W})E[\tilde{R}_2 - R_1]$$

This is positive if and only if the expected yield on the risky asset exceeds the yield on the riskless asset.

Thus, no matter how risk averse an individual is, he will always want to hold some amount of the risky asset if its expected yield is even slightly higher than the riskless yield. While this may at first seem puzzling, the explanation is simple. As long as the risk holding is sufficiently small, the individual's final consumption distribution is nearly riskless, and so marginal utilities are almost the same across states. His behavior toward a very small favorable gamble is therefore essentially that of a risk-neutral agent.

We now suppose that $E[\tilde{R}_2] > R_1$ so that the optimal asset holding, q_2^*, is strictly positive. From (3.2.7) and (3.2.8), q_2^* satisfies the first-order condition:

$$\bar{U}'(q_2^*) = P_2^A E[(\tilde{R}_2 - R_1)v'(\tilde{c}^*)] = 0 \qquad (3.2.9)$$

What happens to demand for the risky asset as wealth increases? From the previous section, we would anticipate that an individual characterized by decreasing absolute risk aversion (DARA) should want to hold more of the risky asset. We now show that this intuition is correct.

The analysis proceeds by asking what happens to the marginal utility of q_2 as $\bar{W}$ increases. At the asset-holding optimum for the initial wealth level, we have seen, $U'(q_2^*) = 0$. If the effect of an increase in wealth is to raise this marginal utility, the new optimum will have to be at a higher level of q_2.

Differentiating (3.2.9) by $\bar{W}$ and making use of (3.2.8) we obtain:

$$\frac{d}{d\bar{W}}\bar{U}'(q_2) = P_2^A(1 + R_1)E[(\tilde{R}_2 - R_1)v''(\tilde{c}^*)]$$

$$= -P_2^A(1 + R_1)E[(\tilde{R}_2 - R_1)v'(\tilde{c}^*)A(\tilde{c}^*)] \qquad (3.2.10)$$

where $A(\tilde{c}) \equiv -v''(\tilde{c})/v'(\tilde{c})$ is the degree of absolute risk aversion.

If $A(c) = \bar{A}$ is constant, this can be rewritten as:

$$\frac{d}{d\bar{W}}\bar{U}'(q_2) = -P_2^A(1 + R_1)\bar{A}E[(\tilde{R}_2 - R_1)v'(\tilde{c}^*)]$$

From (3.2.9) the expectation is zero. Therefore, under Constant Absolute Risk Aversion (CARA), demand for the risky asset is independent of wealth.

Under the normal assumption of decreasing $A(c)$, the analysis is only a bit more complicated. If $R_2 = R_1$ then, from (3.2.8), $c = (1 + R_1)\bar{W}$ and so $A(c) = A((1 + R_1)\bar{W})$. If $R_2 > R_1$, c is larger and so $A(c) < A((1 + R_1)\bar{W})$. Then:

$$(R_2 - R_1)A(c) < (R_2 - R_1)A((1 + R_1)\bar{W})$$

If $R_2 < R_1$, c is smaller and so $A(c) > A((1 + R_1)\bar{W})$. Then again:

$$(R_2 - R_1)A(c) < (R_2 - R_1)A((1 + R_1)\bar{W})$$

Since this is true for all c, it follows from (3.2.10) that:

$$\frac{d}{d\bar{W}}\bar{U}'\left(q_2^*\right) > -P_2^A(1 + R_1)E[(\tilde{R}_2 - R_1)v'(\tilde{c}^*)A((1 + R_1)\bar{W})]$$
$$= -P_2^A(1 + R_1)A((1 + R_1)\bar{W})E[(\tilde{R}_2 - R_1)v'(\tilde{c}^*)]$$

Again, from (3.2.9), the right-hand side of this inequality is zero. Therefore, at the initial optimum, an increase in wealth raises the expected marginal utility of investing in the risky asset and so raises demand for the asset.

Returning to Figure 3.3, it follows that the wealth expansion path in asset space is upward sloping.[2] As depicted, it bends forward so that, as wealth increases, there is a less-than-proportional increase in demand for the risky asset. You are asked to confirm in an exercise at the end of this section that this will be the case under Increasing Relative Risk Aversion (IARA).

In conclusion, in a regime of incomplete markets with a single risky asset, the wealth effect upon the demand for that asset will be positive, zero, or negative according as *absolute* risk aversion $A(c)$ is decreasing (DARA), constant (CARA), or increasing (IARA). So the uncompensated demand for the risky asset, in the region where the individual is a net buyer, will surely have negative slope under DARA or CARA but not necessarily so under IARA. As for the *riskless* asset, its demand (once again, in the region where the individual is a net buyer) must always have negative slope – since the wealth effect is surely positive. (A richer individual will always want to increase his contingent consumption in each and every state of the world.)

---

[2] It is tempting to generalize from this and conjecture that, with one riskless asset and several risky assets, total spending on the latter would rise with wealth. However, as Hart (1975) has shown, special cases can be constructed for which this is not the case. Despite this, there remains the presumption that wealth and total spending on risky assets will be positively related.

Exercises and Excursions 3.2.2

1 Concavity of the Derived Utility Function

Let $q = (q_1, \ldots, q_A)$ be an individual's holdings of A assets. In state s the return on each of these assets is $z_s = (z_{1s}, \ldots, z_{AS})$ so that the total state-s income is:

$$q \cdot z_s = \sum_{a=1}^{A} q_a z_{as}$$

Expected utility is then:

$$U(q) = \sum_{s=1}^{S} \pi_s v(q \cdot z_s)$$

where v is an increasing strictly concave function.

(A) Show that $U(q)$ is also strictly concave, that is, for any pair of vectors q^α, q^β:

$$U(\lambda q^\alpha + (1 - \lambda) q^\beta) > U(q^\alpha) + (1 - \lambda) U(q^\beta), \quad 0 < \lambda < 1$$

(B) Hence confirm that preferences are convex, as depicted in Figure 3.3.

2 Asset Demand with Constant Absolute Risk Aversion

Suppose $v(c) = \kappa_1 - \kappa_2 e^{-Ac}$, $\kappa_1, \kappa_2 > 0$. There are M assets, all of which are risky except asset 1.

(A) Write down the individual's optimization problem and then substitute for q_1, the demand for the riskless asset, using the wealth constraint.

(B) Write down the necessary conditions for an optimal portfolio and confirm that demands for risky assets are independent of initial wealth $\bar{W}$.

3 Demand for a Risky Asset under Increasing Relative Risk Aversion

Let κ_2 be the proportion of initial wealth invested in the risky asset in the portfolio problem described in this section.

(A) Obtain an expression for $U(\kappa_2)$, expected utility as a function of κ_2, and hence show that under constant relative risk aversion (CRRA) the optimal proportion κ_2^* is independent of wealth ($\partial U'(\kappa_2^*)/\partial \bar{W} = 0$).

(B) Apply methods similar to those used in Section 3.2 to establish that, under increasing relative risk aversion (IRRA), κ_2^* declines with wealth.

(C) What occurs under DRRA?

4 Demand for a Risky Asset with Different Attitudes towards, Risk (Pratt 1964)

Suppose that individual J is everywhere more risk averse than K, so that (in accordance with an earlier exercise) J's utility function $v_J(c)$ is an increasing concave transformation of $v_K(c)$:

$$v_J(c) = f(v_K(c)), \quad f(\cdot) > 0, \quad f''(\cdot) < 0$$

(A) Show that, if both individuals face the portfolio-choice problem described in this section, and the prices of the riskless and risky assets are both unity, the optimal holding of the risky asset for J, q_2^J, satisfies:

$$\bar{U}_J'(q_2^J) = P_2^A E[(\tilde{R}_2 - R_1) f'(v_K(\tilde{c})) v_K'(\tilde{c})] = 0$$

where $\tilde{c} = (1 + R_1)\bar{W} + (R_2 - R_1) P_2^A q_2^J$.

(B) Confirm that for each possible realization R_2:

$$(R_2 - R_1) f'(v_K(\tilde{c})) < (R_2 - R_1) f'(v_K(\bar{W}))$$

Hence show that $\bar{U}_K'(q_2^J) > 0$ and therefore that:

$$q_2^J < q_2^K$$

3.3 Changes in the Distribution of Asset Payoffs

The previous section examined the effects of parametric changes in wealth, or in the prices of state claims or of assets, upon the risk-bearing optimum of the individual. For example, we showed that, under a regime of Complete Contingent Markets (CCM), if the individual was previously at an interior optimum, then an increase in wealth would increase his holdings of each and every state claim. Owing to this positive wealth effect, the uncompensated demand curve for any contingent claim is negatively sloped in the region where the individual is a net buyer. An analogous conclusion evidently holds for Complete Asset Markets (CAM). But, with incomplete markets, the uncompensated demand for an asset on the part of a net buyer is unambiguously negatively sloped only if the individual is characterized by decreasing or constant absolute risk aversion (DARA or CARA).

This section represents a shift in point of view. Here the parametric changes impacting upon the individual take the form of shifts in the distribution of the contingent returns or payoffs z_{as} of some particular asset a. Let us reconsider the example of the previous section, in which an individual chooses to hold q_1 units of the riskless asset with payoff z_1 and q_2 units of the risky asset with state s return z_{2s} for $s = 1, \ldots, S$. For simplicity, assume that the endowment is entirely in units of the riskless asset. Then, with endowed wealth $\bar{W} = P_1^A \bar{q}_1$ the utility-maximizing portfolio choice (q_1 and q_2) is the solution to:

$$\underset{q_1, q_2}{\text{Max}} \left\{ U(q_1, q_2) \equiv \sum_{s=1}^{S} \pi_s \nu(q_1 z_1 + q_2 z_{2s}) \,\middle|\, P_1^A q_1 + P_2^A q_2 = \bar{W} \right\}$$

For simplicity, let $P_1^A = P_2^A = 1$ so that the budget constraint becomes $q_1 + q_2 = \bar{W}$. Then if the individual purchases q_2 units of the risky asset, his final state-s consumption is:

$$c_s = (\bar{W} - q_2)z_1 + q_2 z_{2s} = \bar{W} z_1 + q_2(z_{2s} - z_1) \tag{3.3.1}$$

As a first illustration of a parametric change, suppose the return to the risky asset 2 declines in one state of the world but is otherwise unaltered. (In the market as a whole, such a shift would tend to change P_2^A, or more generally, the entire pattern of asset prices – a topic to be covered in Chapter 4. But in this chapter we are continuing to focus upon a single individual so that asset prices are assumed constant.) It is tempting to conclude that the individual would then respond by investing less in the risky asset. However, this intuitively appealing argument is not in general true!

Continuing to assume a single riskless and a single risky asset, suppose there are only two states ($S = 2$) as depicted in Figure 3.4. (This is therefore a situation of CAM.) Since the individual's endowment holding consists only of the riskless asset 1, in state-claim space the endowment point is $\bar{C} = (\bar{W} z_1, \bar{W} z_1)$ on the 45° certainty line. If the individual invests everything in the risky asset instead (so that $q_2 = \bar{W}$), his income claims are represented by the point $R = (\bar{W} z_{21}, \bar{W} z_{22})$. Before the postulated parametric change occurs, then, the set of feasible contingent incomes consists of all the weighted averages of $\bar{C}$ and R yielding non-negative consumptions in both states. Geometrically, this is the line LL' through $\bar{C}$ and R, extending to the axes (since short sales are allowed within the first quadrant). Along this line the optimum position is the tangency at C*.

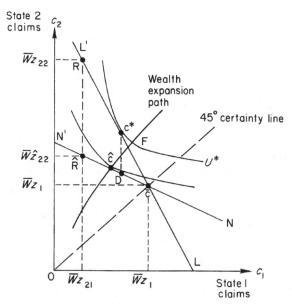

Figure 3.4. Demand for a risky asset.

As depicted, $z_{22} > z_{21}$. That is, the risky asset yields more in state 2 than in state 1. Now suppose that the state-2 yield of the risky asset declines, from z_{22} to $\hat{z}_{22}$. This is equivalent, from the individual's point of view, to a rise in the effective price P_2 of state-2 claims. On the basis of the discussion in the preceding Section 3.2.1, we know that for a net buyer of the risky asset there will be a *substitution effect* away from state-2 consumption and toward state-1 consumption, together with an *income effect* tending to reduce consumption in both states. So the result is unambiguous that at the new risk-bearing optimum there will be a reduction of consumption in state 2, i.e., that $\hat{c}_2 < c_2^*$. Nevertheless, it does not necessarily follow that there will be a reduction in purchases of the risky asset. Since each unit of asset 2 now yields fewer units of state-2 return ($\hat{z}_{22} < z_{22}$) than before, it *may* be the case that the individual would have to buy more units of asset 2 even to generate the reduced quantity of c_2 that he wants to consume.

In Figure 3.4, note that the postulated shift in the risky asset's payoff does not affect the endowment position $\bar{C}$ (which consists of holdings of the *riskless* asset only). So the feasible consumption vectors in Figure 3.4 are now the points on the flatter market line NN' through $\bar{C}$ and $\hat{R}$. Also, it follows from (3.3.1) that, for any given portfolio (q_1, q_2), the shift in z_{22} leaves income in state 1 unchanged. Geometrically, the new income vector generated by any portfolio lies vertically below the old. In particular, $\hat{R}$ lies vertically below R and the state-income yield vector C^* corresponding to the original asset-holding optimum becomes D.

Whether the individual buys more or less of the risky asset then hinges upon whether his indifference-curve tangency lies to the northwest or southeast of D along the line NN'. Specifically, if (as shown in the diagram) the new risk-bearing optimum $\hat{C}$ lies northwest of D, there will be *increased purchases* of asset $2 (\hat{q}_2 > q_2^*)$ even though there is *decreased contingent consumption* in the event of state 2 occurring $(\hat{c}_2 < c_2^*)$. As an obvious corollary, whenever this occurs there will also be a reduction in state-1 consumption. Thus, the reduced state-2 yield of the risky asset "spills over" into reduced consumption in both states. On the other hand, should the new optimum $\hat{C}$ lie southeast of C^*, there will be *reduced purchases* of asset 2 (as well as *reduced consumption* of state 2), hence increased holdings of asset 1 and increased consumption in state 1.

The more rapidly the slope of the indifference curve changes, the smaller is the substitution effect away from c_2-consumption. Hence the more likely it is that the wealth effect of the implicit increase in P_2 dominates, so that the individual's purchase of the risky asset increases. Referring back to Section 3.1 we see that the curvature of the indifference curve is greater the larger is the individual's aversion to risk. So the seemingly paradoxical result, that demand for the risky asset (after a decline of z_{22} to $\hat{z}_{22}$) can increase, is more likely if an individual exhibits a high degree of risk aversion. (From another point of view, however, this is not paradoxical at all. The shift from z_{22} to $\hat{z}_{22}$ has made the risky asset "less risky" – has reduced the gap between z_{22} and z_{21} – which has to some extent increased its attractiveness for highly risk-averse individuals.)

In conclusion, in a simplified regime of two tradable assets (one risky, the other riskless) and two states of the world, a reduction in one of the contingent payoffs z_{as} for the risky asset is equivalent, from the individual's point of view, to an increase in the price P_s of the corresponding state claim. It follows that at the new optimum the individual will reduce his contingent consumption c_s in that state of the world. But he will not necessarily reduce his portfolio holding of the risky asset. And, in particular, if z_{as} declines for the higher-yielding state, a highly risk-averse individual's optimal holding of the risky asset may actually increase – since that asset has in effect become "less risky."

Exercise 1 below proves a related proposition, that if z_{as} falls then the demand for the risky asset will decline if the degree of relative risk aversion, R, is not greater than unity.

Exercises and Excursions 3.3

1 State Returns and Relative Risk Aversion

Choosing units so that $P_1^A = P_2^A = 1$, a risk-averse individual is endowed with $\bar{W}$ units of a riskless asset 1 returning z_1 in each state. He can also make purchases of a risky asset 2 whose payoff is z_{2s} in state s. Initially his optimum holding of the risky asset is positive. Show that if the return z_{2s} on asset 2 rises in some state s, and if the individual's constant relative aversion to risk CRRA is no greater than unity, then his optimal holding of this asset will rise.

2 Parametric Change Lowering Mean and Raising Variance of Asset Payoff

An individual with an initial wealth of $50 must choose a portfolio of two assets, both of which have a price of $50. The first asset is riskless and pays off $50 in each of the two possible states. The second returns z_{2s} in state s, for $s = 1, 2$. The probability of state 1 is π.

(A) If the individual splits his wealth equally between the two assets, confirm the correctness of the following table, where the risky asset returns may have the form of α, β, or γ.

(B) Suppose the individual has a utility function:

$$v(c) = -e^{-Ac}$$

where $A = \frac{\ln 4}{30}$ (and hence $e^{30A} = 4$). Confirm that the individual's preference ranking of the three risky assets is $\gamma > \alpha > \beta$.

	Risky asset returns (z_{21}, z_{22})	Probability of state 1	Final consumption (c_1, c_2)	E(c)	$\sigma^2(c)$
α	(20,80)	1/5	(35,65)	59	144
β	(38,98)	1/2	(44,74)	59	225
γ	(30,90)	1/3	(40,70)	60	200

(C) With preferences as given in (B) show that in each case the individual's optimal decision is to spend an equal amount on each of the two assets.

3.4 Stochastic Dominance

From the exercises at the end of Section 3.3 it is clear that, to derive strong qualitative predictions as to asset holdings in response to parametric changes in payoff distributions, we must introduce additional restrictions – either upon probability distributions or upon preferences. In the following section we describe some restrictions that do have general implications.

3.4.1 Comparison of Different Consumption Prospects

This section adopts a somewhat different approach to the risk-bearing decision. Instead of considering the specific effects of changes in wealth, in state-claim prices, in asset payoffs, etc., we ask under what general conditions it is possible to assert that one prospect or state-distributed consumption vector is preferred over another. We want to be able to answer this question by comparing the probability distributions of consumption alone, while calling only upon standard properties of individuals' preferences – to wit, positive marginal utility of income ($v'(c) > 0$) and risk aversion ($v''(c) < 0$). In this section it will be more convenient to deal with continuous distributions, equivalent to assuming a continuum rather than a finite or countably infinite number of states of the world.

Let $\tilde{c}_1$ and $\tilde{c}_2$ be two consumption prospects and suppose that an individual with utility function $v(c)$ prefers the former. That is:

$$E[v(\tilde{c}_1)] > E[v(\tilde{c}_2)] \tag{3.4.1}$$

We can write the two cumulative distribution functions as:

$$F(c) = \text{Prob}[\tilde{c}_1 \leq c]$$
$$G(c) = \text{Prob}[\tilde{c}_2 \leq c]$$

Let us assume that both $\tilde{c}_1$ and $\tilde{c}_2$ lie between the limits α and β and that both F and G are continuously differentiable. Then for the two distributions there are associated density functions, $F'(c)$ and $G'(c)$. We can rewrite (3.4.1) as:

$$\mathop{E}_{F}[v(\tilde{c})] \equiv \int_{\alpha}^{\beta} v(c)F'(c)dc > \int_{\alpha}^{\beta} v(c)G'(c)dc \equiv \mathop{E}_{G}[v(\tilde{c})] \tag{3.4.2}$$

In general, two individuals with different preferences will have different rankings of these two consumption prospects. However, in some cases it is possible to obtain an ordering that holds for all individuals regardless of their preferences (subject only to the standard properties of positive

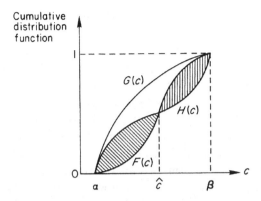

Figure 3.5. First- and second-order stochastic dominance.

marginal utility and risk aversion). In other words, we want to see how far we can get looking only at the probability distributions. When a choice between two prospects can be made using this information alone, it will be said that one distribution *stochastically dominates* the other.

Definition 3.1: First-order stochastic dominance

If, for all c, $F(c) \leq G(c)$ and the inequality is strict over some interval, the distribution F exhibits first-order stochastic dominance over G.

This definition leads immediately to:

Ranking Theorem I
For all increasing, piecewise differentiable functions $v(c)$, if F exhibits first-order stochastic dominance over G, then:

$$\mathop{E}_{F}[v(\tilde{c})] > \mathop{E}_{G}[v(\tilde{c})]$$

Consequently, if the prospect or distribution F is first-order stochastically dominant over G, then any individual with positive marginal utility of income will prefer F to G.

The property of the distribution functions leading to first-order dominance is evident from inspection of Figure 3.5. Here F and H are both first-order stochastically dominant over G but neither F nor H is first-order dominant over the other. Diagrammatically, the F and H curves both lie always below (and so also to the right of) G, but the F and H curves cross.

Following our usual practice, we will emphasize the intuitive meaning of this condition. (More rigorous statements are left as exercises.) First, compare the F and G curves. F being always below G means that, for each and every income level $c°$ between α and β, the cumulative probability that

c is smaller than that income, that $c \leq c^o$, is greater for G than for F. Thus, no matter what level of income we look at between these limits, G always has a greater probability mass in the lower tail than does F. Alternatively, we could express this in terms of the income associated with any given probability level. For example, a lower-tail cumulative probability of, say, 0.5 occurs at a higher income for F than for G. In other words, the distribution F has a higher median (50th percentile) income than G. And, similarly, each and every percentile of the F distribution is at a greater income than the corresponding percentile of the G distribution. So we can confidently say (provided only that the marginal utility of income $v'(c)$ is always positive) that F will surely be preferred. We cannot make a similar comparison of F and H, however. Since F and H cross, comparisons of probability masses in the lower tail (or of income levels associated with any percentile of probability) will not always point the same way.

Only under quite stringent conditions will one distribution ever exhibit first-order stochastic dominance over another. So Ranking Theorem I is not very far reaching. This is not surprising, because only the first standard property of the utility function, that $v'(c) > 0$, has been exploited. A more powerful theorem, involving the concept of *second-order* stochastic dominance, also makes use of the risk-aversion property $- v''(c) < 0$.

Definition 3.2: Second-order stochastic dominance

If for all c:

$$\int_{-\infty}^{c} F(r)dr \leq \int_{-\infty}^{c} H(r)dr \qquad (3.4.3)$$

with the inequality holding strictly over some part of the range, then the distribution F exhibits second-order stochastic dominance over H.

Geometrically, F is second-order dominant over H if, over every interval $[\alpha, c]$, the area under $F(c)$ is never greater (and sometimes smaller) than the corresponding area under $H(c)$. This is equivalent, of course, to the diagonally shaded area in Figure 3.5 being greater than the vertically shaded region.

Definition 3.2 leads directly to:

Ranking Theorem II
For all *increasing concave* twice-piecewise-differentiable functions $v(c)$, the concavity being strict somewhere, if F exhibits second-order stochastic dominance over H, then:

$$\mathop{E}_{F}[v(c)] > \mathop{E}_{H}[v(c)]$$

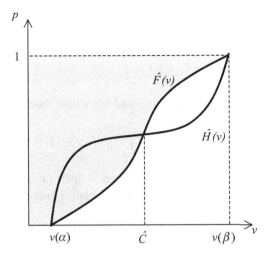

Figure 3.6. Cumulative distribution and expected value.

The intuitive interpretation of second-order stochastic dominance parallels the interpretation of first-order stochastic dominance. As a first step, it is useful to define $\hat{F}(v)$ to be the cumulative distribution function for *final utility* v, when c has the distribution $F(c)$. Note then that:

$$\hat{F}(v(c)) \equiv \text{Prob}\,[\tilde{v} \le v(c)] = \text{Prob}\,[v(\tilde{c}) \le v(c)] = \text{Prob}\,[\tilde{c} \le c] = F(c)$$

That is, at the specific value c° located at any given percentile of the distribution of $\tilde{c}$, the corresponding $v(c^{\circ})$ is at the same percentile of the distribution of v. Similarly, we define $\hat{H}(v)$ to be the cumulative distribution function for v when c has the distribution $H(c)$.

The key point to appreciate is that, as pictured by the dotted region in Figure 3.6, the area lying to the left of the cumulative distribution $\hat{F}(v)$ represents the expected value of v – that is, expected utility $U = \text{E}[v(c)]$ – under the distribution F. To see this, define $p = \hat{F}(v)$ to be the cumulative probability, so that:

$$dp = \hat{F}'(v)dv$$

The mean of $\hat{F}$ is, of course, defined by:

$$\text{E}\,[v] = \int_{v(\alpha)}^{v(\beta)} v\hat{F}'(v)dv = \int_{0}^{1} v\,dp = \int_{0}^{1} \hat{F}^{-1}(p)dp$$

Geometrically, this corresponds to finding the dotted area by integrating along the vertical rather than the horizontal axis in Figure 3.6. Equivalently, the expected value of v is the area of the rectangle less the area under $\hat{F}(v)$. That is:

$$E[v] = v(\beta) - \int_{v(\alpha)}^{v(\beta)} \hat{F}(v)dv$$

Then, to compare two distributions F and H we note that:

$$\mathop{E}_{F}[v(\tilde{c})] - \mathop{E}_{H}[v(\tilde{c})] = - \int_{v(\alpha)}^{v(\beta)} [\hat{F}(v) - \hat{H}(v)]dv$$

That is, the difference in the expected utilities of distributions F and H is just the difference in areas under the implied cumulative distribution functions $\hat{F}$ and $\hat{H}$.

Finally, we can rewrite this integral as:

$$\mathop{E}_{F}[v(\tilde{c})] - \mathop{E}_{H}[v(\tilde{c})] = - \int_{\alpha}^{\beta} [\hat{F}(v(c)) - \hat{H}(v(c))] \frac{dv}{dc}dc$$

$$= - \int_{\alpha}^{\beta} [F(c) - H(c)]v'(c)dc$$

Returning now to Figure 3.5 and looking at the $F(c)$ and $H(c)$ probability distributions, remember that the condition for second-order stochastic dominance requires that the diagonally shaded area (representing the superiority of F over H at low values of c) exceed the vertically shaded area (representing the superiority of H over F at high values of c). But, as we have seen:

$$\mathop{E}_{F}[v(\tilde{c})] - \mathop{E}_{H}[v(\tilde{c})] = \int_{\alpha}^{\hat{c}} [H(c) - F(c)]v'(c)dc$$

$$- \int_{\hat{c}}^{\beta} [F(c) - H(c)]v'(c)dc$$

As long as $v(c)$ is concave so that $v'(c)$ is declining, $v'(c) \geq v'(\hat{c})$ for $c \leq \hat{c}$ and $v'(c) \leq v'(\hat{c})$ for $c > \hat{c}$. It follows that:

$$\mathop{E}_{F}[v(\tilde{c})] - \mathop{E}_{H}[v(\tilde{c})] > \int_{\alpha}^{\hat{c}} [H(c) - F(c)]v'(\hat{c})dc$$

$$- \int_{\hat{c}}^{\beta} [F(c) - H(c)]v'(\hat{c})dc$$

$$= v'(\hat{c}) \int_{\alpha}^{\beta} [H(c) - F(c)]dc$$

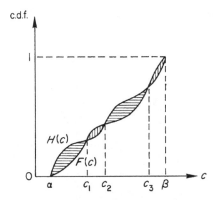

Figure 3.7. Multiple crossings.

From the definition of second-order stochastic dominance, the last integral is positive, and so expected utility is indeed higher under F.

With multiple crossings of F and H the argument is only slightly more complicated. Consider the case of three crossings as in Figure 3.7. Arguing exactly as above, the concavity of $v(c)$ implies that:

$$\int_\alpha^{c_2} (H - F)v'(c)dc > v'(c_1) \int_\alpha^{c_2} (H - F)dc \qquad (3.4.4)$$

and

$$\int_{c_2}^\beta (H - F)v'(c)dc > v'(c_3) \int_{c_2}^\beta (H - F)dc \qquad (3.4.5)$$

Second-order stochastic dominance implies that the integral on the right-hand side of (3.4.4) is positive. Therefore, from the concavity of $v(c)$:

$$\int_\alpha^{c_2} (H - F)v'(c)dc > v'(c_3) \int_\alpha^{c_2} (H - F)dc \qquad (3.4.6)$$

Adding (3.4.5) and (3.4.6) we have, at last:

$$\mathop{E}_F[v(\tilde{c})] - \mathop{E}_H[v(\tilde{c})] = \int_\alpha^\beta (H - F)v'(c)dc > v'(c_3) \int_\alpha^\beta (H - F)dc$$

Again, given second-order stochastic dominance, the last integral is positive and so F is the preferred distribution.

The limiting case where the two distributions have the same mean, but F exhibits second-order stochastic dominance over H, represents a formalization of the idea that one random variable can be more risky than another. This is illustrated in Figure 3.5 where the diagonally shaded region has the

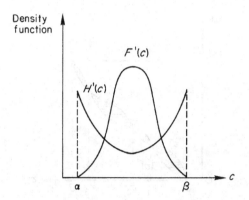

Figure 3.8. Density functions and spread.

same area as the vertically shaded region. Note that the slope of H is greater than the slope of F at both tails of the distribution, while F has a greater slope toward the middle.

From Figure 3.5 we can map the density functions $F'(c)$ and $H'(c)$. These are depicted in Figure 3.8. As already noted, $H'(c) > F'(c)$ toward the ends of the income distribution while $F'(c) > H'(c)$ toward the middle. Then H must have more probability weight in both tails than F. This case, in which probability weight is shifted toward the tails but in such a way that the old and new distributions cross only once, is often referred to as a *simple mean-preserving spread* (Rothschild and Stiglitz, 1971).

As is intuitively clear from Figure 3.8, in the special case where the distribution H represents a simple mean-preserving spread of F it must be that H has higher variance. However, a more powerful result (which is not limited to the single-crossing case) also holds: if F and H have the same mean but F exhibits second-order stochastic dominance over H, then H must have higher variance. This is a direct implication of the following proposition, which follows directly from Ranking Theorem II:

Ranking Theorem III
For all concave functions $v(c)$, the concavity being strict somewhere, if F and H have the same mean and F exhibits second-order stochastic dominance over H then:

$$\underset{F}{\mathrm{E}}[v(\tilde{c})] > \underset{H}{\mathrm{E}}[v(\tilde{c})]$$

Notice that we need not necessarily interpret $v(c)$ as a utility function here (or, for that matter, in the preceding Ranking Theorems). Specifically, we can choose here to let $v(c) = -(c - \mu)^2$, which is, of course, concave in the sense required. Then:

$$-\underset{F}{E}\left[(\tilde{c} - \mu)^2\right] > -\underset{H}{E}\left[(\tilde{c} - \mu)^2\right]$$

That is:

$$-\sigma_F^2 > -\sigma_H^2$$

So if F and H have the same mean μ and F is second-order stochastically dominant, then F has smaller variance.

Thinking now of $v(c)$ as a utility function, we have seen that (i) if F is second-order stochastically dominant over H, then F is strictly preferred, and (ii) if in addition F and H have the same mean, then F has smaller variance. But it does not in general follow that, if two distributions $\tilde{c}_1$ and $\tilde{c}_2$ have the same mean and $\tilde{c}_1$ has smaller variance, then $\tilde{c}_1$ is preferred, for $\tilde{c}_1$ might not be stochastically dominant.

Example:

$$\tilde{c}_1 = \begin{cases} 0.4, & \text{with probability } 1/2 \\ 2.1 & \text{with probability } 1/2 \end{cases}$$

$$\tilde{c}_2 = \begin{cases} 0.25, & \text{with probability } 1/9 \\ 1, & \text{with probability } 7/9 \\ 4, & \text{with probability } 1/9 \end{cases}$$

It is readily confirmed that $E[\tilde{c}_1] = E[\tilde{c}_2]$ and $\text{var}[\tilde{c}_1] < \text{var}[\tilde{c}_2]$. However, with $v(c) = \ln c$, expected utility is negative in the first case and zero in the second, that is, $E[v(\tilde{c}_2)] > E[v(\tilde{c}_1)]$ so that the second prospect is preferred. It is left to the reader to graph the cumulative distribution functions for $\tilde{c}_1$ and $\tilde{c}_2$ and hence to confirm that neither stochastically dominates the other. □

Exercises and Excursions 3.4.1

1 First-Order Stochastic Dominance
For any pair of distributions F and H and differentiable function $v(c)$, integrate by parts to establish that:

$$\underset{F}{E}[v(\tilde{c})] - \underset{H}{E}[v(\tilde{c})] = \int_\alpha^\beta v(c)[F'(c) - H'(c)]dc$$
$$= \int_\alpha^\beta v'(c)[H(c) - F(c)]dc$$

Hence establish Ranking Theorem I.

2 Second-Order Stochastic Dominance

Appealing to Exercise 1, and integrating by parts a second time, establish Ranking Theorem II.

3 Mean-Preserving Spreads

Use your answer to Question 2 to establish Ranking Theorem III.

4 Stochastic Dominance as a Necessary Condition

(A) In the text it was shown that, if $G(c) \geq F(c)$, then for any non-decreasing function $v(c)$:

$$\mathop{E}_{F}[v(\tilde{c})] > \mathop{E}_{G}[v(\tilde{c})]$$

By considering the example:

$$v_1(c) = \begin{cases} -1, & c < r \\ 0, & c \geq r \end{cases}$$

establish that, if the condition for first-order stochastic dominance does not hold, there are some non-decreasing utility functions for which the ranking is reversed. That is, for the entire class of non-decreasing utility functions to rank F over G (at least weakly), first-order stochastic dominance is a necessary condition.

(B) By considering the example:

$$v_2(c) = \begin{cases} c - r, & c < r \\ 0, & c \geq r \end{cases}$$

establish the necessity of the second-order stochastic dominance condition (3.4.3) for Ranking Theorem III to hold for all concave functions.

3.4.2 Responding to Increased Risk*

We conclude this chapter by asking how a change in the probability distribution of income that satisfies the conditions of second-order stochastic dominance affects decisions.

Let $c = c(x, \theta)$ be the consequence of taking action x when some exogenous variable takes on the value θ. Moreover, suppose that this exogenous

---

* Starred sections represent more difficult or specialized materials that can be omitted without significant loss of continuity.

variable is state dependent. Then, given the underlying beliefs about the likelihood of different states and the way θ varies across states, there is some derived distribution function for θ, $F_1(\theta)$. For expositional convenience let θ be distributed continuously. Then, one can write the expected utility of taking action x as:

$$U_1(x) = \int_{-\infty}^{\infty} v(c(x, \theta))F_1'(\theta) \, d\theta$$

A simple illustration is provided by the portfolio choice problem analyzed in Section 3.2. Suppose an individual invests x in a risky asset with gross yield of $1 + \theta$ per dollar and his remaining wealth $W - x$ in a riskless asset returning 1 per dollar. His final income is:

$$c(x, \theta) = (W - x)1 + x(1 + \theta) = W + x\theta \qquad (3.4.7)$$

The question we wish to address is how the individual's portfolio decision is affected by a change in the distribution of the random variable θ.

Returning to the general formulation, suppose that, with distribution function F_1, expected utility is maximized by taking action x_1^*. That is, the rate at which expected utility changes with x:

$$U_1'(x) = \int_{-\infty}^{\infty} \frac{\partial v}{\partial x}(c(x, \theta))F_1'(\theta) d\theta$$

is zero at $x = x_1^*$.

Suppose next that there is a change in the way θ varies with the underlying state of nature. In particular, suppose that the old and new distribution functions for θ, F_1 and F_2, have the same mean and that F_1 exhibits second-order stochastic dominance over F_2.

From Ranking Theorem III it follows immediately that, if $\partial v/\partial x$ is a strictly concave function of θ, then:

$$U_1'(x) = \mathop{E}_{F_1}\left[\frac{\partial v}{\partial x}(c(x, \theta))\right] > \mathop{E}_{F_2}\left[\frac{\partial v}{\partial x}(c(x, \theta))\right] = U_2'(x)$$

In particular, this inequality holds at x_1^*. Therefore:

$$0 = U_1'(x_1^*) > U_2'(x_1^*)$$

It follows that the individual can increase his expected utility by choosing an action $x_2 < x_1^*$. Thus, assuming $U_2(x)$ has a unique turning point under the new (second-order dominated) probability distribution of returns on the risky asset, the individual will reduce his risky investment.

Note that the requirement that $\partial v/\partial x$ should be concave introduces a restriction on the third derivative of the utility function v. As we shall see in the exercises, this may be satisfied by imposing plausible restrictions on the way absolute and relative risk aversion vary with wealth.

Developing the arguments above only a little bit more yields the following result:

Optimal Response Theorem I (Rothschild and Stiglitz 1971):

Suppose that the distribution functions $F_1(\theta)$ and $F_2(\theta)$ have the same mean and F_1 exhibits second-order stochastic dominance over F_2. Let x_i^* be the solution to:

$$\text{Max}_x U_i(x) = \int_{-\infty}^{\infty} v(c(x,\ \theta))F_i'(\theta)\, d\theta, \quad i = 1, 2$$

Suppose further that x_i^* is the unique turning point of $U_i(x)$. Then if $\partial v/\partial x$ is a concave (convex) function of θ, x_1^* is greater than (less than) x_2^*.

While this proposition has been widely used in attempts to analyze the effects of mean-preserving increases in risk, results have been somewhat limited. The analysis of Section 3.3 suggests the reason. Mean-preserving increases in risk have both income and substitution effects, and these are often offsetting.

In an effort to overcome this problem, Diamond and Stiglitz suggested considering the effect of a change to a more risky distribution of returns that keeps expected utility constant. To be precise, suppose that the new distribution leaves expected utility constant at the old optimum x^* but the new distribution of *utility* is more risky in the sense of second-order stochastic dominance. The following theorem provides conditions to sign the effect of such a mean-preserving increase in risk.

Optimal Response Theorem II (Diamond and Stiglitz, 1974)

Suppose that $c \in [\alpha, \beta]$ has a continuously differentiable distribution function $F(c)$. Suppose, furthermore, that the solution x^* of the following problem is the unique turning point of $U_F(x)$:

$$\text{Max}_x U_F(x) = \int_{\alpha}^{\beta} v(x, c)F'(c)dc, \quad \text{where } \frac{\partial v}{\partial c} > 0$$

Then if the distribution shifts from F to G in such a way that, at $x = x^*$, expected utility is unchanged but the new distribution of utility is more risky (in the sense of second-order stochastic dominance), the new optimum x^{**} is less than x^* if:

$$\frac{\partial^2}{\partial c \partial x} \ln \frac{\partial v}{\partial c} < 0$$

Moreover, if the last inequality is reversed, x^{**} exceeds x^*.

The derivation of this result is only a bit more complicated than that of Optimal Response Theorem I. The interested reader will find a sketch of the proof in the exercises at the end of this section. From these exercises it will become clear that significantly stronger results are possible using Optimal Response Theorem II.

Exercises and Excursions 3.4.2

1 *Optimal Responses to a Change in Risk*
(A) In Optimal Response Theorem I, suppose that the assumption that F_1 and F_2 have the same mean is replaced by the assumption that $\partial v/\partial x$ is an increasing function of θ. Show that the theorem continues to hold.
(B) What conclusions can be drawn if $\partial v/\partial x$ is a *convex* function of θ?

2 *Life-Cycle Saving with Future Income Uncertainty (Leland, 1968)*
(A) Show that a sufficient condition for $v'''(c) > 0$ is that absolute risk aversion, $A(c) \equiv -v''(c)/v'(c)$, is decreasing with wealth.
(B) An individual with current income I_0 and uncertain future income $\tilde{I}_1$ can earn $1 + r$ dollars on each dollar saved. His life-cycle utility is given by the intertemporally additive utility function:

$$v(c_0, c_1) = v_0(c_0) + v_1(c_1)$$

where c_0 is current consumption and c_1 is future consumption. Show that, if the distribution of future income becomes less favorable in the sense of second-order stochastic dominance and if $v_1'''(c_1) > 0$, the optimal level of savings increases.

3 *Portfolio Choice*
(A) Show that:

$$\mu x \frac{v''(\lambda + \mu x)}{v'(\lambda + \mu x)} = -R(\lambda + \mu x) + \lambda A(\lambda + \mu x)$$

where $A(c) = -v''(c)/v'(c)$ and $R(c) = -cv''(c)/v'(c)$.

(B) An individual with wealth $\bar{W}$ invests x in a risky asset with a return of $\tilde{z}_2$ and the rest of his wealth in a riskless asset with yield $z_1 = 1$.

If $A(c)$ is decreasing and $R(c)$ is less than unity and non-decreasing, apply Optimal Response Theorem I to establish the impact on x of a change in the distribution of risky returns that is strictly less favorable in the sense of second-order stochastic dominance.

(C) Analyze also the effect of a mean-utility-preserving increase in risk under the assumptions of decreasing absolute and increasing relative risk aversion.

4 Mean-Utility-Preserving Increase in Risk

(A) Under the hypothesis of Optimal Response Theorem II, let $c = \phi(x, v)$ be the inverse of the mapping $V = v(x, c)$, that is, $\phi(x, v) = v^{-1}(x, V)$. Furthermore, let $\hat{F}(V)$ be the implied distribution of V. Confirm that:

$$U_F'(x) = \int_{V_\alpha}^{V_\beta} \frac{\partial v}{\partial x}(x, \phi(x, V))\hat{F}'(V)dV$$

(B) Let x^* be the optimum under the distribution F. Write the corresponding expression for a new distribution G that has the property that, at $x = x^*$, $\hat{G}(V)$ is a mean-preserving spread of $\hat{F}(V)$.

(C) Let x^{**} be the optimum under the new distribution G. Appeal to Ranking Theorem II to show that x^{**} is less than x^* if $\partial v(x^*, \phi(x^*, V))/\partial x$ is a concave function of V.

(D) Define $y(V) \equiv \partial v(x, \phi(x, V))/\partial x$, i.e.:

$$y(v(x, c)) = \frac{\partial v}{\partial x}(x, c)$$

Differentiate by c and hence show that $y'(V)$ can be expressed as follows:

$$y'(v(x, c)) = \frac{\partial v}{\partial x} \ln \frac{\partial v}{\partial c}(x, c)$$

(E) Differentiate this expression again and hence establish Optimal Response Theorem II.

5 Owner-Operated Firms Facing Demand Uncertainty (Sandmo, 1971)

Each firm in an industry is owned and operated by a single agent whose best alternative is working elsewhere at wage w. In the production of q units of output, the cost to firm i of all other inputs, $C(q)$, is an increasing convex function, with $C(0) = 0$. Each owner must choose his output level q^* before knowing the final product price $\tilde{p}$. There is free entry into, and exit from, the industry.

(A) If owners are risk neutral, show that the equilibrium expected price denoted as $\bar{p}_n$ must satisfy:

(i) $\bar{p}_n = C'(q^*)$ (ii) $\bar{p}_n q^* - C(q^*) - w = 0$

(B) If owners are risk averse show, that the equilibrium expected price $\bar{p}_a$ exceeds $\bar{p}_n$.

(C) Suppose that initially there is no uncertainty so that the equilibrium price is $\bar{p}_n$ and output per firm is q^*. If prices become uncertain, apply Optimal Response Theorem II to establish that the output of firms remaining in the industry will decline if the following expression is a decreasing function of p:

$$\phi(q, p) = [pq - qC'(q)]\frac{v''(pq - C(q))}{v'(pq - C(q))}$$

(D) Show that, for all $q > 0$, $qC'(q) > C'(q)$. Hence establish that, under the assumptions of decreasing absolute and non-decreasing relative risk aversion, the equilibrium output per firm declines.

[HINT: Appeal to Optimal Response Theorem II and (A) of Exercise 3.]**

SUGGESTIONS FOR FURTHER READING: For an in-depth exposition of risk-aversion, including an extension to inter-temporal models, see Gollier (2001).

References

Arrow, Kenneth J., "The Theory of Risk Bearing," in *Aspects of the Theory of Risk Bearing*, Helsinki: Yrjö Jahnssonin Säätio, 1965. Reprinted in *Essays in the Theory of Risk Bearing*, Chicago: Markham, 1971.

Diamond, Peter A. and Stiglitz, Joseph E., "Increases in Risk and in Risk Aversion," *Journal of Economic Theory*, 8 (1974), 337–360.

Gollier, Christian, *The Economics of Risk and Time*, Cambridge, MA: MIT Press, 2001.

Hart, Oliver D., "Some Negative Results on the Existence of Comparative Statics Results in Portfolio Theory," *Review of Economic Studies*, 42 (1975), 615–621.

Leland, Hayne E., "Savings and Uncertainty: The Precautionary Demand for Saving," *Quarterly Journal of Economics*, 82 (1968), 465–473.

** End of starred section.

Machina, Mark J., "A Stronger Characterization of Declining Risk Aversion," *Econometrica*, 50 (1982), 1069–1080.

Pratt, John W., "Risk Aversion in the Small and in the Large," *Econometrica*, 32 (1964), 122–136.

Rothschild, Michael and Stiglitz, Joseph E., "Increasing Risk I: A Definition," *Journal of Economic Theory*, 2 (1970), 225–243 and "Increasing Risk II: Its Economic Consequences," *Journal of Economic Theory*, 3 (1971), 66–84.

Sandmo, Agnar, "On the Theory of the Competitive Firm under Price Uncertainty," *American Economic Review*, 61 (1971), 65–73.

4

Market Equilibrium under Uncertainty

We have so far considered only the decisions of the individual. In this chapter the level of analysis shifts to market interactions and the conditions of equilibrium. The *firm* will be introduced as an agency of individuals engaged in the process of production. We continue to deal only with *event uncertainty* under "perfect markets" – ruling out *market uncertainty* with its characteristic attendant phenomena of search and of trading at non-clearing prices. But account will be taken of possibly incomplete regimes of markets; i.e., we will not always assume that each distinct state claim is, directly or indirectly, tradable. In Section 4.3, we build on Section 2.2 to flesh out the capital asset pricing model, which is the cornerstone of asset pricing in financial economics.

4.1 Market Equilibrium in Pure Exchange

In the regime of Complete Contingent Markets (CCM), where claims to a generalized consumption good C under each and every state contingency are separately tradable, as shown in Chapter 2, Equation (2.1.6), the individual's optimum position can be expressed as the Fundamental Theorem of Risk Bearing:

$$\frac{\pi_1 v'(c_1)}{P_1} = \frac{\pi_2 v'(c_2)}{P_2} = \cdots = \frac{\pi_s v'(c_s)}{P_s} \qquad (4.1.1)$$

(This form of the theorem is valid only for interior solutions.[1]) At this point, we call attention to the fact that, in principle at least, all of the following elements may differ among the various individuals $j = 1, \ldots, J$:

---

[1] Unless otherwise indicated, it will be assumed throughout that interior (and not corner) solutions apply for all economic agents.

the probability beliefs π_s^j, the consumption quantities c_s^j, and the utility functions $v_j(c^j)$. However, the prices P_s will be the same for all market participants.

In moving from individual optimization to market equilibrium under CCM, Equation (4.1.1) must hold for each and every market participant. It follows immediately that, for any two individuals j and k, and comparing state 1 with any other state s:

$$\frac{\pi_s^j v_j'(c_s^j)}{\pi_1^j v_j'(c_1^j)} = \frac{P_s}{P_1} = \frac{\pi_s^k v_k'(c_s^k)}{\pi_1^k v_k'(c_1^k)} \tag{4.1.2}$$

Thus, for each and every individual (at an interior solution), the price ratio between any two state claims will equal the ratio of expected marginal utility of incomes in the two states. As an evident corollary, if in addition individuals j and k have the same beliefs, then for all s:

$$\frac{v_j'(c_s^j)}{v_k'(c_s^k)} = \xi \quad \text{(a constant)}$$

In words: for any individuals j and k, the ratio of j's marginal utility of contingent income to k's corresponding marginal utility is the same over all states.

The other conditions required for equilibrium represent market clearing. In equilibrium under pure exchange, for each and every traded state claim the sum of the desired holdings (demand quantities) must equal the sum of the endowment amounts (supply quantities):

$$\sum_{j=1}^{J} c_s^j = \sum_{j=1}^{J} \bar{c}_s^j, \quad \text{for } s = 1, \dots, S$$

Example 4.1: In a world of two equally probable states ($\pi_1 = \pi_2 = 1/2$), suppose there are two equally numerous types of individuals: j and k. The j types have endowment $\bar{C}^j = (\bar{c}_1^j, \bar{c}_2^j) = (40, 40)$ while the k types have endowment $\bar{C}^k = (20, 140)$. The respective utility functions are $v_j = \ln c^j$ and $v_k = (c^k)^{1/2}$. Find the equilibrium price ratio and the optimum risky consumption vectors $\hat{C}^j$ and $\hat{C}^k$.

Answer: One way of solving the system is to consider the respective demands for c_2 claims as a function of the unknown P_2. For the type j

individuals, the Fundamental Theorem of Risk Bearing can be expressed as:

$$\frac{0.5(1/c_1^j)}{P_1} = \frac{0.5(1/c_2^j)}{P_2}$$

or:

$$P_1 c_1^j = P_2 c_2^j$$

And the budget equation is:

$$P_1 c_1^j + P_2 c_2^j = 40P_1 + 40P_2$$

Setting $P_1 = 1$ as numeraire, the type j demand for state 2 claims becomes:

$$c_2^j = 40(1 + P_2)/2P_2$$

An analogous development for the type k individuals leads to:

$$c_2^k = (20 + 140P_2)/(P_2^2 + P_2)$$

Making use of the clearing condition that $c_2^j + c_2^k = 40 + 140 = 180$, it may be verified that the equilibrium price is $P_2 = 1/2$. The associated optimal consumption vectors are $\hat{C}^j = (30, 60)$ and $\hat{C}^k = (30, 120)$. □

Instead of contingent-claims trading, more generally there might be trading of *assets* ($a = 1, \ldots, A$) at prices P_a^A, where a unit of each asset represents a fixed bundle of state-claim payoffs z_{as}. The corresponding Risk-Bearing Theorem for Asset Markets is the individual optimum condition for holdings of assets q_a, applicable under regimes of Complete Asset Markets (CAM) and even for incomplete asset-market regimes:[2]

$$\frac{\sum_s \pi_s v'(c_s)z_{1s}}{P_1^A} = \frac{\sum_s \pi_s v'(c_s)z_{2s}}{P_2^A} = \cdots = \frac{\sum_s \pi_s v'(c_s)z_{As}}{P_A^A}, \quad c_s = \sum_a q_a z_{as}$$

---

[2] As indicated in Chapter 2, an asset-market regime is "complete" if the set of available assets $a = 1, \ldots, A$ allows each individual to achieve the same contingent consumption vector as under CCM. A necessary, though not sufficient, condition for complete asset markets is $A \geq S$.

At an interior optimum, this equation will hold in asset-market equilibrium for each and every economic agent. The equilibrium price ratio between asset 1 and asset a will be such that, for any pair of individuals j and k:

$$\frac{\sum_s \pi_s^j v_j'(c_s^j) z_{as}}{\sum_s \pi_s^j v_j'(c_s^j) z_{1s}} = \frac{P_a^A}{P_1^A} = \frac{\sum_s \pi_s^k v_k'(c_s^k) z_{as}}{\sum_s \pi_s^k v_k'(c_s^k) z_{1s}}$$

Notice once again that not only the asset prices P_a^A are taken as given and thus the same for all individuals, but also the asset state payoffs z_{as}. That is, there is no disagreement among individuals about what each asset will return in each and every state. So, the only possible disagreement allowed for in this simple model concerns the *probabilities* of the different states.[3]

Finally, of course, in asset-market equilibrium there must also be market clearing:

$$\sum_{j=1}^J q_a^j = \sum_{j=1}^J \bar{q}_a^j, \quad \text{for } a = 1, \ldots, A$$

Example 4.2: Under the conditions of the previous example, imagine now that the same endowments are expressed as asset holdings $\bar{q}_a$. Thus, suppose the type j endowment consists of 40 units of asset 1 with state-return vector $(z_{11}, z_{12}) = (1, 1)$ while k's endowment consists of 20 units of asset 2 with return vector $(z_{21}, z_{22}) = (1, 7)$. Find the equilibrium asset price ratio P_1^A/P_2^A and the associated optimum asset holdings $\hat{q}_a$.

Answer: This is evidently a CAM regime. Using the Risk-Bearing Theorem for Asset Markets from Section 2.1.2 of Chapter 2, and since $c_s = \Sigma_a q_a z_{as}$, following the method of the previous example we could develop the parties' demands for one of the assets as a function of its unknown price. An easier analysis suffices here, however, since we know that under the CAM condition the same consumption vectors can be attained as under the CCM assumption of the previous example. We also know from the development in Chapter 2 that the asset prices P_a^A are related to the contingent-claim prices P_s by:

$$P_a^A = \sum_s z_{as} P_s$$

---

[3] This is, of course, a very drastic idealization of individuals' portfolio-holding choice situations in the real world.

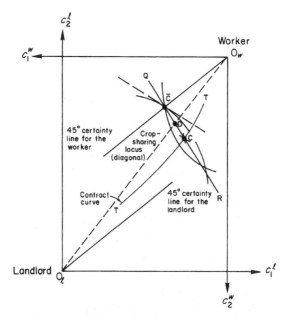

Figure 4.1. Risk sharing via state-claim trading.

Letting the state-claim price $P_1 = 1$ be the numeraire as before, it follows immediately that $P_1^A = 1(1) + 1(0.5) = 1.5$, while $P_2^A = 1(1) + 7(0.5) = 4.5$. And knowing the optimal $\hat{c}_2$ for each type of individual, the equations $c_s = \Sigma_a q_a z_{as}$ can be inverted, leading to the optimum asset holdings $\hat{Q}^j = (\hat{q}_1^j, \hat{q}_2^j) = (25, 5)$ while $\hat{Q}^k = (\hat{q}_1^k, \hat{q}_2^k) = (15, 15)$.   □

4.1.1 Application to Share Cropping

In an agricultural situation, assume there are two decision makers: landlord l owns land but no labor, while worker w owns labor but no land. There are two states of the world: $s = 1$ (loss state, or "bad weather") versus $s = 2$ (non-loss state, or "good weather"). The respective agreed probabilities are π_1 and $\pi_2 \equiv 1 - \pi_1$. For the sake of the argument, assume that all productive decisions have been made so that the only choices remaining are how to share the contingent outputs and the associated risks.

Figure 4.1 is an Edgeworth box, on axes representing c_1 (income in the loss state) and c_2 (income in the non-loss state). Because of the difference in the social totals, the box is vertically elongated. The two parties' 45° certainty lines cannot coincide; it is impossible for *both* individuals to attain certainty positions, though either one could do so if the other were to bear all the risk. For individual h (where $h = l, w$), the absolute indifference-curve slope (the Marginal Rate of Substitution M^h) at any point in the Edgeworth box is given by $\pi_1 v'_h(c_1^h)/\pi_2 v'_h(c_2^h)$. Along the worker's 45° line, $M^w = \pi_1/\pi_2$ since $c_2^w = c_1^w$. But at any such point the landlord's $c_1^l < c_2^l$, hence $v'_l(c_1^l) > v'_l(c_2^l)$, so the landlord's indifference curves must all be steeper than the worker's along the latter's 45° line. Reasoning similarly for the landlord's 45° line, we see that the indifference curves must be shaped as shown in the diagram. It follows that the Contract Curve TT, connecting all the mutual-tangency points where the two parties' indifference-curve slopes are equal, must lie between the two 45° lines. This means that in equilibrium the parties will share the risk.

Assuming price-taking behavior – which would be applicable if there were a large number of competing individuals on both sides of the market – the equilibrium point would depend upon the endowment position. In the diagram, suppose this endowment is $\bar{C}$: the worker is initially receiving a fixed wage while the landlord is bearing all the risk. Under CCM there will then be trading in state claims c_1 and c_2, leading to the CCM equilibrium price ratio P_1/P_2. Specifically (4.1.2) takes the form:

$$\frac{\pi_1 v'_w\left(c_1^w\right)}{\pi_2 v'_w\left(c_2^w\right)} = \frac{P_1}{P_2} = \frac{\pi_1 v'_l\left(c_1^l\right)}{\pi_2 v'_l\left(c_2^l\right)}$$

The solution point is, of course, on the Contract Curve, as indicated by point C in the diagram. Note the following properties of the equilibrium position:

1 The parties have shared the risk, and will in fact do so regardless of the endowment position.
2 Since $c_1 < c_2$ for each party at equilibrium, it follows that $v'(c_1) > v'(c_2)$ for both l and w, and hence that $P_1/P_2 > \pi_1/\pi_2$. That is, the price of contingent income in the loss state is high *relative* to the corresponding probability. This is, of course, what we would expect: apart from the probability weighting factor, claims to income in an affluent state of the world should be cheap in comparison with claims to income in an impoverished state.

We digress now to make some remarks on contract structures. If the worker initially receives a contractually fixed wage placing him on his 45° line, we have seen that a certain amount of trading of contingent claims is necessary to achieve an efficient distribution of risk. The same holds if the landlord initially receives a fixed contractual rent placing her on her 45°

line. Since such trading is costly, we would expect to observe a tendency to avoid these extreme contractual forms. And, in fact, the worker and land-lord functions are very commonly combined in owner-operated farms. An important element affecting the cost of trading is the problem of enforce-ment of contract. For instance, the landlord may find it difficult to control shirking by workers or the two parties might not be able to unambigu-ously identify which state of the world has occurred in order to distribute the contingent payoffs. The potential for trouble and disagreement on that score is all the greater since in practical situations the number of states S is large. (Consider how many states would have to be distinguished within the general category of "good weather.") One way of reducing the difficulty is a *share-cropping* arrangement in which the parties need only decide in what fixed proportions to divide the crop, whatever its size.

In Figure 4.1, the possible proportional divisions of the product would be represented by points along the main diagonal of the Edgeworth box (dashed line). In general, no such division could exactly reproduce the CCM solution along the Contract Curve TT in the diagram. Thus, Equation (4.1.2) would not be satisfied. But a point like D, on the main diagonal of Figure 4.1, may be a reasonably good approximation of the CCM solution at point C. (It would be possible to reproduce the *exact* state-claim solution by combining share cropping with side-payments; for example, if there are only two states as in the diagram, the landlord might receive $x\%$ of the crop less a side-payment of $\$y$ in each state. However, with more than two states, it would in general be necessary to have a different side-payment for each of $S - 1$ distinct states, which would involve essentially the same high transaction costs as full state-claim trading.)

Alternatively, consider a CAM regime. In Figure 4.2, the endowment point $\bar{C}$ could be regarded as representing (i) the worker's initial holding $\bar{q}_a^w$ of a certainty asset a, i.e., an asset with payoffs $(Z_{a1}, Z_{a2}) = (1,1)$, which is reflected by the 45° slope of the line from 0_w to $\bar{C}$ or (ii) the landlord's initial holding $\bar{q}_b^l$ of a risky asset b, the ratio of whose returns (Z_{b1}, Z_{b2}) is reflected in the steeper slope of the line from 0_l to $\bar{C}$. We are free to choose units for each asset, so suppose that a unit of asset a is represented by the unit vector parallel to $0_w\bar{C}$ while a unit of asset b is represented by the unit vector parallel to $0_l\bar{C}$. Then the length of the line $0_l\bar{C}$ is the number of units of asset b initially held by the landlord.

Any exchange of assets by the landlord is a move back along the line $0_l\bar{C}$ and out along a line parallel to $0_w\bar{C}$. By exchanging assets in such quantities as to move to a point on the contract curve such as C^*, each party is satisfying the Risk-Bearing Theorem for Asset Markets, plus, of course, the

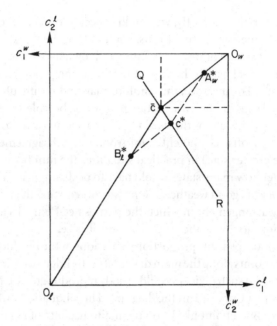

Figure 4.2. Risk sharing via asset trading.

market clearing guaranteed by the fixed size of the Edgeworth box. Once again, however, for $S > 2$ the ideal CCM solution at C^* cannot in general be attained by trading in only two assets a and b.

As an interesting interpretation, we can think of this type of risk-sharing as the exchange of "equity shares" in the two parties' endowments. This interpretation will be developed further later in the chapter.

4.1.2 Application to Insurance

The Edgeworth box of Figure 4.1 can be given another interpretation: the risk-sharing that takes place there can be regarded as "mutual insurance." Indeed, all insurance is best thought of as mutual. Insurance companies, since they do not dispose of any resources other than those possessed by their owners, creditors, and policy holders, are only intermediaries in the risk-sharing process.

Once again, imagine "loss" and "non-loss" states of the world. For example, an earthquake might or might not occur. The Edgeworth box will again be vertically elongated, the social total of income being smaller in the loss state (state 1). From any endowment point like $\bar{C}$ in Figure 4.1, price-taking traders under CCM would arrive at a risk-sharing equilibrium like C* on the Contract Curve TT. As before, the absolute slope P_1/P_2 of the equilibrium market line QR exceeds the absolute slope of the dashed line representing the "fair" price ratio (equal to the probability ratio π_1/π_2). That is, claims to income in the less affluent state of the world command a relatively high price. This "social risk" helps explain why insurance is not offered at strictly fair (or "actuarial") terms.[4] But the influence of social risk depends upon a number of factors, as will be worked out in detail in what follows.

As an instructive special case, imagine there are two individuals j and k with equal initial gross incomes $\bar{c}$, each being subject to a fixed loss hazard L with the same probability p. Thus, each person faces the prospect $(\bar{c}, \bar{c} - L; 1 - p, p)$. Here, p is the probability of an independent private event. Four possible social states can be defined, according as loss is suffered by (1) neither party; (2) j only; (3) k only; or (4) both parties. The corresponding state probabilities are:

$$\pi_1 = (1 - p)^2$$
$$\pi_2 = p(1 - p) = \pi_3$$
$$\pi_4 = p^2$$

It is evident that, even under CCM, there is no possibility of risk-sharing in states 1 and 4. So the only trading that can take place will be exchanging state-2 for state-3 claims. From the symmetry of the situation, such exchange will occur in a 1:1 ratio, so that the equilibrium condition (4.1.1) takes the form, for each individual:

$$\frac{\pi_1 v'(\bar{c})}{P_1} = \frac{\pi_2 v'(\bar{c} - L/2)}{P_2} = \frac{\pi_3 v'(\bar{c} - L/2)}{P_3} = \frac{\pi_4 v'(\bar{c} - L)}{P_4}$$

where, of course, $P_4/\pi_4 > P_3/\pi_3 = P_2/\pi_2 > P_1/\pi_1$.

The equilibrium condition would not take quite so simple a form if inter-individual differences were permitted – as between the losses L^j and L^k, the loss probabilities p_j and p_k, initial incomes $\bar{c}^j$ and $\bar{c}^k$, and the utility functions $v^j(c^j)$ and $v^k(c^k)$. But it nevertheless remains true that, after trading, $c_1 > c_2, c_3 > c_4$ for each individual and that in equilibrium:

$$\frac{P_4}{\pi_4} > \frac{P_3}{\pi_3} \text{ and } \frac{P_2}{\pi_2} > \frac{P_1}{\pi_1}$$

---

[4] In actual insurance practice, transaction costs place a "loading" upon the premiums offered purchasers of policies. In accordance with our assumption of perfect markets, transaction costs will be set aside here.

Any actual system of contractual insurance arrangements will only approximate the ideal results under CCM. One possible arrangement might be a mutual-insurance system with no stated premiums. Instead, policy holders would be proportionately assessed for the amounts required to match the aggregate of losses experienced. In our fully symmetrical example above, in state 1 there would be no loss and no assessment; in state 2 the assessment would be $L/2$ to each party, summing to the full L required to indemnify individual j; similarly in state 3, except that the indemnity would go to individual k; and in state 4, each party would be assessed L and indemnified L, so that no actual transfer of funds would take place. Thus, the assessment system would replicate the results of CCM. More generally, however – allowing for inter-individual differences in loss magnitudes L, loss probabilities p, endowments, etc. – such an assessment arrangement would diverge from results under CCM. But, if only the loss magnitudes varied among individuals, proportionate assessment would be similar to share cropping. An individual whose risk is $x\%$ of the total would be assessed $x\%$ of the loss *ex post*, so that the outcome would lie along the main diagonal of an Edgeworth box in four-dimensional space.

Coming closer to conventional insurance arrangements, standard practice would be to quote (say, for individual j) a fixed premium H^j to be paid into the pool regardless of which state obtains, while a fixed indemnity I^j will be receivable from the pool in either state 2 or state 4. Inability to provide for differential net payments in these two states, together with the corresponding failure in the case of individual k to distinguish state 3 from state 4, represents a serious incomplete-markets problem. Indeed, under mutual insurance the problem is an impossible one, since owing to social risk the totals of premiums paid in could not always match the totals of indemnities payable. For example, if any premiums at all are collected, should state 1 occur, there would be no losses to absorb them. But a zero premium would be absurd, providing no funds for the indemnity payments required in all other states of the world. In practice, this difficulty is avoided by having mutual-insurance pools take on a legal personality, e.g., via the corporate form. Then, premium levels H^j and H^k might be set, for example, to cover indemnities in state 4, the most adverse possibility. Should any other state actually come about, the corporation will show a "profit" that can be rebated back to its owners, the policy holders. (Alternatively, the corporation might engage in time averaging, reinvesting profits in good years to accumulate "reserves" to help cover losses in bad years and thus permit a lower level of premiums.) It will be evident that such a system is essentially equivalent to assessable premiums.

Social risk comes about whenever private risks are not perfectly offsetting. It is sometimes thought that the variability of the per-capita social risk is only a result of small numbers. If so, for pools with a sufficiently large membership N, mean income could be regarded as effectively constant. It follows that, for large N, insurance premiums would become practically actuarial (fair) – apart from transaction costs, of course.

Instead of a fixed loss L^j, assume more generally now that each individual faces a loss-probability distribution $f^j(\tilde{L}^j)$, and for simplicity suppose all the distributions are identical. Then the question is whether the per-capita loss $\tilde{\lambda} = (1/N)\Sigma_{j=1}^{N}\tilde{L}^j$ becomes approximately constant over states as N grows large. In accordance with the Law of Large Numbers, as N increases, the variance of $\tilde{\lambda}$ does decline, hence the error committed by ignoring social risk does diminish. Nevertheless, this error does *not* tend toward zero as N increases, unless indeed the separate risks are on average uncorrelated.[5]

Suppose that the individual L^j distributions all have the same mean μ and variance σ^2, and suppose, also, that the correlations between all pairs of risks equal some common r (which, of course, can be possible only for $r \geq 0$). That is, for any pair L^j, L^k:

$$E[(L^j - \mu)(L^k - \mu)] = r\sigma^2$$

The mean average loss $E[\tilde{\lambda}]$ is then just μ. The variance of the average loss is:

$$\sigma_{\lambda}^2 = E[(\tilde{\lambda} - \mu)^2]$$

$$= \frac{1}{N^2}E\left[\left(\sum_{j=1}^{N}(L^j - \mu)\right)^2\right]$$

$$= \frac{1}{N^2}\sum_{j=1}^{N}E\left[\sum_{k=1}^{N}(L^j - \mu)(L^k - \mu)\right]$$

$$= \frac{1}{N^2}\sum_{j=1}^{N}[\sigma^2 + (N-1)r\sigma^2]$$

$$= \sigma^2\left[\frac{1 + r(N-1)}{N}\right]$$

In the limit as N increases, the variance of per-capita loss approaches $r\sigma^2$, and thus always remains positive unless $r = 0$.

---

[5] See Markowitz (1959), p. 111.

We see, therefore, that social risk is not exclusively due to small numbers; it persists even with large numbers if risks are positively correlated. Somewhat offsetting this consideration is the possibility of time averaging via the accumulation of reserves. Doing so is to employ the Law of Large Numbers in a different dimension: the law tends to operate over time as well as over risks at any moment in time. If risks that are correlated at any point in time are serially uncorrelated over time, aggregated over a number of time periods, the variance of per-capita losses will diminish. (The power of the Law of Large Numbers over time will be weakened to the extent that positive serial correlation exists, that is, if high-social-loss states tend to be followed by similar high-loss states.)

Interpreting the main result of this section in terms of the language of portfolio theory, risks have a "diversifiable" element that can be eliminated by purchasing shares in many separate securities (equivalent to mutual insurance among large numbers of individuals), and an "undiversifiable" element due to the average correlation among risks. It follows then that a particular asset will be more valuable the smaller is the correlation of its returns over states of the world with the aggregate returns of all assets together – the variability of which is the source of undiversifiable risk.[6]

Social risk, therefore, provides two reasons why insurance prices may not be fair or actuarial: (i) if the number of risks in the insurance pool is small, the Law of Large Numbers cannot work very fully; (ii) if the separate risks are on average positively correlated, then even with large numbers the variance of the per-capita return does tend to diminish but does not approach zero. In either case there will still be relatively poor social states for which claims to income will command prices that are disproportionately high relative to the corresponding probabilities (with the reverse holding for relatively affluent social states).

In addition, other factors may help bring about non-actuarial terms of insurance: (1) as mentioned in footnote 4, insurance premiums are "loaded" in order to cover transaction costs, and (2) *adverse selection and moral hazard*, phenomena essentially due to information asymmetries between buyers and sellers, may tend to affect the terms of insurance transactions.

---

[6] In modern investment theory, the correlation of a particular security's return with that of the market as a whole – which represents the returns on all securities together – is measured by a "beta" parameter. Securities with low or, even better, negative betas tend to trade at relatively high prices. That is, investors are satisfied with relatively low expected rates of return on these assets, since they tend to provide generous returns in just those states of the world where aggregate incomes are low (and, therefore, marginal utilities are high). We analyze this topic in detail in Section 4.3.

Exercises and Excursions 4.1

1 Complete versus Incomplete Asset-Market Equilibria

(A) In a world of three equally probable states, with equally numerous individuals of types j and k, the endowments are $\bar{C}^j = (45, 45, 45)$ and $\bar{C}^k = (15, 67.5, 315)$. The utility functions are $v^j = \ln c^j$ and $v^k = (c^k)^{1/2}$. Verify that under CCM the equilibrium price ratios are $P_1:P_2:P_3 = 3:2:1$. Find the individual optimum positions.

(B) Suppose the same endowment positions are expressed in terms of asset holdings. Thus, j holds 45 units of asset a with state returns (1, 1, 1) while k holds 1 unit of asset b with state returns (15, 67.5, 315). Verify that the CCM equilibrium cannot be attained if the parties can exchange only assets a and b.

2 Efficiency of Proportional Sharing

In the landlord-worker problem, show that, if the two parties have common probability beliefs and identical utility functions $v(c^w)$ and $v(c^l)$ characterized by constant relative risk aversion R, then – for any finite number of states S – the CCM solution will lie along the main diagonal of the S-dimensional Edgeworth box. (Hence simple proportional sharing of the crop will be efficient.)

3 Risk Sharing with μ, σ Preferences

Suppose preferences are given by:

$$U^i = \mu(c^i) - \alpha^i \sigma^2(c^i), \quad i = w, l$$

The aggregate output in state s is y_s. The worker, individual w, is to be paid a fixed "wage" ω plus a share y of the residual $y_s - \omega$.

(A) Obtain expressions for $\mu(c^i)$ and $\sigma^2(c^i)$ in terms of ω, y, and the mean and variance of y.

(B) Write down a first-order condition for the Pareto-efficient choice of ω. Hence show that along the Pareto frontier $dU^w/dU^l = -1$.

(C) Hence, or otherwise, establish that the worker's efficient share of aggregate risk is:

$$\gamma^* = \frac{\alpha^l}{\alpha^l + \alpha^\omega}$$

(D) Is it surprising that this share is constant along the Pareto frontier?

(E) Would a similar result hold if there were M workers and N landlords?

4 Insurance with Transaction Costs

Suppose each individual faces the risk of a loss L, the different risks being independent (uncorrelated). Also, there are sufficiently large numbers that the per-capita risk is negligible and so insurance is offered on actuarily fair (i.e., zero profit) terms.

What would be the equilibrium insurance policy if, whenever a loss takes place, the insurance company incurs a transaction cost c?

5 Complete Contingent Markets (CCM) with Constant Absolute Risk Aversion

Suppose each of N individuals exhibits constant absolute risk aversion. All have the same probability beliefs. Under a CCM regime, let P_s denote the equilibrium price in state s ($s = 1, \ldots, S$).

(A) If individual i's degree of absolute risk aversion is A_i show that his optimum claims in states s and t must satisfy:

$$A_i\left(c_s^i - c_t^i\right) = \ln\left(\pi_s/\pi_t\right) - \ln\left(P_s/P_t\right)$$

(B) Hence obtain an expression for the logarithm of relative prices in terms of the average endowments in states s and t, $\bar{c}_s$ and $\bar{c}_t$.

(C) Let A^* be the harmonic mean of the degrees of absolute risk aversion, that is:

$$A^* = N\left[\sum_{i=1}^{N}\frac{1}{A_i}\right]^{-1}$$

Show that the difference between the price ratio P_s/P_t and the ratio of probabilities π_s/π_t is positive if and only if $\bar{c}_t > \bar{c}_s$.

(D) Discuss also the effect of changes in the distribution of endowments, and of an increase in A^*, upon P_s/P_t.

6 Insurance Premiums with State-Dependent Utility

Suppose that health risks are independently distributed for all individuals. Suppose, furthermore, that numbers are sufficiently large so that insurance against a deterioration in health is offered on actuarily fair terms.

(A) Suppose an individual has a utility function $v(c, h) = (ch)^{\frac{1}{2}}$, his health level h being either h_b or h_g (where $h_b < h_g$). Would this individual wish to buy insurance against bad health?

(B) Suppose bad health also reduces income by 50%. Would the individual now wish to buy insurance? If not necessarily, under what conditions would this be the case? Would the individual ever buy enough insurance to completely offset his income loss?

(C) Another individual has a utility function $\bar{v}(c, h) = \ln(ch)$. Confirm that there is a function $u(\cdot)$ such that:

$$\bar{v}(c, h) = u(v(c, h))$$

Hence draw a conclusion as to which individual is more risk averse.

(D) Repeat (A) and (B) with the new utility function.

(E) What can you say about an individual who is more risk averse than both these individuals but again has the same indifference map?

[HINT: You might refer back to Section 2.3 in Chapter 2 before attempting to answer this question.]

4.2 Production and Exchange

The previous section examined regimes of complete and incomplete markets in a pure-exchange economy with a single generalized consumption good C. We showed that the analysis of market equilibrium can be interpreted in terms of an S-dimensional Edgeworth box diagram with one axis for each state claim c_s. Just as goods are allocated efficiently in the traditional commodity-market equilibrium under certainty so, under uncertainty, a complete-market equilibrium (i.e., the CCM case where there are markets in all S states, or else the CAM case where an equivalent regime of asset markets exists) distributes social risk efficiently.

We will now generalize this conclusion. In Section 4.2.1 we show that, even in a world of production, and allowing for many commodities G as well as any number of states S, a complete-market equilibrium allocation is Pareto efficient. Of course, the assumption of complete markets is a strong one. Section 4.2.2 takes up production decisions in a special regime of incomplete markets called a "stock market economy." Conditions are derived under which shareholders unanimously agree upon value maximization as the objective of the firm.

4.2.1 Equilibrium with Production: Complete Markets

Suppose there is a single commodity (corn), a single firm, and two states of the world (rain or no rain). By varying the production process the firm

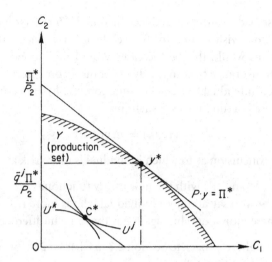

Figure 4.3. Equilibrium and efficiency.

chooses a state-distributed vector of production levels $y = (y_1, y_2)$. The set of possible production vectors or "production set" Y is illustrated in Figure 4.3.[7] We assume that this set is convex.

To illustrate, suppose that when rows of corn are planted close together there will be an especially big harvest *if* the weather is hot. However, if the weather is cool, a better yield is obtained by planting at lower densities. As a special case, let:

$$y_1(x) = 20x, \quad y_2(x) = 100x - 10x^2$$

be the state-dependent outputs associated with a crop density of x. Eliminating x yields the production frontier:

$$y_2 - 5y_1 + \frac{y_1^2}{40} = 0$$

The production set Y consists of the production vectors $y = (y_1, y_2)$ on or inside the production possibility frontier.

Given state-claim prices P_1 and P_2, the profit of the firm (since there are no purchased factors of production) is the revenue $P_1 y_1 + P_2 y_2$. Writing the price vector as $P = (P_1, P_2)$, a profit-maximizing price-taking firm chooses y^* and hence profit level Π to satisfy:

$$\Pi^* = P \cdot y^* \geq P \cdot y, \quad \text{for all } y \in Y$$

---

[7] In a more complete model, inputs would be purchased at $t = 1$ and output produced at $t = 2$, as in Exercise 3 at the end of this section.

(Here and henceforth, we will assume a unique solution exists.) The isoprofit line $P \cdot y = \Pi^*$ is also depicted in Figure 4.3 along with the profit-maximizing production vector y^*.

We now examine the consumer-shareholders' demands for state-contingent corn. With just two individuals j and k, we can illustrate via the Edgeworth box formed in Figure 4.3 with corners at the origin and at y^*. Suppose the two proportionate shareholdings in the firm are $\bar{q}_f^j$ and $\bar{q}_f^k \equiv 1 - \bar{q}_f^j$.[8] With 0 as the origin for j, his budget constraint is:

$$P_2 c_1^j + P_2 c_2^j = \bar{q}_f^j \Pi^* \tag{4.2.1}$$

This is, as depicted, parallel to $\Pi^* = P \cdot y$ but with vertical intercept $\bar{q}_f^j \Pi^* / P_2$. Then the risk-bearing optimum for individual j is point C^* where $U^j(c_1^j, c_2^j)$ is maximized subject to the budget constraint (4.2.1).

Of course, this budget line can also be viewed as the budget line for individual k, using the point y^* as her origin. As depicted, the state-claim prices P_1 and P_2 are such that aggregate consumption equals aggregate production in each state – markets are cleared. Since neither individual can do any better without making the other worse off, the competitive equilibrium is Pareto efficient. And, specifically, price-taking behavior and profit maximization result in an allocation in which the Marginal Rate of Substitution of state-1 claims for state-2 claims, $M \equiv -dc_2 / dc_1$, is, for each individual, equal to his or her marginal rate of productive transformation $-dy_2 / dy_1$.

Note that, just as in the pure-exchange case, the analysis is formally equivalent to the traditional certainty model. However, whereas in the standard certainty model y is a vector of outputs of different commodities, y here becomes a state-contingent output vector. This suggests a way of demonstrating the efficiency of a CCM regime in a much more general setting. All we have to do is to show that the description of individual optimization and market clearing is formally equivalent to that in the traditional certainty model, where the efficiency of competitive equilibrium is a standard result.

As a first step, let us briefly review the traditional general-equilibrium model. Suppose the economy consists of I individuals indexed by i, F firms indexed by f, and G commodities indexed by g. Firm f chooses a vector of inputs and outputs $y^f = (y_1^f, \ldots, y_G^f)$ from the set Y^f of feasible vectors.

---

[8] In Chapter 2 and elsewhere, q_a^i, denoted the *number of units* of asset a held by individual i. Here, the total number of shares in firm f is defined as unity, so each individual's shareholding q_f^i will represent a fractional number of units.

We assume that a firm can always choose not to produce so that the zero vector is in Y^f. A positive y_g^f indicates that the firm produces more than it purchases of commodity g while a negative y_g^f indicates that the firm is a net purchaser of the commodity. With commodity prices $P = (P_1, \ldots, P_G)$, the firm chooses y_*^f to maximize profit,[9] that is:

$$y_*^f \text{ solves } \underset{y^f}{\text{Max}}\{P \cdot y^f | y^f \in Y^f\}$$

Since firm f can always choose not to produce, maximized profit Π^f is non-negative.

Each individual i, with utility function $U^i(c^i)$ where $c^i \equiv (c_1^i, \ldots, c_G^i)$, has some initial endowment of commodities $\omega^i \equiv (\omega_1^i, \ldots, \omega_G^i)$ and owns a proportion $\bar{q}_f^i$ of firm f. The individual then chooses c_*^i to maximize utility subject to the constraint that total expenditure on commodities does not exceed the value of his endowment plus profit shares. That is, c_*^i is the solution of:

$$\text{Max}\left\{U^i(c^i) \Big| P \cdot c^i \leq P \cdot \omega^i + \sum_f \bar{q}_f^i \Pi^f\right\}$$

For P to be a market equilibrium price vector, supply must equal demand in every market,[10] that is:

$$\sum_f y_*^f + \sum_i \omega^i = \sum_i c_*^i$$

And on the assumption that each individual, regardless of his consumption vector, always strictly prefers more of some commodity we know also – from the first theorem of welfare economics (Debreu, 1959) – that this market equilibrium is Pareto efficient.

We now seek to extend this result to include uncertainty. Instead of just G markets, one for each commodity, we introduce markets for each

[9] For example, the production set of the neoclassical firm producing Q units of output with capital and labor according to the production function $Q = \Phi(K, L)$ is:

$$Y^f = \{(Q, -K, -L) | Q \leq \Phi(K, L), K, L \geq 0\}$$

With prices $(P_1, P_2, P_3) = (p, r, w)$, the firm chooses $y^f \in Y^f$ to maximize:

$$P \cdot y^f = pQ + r(-K) + w(-L) = pQ - (rK + wL).$$

[10] As a more general statement (allowing also for corner solutions), supply must at least equal demand, and the price must be zero for any market in which there is excess supply.

commodity in each state of the world – $G \times S$ markets in all. The price P_{gs} is then the price of purchasing a unit of commodity g for delivery if and only if state s occurs.

Each firm makes a decision as to its purchases and sales in each state. For example, a firm producing commodity 1 using commodities 2 and 3 as inputs might have a state-dependent production function:

$$y_{1s}^f = \phi_s^f \left(- y_{2s}^f, -y_{3s}^f \right)$$

The firm then contracts to purchase contingent inputs and deliver contingent outputs in order to maximize its profit:

$$\Pi^f = \left(P_{1s} y_{1s}^f + P_{2s} y_{2s}^f + P_{3s} y_{3s}^f \right) = P \cdot y^f$$

In general, just as in the certainty case, firm f chooses y_*^f so that:

$$\Pi^f = P \cdot y_*^f \geq P \cdot y^f, \quad y^f \in Y^f$$

In the same way, individual i with endowment ω^i and utility function $v^i(c_s^i)$, where $c_s^i = (c_{1s}^i, \ldots, c_{Gs}^i)$, chooses his final consumption bundle to maximize expected utility:

$$U^i(c^i) = \sum_s \pi_s^i v^i(c_s^i)$$

This maximization is, of course, subject to the budget constraint:

$$P \cdot c^i \leq P \cdot \omega^i + \sum_f \bar{q}_f^i \Pi^f$$

Viewed in this way, it is clear that any conclusions about the certainty model must carry over. In particular the equilibrium allocation must lead to a Pareto-efficient allocation of risk bearing.

Several aspects of the equilibrium are worthy of note:

1 Under complete markets, the efficient allocation is achieved when firms simply maximize profit (net market value). Profit being deterministic rather than stochastic, there is no need to consider expected profit or to adjust for some concave function of profit representing owner risk aversion. The point is that, at the time a production decision is made, the firm can also complete all sales of its *contingent* outputs at the ruling state-claim prices. Net earnings or profit can then be handed

over to stockholders. Of course, actual input and output levels will be uncertain. However, the market equilibrium state-claim prices already provide the correct adjustments for the risk factor, so owners are best served when the chosen production vector maximizes net market value. It follows also that stock markets and stock trading have no special role. Indeed, no one has any incentive to trade his initial asset endowment except to make final consumption purchases.

2 Different consumers need not have the same beliefs about the likelihood of different states. The CCM equilibrium is efficient with respect to beliefs *actually held.*

3 All trading in this economy takes place prior to learning which state s has occurred. This raises the question as to whether any individual might wish to engage in posterior trading after the state of the world is revealed. To answer this question, suppose that all prior trading takes place on the anticipation that markets will *not* reopen after the state is revealed. Consumer i will then initially select his state-distributed consumption vector so that his Marginal Rate of Substitution of commodity 1 for commodity g in a particular state is equal to the price ratio:

$$\frac{\dfrac{\partial U^i}{\partial c_{1s}}}{\dfrac{\partial U^i}{\partial c_{gs}}} = \frac{\pi^i_s \dfrac{\partial v^i}{\partial c_{1s}}}{\pi^i_s \dfrac{\partial v^i}{\partial c_{gs}}} = \frac{P_{1s}}{P_{gs}} \qquad (4.2.2)$$

Now suppose that the state is revealed to be s, and that, unexpectedly, markets do in fact reopen for posterior trading. If the state-s market-price *ratios* among the G commodities were to remain unchanged from the prior ratios of (4.2.2), individual i, now with utility function $v^i(c_s)$, will wish to trade so that his new Marginal Rate of Substitution of commodity 1 for commodity j will equal the unchanged price ratio, that is:

$$\frac{\dfrac{\partial v^i}{\partial c_{1s}}}{\dfrac{\partial v^i}{\partial c_{gs}}} = \frac{P_{1s}}{P_{gs}} \qquad (4.2.3)$$

Comparing (4.2.2) and (4.2.3), it follows immediately that individual i will have no need to trade again. Thus, the prior-trading price ratios for the state-s commodity claims dictate a posterior equilibrium in which no retrading occurs.[11] This proposition will play an important role when we consider the topic of speculation in Chapter 6.

So far, we have considered only the *unanticipated* opportunity for retrading after the state is revealed. If the possibility of posterior trading is indeed *anticipated*, consumers must form beliefs about prices in future states ("future spot prices"). Our argument indicates that, as long as everyone believes that relative future spot prices in the state that actually occurs will be the same as relative prior contingent prices, there will be no gains to multiple rounds of trading. Moreover, such beliefs will be self-fulfilling – the market-clearing future spot price ratios will indeed equal the corresponding contingent price ratio.[12]

4 We have implicitly been assuming that production, consumption, and exchange all occur at a single date in time. This also is an expositional simplification that can easily be generalized. The same equation format for a CCM regime can allow for specifying the commodity, the state, and also the date. The price P_{gst} is then the price paid, in the current period, for commodity g to be delivered at time t in the eventuality that state s occurs. As in the one-period model, firm f chooses $y^f = (y^f_{111}, \ldots, y^f_{GST})$ from its production set Y^f to maximize $P \cdot y^f$ – which is the net present value of the production plan or, more simply, the *value of the firm* at today's prices. It should be noted that the firm's plan will, in general, be a contingent plan. That is, some farther future decisions may be contingent upon some still uncertain nearer-future events.

Exercises and Excursions 4.2.1

1 Exchange Equilibrium with Complete Markets
Consider an economy with two states. Every individual has the same utility function $v(c) = \ln(c)$ and believes that state 1 will occur with probability π.

(A) Show that the CCM equilibrium price ratio satisfies:

$$\frac{P_1}{P_2} = \frac{\pi}{1 - \pi} \left(\frac{y_2}{y_1} \right)$$

where y_s is the aggregate endowment of claims in state s.

---

[11] It is left to the reader to confirm that no firm will wish to change its production plan in state s either.

[12] Beliefs may then be called "rational," as in the common but confusing term "rational expectations equilibrium" – a more accurate term would be "self-fulfilling beliefs equilibrium." In the absence of such concordant beliefs about future spot prices, those agents whose beliefs were incorrect will wish to re-enter the market. This in turn opens up opportunities for sophisticated traders to "speculate." We shall have more to say on this topic in Chapter 6.

(B) If the price of a riskless asset yielding 1 unit in each state is 1, show that the state-claim prices are:

$$P_1 = \frac{\pi y_2}{\pi y_2 + (1 - \pi)y_1} \quad \text{and} \quad P_2 = \frac{(1 - \pi)y_1}{\pi y_2 + (1 - \pi)y_1}$$

(C) Suppose there are two types of asset in the economy. A unit of the riskless asset (asset 1) pays off 1 in each state and has market price $P_1^A = 1$. A unit of the risky asset (asset 2) returns $z_{21} = \frac{1}{2}$ in state 1 and $z_{22} = 2$ in state 2. Aggregate supplies of the two assets are q_1 and q_2. If the two states are equally likely, show that the price of the risky asset is:

$$P_2^A = \frac{5q_1 + 4q_2}{4q_1 + 5q_2}$$

(D) Suppose initially there are no units of the risky asset. However, there is a technology that will create units of the risky asset at the cost of one unit of the riskless asset. There is free entry into the industry.

What will be the equilibrium price of the risky asset? What will be the equilibrium supply of the risky asset, expressed as a proportion of the equilibrium supply of the riskless asset?

2   Complete-Market Equilibrium with Production

Consider an economy in which a single firm produces a single commodity. There are two states of the world, state 1 and state 2. The n-th plant in the firm can produce any state-dependent output vector $y = (y_1, y_2)$ lying in the production set $Y^n = \{(y_1, y_2) | y_1^2 + y_2^2 \leq 2\}$. There are two individuals in the economy, each of whom has a 50% share in the firm, and who behave as price takers.

(A) If there are two plants, confirm that the aggregate production set is $Y = \{(y_1, y_2) | y_1^2 + y_2^2 \leq 8\}$. Hence, or otherwise, show that with state-claim prices $(P_1, P_2) = (1,1)$ the firm will produce an output vector $(y_1^* + y_2^*) = (2, 2)$.

(B) If individual 1 believes that state 1 will occur with certainty, explain why, *at the above prices*, his final consumption vector is $(c_1^1, c_2^1) = (2, 0)$.

(C) If the second individual believes that state 2 will occur with certainty, confirm that $P = (1,1)$ is the complete-market equilibrium price vector.

(D) In the absence of trading possibilities the stockholders are no longer able to place an explicit market value on the firm. They must therefore evaluate the firm directly, in terms of its final output. One possible bargaining agreement would be to split the firm with each stockholder becoming sole owner of one plant. Given such an agreement, would individual 1 produce only output in state 1 and individual 2 only output in state 2?

3 Production in a Two-Period Economy with Complete Markets
In a one-commodity, two-state, two-period economy, a firm can use $-y_1$ units of input at $t = 1$ to produce y_{2s} units of output at $t = 2$ in state s, where (y_1, y_{21}, y_{22}) is in the production set:

$$Y = \{(y_1, y_{21}, y_{22}) | y_1 + (y_{21})^2 + (y_{22})^2 \leq 0\}$$

(A) Depict cross sections of the production set in (y_1, y_2) space – assuming $y_{21} = y_{22}$ – and in (y_{21}, y_{22}) space. Use these to draw the production set in a three-dimensional diagram.
(B) With prices (P_1, P_{21}, P_{22}) assumed to be ruling at date 1, solve for the profit-maximizing production vector.

4.2.2 Stock Market Equilibrium*

As argued in Chapter 2 (Section 2.1.2), if the state-contingent returns of the F firms in the economy span the full S-dimensional space of contingent claims, then trading in the F "equity" shares suffices for Complete Asset Markets (CAM). In this section we consider trading in equity shares where there may be fewer firms (assets) than states ($F \leq S$). Once again, consider an economy with a single income commodity ("corn"). Before the state is revealed, firm f makes a production decision yielding a state-contingent output vector $y^f = (y_1^f, \ldots, y_S^f)$, where y^f belongs to the firm's set of feasible output levels y^f. Initial proportionate holdings in firm f are $\bar{q}_f^i$ (for individuals $i = 1, \ldots, I$), where $\Sigma_{i=1}^I \bar{q}_f^i = 1$. Individual i can trade shares in the stock market subject to his portfolio budget constraint:

$$\sum_f P_f^A q_f^i = \sum_f P_f^A \bar{q}_f^i \tag{4.2.4}$$

---

* Starred sections represent more difficult or specialized materials that can be omitted without substantial loss of continuity.

where P_f^A is the market price of firm f (asset f). After having chosen a portfolio, his final consumption will be:

$$c^i = \sum_f q_f^i y^f, \text{ where } c^i = (c_1^i, \ldots, c_S^i)$$

To find the optimal portfolio, the individual solves:

$$\text{Max}\left\{\sum_s \pi_s^i v_i(c_s^i) \,\middle|\, c_s^i = \sum_f q_f^i y_s^f\right\}$$

subject, of course, to the portfolio budget constraint (4.2.4). These considerations lead, as in Chapter 2, to the Risk-Bearing Theorem for Asset Markets: the optimal asset holdings equate the expected marginal utility of investing an additional dollar in each asset.

$$\frac{\sum_s \pi_s^i v_i'(c_s^i) y_s^f}{P_f^A} = \lambda_i \text{ for } f = 1, \ldots, F \tag{4.2.5}$$

Here, the Lagrange multiplier λ_i is his marginal utility of wealth.

Example 4.3: Imagine there are three equally probable states and two firms. Firm 1 produces the certainty output vector $y^1 = (1,1,1)$ while firm 2 produces $y^2 = (2,0,0)$. There are two individuals j and k, each initially endowed with 50% of each firm, and each having the utility function $v = \ln c$.

The individual's decision problem can be expressed (for $i = j, k$):

$$\text{Max } \Sigma_s \pi_s v(c_s^i) = (1/3) \ln \left(q_1^i + 2q_2^i\right) + (1/3) \ln \left(q_1^i\right) + (1/3) \ln \left(q_1^i\right)$$
subject to $P_1^A q_1^i + P_2^A q_2^i = P_1^A \bar{q}_1^i + P_2^A \bar{q}_2^i$.

But by symmetry we know that the equilibrium solutions for the shareholdings are $q_1^i = q_2^i = 1/2$. Letting the value of asset 1 (firm 1) be the numeraire, so that $P_1^A = 1$, by straightforward steps Equation (4.2.5) becomes:

$$\frac{14/9}{1} = \frac{4/9}{P_2^A}$$

So the price of firm 2 is $P_2^A = 2/7$, and the marginal utility of wealth is $\lambda_i = 14/9$ for $i = j, k$. $\quad\square$

We now want to consider the conditions under which shareholders will unanimously agree upon *maximization of value* as the criterion for the firm's productive decisions.

From Equation (4.2.5), in stock market equilibrium we have:

$$P_f^A = \Sigma_s \left[\frac{\pi_s v_i'(c_s^i)}{\lambda_i} \right] y_s^f$$

The expression in brackets is the expected marginal utility of consumption in state s, divided by the individual's marginal utility of income. This is the consumer's implicit valuation of state-s claims.

Now suppose the production vector for firm f were to change from y^f to $y^f + dy^f$, but that *there is only a negligible effect upon the consumers' marginal utilities of income in the various states*. This means that a kind of "large-numbers condition" holds – that no single firm produces such a substantial fraction of the social income in any state as to noticeably affect the consumers' implicit valuations thereof. Then:

$$dP_f^A = \Sigma_s [\pi_s^i v_i'(c_s^i)/\lambda_i] dy_s^f \qquad (4.2.6)$$

Turning to the corresponding effect upon shareholders' utility:

$$U^i = \Sigma_s \pi_s^i v_i(c_s^i) = \Sigma_s \pi_s^i v_i(\Sigma_f q_f^i y_s^f)$$

$$dU^i = q_f^i \Sigma_s \pi_s^i v_i'(c_s^i) dy_s^f$$

Dividing both sides of the equation by λ_i and substituting from (4.2.6), we finally obtain:

$$dU^i/\lambda_i = q_f^i dP_f^A$$

Thus, since in the absence of any substantial effect upon marginal utilities λ_i must remain unchanged, the implication is that any change in firm value P_f^A will shift shareholders' utilities in the same direction.

Following Baron (1979), De Angelo (1981), and Makowski (1983) we call the conjectures of the owners of firm f *competitive* if all believe that a change in the firm's production plan will have negligible effects upon individual agents' shadow prices. We have therefore derived:

Proposition 1: Unanimity over Value Maximization If all individuals have competitive conjectures with respect to the production decisions of firm f, they will unanimously agree on value maximization as the objective function for this firm.

Notice that the condition for "large numbers" or *competitive* behavior is entirely separate from the question of whether or not markets are complete. Even under CCM, a single firm might be perceived by its owners as having some degree of monopoly power over the aggregate supply of claims in one or more states s. Conversely, markets could be seriously incomplete in terms of the number of state claims explicitly or implicitly traded, and yet there might be so many firms that no single one can substantially affect the supply in any state or set of states.

When asset markets are incomplete (as must happen if there are fewer firms than states), a competitive stock market equilibrium cannot in general be Pareto efficient in the sense of Section 4.2.1, even when firms all maximize market values. However, a limited efficiency property of the equilibrium allocation holds:

Proposition 2: Constrained Pareto Efficiency If conjectures by all individuals about all firms are competitive, and denoting $(\hat{q}, \hat{z}, \hat{c})$ as the stock market equilibrium allocation of shares $\hat{q}^i_f$, output levels $\hat{z}^f$, and consumption vectors, $\hat{c}^i$, then there is no alternative feasible allocation (q, z, c) that Pareto dominates $(\hat{q}, \hat{z}, \hat{c})$ when, for all i, $c^i = \Sigma_f q^i_f z^f$.

The theorem says that the equilibrium is an optimum, subject to the constraint that the asset returns must be shared using a rule that is independent of the state. This is equivalent to assuming trading in pure equity shares only (see Diamond, 1967).

Exercises and Excursions 4.2.2

1 Stock Market Equilibrium with Multiple Goods
An economy consists of two firms and two individuals. Firm f produces 1 unit of x in state 1 and 2 units of x in state 2. Firm g produces 1 unit of y in state 1 and 2 units of y in state 2.

Individuals I and II have utility functions:

$$v^I = \ln x + 3 \ln y \text{ and } v^{II} = 3 \ln x + \ln y$$

Individual I assigns a probability of 1/3 to state 1, while individual II assigns a probability of 2/3. Each has a 50% share in the two firms.

(A) Confirm that, if the price vector in a complete market regime is $P = (P_{x1}, P_{x2}, P_{y1}, P_{y2}) = (14, 5, 10, 7)$, individual I maximizes expected utility by choosing the consumption vector $(x^I_1, x^I_2, y^I_1, y^I_2) = (1/7, 4/5, 3/5, 12/7)$. Solve also for the optimum for individual II and hence confirm that P is an equilibrium price vector.

(B) Show also that the two stocks have the same equilibrium value.

(C) Suppose that there are no state-contingent markets. However, the two individuals can trade initially in the stock market and later, after the state is revealed, in commodity markets. Suppose furthermore that the two firms continue to have the same value and that the future spot prices $(\bar{P}_{xs}, \bar{P}_{ys})$ in state s equal the contingent prices (P_{xs}, P_{ys}).

Show that, if individual I sells his holdings in firm f and then sells short one-half of firm f, his final consumption is exactly as in (A). Establish also that, by entering into such a trade in the asset markets, individual II attains the same consumption in (A).

(D) Explain why, at these prices, there can be no better final consumption vector for either individual. That is:

$$P_f^A = P_g^A, \quad (\bar{P}_{x1}, \bar{P}_{y1}) = (14, 10), \quad (\bar{P}_{x2}, \bar{P}_{y2}) = (5, 7)$$

are equilibrium prices in an economy with a stock market and a future spot market.

2 Pareto-Dominated Stock Market Equilibrium (Hart, 1975)

Consider again the stock market economy of the previous question. Suppose both individuals believe that the prices in the future spot markets will be:

$$\left(\bar{P}_{xs}^F, \bar{P}_{ys}^F\right) = (1, r), \quad s = 1, 2$$

(A) Obtain expressions for the future spot values of the two firms in each state. Hence explain why the price of firm g in the stock market will be r times the price of firm f.

(B) Explain also why, under such beliefs, there is no gain to trading in the stock market.

(C) Assuming individuals do not trade in the stock market, show that, if $r = 1$, the final consumption of individual I will be $(x_1^I, x_2^I, y_1^I, y_2^I) = (1/4, 1/2, 3/4, 3/2)$. Solve also for individual II's optimum and hence show that all future spot markets clear, that is:

$$P_a^A = P_{as}^A, \quad (\bar{P}_{xs}, \bar{P}_{ys}) = (1, 1), \quad s = 1, 2$$

is a stock market equilibrium.

(D) Confirm that both individuals are worse off in this equilibrium than in the stock market equilibrium characterized in the previous question.

[Note: See Hart (1975) for other illustrations of constrained Pareto-*in*efficient equilibria with multiple goods.]**

4.2.3 Monopoly Power in Asset Markets*

The analysis above was based on the assumption that all agents are price-takers. In the pure-exchange economy where each agent's wealth is small relative to aggregate wealth, this is a natural assumption. Similarly, if every firm's output is small relative to aggregate output in each state, it seems reasonable to model firms as price-takers also. However, the situation is more complicated if agents spread risk by trading in asset markets rather than contingent-claims markets. For then, even if a firm is small, it will retain monopoly power if it offers a distribution of returns for which there are few close substitutes.

To clarify this result, consider two examples. In the first there are two assets, one of which is riskless, and two states. The asset payoff vectors then span the state-claim space (the regime is CAM), so there is a 1:1 mapping from state-claim prices to asset prices. In the second example there are again two assets, one of which is riskless, but a continuum of states. In each case we examine the incentive for a monopolist supplier of the risky asset to *underproduce*.

For the first example, suppose there are two individuals j and k.[13] Each has the same utility function $v^h(c) = \ln c$, and each owns half the assets of the economy, that is:

$$\left(\bar{c}_1^h, \bar{c}_2^h\right) = \left(\tfrac{1}{2}\bar{c}_1, \tfrac{1}{2}\bar{c}_2\right), \quad h = j, k$$

The two individuals differ, however, in their beliefs: individual j assigns a probability of 3/4 to state 1, and individual k a probability of 1/4.

We now show that the equilibrium state-claim prices are a function of the ratio of aggregate endowments $(\bar{c}_1, \bar{c}_2)$. Let (π_1^h, π_2^h) be the probability vector for individual h. Since he owns half the aggregate endowment, he chooses a consumption bundle that solves:

$$\underset{c_1, c_2}{\text{Max}}\left\{\pi_1^h \ln c_1^h + \pi_2^h \ln c_2^h \,\middle|\, P_1 c_1^h + P_2 c_2^h = \tfrac{1}{2}(P_1\bar{c}_1 + P_2\bar{c}_2)\right\}$$

** End of starred section.

* Starred sections represent more difficult or specialized materials that can be omitted without substantial loss of continuity.

13 In an exercise at the end of this section you are asked to show that the results continue to hold for any number of individuals, with possibly differing beliefs and different shares in the aggregate endowment.

Form the Lagrangian, differentiate, and then rearrange to obtain the following necessary conditions:

$$\frac{\pi_1^h}{P_1 c_1^h} = \frac{\pi_2^h}{P_2 c_2^h} = \frac{1}{P_1 c_1^h + P_2 c_2^h} = \frac{1}{\frac{1}{2}(P_1 \bar{c}_1 + P_2 \bar{c}_2)}$$

Then:

$$P_1 c_1^h = \tfrac{1}{2} \pi_1^h (P_1 \bar{c}_1 + P_2 \bar{c}_2) \tag{4.2.7}$$

Since this is true for both individuals, we can sum over h to obtain:

$$P_1 \bar{c}_1 = P_1 \left(c_1^j + c_1^k \right) = \left(\tfrac{1}{2}(3/4) + \tfrac{1}{2}(1/4) \right) (P_1 \bar{c}_1 + P_2 \bar{c}_2) \tag{4.2.8}$$

A convenient normalization of the state-claim prices is to set:

$$P_1 + P_2 = 1 \tag{4.2.9}$$

That is, a riskless asset yielding 1 unit in each state has a market value of 1. Solving for P_1 and P_2 from (4.2.8) and (4.2.9) leads to:

$$P_1 = \frac{1}{1 + \bar{c}_1/\bar{c}_2} \text{ and } P_2 = \frac{\bar{c}_1/\bar{c}_2}{1 + \bar{c}_1/\bar{c}_2} \tag{4.2.10}$$

These are the equilibrium state-claim prices.

Suppose that each individual's initial endowment is riskless. Then the aggregate endowment in each state is $\bar{c}_s = \bar{c}$ and so $P_1 = P_2 = 1/2$. If there were markets in state claims, individual j, who believes state 1 is more likely, would purchase state-1 claims from individual k. Indeed, from (4.2.7) it can be confirmed that:

$$c_1^j = 3\bar{c}/4 \text{ and } c_1^k = \bar{c}/4$$

Now, imagine instead that the riskless endowments consist of holdings of a single riskless asset a, with no trading opportunities at all. Each individual is therefore forced to consume his own endowment, that is:

$$\bar{c}_1^j = \bar{c}_1^k = \bar{c}/2$$

It follows that the introduction of *any* new non-riskless asset generates very significant risk-spreading gains. As long as there are no arbitrary limits on short sales, each individual adjusts his portfolio until his holdings are such that he can achieve his optimal consumption bundle.

Notice that monopoly power here is not derived purely from ability to produce assets that increase risk-spreading opportunities. Suppose someone was able to convert, via a productive transformation, x units of the riskless asset a into x units each of risky assets with state claim yield vectors $(1,0)$

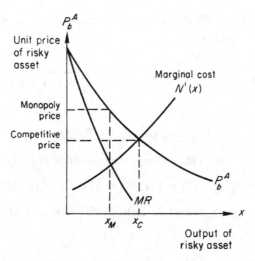

Figure 4.4. Monopoly asset supply.

and $(0,1)$. Clearly, the state space would now be spanned. However, the aggregate endowment ratio $\bar{c}_1/\bar{c}_2$ is unaffected. Hence the value of these two new assets (given by (4.2.10)) would be independent of x.

In this limiting case, therefore, the innovator who introduces the new assets has no monopoly power. More generally, however, let $(\bar{c}_1(x),\ \bar{c}_2(x))$ be the aggregate endowment resulting from the production of x units of a risky asset b. Let the payoff per unit of the asset be $(z_1^b,\ z_2^b)$. Then the price will be:

$$P_b^A = P_1 z_1^b + P_2 z_2^b = \frac{z_1^b + \frac{\bar{c}_1(x)}{\bar{c}_2(x)} z_2^b}{1 + \frac{\bar{c}_1(x)}{\bar{c}_2(x)}}$$

Let $N(x)$ be the number of units of the riskless asset used up in the production of the x units of the risky asset. The new aggregate endowments are therefore:

$$\begin{cases} \bar{c}_1 = \bar{c} - N(x) + xz_1^b \\ \bar{c}_2 = \bar{c} - N(x) + xz_2^b \end{cases} \tag{4.2.11}$$

It is readily confirmed that P_b^A decreases as x increases, as depicted in Figure 4.4. Also depicted in the figure is the marginal cost $N'(x)$ of producing additional units of the risky asset.

Thus, if there were only one potential producer of this new asset, we would have a standard monopoly problem. The single producer chooses an output of the risky asset x_M so as to set marginal revenue equal to marginal cost rather than unit price equal to marginal cost. However, the extent of monopoly power hinges upon the sensitivity of the asset price to output changes. From (4.2.11), if the new asset is a close substitute for a riskless asset, that is, if $z_1/z_2 \approx 1$, then the aggregate endowment ratio varies only very slowly with x. Monopoly power is therefore negligible if the new asset is sufficiently similar to other tradable assets (or combinations of assets).

Finally, the example suggests that if supply of the new asset is small relative to the aggregate endowment, monopoly power will be small even if the new asset is *not* a close substitute.

Mathematically, from (4.2.11):

$$\lim_{\bar{c} \to \infty} \left[\frac{\bar{c}_1(x)}{\bar{c}_2(x)} \right] = \lim_{\bar{c} \to \infty} \left[\frac{\bar{c} - N(x) + xz_1}{\bar{c} - N(x) + xz_2} \right] = 1$$

Whether this result holds under much weaker assumptions remains an open question. As the next example shows, the result is certainly not a completely general one.

We now turn from the two-state example to one with a continuum of states. There are $\bar{q}_a$ units of a riskless asset yielding 1 in each state. There is also a single risky asset b, each unit of which has a random payoff $\tilde{z}$, where z is distributed according to the exponential density function:

$$f(z) = \frac{1}{\gamma} e^{-\gamma z}$$

And there is a single representative consumer in the economy with utility function:

$$v(c) = 1 - e^{-\alpha c}$$

Let (q_a, q_b) be the portfolio of a single consumer, where q_a is the number of units of the riskless asset and q_b the number of units of the risky asset held. His expected utility is then:

$$U(q_a, q_b) = E[v(c)] = \frac{1}{\gamma} \int_0^\infty (1 - e^{-\alpha(q_a + q_b z)}) e^{-\gamma z} dz$$

$$= 1 - \frac{1}{\gamma} e^{-\alpha q_a} \int_0^\infty e^{-(\alpha q_b + \gamma)z} dz$$

$$= 1 - \frac{e^{-\alpha q_a}}{\gamma(\alpha q_b + \gamma)} \tag{4.2.12}$$

As in the previous example, let the price of the riskless asset be $P_a^A = 1$. Then the consumer solves:

$$\underset{q_a, \, q_b}{\text{Max}}\{U(q_a, q_b) \,|\, q_a + P_b^A q_b = W\}$$

From (4.2.12) the first-order condition can be expressed as:

$$\frac{\frac{\partial U}{\partial q_b}}{\frac{\partial U}{\partial q_a}} = \frac{1}{\alpha q_b + \gamma} = \frac{P_b^A}{1}$$

But, in equilibrium, $q_b = x$. Then the unit price of the risky asset is:

$$P_b^A = \frac{1}{\alpha x + \gamma}$$

Note that demand for the risky asset is independent of aggregate wealth. Therefore, in contrast with the earlier example, monopoly power does not decline as the number of units of the riskless asset grows large.

Of course, this result depends critically upon the nature of the utility function. The assumed exponential form indicates that the representative individual exhibits constant absolute risk aversion ($\alpha = $ constant). Together then, the two examples suggest that monopoly power in the production of risky assets will be small as long as (i) the asset is small relative to the total supply of assets in each state and (ii) individuals exhibit approximately constant relative risk aversion.[14]

As has been seen, where monopoly power in asset markets is non-negligible, firms will have an incentive to underproduce, just as in a world of certainty. However, the choice of a criterion for the firm manager is far from clear. If greater production reduces the price of state-s claims, those stockholders who are larger purchasers of such claims will want a higher output than those who believe state s is less likely. This raises the possibility of coalition formation within the firm to buy out other stockholders or to seek a friendly takeover (see Drèze, 1974 and Hart, 1977).

Summing up, this section has provided a theoretical foundation for the value maximization criterion on the part of the firm, and explored the risk-spreading properties of a stock market equilibrium. It also indicated how a change in a firm's input decision, and hence in the probability distribution of its output, would affect its equity value.

---

[14] We are relying here on the fact that, with concordant beliefs and constant relative risk aversion, complete-market prices are a function of aggregate endowments.

Exercises and Excursions 4.2.3

1 Equilibrium State-Claim Prices

There are two states and H consumers, each with utility function $v(c) = \ln c$. Consumer h believes state 1 will occur with probability π_1^h. His endowment is a fraction γ^h of the aggregate endowment $(\bar{c}_1, \bar{c}_2)$.

(A) If state-claim prices are P_1 and P_2, show that consumer h will have state-1 consumption:

$$P_1 c_1^h = \pi_1^h \gamma^h (P_1 \bar{c}_1 + P_2 \bar{c}_2)$$

(B) Summing over h, show that in equilibrium:

$$\frac{P_1}{P_2} = \left(\frac{\displaystyle\sum_{h=1}^{H} \pi_1^h \gamma^h}{\displaystyle\sum_{h=1}^{H} \pi_2^h \gamma^h} \right) \frac{\bar{c}_2}{\bar{c}_1}$$

(C) If all individuals have the same beliefs, show that there will be no trade in this economy.

(D) Is the converse also true? That is, if beliefs differ there will be trade?

(E) If individuals can trade two linearly independent *assets* but cannot exchange contingent claims, will the outcome be the same?

2 Equilibrium Asset Prices

Continuing with the model analyzed in Exercise 1, suppose there are two assets in the economy, both risky. Each unit of asset a yields 1 in state 1 and α in state 2. Each unit of asset b yields β in state 1 and 1 in state 2, where $0 < \alpha, \beta < 1$.

(A) Solve for the equilibrium state-claim price ratio P_1/P_2 in terms of π, α, β and the aggregate endowments of the two assets $\bar{q}_a$ and $\bar{q}_b$.

(B) Hence, or otherwise, obtain an expression for the equilibrium asset price ratio P_a^A/P_b^A.

(C) Under what conditions is the general-equilibrium asset price ratio insensitive to changes in asset supply?

(D) Suppose $\bar{\pi} = 1/2$, $\alpha = \beta$ and there is a constant-returns-to-scale technology that transforms a unit of asset 1 into a unit of asset 2. With free entry into this industry, what will the equilibrium prices of the two assets be? If initially there are 1,000 units of asset a and no

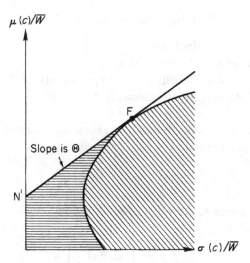

Figure 4.5. Opportunity set per dollar of wealth.

units of asset b, what will be the equilibrium number of each type of asset?**

4.3 The Capital Asset Pricing Model

We now return to the capital asset pricing model introduced in Chapter 2 (Section 2.2), where individuals are concerned only with the *mean* and *standard deviation* of the final wealth (consumption) generated by their portfolio holdings. Making the additional simplifying assumptions that all individuals have agreed beliefs as to the payoff distributions $\tilde{z}_a$ of each and every asset a, and that a riskless asset is available, the Mutual-Fund Theorem was derived. Suppose we imagine a single mutual fund F holding all the risky assets in the economy. Then, the theorem indicates, each investor can maximize utility by holding a particularly simple portfolio: to wit, he can place a fraction of his wealth in that mutual fund and the remainder in the riskless asset. Thus, whether or not such a fund F is explicitly traded, the implication is that every individual will hold his risky assets in the same proportions as exist economy-wide. (However, individuals will still generally vary in how they divide their wealth between the risky fund and the riskless asset.)

Starting with Figure 2.8 in Chapter 2, we can adjust the scales along the two axes, dividing through by the individual's endowed wealth $\bar{W}$. The result is the very similar-looking diagram shown here as Figure 4.5. Using the same notion as in Chapter 2, the vertical axis now represents $\mu(c)/W$ and the

** End of starred section.

horizontal axis $\sigma(c)/\bar{W}$ – mean portfolio income and standard deviation of portfolio income, both measured per dollar of endowed wealth. The point of this adjustment is that, as explained in the earlier chapter, *in per-dollar units each and every investor has the same market opportunities.* Thus, the line N′F that represented the budget line for an individual with specific endowed wealth $\bar{W}$ in Figure 2.11 translates, in the per-dollar units of Figure 4.5, into the budget line of each and every individual in the economy. We will call it the Portfolio Market Line. (The indifference-curve map is not shown in Figure 4.5 because, while the *opportunities* can be expressed in terms of trading μ per dollar for σ per dollar, in general an individual's *preferences* cannot be expressed in terms of willingness to substitute μ per dollar of wealth for σ per dollar of wealth, independently of the level of endowed wealth $\bar{W}$.)[15]

Recall that, in the notation of Chapter 2, μ and σ represent *portfolio* parameters (functions of the individual's consumption). The underlying *asset* parameters are symbolized:

$$\mu_a \equiv \mathrm{E}\left[\tilde{z}_a\right] \qquad\qquad \text{Mean of } \tilde{z}_a$$
$$\sigma_a \equiv \left(\mathrm{E}\left[(\tilde{z}_a - \mu_a)^2\right]\right)^{\frac{1}{2}} \qquad \text{Standard deviation of } \tilde{z}_a$$
$$\sigma_{ab} \equiv \mathrm{E}\left[(\tilde{z}_a - \mu_a)(\tilde{z}_b - \mu_b)\right] \qquad \text{Covariance of } \tilde{z}_a \text{ and } \tilde{z}_b$$

If the riskless asset is $a = 1$, of course, $\sigma_1 = \sigma_{1b} = 0$.

The individual's portfolio parameters are determined in terms of the asset parameters and his individual asset holdings q_a:

$$\mu \equiv \sum_{a=1}^{A} q_a \mu_a$$

$$\sigma \equiv \left(\sum_{a=1}^{A} \sum_{b=1}^{A} q_a q_b \sigma_{ab}\right)^{1/2}$$

And for the mutual fund F that holds the *economy-wide* quantities q_a^F of the risky assets $a = 2, \ldots, A$:

$$\mu_F \equiv \sum_{a=2}^{A} q_a^F \mu_a$$

$$\sigma_F \equiv \left(\sum_{a=2}^{A} \sum_{b=2}^{A} q_a^F q_b^F \sigma_{ab}\right)^{1/2}$$

---

[15] For given wealth $\bar{W}$ and utility function $U(\mu, \sigma)$, the individual will have a well-defined utility function in per dollar of wealth terms: $\hat{U}(\mu/\bar{W}, \sigma/\bar{W})$. However, unless his U function is homothetic, the indifference curves of the $\hat{U}$ function will generally change as $\bar{W}$ changes.

The covariance between any asset a and the mutual fund F is:

$$\sigma_{aF} \equiv E\left[(\tilde{z}_a - \mu_a)\left(\sum_{b=2}^{A} q_b^F(\tilde{z}_b - \mu_b)\right)\right] \equiv \sum_{b=2}^{A} q_b^F \sigma_{ab}$$

The slope of the Portfolio Market Line, the *price of risk reduction* or the *Sharpe ratio* symbolized as Θ, was derived in Equation (2.2.4):

$$\Theta \equiv \frac{d(\mu/\bar{W})}{d(\sigma/\bar{W})} \equiv \frac{d\mu}{d\mu} = \frac{\mu_F/P_F^A - \mu_1/P_1^A}{\sigma_F/P_F^A} = \frac{\mu_F/P_F^A - (1 + R_1)}{\sigma_F/P_F^A} \quad (4.3.1)$$

As before, the "rate of return" $\tilde{R}_a$ on any asset a is defined in:

$$\tilde{z}_a/P_a^A \equiv 1 + \tilde{R}_a$$

The price of risk reduction is the crucial endogenous variable determined in equilibrium, as the separate individuals buy and sell assets with the aim of optimizing their portfolio holdings. And specifically, Θ is the rate at which the market permits anyone to achieve higher portfolio return per dollar in return for higher standard deviation per dollar. As shown in Chapter 2, each individual will be setting his indifference-curve slope or Marginal Rate of Substitution – the rate at which he *is willing* to trade μ for reduced σ – equal to Θ.

Our aim here is to show how the prices P_a^A of the various assets or securities depend upon the price of risk reduction together with the security parameters defined above.

We know that, in equilibrium, the individual simply purchases some quantity q_F of the market fund. Consider then a portfolio that contains the riskless asset, the market fund, and a risky asset a:

$$\mu = q_1(1 + R_1) + q_a\mu_a + q_F\mu_F$$

$$\sigma^2 = q_a^2\sigma_a^2 + 2q_a q_F \sigma_{aF} + q_F^2\sigma_F^2$$

To increase holdings of risky asset a by dq_a, the individual can sell $(P_a^A/P_1^A)dq_a$ units of the riskless asset. The net change in mean return is then:

$$dµ = (q\mu_a - (P_a^A/P_1^A)\mu_1)dq_a$$
$$= (\mu_a - P_a^A(1 + R_1))dq_a$$

This increases the variance of his portfolio according to:

$$d(\sigma^2) = 2\sigma\,d\sigma = 2(q_a\sigma_a^2 + q_F\sigma_{aF})dq_a$$

Also, in equilibrium, $q_a = 0$. It follows that $\sigma = q_F \sigma_F$. Substituting, we obtain:

$$2q_F \sigma_F d\sigma = 2q_F \sigma_{aF} dq_a$$

Hence:

$$d\sigma = \sigma_{aF} dq_a$$

Combining these results, it follows that the individual's Marginal Rate of Substitution between μ and σ is:

$$\frac{d\mu}{d\sigma} = \frac{\mu_a - (1 + R_1)P_a^A}{\sigma_{aF}/\sigma_F}$$

At his optimum, this must be equal to the steepness of the Portfolio Market Line or *price of risk reduction*, given in Equation (4.3.1). Combining these expressions:

CAPITAL ASSET PRICING RULE[16]

$$\frac{\mu_a - (1 + R_1)P_a^A}{\sigma_{aF}} = \Theta = \frac{\mu_F - (1 + R_1)P_F^A}{\sigma_F} \qquad (4.3.2)$$

From (4.3.2) the price of any asset is determined by its mean return μ_a, its covariance with the market portfolio σ_{aF}, and the price of risk reduction Θ.

Example 4.4: Suppose each of J individuals has the same utility function:

$$U^j(\mu, \sigma) = \mu - \tfrac{1}{2}\alpha\sigma^2$$

The riskless asset has price $P_1^A = 1$ and yield $1 + R_1$. The market fund has mean μ_F, standard deviation σ_F, and price P_F^A.

If individual j with initial wealth W_j purchases q_F units of the riskless asset and holds the rest of his portfolio in riskless bonds, the mean and variance of his final wealth are:

$$\mu = \bar{W}^j(1 + R_1) + (\mu_F - P_F^A(1 + R_1))q_F$$
$$\sigma^2 = q_F^2 \sigma_F^2$$

---

[16] This relationship is known in the finance literature as the Capital Asset Pricing Model (CAPM).

Substituting these into his utility function and maximizing with respect to q_F leads to his optimal fund holding:

$$\hat{q}_{jF} = \frac{\mu_F - (1+R)P_F^A}{\alpha \sigma_F^2}$$

From the Mutual-Fund Theorem we know that, in equilibrium, all J individuals will hold the market fund. Also, in equilibrium, demand for the market fund must equal supply:

$$\sum_{j=1}^{J} \hat{q}_{jF} = \left(\frac{J}{\alpha \sigma_F}\right) \left[\frac{\mu_F - (1+R)P_F^A}{\sigma_F}\right] = 1$$

This equation can be solved for the equilibrium price of the market fund. Note also that the bracketed expression is the equilibrium price of risk reduction. Therefore:

$$\Theta = \frac{\alpha \sigma_F}{J}$$

From (4.3.2) the price of asset a, $a = 1, \ldots, A$ satisfies:

$$\mu_a - (1+R_1)P_a^A = \left(\frac{\sigma_{aF}}{\sigma_F}\right)\Theta$$

Then, for this example:

$$P_a^A = \frac{1}{1+R_1}\left(\mu_a - \frac{\alpha}{J}\sigma_{aF}\right)$$

Thus the price of asset a is a decreasing function of the risk-aversion parameter α and of the covariance between $\tilde{z}_a$ and the market fund $\tilde{z}_F$. $\square$

In the finance literature it is more common to rewrite (4.3.2) in terms of rates of return. Since $1 + \tilde{R}_a \equiv \tilde{z}_a/P_a^A$ and $\mu(\tilde{R}_a) \equiv \mu_a/P_a^A$, we have:

$$\sigma(\tilde{R}_a) = \sigma_a/P_a^A \text{ and } \sigma(\tilde{R}_a, \tilde{R}_b) = \sigma_{ab}/P_a^A P_b^A$$

Substituting these expressions into (4.3.2) and rearranging:

$$\mu(\tilde{R}_a) = R_1 + \Theta\frac{\sigma(\tilde{R}_a, \tilde{R}_F)}{\sigma(\tilde{R}_F)}$$

Hence:

SECURITY VALUATION LINE (I)

$$\mu(\tilde{R}_a) = R_1 + \Theta\rho(\tilde{R}_a, \tilde{R}_F)\sigma(\tilde{R}_a) \tag{4.3.3}$$

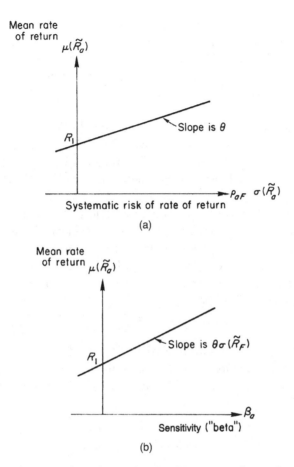

Figure 4.6. (a) Security valuation line (I). (b) Security valuation line (II).

where $\rho(\tilde{R}_a, \tilde{R}_F) \equiv \sigma(\tilde{R}_a, \tilde{R}_F)/\sigma(\tilde{R}_a)\sigma(\tilde{R}_F)$ is the correlation between the rates of return on asset a and the market portfolio.

Figure 4.6a plots Security Valuation Line (I), where the vertical axis is the mean rate of return $\mu(\tilde{R}_a)$ and the horizontal axis is the security's "systematic risk" $\rho_{aF}\sigma(\tilde{R}_a)$ – the fraction of the standard deviation of the security's rate of return represented by its correlation with the mutual fund. In this model, each and every security in the economy, in equilibrium, will fall on the Security Valuation Line. That is, its price P_a^A must be such as to make the security's mean rate of return and its systematic risk the coordinates of a point on the line. Or, we can say, each security will earn a mean rate of return whose excess over the rate of return on the riskless security represents the degree to which the holder of a security incurs a risk correlated with the overall economy-wide risk of the mutual fund. Putting the emphasis the other way, each security's uncorrelated or idiosyncratic risk *not* associated with the variability of the mutual fund is not reflected in price, because that risk has been diversified away through the Law of Large Numbers.

There is an evident parallel between the individual's portfolio choices of $\mu(c)$ and $\sigma(c)$, as shown in the Portfolio Market Line, and the pricing of securities in terms of their mean rate of return and systematic risk as shown by Security Valuation Line (I). In fact, both lines have the same slope, equal to the price of risk reduction Θ.

However, it has become standard practice to picture the Security Valuation Line in a slightly different way. On the horizontal axis, instead of the "systematic risk" $\rho_{aF}\sigma(\tilde{R}_a)$, a closely related measure is customarily employed: to wit, the security's b_{aF}, which we will term its "sensitivity." This is a regression coefficient, logically related to the correlation coefficient ρ_{aF} by the standard formula:

$$b_{aF} \equiv \rho_{aF}\sigma(\tilde{R}_a)/\sigma(\tilde{R}_F)$$

where $\sigma(\tilde{R}_F) \equiv \sigma_F/P_F^A$ is the standard deviation of the rate of return on the mutual fund. The sensitivity b_{aF} is commonly called the "beta" β_a of risky security a. Rewriting (4.3.3), we thus have as a second form of the Security Valuation Line:

SECURITY VALUATION LINE (II)
$$\mu(\tilde{R}_a) = R_1 + \Theta\sigma(\tilde{R}_F)\beta_a$$

As indicated in Figure 4.6b, with β_a on the horizontal axis the slope of the Security Valuation Line becomes $\Theta\sigma(\tilde{R}_F)$.

The interpretation is essentially the same, however. The price of each risky security must adjust until its mean rate of return, over and above the rate of return yielded by the riskless security, reflects its additional riskiness as measured here by volatility. The advantage of this formulation is that the sensitivity β_a can readily be statistically estimated, using historical data, by regressing the security's rate of return upon the rate of return on the market portfolio.

Finally, the way in which security price is determined by the balance between mean return and systematic risk or volatility has implications for the productive decisions of the firm. In Figure 4.7, firm a has an opportunity set showing the combinations of mean payoff μ_a and correlated standard

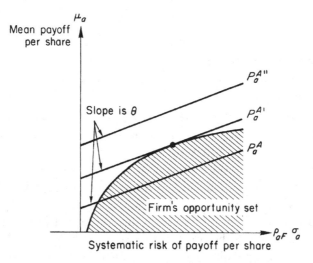

Figure 4.7. Firm's share-price maximization.

deviation $\rho_{aF}\sigma_a$ of payoff it can achieve per share. (We are assuming that firm a has a simple financial structure consisting of a fixed number of shares of security a.) On these axes, there is a family of "iso-price lines" P_a^A, $P_a^{A'}$, ... as illustrated in the diagram. Thus, the firm can achieve a higher share price, other things equal, by *raising* its mean payoff μ_a or by *reducing* either its standard deviation of payoff σ_a or else the correlation ρ_{aF} between its payoff distribution and that of the mutual fund.

The general equation of the iso-price lines, derived from (4.3.3) above, and using the fact that $P_1^A = 1$, is:

$$\mu_A = \mu_1 P_a^A + \Theta \rho_{aF} \sigma_a$$

Evidently, the firm does best (maximizes its share price) at the point of tangency. Thus, we see again that the price of risk reduction Θ is the crucial endogenous variable of this system. On the one hand, each and every individual finds his indifference-curve tangency by setting his Marginal Rate of Substitution $d\mu/d\sigma$, reflecting his degree of risk aversion, equal to Θ. And on the other hand, each and every firm finds its productive optimum, selecting the characteristics of its payoff distribution $\tilde{z}$, by making the marginal trade-off between its mean payoff and the correlated standard deviation of its payoff also equal to Θ.

Exercises and Excursions 4.3

1 Equilibrium Prices in a μ, σ Model

Continuing with the numerical example of Exercise 4 in Exercises and Excursions 2.2, now suppose that the asset prices are not given but remain to be determined.

(A) Nevertheless, under the stated assumptions that all individuals are alike, it is possible to determine immediately that the price of risk reduction is $\Theta = 3/10$. Why?

(B) Knowing Θ, and since by assumption $P_1^A = 1$, verify that the prices P_2^A and P_3^A are as tabulated in the exercise of Chapter 2. Find the corresponding $\mu(\tilde{R}_a)$ and $\sigma(\tilde{R}_a)$ for each asset.

(C) Find the equation for Security Valuation Line (I), showing $\mu(\tilde{R}_a)$ as a function of the correlated riskiness $\rho_{aF}\sigma(\tilde{R}_a)$, and locate the points corresponding to each of the three securities.

(D) Do the same for the Security Valuation Line (II), showing $\mu(\tilde{R}_a)$ as a function of "beta" β_a.

2 The Effect of Large Numbers on the Price of Risk Reduction

Suppose that utility $U(\mu, \sigma)$ is a function of the mean and variance of an individual's portfolio (as is the case with normally distributed returns). Assume that $\partial U(\mu, \sigma)/\partial \sigma \to 0$ as $\sigma \to 0$.

(A) Holding fixed the aggregate market risk, suppose the number of individuals in the economy, N, becomes large. Given the hypothesis of (A), show that the price of risk reduction declines toward zero.

(B) Suppose each firm produces an independent risk of similar mean and variance. Show that, as the number of firms and individuals rises in proportion, the price of risk reduction again declines toward zero.

(C) What do these results tell us about the ability of insurance companies to offer actuarialy fair insurance on independent risks? What about insuring against earthquake losses in Los Angeles?

3 Pricing an Uncorrelated Asset

An individual with utility function $U^j(\mu, \sigma^2) = \mu - \frac{1}{2}\alpha_j\sigma^2$ has current wealth W_j. Each dollar invested in the riskless asset yields $1 + R$. There is also a risky asset with price P_F and payoff distribution $\tilde{z}_F$.

(A) If the individual purchases q units of the risky asset, write an expression for his expected wealth and variance of wealth in terms of r, P_F^A, μ_F, and σ_F^2.

(B) Hence show that his optimal holding of the risky asset is:

$$q_j = \frac{\mu_F - (1 + R)P_F^A}{\alpha_j \sigma_F^2}$$

(C) If differences in tastes can be represented by differences only in the parameter α_j, show that the equilibrium price of the risky asset is:

$$P_F = \frac{1}{1 + R}\left(\mu_F - \frac{\bar{\alpha}}{J}\sigma_F^2\right)$$

where $\bar{\alpha} \equiv J/(\Sigma_j 1/\alpha_j)$ is the harmonic mean of the taste parameters.

(D) Show also that the equilibrium price of risk reduction is:

$$\Theta = \frac{\bar{\alpha}}{J}\sigma_F$$

(E) By appealing to the asset pricing Equation (4.3.2), show that, if F is the market portfolio, the price of asset a satisfies:

$$\mu_a - (1 + R)P_a^A = \frac{\sigma_{aF}\bar{\alpha}}{J}$$

(F) Suppose asset a is uncorrelated with all the other assets. Show that the equilibrium price of asset a is:

$$P_a^A = \frac{1}{1 + R}\left(\mu_a - \frac{\bar{\alpha}}{J}\sigma_a^2\right)$$

4 Correlated Assets and Monopoly Power

Suppose the assumptions of Exercise 3 are modified as follows. There are A risky assets each with mean return μ and variance σ^2. The covariance between pairs of asset returns is $\rho\sigma^2$.

(A) Show that the equilibrium price of asset a is:

$$P_a^A = \frac{1}{1 + R}\left(\mu - \frac{\bar{\alpha}}{J}((A - 1)\rho + 1)\sigma^2\right)$$

(B) Suppose that asset a is replicated q times. That is, there are $q - 1$ new assets, each with a return identical to asset a. Show that the equilibrium price of asset a is:

$$P_a^A = \frac{1}{1 + R}\left(\mu - \frac{\bar{\alpha}}{J}((A - 1)\rho + q)\sigma^2\right)$$

(C) Hence establish that, if asset a is replicable by the owners at a cost $c(q)$, the profit-maximizing supply will be lower than the efficient supply.

(D) What happens to monopoly power as the number of risky assets A and the number of individuals N grow proportionally large?

SUGGESTIONS FOR FURTHER READING: See Hirshleifer (1970) for extensive coverage of intertemporal choice. An advanced treatment of asset-pricing models can be found in LeRoy and Werner (2000) and Duffie (2001).

References

Baron, David P., "Investment Policy: Optimality, and the Mean-Variance Model," *Journal of Finance*, 34 (1979), 207–232.

De Angelo, Harry, "Competition and Unanimity," *American Economic Review*, 71 (1981), 18–27.

Debreu, Gerard, *Theory of Value*, New York: Wiley, 1959.

Diamond, Peter A., "The Role of the Stock Market in a General Equilibrium Model with Technological Uncertainty," *American Economic Review*, 57 (1967), 759–776.

Drèze, Jacques, "Investment under Private Ownership: Optimality, Equilibrium and Stability," chapter 9 in J. Drèze (ed.), *Allocation under Uncertainty: Equilibrium and Optimality*, London: Macmillan, 1974.

Duffie, Darrell, *Dynamic Asset Pricing Theory*, Princeton University Press: Princeton University Press, 2001.

Hart, Oliver D., "On the Optimality of Equilibrium When the Market Structure Is Incomplete," *Journal of Economic Theory*, 11 (1975), 418–443.

————, "Take-Over Bids and Stock Market Equilibrium," *Journal of Economic Theory*, 16 (1977), 53–83.

Hirshleifer, Jack, *Investment, Interest, and Capital*, Englewood Cliffs, NJ: Prentice-Hall, 1970.

LeRoy, Stephen and Werner, Jan, *Principles of Financial Economics*, Cambridge: Cambridge University Press, 2000.

Makowski, Louis, "Competition and Unanimity Revisited," *American Economic Review*, 73 (1983), 329–339.

Markowitz, Harry M., *Portfolio Selection: Efficient Diversification of Investments*, Cowles Foundation for Research in Economics, Yale University, Monograph 16, New York: Wiley, 1959.

PART II

5

Information and Informational Decisions

In Part I of this book, covering *the economics of uncertainty*, the key topics addressed were (1) individuals' optimizing "terminal" choices with regard to the bearing of risk, and (2) the market equilibrium determined by the aggregate of such individual decisions. In turning here in Part II to *the economics of information*, we will similarly be considering issues on individual and on group decision making. On the individual level, the central question is: supposing you could get additional information before having to make a terminal decision, how ought you to decide whether and how much information to collect? On the group level, the main question is: what is the nature of the overall equilibrium that arises when some or all individuals undertake such "informational" actions?

After some introductory discussions, the present chapter first analyzes individuals' decisions as to the acquisition of information. We then consider the informational choices of groups, since the necessity to act as a collectivity has significant consequences for the nature and amount of information desired. Later chapters take up the implications for market equilibrium.

5.1 Information – Some Conceptual Distinctions

"Information" is a word with many meanings. Some of the distinctions to be brought out here will be useful in what follows.

Information as knowledge versus information as news

Information is sometimes taken to mean *knowledge* – an accumulated body of data or evidence about the world. From this point of view, information is a stock magnitude. But the word may also denote an increment to this stock of knowledge, in the form of a *message* or an item of *news*.

Information versus beliefs

Terms like knowledge, information, news, etc., are generally understood to refer to objective evidence about the world. *Belief* is the subjective correlate of knowledge. In this chapter we will be seeing how increments of objective knowledge (news or messages) lead rational individuals to revise their beliefs. Ultimately, however, decisions must be based upon subjective beliefs.

News and message – messages versus message service

The term "message" is generally taken to mean an intended communication from one to another person. "News" is somewhat more general and may refer to evidence or data arrived at by some process other than interpersonal communication, for example, by observing the weather. (This is receiving a message from nature, so to speak.) But we will be treating the words "news" and "message" as synonymous. A more essential distinction for our purposes, one that we will be insisting upon, is between a "message" and a "message service" (or between "news" and a "news service"). Rothschild's legendary carrier pigeon, which supposedly brought him early news of the outcome at Waterloo, was a message service; the report of Napoleon's defeat was the message. Since you can never know in advance what you will be learning, you can never purchase a *message* but only a message service – a set of possible alternative messages.[1]

Communication: intended versus inadvertent, inaccurate versus deceptive

Apart from intended messages, there may, of course, be unintentional communications of various types: (i) a report intended for one party may be overheard by another (or even intercepted so as never to arrive at its intended destination). More important for our purposes is: (ii) attempting to use your knowledge may inadvertently reveal it. If you purchase stock in Universal Petroleum on the basis of information that they have just discovered a new oil field, your action tends to drive up the price of Universal stock, thereby providing a signal to other traders.

As for accuracy, the content of a message may, of course, be more or less incorrect. Or, even if fully accurate as sent, it may be garbled in transmission before receipt. (It may even be *intentionally* inaccurate as sent, which need not imply a deceptive purpose; the inaccuracy may even be necessary for

---

[1] We sometimes use "signal" to mean a "message" and "information signal" to mean a "message service."

conveying the truth, as when the laws of visual perspective require that lines be made to converge if they are to be perceived as parallel.)[2]

Public versus private information

One of the crucial factors affecting the economic value of information is its *scarcity*. At one extreme, a particular datum may be possessed by only a single individual (private information); at the other extreme, it may be known to everyone (public information). *Publication* is the conversion of information from private to public status. All dissemination, even confidential communication to a single other person, involves some loss of privacy and thus of any value attaching thereto. (It would be possible to transmit purely private information only if a technology were to emerge whereby *forgetting* could be reliably effectuated. Then, for a price, I might give you some news while arranging to forget it myself!)

Public versus private *possession* of information must not be confused with quite another point, how narrow or widespread is the *relevance* of a bit of news. Whether or not there is oil under my land is of special private relevance to me, but discovery of a cheaper oil-extraction process may affect almost everyone.

First-order information versus second-order information

First-order information is about events – the outcome of the battle of Waterloo, or the result of tossing a die. In contrast, higher-order information relates to the message or information itself. There are many different aspects of an item of news about which we might like to become informed, quite apart from its content: for example, its source (which may be a clue to accuracy), or its privacy (how many people already know it).

We can distinguish an *overt secret* from a *covert secret*. Someone interested in marketing an item of news – or, to state things more carefully, in selling a message service that will emit a not-yet-known news item as its message – of course, needs to keep the actual message quite secret in advance of sale. But he will be broadcasting the higher-order information that he has such a secret. In contrast, someone engaged in espionage may be as urgently concerned to conceal the higher-order information (his possession of a secret) as the content of the secret itself.

One special case of higher-order information is the condition called "common knowledge." This is said to exist, say, when two persons both

---

[2] See also Section 12.1.1, where the purpose of sending a garbled message is deception.

Table 5.1. *Consequences of terminal choices*

		States (s)			
		1	2	...	S
	1	c_{11}	c_{12}	...	c_{1S}
	2	c_{21}	c_{22}	...	c_{2S}
Acts (x)	...	...	...	...	...
	X	c_{x1}	c_{x2}	...	c_{xS}
	Beliefs:	π_1	π_2	...	π_S

know a certain fact, each knows the other knows it, each knows that the other knows he knows it, and so forth (Aumann, 1976). We will see below that having "concordant beliefs" (agreed estimates of the probabilities of different states of the world) does not in general lead to the same economic consequences as having those same beliefs as "common knowledge."

5.2 Informational Decision Analysis

This section analyzes an individual's optimizing choice between the alternatives of: (1) taking immediate terminal action, versus (2) acquiring better information first, with the aim of improving the ultimate terminal decision to be made.

5.2.1 The Use of Evidence to Revise Beliefs

Table 5.1 is a generalized version of the simple picture of Table 1.1 in the opening chapter. For a set of available *terminal* actions $x = (1, \ldots, X)$ and a set of states of the world $s = (1, \ldots, S)$, the individual's choice of action and nature's selection of the state interact to determine the associated consequence c_{xs}. The bottom margin of the table shows the distribution of the individual's current probability beliefs, where π_s is the probability attached to the occurrence of state s, and, of course, $\sum_s \pi_s = 1$.

In taking terminal action, a person will choose whichever act x has the highest expected utility for him:

$$\underset{(x)}{\text{Max}}\, U(x) \equiv \sum_s \pi_s v(c_{xs}) \tag{5.2.1}$$

Here $v(c)$ is, as before, the elementary utility function.

Table 5.2. *Joint probability matrix* $(J = [j_{sm}])$

		Messages (m)			M	Probabilities for states
	J	1	2	$\cdots$		
	1	j_{11}	j_{12}	$\cdots$	j_{1M}	π_1
States	2	j_{21}	j_{22}	$\cdots$	j_{2M}	π_2
(s)	$\cdots$	$\cdots$	$\cdots$	$\cdots$	$\cdots$	
	S	j_{S1}	j_{S2}	$\cdots$	j_{SM}	π_S
Probabilities for messages		q_1	q_2	$\cdots$	q_M	1.0

Receipt of any particular message m will generally lead to a revision of probability beliefs, and thus may possibly imply a different choice of best terminal action. We now ask how the individual's probability estimates should be revised in the light of new information, that is, how he should convert his *prior* probabilities into *posterior* probabilities.

In this belief revision process, five different probability measures may be involved:

π_s = the unconditional or marginal (prior) probability of state s

q_m = the unconditional probability of receiving message m

j_{sm} = the joint probability of state s and message m

$q_{m \cdot s}$ = the conditional probability (or "likelihood") of message m, given state s

$\pi_{s \cdot m}$ = the conditional (posterior) probability of state s, given message m

There are a number of ways of displaying the interaction among the various probability distributions involved. The clearest is to start with the *joint probability matrix J* pictured in Table 5.2. In the main body of the table, j_{sm} is the joint probability of the state being s and the message being m. (For example, the state might be "rain tomorrow" and the message "barometer is falling.")

The sum of all these joint probabilities, taken over all the messages and states, is, of course, unity: $\sum_{s,m} j_{sm} = 1$. For each given state s, summing over the messages m (i.e., summing the j_{sm} horizontally in each row of the J matrix) generates the corresponding prior "marginal" state probabilities π_s shown in the adjoined column at the right of Table 5.2. This corresponds to the probability identity:

$$\sum_m j_{sm} \equiv \pi_s$$

Table 5.3. *Likelihood matrix* $(L \equiv [l_{sm}] \equiv [q_{m \cdot s}])$

		Messages (m)				
	L	1	2	...	M	
	1	$q_{1 \cdot 1}$	$q_{1 \cdot 1}$	...	$q_{M \cdot 1}$	1.0
	2	$q_{1 \cdot 2}$	$q_{2 \cdot 2}$	...	$q_{M \cdot 2}$	1.0
States(s)	...	...	...	...	...	...
	S	$q_{1 \cdot S}$	$q_{2 \cdot S}$	...	$q_{M \cdot S}$	1.0

Similarly, of course, summing over the states s (i.e., adding up the j_{sm} vertically in each column) generates the "marginal" message probabilities q_m, as shown in the row adjoined at the bottom of Table 5.2:

$$\sum_s j_{sm} \equiv q_m$$

The q_m are the prior probabilities that the individual attaches to receiving the different messages. Since the state probabilities and the message probabilities each make up a probability distribution – the grand sum taken either over the π_s or over the q_m – must again be 1.0, as indicated in the lower-right corner of the table.

Two other important matrices are readily derived from the underlying joint probability matrix J. We will call them the *likelihood matrix L* and the *potential posterior matrix* Π.

The likelihood matrix $L = [l_{sm}]$ (Table 5.3) shows the *conditional* probability of any message given any state, which will be denoted $q_{m \cdot s}$. Thus:

$$l_{sm} \equiv q_{m \cdot s} \equiv \frac{j_{sm}}{\pi_s} \qquad (5.2.2)$$

Numerically, the elements of the L matrix are obtained from the J matrix by dividing the j_{sm} in each row through by the adjoined π_s. For any row of the L matrix, these conditional probabilities must, of course, sum to unity, since:

$$\sum_m q_{m \cdot s} \equiv \frac{1}{\pi_s} \sum_m j_{sm} \equiv \frac{1}{\pi_s} \pi_s \equiv 1$$

(But note that the *column* sums in the L matrix do not sum to unity, except by accident, and in fact these column sums have no meaning so far as our analysis is concerned.)

Table 5.4. *Potential posterior matrix* ($\Pi \equiv [\pi_{s \cdot m}]$)

		Messages (m)			
	Π	1	2	...	M
	1	$\pi_{1 \cdot 1}$	$\pi_{1 \cdot 2}$	...	$\pi_{1 \cdot M}$
	2	$\pi_{1 \cdot 2}$	$\pi_{2 \cdot 2}$	...	$\pi_{2 \cdot M}$
States (s)	...	...	...	...	...
	S	$\pi_{S \cdot 1}$	$\pi_{S \cdot 2}$	...	$\pi_{S \cdot M}$
		1.0	1.0	...	1.0

The potential posterior matrix Π (Table 5.4) shows the conditional probability of each state given any message m, which is denoted $\pi_{s \cdot m}$ and defined in:

$$\pi_{s \cdot m} \equiv \frac{j_{sm}}{q_m} \qquad (5.2.3)$$

The elements of the Π matrix are obtained numerically from the underlying J matrix by dividing all the j_{sm} in each column through by the adjoined q_m below. The *column* sums must then all be unity, since:

$$\sum_s \pi_{s \cdot m} \equiv \frac{1}{q_m} \sum_s j_{sm} \equiv \frac{1}{q_m} q_m \equiv 1$$

(Here the *row* sums do not in general equal unity, and in fact have no relevant meaning for our purposes.) Why we term this the potential posterior matrix should be evident. Each separate column shows the "posterior" probability distribution for states of the world that a person with a given J matrix should logically adopt, after having received the particular message m. The entire Π matrix therefore gives us an *ex ante* picture of *all* the alternative posterior distributions that could come about, depending upon which of the possible messages is received.

Looking at this in a somewhat different way, the prior probability π_s of state s is an average, weighted by the message probabilities q_m, of the posterior probabilities $\pi_{s \cdot m}$ for state s:

$$\pi_s = j_{s1} + \cdots + j_{sM} = q_1 \pi_{s \cdot 1} + \cdots + q_M \pi_{s \cdot M}$$

Or, expressing the relation between the prior state-probability vector $\pi = (\pi_1, \ldots, \pi_s)$ and the message-probability vector $q = (q_1, \ldots, q_M)$ in matrix notation:

$$\pi = \Pi q \qquad (5.2.4)$$

And analogously, the message probability q_m is an average of the prior state probabilities weighted by the likelihoods:

$$q_m = j_{1m} + \cdots + j_{sm} = \pi_1 q_{m \cdot 1} + \cdots + \pi_S q_{m \cdot S}$$

So that, in matrix notation:

$$q = L'\pi$$

Example 5.1: There may be oil under your land. The alternative terminal actions are to undertake a major investment to develop the field or not to do so, and this decision will, of course, depend upon your estimate of the chance of oil really being there. The underlying "states of the world" are three possible geological configurations: state 1 is very favorable, with 90% chance that oil is there; state 2 is much less favorable, with 30% chance; state 3 is hopeless, with 0% chance.

In order to improve your information before taking terminal action, you have decided to drill a test well. The two possible sample outcomes or messages are that the test well is either "wet" or "dry." On the assumption that the test well is a random sample, then, if the true state is really state 1, there is a 90% chance of the message "wet"; if it is state 2, there is a 30% chance; and if it is state 3, no chance. So the given data specify the likelihood matrix $L \equiv [q_{m \cdot s}]$ shown below.

Suppose that, in addition, you initially attach probabilities $(\pi_1, \pi_2, \pi_3) = (0.1, 0.5, 0.4)$ to the three states. Multiplying each likelihood $q_{m \cdot s}$ in the L matrix by the prior probability π_s yields the joint probability matrix $J \equiv [j_{sm}]$. The column sums are then the message probabilities $q_1 = 0.24$ and $q_2 = 0.76$. Using these you can easily compute your potential posterior matrix $\Pi = [\pi_{s \cdot m}]$.

		$L \equiv [q_{m \cdot s}]$ Messages (m)				$J \equiv [j_{sm}]$ Messages (m)				$\Pi \equiv [\pi_{s \cdot m}]$ Messages (m)	
		Wet	Dry			Wet	Dry			Wet	Dry
	L	1	2	J		1	2	π_s	Π	1	2
	1	0.9	0.1	1.0	1	0.09	0.01	0.1	1	0.375	0.013
States	2	0.3	0.7	1.0	2	0.15	0.35	0.5	2	0.625	0.461
(s)	3	0	1.0	1.0	3	0	0.40	0.4	3	0	0.526
					q_m	0.24	0.76	1.0		1.0	1.0

Notice that the message "wet" shifts your prior distribution $(\pi_1, \pi_2, \pi_3) = (0.1, 0.5, 0.4)$ to the much more favorable posterior distribution $(\pi_{1\cdot1}, \pi_{2\cdot1}, \pi_{3\cdot1}) = (0.375, 0.625, 0)$. The message "dry" leads, of course, to a much less hopeful posterior distribution $(\pi_{1\cdot2}, \pi_{2\cdot2}, \pi_{3\cdot2}) = (0.013, 0.461, 0.526)$.[3]   □

So far as pure logic is concerned, the relevant data might equally well be presented or summarized in three different ways: (1) by the joint probability matrix J; (2) by the prior probability distribution for *states* (the right-hand margin of the J matrix) together with the likelihood matrix L; and, (3) by the prior probability distribution for *messages* (the bottom margin of the J matrix) together with the potential posterior matrix Π. But from the operational point of view, a decision maker will usually find it most convenient to use method 2. As in the example above, he is likely to think in terms of having a prior probability distribution for the underlying states together with a likelihood matrix L describing the message service being employed.

Prior beliefs are always *subjective*, while the likelihood matrix summarizing the possible message outcomes may often (though not necessarily) be *objective*. Suppose the message service represents the outcome of two tosses of a coin. For the state of the world that the coin is fair, with unbiased sampling the likelihood of the message "two heads" is objectively calculable from the laws of probability as 1/4. But someone who is not sure that the sampling is unbiased might subjectively assign a somewhat different likelihood to the message "two heads."

This process of revision of probabilities is called *Bayesian*, after Bayes' Theorem. The derivation is simple. First, the joint probability j_{sm} can be expressed in two ways in terms of the conditional probabilities defined in (5.2.2) and (5.2.3):

$$\pi_s q_{m\cdot s} \equiv j_{sm} \equiv q_m \pi_{s\cdot m}$$

---

[3] Random or "unbiased" sampling was assumed here, e.g., in state 1 (defined in terms of a 90% chance of oil being there) the likelihood matrix L indicates a 90% probability $q_{1\cdot1}$ of receiving the message "wet." The underlying method is, however, sufficiently general to allow even for biased sampling. Thus, if state 1 is the true state of the world, conceivably the well (perhaps because it will not be drilled to full depth) could still have only an 80% chance of showing "wet." Whatever the likelihoods are, they can be displayed in the L matrix (and equivalently reflected in the J and Π matrices as well).

(Note how these three formulations relate to the information contained in the L, J, and Π matrices, respectively.) Solving for the posterior probability $\pi_{s \cdot m}$:

Bayes' Theorem (I)

$$\pi_{s \cdot m} \equiv \frac{j_{sm}}{q_m} \equiv \pi_s \frac{q_{m \cdot s}}{q_m} \qquad (5.2.5)$$

In words: The posterior probability that an individual should attach to state s, after receiving message m, is equal to the prior probability π_s multiplied by the likelihood $q_{m \cdot s}$ of message m, and then divided by a normalizing factor, which is the overall probability q_m of receiving message m. Since the latter is the "marginal" probability of m, we can also write Bayes' Theorem in the alternative forms:

Bayes' Theorem (II)

$$\pi_{s \cdot m} \equiv \pi_s \frac{q_{m \cdot s}}{\sum_{s'} j_{s'm}} \equiv \pi_s \frac{q_{m \cdot s}}{\sum_{s'} \pi_{s'} q_{m \cdot s'}} \qquad (5.2.5)$$

The Bayesian belief-revision process is illustrated in Figure 5.1. For diagrammatic convenience, the pictorial representation assumes a continuous rather than a discrete state-defining variable, running from a lower limit $s = 0$ to an upper limit $s = S$. The "prior probability" curve in the diagrams is the given initial probability density function $\pi(s)$, where, of course, $\int_0^S \pi(s)\,ds \equiv 1$. By assumption here, this density shows some humping toward the middle; i.e., prior beliefs are such that middling values of s are regarded as more likely than extreme ones.

There are two alternative messages: $m = 1$ has much greater likelihood if the true state of the world is toward the high end of the range (upper diagram), while $m = 2$ has greater likelihood if s is small (lower diagram). Although the prior probability distributions are the same in the upper and lower panels, the differing "likelihood function" curves lead to differing "posterior probability" density functions. In each panel, the posterior distribution is a kind of compromise or average of the other two curves. More specifically, for any s, the height $\pi_{s \cdot m}$ along the posterior probability density curve is the product of the height along the prior density curve (π_s) times the height along the likelihood function $(q_{m \cdot s})$ – adjusted by a normalization or re-scaling factor to make the new integrated probability equal to unity. (This normalization corresponds to dividing through by the message probability q_m, as indicated in Equation (5.2.5).)

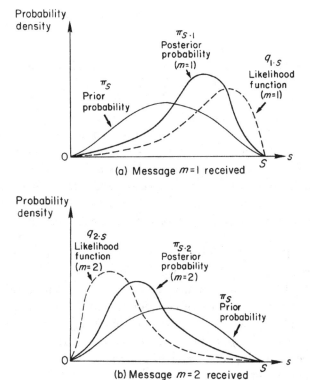

Figure 5.1. Bayesian revision of probability beliefs.

Three useful propositions are implicit in the Bayesian belief-revision process:

(1) Recall our discussion in the initial chapter about the individual's *confidence* in his beliefs, and how this would affect his decision whether or not to acquire more information. Confidence is indicated in Figure 5.1 by the "tightness" of the prior probability distribution – the degree to which a person approaches assigning 100% probability to some single possible value of *s*. The corresponding proposition is: other things equal, the higher the prior confidence, the more the posterior distribution will resemble the prior distribution for any given message or weight of evidence. This is intuitively clear if we go to the limit. An individual with "absolute" prior confidence, who attaches 100% probability to some particular value $s = \hat{s}$, can learn nothing from new evidence. From Equation (5.2.4), if the prior probabilities π_s all

equal zero for any $s \neq \hat{s}$, the corresponding posterior probabilities $\pi_{s \cdot m} = 0$ also.

(2) Other things equal, the greater the mass of new evidence the more the posterior distribution will resemble the likelihood function rather than the prior probabilities. A large sample size, for example, will be reflected in a very "tight" likelihood curve in the diagrams. Suppose that, in tossing a coin, P is the unknown true probability of obtaining heads while p is the sample proportion of heads observed in n tosses. Then $p = 0.5$ in a sample of two tosses would be reflected in a "loose" likelihood curve with only a mild peak around $P = 0.5$ – whereas $p = 0.5$ in a sample of 100 tosses would produce a very tight likelihood curve with a sharp peak around $P = 0.5$. As before, the tighter the curve, the more pull it has upon the shape of the posterior probability distribution.

(3) Other things equal, the more "surprising" the evidence, the bigger the impact upon the posterior probabilities. Intuitively, this is obvious: only when a message is surprising does it call for any drastic change in our beliefs. In terms of Equation (5.2.5), a "surprising" message would be one with low message probability q_m. Other things equal, the smaller the q_m in the denominator on the right-hand side, the bigger the multiplier causing the posterior probability $\pi_{s \cdot m}$ to diverge from the prior π_s.

Exercises and Excursions 5.2.1

1 *The Game Show*

A contestant on a television game show may choose any of three curtained booths, one of which contains a valuable prize. Lacking any prior information, she arbitrarily selects one of the booths, say, no. 1. But before the curtain is drawn revealing whether she wins or loses, the Master of Ceremonies says: "Wait, I'll give you a chance to change your mind." He then draws the curtain on one of the *other* booths, say, no. 2, which is revealed to be empty. The M.C. then asks if the contestant cares to change her choice. Should she do so?

2 *Joint (J), Likelihood (L), and Potential Posterior (Π) Matrices*

(A) There are two states s_1 and s_2 and two messages m_1 and m_2. The prior probability distribution over states is $\pi = (0.7, 0.3)$. The posterior probabilities $\pi_{s \cdot m}$ include $\pi_{1 \cdot 1} = 0.9$ and $\pi_{2 \cdot 2} = 0.8$. Calculate the Π, L, and J matrices.

(B) (i) If you have the J matrix, what additional data (if any) are needed to construct each of the other two matrices?
   (ii) Same question, if you have the L matrix.
   (iii) Same question, with the Π matrix.
(C) For the prior probability distribution π above, and still assuming only two possible messages, show (if it is possible to do so):
   (i) An L matrix representing a *completely conclusive* message service. (That is, a matrix leaving no posterior uncertainty whatsoever.) If it exists, is it *unique*, or are there other such L matrices? Also, does any such matrix depend at all upon π?
   (ii) An L matrix that is *completely uninformative*. Answer the same questions.
   (iii) An L matrix that (if one message is received) will conclusively establish that one of the states will occur but (if the other message is received) will be completely uninformative. Same questions.

5.2.2 Revision of Optimal Action and the Worth of Information

If immediate terminal action is to be taken, the individual will choose whichever act has highest expected utility, as indicated in Equation (5.2.1). In condensed notation:

$$\underset{(x)}{\text{Max}}\, U(x; \pi) \equiv \sum_s \pi_s v(c_{xs}) \qquad (5.2.6)$$

Denote as x_0 the optimal immediate terminal action, which, of course, must be calculated in terms of the prior probabilities π_s. What we are concerned with here is the value of an *informational action*, that is, the expected utility gain from using an information service.

After a particular message m has been received from such a service, the decision maker would use (5.2.6) once again, employing now the *posterior* probabilities $\pi_{s \cdot m}$. This recalculation could well lead to a choice of a different optimal terminal action x_m. Then ω_m, the value in utility units of the message m, can be defined as:

$$\omega_m \equiv U(x_m; \pi_{\cdot m}) - U(x_0; \pi_{\cdot m})$$

This is the expected gain from the revision of optimal action, calculated in terms of the individual's *revised* probabilities $\pi_{\cdot m} \equiv (\pi_{1 \cdot m}, \ldots, \pi_{S \cdot m})$. Evidently, the expected utility gain must be non-negative, else x_m could not have been the optimal act using the posterior probabilities. (But message m

could lead to *no change* of best action despite the revision of probability beliefs, in which case $\omega_m = 0$ – such a message has zero value.)

However, one cannot purchase a given message but only a *message service*. So it is not the ω_m associated with some particular message that is relevant but rather the expectation of the utility gain from all possible messages weighted by their respective message probabilities q_m. More specifically, for a message service μ characterized by a particular likelihood matrix L and prior beliefs, π, the expected value of the information (the worth of the message service) is:

$$\Omega(\mu) = \mathop{\mathrm{E}}_m[\omega_m] = \sum_m q_m[U(x_m; \pi_{\cdot m}) - U(x_0; \pi_{\cdot m})]$$

Since each ω_m is non-negative, we know that a message service can never lower the agent's expected utility (before allowing for the *cost* of the service).[4]

Let c^*_{sm} denote the income in state s associated with the best action x_m after receiving message m, and c^*_{s0} the corresponding income for the best uninformed action x_0 (that is, the best action in terms of the prior beliefs):

$$\Omega(\mu) = \sum_m q_m \sum_s \pi_{s \cdot m} v\left(c^*_{sm}\right) - \sum_m \sum_s \pi_{s \cdot m} q_m v\left(c^*_{s0}\right)$$

$$= \sum_m \sum_s \pi_{s \cdot m} q_m v\left(c^*_{sm}\right) - \sum_s \pi_s v\left(c^*_{s0}\right) \qquad (5.2.7)$$

Thus the value of the message service is just the difference between expected utility with and without the service.

For a simplified model with only two states of the world ($s = 1, 2$), Figure 5.2 illustrates a situation with three available terminal actions ($x = 1, 2, 3$). In this three-dimensional diagram, utility is measured vertically, while the probabilities of the two states are scaled along the two horizontal axes. Each possible assignment of probabilities to states is represented by a point along AB, a line in the base plane whose equation is simply $\pi_1 + \pi_2 = 1$.

Suppose state 1 occurs. Then the cardinal preference-scaling values (the elementary utilities) associated with the consequences c_{x1} attaching to the different actions x are indicated by the intercepts labeled $v(c_{11})$, $v(c_{21})$, and $v(c_{31})$ lying vertically above point B in the diagram. Similarly, $v(c_{12})$, $v(c_{22})$, and $v(c_{32})$, the elementary utilities of outcomes in state 2, are the

---

[4] This is true only in single-person settings. As we shall see in Section 5.3, in multi-person settings, one person's decision to acquire a message service may change another person's behavior. This can lead to a smaller expected utility to the person who acquires the message services.

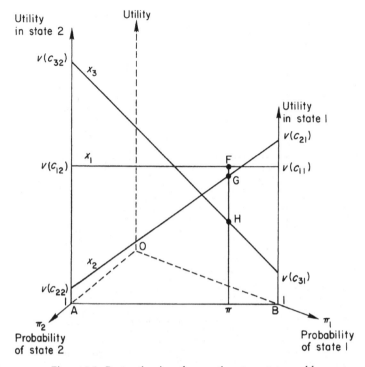

Figure 5.2. Best action in a three-action, two-state world.

corresponding intercepts above point A. (Note that x_1 is a certainty action, since it yields the same elementary utility in either state.) The expected utility $U(x_i, \pi) = \pi_1 \, v(c_{i1}) + \pi_2 \, v(c_{i2})$ of any action x, given any probability vector π, is shown by the vertical distance from the point $\pi = (\pi_1, \pi_2)$ along AB to the line joining $v(c_{x1})$ and $v(c_{x2})$ for that action. In the diagram, if π is the prior probability vector then the best immediate *terminal action* is the certainty action $x = 1$ whose expected utility is indicated by the height of point F above the base plane.

In Figure 5.2, everything of interest takes place in the vertical plane overlying the line AB. So we can simplify matters by shifting to a two-dimensional diagram, as in Figure 5.3, where the line AB becomes the horizontal axis along which π_1 varies from zero to unity. In this simplified diagram, we see once more the expected utilities of actions $x = 1, 2, 3$ as functions of the prior probability vector $\pi = (\pi_1, \pi_2)$, leading to the choice of $x = 1$ as the best terminal action in terms of the prior probabilities.

We now want to picture the effects of receiving information. Suppose an information service μ can generate two possible messages $m = 1, 2$. Either

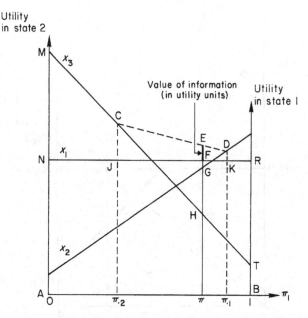

Figure 5.3. The value of information.

message will lead to a revised (posterior) probability vector $\pi_{.m} \equiv (\pi_{1 \cdot m}, \pi_{2 \cdot m})$. If message $m = 2$ is received, by construction the revised choice of action in terms of the posterior probability vector $\pi_{.2} \equiv (\pi_{1.2}, \pi_{2.2})$ is $x = 3$, with expected utility indicated by the height of point C. The *ex post* expected-utility gain over $x = 1, \omega_1$, is therefore equal to the vertical distance CJ (the probability-weighted average of the *gain* MN if state 2 occurs and the *loss* RT if state 1 occurs). If, on the other hand, the message received is $m = 1$, the best action in the diagram is $x = 2$ (expected utility indicated by point D), so $\omega_2 = $ DK. Then $\Omega(\mu)$, the value of the information service in terms of the gain in expected utility, is represented by the vertical distance EF above the point π along the line AB.

Example 5.2: In an oil-drilling situation, suppose there are just two possible states: "wet" (with prior probability $\pi_1 = 0.24$) and "dry" (with prior probability $\pi_2 = 0.76$).[5] If you take action $x = 1$ (drill the well) and it is wet, you gain \$1,000,000. If it is dry, you lose \$400,000. Action $x = 2$

---

[5] These numbers are consistent with those in the previous example. Although in that example there were three states, associated with three different possible geological formations, the implied overall probabilities worked out to 0.24 for wet and 0.76 for dry, as shown in the bottom row adjoined to the J matrix.

(not drilling) involves a $50,000 cost in relocating your rig. Suppose your utility function is simply linear in income (you are risk neutral), so we can write $v(c) = c$. A message service, taking the form of a geological analysis in advance of drilling, is characterized by the following likelihood matrix *L*. How much should you be willing to pay for it?

		Message		
$L = [q_{m \cdot s}]$		Wet	Dry	
State	Wet	0.6	0.4	1.0
	Dry	0.2	0.8	1.0

Answer: In terms of your prior probabilities, action $x = 1$ involves an expected gain of 0.24 ($1,000,000)$-$0.76($400,000) = -$64,000$, whereas action $x = 2$ leads to a loss of only $50,000. So the optimal prior action x_0 is $x = 2$. As for the value of the message service, straightforward computations lead to the Potential Posterior Matrix shown below.

		Message	
$\Pi = [\pi_{s \cdot m}]$		Wet	Dry
State	Wet	0.486	0.136
	Dry	0.514	0.864
		1.0	1.0

Using the posterior probabilities, if the message is "dry", the best action remains $x = 2$ (not drilling). But if the message is "wet," the expected gain from drilling (action $x = 1$) becomes $0.486($1,000,000) - 0.514($400,000)$ $= $280,400$. So the expected value of the information is $0.296 ($280,400) + 0.704 (-$50,000) - (-$50,000) = $97,798$. This is the value of the message service, where 0.296 and 0.704 are the message probabilities q_1 and q_2. □

We have already seen, in discussing Bayes' Theorem, that higher prior confidence implies smaller revision of beliefs from given messages. It follows that higher confidence also implies lower value of information. With more confident prior beliefs, in Figure 5.3 the posterior probability vectors $\pi_{.1}$ and $\pi_{.2}$ would both lie closer to the original π. It is evident that the effect (if any) of greater prior confidence can only be to shrink the distance EF that represents the value of acquiring more evidence.

So far, we have discussed the value of information in utility units. The natural next step is to calculate what a message service is worth in income (corn) units – i.e., the maximum fee ξ that someone with utility function $v(c)$ would be willing to pay for the information.

As follows directly from Equation (5.2.7), the fee is determined in:

$$\sum_m \sum_s \pi_{s \cdot m} q_m v(c_{sm}^* - \xi) = \sum_s \pi_s v(c_{s0}^*) \qquad (5.2.8)$$

That is, the maximum fee ξ that a person would pay, in advance of receiving the message, is such as to make the expected utility of the best informed action exactly equal to the expected utility of the best uninformed action.

Suppose that $x_m = x_0$ for all messages m. Then $c_{sm}^* = c_{s0}^*$ for all messages m, and $\xi = 0$ is the solution to (5.2.8). Thus, as one would expect, if the optimal action remains the same regardless of the message received, then the information service is worthless.

Example 5.3: In a two-state world, suppose the contingent-claim prices for corn in states 1 and 2 are numerically equal to the prior state probabilities: $p_1 = \pi_1$ and $p_2 = \pi_2$, where $\pi_1 + \pi_2 = 1$. (Thus, the prices are "fair.") Specifically, suppose the states are equally probable. Consider an individual with utility function $v(c) = \sqrt{c}$ and endowment $(\bar{c}_1, \bar{c}_2) = (50, 150)$.

Before acquiring any additional information, there are an infinite number of possible actions the individual might take, representing the possible amounts of his endowed c_1 he might trade for c_2, or vice versa. But, since the prices are fair, in accordance with Fundamental Theorem of Risk Bearing we know that the optimal action will be to trade to the certainty position $(c_{10}^*, c_{20}^*) = (100, 100)$. (The 0 subscript here signifies, as before, the best *uninformed* action.) In terms of a picture like Figure 5.3, the "null action" $\bar{x}$ – remaining at the endowment position – would be represented by a line with negative slope, the left intercept being at $\sqrt{150}$ and the right intercept at $\sqrt{50}$. The optimal uninformed action x_0^* would be a horizontal line at $v(100) = \sqrt{100} = 10$. The expected utility of the endowment position is $(\sqrt{150} + \sqrt{50})/2$ or about 9.66, while the expected utility of x_0^* is, of course, 10. So 0.34 is the utility gain, over the endowment position, of the best action under uncertainty.

Now suppose a message service μ, whose output will be *conclusive* as to which state is going to obtain, becomes available in time for the individual to engage in state-claim trading at the same fair prices. To determine the value of μ in utility units we first have to find, for each possible message m, the individual's best informed action. If message 1 is received, obviously the individual will convert all of his endowed wealth into 200 units of c_1, and similarly into 200 units of c_2 if message 2 is received. Thus his expected utility will be $\sqrt{200}$ or 14.14 approximately.

To determine the maximum fee ξ he would be willing to pay, we can use Equation (5.2.8), which reduces here to the simple form:

$$v(200 - \xi) = v(100)$$

The solution is $\xi = 100$. Thus, the individual here would be willing to pay up to half of his endowed wealth for a conclusive message, arriving in time for market trading, telling him which state is going to obtain. □

Exercises and Excursions 5.2.2

1 Value of Information in a Simple Betting Problem
You have an opportunity to gamble on the toss of a coin. If your choice is correct, you win $30, but if it is wrong, you lose $50. Initially, you think it equally likely that the coin is two-headed, two-tailed, or fair. If you are risk neutral, so that your utility function can be written $v(c) = c$, how much should you be willing to pay to observe a sample of size 1?

2 Value of Information in a Two-Action Problem with Linear Costs
You are the receiving officer of a company that has received a large shipment of ordered goods. You must decide whether to accept (action $x = A$) or reject (action $x = R$) the shipment. Which you will want to do depends upon the unknown proportion defective P in the shipment (population). Your loss function is:

$$L(R.P) = \begin{cases} 0, & \text{for} \quad P \geq 0.04 \\ 100(0.04 - P), & \text{for} \quad P < 0.04 \end{cases}$$

$$L(A.P) = \begin{cases} 0, & \text{for} \quad P \leq 0.04 \\ 200(P - 0.04), & \text{for} \quad P > 0.04 \end{cases}$$

Your prior probability distribution is defined over four discrete values of P (states of the world):

Fraction defective (P)	Prior probability (π_s)
0.02	0.7
0.04	0.1
0.06	0.1
0.08	0.1
	1.0

(A) What is your best *prior* decision, in the absence of sample information? Assume that you are risk neutral, with utility function $v(c) = c$.

(B) How much should you be willing to pay for a sample of size 1?

3 Value of Information with Logarithmic Utility

Two individuals with endowed wealths W_1 and W_2 have the same utility function $v = \ln(c)$, the same probability beliefs π_s, and face the same state-claim prices P_s.

(A) Individual 1 will receive no additional information, but individual 2 will be receiving conclusive information revealing the true state before trading takes place. Show that the utility difference between them is given by:

$$U_2 - U_1 = \ln W_2 - \ln W_1 - \sum_s \pi_s \ln \pi_s$$

[HINT: Make use of a simple relationship between W and c_s that holds for the logarithmic utility function.]

(B) Using this result, show that an uninformed individual with this utility function would be willing to give up a fraction K^* of his wealth to receive conclusive information before trading takes place, where:

$$K^* = 1 - (\pi_1)^{\pi_1}(\pi_2)^{\pi_2} \cdots (\pi_S)^{\pi_S}$$

(C) Show that he will pay the most when he initially assigns equal probabilities to all states.

4 Value of Less-than-Conclusive Information

Under the conditions of Example 5.3, suppose the message service μ does not provide a fully conclusive message as to which state is going to obtain. Instead, suppose message m_1 is such as to lead to the posterior distribution $(\pi_{1.1}, \pi_{2.1}) = (0.75, 0.25)$ while message m_2 leads to $(\pi_{1.2}, \pi_{2.2}) = (0.25, 0.75)$.

(A) Compute the likelihood matrix L associated with this message service.

(B) Show that the individual with the utility function in the text example, $v(c) = \sqrt{c}$, would be willing to pay a fee ξ equal to 20 units of corn for this information, provided as before that the message arrives in time for market trading.

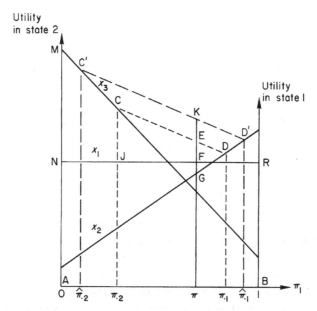

Figure 5.4. More informative and less informative message services.

5.2.3 More Informative versus Less Informative Message Services*

In general, the value of a message service for any individual will depend upon: (1) the set of actions available, (2) his utility function $v(c)$, and (3) his probability beliefs over messages and states. We will be inquiring here into the circumstances in which, regardless of his utility function and range of available actions, an individual with given prior probability beliefs will be able to rank different message services in terms of their "informativeness." (How the value of a message service also responds to differing utility functions and to different action sets will be taken up in the sections following.)

A message service $\hat{\mu}$ is defined as *more informative* than another service μ, for an individual with given prior probability vector π, if using $\hat{\mu}$ provides him with a greater utility gain than using μ regardless of his utility function $v(c)$ and action set. More specifically, if for some individual i the possible belief revisions brought about by $\hat{\mu}$ will lead him to choose corresponding terminal actions whose expected utility gain $\hat{\Omega}_i$ is higher than the improvement Ω_i achievable using message service μ.

Figure 5.4 provides an intuitive illustration. The shorter dashed lines represent an information service μ that generates two possible messages

---

* Starred sections represent more difficult or specialized materials that can be omitted without significant loss of continuity.

1 and 2, leading to posterior probability vectors $\pi_{.1}$ and $\pi_{.2}$ as in the previous Figure 5.3. The alternative information service $\hat{\mu}$, indicated here by the longer dashed lines, also generates two messages 1 and 2. As shown, the additional utility improvement due to using $\hat{\mu}$ rather than μ is the length KE in the diagram.

Recall that the individual's prior probability vector π can always be expressed as the message-probability-weighted average of the posterior probability vectors $\pi_{.m}$ associated with any message service employed, that is:

$$\pi = q_1\pi_{.1} + q_2\pi_{.2} = \hat{q}_1\hat{\pi}_{.1} + \hat{q}_2\hat{\pi}_{.2}$$

In the diagram, $\hat{\pi}_{.1}$ lies to the right of $\pi_{.1}$ and $\hat{\pi}_{.2}$ lies to the left of $\pi_{.2}$, so the posterior vectors of the alternative service $\hat{\mu}$ are a mean-preserving spread of those of μ. When this holds, so that the posterior vectors associated with $\hat{\mu}$ bracket those of μ as in the diagram, we can say that message 1 under $\hat{\mu}$ is *more conclusive* than the corresponding message under the original service μ as to the occurrence of state 1, while message 2 under $\hat{\mu}$ is more conclusive as to state 2. This is the essential interpretation of the "informativeness" property.

One point is worth special note: when the bracketing condition holds as in Figure 5.4, *the more informative message service $\hat{\mu}$ leads to higher expected utility even when, as shown, the posterior actions associated with all of the possible messages are unchanged from μ.* The reason is that, both messages being more conclusive, even when the actions are unchanged there is a smaller risk of posterior error (choosing the wrong action) no matter which message is received. Of course, if $\hat{\mu}$ actually implies some change in one or more of the best conditional actions, in comparison with μ, the utility gain will be even larger.

To formalize the argument about the conclusiveness of messages, suppose that for an individual with prior beliefs π each possible posterior probability vector $\pi_{.m}$ under message service μ is a convex combination of the posterior probabilities under the superior message service $\hat{\mu}$, that is:

$$\begin{bmatrix} \pi_{1 \cdot m} \\ \pi_{2 \cdot m} \end{bmatrix} = \begin{bmatrix} \hat{\pi}_{1 \cdot 1} \\ \hat{\pi}_{2 \cdot 1} \end{bmatrix} a_{1 \cdot m} + \begin{bmatrix} \hat{\pi}_{1 \cdot 2} \\ \hat{\pi}_{2 \cdot 2} \end{bmatrix} a_{2 \cdot m}$$

where $a_{\hat{m} \cdot m}$ are linear weights. In matrix notation:

$$\Pi = \hat{\Pi}A, \quad \text{where } A = [a_{\hat{m} \cdot m}] \tag{5.2.9}$$

For the columns of Π to be convex combinations of the columns of $\hat{\Pi}$, it must be the case that the matrix A is non-negative and has columns summing to 1:

$$\sum_{\hat{m}} a_{\hat{m}\cdot m} = 1, \qquad a_{\hat{m}\cdot m} \geq 0 \qquad (5.2.10)$$

As Blackwell (1953) first noted, there is a useful interpretation of the elements of A. One can think of the message service μ as representing the result of receiving message $\hat{\mu}$ except that some information has been "garbled" in transmission.[6] To be precise, $a_{\hat{m}\cdot m}$ can be interpreted as the conditional probability that, when message m is received, message $\hat{m}$ was actually sent. Since probabilities must sum to 1, condition (5.2.10) must then hold.

Under this interpretation, there is a further relationship between the message probability vectors q and $\hat{q}$:

$$q_{\hat{m}} = \sum_m a_{\hat{m}\cdot m} q_m$$

$$\begin{bmatrix} \text{probability} \\ \text{message } \hat{m} \\ \text{was sent} \end{bmatrix} = \sum_m \begin{bmatrix} \text{probability } \hat{m} \\ \text{was sent if} \\ m \text{ is received} \end{bmatrix} \cdot \begin{bmatrix} \text{probability} \\ \text{message } m \\ \text{was received} \end{bmatrix}$$

In matrix notation:

$$\hat{q} = Aq \qquad (5.2.11)$$

Returning to Figure 5.4, we have argued that the crucial requirement for an individual with prior beliefs π to be able to rank the two services, regardless of his preferences, is that the posterior probability vectors $\pi_{\cdot m}$ of message service μ must be convex combinations of the posterior probability vectors $\pi_{\cdot \hat{m}}$ of $\hat{\mu}$. Equation (5.2.11) appears to be a second restriction on probabilities. However, the following relationship between the message probabilities and prior probabilities must hold:

$$\begin{bmatrix} \hat{\pi}_{1\cdot 1} & \hat{\pi}_{1\cdot 2} \\ \hat{\pi}_{2\cdot 1} & \hat{\pi}_{2\cdot 2} \end{bmatrix} \begin{bmatrix} \hat{q}_1 \\ \hat{q}_2 \end{bmatrix} = \begin{bmatrix} \pi_1 \\ \pi_2 \end{bmatrix} = \begin{bmatrix} \pi_{1\cdot 1} & \pi_{1\cdot 2} \\ \pi_{2\cdot 1} & \pi_{2\cdot 2} \end{bmatrix} \begin{bmatrix} q_1 \\ q_2 \end{bmatrix}$$

Then, appealing to (5.2.9):

$$\begin{bmatrix} \hat{\pi}_{1\cdot 1} & \hat{\pi}_{1\cdot 2} \\ \hat{\pi}_{2\cdot 1} & \hat{\pi}_{2\cdot 2} \end{bmatrix} \begin{bmatrix} \hat{q}_1 \\ \hat{q}_2 \end{bmatrix} = \begin{bmatrix} \hat{\pi}_{1\cdot 1} & \hat{\pi}_{1\cdot 2} \\ \hat{\pi}_{2\cdot 1} & \hat{\pi}_{2\cdot 2} \end{bmatrix} \begin{bmatrix} a_{1\cdot 1} & a_{1\cdot 2} \\ a_{2\cdot 1} & a_{2\cdot 2} \end{bmatrix} \begin{bmatrix} q_1 \\ q_2 \end{bmatrix}$$

---

[6] See also Marschak and Miyasawa (1968).

Since the columns of $\hat{\Pi}$ sum to 1 and differ, the matrix $\hat{\Pi}$ has rank equal to 2. Hence we can pre-multiply by the inverse $\hat{\Pi}^{-1}$ to obtain:

$$\begin{bmatrix} \hat{q}_1 \\ \hat{q}_2 \end{bmatrix} = \begin{bmatrix} a_{1\cdot1} & a_{1\cdot2} \\ a_{2\cdot1} & a_{2\cdot2} \end{bmatrix} \begin{bmatrix} q_1 \\ q_2 \end{bmatrix}$$

Thus, in the 2×2 case, Equation (5.2.11) is not a separate condition but an implication of Equation (5.2.9).

Let us now reinterpret these equations in more general terms. Let $\hat{m}$ be one of $\hat{M}$ messages under message service $\hat{\mu}$ and let m be one of M messages under service μ. As before, condition (5.2.9) indicates that each message under μ can be interpreted as a "garbling" of the message sent under $\hat{\mu}$. Moreover, arguing as above:

$$\hat{\Pi}\hat{q} = \pi = \Pi q = \hat{\Pi}Aq \qquad (5.2.12)$$

As long as the columns of $\hat{\Pi}$ are linearly independent, it follows from (5.2.12) that $\hat{q} = Aq$. Thus that condition (5.2.11) is an implication of (5.2.9) holds not only for the 2×2 case but quite generally, given linear independence. On the other hand, in the absence of linear independence, there are many possible message probability vectors that are solutions to the system of equations $\hat{\Pi}\hat{q} = \pi$.

As a specific example, consider the following matrices:

$$\hat{\Pi} = \begin{bmatrix} 1 & \frac{1}{2} & 0 \\ 0 & \frac{1}{2} & 1 \end{bmatrix}, \quad \Pi = \begin{bmatrix} \frac{3}{4} & \frac{1}{4} \\ \frac{1}{4} & \frac{3}{4} \end{bmatrix}, \quad A = \begin{bmatrix} \frac{1}{2} & 0 \\ \frac{1}{2} & \frac{1}{2} \\ 0 & \frac{1}{2} \end{bmatrix}, \text{ and } q = \pi = \begin{bmatrix} \frac{1}{2} \\ \frac{1}{2} \end{bmatrix}$$

Here we do not have enough data to uniquely compute the message probabilities $\hat{q}$ from $\hat{\Pi}$ and π. One possible solution is $\hat{q} = Aq$, so that $\hat{q} = (\frac{1}{4}, \frac{1}{2}, \frac{1}{4})$, which suggests that message service μ is a garbling of $\hat{\mu}$. On the other hand, an alternative possibility is that $\hat{q} = (0, 1, 0)$. In this case, message service μ has no value since neither of the two helpful messages are ever sent. Absent linear independence, therefore, conditions (5.2.9) and (5.2.11) are both needed before one message service can be described as a "garbling" of the other.

Since the posterior beliefs mix prior beliefs and likelihoods, the two conditions may hold for one individual but not for another, unless their beliefs are the same. Indeed, as the following example indicates, two individuals with different priors may rank two information services differently regardless of their preferences.

Example 5.4: Suppose that the message services $\hat{\mu}$ and μ have the following likelihood matrices:

$$\hat{L} = \begin{bmatrix} \frac{3}{4} & \frac{1}{4} \\ \frac{1}{4} & \frac{3}{4} \\ \frac{1}{4} & \frac{3}{4} \end{bmatrix} \text{ and } L = \begin{bmatrix} \frac{5}{3} & \frac{3}{8} \\ \frac{3}{8} & \frac{5}{8} \\ 1 & 0 \end{bmatrix} \begin{matrix} s = 1 \\ s = 2 \\ s = 3 \end{matrix}$$

If Alex believes that states 1 and 2 each occur with probability $\frac{1}{2}$ while state 3 never occurs, the third row of the likelihood matrices is irrelevant for him. Comparing the first two rows, it is intuitively clear that service $\hat{\mu}$ is more valuable to Alex. In fact, it is easy to check that the posterior matrices $\hat{\Pi}$ and Π are:

$$\hat{\Pi} = \begin{bmatrix} \frac{3}{4} & \frac{1}{4} \\ \frac{1}{4} & \frac{3}{4} \end{bmatrix} \text{ and } \Pi = \begin{bmatrix} \frac{5}{8} & \frac{3}{8} \\ \frac{3}{8} & \frac{5}{4} \end{bmatrix}$$

Thus, for Alex, the posterior probability vectors associated with $\hat{\mu}$ (the columns of the $\hat{\Pi}$ matrix) bracket those associated with μ.

On the other hand, suppose Bev believes that state I will never occur while states 2 and 3 are equally likely. For her, the top row of each of the likelihood matrices is irrelevant. For likelihood matrix $\hat{L}$, the second and third rows are identical. Receiving a message therefore conveys no information. It follows immediately that Bev will prefer L to $\hat{L}$. □

This raises the question as to whether there are circumstances under which different individuals will *always* agree on a ranking of alternative message services, regardless of possibly differing prior beliefs. We now show that there are such conditions.

Suppose it is the case that each service does have an objectively calculable (or, at least, interpersonally agreed) likelihood matrix. Following the terminology of Blackwell, one likelihood matrix $\hat{L}$ is *more informative* than another matrix L if there exists a non-negative $\hat{M} \times M$ matrix B, each of whose rows sum to unity, such that:

$$\begin{matrix} (S \times \hat{M}) & (\hat{M} \times M) & (S \times M) \\ \hat{L} & B & = & L \end{matrix}$$

That is:

$$\sum_{\hat{m}} \hat{l}_{s \cdot \hat{m}} b_{\hat{m} \cdot m} = l_{s \cdot m} \tag{5.2.13}$$

$$\sum_{m} b_{\hat{m} \cdot m} = 1, \quad b_{\hat{m} \cdot m} \geq 0$$

As before, we can interpret the relationship between L and $\hat{L}$ in terms of transmission garbling. We can think of $b_{\hat{m}\cdot m}$ as the probability that, if message m is received, it was message $\hat{m}$ that was sent. Equation (5.2.13) can then be understood as the statement that:

$$
\begin{bmatrix} \text{the likelihood} \\ \text{of message } m \\ \text{given state is } s \end{bmatrix} = \sum_{\hat{m}} \begin{bmatrix} \text{probability of} \\ \text{receiving message } m \\ \text{when } \hat{m} \text{ was sent} \end{bmatrix} \cdot \begin{bmatrix} \text{the likelihood} \\ \text{of message } \hat{m} \\ \text{given state is } s \end{bmatrix}
$$

If condition (5.2.13) holds, it follows almost immediately that there must be a matrix A satisfying (5.2.9) and (5.2.11). First, given the definition of $B = [b_{\hat{m}\cdot m}]$, we can compute the corresponding A matrix using Bayes' Theorem:

$$
a_{\hat{m}\cdot m} q_m = b_{\hat{m}\cdot m} \hat{q}_{\hat{m}}
$$

$$
\begin{bmatrix} \text{probability that} \\ \hat{m} \text{ was sent when} \\ m \text{ is received} \end{bmatrix} \begin{bmatrix} \text{probability} \\ \text{that } m \text{ is} \\ \text{received} \end{bmatrix} = \begin{bmatrix} \text{probability that} \\ m \text{ is received} \\ \text{when } \hat{m} \text{ was sent} \end{bmatrix} \begin{bmatrix} \text{probability} \\ \text{that } \hat{m} \\ \text{was sent} \end{bmatrix}
$$

Moreover, summing over the messages received:

$$
\sum_m a_{\hat{m}\cdot m} q_m = \hat{q}_{\hat{m}}
$$

or, in matrix notation:

$$
Aq = \hat{q}
$$

Let U_m be maximized expected utility given message m from information service L and let $\hat{U}_{\hat{m}}$ be maximized expected utility given message $\hat{m}$ from information service $\hat{L}$. Then we wish to show that, if $\hat{L}$ is more informative:

$$
\sum_m q_m U_m \leq \sum_{\hat{m}} \hat{q}_{\hat{m}} \hat{U}_{\hat{m}}
$$

If x_m^* is the optimal action, given m:

$$
U_m = \sum_s \pi_{s\cdot m} v(c_s(x_m^*))
$$

From (5.2.13):

$$U_m = \sum_{\hat{m}} a_{\hat{m} \cdot m} \left(\sum_s \hat{\pi}_{s \cdot \hat{m}} v(c_s \left(x_m^* \right)) \right)$$

Since x_m^* is a feasible (but not necessarily optimal) action given message $\hat{m}$, we know that:

$$\sum_s \hat{\pi}_{s \cdot \hat{m}} v(c_s \left(x_m^* \right)) \leq U_{\hat{m}}$$

Therefore:

$$U_m \leq \sum_{\hat{m}} a_{\hat{m} \cdot m} U_{\hat{m}} \tag{5.2.14}$$

In words, expected utility given message m of the garbled service μ is no greater (and generally less) than the probability-weighted expected utility of the best actions associated with the various messages $\hat{m}$ of the ungarbled information service that m garbles together.

This is not, by itself, enough to rank the two services. But multiplying (5.2.14) by q_m, summing over m and then appealing to (5.2.13), we obtain:

$$\sum_m q_m U_m \leq \sum_m q_m \sum_{\hat{m}} a_{\hat{m} \cdot m} U_{\hat{m}} = \sum_{\hat{m}} \left[\sum_m a_{\hat{m} \cdot m} q_{\hat{m}} \right] U_{\hat{m}} = \sum_{\hat{m}} \hat{q}_{\hat{m}} U_{\hat{m}}$$

where the expression at the extreme left represents the expected utility under L while the expression at the extreme right represents the expected utility under $\hat{L}$.

Example 5.5: A message service $\hat{\mu}$ taking the form of a random sample of size 2 is surely more informative than an alternative message service μ representing a sample of size 1. To take a specific case, suppose a coin is either fair (state 1) or two-headed (state 2). Suppose Alex attaches prior probability $3/4$ to state 1 and $1/4$ to state 2, while Bev has the reversed prior probabilities. First, find the B matrix in Blackwell's condition to show, in terms of the likelihood matrices, that μ is a garbling of $\hat{\mu}$. Then, for both Alex and Bev find the A matrix of equation (5.2.9), and the associated message probabilities, which demonstrate that the posterior probability vectors of μ are a garbling of those of $\hat{\mu}$.

Answer: The likelihood matrices $\hat{L}$ and L are:

		MESSAGE (No. of heads)					
State	L	0	1	$\hat{L}$	0	1	2
1 = Fair	1	0.5	0.5	1	0.25	0.5	0.25
2 = Two-headed	2	0	1	2	0	0	1

By straightforward computation, it can be shown that Blackwell's condition holds in the form:

$$
\begin{array}{ccccc}
L & = & \hat{L} & & B \\
\begin{bmatrix} 0.5 & 0.5 \\ 0 & 1 \end{bmatrix} & = & \begin{bmatrix} 0.25 & 0.5 & 0.25 \\ 0 & 0 & 1 \end{bmatrix} & & \begin{bmatrix} 1 & 0 \\ 0.5 & 0.5 \\ 0 & 1 \end{bmatrix}
\end{array}
$$

So L is a garbling of $\hat{L}$.

Alex's joint probability matrices (J and $\hat{J}$) and potential posterior matrices (Π and $\hat{\Pi}$) for message service μ (sample of size 1) and message service $\hat{\mu}$ (sample of size 2) are:

J	0	1		Π	0	1
1	0.375	0.375	0.75	1	1	0.6
2	0	0.25	0.25	2	0	0.4
	0.375	0.625			1.0	1.0

$\hat{J}$	0	1	2		$\hat{\Pi}$	0	1	2
1	0.1875	0.375	0.1875	0.75	1	1	1	0.429
2	0	0	0.25	0.25	2	0	0	0.571
$\hat{q}$	0.1875	0.375	0.4375			1.0	1.0	1.0

The message probabilities are the column sums of J and $\hat{J}$. The A matrix can then be determined by applying Bayes' Theorem $a_{\hat{m} \cdot m} q_m = b_{\hat{m} \cdot m} \hat{q}_{\hat{m}}$.

$$
A = \begin{bmatrix} 0.5 & 0 \\ 0.5 & 0.3 \\ 0 & 0.7 \end{bmatrix}
$$

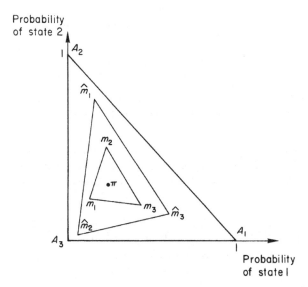

Figure 5.5. Ranking information services with three states and three messages.

Straightforward computation reveals that $\hat{\Pi}A = \Pi$ and that $Aq = \hat{A}$. Therefore Π is a garbling of $\hat{\Pi}$. Determination of the corresponding A matrix for Bev is left as an exercise for the reader. ☐

Exercises and Excursions 5.2.3

1 Generalization of the "Bracketing" Condition

(A) Figure 5.4 pictured a situation where, with $S = 2 = M$, message service $\hat{\mu}$ was interpreted as "more informative" than μ if the posterior probability vectors of $\hat{\mu}$ bracketed those of μ. Show that there is a geometrical interpretation of the bracketing condition if $S = 3 = M$.

[HINT: Figure 5.5 will be helpful.]

(B) What if $S = 2$, $M = 3$?

(C) Explain also why the geometrical analysis of (A) does not generalize to the case of $S = 3$, $M = 4$.

2* Comparison of Information Matrices

Two information services $\hat{\mu}$ and μ have potential posterior matrices $\hat{\Pi}$ and Π where:

$$\hat{\Pi}A = \Pi$$

---

* Starred questions or portions of questions may be somewhat more difficult.

and A is an $\hat{M} \times M$ non-negative matrix whose columns sum to unity. Assume that both Π and $\hat{\Pi}$ have full rank (M and $\hat{M}$, respectively).

    (A) Confirm that each column of $\Pi(\pi._m)$ can be expressed as a convex combination of the $\hat{M}$ columns of $\hat{\Pi}$.

    (B) Does it follow that all individuals will prefer $\hat{\Pi}$ to Π?

[HINT: Consider a case in which there are two states. Information service $\hat{\mu}$ sends one of three messages while information service μ sends one of two messages. For the former let one of the messages be "stay with your prior beliefs."]

    (C) Suppose that $S \geq \hat{M} \geq M$. If $\hat{\Pi}A = \Pi$ and A has rank M does it follow that $\hat{\mu}$ is necessarily preferred over μ?

[HINT: Show that $\hat{q}$ and q are unique and satisfy $Aq = \hat{q}$.]

3 Ranking Information Services

An individual believes that each of two states is equally likely. He has available a message service that will send him one of two messages. If the true state is $s = 1$, the message $m = 1$ is received with probability $\frac{7}{8}$. If the true state is $s = 2$, the message $m = 1$ is received with probability $\frac{5}{8}$.

    (A) Write down the likelihood matrix and the (unconditional) message probabilities. Use these to compute the potential posterior matrix II.

    (B) The individual is offered an alternative message service that will also send him one of two messages. If the true state is $s = 1$, the message $\hat{m} = 1$ is received with probability $\frac{3}{4}$. If the true state is $s = 2$, the message $\hat{m} = 1$ is received with probability $\frac{1}{4}$. Intuitively, why is this message service more valuable?

    (C) Write the likelihood matrix L for this new information service and compute the potential posterior matrix.

    (D) Confirm that the posterior probabilities for the first service are convex combinations of the posterior probabilities for the second service.

    (E) Show that this conclusion holds regardless of the prior probabilities. That is, all individuals, regardless of preferences and beliefs, will prefer the second service.

4   A Non-Concavity in the Value of Information (Stiglitz and Radner, 1984)
An individual with initial wealth $\overline{W}$ faces state-claim prices P_s, for $s = 1, 2$.
His utility function is $v(c) = \log (c)$.

(A) If he believes that state 1 will occur with probability π and state
2 with probability $(1 - \pi)$, obtain an expression for his maximized
expected utility $U(\pi)$ as a function of π. Depict this in a diagram for
$0 \leq \pi \leq 1$.

(B) Is $U(\pi)$ convex? Discuss whether your answer holds in general.

(C) Suppose his prior probability of state 1 is $\bar{\pi}$ and that he expects
to receive one of two messages that will change his probability of
state 1 either to $\bar{\pi} + \theta$ or $\bar{\pi} - \theta$. Explain why the probability of each
message must be 0.5, and hence show that the gain in expected utility
from having this information prior to trading is:

$$\Omega(\theta) = \frac{1}{2}(\bar{\pi} + \theta) \log (\bar{\pi} + \theta) + \frac{1}{2}(\bar{\pi} - \theta) \log (\bar{\pi} - \theta) - \bar{\pi} \log \bar{\pi}$$

$$+ \frac{1}{2}(1 - \bar{\pi} - \theta) \log (1 - \bar{\pi} - \theta)$$

$$+ \frac{1}{2}(1 - \bar{\pi} + \theta) \log (1 - \bar{\pi} + \theta) - (1 - \bar{\pi}) \log (1 - \bar{\pi})$$

(D) Hence show that the marginal gain in utility from a "little bit" of
information is zero. Also show that for all $\theta > 0$ the marginal value
$\Omega'(\theta)$ of θ is positive and increasing.

(E) Obtain the dollar value of the information, $k(\theta)$.

(F) Using your answers to parts (D) and (E), show that $k(\theta)$ is convex in
the neighborhood of $\theta = 0$.**

5.2.4   Differences in Utility Functions and the Worth of Information

In the previous section, we saw how in some circumstances it is possible to
rank information services independently of the individual's utility function
$v(c)$ and action set $x = 1, \ldots, X$. In this and the following sections we will
be showing how preferences and the set of actions available affect the worth
of information. More specifically, the question examined here is whether or

** End of starred section.

in what circumstances a *more risk-averse* individual is willing to pay more for information.

Intuitively, it might be thought that a more risk-averse individual will always be more anxious to reduce his uncertainty by acquiring more information. But it turns out that this is not valid in general. Whether or not a more risk-averse individual will pay more for a message service depends upon the *comparative riskiness of the decisions that would be made without the information and with the information.*

Consider first a situation in which the optimal prior action x_0 for some individual i would generate sure income c^o for him. If he invests in information, each possible message m will be associated with some best terminal action x_m. Suppose that x_m is a risky action for at least one possible message m, the associated consequence distribution being $(c_{sm}; \pi_{s \cdot m})$. Since there has been some change of optimal action, the information is surely valuable. So there must be some positive maximum fee ξ that the individual would be willing to pay for the information. Thus, as a special case of Equation (5.2.8), this maximum fee is determined in:

$$v^i(c^o) = \Sigma_m \Sigma_s \pi_{s \cdot m} q_m v^i(c_{sm} - \xi) \qquad (5.2.24)$$

In Chapter 3 we saw that, if individual j is everywhere more risk averse than individual i, then j's utility function $v^j(c)$ could be expressed as a strictly concave function $f(\cdot)$ of $v^i(c)$. So, we can write:

$$v^j(c^o) = f(v^i(c^o)) = f(\Sigma_m \Sigma_s \pi_{s \cdot m} q_m v^i(c_{sm} - \xi))$$

$$> \Sigma_m \Sigma_s \pi_{s \cdot m} q_m f\left(v^i(c_{sm} - \xi)\right), \quad \text{by Jensens inequality}$$

$$= \Sigma_m \Sigma_s \pi_{s \cdot m} q_m v^j(c_{sm} - \xi)$$

Thus the more risk-averse individual j would be strictly worse off purchasing the information at a price of ξ. In other words, the information in this case is *less valuable* for the more risk-averse individual.

The key premise here was that the optimal uninformed action was riskless. While the message service was indeed a valuable one, it involved some chance of leading the recipient of the information to choose a risky action. Given that fact, the worth of the service was smaller for the more risk-averse decision maker. Figure 5.3 illustrated such a situation. The riskless action x_1 is the best choice, in the absence of information, for an individual with prior belief vector π. As illustrated, while acquiring the message service leading to the posterior probability vectors $\pi_{\cdot 1}$ or $\pi_{\cdot 2}$ (the dashed lines) provides a utility increment EF, it does entail shifting from a riskless action

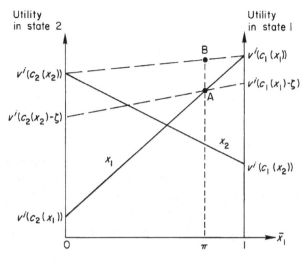

Figure 5.6. Risk aversion and the value of perfect information.

to a risky situation (with conditional utility levels indicated by points D and C). For an individual with the same beliefs but characterized by a more risk-averse utility function, the vertical scaling would change so that the utility increments CJ and EF both become smaller. (The marginal utility of additional income falls faster as risk aversion increases.) Thus, a more risk-averse individual would not be willing to pay as much for the service.

The opposite case is pictured in Figure 5.6. Here x_0, the best uninformed choice for individual i, is action x_1 which is highly risky. To keep matters simple, suppose that the information service reveals the state with certainty. It is clear from Figure 5.6 that if message 1 is received, the optimal action remains x_1, but if message 2 is received, the new optimal action becomes x_2. Then, if the information were costless, i's expected utility would rise by the amount AB. As before, let ξ be the maximum that individual i would pay for the message service. That is:

$$\pi_1 v^i(c_1(x_1)) + \pi_2 v^i(c_2(x_1)) = \pi_1 v^i(c_1(x_1) - \xi) + \pi_2 v^i(c_2(x_2) - \xi)$$

$$(5.2.25)$$

Let c_{s0} and v^i_{s0} be the consumption and the utility in state s with the best uninformed action, and c_{sI} and v^i_{sI} the consumption and utility in state s given the corresponding conclusive message, after deducting the cost ξ. (In general, any message m may imply a different best action x_m and so each c_{sI} would be a vector with m elements. But, as defined here, c_{1I} is unique since it is the consumption in state 1 when the message reveals state 1 *with certainty*, and similarly for c_{2I}.)

As depicted in Figure 5.6, $c_{10} \equiv c_1(x_1) > c_{1I} \equiv c_1(x_1) - \xi$, so that $v^i_{10} > v^i_{1I}$. But $c_{20} \equiv c_2(x_1) < c_{2I} \equiv c_2(x_2) - \xi$, so that $v^i_{20} < v^i_{2I}$. Also, by construction, $c_{1I} > c_{2I}$. It follows that:

$$v^i_{10} > v^i_{1I} > v^i_{2I} > v^i_{20}$$

But the expected utilities of the distributions $(c_{1I}, c_{2I}; \pi_1, 1 - \pi_1)$ and $(c_1(x_1), c_2(x_1); \pi_1, 1 - \pi_1)$ are the same, as indicated in Equation (5.2.25) and pictured in Figure 5.6 by the intersection at point A. Thus, the no-information distribution of utilities is a *mean-preserving spread* of the full-information distribution attained after paying the maximum fee ξ.

From Chapter 3 it follows immediately that, for any concave function $f(\cdot)$:

$$\Sigma_s \pi_s f\left(v^i_{sI}\right) > \Sigma_s \pi_s f\left(v^i_{s0}\right)$$

But, as noted above, if individual j is more risk averse there is some concave function $f(\cdot)$ such that $v^j(c) = f(v^i(c))$. Then:

$$\Sigma_s \pi_s v^i_{sI} = \Sigma_s \pi_s v^i_{s0} \quad \text{implies} \quad \Sigma_s \pi_s v^j_{sI} > \Sigma_s \pi_s v^j_{s0}$$

That is, if a less risk-averse individual i is just indifferent as to receiving information that costs ξ, a more risk-averse individual j would strictly prefer to receive the information at that price. Or, j would be willing to pay strictly more for the information.

The key point is that, in this second example, receipt of the information is associated with shifting to a *less risky* consumption prospect. Therefore, the more risk-averse individual is willing to pay more for the message service.

Exercises and Excursions 5.2.4

1 *The Value of Information*
  (A) An individual with logarithmic utility function believes each of two states to be equally likely. He can purchase state claims at prices $P_1 = P_2 = 1$. Show that he will be willing to pay up to half of his wealth for conclusive information as to which state will occur.
  (B) Would a more risk-averse individual be willing to pay as much?

[HINT: It might help to draw the individual's budget constraint and indifference curves in state-claim space.]

2 The Value of Risky Information

As in the previous exercise, there are two states. However, now the price of state 1 claims is higher $(P_1 > P_2)$.

(A) If the odds of state 1 satisfy:

$$\frac{\pi_1}{1 - \pi_1} = \frac{P_1}{P_2}$$

confirm that an uninformed individual would take no risk.

(B) Using a diagram, depict his final consumption if he is given conclusive information about the state. Illustrate also the maximum amount that he would be willing to pay for this information.

(C) Hence, or otherwise, show that a more risk-averse individual would not be willing to pay as much for the information.

(D) Suppose the odds of state 1 instead satisfy:

$$1 < \frac{\pi_1}{1 - \pi_1} < \frac{P_1}{P_2}$$

Confirm that an uninformed individual would accept some risk. Confirm also that, if he were to pay his reservation price for conclusive information, the riskiness of his final consumption bundle would be greater.

(E) Hence, or otherwise, draw a general conclusion regarding the effect of increased risk aversion upon the value of information.

3 Changes in Wealth

A risk-averse individual is just on the borderline of being willing to buy an information service. Suppose he becomes wealthier than before, in the sense that he now has a positive riskless endowment c^o *in addition to* the payoffs of the various terminal actions available to him. Does being richer make him more or less willing to purchase the information service?

[HINT: Does the answer have something to do with whether he has increasing, decreasing, or constant absolute risk aversion (IARA, DARA, or CARA)?]

5.2.5 The Worth of Information: Flexibility versus Range of Actions

In the discussion above we thought of information as being newly generated by an informational action like a sampling experiment or, alternatively, as

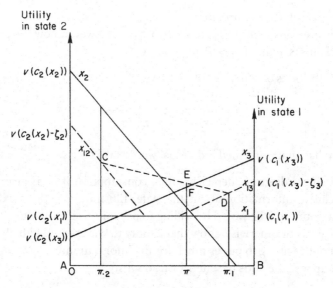

Figure 5.7. The value of flexibility.

acquired from others via a transaction like the purchase of expert opinion. But in some cases information may autonomously *emerge* simply with the passage of time, without requiring any direct action by recipients. Tomorrow's weather is uncertain today, but the uncertainty will be reduced as more meteorological data flow in, and will in due course be conclusively resolved when tomorrow arrives. Direct informational actions might still be useful, by providing knowledge *earlier.* So under conditions of emergent information a kind of indirect informational action may become available – adopting a flexible position and *waiting* before taking terminal action.

Suppose a choice must be made now between immediate terminal action and awaiting emergent information. This choice can only be interesting where there is a tradeoff between two costs: (1) a cost of waiting versus (2) an "irreversible" element in the possible loss suffered from mistaken early commitment (see Jones and Ostroy, 1984).

The essential idea is pictured in Figure 5.7. The individual, if he decides upon immediate terminal action, has a choice among x_1, x_2, or x_3. As the diagram is drawn, he would never select x_1 as his immediate terminal action, since either x_2 or x_3 has higher expected utility for any π. Given his illustrated beliefs π, the best immediate terminal choice is x_3 yielding expected utility F. But suppose that x_1 has a "flexibility" property. To wit, *after* receiving emergent information the individual can shift from x_1 to x_2, at a cost of ξ_2, achieving the intermediate overall utility indicated by the dashed line

x_{12} – or, should the information point the other way, he can shift from x_1 to x_3 at a cost of ξ_3 with overall utility payoff indicated by the dashed line x_{13}. As shown in the diagram, if message 1 is received (leading to the posterior probability vector $\pi_{.1}$), the individual would shift to x_3, thus attaining overall utility indicated by point D on line x_{13}. Similarly, message 2 would allow him to attain point C on line x_{12}. His expected utility is then E, exceeding the utility of the best immediate terminal action x_3 by an amount indicated by the distance EF.

The element of "irreversibility" appears here in the fact that line x_{12} lies below x_2 in the range where both of these are preferred to x_1, and similarly x_{13} lies below x_3 in the corresponding range. One has to pay a price to retain flexibility, the price being that you cannot do as well as if you had made the best choice among the "irreversible" actions in the first place.

After examining the relative advantages of remaining "flexible" (of initially choosing action x_1 in Figure 5.7) versus higher immediate return (choosing action x_2 or x_3), natural next questions to ask are: (1) Does the value of remaining flexible tend to increase or decrease as the message service employed becomes more informative? And conversely: (2) Is the value of information greater for someone having taken a flexible position? Intuitively, we would expect the answers to both questions to be affirmative. Remaining flexible is in effect like buying an option as to what later action will be taken. The more informative the message service, or the more flexible the position chosen, the greater is the value of the option. With regard to question 1, in Figure 5.7 we can see immediately that a more informative message service – for which $\pi_{.1}$ would be shifted to the right and $\pi_{.2}$ to the left – would increase the height of point E (which represents the expected utility of remaining flexible) while leaving point F (which represents the expected utility of the best immediate action) unaffected. And for the converse question 2, the affirmative answer is trivially true, since having chosen either of the immediately more remunerative but "inflexible" actions x_2 or x_3 entirely eliminates the option value of later information.

Parallel questions can be asked about the effects of increasing the *range* of possible actions. We might expect the answers to be affirmative once again, since having a greater range of actions is somewhat akin to being in a more flexible position. But, it turns out, the answers as to flexibility and as to range are not at all the same. Consider first the analog of question 2 above: Does increasing the range of possible actions raise the value of information? Intuitively, we might at first think that the greater the range of actions that can be taken, the greater the value of having better information before deciding. But this overlooks a crucial difference between increasing

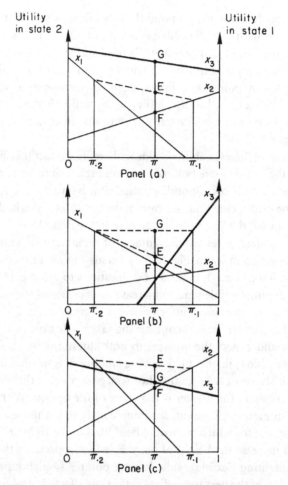

Figure 5.8. Range of actions and the value of information.

flexibility and increasing range: when flexibility increases, the expected utility of the best "uninformed" decision remains unaffected – but an increase in the range of action can modify the results of the best *uninformed* as well as of the best *informed* decision.

The three panels of Figure 5.8 illustrate some of the possibilities. In each case, to begin with, there are only actions x_1 and x_2, the best initial choice yielding the expected utility indicated by point F. As before, the message service μ leads to an improved expected utility E, so that the value of information is EF. In the top panel (a), a new action x_3 has been introduced that totally dominates the other two actions for any probability beliefs whatsoever. Since x_3 would be chosen in any case, this extension of the range of choice reduces the value of any message service to zero! Somewhat less extreme cases are illustrated in the other two panels. Summarizing briefly, the middle panel (b) suggests that, if the new action x_3 is very superior toward either boundary (e.g., when one state or the other is initially nearly certain), enlarging the range of action will indeed tend to *increase* the value of information (from EF to GF here). On the other hand, the bottom panel (c) indicates that, if the new action x_3 is superior mainly in the interior (i.e., when it remains very uncertain which state will obtain), the enlargement of the range tends to *reduce* the value of information. (The presence of an action that is very rewarding even under uncertainty makes it less essential to acquire information aimed at reducing uncertainty.)

The upshot, therefore, is that the effect upon the value of information of increasing the range of available actions is highly situation dependent. It will be evident that the same holds also for the analog of question 2: having a more informative message service may either increase or decrease the value of extending the range of available actions.

Summary of Section 5.2
In this section, we analyzed the optimal use of information by an individual. Bayes' Theorem tells us how to revise prior beliefs after the arrival of a message from a message service. An individual's expected utility does not decrease with a message service. The value of a message service to the individual is the amount he would pay for it and just be indifferent between buying the message service or not. If a message service has a strictly positive value to an individual then the individual's optimal action must change after the arrival of at least one of the messages of this message service.

Next, we turned to the question of ranking message services. A message service $\hat{\mu}$ is preferred to message service μ by any individual (regardless of his utility function or prior beliefs) if and only if the messages in μ are obtained by adding noise to the messages in $\hat{\mu}$; the process of "adding noise" is summarized in Equation (5.2.13). A different question is the worth of a message service to two different individuals, one more risk averse than the other. If the message service is associated with shifting to a less risky consumption prospect then the more risk-averse individual is willing to pay more for the message service. We closed this section with an analysis of the costs and benefits of maintaining a flexible position.

In the next section, we turn to the use of information in a multi-person setting.

Exercises and Excursions 5.2.5

1   The Value of Remaining Flexible

In the absence of information, x_3 is the optimal action. By waiting for information an individual forfeits action x_3 but may still choose between x_1 and x_2.

Suppose he is just indifferent between choosing x_3 or waiting for the information to arrive.

(A) What would an everywhere more risk-averse individual do?

(B) What about an individual who has a higher initial riskless wealth?

2   Adding to the Range of Options

(A) For the general two-state case, show that, if a new action is added that is "more risky" than any of the initial feasible set, its value is higher (or at least no lower) if information is better.[7]

(B) Again for the two-state case, suppose that the initial set consists of actions that are all risky. A new action is added that yields the same utility in each state. Is it true that the change in expected utility due to the new action is either strictly *lower* or no higher under superior information?

5.3 Multi-Person Decisions

Suppose a group of people must act together to make a collective decision. For the multi-personal aspect to be at all interesting there has to be some disagreement among the individuals involved as to the best choice of action. As we shall see, such disagreement may stem from (a) conflict of interests, (b) divergence of beliefs, or (c) both together.

In Section 5.3.1 the choice to be made (the action to be undertaken) is wholly within the power of a single decision maker. However, the decision maker is in a position of possibly wanting to use information at the disposal of an *expert* – a circumstance typically involving both divergence of beliefs and conflict of interest between the expert and his client. In Section 5.3.2 we turn to group decisions in the proper sense, that is, where more than one person has some "constitutional" power over the ultimate decision to be made.

---

[7] An action x_1 is "more risky" than several other actions if in one state x_1 yields a higher utility than the other actions and in the other state x_1 yields a lower utility than the other actions. Thus, in Figure 5.8(c), x_1 is more risky than x_2 and x_3.

5.3.1 The Use of Experts

For concreteness, suppose a decision maker employs a weather forecaster as expert, where the two relevant states of the world are "rain" (R) or "shine" (S). The expert's report may take any of a number of forms, among them:

(i) "My barometer reads 30.52." Here the expert is merely reporting his data or evidence. Assuming there is no reason to doubt the accuracy of the report (more on this below), the client should treat this evidence just as if she had observed the barometer herself. Given her own prior beliefs (π_R, π_S), where, of course, $\pi_S \equiv 1 - \pi_R$, and given her likelihood matrix L for the different possible barometer readings (messages) in each possible state of the world, the decision maker should employ Bayes' Theorem (5.2.5) to obtain her posterior probabilities ($\pi_{R \cdot m}, \pi_{S \cdot m}$). These revised probabilities would then be used in Equation (5.2.1) to determine the best (utility-maximizing) terminal action.

(ii) "My probability estimate for rain is 45%." Assuming once again that there is no question about accuracy or sincerity, the expert here is providing a probability distribution that, let us suppose, is *his own* posterior distribution after reading the barometer and applying Bayes' Theorem. Thus, ($\pi^e_{R \cdot m}, \pi^e_{S \cdot m}$) = (0.45, 0.55). In comparison with (i) above, the client is now getting the benefit of certain additional information in the form of the expert's priors and likelihood function, with which the expert's actual new evidence has been integrated. However, if as indicated here, the expert reports *only* his posterior probabilities, all this information has been confounded together in such a way that the decision maker cannot in general uniquely infer just what barometer reading occurred. So, something has been lost as well as gained in comparison with the first type of report.

(iii) "My recommendation is, wear a raincoat." Here the expert has taken it upon himself to indicate the *action* with highest expected utility for his client, implying that he knows the decision maker's consequence matrix c_{xs} and utility function $v(c)$ as well as the appropriate posterior probabilities. Once again, the question of sincerity apart, the client is getting the benefit of additional information – conceivably, the expert might know the decision maker's consequence matrix and utility function better than the latter does herself. But all this information has now been confounded together into a very bare and stark message, from which the decision maker cannot in general separately extract either the expert's barometer reading or the expert's posterior probability beliefs.

Thus the expert's report might be a rather modest one, as in (i) above, which leaves the decision maker still in the position of having to do the work of determining her posterior probabilities and ultimately the best action to undertake. Or, the report might be more ambitious and purport to integrate and digest all the information needed to determine the posterior probabilities as in (ii) above or even the best action as in (iii) above.

Nevertheless, ultimately it is the client who must make the decision. If she is rational, and especially since the questions of sincerity and accuracy do always arise, cases (ii) and (iii) above are really not that different from case (i). *Any* report on the part of the expert, whatever its purported content, is really only a "message" that the decision maker still has to weigh in accordance with her prior beliefs and likelihood matrix.[8] (In the case where an expert is being used, the likelihood matrix can more specifically be termed the client's *credence matrix* for the expert's report.) But it remains true that the actual content of the report is irrelevant for the Bayesian calculation of posterior probabilities – all the useful information that any message can provide is summarized by the likelihood matrix. An example will make this clear.

Example 5.6: Suppose the expert will be giving a report that purports to be his posterior estimate $\pi^e_{R \cdot m}$, after consulting his private barometer, for the probability of rain (to the nearest quartile). The decision maker still would rationally have to construct a credence matrix before she can use such a message. Matrix L_1 below is a possible credence matrix. In L_1 the client believes that when the true state is shine the expert will never fail to predict it, but that his predictions are somewhat less perfect indicators when the true state is rain. (Thus, the client believes that $\Pr(L_1 = 0|R) = \frac{1}{15}$, $\Pr(L_1 = 0|S) = 1$, etc.) What is the basis for such beliefs? No simple answer can be given. The credence matrix would presumably depend upon the client's opinions as to the expert's character, his possible conflicting interests, prior knowledge, reliability of his barometer, etc. However arrived at, a

---

[8] It might even be the case that the "expert" is producing gibberish noises, as in some of the ancient Greek oracles, or perhaps not intending to convey a message at all. Thus it was once widely believed that the author of the "Maggie and Jiggs" comic strip was providing useful stock market up/down predictions, via the tilt of Jiggs' cigar.

decision maker cannot rationally use an expert without implicitly having some such set of beliefs.

			Message				
L_1		0	0.25	0.50	0.75	1.0	
	R	$\frac{1}{15}$	$\frac{2}{15}$	$\frac{3}{15}$	$\frac{4}{15}$	$\frac{5}{15}$	1.0
State	S	1.0	0	0	0	0	1.0

Alternatively, suppose the expert will simply be advising the decision maker to leave her raincoat at home (action x_1) or to wear one (action x_2). While we would expect there to be some correlation, the recommendation x_2 is not exactly equivalent to predicting a high probability of rain. What is the significance of such a recommendation for the client's decision? Again, the expert's report is only a *message*. Its weight in the final decision depends upon the client's credence matrix for this type of message, which might take a form like L_2 below:

		Message		
L_2		$x = 1$	$x = 2$	
	R	0.4	0.6	1.0
State	S	1.0	0	1.0

□

Two factors are generally very important in the client's estimate of the evidential significance of an expert's report: (1) the motivation for the expert to be *sincere* (to tell the truth as he sees it) and (2) the expert's motivation to invest the effort necessary to be *accurate*. These factors are, to some extent at least, subject to influence via the contractual reward structure. We will first examine here how such a reward structure can influence the sincerity of the expert's report.

Consider as before a situation where the true states of the world are rain and shine. Adopting a simplified notation for convenience here, let the *expert's belief* (posterior to any evidence he may have collected) as to the probability of rain be p. We will suppose that he is asked to report this probability belief; his actual report will be denoted q.

Let the expert's reward structure (sometimes called a "scoring rule") take the linear form:

$$\begin{cases} \rho_R = A + Bq & \text{Payoff in the event of rain} \\ \rho_S = A + B(1-q) & \text{Payoff in the event of shine} \end{cases}$$

where $B > 0$. Assuming risk neutrality, a self-interested expert will choose the q that maximizes his own mean reward $\bar{\rho}$:

$$\begin{aligned} \underset{(q)}{\text{Max}} \; \bar{\rho} &= p(A + Bq) + (1-p)\,(A + B(1-q)) \\ &= A + (1-p)B + B(2p-1)q \end{aligned}$$

Since the final term is positive if and only if $p > \frac{1}{2}$, the maximizing strategy for the expert is:

If $p > \frac{1}{2}$, report $q = 1$
If $p < \frac{1}{2}$, report $q = 0$

Thus, this scoring rule does not induce sincerity on the part of a risk-neutral expert.

There are three classes of scoring rules that induce a risk-neutral expert to deliver a sincere report (see Winkler, 1996 for a survey of scoring rules). To wit, if q_s is the reported probability estimate for state s:

$$\begin{aligned} \rho_s &= \ln q_s & \text{Logarithmic} \\ \rho_s &= 1 - (1 - q_s)^2 & \text{Quadratic} \\ \rho_s &= \frac{q_s}{\sqrt{\sum_s q_s^2}} & \text{Spherical} \end{aligned} \qquad (5.3.1)$$

For example, if the expert provides a report q for the probability of rain, the quadratic scoring rule of (5.3.1) reduces to:

$$\begin{cases} \rho_R = 2q - q^2 \\ \rho_S = 1 - q^2 \end{cases}$$

Maximizing $\bar{\rho}$, it may be verified that if the expert's true belief of the probability of rain is p, then this rule leads the expert to report $q = p$.

As we have seen, the decision maker will in general not simply *adopt* the expert's probability beliefs. Rather, she will be revising her own probabilities in the light of her credence matrix. But, if the reward structure is such that the client can at least accept the expert's report as sincere, one source of uncertainty will have been eliminated.

The scoring rules discussed so far are appropriate for reports of the form (ii) described above, i.e., the expert's message purports to be his posterior probability distribution over states of the world. Alternatively, imagine that the report is to be of type (iii), consisting simply of a recommendation as to the best action x. Let us make the following assumptions: (1) client and expert are both risk-neutral, and (2) the expert knows that the client will indeed be adopting his recommendation. Then a very simple reward structure is appropriate:

$$\rho_s = \alpha c_{xs} \ (\alpha > 0) \tag{5.3.2}$$

This amounts to giving the expert a "slice of the action," so that he maximizes his own expected income by recommending the action that maximizes the client's expected income.

Of course, deviations from risk neutrality would require some revision of the optimal reward structure indicated by (5.3.2). And also, even if she thinks the expert's recommendation is sincere, the decision maker will not always simply be adopting the recommended action. Hence the expert might be motivated to diverge from the rule in (5.3.2), in order to "fool" his client into taking what the expert believes to be the best action for both of them (in terms of maximizing expected income).

We can also see immediately that, even if the requisite conditions are met for *sincerity*, the expert may not be induced to undertake the ideal investment for achieving *accuracy*. Since the expert's slice α would in general be less than unity, the rule (5.3.2) would give him less than a dollar for each dollar's worth of information provided – measuring the worth to the client in terms of the increase in her expected income $\Delta E(c_{xs})$. An "ideal" effort-inducing reward structure would have to be such that, on the margin, the expert reaps the full value of his final increment of effort.

5.3.2 Group Choices[9]

A group, for our purposes, is defined by the requirement that the members are required to undertake some *joint action*. How the collective choice emerges from the preferences of the separate members depends upon the group's "constitutional" decision procedure. This might, for example, be a unanimity rule, or simple majority voting, or a weighting system that gives some members more power than others. As already indicated, the possible disagreements that can cause problems for group decision may be due

---

[9] This section depends substantially upon the discussion in Raiffa (1968), chapter 8.

to *differing beliefs* (the members hold different probability distributions for states of the world),[10] to *conflicts of interest* (the individuals derive differing benefits and costs from alternative group actions), or to both of the above. We will be showing in more detail here how the decisions of a group with regard to the acquisition and use of information are affected by disagreements on these scores.

Conflicts of interest may stem from differences in payoffs, differences in personal utility functions, or differences in endowments. If the available group actions distribute the payoffs differently over individuals, disagreements are evidently likely. And, even if all the actions at issue involve identical payoffs to each group member under all circumstances, there may still be disagreement owing to divergences in utility functions $v(c)$. For example, some individuals may be more risk averse than others. Furthermore, even with equal division of payoff and the same $v(c)$ functions, members could still differ in utilities assigned to group actions if they possess different amounts of (or different probability distributions of) *endowed income from other sources*. For example, a risky prospect may be valued differently by two equally risk-averse group members, if for one of them the prospect is a risk-widening gamble while for the other it amounts to a risk-offsetting insurance arrangement.

One question that arises is whether there is some way of aggregating or averaging individual beliefs on the one hand, and individual utility assignments on the other hand, so that the best group action may be chosen by a collective analog of the individual expected-utility equation (5.2.1). That is, can we somehow find a *group utility function* and a *group probability estimate* permitting use of the expected-utility rule? The answer to this is generally negative. The following is a simple illustration.[11]

Table 5.5 consists of two matrices, one for individual j and another for k. The matrices are in the form of Table 1.1 of Chapter 1, except that in the body of the matrices the consequences c_{xs} have been replaced by the individual

---

[10] Consistent with our previous discussions, differences of belief have been defined solely in terms of diverging probability distributions for states of the world. But what of possible variety of opinion among group members as to the *consequences* c_{xs}? We need not consider these as a separate category, since any such divergences can be reduced ultimately to assigning differing probability weights to states of the world. Suppose two individuals agree in assigning probability π_s to state s, but individual i says the state s consequence for the group is c'_{xs} while individual j says it is c''_{xs}. Then we should think in terms of there being two distinct states s' and s''. Both members can now agree on describing the respective consequences as c'_{xs} and c''_{xs}, the disagreement being that individual i assigns the entire probability π_s to the new state s' (and assigns zero probability to s'') – while the reverse of course applies for individual j.

[11] Based on Dalkey (1972).

Table 5.5.

		Individual j's utility for consequences					Individual k's utility for consequences		
		States					States		
		(0.8)	(0.2)				(0.2)	(0.8)	
	I	s_1	s_2	E(v)		i	s_1	s_2	E(v)
Actions	x_1	10	5	9*	Actions	x_1	4	8	7.2*
	x_2	7	9	7.4		x_2	8	6	6.4

utility evaluations thereof, $v^j(c_{xs}^j)$ and $v^k(c_{xs}^k)$. This notation indicates that, in a choice among group actions, each self-interested individual will take note only of his own personal consequence c_{xs}^i – which would be some share, though not necessarily a constant proportionate share, of the overall group payoff $\Sigma_i c_{xs}^i$ – in the light of his personal utility function $v^i(c^i)$. In the specific numerical illustration here, action x_1 is preferred in expected-utility terms over action x_2 by both individuals, using their respective probability assignments for the two states as indicated in the upper margin.

Table 5.6 is constructed in similar form, but now the body of the matrix indicates the *averaged* utilities (using equal weights) while the similarly *averaged* probability estimates are shown in the upper margin. In terms of these averages, in expected-utility terms the group seemingly prefers action x_2 over action x_1! While this is only a numerical instance, a similar example can be constructed to defeat any pre-assigned mode of averaging that purports to generate a group utility and a group probability for use in choosing among actions via the expected-utility rule.

Our interest here however is not the general problem of group decision under uncertainty, but rather the analysis of a group's *informational actions*. Can we say whether groups will invest too much or too little in acquiring information? In what follows we will first examine the consequences of differences in beliefs, and afterward turn to conflict of interests.

Table 5.6. *Average probabilities and utilities from Table 5.5*

		States		
		(0.5)	(0.5)	
		s_1	s_2	E(v)
Actions	x_1	7	6.5	6.75
	x_2	7.5	7.5	7.5*

Differences of Opinion

If differences of opinion are the *only* source of disagreement, there is a clear result that can be stated as follows:

Suppose states of the world are characterized by a single defining parameter (e.g., a continuous variable like a barometer pressure reading or a discrete one like election of a Republican or Democrat as President), and there are differences of belief but no conflicts of interest involved in the decision to be made. Then groups tend to invest "too much" in information (in a sense to be made explicit below).

The underlying idea is this. Consider any individual who, under the group's constitutional decision rule, is not a sole dictator. In general, then, to influence the collective choice in the direction he thinks best for the group, he will have to persuade some of the others. He might be able to persuade them, to some degree, simply by revealing his own beliefs – as in the case of the expert discussed in the previous section. But we will assume that any such mode of influence (on which, more below) has already been exploited as far as it will go, still leaving some differences of opinion. And in fact, we will assume, the only method of persuasion is through acquiring more evidence. More specifically, the question at issue is a group decision whether or not to postpone terminal action while acquiring more evidence.

In this context, we can now indicate the sense in which the group may invest "too much" in acquiring information. Assuming for simplicity a unanimity constitutional rule, the group may unanimously agree to obtain information that each and every member of the group would have thought not worth purchasing if he were the sole dictator, i.e., the information is acquired *solely* because, in the estimate of each and every member, it is needed in order to bring the others around to his own prior views – the key point being, of course, that each member believes that the new evidence will tend to show that his own initial beliefs were correct.

Example 5.7: Two identically endowed individuals j and k have the opportunity of making a joint bet of $200 in total ($100 each) either on Seabiscuit (action x_1) or on War Admiral (action x_2) in their famous match race. The constitutional rule is unanimity, failing which the default action x_3 is not to bet at all. Payoffs are to be equally divided, and j and k each have a risk-neutral utility function so there is no conflict of interest. The racetrack is offering even money odds.

The consequence matrix C envisaged by each is shown in Table 5.7. If, for example, j and k agree to bid on Seabiscuit ($x = x_1$) and the horse wins ($s = s_1$) the payment is $400 and so each individual nets $100. If the horse loses ($s = s_2$), each individual loses his $100 bet. However, their prior probability estimates diverge as indicated: j has 80% belief in a Seabiscuit

Table 5.7.

C	s_1	s_2	$E[v^j(c)]$	$E[v^k(c)]$
π_s^j :	(0.8)	(0.2)		
π_s^k :	(0.2)	(0.8)		
x_1	100	−100	60*	−60
x_2	−100	100	−60	60*
x_3	0	0	0	0

victory (state s_1) while k assigns 80% probability to War Admiral winning (state s_2). Since the two individuals are risk neutral, we can set $v(c)$ for each of them, and thus derive the respective expected utilities of the different actions shown on the right. Since there is no unanimity, the default no-bet action x_3 would be the group choice.

Suppose now that a *perfect* information service becomes available, as shown by the likelihood matrix L in Table 5.8. Were j and k each in a position to bet \$100 independently of one another, each would have been willing to pay only up to \$100−\$60 = \$40 to receive the message. But, if collective bets are the only ones possible, the perfect information is worth a full \$100 each. For it leads to that amount of per-capita profit as against the zero payoff of the default action. Thus, even if the price to the group of the information service were as high as \$199, the individuals would unanimously agree to make the purchase. □

The tendency toward overinvestment in information may be reversed if uncertainty has more than one dimension (see Raiffa, 1968, p. 231). Suppose, for example, that individual j is pretty sure that the track will be muddy, *and* also that Seabiscuit does better in mud. Individual k might be equally sure that the track will be dry, and that a dry track is just what Seabiscuit needs. Hence the two members may unanimously agree upon the action x_1, bet on Seabiscuit, as a result of compensating disagreements as to the reasons why! Resolving just *one* of the disagreements, as by investing in a message service that would conclusively indicate whether the track will be muddy, will then make it impossible to achieve unanimity as to the bet. So the parties might well unanimously refuse information that would resolve

Table 5.8.

L	m_1	m_2	
s_1	1.0	0	1.0
s_2	0	1.0	1.0

the disagreement in one dimension only, even if such information were fully accurate and free of charge.

We now turn to an issue alluded to earlier, to wit, whether in the absence of conflict of interest there is a way for initial divergences of opinion to be resolved without investing in new evidence. Divergences of beliefs at any moment of time can only result from: (i) differences in prior probability distributions, (ii) differences in the private data in hands of individuals, and/or (iii) differences in the likelihood functions for data observed in common. Suppose there are "objective" grounds for agreed prior beliefs and likelihood functions, so only element (ii) remains as the source of disagreement. Take a coin, for example. In the absence of any knowledge at all there is no basis for choosing heads over tails or vice versa – hence by an "equal ignorance" argument an *agreed prior distribution* (one assigning 50% probability each to heads and tails) seems warranted. And, if sample evidence is acquired and there is no reason to believe that it is not a random sample from all possible tosses of the coin, an *agreed likelihood function* is required by the laws of probability. It follows then that if members of the group were to disclose all the private evidence each has at his disposal, they should ultimately end up with agreed posterior probability beliefs.

A much stronger proposition has received attention in the literature (see Aumann, 1976). The underlying idea is that each member of the group discloses to the others not the *evidence* at his disposal, but rather his own *personal posterior distribution in consequence of having seen his private evidence*. Then assuming that the members' priors are "common knowledge" (which means that the priors are agreed, each individual knows they are agreed, knows that the others know he knows this, etc.), it is in principle possible to work back from the disclosed posteriors to the private evidence incorporated therein.

The process can be illustrated as follows. Two individuals i and j are seeking consensus as to the probability p of head on the next toss of a coin. They have common knowledge prior distributions over the possible values for p, and specifically let the distributions assign equal prior probabilities of $\frac{1}{3}$ each to $p = 0$, $p = \frac{1}{2}$, and $p = 1$. Each person also has private evidence in the form of a single toss of the coin, and the fact that each has such private evidence is also common knowledge. (The private evidence that each possesses is an "overt secret.") Suppose that i has actually observed a head and j a tail. By Bayes' Theorem, i's revised or posterior estimate for the probability of head on the next toss of the coin will equal $\frac{2}{3}$ while j's will equal $\frac{1}{3}$. When they reveal these "first-round" posteriors to one another, each can then immediately infer the content of his partner's private evidence. In this way each comes to know that the combined sample results are one head and one tail. Using that knowledge leads them to an agreed "adjusted" posterior estimate – to wit, a 50% chance of head on the next toss.

What if the respective sample sizes were unknown to the other party? Here each must have a prior probability distribution for the other's sample size as well, which (if these are also "common knowledge") makes for a more complicated but still in principle feasible second-round set of posterior estimates. In general, these will not yet be in agreement. However, from the respective weight each person attaches to his own observations in going from the direct Bayesian first-round posteriors to the combined or second-round posterior estimates, each reveals something to the other about the magnitude of his own sample. Eventually, it has been shown, this process leads to agreed final posterior estimates.

Example 5.8: Individuals i and j have "common knowledge" that, with equal probabilities of $\frac{1}{3}$, a coin is either two-headed ($p = 1$), fair ($p = \frac{1}{2}$), or two-tailed ($p = 0$). Also with equal probabilities, either may draw a sample of sizes 0, 1, or 2. Individual i in fact draws a sample of size 1, and observes a head. Individual j draws a sample of size 2, and observes a head and a tail.

After making his Bayesian calculation, i will reveal his first-round posterior distribution (head, tail; $\frac{2}{3}, \frac{1}{3}$). And j (who, of course, now knows for sure that the coin is fair) will reveal hers as (head, tail; $\frac{1}{2}, \frac{1}{2}$). Individual j can infer, with 100% confidence, that i's sample size must have been 1 (since only a head in a sample of 1 could have led to i's revealed initial posterior distribution). But this hardly matters for j, who already knows for sure that the coin is fair. So j's *revised* posterior distribution, on the basis of knowing the merged evidence, remains (head, tail; $\frac{1}{2}, \frac{1}{2}$). As for individual i, upon seeing j's initial posterior distribution he cannot be sure whether j has observed nothing at all (sample of size 0) or else has obtained 1 head and 1 tail in a sample of size 2. But upon seeing j's *revised* distribution, and noticing that j has made no change to take account of j's first-round posterior distribution, individual i will also realize that the latter must have been the case. So i will come into agreement with j's revised posterior solution. □

Let us re-examine Example 5.7 in light of the above discussion. Suppose that individuals j and k start with a common prior and agree on a likelihood function of observed information; the divergence of opinion between them is entirely due to differences in observed information. Then, if they report their probability beliefs to each other, update their beliefs, report their new beliefs, and so on, then ultimately they will converge to the same posterior beliefs. However, unlike in Example 5.8, there is no compelling reason to believe that the two individuals in Example 5.7 will start with a common prior about the prospects of the two horses or that they will agree on a likelihood function of observed information.[12]

There is one puzzling aspect of the process described in the above examples. It requires complete sincerity on the part of each member, which could scarcely occur unless their interests are entirely harmonious. But, if so, surely it would have been more efficient and economical for each person simply to disclose his own private sample evidence to his partner! It is only when conflict of interest plays a role that inferring the other party's private evidence from his actions – a process that may be called "information leakage" – really becomes an interesting issue.

Conflicts of Interest

When conflicts of interest are present, an enormous range of possibilities arise, even if we keep things simple by excluding any initial divergences of belief. Two possibilities will be illustrated here: in the first, there is unanimous agreement to reject perfect *public* information, even if free, while in the second, *private* information is similarly rejected.

Example 5.9: Suppose a community of 1,000 identical individuals is offered the following deal. Provided there is unanimous agreement to the proposal, 999 of them will receive unlimited wealth and glory, but one single member of the group must die. And, no one can know in advance who the unlucky person will be. This deal *might* (see our discussion of the "value of life" in Chapter 2) win unanimous acceptance, and let us suppose that such is the case. But, before that decision is actually effectuated, the members of the community are offered another option: they can now choose to be informed in advance, without charge, as to who the unlucky person would be. Evidently, if the members of the community were unanimously willing to accept the initial gamble, they must now be unanimously *unwilling* to accept the information even if free – since receiving it would destroy the possibility of unanimous agreement upon the gamble.   □

In the example just given there was no prior difference of opinion, and – the information being perfect and public – there could be no posterior difference of opinion either. The information would be rejected because, while there is a *latent* conflict of interest among the members, that conflict is not relevant for the gamble made in a state of ignorance. Disclosure of

---

[12] Morris (1995) provides an interesting discussion of the origins of the common prior assumption in economics and discusses settings where it can be dispensed with.

the information makes the latent conflict of interest an actual one, thereby (under the group's constitutional rule of unanimity) precluding acceptance of a desired gamble.

Example 5.10: Two individuals i and j are to predict whether the top card of a shuffled deck is black or red. The predictions are made in sequence: i guesses first, and then j (after hearing i's guess). If they make the same prediction each wins \$1, whether their prediction turns out correct or not. If they disagree, the one who is correct wins \$3, and the other nothing. Risk neutrality is assumed.

Since i has no basis for preferring one or the other color, he will choose at random. Then j will choose the opposite color, so each will have an expected gain of \$1.50.

Now suppose someone offers, without charge, an arrangement whereby the first-mover i can know the actual color of the top card before he makes his prediction. Evidently, the parties would be unanimous in rejecting that arrangement – even i as the "beneficiary." For, with that information individual i would choose the correct color, j would then make the same choice, and they would each gain only \$1 rather than an expectation of \$1.50. □

In this latter example, there was no prior difference of opinion. Furthermore, even though, under the arrangement proposed, the evidence would be privately conveyed only to the first chooser, its content could readily be inferred by the other party. Thus, the second example is not really different from the first. In the absence of information the conflict of interest – the (3,0) versus (0,3) payoff possibilities if opposite colors are chosen – remains only latent, since in a state of ignorance each party expects to earn the same \$1.50 on average. Supplying the information once again makes the conflict of interest actual, leading to a revised group action in which they both can reap only their second-best payoffs of \$1 each.

Finally, let us consider the *interaction* of conflict of interest with differences of belief. Here also a proposition of some generality can be stated, somewhat to the opposite effect of the earlier proposition that applied when *only* differences of opinion are involved:

In groups characterized by conflicts of interest as well as differences of belief, the acquisition of information tends to be avoided.

This proposition can only be stated in "tends to" form, since the actual choice to avoid acquiring information will depend upon the constitutional decision rule as well as upon the specifics of the situation. The following example will illustrate.

Example 5.11: Returning to the match race between Seabiscuit and War Admiral, suppose now that individuals j and k will simply be betting $100 at even money against one another. Since j attaches 80% probability to Seabiscuit winning, and k similarly for War Admiral, each has a $60 expectation of gain. The group decision is whether or not to collectively incur the cost of staging the race, with the cost to be evenly split. Evidently, the decision would be unanimous in favor of doing so at any per-capita cost less than $60. Returning once again to a theme familiar from the examples above, free information in the form of an infallible public forecast (as to which horse will win) would be unanimously rejected.   □

This example represents an interesting twist in comparison with the preceding. In the earlier examples, despite a latent conflict of interest, under conditions of ignorance the parties were nevertheless able to agree upon a risky action that (in an *ex ante* sense) was "really" advantageous to all. While in actuality not all would gain – one person out of the 1,000 would lose his life in the "unlimited wealth and glory" example, and there would be a loser as well as a winner if opposite colors were chosen in the card-color example – *viewed in advance* the gain was worth the risk, in everyone's estimate. The twist here is that, while it remains the case that each regards the gain as worth the risk, even viewed in advance the risky action cannot be "really" advantageous to all. In the Seabiscuit–War Admiral match, if anything is paid for information, the group as a whole must lose. In fact, if the true probabilities were known, and assuming some degree of risk aversion, one or both of them would refuse to bet. Knowing this, the parties would, of course, unanimously agree not to undertake the cost of staging the race. The upshot then is that, where there are conflicts of interest, each member of a group might prefer not receiving information that would destroy his chance to exploit (what he perceives to be) the erroneous beliefs of others.

Recalling that these examples do not purport to cover all the issues involved, we can nevertheless summarize the indications provided:

1 "Excessive" group investment in information tends to take place (in comparison with what each and every member of the group regards as optimal) when, given differences of belief but no conflicts of interest, each member believes that the additional evidence is likely to convince others of the correctness of his own opinions (as to what is best for the group).

2 "Insufficient" investment in information tends to take place (as illustrated by our examples in which even perfect and free evidence would be unanimously refused) in a number of cases, among them: (a) in the absence of conflict of interests, where agreements as to the best

group action are grounded upon *compensating disagreements* in different dimensions of uncertainty; (b) where, with agreed beliefs as to an uncertain event, resolving the uncertainty makes it impossible for the group to undertake an *ex ante* unanimously preferred risky action; (c) where, with differences of opinion and conflicts of interest as well, elimination of the differences of opinion would make it impossible to undertake a group action whereby each expects to profit at the expense of the others.

SUGGESTIONS FOR FURTHER READING: Blackwell's sufficiency, which is used to rank message services in Section 5.2.3, is a very strong requirement. There are other less restrictive orderings of message services; an overview of these may be found in Jewitt (2007). The idea of paying for flexibility, which underlies the analysis in Section 5.2.5, is also found in the option value literature in finance. A good introduction to this finance literature is Trigeorgis (1996). It is important for several of the examples in Section 5.3.2 that participants not have common knowledge prior distributions. In Chapters 6 and 12, we return to some of the questions addressed in Section 5.3.

References

Aumann, Robert J., "Agreeing to Disagree," *Annals of Statistics*, 4 (1976), 1236–1239.

Blackwell, David, "Equivalent Comparison of Experiments," *Annals of Mathematics and Statistics*, 24 (1953), 265–272.

Dalkey, Norman, "An Impossibility Theorem for Group Probability Functions," RAND Corporation Paper, P-4862 (1972).

Jewitt, Ian, "Information Order in Decision and Agency Problems," working paper, Nuffield College, Oxford (2007).

Jones, Robert A. and Ostroy, Joseph M., "Flexibility and Uncertainty," *Review of Economic Studies*, 51 (1984), 13–32.

Marschak, Jacob and Miyasawa, Koichi, "Economic Comparability of Information Systems," *International Economic Review*, 9 (1968), 137–174.

Morris, Stephen, "The Common Prior Assumption in Economic Theory," *Economics and Philosophy*, 11 (1995), 227–253.

Raiffa, Howard, *Decision Analysis*, Reading, MA: Addison-Wesley, 1968.

Stiglitz, Joseph E. and Radner, Roy, "A Nonconcavity in the Value of Information," in Marcel Boyer and Richard Kihlstrom (eds.), pp. 33–52 *Bayesian Models in Economic Theory*. Amsterdam: North-Holland, 1984.

Trigeorgis, Lenos, *Real Options: Managerial Flexibility and Strategy in Resource Allocation*, Cambridge, MA: MIT Press, 1996.

Winkler, Robert L., "Scoring Rules and the Evaluation of Probabilities," *Test*, 5 (1996), 1–60.

6

Information and Markets

In Part I, dealing with the *economics of uncertainty*, after covering the "terminal" decisions of the individual in Chapters 1 through 3 we moved on in Chapter 4 to consider market equilibrium. And similarly here in the realm of the *economics of information*: having examined individuals' "nonterminal" (informational) decisions in Chapter 5, we now turn to the analysis of the market equilibrium generated thereby.

A first key distinction is between *public* and *private* information. If an information service provides public information, decision makers throughout the economy will be attempting to revise their portfolios in the light of their changed beliefs. Consequently, asset prices will adjust. In particular, market values will rise for those assets paying off more handsomely in states of the world now regarded as more likely. If, on the other hand, the message provided is strictly private, an informed party may be able to profit in various ways without any noticeable effect upon prices. However, as we shall see, almost always there are processes at work tending to "publicize" private information. Sometimes this occurs because the informed individual can gain by intended disclosure of his data, for example, if he sells it to others. Or sometimes there may be unintended leakage into the public domain – owing, perhaps, to the fact that the uninformed can monitor the behavior of those who are informed. These more difficult problems are reserved for later in this chapter; only fully public information will be examined initially.

A second distinction is between *produced* and *emergent* information. Information is produced when, for example, new evidence is generated by a sampling experiment conducted by the agent himself or by an expert on his behalf. Ordinarily, some cost is incurred in producing such data, i.e., in acquiring such a "message service." But it may also be that information emerges costlessly, simply with the passage of time. Tomorrow's weather is uncertain today, but the uncertainty will be reduced as more meteorological data flow in and will in due course be conclusively resolved when tomorrow arrives. Where emergent information is anticipated, an individual might choose a kind of passive informational action – simply waiting before making his terminal move. Just such a choice was examined in Chapter 5 under the heading of "flexibility."

Sections 6.1 and 6.2 are devoted to the market consequences of emergent public information. When such information is anticipated, economic agents may have to contemplate market exchanges in two distinct rounds: trading that takes place *prior to* and trading *posterior to* announcement of the news. The equilibria of the two trading rounds will generally be interrelated, but the form of the relationship depends importantly upon the completeness of the prior and the posterior market regimes. In Section 6.3 the impact of some traders having access to private information is analyzed. The possibility of leakage of private information through movements in price is examined. We end with a discussion of the rational expectations hypothesis in Section 6.4.

6.1 The Inter-related Equilibria of Prior and Posterior Markets

6.1.1 Complete Contingent Markets

In dealing with the *economics of uncertainty* in Part I, we mainly considered models with S states of the world and a single consumption good C ("corn"). A regime of Complete Contingent Markets (CCM) was said to exist when all the distinct contingent claims c_s are separately tradable at prices P_s. Alternatively, a regime of Complete Asset Markets (CAM) – for which a sufficient condition is that there exist $A = S$ distinct assets characterized by linearly independent state payoff vectors – can, of course, generate the same results as CCM regimes, but this complication will generally be set aside in the current chapter.

Assuming an interior solution, the familiar optimality condition for the individual (the Fundamental Theorem of Risk Bearing) and the consequent equilibrium condition for prices take the form:

NON-INFORMATIVE EQUILIBRIUM (Single Good)

$$\pi_s^i v_i' \left(c_s^i \right) / \pi_{\hat{s}}^i v_i' \left(c_{\hat{s}}^i \right) = P_s / P_{\hat{s}} \tag{6.1.1}$$

where s and $\hat{s}$ are any two states and v_i' is the marginal utility of individual i evaluated at the indicated consumption quantity for each state. Equation (6.1.1) holds for each individual in the market. To achieve this condition, individuals in a world of uncertainty will generally have undertaken both productive transformations and market exchanges, with the effect of modifying the aggregate economy-wide risk and also redistributing it among the various agents.

But now we will be assuming that emergent public information is expected to arrive before the close of trading. Let us call this an "informative situation." In general, in an informative situation, market exchanges may take place both prior to and posterior to receipt of the message. Thus the prospective arrival of public information divides trading into a prior round and a posterior round. In the prior round, the individual makes exchanges toward a "trading portfolio"; in the posterior round, he will be making any other exchanges required to convert his trading portfolio into an optimal "consumption portfolio." We will generally be assuming, however, that the message is not timely enough to permit *productive* adaptations to the changed probability beliefs. For example, a message as to increased flood danger in the rainy season may come in time to affect the market terms of flood-insurance transactions, but not in time to permit construction of dams or dikes.

There is a remarkable theorem about the relationship between the prior-round and the posterior-round equilibria for informative situations in CCM trading, which we will approach in easy stages.

Model 1 (single consumption good, conclusive information): Suppose it is known that the arriving message will be *conclusive* as to which state of the world will obtain, and also *exhaustive* in the sense that to each and every state s corresponds exactly one message m. (In what follows, the term "conclusive" will be taken to mean "conclusive and exhaustive.") Notice, first, that, if there really were only a single consumption good C, there would be no scope at all for trading in the posterior round. Once it becomes known that some particular state s will obtain, income claims $c_{\hat{s}}$ for any other state $\hat{s} \neq s$ lose all value. In these circumstances, it is evident, all desired portfolio adjustments must be undertaken in the prior round of trading. In other words, one's trading portfolio will necessarily be his consumption portfolio. Assuming everyone can draw this logical inference, Equation (6.1.1), which applied for the economics of uncertainty (i.e., in a non-informative situation), remains applicable here even though now we are dealing with an informative situation.

The symbols P^o and P^1 will be used here to distinguish the *prior-round* and *posterior-round* prices determined in informative situations, while P without a superscript signifies the price vector associated with a non-informative situation. Then, with a single consumption good C and anticipated arrival of conclusive information, the condition for *prior-round* equilibrium in an informative situation is (where s and $\hat{s}$ are any two states):

INFORMATIVE EQUILIBRIUM (Single Good)

$$\pi_s^i v_i' \left(c_s^i\right) / \pi_{\hat{s}}^i v_i' \left(c_{\hat{s}}^i\right) = P_s^o / P_{\hat{s}}^o = P_s / P_{\hat{s}} \qquad (6.1.1')$$

Result of Model 1: In an informative situation, given the conditions: (i) Complete Contingent Markets (CCM), (ii) anticipated conclusive information, and (iii) a single consumption good, there can be no posterior-round trading. The equilibrium prior-round state-claim price ratio $P_s^o / P_{\hat{s}}^o$ will therefore be the same as the ratio $P_s / P_{\hat{s}}$ that would have obtained in a non-informative situation where no message at all was expected.[1]

Example 6.1: An economy consists of two equally numerous types of individuals under pure exchange. Everyone has the utility function $v(c) = \ln c$, where c represents the quantity of a single consumption good C ("corn"). There are just two states ($s = 1$, 2) with probabilities $(\pi_1, \pi_2) = (0.6, 0.4)$. That is, all individuals have the same beliefs about the likelihood of the two states. For type-i individuals the state-distributed endowment is $(\bar{c}_1^i, \bar{c}_2^i) = (400, 0)$; for type-$j$ individuals it is $(\bar{c}_1^j, \bar{c}_2^j) = (0, 160)$. In a non-informative situation under pure exchange, Equation (6.1.1) becomes:

$$\frac{0.4 \left(1/c_2^i\right)}{0.6 \left(1/c_1^i\right)} = \frac{P_2}{P_1} = \frac{0.4\left(1/c_2^j\right)}{0.6\left(1/c_1^j\right)}$$

Making use also of the budget equations on each side, it is easy to verify that the solution is:

$$\left(c_1^i, c_2^i\right) = (240, 96), \left(c_1^j, c_2^j\right) = (160, 64),$$
$$P_2/P_1 = 5/3$$

Also, of course, $P_2^o / P_1^o = P_2/P_1$. $\qquad\qquad \square$

As indicated in the example, since everyone realizes that no *posterior* exchanges will be possible, in the prior round each person trades to his optimal risk-bearing portfolio.

Model 2 (G consumption goods, conclusive information): Still assuming that the emergent information will be conclusive as to which state of the world is going to obtain, consider now the more general case of multiple consumption goods $g = 1, \ldots, G$. In a *non-informative* situation under

---

[1] We are assuming here that the equilibrium of the equation system is unique. Otherwise, it is conceivable that a non-informative situation would lead to one of the set of possible equilibria, and an informative situation to a different member of the same set. This complication is set aside in our analysis.

a CCM regime there would be trading in the *GS* different claims c_{gs} – entitlements to a unit of good g contingent upon the occurrence of state s – at prices P_{gs}. The equilibrium conditions would include ratios of the following two types, where s and $\hat{s}$ are any two states and g and $\hat{g}$ are any two goods:

NON-INFORMATIVE EQUILIBRIUM CONDITIONS (*G* goods)

$$\frac{\pi_s^i \partial v_i \left(c_{1s}^i, \ldots, c_{Gs}^i \right) / \partial c_{gs}^i}{\pi_{\hat{s}}^i \partial v_i \left(c_{1\hat{s}}^i, \ldots, c_{G\hat{s}}^i \right) / \partial c_{g\hat{s}}^i} = \frac{P_{gs}}{P_{g\hat{s}}}$$

$$\frac{\partial v_i \left(c_{1s}^i, \ldots, c_{Gs}^i \right) / \partial c_{gs}^i}{\partial v_i \left(c_{1s}^i, \ldots, c_{Gs}^i \right) / \partial c_{\hat{g}s}^i} = \frac{P_{gs}}{P_{\hat{g}s}} \qquad (6.1.2)$$

Turning to the *informative* situation, a CCM regime in the prior round would again involve trading in the *GS* different claims c_{gs} – now determining a set of equilibrium prior prices P_{gs}^o. After the conclusive message arrives that some particular state s will obtain, *posterior* trading among the G commodity claims c_{gs} that remain valid could now take place, leading to a set of equilibrium prices P_{gs}^l. (Whereas in the case of a single consumption good, in contrast, posterior trading was impossible – since only the single claim c_s remain valid.)

Nevertheless, an analogous two-part result continues to hold for the equilibrium of the informative situation: (1) The prior-round equilibrium price ratios will be the same as those which would have been arrived at in a non-informative situation, and (2) all the needed portfolio adjustments will occur in the prior round, i.e., there will be no posterior-round trading.[2] Thus at the prior-round equilibrium:

INFORMATIVE EQUILIBRIUM (*G* Goods, Prior-Round Trading)

$$\frac{\pi_s^i \partial v_i \left(c_{1s}^i, \ldots, c_{Gs}^i \right) / \partial c_{gs}^i}{\pi_{\hat{s}}^i \partial v_i \left(c_{1\hat{s}}^i, \ldots, c_{G\hat{s}}^i \right) / \partial c_{g\hat{s}}^i} = \frac{P_{gs}^o}{P_{g\hat{s}}^o} = \frac{P_{gs}}{P_{g\hat{s}}}$$

$$\frac{\partial v_i \left(c_{1s}^i, \ldots, c_{Gs}^i \right) / \partial c_{gs}^i}{\partial v_i \left(c_{1s}^i, \ldots, c_{Gs}^i \right) / \partial c_{\hat{g}s}^i} = \frac{P_{gs}^o}{P_{\hat{g}s}^o} = \frac{P_{gs}}{P_{\hat{g}s}} \qquad (6.1.2')$$

These are identical with Equations (6.1.2) except for the explicit indication that the price ratios with superscript O (the equilibrium ratios for

---

[2] As indicated in the preceding footnote, we are setting aside the possibility that the equilibrium may not be unique. Henceforth, this qualification will be taken as understood without further repetition.

prior-round trading in an informative situation) are the same as those without superscript (the equilibrium price ratios for a non-informative situation).

To get at the intuition underlying these results, let us first step back a moment. Imagine that the parties had all calculated and traded in the belief that the situation was a *non-informative* one, and thus had arrived at the equilibrium indicated by conditions (6.1.2) above. Now, quite unexpectedly, new conclusive information that some particular state *s* is going to obtain is, in fact, publicly revealed. At this point, it would be possible for any or all of the parties to engage in re-trading, on the basis of their changed probability beliefs in the light of the information received. But the equilibrium condition represented by the lower equation of (6.1.2) evidently continues to hold *if* the price ratios $P_{gs}/P_{\hat{g}s}$ all remain unchanged and the parties engage in no further trading.

Looking at this in more detail, the upper row of Equations (6.1.2) represents, for some single good *g*, the conditions for optimal balance between contingent claims valid under different states of the world. Evidently, all these claims will now have become worthless except for those involving the specific state *s*. Hence, $c_{g\hat{s}}$ claims for any $\hat{s} \neq s$ will be non-tradable; anyone stuck with them will be unable to get anything valuable in exchange. As for the lower row, those equations represent the balance between any two goods *g* and $\hat{g}$, given the particular state *s*. The point to notice is that in these equations no probabilities appear. Hence, if the initial trading satisfied the conditions in the lower equations, knowing now that the probability of the specific state *s* has become unity in no way calls for additional trading.

We have seen that the *unanticipated* arrival of conclusive information, no matter what its content, cannot lead to any posterior trading. It then follows that, even when the arrival of such public information is *anticipated in advance*, rational individuals would not expect to be able to make advantageous use of it for posterior trading. The equations in the lower row of (6.1.2′) represent how each person would balance in advance between holdings of different goods, *contingent upon* some state *s* having obtained. Knowing afterward that state *s* had in fact obtained leaves the situation unchanged since all individuals had already contemplated and allowed for that contingency in their prior-round trading.

Thus, if all individuals have chosen their prior-round trading portfolios in accordance with (6.1.2′), these conditions remain satisfied without anyone revising his portfolio in the posterior round of trading. So:

$$\frac{P_{gs}^I}{P_{\hat{g}s}^I} = \frac{P_{gs}^O}{P_{\hat{g}s}^O} = \frac{P_{gs}}{P_{\hat{g}s}} \tag{6.1.3}$$

Result of Model 2: Given the conditions: (i) CCM, (ii) anticipated conclusive information, and (iii) G consumption goods, once again there will be no posterior-round trading. Also, the posterior-round price ratios and the prior-round price ratios will again be the same as the price ratios that would have held in a non-informative situation.

However, this conclusion is based on a crucial implicit assumption: that all the traders in their prior-round decisions *correctly forecast* what the equilibrium posterior price ratio will be. Such forecasts will be termed "self-fulfilling predictions" (SFP). SFP forecasts are easy to make here, since Equation (6.1.3) tells us that the price *ratio* between any pair of goods g and $\hat{g}$ contingent upon state s will remain unchanged after receipt of the message that state s will obtain. However, if traders mistakenly thought that posterior price ratios would diverge from those in the prior round, they would be led to make "erroneous" prior-round transactions, affecting the prior-round market equilibrium and thus requiring corrective posterior-round trading. In short, the price ratios will remain unchanged in posterior-round trading *if* in the prior round everyone believed that would be the case. The SFP forecast will be correct, provided that everybody joined in making it. (This corresponds to one of the meanings of the mysterious phrase "rational expectations" to be discussed below.)

Example 6.2: There are two consumption goods: a risky commodity F ("fruit") and a non-risky commodity N ("nuts"). Let everyone have the utility function $v(c_n, c_f) = \ln(c_n c_f)$ or, in more compact notation, $v(n, f) = \ln(nf)$. And all agree on the state probabilities $(\pi_1, \pi_2) = (0.6, 0.4)$.

Once again assume there are two equally numerous types of individuals. Individuals of type i have only a non-risky "nuts" endowment that is constant over states: $\bar{n}_1^i = \bar{n}_2^i = 200$. And those of type j have only a risky "fruit" endowment, varying over states: $\bar{f}_1^j = 400$, $\bar{f}_2^j = 160$. Equations (6.1.2) become:

$$\frac{\pi_1 \dfrac{\partial v^k}{\partial n_1^k}}{P_{n1}} = \frac{\pi_2 \dfrac{\partial v^k}{\partial n_2^k}}{P_{n2}} = \frac{\pi_1 \dfrac{\partial v^k}{f_1^k}}{P_{f1}} = \frac{\pi_2 \dfrac{\partial v^k}{\partial f_2^k}}{P_{f2}}, \quad \text{for } k = i, j$$

For our example with logarithmic preferences:

$$\frac{0.6}{P_{n1} n_1^k} = \frac{0.4}{P_{n2} n_2^k} = \frac{0.6}{P_{f1} f_1^k} = \frac{0.4}{P_{f2} f_2^k}, \quad \text{for } k = i, j \qquad (6.1.4)$$

These equations are satisfied, and supply and demand equated, if each and every individual trades to the consumption portfolio $(n_1^k, n_2^k, f_1^k, f_2^k) = (100, 100, 200, 80)$. Substituting in the preceding equation, and inverting:

$$\frac{P_{n1}100}{0.6} = \frac{P_{n2}100}{0.4} = \frac{P_{f1}200}{0.6} = \frac{P_{f2}80}{0.4}$$

Choosing the normalization $P_{n1} + P_{n2} = 1$, so that the numeraire is a certainty claim to good N, the equilibrium contingent-claims price vector for non-informative trading is $P = (P_{n1}, P_{n2}, P_{f1}, P_{f2}) = (0.6, 0.4, 0.3, 0.5)$.

Now consider an *informative* situation, where a conclusive message is anticipated as to which state will obtain, and let us assume all traders make the correct "self-fulfilling predictions" SFP as to the posterior prices. If the prior-round informative price vector P^o is exactly the same as the non-informative price vector P, then everyone can achieve in prior-round trading the same portfolios as in the non-informative situation. Thus: $P^o \equiv (P_{n1}^o, P_{n2}^o, P_{f1}^o, P_{f2}^o) = (0.6, 0.4, 0.3, 0.5) = P$.

As for the *posterior* price ratios under each of the two contingencies, the equilibrium solutions are:

In the event that state 1 obtains:

$$\frac{\partial v(n_1, f_1)/\partial f}{\partial v(n_1, f_1)/\partial n} = \frac{1/200}{1/100} = 0.5 = \frac{P_{f1}^I}{P_{n1}^I} = \frac{P_{f1}^o}{P_{n1}^o}$$

In the event that state 2 obtains:

$$\frac{\partial v(n_2, f_2)/\partial f}{\partial v(n_2, f_2)/\partial n} = \frac{1/80}{1/100} = 1.25 = \frac{P_{f2}^I}{P_{n2}^I} = \frac{P_{f2}^o}{P_{n2}^o}$$

One or the other of these conditions would be applicable in posterior trading. Since under the SFP assumption *these posterior price ratios are correctly forecast when the parties make their prior-round trading decisions*, no utility-improving portfolio revision will be needed or possible in the posterior round.   □

Suppose now that the above equilibrium fails to hold, owing to individuals not making the correct self-fulfilling predictions SFP. Would that imply a loss of Pareto-efficiency? In a world of pure exchange, there can be no change in the social aggregates. So, to the extent that "erroneous" transactions take place in the prior round, such trading will lead only to wealth redistributions. In that case the availability of posterior markets, among the G claims c_{gs} still valid after state s is known to obtain, suffices to ensure that efficient portfolio revision will still occur. But if *production* could be taking place before the message arrives, the erroneous prior-round prices caused by the failure of individuals to make the correct SFP would also imply mistaken prior-round productive decisions, and thus a real efficiency loss. In light of this, we shall at times refer to the equilibrium attained under CCM, given self-fulfilling predictions, as the "efficient" equilibrium. (Recall, however, that we are ruling out productive adaptations *after* the message arrives, such as building a dam upon learning that a flood will occur.)

We can now state the theorem proper, which holds also in the much more general case of messages that are not "conclusive."

Proposition 6.1: Under conditions of emergent public information, with a CCM regime in the prior round of trading and assuming self-fulfilling predictions SFP, after arrival of the message all the still-relevant price ratios will remain unchanged, so that no posterior-round trading need take place. Furthermore, these prior-round prices provide the correct guidance for efficient prior-round productive decisions.

The generalization to the case of non-conclusive messages follows very easily from the above, except that we must now redefine prior-round Complete Contingent Markets to mean trading in the *GSM* distinct claims c_{gsm} – each being an entitlement to a particular good *g* in state *s* provided that message *m* was received. After the close of prior-round trading some particular message $\hat{m}$ will have arrived, so that only the *GS* claims of type $c_{gs\hat{m}}$ retain any value. It is not difficult to verify, once again assuming that traders correctly forecast that all the relevant posterior-round price ratios will remain unchanged, that no one will be able to engage in any advantageous posterior revision of the portfolios chosen in prior-round trading.

The practical implications of this proposition may seem disturbing. Can it really be the case that, in an informative situation, a posterior round of trading is never necessary? Such a conclusion would be unwarranted, because the results obtained to this point have been conditioned upon the assumption of a regime of Complete Contingent Markets in both prior and posterior rounds of trading. This assumption will be relaxed in the sections following.

6.1.2 Incomplete Regimes of Markets

Admittedly, it was rather unrealistic of us to keep multiplying the number of tradable commodities, as required by the CCM assumption. Starting with the "natural" case of markets in *G* goods (that is, markets for certainty claims only), we then allowed *GS* markets for goods × states and finally *GSM* markets for goods × states × messages. Issues of great practical importance arise when we consider less complete regimes of markets. However, to maintain simplicity, when we examine different market regimes in what follows we will limit the discussion to the special case of fully *conclusive* information. Then the set of *M* messages collapses into the set of *S* states, so that a complete market regime would require trading only in the *GS* claims c_{gs}.

Several possible patterns of market incompleteness will be discussed here:

Numeraire Contingent Markets (NCM)

Suppose that, with *G* goods and *S* states, prior-round trading can take place but only in contingent claims to the single good $g = 1$, which we can select to be the numeraire good. Thus, in the prior round there are *S* tradable c_{1s} entitlements. After receipt of a conclusive message that some particular state *s* will obtain, in the posterior round everyone will be choosing a preferred consumption basket by trading among the *G* remaining valid entitlements c_{gs}.

Proposition 6.2: Under conditions of emergent conclusive information, in an NCM regime of trading the same efficient allocation as under CCM can be achieved, provided that self-fulfilling predictions SFP may be assumed (Arrow, 1964). However, in general, posterior as well as prior trading will be required.

Since the NCM regime has only *S* tradable claims in the prior round and *G* in the posterior round, while the CCM regime had (assuming conclusive information) *GS* claims in the prior round and *G* again in the posterior round, this proposition correctly suggests that the CCM regime provided more than the minimally necessary trading opportunities for efficiency.

To understand Proposition 6.2, consider the budget constraints in the NCM regime. In the prior round each individual can trade only numeraire (commodity 1) claims. Let $\bar{c}_{gs}^i$ denote individual *i*'s initial endowment (of good *g* in state *s*) and let c_{gs}^{oi} denote the typical element of individual *i*'s *trading portfolio*: his holdings at the end of the prior round. If the prior-round price vector is $P_1^o = (P_{11}^o, \ldots, P_{1s}^o)$ his prior-round budget constraint is:

$$\sum_s P_{1s}^o c_{1s}^{oi} = \sum_s P_{1s}^o \bar{c}_{1s}^{oi} \tag{6.1.5}$$

$$c_{gs}^{oi} = \bar{c}_{gs}^{i}, \text{ for } g \neq 1$$

In the posterior round, when the state is revealed, each individual can then re-trade between his claims to commodity 1 and his claims to other commodities. If the posterior price vector in any state s is $P_s^I = (P_{1s}^I, \ldots, P_{gs}^I)$, then if state s obtains individual i has the posterior budget constraint (where c_{gs}^i denotes the typical element of his *consumption portfolio*):

$$\sum_{g=1}^{G} P_{gs}^I c_{gs}^i = \sum_{g=1}^{G} P_{gs}^I c_{gs}^{oi}, s = 1, \ldots, S \qquad (6.1.6)$$

Whatever state of the world s obtains, in the posterior market prices can be normalized by setting the price of numeraire (good 1) claims equal to the prior-round price, that is:

$$P_{1s}^o = P_{1s}^I, \; s = 1, \ldots, S$$

Under this normalization, P_{1s}^I can be substituted for P_{1s}^o in the prior-round budget constraint (6.1.5). Then, summing (6.1.6) over s:

$$\sum_g \sum_s P_{gs}^I c_{gs}^i = \sum_g \sum_s P_{gs}^I \bar{c}_{gs}^i$$

This is the budget constraint for the CCM regime where, for each s, the state-claim price vector P_s^o has been replaced by the relevant P_s^I. Thus the CCM regime can indeed be replicated by a NCM regime in which $P^I = P$. (That is, where the posterior-round prices, in those markets that remain active, are the CCM equilibrium prices.)

The intuition behind Proposition 6.2 should now be clear. In the prior round each individual is able to transfer wealth across states. As long as prices in the prior round equal the CCM prices for the numeraire good in a non-informative situation, the exchange rates across states are the same in the two regimes. Then, in the posterior market, if prices are once again equal to the contingent-claim prices, each individual can purchase the same final consumption bundle as in the CCM regime.

Three separate factors mainly affect the parties' trading portfolios, i.e., their desired holdings of c_{1s}^o claims, and thereby motivate prior-round trading in the NCM regime: (1) *belief disparities*: an individual attaching a relatively high probability to any particular state $\hat{s}$ will, of course, want to end up holding a relatively large amount of $c_{1\hat{s}}^o$ claims; (2) *endowment disparities*: an individual whose endowment of goods in general is disproportionately weighted toward some $\hat{s}$ will attempt to balance his contingent posterior wealths by selling off some of his $\bar{c}_{1\hat{s}}$ claims, i.e., by trading to make

$c_{1\hat{s}}^o < \bar{c}_{1\hat{s}};^3$ (3) *preference disparities:* even if two individuals have the same beliefs and endowments, they may still want to trade if their preferences are different, e.g., one may prefer nuts and the other fruit.

In what follows, it will be convenient to concentrate attention upon an illuminating special case in which (i) all beliefs are agreed, (ii) the numeraire (good 1) is riskless (that is, each person's numeraire endowment is uniform over states), and (iii) there is a common utility function that is additively separable in the numeraire and non-numeraire goods. The last assumption implies that the marginal utility of each good in any state will depend only upon its own quantity in the consumption portfolio; i.e., there is no complementarity in preference among goods.

The following example illustrates a case where a CCM regime equilibrium is replicated in a NCM regime even though no *prior-round* trading takes place in the NCM regime. There are no belief or preference disparities and endowments values, computed at prices of the CCM regime, of all individuals are identical.

Example 6.3: Return to the conditions of Example 6.2, with type-i individuals possessing a non-risky endowment $(\bar{n}_1, \bar{n}_2) = (200, 200)$ of good N ("nuts"), where N is the numeraire (so that $P_{n1} + P_{n2} = 1$), while type-j individuals have a risky endowment $(\bar{f}_1, \bar{f}_2) = (400, 160)$ of good F ("fruit"). Each person has utility function $v = \ln(nf)$ and probability beliefs $(\pi_1, \pi_2) = (0.6, 0.4)$ as before.

From Proposition 6.2 we know that the NCM regime can replicate the CCM regime. But, assuming self-fulfilling predictions, what trading if any will occur in the prior round?

From Example 6.2, the equilibrium CCM prices are:

$$(P_{n1}, P_{n2}, P_{f1}, P_{f2}) = (0.6, 0.4, 0.3, 0.5)$$

In addition, we saw there that the first-order conditions for expected-utility maximization by any individual k can be written:

$$\frac{0.6}{P_{n1}n_1^k} = \frac{0.4}{P_{n2}n_2^k} = \frac{0.6}{P_{f1}f_1^k} = \frac{0.4}{P_{f2}f_2^k}, \quad \text{for } k = i, j$$

It follows that expenditure on each commodity in state 1 is $(0.6)/(0.4) = 1.5$ times expenditure on each commodity in state 2. So total wealth allocated to state-1 expenditure is 1.5 times wealth allocated to state-2 expenditure.

---

[3] He may even find it optimal to set $c_{1\hat{s}}^o < 0$; that is, he can take a short position in good 1.

Suppose that prices are the same in the active markets of the NCM regime – the prior-round markets for good N in all states and the posterior-round markets for all goods in whatever state s obtains. Suppose that there is no trading in the prior round. A type-i individual with endowment $(\bar{n}_1^i, \bar{n}_2^i, \bar{f}_1^i, \bar{f}_2^i) = (200, 200, 0, 0)$ then has a state-1 wealth of $P_{n1}\bar{n}_1^i = 120$ and a state-2 wealth of $P_{n2}\bar{n}_2^i = 80$. Similarly, a type-j individual with endowment $(\bar{n}_1^j, \bar{n}_2^j, \bar{f}_1^j, \bar{f}_2^j) = (0, 0, 400, 160)$ has a state-1 wealth of $P_{f1}\bar{f}_1^j = 120$ and a state-2 wealth of $P_{f2}\bar{f}_2^j = 80$. So, in the absence of any prior-round trading, each individual would be allocating his wealth over states exactly as in the CCM regime. It follows that under the conditions of this example no prior-round trading is necessary to achieve the equilibrium of the NCM regime, which in turn replicates the equilibrium of the CCM regime. □

More generally, however, under the constrained NCM regime individuals will need to trade in both rounds. The next example will illustrate. Note that in this example there are endowment value disparities at CCM prices.

Example 6.4: Holding to the other conditions of example 6.3, assume now the following initial endowments:

Type i : $(\bar{n}_1, \bar{n}_2, \bar{f}_1, \bar{f}_2,) = (0, 90, 280, 160)$
Type j : $(\bar{n}_1, \bar{n}_2, \bar{f}_1, \bar{f}_2,) = (200, 110, 120, 0)$

Note that the individual endowments of commodity N ("nuts") are no longer riskless. However, the social totals of endowed claims are the same as in Examples 6.2 and 6.3 – $(\bar{N}_1, \bar{N}_2, \bar{F}_1, \bar{F}_2,) = (200, 200, 400, 160)$. So the *aggregate* N-endowment remains riskless.

With CCM trading in a *non-informative* situation, the price vector would remain $(P_{n1}, P_{n2}, P_{f1}, P_{f2}) = (0.6, 0.4, 0.3, 0.5)$ as in Example 6.2. Moreover, since the overall wealths are the same as in the previous examples, the CCM equilibrium consumption portfolios must be the same. So, in accordance with the earlier examples, the market value of consumption in state 1 is 1.5 times that in state 2, for both type-i and type-j individuals.

Now consider a NCM regime. Suppose a type-i individual moves in the prior round to a trading portfolio (n_1^{oi}, n_2^{oi}) in N-claims. (Of course, he cannot modify his endowment of F-claims in the prior round.) If the prior-round state-contingent prices of N remain the same as in the CCM regime, then $P_{n1}(n_1^{oi} - \bar{n}_1^i) = P_{n2}(\bar{n}_2^i - n_2^{oi})$, or $0.6\,n_1^{oi} = 0.4(90 - n_2^{oi})$.

Given such a trade, if a type-i individual is to replicate the CCM outcome, his wealth in state 1 must be 1.5 times his wealth in state 2. Thus:

$$\frac{0.6n_1^{oi} + 0.3(280)}{0.4n_2^{oi} + 0.5(160)} = 1.5$$

Solving simultaneously with the preceding equation leads to the type-i individual's trading portfolio:

$$\left(n_1^{oi},\ n_2^{oi},\ \bar{f}_1^i,\ \bar{f}_2^i\right) = (60, 0, 280, 160)$$

For the type-j individual on the other side of this trade, the trading portfolio will be:

$$\left(n_1^{oi},\ n_2^{oi},\ \bar{f}_1^j,\ \bar{f}_2^j\right) = (140, 200, 120, 0)$$

This also meets the condition that wealth in state 1 is 1.5 times wealth in state 2. The NCM therefore once again replicates the results of the CCM regime. However, as this example indicates, if individuals' endowed portfolios differ in such a way that one person's endowment is weighted toward state 1 and the other's toward state 2, prior-round trading under NCM will be required to replicate the CCM equilibrium. □

We can now consider the question of what constitutes a minimally sufficient range of markets to achieve efficiency (continuing to assume, for simplicity, that the emergent information is conclusive). With a CCM regime in the prior round, the range of markets (GS tradable claims) is so ample that no *posterior* trading is needed at all. The NCM regime, in contrast, having provided only the minimally necessary S tradable claims in the prior round, must still generally allow for trading among the G surviving claims in the posterior round.

It might seem from this discussion that CCM in the prior round provides a wastefully "excessive" number of markets in comparison with the minimally sufficient NCM: $SG + G$ in comparison with $S + G$. However, such a conclusion is not really warranted when we take into account the plausibility of the SFP assumption in each of the two regimes. Under CCM, the SFP forecasts are easy to make, being simply "no change." That is, the prediction for any state $\hat{s}$ is that the posterior price ratios will be the same as the corresponding prior contingent-claim price ratios. But, under NCM, even when probability beliefs are agreed, the correct forecasts *are not in general computable from data available to traders in the prior round* (Radner, 1968). Thus, while technically possible, it is really quite implausible that the NCM regime could reproduce the efficient outcomes achievable under CCM.

Absent self-fulfilling predictions under the NCM regime, what would be the actual outcome for the prior-round and posterior-round equilibrium? In our model, we simply cannot say. In contrast with the CCM regime where there is a theoretical basis for predicting the posterior price ratios, under NCM we do not as yet have a theory for forming the required prior expectations as to posterior prices. (This question will be reconsidered when the topic of "rational expectations" is taken up later in the chapter.)

No Prior-Round Markets

What if prior-round markets do not even exist? This corresponds to the case where information arrives before any exchanges at all have taken place, i.e., while the parties are all still at their endowment positions. The clearest instance of such a situation is where the arrival of news is totally "unanticipated."[4]

This situation has aroused considerable interest, in view of the surprising implication that incoming public information could be socially disadvantageous, in the sense that everyone in the economy might be willing to pay something *not* to have the message revealed! Think of a group of traders who, in prior-round trading, would have balanced their risks by mutually insuring one another against fire. If they have not yet done so, a message service offering conclusive but "premature" information as to whose houses would burn down might well be rejected by everyone, even if free. In effect, the arrival of the message before the opening of markets would make it impossible for people to diversify their risks. (On the other hand, if the early arrival of the information permitted more effective *productive* adaptations, for example, protective measures against fire, this socially valuable consequence of timely information must be weighed against the adverse effect upon individuals' ability to spread risks.)

Futures and Spot Markets (F&SM)

The CCM and NCM regimes both allow trading in state-contingent claims. Such trading does take place to some extent in the actual world, directly as in some insurance transactions or indirectly via trading in assets like corporate shares, which can be regarded as packages of state-claims. But most trading represents exchange of *unconditional* commodity claims – rights to receive one or more units of some good regardless of the state of the world. For

---

[4] Note that this interpretation does not refer to the *content* of the news or to the message probability q_m. "Unanticipated" means that no one had expected any message at all to arrive.

such unconditional trading in commodities, the prior-round transactions correspond to dealings in "futures" markets and the posterior exchanges after arrival of the information to dealings in later "spot" markets.

Under such a Futures and Spot Markets (F&SM) regime, it will be assumed, in the prior round futures trading takes place in all the G unconditional claims for the various goods,[5] while the posterior round allows for re-trading of the same claims in spot markets. Since it is reasonable to assume that $G < S$ (there are many more conceivable contingencies than goods), it is evident that the $G + G$ markets in two rounds of trading under F&SM cannot in general achieve the same efficiency as the $S + G$ markets under NCM – not to mention the $GS + G$ markets under CCM.

This negative conclusion is mitigated by two considerations, however. First, since society incurs costs when more markets are provided, the inefficiency due to incompleteness of markets will to some extent be counterbalanced by the savings in transaction costs. And, second, our analysis has been oversimplified in assuming just a single prior and a single posterior round, i.e., that message arrival is a one-time event. More generally, less-than-conclusive bits of information will be emerging repeatedly as time progresses, permitting multiple rounds of trading before the final realization of the state of the world. (These two problems – the efficient number of markets to provide, and the degree to which multiple rounds of markets can overcome market incompleteness in any single round – post formidable intellectual difficulties, which we will not attempt to address here.)

Several important features of the F&SM regime will be clarified in the discussion of *speculation* that follows.

Exercises and Excursions 6.1

1 Trading in Anticipation of Partial Information
Write down the *non-informative* and the *informative* equilibrium conditions if the information provided by the message service is less than conclusive. Can you justify Proposition 6.1 for this case?

2 The Value of Withholding Public Information
Given the endowments and other assumptions of Example 6.1, would individuals of type i or type j be willing to pay something *not* to

---

[5] In actuality, effective futures markets exist only for a small subset of the commodities traded in spot markets.

have the information as to what state of the world will obtain revealed "prematurely" (before prior-round trading)? What about the circumstances of the other text examples?

3 Differences of Belief

In Examples 6.3 and 6.4, individuals had diverging endowments but agreed beliefs. Consequently their motivation to engage in prior-round NCM trading was solely to balance endowment risks over states. Holding to the assumption that they share the same utility function $v(n,f) = \ln(nf)$, suppose now they all have identical nuts-fruit endowments $(\bar{n}_1, \bar{n}_2, \bar{f}_1, \bar{f}_2) = (100, 100, 200, 80)$ but their probability beliefs diverge. In particular, let type-i individuals attach probability 0.5 to state 1 while type-j individuals attach probability 0.6 to that state. So the parties, if they trade at all in the prior round, do so only in order to reflect their differing beliefs as to the likelihood of the two states.

Maintaining the other assumptions of the text examples, would the *posterior*-round prices remain the same as before? What prior-round NCM trading, if any, will take place? Will each individual still be attempting to equalize contingent posterior wealths over states?[6]

6.2 Speculation and Futures Trading

Up to this point we have assumed that individuals merely *adapt* to present and predicted future prices in choosing utility-maximizing consumption portfolios. In some cases, however, individuals can do even better, or at least might believe they can do so, by adopting *speculative* trading positions before emergence of the anticipated public information.

The theory of speculation has been subject to considerable controversy. One of the difficulties is that some authors use the term "speculation" for what is really *arbitrage* – that is, commitments taking advantage of momentary price differentials over space or time, under conditions of market disequilibrium. Consider, for example, the debate over the question "Does speculation tend to stabilize prices?" A premise underlying much of this debate is that prices are initially moving along some arbitrarily specified price path, e.g., a sine curve, before speculators enter. According to one side

---

[6] In this question we assume that an individual does not change his beliefs after observing the trading behavior of others (in prior rounds). However, it is conceivable that an individual who initially believes that state s is much more likely than state $\hat{s}$ may revise this belief after observing others sell state s contingent goods and buy state $\hat{s}$. We shall consider this possibility in Section 6.4.

of the debate, speculators will buy when the price is *low* and sell when it is high, thus tending to smooth out the sine wave. Alternatively, it might be postulated that they buy when the price path is *rising* and sell when it is falling, in which case the effect could be to increase the amplitude of the price fluctuations.[7]

But where does the initial price path, postulated by both sides of the debate, come from? It seems to represent an arbitrary transient pattern without any basis in economic fundamentals. In terms of the comparative-statics *equilibrium* approach employed in our analysis throughout, an initial price path can never come out of thin air. Any time-pattern of prices must be the resultant of underlying economic fundamentals, of supply-demand forces. One possibility might be seasonal variation of supply. If the sine wave represents a continuous moving equilibrium of prices as supply varies over the annual cycle, there is no basis for speculators to enter the market at all – either to smooth or to amplify the price fluctuations. Thus the price path postulated in this debate, a "bubble" that does not reflect any economic fundamentals, may generate *arbitrage* opportunities, but these must not be confused with speculative commitments in an equilibrium model.

A second type of error is to confuse speculation with storage over time or carriage over space. Storage and transportation are productive processes, whereas speculation is purely an exchange activity.[8] A party engaged in production might sometimes also want to take a speculative position, but the two activities are not the same.

For our purposes, speculation is purchase with the intention of re-sale or sale with the intent of re-purchase – where the uncertainty of the later spot price is the source of possible gain or loss. An F&SM regime will be assumed, the two rounds of trading being separated by the anticipated arrival of new public information. Thus speculation is trading in the prior round (in "futures markets"), with a view to re-trading in the posterior round (in subsequent "spot markets"). However, it turns out that distinguishing the speculative motive proper from other possible reasons for engaging in futures trading raises some subtle issues that are not dealt with here. Our emphasis will be on the determinants of *participation in futures markets* generally.[9]

---

[7] See, for example, Friedman (1960) and Baumol (1957).

[8] In the former Soviet Union, newspapers used to report the imposition of jail sentences for the crime of "speculation." In most cases, it appears, these illegal activities were forms of production: carrying goods over time or distance, or breaking bulk, to the advantage of the final consumers.

[9] The analysis that follows is based in part upon Hirshleifer (1977).

In an F&SM regime, on the basis of their beliefs as to what the incoming message is going to reveal, in the prior round of trading individuals exchange unconditional claims to commodities $g = 1, \ldots, G$ in order to arrive at optimal *trading portfolios*. This prior trading is associated with and determines a set of equilibrium futures prices P_g^o. (Notice that, while decision makers engaging in prior trading necessarily have beliefs about what the later spot prices are going to be, such traders are not envisaging a single arbitrary initial price path. Rather, in an uncertain world they must contemplate *alternative* contingent price paths, each such pattern being the consequence of the supply/demand fundamentals characterizing one of the possible states of the world.) After arrival of the anticipated message, the parties revise their beliefs and then possibly engage in further posterior exchanges in the spot markets in order to arrive at their final *consumption portfolios*. This posterior trading will, of course, determine the vector of equilibrium posterior-round or spot prices P_g^I.

The best-known theory of futures markets is due to Keynes (1930) and Hicks (1946), who emphasized the *price risk* faced by economic agents and their *differential risk aversion* with regard to bearing that risk. In the prior round (futures trading), they argued, relatively risk-tolerant "speculators" enter to accept the price risk that relatively risk-averse "hedgers" want to divest. For example, a grower of wheat does not know whether the ultimate spot price of wheat will be high or low. So he hedges his price risk by selling his crop today in the futures market, realizing a known futures price from a speculator. Technically, the speculator takes a "long" position in the futures market, while the grower goes "short" in futures (though, of course, he is "long" the underlying good). Assuming normal risk aversion, the Keynes-Hicks analysis implies that over time speculators will benefit from a mean positive excess of spot price over futures price – so-called "normal backwardation" – as their reward for bearing the price risk.

Controversy persists as to whether or not the statistical evidence confirms the presence of normal backwardation. Later researchers in the Keynes-Hicks tradition have, however, brought out that hedgers can in principle be on either side of the futures market. Instead of a grower, consider a miller facing an uncertain purchase price for wheat. To hedge his price risk, a miller would *buy* futures (take a long position). Then speculators need bear only the imbalance between the commitments of "short hedgers" and "long hedgers." Since this imbalance could go either way, the risk-compensating average price movement between futures and spot markets could similarly go either way.

On the other hand, in fundamental opposition to the Keynes-Hicks tradition, Holbrook Working (1953, 1962) denied that there need be any systematic difference as to risk tolerance between so-called speculators and hedgers, or even that these categories could be strictly distinguished at all. In Working's view, *differences of belief* rather than *differences in risk tolerance* are the primary motivators of futures trading.

Both of these elements, risk transfer and belief differences, may play a role in futures trading, though sometimes interacting in rather unexpected ways. In addition, there are at least two other crucially important factors: *divergences in endowments* and the *elasticity of demand* for the final product.

As a crucial analytical point, the Keynes-Hicks tradition is seriously in error in its sole concentration upon the risk of price fluctuations. For the economy as a whole, the ultimate source of risk is, mainly, the stochastic variability of supply under alternative states of the world. Turning to the individual agents, it follows that their trading decisions will generally be governed by *quantity risk* (the variability of crops in the different states of the world) as well as by *price risk* (the corresponding variability of crop prices) (McKinnon, 1967). Indeed, it is evident that price risk is for the most part only a derivative consequence of the underlying uncertainty as to the actual supply quantity (whether the crop will be good or bad).[10] Furthermore, for the economy as a whole, price and quantity risks always tend to be offsetting. For example, when the crop of a representative wheat-grower is big (good news), the wheat price he receives will be low (bad news). As a result, a grower with an endowed quantity risk might well find it preferable *not* to hedge in the futures market against the offsetting price risk.

Analytically, the crucial differences among the CCM, NCM, and F&SM regimes are reflected in the prior-round individual budget constraints. As before, we let superscript o signify prior-round quantities (elements of the "trading portfolio") or prices, and the budget equations take the respective forms:

PRIOR-ROUND BUDGET CONSTRAINTS

$$\sum_g \sum_s P_{gs}^o c_{gs}^{oi} = \sum_g \sum_s P_{gs}^o \bar{c}_{gs}^i \qquad \text{CCM}$$

[10] Of course, price risk could also reflect uncertainties on the demand side, e.g., whether or not consumers' tastes are shifting away from wheat bread.

$$\sum_s P^o_{1s} c^{oi}_{1s} = \sum_s P^o_{1s} \bar{c}^{-i}_{1s} \qquad \text{NCM } (g = 1 \text{ is numeraire})$$

$$\sum_g P^o_g g^{oi} = 0 \qquad \text{F\&SM}$$

In the F&SM equation, g^{oi} represents the quantity of good g *purchased* by individual i in the prior round (or *sold*, if $g^{oi} < 0$), this amount being the same regardless of state of the world. Thus, for each and every state:

$$c^{oi}_{gs} \equiv \bar{c}^i_{gs} + g^{oi}$$

In contrast with (6.1.2) or (6.1.2') for the CCM regime, the F&SM optimality conditions reduce to the $G - 1$ equations:

$$\frac{\sum_s \pi^i_s \partial v_i \left(c^i_{1s}, \dots, c^i_{Gs} \right) / \partial c^{oi}_{gs}}{\sum_s \pi^i_s \partial v_i \left(c^i_{1s}, \dots, c^i_{Gs} \right) / \partial c^{oi}_{\hat{g}s}} = \frac{P^o_g}{P^o_{\hat{g}}}$$

Example 6.5: Returning again to the conditions of Example 6.3, assume now an F&SM regime. That is, individuals are permitted to exchange only certainty claims to commodities. Given an informative situation in such a world, the individuals of type j, with endowment $(\bar{f}_1, \bar{f}_2) = (400, 160)$ – suppliers of "fruit" F – face both quantity risk and price risk. However, since the fruit price will be high when the fruit quantity they have available to sell is small, and vice versa, these risks are more or less offsetting. The type-i individuals with riskless "nuts" endowment $(\bar{n}_1, \bar{n}_2) = (200, 200)$ face no quantity risk but still have price risk, since the posterior price ratio of nuts versus fruit will depend upon which state ultimately obtains.

Just as for the NCM regime of Example 6.3, here also the F&SM equilibrium involves zero prior-round trading – in this case, zero trading of certainty commodity claims (futures) rather than of contingent numeraire claims. The logic is very similar. As before, given the homothetic utility function $v(n\ f) = \ln\ (nf)$, the posterior-round equilibrium price ratios (which are also the correct SFP forecasts for guiding prior-round trading decisions) are $P^I_{f1}/P^I_{n1} = 0.5$ and $P^I_{f2}/P^I_{n2} = 1.25$ for the two possible posterior states of the world. Since the parties already have state-balanced endowment distributions, if they refrain from trading in the prior (futures) round they will, in posterior-round (spot) trading, be able to achieve the same consumption portfolios as under CCM in Example 6.2. Specifically, i and j can both achieve $(n_1, n_2, f_1, f_2) = (100, 100, 200, 80)$. Thus, in this case again a restricted trading regime leads everyone to the same efficient final consumption portfolios as the efficient CCM regime.

Of course, for this to come about the prior-round (futures) price ratio between fruit and nuts will have to be such that neither party wants to trade. It turns out that this equilibrium price ratio (where supply and demand are equal at zero trading) is $P_f^o/P_n^o = 0.8$ – or, letting N be the numeraire so that $P_n^o = 1$, then $P_f^o = 0.8$ is the equilibrium futures price of the risky commodity F. Why? Recall that, in the CCM regime of Example 6.2, the prior-round prices were $(P_{n1}^o, P_{n2}^o, P_{f1}^o, P_{f2}^o) = (0.6, 0.4, 0.3, 0.5)$. Thus a certainty claim to nuts could be bought or sold for $P_{n1}^o + P_{n2}^o = 0.6 + 0.4 = 1.0$, while a certainty claim to fruit could be bought or sold for $P_{f1}^o + P_{f2}^o = 0.3 + 0.5 = 0.8$. Since the prior-round price ratio $(P_{f1}^o + P_{f2}^o)/(P_{n1}^o + P_{n2}^o) = 0.8$ supported a no-trading prior-round equilibrium even when the very ample CCM trading regime was available, the same price ratio will also be consistent with zero prior-round ("futures") trading in the less complete F&SM regime. ☐

The possibly puzzling feature of this example, that a no-prior trading result is achieved even though the F&SM regime is not in general minimally sufficient to replicate the efficient solution of a CCM regime, calls for further comment. Note that, while the F&SM regime provides only $G + G$ markets whereas the minimally sufficient NCM provides $S + G$ markets, in our numerical examples $G = S = 2$. Thus, in the situation of the example (but not in general) even the F&SM regime was minimally complete. Had we considered, say, an example with two goods but three states of the world, then even under the SFP assumption it would not have been generally possible to achieve the efficient CCM portfolios under F&SM.

While Example 6.5 is a special case, it demonstrates that the presence of price risks on one or both sides of the market need not dictate futures trading. For the suppliers of the risky commodity F in this example, the price risks and quantity risks are exactly offsetting, the actual revenue (in numeraire units) from sales being the same in either state: $200 \times 0.5 = 100 = 80 \times 1.25$. Put another way, the postulated preference functions implied an aggregate demand curve for "fruit" with unitary elasticity. Thus, there is price risk and quantity risk, but the two offset so as to eliminate all *revenue* risk.

The general-equilibrium model described above is unrealistic in a number of significant respects. A more realistic model, making use of some strategic simplifications that correspond to known features of actual markets, would cast additional light upon the forces governing futures-market participation. In the actual world, some (in fact, the overwhelming majority of) potential traders are effectively excluded from futures markets by *transaction costs*. In this respect, there is a crucial asymmetry between the situations of typical consumers and typical suppliers of goods. Suppliers tend to be specialized in producing some particular commodity, while consumers generally are rather diversified purchasers of a great many commodities. Transaction costs with a substantial fixed component, independent of the size of transaction,[11] will therefore deter the smaller-scale futures trading of consumers more than the larger-scale futures trading of suppliers. This fact may open up a niche for speculators, to compensate for the absence of consumers on the demand side of futures markets. A model that incorporates these features may be found in Hirshleifer (1990).

Exercises and Excursions 6.2

1 Futures Trading

Suppose Example 6.5 is modified so that type-i individuals have endowments $(n_1, n_2, f_1, f_2) = (0, 150, 200, 160)$ while type-j individuals have endowments $(n_1, n_2, f_1, f_2) = (200, 50, 200, 0)$.

(A) Confirm that, in a CCM regime, final consumption will be exactly as in Examples 6.2 and 6.5.

(B) Suppose that the futures (prior-round) price of fruit is 0.8 in terms of nuts as numeraire ($P_f^o = 0.8$ and $P_n^o = 1$). Confirm that, if a type-i buyer purchases $800/3$ units of nuts on the futures market and sells $1000/3$ units of fruit, his budget constraints in the spot market after the information is revealed are:

state 1: $0.3f + 0.6n = 120$
state 2: $0.5f + 0.4n = 80$

(C) Hence, or otherwise, confirm that such trades are equilibrium trades.

(D) How can it be feasible for a type-i buyer to sell an amount on the futures market which exceeds his endowment in any state?

2 The Martingale Property of Prices

In Example 6.5, the prior-round equilibrium price ratio P_f^o/P_n^o is the *mathematical expectation* of the posterior ratios P_{fs}^1/P_{ns}^1 – specifically here, $0.8 = 0.6 (0.5) + 0.4 (1.25)$. (This is sometimes called the "martingale" property

---

[11] Even if explicit brokerage charges are strictly proportional to volume, the costs of learning and of establishing trading connections will necessarily have a large fixed component.

of prices.) Would you expect the martingale property to hold generally? In particular, maintaining the conditions of this example except for letting the utility function take a different form, would the martingale property remain valid? Also, what would happen if the numerators and denominators were interchanged in the price ratios?

6.3 The Production and Dissemination of Information

According to the traditional analysis,[12] already produced information is a "public good"; it can be made concurrently available to any and all members of the community. If so, it is sometimes said, any barriers to use, for example, patents or copyrights or property in trade secrets, are inefficient. On the other hand, if researchers cannot gain property rights in their discoveries, there may be inadequate motivation to invest in the production of information.

In principle at least, there is an efficient solution to these two problems. *First*, the motivation to produce new ideas would be optimal if the discoverer could be granted a perfectly enforced, perpetual, and exclusive right to his discovery. And, *second*, there would be no hampering of efficient use if the owner of the property right could establish a profit-maximizing perfectly-discriminating fee schedule, since on the margin the optimal fee would be zero. But in actuality owners of copyrights or patents cannot impose perfectly discriminating royalty fee structures (or their equivalent in terms of lump-sum charges), hence some loss of efficiency in this regard is bound to occur. On the other side of the picture, property rights in ideas can never be perfectly defined or enforced. So the legal protection of patents and copyrights is inevitably incomplete, and that of trade secrets not covered by patents or copyrights is even more deficient.

In practice, there is something of a trade-off: greater legal protection to discoverers will ameliorate the underproduction problem, but tend to aggravate the underutilization problem.[13] Thus, the traditional analysis suggests, current legal arrangements – patents, copyrights, and protection of trade secrets that amount to only imperfect and partially effective property

[12] See, for example, Arrow (1962) and Machlup (1968).
[13] There are exceptions to this generalization. Suppose that stronger legal enforcement leads some consumers to shift from unauthorized use (copying) to licensed use. There is likely to be an efficiency gain, since the cost of illegal copying of ideas is generally greater than the social cost of extending licensed use. Note that in this case the *extent* of utilization of the information may be unaffected, but a lower-cost is substituted for a higher-cost *mode* of utilization (see Novos and Waldman, 1987).

Table 6.1. *Forces affecting inventive activity*

Tending to induce underinvestment
Public good effect: Free riders can reap benefits.
Tending to induce overinvestment
Commons effect: Entrants receive average product (>marginal product) of inventive activity.
Speculative effect: Private benefit of invention is, in part, merely redistributive

rights in ideas – may constitute a defensible compromise between the two competing goals.

This analysis does not capture all the important elements of the picture. In contrast with the "public good effect" that discourages investment in research and invention, there are pressures tending to induce *over* investment in the production of ideas. As indicated in Table 6.1, two main forces are involved. First, undiscovered knowledge is a common-property resource; entry into such a commons tends to continue so long as the *average* yield (rather than, as efficiency dictates, the *marginal* yield) is remunerative.[14] This might be called the "commons effect." Second, even if the information itself is of little or no socially productive significance, it may have private value as a means of transferring wealth from uninformed to informed traders. This will be called the "speculative effect."[15]

In sum, a divergence between an individual's private benefit from inventive activity and social surplus of inventive activity leads to overinvestment or underinvestment. If the private benefit is less than social surplus, then there is underinvestment in inventive activity, and if the private benefit exceeds social surplus, there is overinvestment.

6.3.1 Private Information and the Leakage Problem

Let us now shift attention to unintended dissemination of private information – the problem of leakage. There are two main ways in which information, produced or acquired at some cost, may leak out. "Direct leakage" occurs if, for example, the valuable secret is disclosed by mistake or, alternatively, is uncovered through industrial espionage. "Market leakage" occurs when the very attempt to exploit a discovery, through dealings with other

---

[14] Barzel (1968).
[15] Fama and Laffer (1971); Hirshleifer (1971). See also Bergemann and Valimaki (2002), which is discussed in Chapter 12.

parties, necessarily entails some degree of disclosure. As soon as a new product embodying a discovery is offered to consumers, for example, competitors may start trying to uncover the secret through reverse engineering.[16] Quite a different form of market leakage will be the center of attention here, however: the possibility that attempting to profit from a discovery may allow free-riders to infer the content of the message *from the impact upon price itself.*

Previously (see Section 5.3) we have assumed that individuals have divergent beliefs as to the likelihood of the possible states of the world, but the *sources* of divergent beliefs were left unexplained. In contrast, here we will be assuming that, while everyone has identical prior beliefs, some parties may have invested in a message service allowing Bayesian updating – for example, a private weather-forecasting service. The informed individuals thus gain an advantage, though, of course, generally at some cost. (We will also initially assume that everyone knows that this is the case, a "common knowledge" assumption to be reconsidered later.) Suppose purchasers of information attempt to profit therefrom by taking a long or short position in crop futures. Then the other parties might to a greater or lesser extent be able to infer the content of the hidden message by observing the movement of futures prices.[17] (This is one more instance of the "public good effect" that tends to reduce the incentive to acquire private information. Conversely, to the extent that such leakage occurs, the "speculative effect" that operates to induce overinvestment in information will be weakened or even eliminated.)

In the interests of simplicity, let us rule out possible monopoly power over price. All traders, informed and uninformed, treat price as parametric. Thus, we can assume, everyone will be submitting a personal excess-demand schedule to a hypothetical auctioneer whose function is to aggregate these and thereby determine the market-clearing equilibrium price.

To illustrate, suppose all individuals have the same utility function $v(c_s) = \ln(c_s)$. There are two states of the world, 1 and 2 (say, no rain versus rain). Each individual initially believes that the probability of state 1 is $\bar{\pi}$. Individual j may be uninformed ($j = U$) or informed ($j = I$).

Initially, suppose the situation is non-informative (as defined in Section 6.1), so that all individuals are uninformed. Assuming a regime of Complete

---

[16] Copyright and patent laws aim at controlling unauthorized use of such disclosures, but, of course, can never do so perfectly.

[17] Grossman and Stiglitz (1976, 1980).

Contingent Markets (CCM), each trader will be choosing a portfolio to satisfy the Fundamental Theorem of Risk Bearing:

$$\frac{\bar{\pi} v'\left(c_1^j\right)}{\bar{P}_1} = \frac{(1 - \bar{\pi})v'\left(c_2^j\right)}{\bar{P}_2}$$

where $\bar{P}_1$ and $\bar{P}_2$ signify the state-claim prices for the non-informative situation.

Given the assumed form of the $v(c)$ function, the marginal utilities are:

$$v'\left(c_1^j\right) = 1/c_1^j \quad \text{and} \quad v'\left(c_2^j\right) = 1/c_2^j$$

So the Fundamental Theorem implies that:

$$\frac{\bar{\pi}}{\bar{P}_1 c_1^j} = \frac{1 - \bar{\pi}}{\bar{P}_2 c_2^j} = \frac{1}{W^j}$$

where the individual's wealth W^j is the value of his endowment:

$$W^j \equiv \bar{P}_1 \bar{c}_1^j + \bar{P}_2 \bar{c}_2^j$$

Therefore the individual state-contingent demands can be written:

$$c_1^j = \frac{\bar{\pi}}{\bar{P}_1} W^j \quad \text{and} \quad c_2^j = \frac{1 - \bar{\pi}}{\bar{P}_2} W^j$$

Summing over all individuals, the aggregate demands are:

$$C_1 = \frac{\bar{\pi}}{\bar{P}_1}(\bar{P}_1 \bar{C}_1 + \bar{P}_2 \bar{C}_2) \quad \text{and} \quad C_2 = \frac{1 - \bar{\pi}}{\bar{P}_2}(\bar{P}_1 \bar{C}_1 + \bar{P}_2 \bar{C}_2) \quad (6.3.1)$$

where $\bar{C}_1$ and $\bar{C}_2$ are the aggregate endowments. These are the supply-demand conditions determining the price ratio $\bar{P}_2/\bar{P}_1$ *for the non-informative case.*[18]

Aggregate Demand of Informed Traders (Speculative Behavior Excluded)
Now we want to consider an informative situation. Specifically, suppose that at a cost (in utility units) of Δ in each state,[19] an individual may purchase

---

[18] Actually, an even simpler result holds here:

$$\frac{\bar{P}_2}{\bar{P}_1} = \frac{\bar{\pi}}{1 - \pi} \frac{\bar{C}_1}{\bar{C}_2}$$

However, the more general form of (6.3.1) is needed later to determine the composite effect of informed and uninformed groups upon the price ratio P_2/P_1.

[19] A fixed cost in utility units is actually a rather unreasonable assumption. Given different consumption levels in different states, a fixed cost in corn units would imply cost in utility

a message service whose output will change $\bar{\pi}$, his prior assessment of the probability of state 1, to some posterior assessment π. Defining $f(\pi)$ to the probability density of the message π, we require:

$$E[\pi] = \int_0^1 \pi f(\pi)d\pi = \bar{\pi}$$

An informed individual then has expected utility:

$$U^1(c^1) = \pi \ln c_1^I + (1 - \pi) \ln c_2^I - \Delta$$

Given the output of his message service, an informed individual can use his superior information simply to choose an improved final consumption portfolio in the light of his changed beliefs and the existing market prices. Alternatively, as explained in Section 6.2, in some circumstances an informed individual may be in a position to *speculate*, that is, to hold a trading portfolio (or futures position) so as to profit from the prospective changes in market prices when his private information becomes public later. For simplicity here, we exclude speculative behavior.

Then, by the same reasoning as before, the informed individuals' demands are:

$$c_1^I = \frac{\pi}{P_1}\left(P_1\bar{c}_1^I + P_2\bar{c}_2^I\right) \quad \text{and} \quad c_2^I = \frac{1 - \pi}{P_2}\left(P_1\bar{c}_1^I + P_2\bar{c}_2^I\right)$$

Of course, the price ratio P_2/P_1 will now in general diverge from the $\bar{P}_2/\bar{P}_1$ of the non-informative situation.

Suppose that the informed individuals begin with a given fraction f of each of the aggregate state endowments $(\bar{C}_1, \bar{C}_2)$. (Ultimately, f will be an endogenous variable to be determined, but for the moment let us take it as given.) Then, summing over the informed individuals' demands:

$$C_1^I = \frac{\pi}{P_1}f\left(P_1\bar{C}_1 + P_2\bar{C}_2\right) \quad \text{and} \quad C_2^I = \frac{1 - \pi}{P_2}f\left(P_1\bar{C}_1 + P_2\bar{C}_2\right)$$

Aggregate Demands of Uninformed Traders (Naive Behavior Assumed)
Exactly the same argument can be applied to the uninformed traders, with endowment equal to the fraction $1 - f$ of the aggregate endowment, on the supposition that these individuals behave "naively." That is, they simply adapt to the ruling market prices in the light of their prior beliefs $\bar{\pi}$ and do *not* attempt to infer the true π from the movement of price itself. By a

units varying from state to state. The assumption is adopted here solely for reasons of tractability.

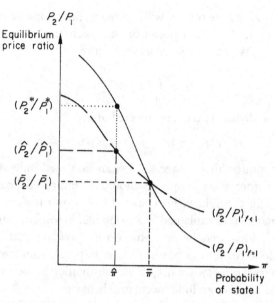

Figure 6.1. Price ratio as a function of informed individuals' message.

parallel argument, the aggregate demands C_1^U of naive uninformed traders in an informative situation will be:

$$C_1^U = \frac{\bar{\pi}}{P_1}(1 - f)\left(P_1\bar{C}_1 + P_2\bar{C}_2\right) \quad \text{and}$$

$$C_2^U = \frac{1 - \bar{\pi}}{P_2}(1 - f)\left(P_1\bar{C}_1 + P_2\bar{C}_2\right)$$

Summing over the two groups:

$$C_1 = \frac{\pi f + \bar{\pi}(1 - f)}{P_1}\left(P_1\bar{C}_1 + P_2\bar{C}_2\right) \quad \text{and}$$

$$C_2 = \frac{(1 - \pi)f + (1 - \bar{\pi})(1 - f)}{P_2}\left(P_1\bar{C}_1 + P_2\bar{C}_2\right) \qquad (6.3.2)$$

In equilibrium, supply equals demand. Then setting $C_s = \bar{C}_s$, $s = 1, 2$ in (6.3.2), we obtain at last:

$$\frac{P_2}{P_1} = \frac{\bar{C}_1}{\bar{C}_2}\frac{(1 - \pi)f + (1 - \bar{\pi})(1 - f)}{\pi f + \bar{\pi}(1 - f)} \qquad (6.3.3)$$

Notice that, for all $f > 0$, as π increases, the numerator on the right-hand side falls while the denominator increases. So, as depicted in Figure 6.1, the equilibrium price ratio P_2/P_1 is a decreasing function of π, the informed individuals' posterior belief that state 1 will occur. This is, of course, what we would expect. The higher is the π implied by the message received by the informed individuals, the greater will be their demands (at any given price ratio) for state-1 claims. (For naive uninformed individuals, of course, the demands remain unaffected.) Thus, a high π implies a low ratio P_2/P_1.

In addition, the equation indicates that P_2/P_1 is increasing in f if and only if $\pi < \bar{\pi}$. More generally, the larger is f, the steeper will be the curve relating P_2/P_1 to π. In other words, the larger the fraction informed, the more sensitive will be the equilibrium price ratio to any divergence of the message π from the prior belief $\bar{\pi}$.

Uninformed Traders – From Naive to Sophisticated Behavior
In the absence of any information gathering (when $f = 0$), the equilibrium price ratio would be $\bar{P}_2/\bar{P}_1$. But, when others are informed about the true probabilities, the uninformed find themselves using the "wrong" beliefs and so at a disadvantage in trading. Ideally, if it were possible to identify the informed individuals, the uninformed should refuse to trade with them; the uninformed group should open a separate market and engage in risk balancing by trading only among themselves, at the equilibrium price ratio $\bar{P}_2/\bar{P}_1$. However, this is generally infeasible. It is difficult or impossible to know whether your trading partner is informed or uninformed, nor can the uninformed parties know *ex ante* what the $\bar{P}_2/\bar{P}_1$ price ratio would have been in the absence of information-gathering activity. So an uninformed individual who engages in trade at all must expect, to some extent, to be dealing at a disadvantage with informed individuals. This disadvantage could be so great that it would be strictly better to withdraw from the market entirely, even though doing so means foregoing the opportunity to balance risks via market trading. Consider the extreme case in which the uninformed all have identical endowments and preferences. Then, in the absence of the informed parties, no trading would take place; the equilibrium prices would be such as to sustain the initial endowment positions. Knowing this, in the presence of informed parties, the uninformed would indeed do better by refusing to trade.

But the uninformed parties have another recourse: they do not have to behave naively. Suppose that the revised state-1 probability for the informed individuals is $\hat{\pi}$. If the fraction informed is some $f < 1$, and the uninformed behave naively as before (use their prior beliefs to trade), the equilibrium price ratio would be some $\hat{P}_2/\hat{P}_1$ as depicted in Figure 6.1. However, if the uninformed understand the model and if they also know f, they might

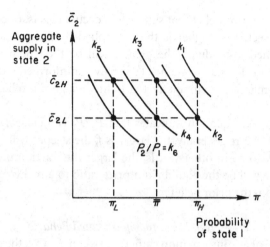

Figure 6.2. Iso-price contours with information and aggregate endowment uncertain.

be able to infer the message $\hat{\pi}$ from the price ratio $\hat{P}_2/\hat{P}_1$.[20] Given such an inference, the fraction informed will rise to unity, and so the equilibrium price ratio rises to P_2^*/P_1^*. But then the uninformed are better off than the informed, not having incurred the utility cost Δ of gaining access to the information!

It is tempting to think that this result follows from the simplicity of the example. However, as Radner (1979) has shown, even if individuals have differing preferences and endowments and there are an arbitrarily large but finite number of states of nature, the information of the informed agents can be inferred from market prices almost certainly.

Radner's argument can be illustrated by a small modification of the example. Suppose that the aggregate endowment in the rainy state $\bar{C}_2$ is itself uncertain. Initially, suppose that all but a negligible fraction of the individuals have become informed and have the posterior probability π. The equilibrium price ratio is then given by (6.3.3), with $f = 1$:

$$\frac{P_2}{P_1} = \frac{\bar{C}_1}{\bar{C}_2}\frac{(1-\pi)}{\pi}$$

Note that this is decreasing in both π and $\bar{C}_2$. Equilibrium price-ratio contours as functions of $\bar{C}_2$ and π are drawn in Figure 6.2. Suppose, as

---

[20] This would be true only under rather extreme assumptions, however. Such computations require knowledge not only of the market-clearing price ratio but also of the entire function $(P_2/P_1)_{f<1}$. We comment on this further below.

depicted, that π can take on three possible values π_L, $\bar{\pi}$, and π_H while $\bar{C}_2$ can take on two possible values $\bar{C}_{2L}$ and $\bar{C}_{2H}$. These generate six possible equilibrium price ratios $k_1, k_2, \ldots, k_6$, where $k_1 < k_2 < \cdots < k_6$, depicted in Figure 6.2. While it would be possible for one of the iso-price contours to go through more than one of the six points, this is an event with zero probability if the parameters are drawn from some underlying continuous probability distribution. Thus, any of the few uninformed individuals can correctly infer π from equilibrium prices. The equilibrium itself may be arrived at through a price-adjustment process facilitated by a Walrasian auctioneer.

Next, suppose that only a fraction f of the population are informed and that they have learned that $\pi = \pi_H$. Suppose, furthermore, that the auction-eer starts out with a price ratio of $P_2/P_1 = k_4$; that is, a ratio consistent with the beliefs of the uninformed. Finally, suppose that the actual aggregate supply is $\bar{C}_{2H}$. In each round of the Walrasian auction, an informed individual submits his true demand, conditional upon the information that he receives. An uninformed individual always bases his beliefs on the hypothesis that the auctioneer has called out the equilibrium price. It follows that in the initial round, the informed will generate an excess supply of state-2 claims, since $\pi = \pi_H$. In response, the auctioneer lowers the price ratio to $P_2/P_1 = k_2$. The uninformed then conclude that $\pi = \pi_H$. However, again, there is excess supply of state-2 claims. The auctioneer then lowers the relative price again to $P_2/P_1 = k_1$ and both markets clear. It follows that all information is revealed via the Walrasian auctioneer.

While we have only examined an example, the underlying conclusion is quite general. Let m_j be the message received by individual j from his information service and let $P(m) = P(m_1, \ldots, m_n)$ be the equilibrium price vector if *every* individual in the economy is provided with all the available information $(m_1, \ldots, m_n)$. If there is a finite number of states and messages, then with probability 1:

$$m' \neq m'' \Rightarrow P(m') \neq P(m'')$$

It follows that, just as in the example, all information is revealed in a Walrasian equilibrium with perfect inference by every agent.

The "generic" existence of a fully revealing equilibrium price raises a disturbing puzzle, as has been seen. If the uninformed behave in a sophisti-cated rather than naive manner, they can infer messages without incurring the cost of purchasing an information service. As a result, no one has an incentive to become informed.

But the puzzle is really an artifact of the assumption that uninformed individuals can make essentially perfect inferences from market prices. Consider instead the limiting case of a continuous distribution of aggregate endowment in state 2 (rain) and a continuous distribution of beliefs (informative messages). Then all the points on an iso-price contour are feasible and so any inference by an uninformed individual would remain incomplete. He could update his beliefs by observing prices but would not be able to perfectly infer the message π. Information leakage is therefore only *partial*; the incentive to invest in information is reduced but not eliminated.

What should be made of the difference between the strong leakage result for the discrete case and the more reasonable partial leakage result for the continuous case? The answer is that, with a large finite set of unpriced states (a large number of dots in Figure 6.2), the price contour through any one pair $(\pi, \bar{C}_2)$ will pass very close to other pairs. Then, unless the uninformed outsider has access to a high-speed computer, a perfectly accurate model of the economy, and an enormous amount of data, he will be unable to infer the insiders' information with any great accuracy. And, in fact, some of the data required are essentially unknowable, being the demand functions of other individuals at price ratios other than those visible in current market trading.

In view of all these limitations, the leakage effect is, realistically speaking, normally rather less important than might initially have appeared.

Exercises and Excursions 6.3.1

1 Fully Revealing Contingent-Claim Prices
Consider an economy in which all individuals have the same utility function $v(c) = \ln c$. There are two states, $s = 1, 2$. Individuals in group ω believe that the probability of state 1 is π^ω. The aggregate endowment of the group is $(\bar{C}_1^\omega, \bar{C}_2^\omega)$.

(A) Show that, if the price of state-s claims is P_s, the group's total demand for state-1 claims is:

$$C_1^\omega = \pi^\omega \left[\bar{C}_1^\omega + (P_2/P_1)\bar{C}_2^\omega \right]$$

(B) Suppose that there are two groups, $\omega = U, I$. Show that the equilibrium price ratio is:

$$\frac{P_2}{P_1} = \frac{(1 - \pi^U)\,\bar{C}_1^U + (1 - \pi^I)\bar{C}_1^I}{\pi^U \bar{C}_2^U + \pi^I \bar{C}_2^I}$$

(C) Suppose group I is the informed group; members of this group receive a message that results in the revised state-1 probability π^I. Confirm that, if the uninformed group behave naively, the information of the informed is fully reflected in the equilibrium price ratio.

(D) Suppose each member of the informed group sacrifices δ_1 units of state-1 claims and δ_2 units of state-2 claims to obtain the information. Is it still the case that information is fully reflected in the equilibrium price ratio?

2 Fully Revealing Asset Prices

Using the data of the previous exercise, suppose that individuals trade in asset markets rather than in state-claim markets. Asset 1, the riskless asset, yields 1 unit of income in each state. Asset 2 yields z_{2s} units in state s, for $s = 1, 2$.

(A) Obtain an expression for the equilibrium ratio of asset prices.
(B) Hence, or otherwise, confirm that again the informed traders' information is fully revealed by the price ratio.

3 Information Leakage with More than One Informed Group

Using the data of Exercise 1, suppose that there are two informed groups. Group A receives a message that results in the revised state-1 probability π^A, while group B's message leads to π^B.

(A) Obtain an expression for the equilibrium ratio of state-claim prices P_2/P_1.
(B) If there are a finite number of messages and hence a finite number of pairs (π^A, π^B), explain why, with probability 1, the beliefs of both informed groups will be fully reflected in market prices.
(C) Explain why your conclusion is not dependent upon the specific assumptions of the model *except* that the number of messages is finite.

6.3.2 Partial Leakage with Constant Absolute Risk Aversion[*]

Without making very strong assumptions, it is extremely difficult to model partial leakage of information from informed to uninformed individuals. However, there is one special case in which strong results are obtainable.

---

[*] Starred sections represent more difficult or specialized materials that can be omitted without significant loss of continuity.

Suppose each of n individuals exhibits constant absolute risk aversion (CARA). These individuals have initial endowments of a riskless asset, each unit of which yields one unit of consumption, and also a risky asset with gross yield $\tilde{R}$ that is normally distributed. Let individual i's endowment of the two assets be $(\bar{q}_{1i}, \bar{q}_{2i})$ and his final portfolio be (q_{1i}, q_{2i}). If the price of the unit of the risky asset is P and the price of the riskless asset is normalized to be 1, individual i's budget constraints and final consumption are:

$$q_{1i} + Pq_{2i} = \bar{q}_{1i} + P\bar{q}_{2i} \quad \text{and} \quad \tilde{c}_i = q_{1i} + q_{2i}\tilde{R}$$

Substituting for q_{1i}, final consumption can be rewritten as:

$$\tilde{c}_i = \bar{q}_{1i} + P\bar{q}_{2i} + q_{2i}(\tilde{R} - P) \tag{6.3.4}$$

Given the assumptions of normality and constant absolute risk aversion, expected utility is proportional to:

$$U_i = \mathrm{E}[\tilde{c}_i] - \tfrac{1}{2}A_i \,\mathrm{Var}[\tilde{c}_i]$$

where A_i is individual i's degree of absolute risk aversion. (See Exercise 2 at the end of Section 2.2 for a derivation of this result.)

Substituting from (6.3.4), we obtain:

$$U_i = \bar{q}_{1i} + P\bar{q}_{2i} + q_{2i}[\mathrm{E}[\tilde{R}|m_i] - P] - \tfrac{1}{2}A_i q_{2i}^2 \,\mathrm{Var}[\tilde{R}|m_i]$$

Note that the mean and variance of the risky return are dependent upon some message m_i received by individual i from an information service. Differentiating by q_{1i} and rearranging, individual i's demand for the risky asset is:

$$q_{1i}^* = \left(\frac{1}{A_i \,\mathrm{Var}[\tilde{R}|m_i]}\right) (\mathrm{E}[\tilde{R}|m_i] - P)$$

Let Q_2 be the aggregate supply of the risky asset. Summing over i and setting supply equal to demand, leads to the pricing rule:

$$\sum_{i=1}^{n} \left(\frac{1}{A_i \,\mathrm{Var}[\tilde{R}|m_i]}\right) (\mathrm{E}[\tilde{R}|m_i] - P) = Q_2 \tag{6.3.5}$$

As an illustration, suppose that a subset I of the population all obtain the same message m, which is an unbiased but noisy estimate of the unknown yield $\tilde{R}$:

$$\tilde{m}_i = \tilde{m} = \tilde{R} + \tilde{\varepsilon}$$

We assume that $\tilde{\varepsilon}$ is independent of $\tilde{R}$ and normally distributed with mean 0 and variance σ_ε^2. Let σ_R^2 be the variance of $\tilde{R}$. Then, from normal distribution theory, the conditional expectation and variance of $\tilde{R}$ can be expressed as:

$$E[\tilde{R} \mid m] = (1 - \alpha_I)\mu + \alpha_I m,$$
$$\text{Var}[\tilde{R} \mid m] = \sigma_I^2$$

The important point to note is that both α_I and σ_I^2 are functions only of the underlying variances σ_R^2 and σ_ε^2 and *not* of the message m.

Following Grossman and Stiglitz (1980), we shall refer to individuals in I as insiders. The remaining individuals or outsiders receive no message. As a final simplification, suppose all individuals have the same degree of absolute risk aversion, that is, $A_i = A$, for $i = 1, \ldots, n$. Then (6.3.5) can be rewritten as follows:

$$\left(\sum_{i \in I} \frac{1}{A\sigma_I^2} \right) ((1 - \alpha_I)\mu + \alpha_i m - P) + \left(\sum_{i \notin I} \frac{1}{A\sigma_R^2} \right) (\mu - P) = Q_2$$

$$(6.3.6)$$

Collecting terms:

$$\theta_0 \mu + \theta_1 m - \theta_2 P = Q_2 \qquad (6.3.7)$$

where $\theta \equiv (\theta_0, \theta_1, \theta_2)$ is a factor of parameters dependent only on the underlying variances.

It follows that, if the aggregate supply of the risky asset is fixed, the equilibrium price increases linearly with the message m. Therefore, as Grossman and Stiglitz (1980) point out, the equilibrium price becomes a perfect predictor of the message received by the informed. Just as in the finite-state example above, complete information leakage is possible. Then, if information is costly and outsiders do make the correct inference, they are better off than insiders. It follows that no individual has an incentive to become informed.

To generate *partial* leakage, and hence to restore the incentive for information gathering, a second source of uncertainty must be introduced. One possibility is aggregate supply uncertainty. Suppose then that Q_2 is independently and normally distributed[21] with mean $\bar{Q}_2$ and variance σ_Q^2. From

[21] As formally modeled, each individual's endowment of the risky asset is independently distributed. Therefore, as long as the population is sufficiently large, the fact that an individual knows his own endowment yields essentially no information about aggregate supply.

(6.3.7) the equilibrium price is now an increasing function of the message m and a decreasing function of aggregate supply Q_2. It follows that outsiders are no longer able to infer m solely by observing P.

Suppose, however, that they *conjecture* a linear equilibrium relationship of the form given by (6.3.7), that is, for some vector of parameters $\gamma = (\gamma_0, \gamma_1, \gamma_2)$:

$$\gamma_0 \mu + \gamma_1 m - \gamma_2 P = Q_2 \tag{6.3.8}$$

Given such a conjecture, it follows that the equilibrium price P is a linear function of two independently-distributed normal random variables and is thus normally distributed as well. From normal distribution theory, the expectation and variance of $\tilde{R}$ conditional upon observing P can be written as:

$$E[\tilde{R}|P] = (1 - \alpha_0)\mu_R + \alpha_0 P$$
$$\mathrm{Var}[\tilde{R}|P] = \sigma_0^2$$

where α_0 and σ_0^2 are functions of the underlying variances and the vector γ. Continuing with the assumption that all individuals have the same degree of absolute risk aversion, and substituting these expressions into (6.3.6) leads to the revised pricing rule:

$$\left(\sum_{i \in I} \frac{1}{A_i \sigma_I^2} \right) ((1 - \alpha_I)\mu_R + \alpha_I m - P)$$

$$+ \left[\sum_{i \notin I} \frac{1}{A_0 \sigma_0^2} \right] ((1 - \alpha_0)\mu_R + \alpha_0 P - P) = Q_2$$

Collecting terms, it follows that there is some vector $\gamma^* = (\gamma_0^*, \gamma_1^*, \gamma_2^*)$ such that:

$$\gamma_0^* \mu + \gamma_1^* m - \gamma_2^* P = Q_2 \tag{6.3.9}$$

Comparing (6.3.8) and (6.3.9), it follows that the form of the pricing rule is the one conjectured. That is, for any linear conjecture with parameter vector γ, there exists an equilibrium pricing rule that is linear with parameters:

$$\gamma^* = f\left(\gamma; \sigma_R^2, \sigma_\varepsilon^2, \sigma_Q^2 \right)$$

What Grossman and Stiglitz were able to show is that there is a unique fixed point of this mapping. That is, there exists a unique linear conjecture that is correct or "rational." They then established that the difference between the expected utility of the insiders and outsiders declines as the proportion of insiders rises. It follows that, if information is costly, the number of individuals purchasing information rises until the expected utility of insiders and outsiders is equated.

Hellwig (1980) considers a model in which each individual receives a different message:

$$\tilde{m}_i = \tilde{R} + \tilde{\varepsilon}_i, \ i = 1, \ldots, n$$

and $\tilde{\varepsilon}_i$ is independently and normally distributed with mean σ_i^2. Suppose, first, that individuals make no use of information contained in market prices. The pricing rule (6.3.5) then becomes:

$$\sum_{i=1}^{n} \frac{1}{A_i \ \text{Var}[\tilde{R}|m_i]} \ ((1-\alpha_i)\mu + \alpha_i(\tilde{R}+\tilde{\varepsilon}_i) - P) = Q_2 \qquad (6.3.10)$$

Suppose the economy is replicated so that there are T individuals of each type and the aggregate endowment is TQ_2. Each individual of type i receives an independent message $\tilde{m}_{it} = \tilde{R}_t + \tilde{\varepsilon}_{it}$, $t = 1, \ldots, T$, with mean zero and variance σ_i^2. From (6.3.10) it follows that the new equilibrium pricing rule is:

$$\sum_{i=1}^{n} \frac{1}{A_i \ \text{Var}[\tilde{R}|m_{it}]} \left((1-\alpha_i)T\mu + \alpha_i \left(T\tilde{R} + \sum_{t=1}^{T} \tilde{\varepsilon}_{it} \right) - TP \right) = TQ_2$$

Dividing by T:

$$\sum_{i=1}^{n} \frac{1}{A_i \ \text{Var}[\tilde{R}|m_{it}]} \left((1-\alpha)\mu + \alpha_i\tilde{R} + \left[\frac{1}{T} \sum_{t=1}^{T} \tilde{\varepsilon}_{it} \right] - P \right) = Q_2$$

In the limit as T becomes large, the variance of the average of the T independent random variables approaches zero. That is, the expression inside the square brackets approaches zero with probability 1. Then, in the limit with probability 1:

$$\sum_{i=1}^{n} \frac{1}{A_i \ \text{Var}[\tilde{R}|m_{it}]} ((1-\alpha_i)\mu + \alpha_i\tilde{R} - P) = Q_2$$

The equilibrium price is then a linear function of the actual return $\tilde{R}$ and the random aggregate supply $\tilde{Q}_2$ and is *independent* of each individual's own message.

Now suppose individuals try to incorporate the information contained in market prices into their own decisions. As in the case considered by Grossman and Stiglitz, suppose individuals all make the same linear conjecture:

$$\gamma_0 \mu + \gamma_1 \tilde{R} - \gamma_2 P = \tilde{Q}_2$$

Individual i, $i = 1, \ldots, n$, then computes a conditional mean and variance. From normal distribution theory, the conditional mean is again a linear function of the private signal m_{it} and the price P. The analysis then proceeds exactly as before, and it can be confirmed that the linear conjecture implies a limiting relationship (as $T \to \infty$) of the form:

$$\gamma_0^* \mu + \gamma_1^* \tilde{R} - \gamma_2^* P = \tilde{Q}_2$$

That is, once again, for any linear conjecture with parameter vector γ there is an equilibrium pricing rule that is linear with parameter vector $\gamma^* = g(\gamma)$. From Hellwig's analysis we know that there is a unique fixed point of this mapping, leading once again to a rational expectations equilibrium with partial leakage. While the algebra is tedious, it is also possible to solve for the equilibrium value of γ.

This relationship has been exploited successfully in contributions to the finance literature. Diamond (1985), for example, characterizes the value of optimal release of public information by firms. Intuitively, the more information released by firms, the lower is the incentive for each individual to obtain private information. Thus, total expenditures on information acquisition are thereby reduced. Verrecchia (1982) focuses on the level of private information acquisition. In his extension of the basic model, the noisiness of individual i's message service, represented by the variance σ_i^2, is a decreasing function of some costly input. Each individual then chooses his optimal message service. He shows, for example, that if two individuals differ only in their degree of risk aversion, the less risk-averse individual will spend more on information acquisition in the "rational expectations" equilibrium. This is intuitively sensible. A less risk-averse individual takes more risky positions based on his information and the return to more accurate information is therefore greater.

We conclude this section with some cautionary remarks. First, the constant absolute risk-aversion/normal distribution model is very special. Second, even within the confines of this model, analytical solutions with partial leakage all hinge on the assumption that the aggregate supply of the risky asset is a random variable. This is hard to justify in many contexts, for example, in a stock market.[22]

More fundamentally, recall that we have been excluding speculative behavior on the part of the informed individuals. While the uninformed are assumed to be enormously competent and well-equipped economists and statisticians, the *informed* are supposed to behave rather simplistically – simply presenting their true demands to the auctioneer. In a more realistic model, an informed individual would have a pretty good idea which way prices will move when his private information becomes public knowledge. So he has an incentive to take an initial speculative position in the market and then wait for prices to adjust before moving to his final consumption bundle, in accordance with the analysis in Section 6.2. This means that the payoff to becoming informed may become quite large after all.

The speculation option available to the informed traders has two different kinds of effects upon the leakage problem. First, it increases the sensitivity of price to the message received. Suppose the message m indicates that state 1 is more probable than was previously believed. Then informed traders who speculate will initially purchase state-1 claims more heavily than if they were merely adapting their consumption portfolios to their revised beliefs. It follows that state-1 claims will be bid up more sharply in the market, thus providing a more visible clue to the uninformed – at least as to the direction of change signaled by the unknown message. On the other hand, as an analytical matter, the speculation option adds another complication to the already difficult problem that uninformed parties face in trying to infer the missing message on the basis of a still more general economic model and the associated econometric calculations.

The equilibrium of such a generalized model will not be addressed here, but it will involve: (i) speculative as well as adaptive behavior on the part of the informed; (ii) sophisticated behavior on the part of the uninformed, as they attempt with partial success to infer the message generated by the information service; and (iii) an equilibrium fraction f of traders who choose to become informed at cost Δ. An even more general model would provide for an information-supplying industry, so that Δ itself would be determined endogenously.

---

[22] An alternative approach is to introduce "noise traders." These are individuals who make trades that are exogenous to the formal model. See Black (1986) and Shleifer and Summers (1990).

Exercises and Excursions 6.3.2

1 Aggregation of Insiders' Information

There are N_I insiders who each pay \$$\delta$ and receive a signal correlated with the true return on a risky asset. The signal received by insider i is $m_i = R + \varepsilon_i$, where R and ε_i $(i = 1, \dots, N_I)$ are $N_I + 1$ independently and normally distributed random variables with means μ and 0 and variances σ^2 and σ_ε^2. There are N_o outsiders who receive no information. All individuals exhibit constant absolute risk aversion.

(A) Show that the expectation of R given the observations $m_1, m_2, \dots, m_{N_I}$ can be expressed in the form:

$$\alpha\mu + (1 - \alpha)\left(\frac{m_1 + m_2 + \cdots + m_{N_I}}{N_I}\right)$$

(B) In a world in which there is a riskless asset and a single risky asset, suppose that in bidding for the risky asset, insiders and outsiders simply use their own endowed or acquired information (i.e., they do not draw inferences from market prices). If all insiders have the same degree of absolute risk aversion, obtain an expression for the market-clearing price. Confirm that it is a function of the sum of the N_I messages received. Compare this price with the price that would clear markets if the N_I insiders were all to receive all N_I messages.

(C) Suppose outsiders are not smart enough to draw inferences from market prices. However, insiders do have this capacity. If inside information is costly to purchase, what incentive is there for any of the insiders to obtain it? Is there an equilibrium number of insiders who purchase the information?

(D) Would your answer to (C) differ significantly if insiders have differing degrees of risk aversion? (Discuss only.)**

6.4 Rational Expectations

In the models of the Section 6.3, uninformed traders are able to infer from market prices some or all of the information held by informed traders. The uninformed traders are said to have "rational expectations."

As originally proposed, rational expectations referred to anticipations that "are essentially the same as the predictions of the relevant economic theory" (Muth, 1961, p. 316). The simplest supply-demand model will serve

** End of starred section.

as example. As is well known, in an actual market there may be trading at "false prices": for any given unit of the good, a buyer might pay more or less, and a seller correspondingly receive less or more, than the theoretical equilibrium price that would be established if the market were an ideal frictionless mechanism. It is true that, starting from any disequilibrium price, a transient "cobweb" path might lead eventually toward a final equilibrium where there is no further tendency to change. However, even so, if some trades have already taken place at false prices, the final equilibrium of price and quantity will not in general be identical with the theoretical supply-demand intersection.

The rational expectations approach to this problem suggests that each trader in the market will make a guess as to the equilibrium price – on the basis of the private information at his disposal, plus his general knowledge of relationships such as the law of supply and demand – and that these guesses balance out to an average that is not far from correct:

allowing for cross-sectional differences in expectations is a simple matter, because their aggregate effect is negligible as long as the deviation from the rational forecast ... is not strongly correlated with those of the others. (Muth, 1961, p. 321)

One important point to note is that two somewhat different types of analyses are involved, corresponding to the professional skills of the *economist* and of the *econometrician*. The economist predicts that the price will be determined by the intersection of the supply and demand curves, while the econometrician provides the actual specific quantitative forms of those curves. Put another way, the economist makes predictions about the endogenous variables of economic systems, and specifically the prices and quantities exchanged or produced, but only *given* the exogenous data. Estimating the actual determining data is a task for the econometrician. So rational expectations corresponds, in effect, to assuming that ordinary individuals can be taken to be both pretty good economists and pretty good econometricians, at least on average.

When it comes to "visible" markets, those involved in trading current goods here and now, rational expectations is a well-validated hypothesis. Innumerable economic studies have successfully employed the assumption that essentially all such trading takes place at the supply-demand intersection. In addition, economic experimentation has verified that, practically always, prices in simulated markets move very rapidly toward the equilibrium – there is very little trading at false prices.[23]

---

[23] See, for example, Smith (1982) and chapter 3 of Davis and Holt (1993).

However, futures trading poses a much more difficult problem. Rational traders have to make conjectures about what prices will be at *later* dates, after the prospective arrival of information. The question is, how reasonable is it to postulate that traders can be good enough economists and econometricians so as to make *self-fulfilling predictions* (SFPs) about the results that would be observed in "invisible" markets that have not yet opened, or that (since these are *contingent* markets) will in the great majority of cases never open?

In some situations, we have seen, the correct SFP prediction for posterior prices may be easy to make. Our theoretical development in Section 6.1 indicated that, given Complete Contingent Markets (CCM) in the prior round of trading, the correct forecast for the posterior round is simply "no change." More specifically, for any state s that might obtain, if all traders forecast that the posterior price ratios among the c_{gs} claims to different goods contingent upon state s will be equal to the prior price ratios, and have made their prior-round trading decisions accordingly, their anticipations will be borne out. So forming "rational" expectations under CCM does not seem difficult. But realistically, we cannot very well call upon results that hold only under the very idealized condition of CCM. And, in particular, we have seen that with *incomplete* regimes of markets in the prior round, traders do not normally have the information for making correct contingent predictions about the price ratios that would be ruling in the alternative possible future states of the world. When some traders have private information, it is even more difficult for traders to make correct inferences about private information of others from price ratios.

One interesting point brought out by Arrow (1978) is that the rational-expectations assumption in effect stands on its head the famous contention by Hayek (1945) about the informational function of the market system. Hayek's view was that prices are marvelously efficient summary statistics, conveying to traders all that they need to know about the vastly detailed particular circumstances of other economic agents which might impinge upon their own decisions. Absent a price system, Hayek argued, a central planner would require an impossibly elaborate data-gathering and data-analyzing scheme to make intelligent economic choices. But rational expectations seems to imply that the price signals from the "invisible" markets are hardly needed. Private traders supposedly can, at least on average, correctly guess what the price signals would have been!

In attempting to replicate the price signals of missing markets contingent upon future events, there are realistic difficulties for both the economist and the econometrician. Even were the data known, it may not be a trivial matter to compute the equilibrium of a complex system. And forecasting *exogenous* data – for example, assigning correct probabilities to good versus bad weather, or to war versus peace – would seem to require somewhat more than the talents we usually ascribe to the econometrician. In such contexts rational expectations requires that individuals be actually clairvoyant (once again, at least on average). For example, in some macroeconomic models, rational expectations has been taken to mean that, in addition to being able to analyze the effects of any given monetary policy, individuals can also decipher the current and future policies of the monetary authorities.

Knight (1921, p. 227) appears to support this view in asserting that: "We are so built that what seems to us reasonable is likely to be confirmed by experience, or we could not live in the world at all." This Lincolnesque idea that "the people can't be fooled" may be based upon viewing the underlying processes that generate observed world events as *stationary*, so that individuals can gradually learn both about the effects of events upon prices and about the probability distribution of events. However, such a learning evolution does not imply that beliefs would be on average correct except in the limit.

While it is difficult to see what an adequate test of the rational expectations hypothesis may be, a number of patterns in the data seem to have been usefully interpreted in these terms. Indeed, in dealing with regimes of incomplete markets, it is difficult to propose any other assumption to deal with individuals' beliefs about future events. Our main concern has been to analyze the theoretical role of SFPs simply as an assumption, and to warn against casual acceptance of the empirical validity of rational expectations as the real-world analog of SFPs.

SUGGESTIONS FOR FURTHER READING: See Newberry (2008) for an overview of the futures markets literature. Duffie (2001) provides an advanced treatment of futures markets within a general framework of asset pricing theory. A good introduction to the rational expectations literature is Bray (1985).

References

Arrow, Kenneth J., "Economic Welfare and the Allocation of Resources for Invention," in *The Rate and Direction of Inventive Activity: Economic and Social Factors*, Universities-NBER Conference Series, Princeton: Princeton University Press, 1962, 609–626.

———, "The Role of Securities in the Optimal Allocation of Risk Bearing," *Review of Economic Studies*, 31 (1964), 91–96. Reprinted in Kenneth J. Arrow, *Essays in the Theory of Risk-Bearing*, Chicago: Markham, 1971.

————, "The Future and the Present in Economic Life," *Economic Inquiry*, 16 (1978), 157–169.

Barzel, Yoram, "Optimal Timing of Innovations," *Review of Economic Statistics*, 50 (1968), 348–355.

Baumol, William J., "Speculation, Profitability, and Stability," *Review of Economics and Statistics*, 30 (1957), 263–271.

Bergemann, Dirk and Valimaki, Juuso, "Information Acquisition and Efficient Mechanism Design," *Econometrica*, 70 (2002), 1007–1033.

Black, Fischer, "Noise," *Journal of Finance*, 41 (1986): 529–543.

Bray, Margaret, "Rational Expectations, Information and Asset Markets: An Introduction," *Oxford Economic Papers*, 37 (1985), 161–195.

Davis, Douglas D. and Charles Holt, *Experimental Economics*, Princeton: Princeton University Press, 1993.

Diamond, Douglas W., "Optimal Release of Information by Firms," *Journal of Finance*, 40 (1985), 1071–1094.

Duffie, Darrell, *Dynamic Asset Pricing Theory*, Princeton University Press: Princeton, 2001.

Fama, Eugene F. and Laffer Arthur B., "Information and Capital Markets," *Journal of Business*, 44, 289–298, (1971).

Friedman, Milton, "In Defense of Destabilizing Speculation," in R. W. Pfouts (ed.), *Essays in Economics and Econometrics*, Chapel Hill: University of North Carolina Press, 1960. Reprinted in Milton Friedman, *The Optimum Quantity of Money and Other Essays*, Chicago: Aldine, 1969.

Grossman, Sanford J. and Stiglitz, Joseph E., "Information and Competitive Price Systems," *American Economic Review*, 66 (1976), 246–253.

————, "On the Impossibility of Informationally Efficient Markets," *American Economic Review*, 70 (1980), 393–408.

Hayek, Friedrich A., "The Use of Knowledge in Society," *American Economic Review*, 35 (1945), 519–530.

Hellwig, Martin F., "On the Aggregation of Information in Competitive Markets," *Journal of Economic Theory*, 22 (1980), 477–498.

Hicks, John R., *Value and Capital*, 2nd edition, London: Oxford University Press, 1946.

Hirshleifer, David, "Hedging Pressure and Futures Price Movements in a General Equilibrium Model," *Econometrica*, 58 (1990), 411–428.

Hirshleifer, Jack, "The Private and Social Value of Information and the Reward to Inventive Activity," *American Economic Review*, 61 (1971), 561–574.

————, "The Theory of Speculation under Alternative Regimes of Markets," *Journal of Finance*, 32 (1977), 975–999.

Keynes, John M., *A Treatise on Money*, London: Macmillan, 1930.

Knight, Frank H., *Risk, Uncertainty, and Profit*, New York: Houghton Mifflin, 1921.

Machlup, Fritz, "Patents," in *International Encyclopedia of the Social Sciences*, New York: Free Press, 1968.

McKinnon, Ronald I., "Futures Markets, Buffer Stocks, and Income Stability for Primary Producers," *Journal of Political Economy*, 75 (1967), 844–861.

Muth, John F., "Rational Expectations and the Theory of Price Movements," *Econometrica*, 29 (1961), 315–335.

Newberry, David M., "Futures Markets, Hedging and Speculation," in *The New Palgrave Dictionary of Economics*, Steven N. Durlauf and Lawrence E. Blume (eds.), 2nd edition, vol. 3, pp. 521–526, New York: Palgrave MacMillan, 2008.

Novos, Ian E. and Waldman, Michael, "The Emergence of Copying Technologies: What Have We Learned?", *Contemporary Policy Issues*, 5 (1987), 34–43.

Radner, Roy, "Competitive Equilibrium under Uncertainty," *Econometrica*, 36 (1968), 31–58.

_____, "Rational Expectations Equilibrium: Generic Existence and the Information Revealed by Prices," *Econometrica*, 47 (1979), 655–678.

Shleifer, Andrei and Lawrence H. Summers, "The Noise Trader Approach to Finance," *Journal of Economic Perspectives*, 4(2) (1990), 19–33.

Smith, Vernon L., "Microeconomic Systems as an Experimental Science," *American Economic Review*, 72 (1982), 923–955.

Verrecchia, Robert E., "Information Acquisition in a Noisy Rational Expectations Economy," *Econometrica*, 50 (1982), 1415–1430.

Working, Holbrook, "Futures Trading and Hedging," *American Economic Review*, 43 (1953), 314–343.

_____, "New Concepts Concerning Futures Markets and Prices," *American Economic Review*, 52 (1962), 431–459.

7

Strategic Uncertainty and Equilibrium
Concepts

For the most part, the analysis to this point has dealt with *event uncertainty*. Individuals were mainly uncertain about nature's choice of state of the world. In the following chapters the focus shifts to *strategic uncertainty*, where the best course of action for individual A depends upon individual B's choice, and vice versa. So the main risks that a person has to deal with concern the actions and reactions of others. A first step is the choice of an equilibrium concept for such an environment, which turns out to be a subtle and still controversial issue. As usual, our discussion will not attempt to address formal issues of existence or uniqueness of equilibrium. Our aim instead is to provide an intuitive interpretation of the key ideas.

7.1 Dominant Strategy

We begin with the Prisoners' Dilemma, a game that is easy to analyze. The story behind this game is as follows. Two accomplices have been arrested on suspicion of committing a major crime. The prosecutor does not have sufficient evidence to convict them of this crime. Without a confession from at least one of the two accomplices the prosecutor can only send them to prison for one year for the lesser charge of illegal possession of weapons. The two accomplices (or prisoners) are locked up in different cells and cannot communicate with each other. The prosecutor approaches each of them separately and says, "If you confess and your friend does not then I will drop all charges against you. On the other hand, if your friend confesses and you do not then you will do 10 years. If you both confess then I'll see to it that you get parole after 5 years in prison. Think hard about what you want to do and let me know tomorrow morning." Each prisoner knows that if both of them remain silent and do not confess then each will be sentenced

Table 7.1. *Prisoners' Dilemma*

		Prisoner k	
		Defect x_1^2	Cooperate x_2^2
Prisoner j	Defect x_1^1	$-5, -5$	$0, -10$
	Cooperate x_2^1	$-10, 0$	$-1, -1$

to only one year of prison on firearms possession charges. What do you think the prisoners' will do?

Assume that each prisoner acts purely in his own self-interest and seeks to minimize his time in prison. Let us call the two choices that each prisoner faces Defect (if he confesses) and Cooperate (if he does not confess).[1] The consequence (i.e., the number of years in prison) for each prisoner depends not only on his own choice but also on the choice of his accomplice. The consequences are shown in Table 7.1. If, for example, prisoner j Defects and prisoner k Cooperates, then j spends 0 years in prison and k spends 10 years. This is represented as $(0, -10)$ in Table 7.1. (We represent payoffs of games so that higher numbers are better.)

First, consider this game from prisoner j's viewpoint. Suppose that prisoner k were to Defect; then prisoner j is sentenced to only 5 years if he Defects whereas he gets 10 years if he Cooperates. Suppose, instead, that prisoner k were to Cooperate; then prisoner j spends no time in prison if he Defects whereas he spends 1 year in prison if he Cooperates. Thus, Defect is the best course of action for prisoner j, *regardless* of prisoner k's choice of action. In the language of game theory, Defect is a *strictly dominant strategy* for prisoner j. A symmetric argument establishes that Defect is a strictly dominant strategy for prisoner k as well. For each prisoner, Cooperate is a *strictly dominated strategy* – it is strictly dominated by Defect.

Thus, each prisoner will Defect and end up spending 5 years in prison. If, instead, each prisoner had selected Cooperate then each would spend only 1 year in prison. However, a choice of Defect by both players is the only strategically stable outcome. To convince yourself that this is the case, suppose that the two prisoners can communicate with each other. They meet and agree to Cooperate so that each is sentenced to only 1 year in prison. After reaching this non-binding agreement they go back to their cells. What

---

[1] By not confessing, a prisoner Cooperates with his accomplice. Confessing betrays the accomplice; it is an act of defection.

Table 7.2. *Prisoners' Dilemma* (general payoffs) (e > f > g > h)

		Defect x_1^2	Cooperate x_2^2
Defect	x_1^1	g, g	e, h
Cooperate	x_2^1	h, e	f, f

do you think each prisoner will do when he meets the prosecutor the next morning? Each prisoner, even if he believes that his accomplice will stick to the agreement, has an incentive to deviate from Cooperate to Defect – better to spend no time rather than 1 year in prison. And if the prisoner believes that his accomplice may renege on their agreement and Defect, then that makes Cooperate all the more attractive.

There are other strategic situations which have a payoff structure similar to the Prisoners' Dilemma. Consider two firms that compete in a market with completely inelastic demand. Each firm chooses between a Low Price and a High Price. As demand is inelastic, the total quantity sold by the two does not change with price. Thus, each firm's profit is higher when both choose High Price (which corresponds to Cooperate) than if they both choose Low Price (which corresponds to Defect). However, if one chooses Low Price and the other High Price, then the former firm corners the market and makes a greater profit than if both firms had selected High Price.

Table 7.2 gives the general form of the Prisoners' Dilemma. The inequalities $e > f$ and $g > h$ on the payoffs ensure that Defect is a strictly dominant strategy. The inequality $f > g$ implies that payoff obtained when the two players choose (Defect, Defect) is Pareto dominated by the payoff under (Cooperate, Cooperate). We shall return to this game in Chapter 11, where we investigate whether repeated interactions between the same two players increases the possibility of cooperation.

In most games, players do not have a strictly dominant strategy, and it is less obvious how they should play. We turn to this issue in the remainder of this chapter.

7.2 Nash Equilibrium

In a *coordination game*, the parties' interests are somewhat parallel. A specific example known as "Stag Hunt" originates in a situation presented by the philosopher Jean-Jacques Rousseau. Two hunters can either hunt hare on their own or cooperate to hunt stag. A stag is more difficult to hunt and

Table 7.3. *Stag Hunt*

		Player k	
		Stag x_1^k	Hare x_2^k
Player j	Stag x_1^j	10, 10	0, 7
	Hare x_2^j	7, 0	6, 6

requires the combined efforts of the two; it also provides more meat for each hunter than a hare. This is reflected in the payoffs in Table 7.3, where if both players (hunters) j and k select Stag they each get a payoff of 10, whereas if each player chooses Hare, the payoff for each is 6. If player j chooses Stag and player k chooses Hare then j gets 0 – he does not succeed in hunting any game – whereas k gets 7.[2] Thus, the two parties both gain by coordinating their activities on a stag hunt. But a trust dilemma arises here. Even if the two hunters were to agree to hunt stag, can each trust the other not to stray from this decision? To quote from Rousseau's *A Discourse on Inequality* (1755):

> If it was a matter of hunting a deer, everyone well realized that he must remain faithfully at his post; but if a hare happened to pass within the reach of one of them, we cannot doubt that he would have gone off in pursuit of it without scruple and, having caught his own prey, he would have cared very little about having caused his companions to lose theirs.

The decision is further complicated by the fact that payoff from Hare (7 if the other player chooses Stag, 6 if the other player chooses Hare) is much less variable than the payoff from Stag (either 10 or 0).

Approaching this problem in terms of game theory, we can view each player as choosing an action without knowledge of the other player's action choice. In effect, the players can be thought of as choosing their actions simultaneously. We can depict this situation with a game tree in Figure 7.1. Player j is represented here as having the first move, but player k must make a decision without knowing j's choice. This is represented by means of the dashed line called the "information set" connecting the two decision nodes of player k. Player j moves first, and then player k gets to move. Player k does

---

[2] When a player is the only one hunting hare, his payoff is slightly higher than when both hunt hare (7 instead of 6).

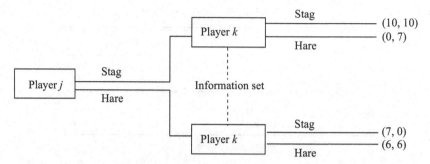

Figure 7.1. Game tree of Stag Hunt.

not know which of the two decision nodes in his information set has been reached; i.e., he does not know player *j*'s action.[3]

The most frequently used solution concept for games is called the Nash non-cooperative solution, or *Nash equilibrium*.[4] The key idea is that there is an equilibrium when, given the strategies of all the other players, each single participant finds that his own strategy is (at least weakly) a best response to their choices. Thus the Nash equilibrium is a "no regret" equilibrium.

Our simple example is a two-player game in which each player simultaneously chooses one of two actions. With simultaneous play, each player is assumed to have made a hypothesis about the strategies of his opponents. His own strategy is then a best response to the others' hypothesized strategies. If, for each player, the chosen action coincides with what the other players have hypothesized about his strategy, a Nash equilibrium exists.[5]

In the Stag Hunt game, it is a best response to always match the action of the other player. If player *k*, say, were to choose Stag, the best response of player *j* is also Stag since it yields a payoff of 10 while Hare gives only 7 to player *j*. Similarly, if *j* were to choose Stag, *k*'s best response is Stag. Hence, the action or strategy pair (Stag, Stag) is a Nash equilibrium in this game. In this equilibrium the parties achieve the mutually preferred outcome (10, 10).

---

[3] We could also have drawn this game tree with the decision nodes of the two players exchanged. That is, player *k* moves first and player *j* has two decision nodes within an information set. This game tree represents exactly the same strategic situation.

[4] Nash (1951). The Nash equilibrium is a generalization of a solution to the oligopoly problem that goes back to Cournot (1838).

[5] Note that the Nash equilibrium is *not* justified by appealing to some plausible dynamic process. Rather, it is a state of affairs in which, if it were somehow to come about, no party would unilaterally want to revise his action.

A similar argument establishes that (Hare, Hare), another mutual best response pair of actions, is also a Nash equilibrium. In this second Nash equilibrium, the parties achieve the inferior outcome (6, 6).

Unlike the Stag Hunt game, many games do not have a Nash equilibrium in simple actions or *pure strategies*. In such situations, a fruitful approach is to extend the range of choice beyond the pure strategies available to each player so as to consider *mixed strategies* as well; that is, the set of probabilistic combinations of the available pure strategies. If there are only two pure strategies, the complete set of pure and mixed strategies available to player i can be expressed (in analogy with the "prospect notation" of chapter 1) as:

$$\bar{X} = \left\{ \left(x_1^i, x_2^i; \pi^i, 1 - \pi^i \right) \middle| 0 \le \pi^i \le 1 \right\}$$

where π^i = probability that player i chooses x_1^i.

More generally, if player i has a set of A^i feasible pure strategies $X^i = \{x_1^i, \ldots, x_{A^i}^i\}$, then player i's complete set of strategies (the set of probability vectors over these pure strategies) can be expressed as:

$$\bar{X}^i = \left\{ \left(x_1^i, \ldots, x_{A^i}^i; \pi_1^i, \ldots, \pi_{A^i}^i \right) \middle| 0 \le \pi_a^i \le 1 \text{ and } \sum_{a=1}^{A^i} \pi_a^i = 1 \right\}$$

where π_a^i is the probability that player i chooses strategy π_a^i.

Returning to the Stag Hunt game tree, recall that there are two Nash equilibria in pure strategies. Either the players coordinate on strategy 1 (Stag) or on strategy 2 (Hare). In each case, either party acting alone can only lose by changing to a different action. But now there is also an equilibrium in mixed strategies. The following condition provides a technique for locating a Nash equilibrium in which at least one player uses a mixed strategy:

Suppose player i has chosen a mixed strategy. For his mixed strategy to be part of a Nash equilibrium, player i must then be indifferent – given the chosen strategies (pure or mixed) of the other players – among all of the pure strategies entering with non-zero probability into his own mixed strategy.

In the Stag Hunt game, suppose the players have chosen respective mixed strategies $(\pi^i, 1 - \pi^i)$, $i = j, k$. We now ask when player j will be indifferent between the pure strategies 1 (Stag) and 2 (Hare). If he chooses Stag, his expected payoff is:

$$\pi^k(10) + (1 - \pi^k)(0) = 10\pi^k$$

Table 7.4. *Chicken*

			Player k	
			Coward x_1^k	Hero x_2^k
Player j	Coward	x_1^j	4, 4	0, 8
	Hero	x_2^j	8, 0	−6, −6

If he chooses Hare, his gain is:

$$\pi^k(7) + (1 - \pi^k)(6) = 6 + \pi^k$$

Player j will be indifferent between Stag and Hare if and only if player k's probability mixture is $(\pi^k, 1 - \pi^k) = (2/3, 1/3)$. Given the symmetry of the game, player k's expected gains are equal when player j's mixture is $(2/3, 1/3)$ also. Evidently, this strategy pair is the only mixed-strategy Nash equilibrium.

Note that while the two pure strategy Nash equilibria here are *strong*, meaning that a player who unilaterally switches to any other strategy will end up actually worse off for having done so, the mixed strategy Nash equilibrium is *weak*. In fact, as follows directly from the condition stated above for finding the mixed strategy solution, if all other parties are playing in accordance with the mixed strategy Nash equilibrium then *any single player could equally well have chosen any of the pure strategies entering into his Nash equilibrium mixture* – or, indeed, any other mixture of them as well. More generally, a Nash equilibrium in pure strategies may be either strong or weak, but a Nash equilibrium in mixed strategies is always weak.

We now consider an alternative payoff environment, the famous game of Chicken[6] (Table 7.4), again under the assumption of simultaneous play. For instance, if j chooses Coward and k chooses Hero, the payoffs to j and k are 0 and 8 respectively.

In the Chicken game, there are once again two pure-strategy Nash equilibria, but in this case they are asymmetrical – at the off-diagonal cells (x_1^j, x_2^k) and (x_2^j, x_1^k). There is a mixed strategy Nash equilibrium as well. Given the specific payoffs of Table 7.4, the equilibrium mixed strategy is symmetrical: each player chooses strategy 1 (Coward) and strategy 2 (Hero) with probabilities 0.6 and 0.4, respectively. At the mixed strategy Nash

---

[6] In the biological literature, the game of Chicken is known as Hawk-Dove (Maynard Smith, 1976).

equilibrium each player's expected return is 2.4, intermediate between the Hero payoff of 8 and the Coward payoff of 0 at each of the pure-strategy Nash equilibria.

The "normal form" matrices of Tables 7.1, 7.3, and 7.4 describe the *payoff environments* of Prisoners' Dilemma, Stag Hunt, and Chicken, respectively. To represent other aspects of the game such as the *procedural rules* (for example, whether the players move simultaneously or in sequence, and if in sequence who moves first) and the *information or beliefs* that the different parties possess, one turns to the game tree or "extensive form."[7] In the next three sections of the chapter we will describe how these procedural and informational aspects of the problem affect possible solutions of a game. And, in particular, we will explore how they provide possible ways of separating more plausible Nash equilibria from those that are less plausible.

Exercises and Excursions 7.2

1 Tender Trap

Another example of a co-ordination game is Tender Trap (Hirshleifer, 1982). The Dvorak typewriter keyboard is, it has been claimed, ergonomically superior to the currently standard "Qwerty" arrangement. But having settled on the current standard keyboard, largely by historical accident, now manufacturers are supposedly reluctant to produce Dvorak keyboards so long as almost all typists are trained on Qwerty, while typists do not want to train on Dvorak when almost all keyboards are Qwerty.[8] Even the inferior keyboard as a matched choice is superior to failing to co-ordinate at all.

		Player k (typist)	
		Dvorak x_1^k	Qwerty x_2^k
Player j (manufacturer)	Dvorak x_1^j	10, 10	4, 4
	Qwerty x_2^j	4, 4	6, 6

The above table shows the payoffs to the two players – manufacturer and typist – in Tender Trap. Draw the game tree corresponding to this payoff

---

[7] Figure 7.1 is an example of a game tree.

[8] Liebowitz and Margolis (1990) claim that this story is mythical and that the Dvorak keyboard is not superior to Qwerty.

table. Find all pure strategy Nash equilibria. Is there a mixed strategy Nash equilibrium in this game?

Tender Trap illustrates the binding force of convention (of having an agreed rule) even allowing for the possibility that the convention is not ideal. We tacitly agree upon many conventions to order our daily lives – rules of the road, rules of language, rules of courtesy. Although better rules might well have been arrived at, it is hard to change a settled convention.

7.3 Subgame-Perfect Equilibrium

While the Nash equilibrium concept remains at least a preliminary guide, frequently there are multiple Nash equilibria. Not only do multiple Nash equilibria create difficulties when it comes to prediction, they also pose problems for the theory itself. A condition of equilibrium is that each player's choice be a best response to the strategy of his opponents. But, if Nash equilibrium is not unique, how will a player know whether a given strategy choice on his part is a best reply when the opponents may be choosing among several different Nash equilibria strategies? Owing to such problems, much effort has gone into "refining" the Nash equilibrium concept (Selten, 1965, Selten, 1975; Myerson, 1978; Kreps and Wilson, 1982; Kohlberg and Mertens, 1986; Grossman and Perry, 1986; Cho and Kreps, 1987). Two widely accepted refinements of Nash equilibrium will be examined in this and the next section.

Consider the following game. One firm, the "entrant," moves first by deciding whether or not to invade a market now occupied solely by an "incumbent" firm. If she chooses to enter, the entrant will quote a price lower than that previously ruling. The incumbent must respond in one of two ways. He can (i) match the entrant's price and hence share the market, or (ii) quote a price still lower than hers so as to drive out the new competitor. In the latter case, the incumbent's profits are further reduced while the entrant suffers a loss.

Figure 7.2 depicts the game tree of this game; Table 7.5 depicts the same game in tabular or normal form. In these diagrams, the first number is the incumbent's payoff and the second is the entrant's payoff; thus, if the entrant stays out the incumbent's payoff is 6 and the entrant's payoff is 0. Looking at the table, there are two Nash equilibria in pure strategies,[9] indicated by the asterisks. (1) If the incumbent is going to choose Undercut, the entrant's best response is to choose Out. And if she chooses Out, the

---

[9] Since this is a sequential-move game, we need not consider mixed strategies.

Table 7.5. *Entry game*

		Player 2 (entrant)	
		Enter	Out
Player 1 (incumbent)	Match	2, 2*	6, 0
	Undercut	0, −1	6, 0*

incumbent loses nothing by being prepared to Undercut. (2) On the other hand, if the entrant chooses Enter, the incumbent's best response is Match. And, given the choice Match, the entrant is indeed better off choosing Enter.

But is the first equilibrium really plausible? In other words, once entry has taken place, will the incumbent carry out this threat or intention to Undercut her price? In terms of the decision sequence or game tree, the entrant might reason as follows: "Once I have chosen Enter, the incumbent will be better off choosing Match. Undercut is an empty threat. I therefore am better off choosing Enter."

Formally, a *subgame* of a game tree starts at a single node that is not in an information set with other nodes. The entry game has the simple subgame depicted in Figure 7.3. Given that fact, instead of requiring only that strategies be best replies for the original game, it seems reasonable to impose the additional condition that the relevant parts of each player's overall strategy be a best response in any subgame as well. In other words, the chosen strategy should not only be rational in the Nash equilibrium "best response" sense but in addition should not involve the player in an irrational choice among available options at any later (decision) node, even nodes that may not be reached if the Nash equilibrium is played. Whenever the Nash equilibrium strategies are rational at any *subgame* starting from a node in a tree, the equilibrium is said to be *perfect*, or, more precisely, *subgame perfect* (Selten, 1965).

The Nash equilibrium (Out, Undercut) involves a suboptimal choice by the incumbent in the event that the entrant deviates from the Nash

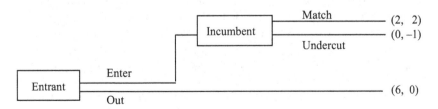

Figure 7.2. Game tree of entry.

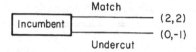

Figure 7.3. Subgame for incumbent.

equilibrium and chooses to Enter. In other words, this Nash equilibrium is supported by a threat by the incumbent to Undercut upon entry, a threat that the incumbent is unlikely to carry out as it is not in his self-interest to do so. The requirement of subgame perfection eliminates Nash equilibria (such as this one) that are supported by non-credible threats.

As another illustration of subgame-perfect equilibrium, consider an auction conducted under the following rules. The auctioneer starts the bidding at $1,000 and will make raises in steps of $1,000. The n bidders draw numbers out of a hat. The buyer drawing number 1 has the first opportunity to accept or reject the initial asking price. If buyer 1 rejects, he is out of the auction and buyer 2 has a chance to bid $1,000. If buyer 1 accepts, the asking price is raised by $1,000 and the auctioneer moves to buyer 2 who then must decide whether to accept at $2,000 or reject (and hence exit). The auction continues until the asking price is rejected by all buyers, in which case the last acceptance becomes the actual sale.

Suppose there the two buyers are bidding for a diamond tiara. Alex, who drew the number 1, values the tiara at $3,500. Bev, who drew the number 2, values the tiara at $2,500.[10] The "sensible" solution is for Alex to accept the opening price of $1,000 while Bev accepts the next asking price of $2,000. Alex then bids $3,000 and wins the tiara. However, there are other Nash equilibria. Consider the following alternative strategy pair as a solution:

Alex's strategy: Reject the initial price.
Bev's strategy: Accept an asking price if and only if it is less than $5,000.

The strategy described for Bev seems rather weird, since it raises the possibility that she could end up paying for the tiara more than her valuation of $2,500. But let us follow the logic of the proposed solution. Given that Alex does reject immediately, Bev will take the tiara for $1,000, getting her maximum net payoff of $2,500 − $1,000 = $1,500. So this strategy for Bev is indeed a best response to Alex. Now consider whether Alex's strategy is a best response to Bev's. If Alex rejects he ends up with nothing. But if he

[10] We are implicitly assuming that the seller does not have full knowledge of the buyers' reservation prices. For, if he did, rather than hold an auction he would simply announce an asking price close to $3,500.

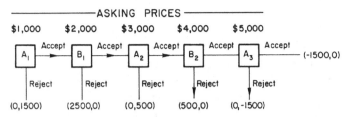

Figure 7.4. Open auction with alternating bids.

accepts, that is, if he follows some strategy *other* than the one considered here, for example, bidding up to his own valuation, the bidding sequence might go as follows:

Alex bids $1,000
Bev bids $2,000
Alex bids $3,000
Bev bids $4,000 (!) and gets the tiara.

No matter what specific strategy Alex chooses (he might, for example, set himself an upper limit of $1,000 or $3,000 or $5,000 or . . .), he will either end up with nothing or, worse, end up paying more for the tiara than it is worth to him. To reject the initial asking price is therefore indeed a best response to Bev's strategy. It follows that the pair of proposed strategies is also a Nash equilibrium.

Just as in the entry game, we can eliminate this "implausible" Nash equilibrium by requiring that the equilibrium be subgame perfect. The tree or extensive form of the game is depicted in Figure 7.4, with initial node A_1. There are four subgames beginning at B_1, A_2, B_2, and A_3. Each is easily analyzed. Starting with the last subgame beginning at A_3, Alex loses $1,500 by accepting once Bev has bid $4,000, so his best response is to reject. This is denoted by the arrow pointing down from A_3.

Next, consider the subgame originating at B_2. If Alex had bid $3,000, Bev's payoff from accepting at $4,000 would be −$1,500 (= $2,500 − $4,000) since, as we have just argued, Alex will reject at his next opportunity. Her optimal move at B_2 is therefore to reject, which would violate the strategy under consideration. It follows that the implausible Nash equilibrium associated with that strategy pair is not subgame perfect.

To confirm that the "sensible" intuitive Nash equilibrium is subgame perfect, consider the subgame with initial node A_2. From our previous argument, if Alex accepts the asking price of $3,000, Bev will reject the asking price of $4,000, and so Alex's net payoff is $500 (= $3,500 − $3,000). It follows that his optimal strategy is to accept. This is depicted by an arrow pointing across from the node A_2.

Now consider the subgame with initial node B_1. Bev is outbid if she accepts and gets nothing if she rejects. Therefore to accept the asking price of $2,000 is a best response. Given this, Alex's optimal strategy in the opening round is to accept also. We conclude therefore that the "sensible" Nash equilibrium (in which Alex will bid up to $3,000 and Bev up to $2,000) is subgame perfect.

Unfortunately, this is not the end of the story. From node B_1, Bev is indifferent between accepting and rejecting. Rejecting $2,000 is therefore also a best response. It follows that there is a second subgame-perfect equilibrium in which Alex accepts the starting offer of $1,000 and Bev then drops out of the bidding. Nor is this an entirely implausible outcome. Intuitively, Bev may note that Alex always has an incentive to outbid her, and so she may well decide not to bother going through the exercise of pushing up the price on the seller's behalf. However, if there is any chance at all that Alex will not continue bidding, Bev is strictly better off staying in and accepting the asking price of $2,000.

This suggests a further approach to "refining" the Nash equilibrium concept. Starting with some game G, one might perturb the payoffs and consider what happens as the perturbation approaches zero. A Nash equilibrium for the original game G that is the limit of Nash equilibria in the perturbed game is surely more credible than if this were not the case. For example, in the previous bidding game suppose that Alex's valuation is $3,500 with probability $1 - \pi_A$ and $1,500 with probability π_A while Bev's valuation is $2,500 with probability $1 - \pi_B$ and $500 with probability π_B. (Here each person's probability distribution is known to the opponent, but only the individual knows his or her own actual realization.) If Alex accepts the initial price of $1,000, he will take the tiara at that price with probability π_B, since Bev will not bid if her valuation is $500. If Bev has a valuation of $2,500, she will accept at $2,000 and win with probability π_A, since Alex will bid $3,000 only if his valuation is $3,500. Of the two subgame-perfect equilibria for the bidding game, the equilibrium in which the price is bid up to $3,000 is therefore more credible than the one in which Bev rejects the asking price of $2,000.

A second approach, also due to Selten (1975), introduces "noisy" strategies. Suppose an individual who intends to select some strategy x_a from his set of feasible pure strategies $(x_1, x_2, \ldots, x_A)$ unintentionally plays some other strategy x_b with probability $\pi_b > 0$, where $\sum_{b \neq a} \pi_b = \varepsilon$ and ε is small. Then an opponent may want to choose her strategy in the light of this "tremble" possibility.

For our alternating-bid auction, the possibility of such trembles may induce each buyer to stay in the bidding until the asking price exceeds his or her reservation price. Again, the reason should be clear. As long as there is a chance that an opponent will make a mistake and drop out, a buyer is better off accepting any asking price below his or her reservation price, since there is a positive probability of winning.

We explore this idea more systematically in the next section.

Exercises and Excursions 7.3

1 *Entry Game with Two Types of Entrant*
Suppose that with probability π the entrant, if she decides to enter, signs a short-term contract with a supplier. If so the payoffs in the game are exactly as in Table 7.5. With probability $1 - \pi$ the entrant, if she decides to enter, signs a long-term contract. In that case payoffs are:

ENTRY GAME WITH A LONG-TERM CONTRACT

		Player 2 (entrant)	
		Enter	Out
Player 1 (incumbent)	Match	3, 1	6, 0
	Undercut	−1, −2	6, 0

The incumbent does not know whether the entrant has signed a short-term or long-term contract.

(A) If $\pi = 1$, we have seen that there are two Nash equilibria, one of which is subgame perfect. Show that the conclusion is the same if $\pi = 0$.
(B) There are two subgame-perfect equilibria if $0 < \pi < 1$. Explain.
(C) Suppose that the entrant "trembles" as she chooses her strategy so that there is a small probability that she will stray from her pure Nash equilibrium strategy. What will be the outcome of such a game?
(D) Does your answer change if the incumbent also "trembles" with small probability?

2   Second-Price Sealed-Bid Auction

Alex has a valuation of $3,500, Bev a valuation of $2,500. Bids must be submitted in hundreds of dollars. Valuations are common knowledge to the two buyers but are unknown to the seller.

Each buyer makes a sealed bid, without knowledge of the opponent's bid. The high bidder is the winner and pays the *second highest* bid.

(A) Explain why bids by Alex and Bev of $3,500 and $2,500, respectively, are Nash equilibrium bids. (Since there are no subgames the solution is also subgame perfect.)

(B) Explain why bids of $0 by Alex and $10,000 by Bev are also Nash equilibrium bids. Are there other equilibria as well?

(C) Appeal to arguments along the line of those at the end of the section to conclude that the Nash equilibrium of (A) is more credible than any other equilibrium.

7.4 Further Refinements

As has been seen, the additional requirement of subgame perfectness can reduce the number of Nash equilibria. But subgame perfectness is applicable only to games in which players move one at a time (and where these moves are public information). And, even when there is a strong subgame structure, there may be multiple subgame-perfect equilibria, some of which seem more credible than others. It would be desirable therefore to find other criteria for ruling out certain of the implausible Nash equilibria.

Consider the following modification of the entry game analyzed in the previous section. The rules are as before except that now the entrant as first mover can enter in two different ways. These affect the outcome if the seller tries to Match. If the entry is Mild, the entrant accepts a price match by the incumbent, whereas, if the entry is Tough, the entrant fights with a further price cut. The incumbent must choose his strategy knowing whether entry has occurred but without knowing whether the entrant has chosen Mild or Tough.

Payoffs in this game are given in Table 7.6 (note that if the entrant chooses Mild, the payoffs are exactly as in the example of Table 7.5). The tree or extensive form of the game is depicted in Figure 7.5. As before, the nodes connected by the dashed line (the information set) indicate that the player at that point must choose without knowing which branch of the tree he or she is on.

Table 7.6. *Entry game with tough entry-I*

		Player 2 (entrant)		
		Mild entry	Tough entry	Out
Player 1 (incumbent)	Match	2, 2	1, 1	6, 0
	Undercut	0, −1	0, 0	6, 0

There are two Nash equilibria in pure strategies: (1) the entrant stays Out and the incumbent chooses Undercut; (2) the entrant chooses Mild Entry and the incumbent chooses Match.

Since there are no subgames of this game, we need to employ some other refinement of Nash equilibrium to rule out one of these equilibria. Consider how the incumbent fares against each possible entry strategy. With Mild entry, the incumbent has a payoff of 2 if he matches and 0 if he undercuts. If the entry strategy is Tough, again the incumbent is strictly better off choosing Match. Therefore, regardless of the type of entry, the incumbent is strictly better off choosing Match.

Undercut is a *weakly dominated strategy.* Once entry has occurred, Undercut yields the incumbent a lower payoff than Match. And of course, if the entrant remains Out, it makes no difference what the incumbent would have done. It thus seems reasonable to conclude that the incumbent will

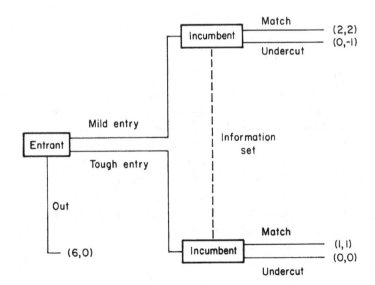

Figure 7.5. Entry game with two entry strategies.

Table 7.7. *Entry game with tough entry-II*

		Player 2 (entrant)		
		Mild entry	Tough entry	Out
Player 1 (incumbent)	Match	2, 2	−1, 1	6, 0
	Undercut	0, −1	0, −1	6, 0

respond to entry with Match. This eliminates the Nash equilibrium in which the entrant stays out because of the (empty) threat of undercutting.

Another very similar example is given in Table 7.7. Here the payoffs in the second column of Table 7.6 (when the entrant chooses Tough) have been changed. Now it is no longer the case that Undercut is a weakly dominated strategy. However, consider the choices of the entrant. If the incumbent matches, the entrant's payoff is higher if she chooses Mild. If the incumbent undercuts, the entrant's payoff is the same whether she chooses Mild or Tough. Tough entry is therefore a weakly dominated strategy for the entrant. By eliminating such a strategy the game is reduced to the original entry game analyzed in the previous section (Table 7.5).

Eliminating (weakly) dominated strategies[11] is a relatively uncontroversial further refinement. However, only in rare cases is the dominance criterion applicable. Consider next the three-player game depicted in tree form in Figure 7.6. Each player chooses either Up or Down. The two nodes for player 3 are connected, indicating that this is an information set. That is, player 3 must select his action without knowing whether it was player 1 or player 2 who made the previous move. The payoffs to the players are specified at the terminal nodes: for instance, if players 1 and 3 each chooses Up, then players 1, 2, and 3 get −1, 0, and 1, respectively.

If player 1 chooses Up, player 3's best response is Down. Player 1 then ends up with a payoff of 3. Since player 1 is certain to have a lower payoff if he chooses Down, this is a Nash equilibrium.

But what if player 1 and player 2 both choose Down? This will occur if player 1 is a pessimist and thinks that player 3 will choose Up. Player 1 therefore chooses Down. If player 2 is also a pessimist he too will choose Down rather than Up, out of fear that player 3 will choose Down.

Note that this outcome occurs because player 1 thinks that player 3 will choose Up while player 2 thinks that player 3 will choose Down. That is, the players have mutually inconsistent beliefs.

---

[11] A somewhat stronger refinement is the *successive* elimination of weakly dominated strategies.

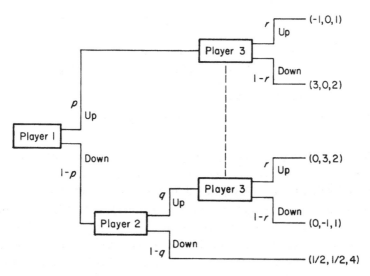

Figure 7.6. Playing against an unknown opponent.

One way of overcoming this problem has been suggested by Kreps and Wilson (1982). Take any strategy vector $s = (s_1, \ldots, s_n)$ for the n players. Consider, for each agent, a completely mixed strategy[12] that is close to s. Since all nodes are reached with completely mixed strategies, Bayes' Theorem can be applied in a straightforward manner to compute beliefs of each information set. Beliefs are then *consistent* if they are the limiting beliefs as the mixed strategies approach s.

For our example, suppose players 1 and 2 choose Down. Then consider this as the limit of mixed strategies in which player 1 chooses Up with small probability p, player 2 chooses Up with small probability q, and player 3 chooses Up with probability r. The probability that player 3 is then called on to play is $p + (1 - p)q$ and the conditional probability that it was player 1 who chose Up is:

Prob(1 chose Up | 3's information set is reached)

$$= \frac{p}{p + (1 - p)q} = \frac{(p/q)}{(p/q) + 1 - p} \qquad (7.4.1)$$

In the limit, as $p \to 0$ this approaches:

$$\frac{p/q}{1 + p/q}$$

---

[12] A completely mixed strategy for a player is a mixed strategy in which every pure strategy of the player is selected with non-zero probability.

If q goes toward zero faster than p, this ratio approaches 1 in the limit. On the other hand, if p goes to zero more quickly than q, this ratio approaches zero. Indeed, any conditional belief is consistent. To see this, set $p/q = \pi /(1 - \pi)$ where $0 < \pi < 1$. Substituting into (7.4.1) and taking the limit we obtain:

$$\lim_{p, q \to 0} \text{Prob}(1 \text{ chose Up} \mid 3\text{'s information set is reached}) = \pi$$

Thus, for this example, consistency imposes no restrictions upon the beliefs of agent 3. However, it still has predictive power since it imposes the restriction that players 1 and 2 must agree about agent 3's beliefs.

For the tree in Figure 7.6, the payoffs of players 1 and 2 for the top pair of terminal nodes are just the mirror image of those for the second pair of terminal nodes. If $\pi > \frac{1}{2}$ so that player 3 is more likely to be at the upper node, his best response is Down. If $\pi < \frac{1}{2}$ player 3's best response is Up. Finally, if $\pi = \frac{1}{2}$, then player 3 is indifferent and so willing to play a mixed strategy.

We can now establish that, for any consistent beliefs, the terminal node $(\frac{1}{2}, \frac{1}{2}, 4)$ will not be reached in equilibrium. For if $\pi > \frac{1}{2}$ player 3 chooses Down and so player 1's best response is Up. And if $\pi < \frac{1}{2}$ player 3's best response is Up, in which case player 2's best response is Up. Finally, if $\pi = \frac{1}{2}$ and player 3 adopts the mixed strategy of choosing Up with probability r, the payoff of player 1 is $3 - 4r$ if he chooses Up. Moreover, if player 1 chooses Down and player 2 chooses Up, player 2 has an expected payoff of $4r - 1$.

For all possible values of r, the larger of these two payoffs is at least 1. It follows that, for all r, either player 1 or player 2 or both have a best response of Up. The terminal node of $(\frac{1}{2}, \frac{1}{2}, 4)$ is therefore never reached if beliefs are consistent.

We now formalize the concept of consistency.

Definition: Consistent Beliefs

Let $\{(s_t^1, \ldots, s_t^n) \mid t = 1, 2, \ldots\}$ be a sequence of completely mixed strategies which converges to $(\bar{s}^1, \ldots, \bar{s}^n)$. Let $\{(H_t^1, \ldots, H_t^n) \mid t = 1, 2 \ldots\}$ be the corresponding beliefs of the n agents at each node of the tree induced by the completely mixed strategies (via Bayes' Theorem). If $(\bar{H}^1, \ldots, \bar{H}^n)$ is the limit of this sequence then these beliefs are consistent with strategy $(\bar{s}^1, \ldots, \bar{s}^n)$.

Having characterized consistent beliefs at every node and information set in the tree, it is then a straightforward matter to work backwards through the tree and determine whether strategies are best responses. If so, the strategies are said to be sequential (that is, sequentially consistent).

Definition: Sequential (Nash) Equilibrium

Let $(\bar{H}^1, \ldots, \bar{H}^n)$ be beliefs that are consistent with the Nash equilibrium strategy $(\bar{s}^1, \ldots, \bar{s}^n)$. If, moving sequentially through the entire tree, the Nash equilibrium strategies are best responses under these beliefs, then the equilibrium is sequential.

The sequential equilibrium concept is a modification of an earlier approach due to Selten (1975). He too begins by considering a sequence of completely mixed strategies that converges to a Nash equilibrium. However, in contrast with the definition of a sequential equilibrium, the beliefs induced by the completely mixed strategies and not just the limit of these beliefs are a part of the definition.

The basic idea is to start with a Nash equilibrium strategy for the n players $(\bar{s}^1, \ldots, \bar{s}^n)$ and then ask whether, for each i, $\bar{s}_i$ is still a best response if each opponent trembles when he tries to play his equilibrium strategy and instead plays each of his other feasible strategies with a small positive probability.

If such a set of trembles can be found, then the equilibrium is said to be trembling-hand perfect. Formalizing our earlier intuitive discussion, we have the following definition:

Definition: Trembling-Hand Perfect Equilibrium

Let $\{(s_t^1, \ldots, s_t^n) | t = 1, 2, \ldots\}$ be a sequence of completely mixed strategies converging to $(\bar{s}^1, \ldots, \bar{s}^n)$ and let $\{(H_t^1, \ldots, H_t^n) | t = 1, 2, \ldots\}$ be the beliefs of the n agents induced by the completely mixed strategies. If for each i and all t sufficiently large, the best response by agent i, given beliefs H_t^i, is $\bar{s}^i$, then $(\bar{s}^1, \ldots, \bar{s}^n)$ is trembling-hand perfect.

While the requirements of a trembling-hand perfect equilibrium are mildly stronger, it is only in rather special cases that a sequential equilibrium is not also trembling-hand perfect.

One of these is the simple bidding game of Exercise 2 at the end of Section 7.3. There Alex had a valuation of $3,500 and Bev a valuation of $2,500. It is a weakly dominant strategy for Alex to remain in the bidding as long as the asking price is less than $3,500. Therefore the belief that Alex will be willing to stay in the bidding beyond Bev's valuation is sequentially rational. Thus it is a sequential equilibrium for Bev to reject the initial asking price of $1,000 and drop out of the bidding. However, if there is a positive probability that Alex will tremble and drop out of the bidding at a price below $2,500,

Bev is strictly better off staying in the bidding. So, dropping out immediately is not a trembling-hand perfect equilibrium strategy for Bev.

At a conceptual level, most people find the trembling-hand analogy quite straightforward. In contrast, consistency as a limit of beliefs seems abstract and difficult to grasp. Given this, it is natural to employ the trembling-hand perfect equilibrium when this proves to be relatively uncomplicated. However, for sophisticated applications it can be significantly easier to check whether there exist sequentially consistent beliefs for a Nash equilibrium.

Exercises and Excursions 7.4

1 Sequential Equilibria

Consider the game depicted in Figure 7.6.

   (A) Show that (Up, Down, Down) is a sequential equilibrium of this game.
   (B) Is (Down, Up, Up) also a sequential equilibrium?
   (C) Are there any sequential equilibria in which player 3 adopts a mixed strategy?

2 Elimination of a Family of Nash Equilibria

Suppose that the payoffs for the game depicted in Figure 7.6 are modified as follows:

	Payoff vector
If player 1 chooses Up and 3 chooses Up	(3, 3, 2)
If player 1 chooses Up and 3 chooses Down	(0, 0, 0)
If player 1 chooses Down, 2 chooses Up and 3 Up	(4, 4, 0)
If player 1 chooses Down, 2 chooses Up and 3 Down	(0, 0, 1)
If players 1 and 2 both choose Down	(1, 2, 1)

Let p be the probability that player 1 chooses Up, q be the probability that player 2 chooses Up, and r be the probability that player 3 chooses Up.

   (A) Show that for $q \leq 2/3$ and $r \leq 1/3$, two Nash equilibria are (Up, q, Up) and (Down, Down, r).
   (B) Show that only one of these two classes of equilibria meets the condition for sequential equilibrium.

3 *Trembling-Hand Perfect Equilibrium*
  (A) Explain why a trembling-hand perfect equilibrium is a sequential equilibrium.
  (B) If the payoff matrix of a simultaneous-move game is as shown below, draw the tree of the corresponding sequential-move game, in which player 1 moves first and player 2 must respond without knowing what player 1 has chosen.

		Player 2	
$(\alpha > 1)$		l	r
Player 1	L	1, 1	1, α
	R	2, 0	$-1, -1$

  (C) Confirm that there are two Nash equilibria. Then let ε_1 be the probability that player 1 takes an out-of-equilibrium action. For each equilibrium confirm that, as long as ε_1 is small, player 2's best response is unaffected.
  (D) Suppose, in addition, that player 2 makes an out-of-equilibrium move with probability ε_2. Show that neither player's best response is affected as long as ε_1 and ε_2 are sufficiently small. That is, the equilibria are trembling-hand perfect.
  (E) Suppose instead that $\alpha = 1$. Show that there is only one trembling-hand perfect equilibrium. However, both the Nash equilibria identified in (C) are sequential.

COMMENT: This example illustrates that it is only for very specific parameter values of the normal-form payoff matrix that a sequential equilibrium is not also trembling-hand perfect.

4 *Open Bidding with Different Valuations*
Section 7.3 took up an example in which Alex and Bev made sequential bids for a tiara. For this game there are two subgame-perfect equilibria.

  (A) Explain why both are sequential equilibria.
  (B) Show that only one is trembling-hand perfect.
  (C) Would any small change in the parameters of the model change your answer to (B)?
  (D) Try to reconcile your answer with the comment at the end of the previous question.

Table 7.8. *To fight or not to fight*

$v^a, v^b \in \{1, -4\}$		Player b (Bev)	
		Aggressive	Passive
Player a (Alex)	Aggressive	v^a, v^b	6, 0
	Passive	0, 6	3, 3

7.5 Games with Private Information

While the "refinements" discussed in the previous sections succeed in excluding some of the implausible Nash equilibria, important difficulties remain. This is especially the case when players have private information but *their actions may signal their type*. Further refinements can be sensibly applied in such games of private information.

Consider the following example. Each of two players simultaneously chooses Aggressive or Passive. If both choose Aggressive so that a fight ensues, for either player the payoff is 1 if he is naturally mean and −4 if he is naturally kind. A player knows whether or not he is himself a mean type of individual, but this information is private.

The normal form of the game is depicted in Table 7.8. If player a (Alex) thinks that player b (Bev) is likely to play aggressively, his best response is to choose Aggressive if $v^a = 1$ and Passive if $v^a = -4$. Since the game is symmetric, the same is true for Bev. On the other hand, if Alex thinks that Bev is likely to choose Passive, then his best response is Aggressive, regardless of his private information.

But what will Alex think about Bev? And what will Alex think Bev will think about Alex? And what will Alex think that Bev will think Alex will think about Bev? . . . . And so on.

Economic theorists have, almost exclusively, chosen to rely on a resolution of this puzzle proposed by Harsanyi (1967–68). Suppose that the uncertain payoffs v^a and v^b are draws from some joint distribution. Moreover, and this is critical, suppose that this joint distribution is *common knowledge*.[13] That is, each player knows the joint distribution, each player knows that the other knows the joint distribution, each player knows that the other knows the joint distribution, and so on. Then each player is able to utilize this information to compute a best response.

---

[13] The concept of common knowledge was discussed in Section 5.3.

For our example, there are four possible payoff pairs when both players choose to be aggressive. Suppose the probability of each payoff-pair is $\frac{1}{4}$. With private information, a complete description of a player's strategy is a description of his strategy (possibly mixed) for each possible private message. We now confirm that it is a Nash equilibrium for each player to choose Aggressive if his or her parameter value is positive and to choose Passive if it is negative.

Suppose Bev behaves in this manner. Given our assumption that each payoff vector is equally likely, there is a probability of 0.5 that Bev will choose Aggressive. If Alex's valuation is v^a, his expected payoff to Aggressive is $(\frac{1}{2})v^a + (\frac{1}{2})6$ while his expected payoff to Passive is $(\frac{1}{2})0 + (\frac{1}{2})3$. The net advantage of Aggressive is therefore $\frac{1}{2}(v^a + 3)$. This is positive if $v^a = 1$ and is negative if $v^a = -4$. Therefore Alex's best response is to behave as proposed. Given the symmetry of the example, it follows that the proposed strategy is a Nash equilibrium.

To reiterate, in a game with private information, a strategy is a description of a player's action (or probabilistic mix of actions) for each possible private information state. As long as the underlying distribution of private informational messages is common knowledge, each player can compute his expected payoff against a particular strategy of his opponent. Equilibrium strategies are then strategies that are best responses, just as in the earlier discussion of Nash equilibrium with no private information. Because of the importance of the common-knowledge assumption, economists sometimes acknowledge the distinction by referring to the equilibrium as a *Bayesian Nash equilibrium*.

As a second example, let us consider an advertising game with private information. In this game, there is an equilibrium in which a seller of high-quality products can signal that fact by costly advertising.

Suppose that a manufacturer is about to introduce a new product that will be of either superior or mediocre quality. These define two "types" of firm. If the product is superior, optimal use by consumers is High. If it is mediocre, optimal use is Low. High rates of consumption generate high revenue and profit for the firm. Before distribution of the new product the firm chooses either Zero advertising, Z, Radio advertising, R, or more expensive TV advertising, T.

It is common knowledge that the odds of a superior product are only 1 to 4. Consumers are not able to observe product quality until it has been used for some time. They do, however, observe the advertising decision of the firm. The firm observes product quality before taking an advertising decision.

Table 7.9. *Advertising game*

			Consumer's choice		
			Low	High	
Type of manufacturer	Mediocre (prob. = 0.8)	T	−3, 1	1, 0	ε
		R	−1, 1	3, 0	ε
		Z	4, 1	8, 0	$1 - 2\varepsilon$
	Superior (prob. = 0.2)	T	−3, 2	5, 4	ε
		R	−1, 2	7, 4	ε
		Z	4, 2	12, 4	$1 - 2\varepsilon$

The payoff matrix for this game is given in Table 7.9. Note that, in switching from Zero advertising to Radio advertising, the manufacturer's payoff declines by 5. This reflects the cost of the advertising. TV advertising costs 7 so there is a further decline of 2 in the manufacturer's payoff if he switches from Radio to TV.

One Nash equilibrium of this game is for consumers to choose a Low rate of consumption and for both types of manufacturers to choose Zero advertising. This is readily confirmed from Table 7.9. With consumers choosing Low, there is no incentive for a manufacturer to incur any advertising costs.

This equilibrium is also sequential (and trembling-hand perfect). To see this, consider the mixed strategies of the two types given by the final column in Table 7.9. Since both types choose Radio advertising with probability ε, the conditional probability that an advertiser is mediocre is equal to the prior probability, that is, 0.8. The expected payoff to consuming at a high rate is therefore $(0.8)(0) + (0.2)(4) = 0.8$, while the expected payoff to consuming at a low rate is $(0.8)(1) + (0.2)(2) = 1.2$. Given such beliefs, consumers will choose the low rate.

Exactly the same argument holds for TV advertising. Therefore the belief that both types of manufacturers will choose Zero advertising is consistent. This "pooling" equilibrium in which the different types are not differentiated is not the only equilibrium, however. There is a second "separating" equilibrium in which a superior manufacturer signals his product's quality via advertising.

Suppose consumers believe that superior manufacturers will choose TV while mediocre advertisers will choose Radio or Zero advertising. From Table 7.9, given such beliefs, the best response to TV is a high rate of use, and the best response to Radio or Zero advertising is a low rate of use. Finally,

Table 7.10. *Equilibrium payoffs in the advertising game*

		Mediocre manufacturer	Superior manufacturer	Consumer
E_1:	Neither type advertises	4	4	1.2
E_2:	Superior chooses TV	4	5	1.6
E_3:	Superior chooses Radio	4	7	1.6

given such choices by consumers, a superior manufacturer has a payoff of 5 if he chooses TV, a payoff of -1 if he chooses Radio, and a payoff of 4 if he chooses Zero advertising. His best response is therefore to advertise on TV. On the other hand, a mediocre manufacturer has a payoff of 4 without advertising and a payoff of 1 if he advertises on TV. It follows that the proposed strategies are Nash equilibrium strategies. Arguing almost exactly as above, it may be confirmed that the consumers' beliefs are consistent. Therefore the Nash equilibrium is also sequential.

But this is far from the end of the story. Suppose consumer beliefs are different, and instead they believe that any manufacturer who advertises on either Radio or TV is of high quality while a manufacturer who does no advertising is of mediocre quality. From Table 7.9, a mediocre manufacturer is still better off not advertising while a superior manufacturer will choose Radio advertising. We therefore have a third Nash (and sequential) equilibrium.

It is instructive to compare the payoffs in the different equilibria, as summarized in Table 7.10. Note that no player is made worse off and at least one is made better off in moving from the first to the second and then to the third equilibrium. In particular, a superior manufacturer has a strong incentive to try to convince players to play the third equilibrium. We shall now argue that such a player, if he is allowed to communicate, can plausibly talk his way out of the other two equilibria. More precisely, we begin by proposing a (sequential) Nash equilibrium and then ask whether the equilibrium beliefs are likely to survive if players can communicate.

Suppose, for example, that the proposed equilibrium has the superior-quality manufacturer choosing TV and the mediocre manufacturer choosing Zero advertising.

The superior firm might send the following message to consumers: "I am a superior firm but I am going to advertise on Radio rather than Television. You should believe me and choose a high rate of usage since a mediocre firm would be worse off if it were to choose Radio and you were to make the same response."

Looking at Table 7.9, we see that this message is correct. With a high rate of usage, the short-run gains for a mediocre firm are offset by the cost of advertising and so profit is 3 – which is less than the equilibrium profit of 4. However, the superior firm is clearly better off. Therefore if consumers recognize that the argument is correct, the Nash equilibrium with TV advertising fails the communication test.

More formally, let $\Theta = \{\theta_1, \ldots, \theta_n\}$ be the set of possible types of player. We will describe an equilibrium as being *weakly communication proof* if no message of the following type is credible:[14]

I am taking an out-of-equilibrium action and sending you the true message that my type is $\theta_i \in \Theta$, and you should believe me. For if you do and respond optimally, I will be better off while any other type of player mimicking me would end up worse off.

This communication test hinges upon the availability of an out-of-equilibrium action that would be in the interests of only one type of player. The following stronger test allows for an out-of-equilibrium action that would be in the interests of a subset of the possible types of player. We describe an equilibrium as being *strongly communication proof* if no message of the following type is credible:

I am taking an out-of-equilibrium action and sending you the true message that my type is in B, a subset of Θ, and you should believe me. For if you do so and respond optimally (using prior beliefs about types), any type in B would be better off while any other type of seller attempting to do the same would end up worse off.

It may be that none of the Nash equilibria survive this strong communication test. Thus, at least so far as we now can tell, game-theoretic methodology will sometimes fail to generate a credible equilibrium. While perhaps regrettable this is, we believe, hardly surprising. In general, games with private information have informational externalities. One player's return yields information about his type and, by inference, information about other players who choose different actions. In the presence of such externalities it would be much more surprising if there were a universal existence theorem for credible equilibria.

Nevertheless, even without equilibrium explanations for every imaginable situation, the Nash equilibrium concept with its refinements has proved to be fruitful for analyzing a wide range of strategic interactions, as will be illustrated further in the chapters to come.

---

[14] This is what Cho and Kreps (1987) refer to rather obliquely as the "intuitive criterion."

Exercises and Excursions 7.5

1 Bayesian Nash Equilibrium with Correlated Beliefs

In the first example considered in Section 7.5, the probability that an opponent has a positive payoff when both are aggressive is 1/2 regardless of a player's type. That is, types are independent. Suppose instead that $v^a = 1$ and $v^b = 1$ with probability $\frac{1}{4}$ while $v^a = 1$ and $v^b = -4$ is β and $v^a = -4$ and $v^b = 1$ is β. That is, the joint probability matrix is symmetric.

(A) Show that types are positively correlated if and only if $\beta < \frac{1}{4}$.
(B) If $\beta \geq \frac{9}{40}$ holds, show that it is a Bayesian Nash equilibrium for a player to choose Aggressive when v^a is positive and Passive when v^a is negative.
(C) Show also that if $\beta < \frac{9}{40}$ then this is no longer a Bayesian Nash equilibrium.
(D) What is the Bayesian Nash equilibrium in this case?

7.6 Evolutionary Equilibrium

The approach outlined in the preceding sections is not useful in exploring the long-run equilibria of games that are played repeatedly in large anonymous populations subject to natural selection. In such cases what can be said about the outcome and what equilibria are likely to emerge? One way of resolving this problem is to introduce evolutionary or natural-selection considerations, as proposed by the biologist John Maynard Smith (1976, 1982). Imagine a large uniform population of organisms that randomly encounter one another in pairwise interactions, with payoffs for each single encounter given by some game matrix. Then, owing to the force of natural selection, over the generations a strategy yielding above-average return will gradually come to be used by larger and larger fractions of the population while strategies with below-average returns will shrink in representation. Among economic players, *imitation* may replace or supplement natural selection, with somewhat similar results (Alchian, 1950; Winter, 1964). If the dynamic evolutionary process leads to a population whose members are fractionally distributed over a set of strategies – or, as a special case, all of whom are following some single strategy – then that distribution is called an *evolutionary equilibrium*, provided that the evolutionary process works to maintain and restore the distribution in the face of all sufficiently small arbitrary displacements of the population proportions ("shocks").

To begin with, consider only pure strategies. Let us assume a symmetrical game (so that the row and column players could be interchanged without affecting the matrix of payoffs).[15] Denote as $V(x_a \mid x_b)$ the expected payoff to an organism playing x_a in an environment where everyone else in the population is playing x_b. Maynard Smith defined what he termed an "evolutionarily stable strategy" (ESS) as follows. Strategy x_a is an ESS if either of these two conditions hold:

(i) $V(x_a \mid x_a) > V(x_b \mid x_a)$

(ii) Or, $V(x_a \mid x_a) = V(x_b \mid x_a)$ and $V(x_a \mid x_b) > V(x_b \mid x_b)$

for any $b \neq a$

The first condition corresponds essentially to the strategy pair (x_a, x_a) being a *strong* Nash equilibrium. If when everyone else is playing x_a, any single player finds that x_a is strictly better for him than any other strategy, then x_a is an ESS. The second condition says that, even if (x_a, x_a) is only a *weak* Nash equilibrium, with x_a yielding the same expected payoff as another strategy x_b, that strategy pair can still be an ESS provided that x_a can defeat any other strategy x_b when the population consists almost entirely of players of x_b. In effect, the first condition says that the home team prevails when it can beat any intruder. The second says that the home team can still win out even if it only ties some intruders, provided it can beat any such intruder on the latter's own home field.

Satisfying the conditions for an ESS does not necessarily suffice for evolutionary equilibrium, however. In the first place, the ESS definition above was pitched in terms of a single evolutionarily stable *strategy* – whereas, more generally, evolutionary stability is a characteristic of a population distribution over a set of strategies. If strategies a, b, and c are being played within a certain population in proportions p_a, p_b, and p_c, respectively, that distribution may or may not be evolutionarily stable – with no implications one way or the other as to whether any of the three component strategies is an ESS standing alone.

It is important not to confuse a *mixed population* with a *uniform population playing a mixed strategy*. A population distribution in the proportions p_a, p_b, and p_c over the pure strategies a, b, and c does not in general have the same stability properties as a population uniformly playing the corresponding probability mixture of the same three strategies. (Except that when there are only two pure strategies, the stability properties are indeed equivalent.)[16]

[15] This amounts to assuming a homogeneous population in which everyone is of one single type.

[16] Maynard Smith (1982), pp. 184–186.

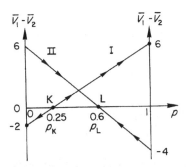

Figure 7.7. Evolutionary equilibria in Tender Trap and Chicken.

Second and more fundamentally, since an evolutionary equilibrium is the stable terminus of a natural-selection process over the generations, it is characterized not only by the payoff elements entering into the definition of the ESS but also by the dynamic formula governing the change in population proportions in response to yield differentials in any generation (Taylor and Jonker, 1978; Zeeman, 1981; Friedman, 1991; Hirshleifer and Martinez Coll, 1988). It may be, for example, that, even if the payoffs remain unchanged, increasing the sensitivity of the dynamic response formula can lead to explosive cycling instead of the damped behavior of a system consistent with ultimate stability.[17]

In what follows, we will generally be employing the evolutionary equilibrium terminology, although in most of the simple cases dealt with the ESS definition originally proposed by Maynard Smith suffices to locate the equilibrium.

Along the lines of the analysis in Hirshleifer (1982), the essentials of the relation between Nash equilibrium and evolutionary equilibrium are pictured in Figure 7.7. On the horizontal axis is plotted p, the proportion of the population playing the first or "more cooperative" strategy in the games Chicken and Tender Trap considered in Section 7.2.[18]

---

[17] Consider the discrete-generation dynamic formula:

$$\Delta p_a = \kappa p_a(\bar{V}_a - V), \quad \text{for all strategies } a = 1, \ldots, A$$

Here p_a is the proportion of the population playing strategy a (where, of course, $\sum_a p_a = 1$), $\bar{V}_a$ is the mean payoff received by a player of strategy a, V is the average mean yield for the population as a whole, and κ is a parameter representing the sensitivity of the dynamic process. Then, if there is an interior Nash equilibrium consisting of a population distributed over a set of pure strategies, whether or not that Nash equilibrium is also an evolutionary equilibrium depends upon κ being sufficiently small (Hirshleifer and Martinez Coll, 1988, pp. 387–390).

[18] Recall that "Dvorak" and "Coward" are the more cooperative strategies in (the simultaneous move version of) Tender Trap and in Chicken, respectively.

On the assumption that each individual will be randomly encountering other members of the population in a one-in-one interaction, let $\bar{V}_1$ denote the average payoff, as a function of p, to an individual choosing the more cooperative strategy 1. Similarly, let $\bar{V}_2$ be the expected payoff to the less cooperative strategy 2 as a function of p. Thus:

$$\bar{V}_1 \equiv pV(x_1|x_1) + (1-p)V(x_1|x_2)$$
$$\bar{V}_2 \equiv pV(x_2|x_1) + (1-p)V(x_2|x_2) \qquad (7.6.1)$$

Evidently, the second strategy will be more successful, and thus over the generations will be naturally selected over strategy 1, whenever $\bar{V}_1 - \bar{V}_2 < 0$. From (7.6.1):

$$\bar{V}_1 - \bar{V}_2 = p[V(x_1|x_1) - V(x_2|x_1)] + (1-p)[V(x_1|x_2) - V(x_2|x_2)]$$

If strategy x_1 is a strong Nash equilibrium so that the first bracketed term is strictly positive, then $\bar{V}_1 - \bar{V}_2$ is necessarily positive when p approaches unity. Moreover, even if the payoffs were such that the first bracket is zero, $\bar{V}_1 - \bar{V}_2$ is still positive if the second bracket is positive. Hence sufficient conditions for an evolutionary equilibrium are indeed those given by (i) and (ii) in the definition of ESS above.[19]

Figure 7.7 indicates that two qualitatively different types of situations associated with the payoff environments of Tender Trap (line I) and Chicken (line II). Line I is positively sloped, owing to the fact that in Tender Trap it is more profitable always to conform to what the great majority of the other players are doing; line II is negatively sloped since in the environment summarized by the Chicken payoff matrix it is more advantageous to do the contrary.

For the Tender Trap example of Exercise 7.2.1, $p = 0$ corresponds to the mutually less profitable "Qwerty" Nash equilibrium at (x_2, x_2); $p = 1$ similarly corresponds to the more profitable "Dvorak" Nash equilibrium at (x_1, x_1); and finally the crossover point K at the population proportions $(p_K, 1 - p_K) = (0.25, 0.75)$ corresponds to the mixed Nash equilibrium. As can be seen, for $p > p_K$, the difference $\bar{V}_1 - \bar{V}_2$ is positive. Then, as indicated by the arrows, the proportion adopting the first strategy will grow over the generations, eventually achieving the extreme at $p = 1$. For any initial proportion $p < p_K$, on the other hand, the evolutionary process over time will go the other way, terminating at $p = 0$. Thus, the mixed-strategy Nash

---

[19] This argument can also be used to show that even when there are more than two pure strategies (i) any strong Nash equilibrium is an evolutionary equilibrium and (ii) a weak Nash equilibrium might not be an evolutionary equilibrium.

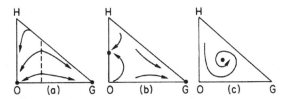

Figure 7.8. Examples of possible evolutionary equilibrium patterns when $A = 3$.

equilibrium[20] represented by point K is not an evolutionary equilibrium (is not "evolutionarily stable"); only the pure-strategy Nash equilibria at $p = 0$ and at $p = 1$ are evolutionary equilibria.

For the Chicken payoff matrix of Table 7.4, there is a mixed Nash equilibrium at the crossover point L, where $(p_L, 1 - p_L) = (0.6, 0.4)$. Since in Chicken it is the *less* prevalent strategy that has the advantage, as indicated by the arrows along line II, the evolutionary progression is always away from the extremes and toward the interior solution at point L. Thus, for Chicken only, the mixed Nash equilibria is an evolutionary equilibrium.

A number of new possibilities emerge when we consider strategy sets where the number of pure strategies, A, exceeds 2.[21] Figure 7.8 is a suggestive illustration for $A = 3$. Any point within each triangle represents a distribution of the population over the three strategy options. The horizontal coordinate represents the proportion p_1 playing strategy 1, the vertical coordinate the proportion p_2 playing strategy 2, while the remaining proportion p_3 is measured by the horizontal (or, equivalently the vertical) distance from the hypotenuse. Thus, the origin is the point where $p_3 = 1$. The arrows show convergence possibilities for a number of different possible cases. Without going into the specific conditions here,[22] it is evident that there may be evolutionary equilibria (as indicated by the heavy dots in the diagrams) at various combinations of: (i) one or more vertices; (ii) an edge and a vertex; or (iii) in the interior.[23] A vertex evolutionary equilibrium corresponds to the situation where only a single strategy is represented in equilibrium; an edge evolutionary equilibrium corresponds to more than

---

[20] Since in both Tender Trap and Chicken only two pure strategies are involved, for purposes of analyzing evolutionary stability we can, as indicated above, deal with a uniform population playing a mixed strategy as if it were a mixed population playing the corresponding distribution of pure strategies.

[21] Here we will always be thinking of *mixed populations*, each member of which plays some pure strategy, rather than *uniform populations playing a mixed strategy*.

[22] On this, see Hirshleifer and Martinez Coll (1988, pp. 379–380).

[23] Some of the possibilities are illustrated in the exercises below.

one, but not all, strategies being represented; an interior evolutionary equilibrium indicates that all strategies are represented. Or, finally, there may be no evolutionary equilibrium at all.

For $A \geq 3$, there are several other interesting implications. First, it may be that each of two or more strategies can defeat all others, but are tied against one another. In such cases, no single one of the winning strategies will meet the conditions for an evolutionary equilibrium, since it is not stable with regard to displacements shifting its proportionate representation as against other members of the winning group. Yet, the group as a whole represents a kind of *evolutionary equilibrium region*, since any given starting point of the evolutionary progression will always be attracted to some terminus along the edge connecting those strategies. Second, it is also possible to have a different kind of attractive region: a closed "limit cycle" toward which the population proportions spiral from within or without – but where, along the curve itself, the proportions cycle perpetually.

Exercises and Excursions 7.6

1 Nash Equilibrium and Evolutionary Equilibrium
Identify the pure-strategy and mixed-strategy Nash equilibria, and the evolutionary equilibria as well, of the following payoff matrices. Show that 1 has evolutionary equilibria at all three vertices; 2 has an evolutionary equilibrium only along an edge; 3 has only an interior evolutionary equilibrium; and 4 has no evolutionary equilibrium at all.

1	a	b	c	2	a	b	c
a	8, 8	3, 2	1, 7	a	3, 3	4, 4	2, 2
b	2, 3	5, 5	4, 0	b	4, 4	3, 3	2, 2
c	7, 1	0, 4	5, 5	c	2, 2	2, 2	1, 1

3	a	b	c	4	a	b	c
a	1, 1	2, 2	3, 3	a	3, 3	3, 3	2, 1
b	2, 2	1, 1	2, 3	b	3, 3	3, 3	2, 2
c	3, 3	3, 2	1, 1	c	1, 2	2, 2	1, 1

2 Evolutionary Dynamics
This exercise is designed to illustrate the dynamics corresponding to the two vertex evolutionary equilibria shown in the first diagram of Figure 7.8.

For the payoff matrix below, let (p_1, p_2, p_3) be the population proportions using strategies a, b, and c, respectively.

	a	b	c
a	2, 2	0, 0	0, 0
b	0, 0	1, 1	0, 2
c	0, 0	2, 0	1, 1

(A) Using the discrete-generation dynamic formula given in footnote 17, show that the population proportions evolve according to:

$$\Delta p_1 = \kappa p_1(2p_1 - V)$$
$$\Delta p_2 = \kappa p_2(p_2 - V)$$
$$\Delta p_3 = \kappa p_3(2p_2 + p_3 - V)$$

(B) Since these changes sum to zero, show that:
$V = 2p_1^2 + p_2^2 + p_3(2p_2 + p_3^2) = 2p_1^2 + (p_2 + p_3)^2 = 2p_1^2 + (1 - p_1)^2$

(C) Hence show that $\Delta p_1 > 0$ if and only if $1 > p_1 > \frac{1}{3}$.

(D) Show that V exceeds $\frac{2}{3}$ for all p_1. Hence explain why $\Delta p_2 < 0$ for all $p_2 < \frac{2}{3}$.

(E) Show that if $p_1 < \frac{1}{3}$ and $p_3 \approx 0$, Δp_2 is strictly positive.

(F) Use these results to explain why the population proportions will evolve as depicted in Figure 7.8a (as long as κ is sufficiently small).

3 *Nash Equilibrium versus Evolutionary Equilibrium, and Evolutionary Equilibrium Region*

(A) For the payoff matrix below, show that there is a weak Nash equilibrium at the (c, c) strategy pair along the main diagonal (corresponding to the c-vertex of the triangle). However, show that this Nash equilibrium cannot be an evolutionary equilibrium.

[HINT: If $p_c = 1 - \varepsilon$, are there any p_a, p_b population fractions, summing to ε, for which strategy a and/or strategy b has higher payoff than strategy c?]

	a	b	c
a	3, 3	3, 3	1, 4
b	3, 3	3, 3	2, 2
c	4, 1	2, 2	2, 2

(B) Show that strategy c will be dominated, even as ε approaches unity, by mixtures of a and b in which the latter has more than 50% representation. Accordingly, identify a range along the a–b edge of the triangle that represents an evolutionary equilibrium region.

4   Interacting Populations

The analysis in the text postulated interactions within a single homogeneous population. But sometimes we want to consider interactions between members of two distinct populations: e.g., males versus females, buyers versus sellers, predators versus prey.

(A) The payoff matrix below is associated with the game known as Battle of the Sexes. What are the three Nash equilibria of this game?

(B) In considering evolutionary equilibria of games with interacting populations, we seek stable vectors of population proportions (p_1, $p_2, \ldots, p_A$; $q_1, q_2, \ldots, q_A$) – where the p's represent the proportions of the first population and the q's are proportions of the second population, both distributed over the A available pure strategies. Find the evolutionary equilibria of the Battle of the Sexes game, if any.

		Player k	
		x_1^k	x_2^k
	x_1^j	10, 8	4, 4
Player j	x_2^j	4, 4	8, 10

(C) In the Chicken game, described earlier in the chapter as taking place within a single homogeneous population, there were three Nash equilibria of which only the single "interior" Nash equilibrium (representing a mixed-strategy or mixed-proportions solution) was an evolutionary equilibrium. Suppose now that the interacting players come from different populations. Do the results differ?

5   The "War of Attrition" (Maynard Smith, 1976; Riley, 1979)

Two animals are competing for a single prize (item of food). As long as they engage in a merely ritualistic (non-damaging) struggle, neither wins the prize and each incurs an opportunity cost of c per unit of time. If player

2 withdraws at time t, the payoffs are:

$$U_1 = V - ct$$

$$U_2 = -ct$$

(A) Explain why no player will, in equilibrium, choose any particular stopping time $\hat{t}$ with positive probability.

(B) Suppose player 2 adopts the continuously mixed strategy of dropping out by time t with cumulative probability $G(t)$. Write the expected payoff to player 1.

(C) Hence, or otherwise, show that the Nash equilibrium strategy of this game is:
$G(t) = 1 - \exp^{-ct/V}$

(D) Explain why it is only a matter of notational convenience to choose a unit of measurement so that $c = V$.

(E) *Under this assumption, show that the expected payoff to playing the Nash equilibrium strategy against a mutant strategy $H(t)$ can be expressed as:

$$V(v|\mu) = \int_0^\infty G'(t)\left[H(t) - t + \int_0^t H(x)dx \right]dt$$

$$= \int_0^\infty [G'(t)(H(t) - t) + H(t)(1 - G(t))]dt$$

[HINT: Integrate $\int_0^\infty G'(t) \int_0^t H(x)\,dxdt$ by parts, using the fact that $G'(t) = -\,d(1 - G(t))/dt.$]

(F) *Show that $V(\mu \mid \mu) - V(v \mid \mu)$ reaches a maximum at $\mu = v$, that is, the Nash equilibrium is also an evolutionary equilibrium.

[HINT: Write the Euler condition and then use the fact that $G'(t) + G(t) - 1 = 0.$]

SUGGESTIONS FOR FURTHER READING: There are several first-rate books on game theory. Friedman (1986) and Gibbons (1992) are excellent introductions to game theory. For more in-depth treatments, the reader should consult Fudenberg and Tirole (1991), Osborne and Rubinstein (1994), or Myerson (1997). For evolutionary game theory, the subject of Section 7.6, see Weibull (1997).

---

* Starred questions or portions of questions may be somewhat more difficult.

References

Alchian, Armen A., "Uncertainty, Evolution, and Economic Theory," *Journal of Political Economy*, 58 (1950), 211–221.

Cho, In-Koo and Kreps, David M., "Signalling Games and Stable Equilibria," *Quarterly Journal of Economics*, 102 (1987), 179–221.

Cournot, Augustin, *Recherches sur les Principes Mathématiques de la Théorie des Richesses*, Paris: Hachette, 1838.

Friedman, Daniel, "Evolutionary Games in Economics," *Econometrica*, 59 (1991), 637–666. Reprinted in Eric Maskin, ed., *Recent Developments in Game Theory*, a volume in the series *The International Library of Critical Writings in Economics*, Northampton, MA: Edward Elgar, 1999.

Friedman, James W., *Game Theory with Applications to Economics*, New York: Oxford University Press, 1986.

Fudenberg, Drew, and Jean Tirole, *Game Theory*, Cambridge, MA: MIT Press, 1991.

Gibbons, Robert, *Game Theory for Applied Economists*, Princeton: Princeton University Press, 1992.

Grossman, Sanford and Perry, Motty, "Perfect Sequential Equilibrium," *Journal of Economic Theory*, 39 (1986), 120–154.

Harsanyi, John G., "Games with Incomplete Information Played by 'Bayesian' Players," *Management Science*, 14 (1967–68), 159–182, 320–334, 486–502.

Hirshleifer, Jack, "Evolutionary Models in Economics and Law: Cooperation versus Conflict Strategies," *Research in Law and Economics*, 4 (1982), 1–60.

Hirshleifer, Jack and Coll, Juan Carlos Martinez, "What Strategies Can Support the Evolutionary Emergence of Cooperation?" *Journal of Conflict Resolution*, 32 (1988), 367–398.

Kohlberg, Elon and Mertens, Jean-François, "On the Strategic Stability of Equilibria," *Econometrica*, 54 (1986), 1003–1038.

Kreps, David M. and Wilson, Robert, "Sequential Equilibrium," *Econometrica*, 50 (1982), 863–894.

Liebowitz, Stan J. and Margolis, Stephen E., "The Fable of the Keys," *Journal of Law and Economics*, 33 (1990), 1–25.

Maynard Smith, John, "Evolution and the Theory of Games," *American Scientist*, 64 (1976), 41–45.

———, *Evolution and the Theory of Games*, Cambridge: Cambridge University Press, 1982.

Myerson, Roger, "Refinements of the Nash Equilibrium Concept," *International Journal of Game Theory*, 7 (1978), 73–80.

———, *Game Theory: The Analysis of Conflict*, Cambridge, MA: Harvard University Press, 1997.

Nash, John F., Jr., "Non-Cooperative Games," *Annals of Mathematics*, 54 (1951), 286–295.

Osborne, Martin J. and Ariel Rubinstein, *A Course in Game Theory*, Cambridge, MA: MIT Press, 1994.

Riley, John G., "Evolutionary Equilibrium Strategies," *Journal of Theoretical Biology*, 76 (1979), 109–123.

Selten, Reinhard, "Spieltheoretische Behandlung eines Oligopolmodells mit Nachfrägetragheit," *Zeitschrift für die gesamte Staatswissenschaft,* 121 (1965), 301–324 and 667–689.

———, "A Reexamination of the Perfectness Concept for Equilibrium Concepts in Extensive Games," *International Journal of Game Theory,* 4 (1975), 25–55.

Taylor, Peter D. and Jonker, Leo B., "Evolutionarily Stable Strategies and Game Dynamics," *Mathematical Biosciences,* 40 (1978), 145–156.

Weibull, Jorgen W., *Evolutionary Game Theory,* Cambridge, MA: MIT Press, 1997.

Winter, Sidney G., "Economic 'Natural Selection' and the Theory of the Firm," *Yale Economic Essays,* 4 (1964), 225–272.

Zeeman, Erik C., "Dynamics of the Evolution of Animal Conflicts," *Journal of Theoretical Biology,* 89 (1981), 249–270.

Informational Asymmetry and
Contract Design

The theme of this chapter is *informational asymmetry*, which is not the same as the *differences of beliefs* considered at various points in earlier chapters. Beliefs may differ without there being a consensus that any single person's opinions are intrinsically superior to anyone else's. In some situations, however, it will be clear to all parties involved that some of them are better informed than others. When a principal employs an agent to carry out actions whose outcomes are uncertain – for example, when an absentee landlord engages a farm manager – the latter will evidently be in a better position to know about any shirking or opportunistic behavior he chooses to engage in. As another example, an expert jeweler will evidently be more familiar with the quality of the diamonds he offers for sale than will an ordinary prospective purchaser. We will be considering the first type of situation in Section 8.1 under the heading of *hidden actions* or *moral hazard*. Sections 8.2 and 8.3 explore aspects of the second type of situation, the problem of *hidden knowledge* or *adverse selection*. In each case the challenge facing the lesser-informed party is to design an incentive scheme (a contract) aimed at mitigating the effects of informational asymmetry.[1]

The primary focus in this chapter will be on the choices made (the contracts designed) by a less well-informed decision maker or principal who has monopoly power. In the case of hidden actions, introducing competition among principals affects the analysis in only a minor way (see Exercise 8.1.2). On the other hand, in the case of hidden knowledge, when a number of less-informed transactors compete with one another, subtle issues arise regarding the nature of equilibrium. For this reason we defer a discussion of competition and hidden knowledge until Chapter 9.

---

[1] In Chapter 5 we considered the situation of a decision maker who employs an expert. That discussion addressed only the problem of sincerity, how to induce the expert to accurately reveal his hidden knowledge.

8.1 Hidden Actions ("Moral Hazard") and Contract Design[2]

Suppose an absentee landlord (the principal) hires a farm manager as his *agent*. The agent's utility function is $v^A(c, x)$, where her action is x (which we may think of as her *effort*) and her income is c. As a result of the agent's choice of action, the gross gain to the principal is the random variable $\tilde{y}(x)$ out of which he must pay the agent the amount r. If the principal is risk neutral, his utility function can be written:

$$v^P = y(x) - r$$

For simplicity, assume there are just two possible outcomes y_1 and y_2, with $y_2 > y_1$. By choosing a higher level of x, agent increases the probability $\pi(x)$ of the favorable outcome or event:[3]

$$d\pi(x)/dx > 0$$

Both principal and agent have the same knowledge of the underlying technology, so there is no disagreement about this probability function. Effort enters negatively into the agent's utility function:

$$\partial v^A(c, x)/\partial x < 0$$

With x not observable, the principal must choose a payment scheme contingent upon the observed outcome or event. Let r_i be the payment if the outcome is y_i, for $i = 1, 2$. Then, if the agent takes action x, the expected utilities of principal and agent are, respectively:

$$U^P = (1 - \pi(x))(y_1 - r_1) + \pi(x)(y_2 - r_2) \qquad (8.1.1)$$

$$U^A = (1 - \pi(x))v^A(r_1, x) + \pi(x)v^A(r_2, x) \qquad (8.1.2)$$

where, by assumption, the agent has no source of income apart from the contingent payments r_1 and r_2.

For any payment scheme $r = (r_1, r_2)$, the agent will respond by choosing the action $x^*(r)$ that maximizes her expected utility. Substituting this action for the agent into (8.1.1) and (8.1.2) yields the derived utility levels $U_*^P(r)$ and $U_*^A(r)$, both explicitly dependent upon the payment scheme r and, implicitly, upon the agent's underlying optimal response function $x^*(r)$.

---

[2] This section relies heavily on Grossman and Hart (1983).

[3] Note that the probabilities of the two possible outcomes y_1 and y_2 are not determined solely by the state of the world, but rather by the interaction between nature's choice of state and the agent's choice of effort.

We now examine the nature of the principal's *optimal contract*, one which, holding constant the expected utility of the agent, maximizes the principal's expected utility.[4]

First, suppose that the agent also is risk neutral so that her utility function can be written as:

$$v^A(r, x) = r - K(x) \qquad (8.1.3)$$

Here $K(x)$ is the agent's "cost of effort" which, by assumption here, is commensurate with the payment r. Thus, $r - K(x)$ is the agent's net income, and she is neutral toward income risk. Equation (8.1.2) can then be rewritten as:

$$U^A = (1 - \pi(x))r_1 + \pi(x)r_2 - K(x) \qquad (8.1.2')$$

Adding (8.1.1) and (8.1.2') and rearranging:

$$U^P = (1 - \pi(x))y_1 + \pi(x)y_2 - K(x)U^A$$
$$\equiv E[\tilde{y}(x)] - K(x) - U^A$$

So, maximizing U^P for given U^A, we see that an optimal contract is also efficient. Because the principal and the agent are risk neutral, an optimal contract induces the agent to maximize the expected value of output less her own cost of effort and that maximizes the sum of their expected utilities. In other words, while acting in their own self-interest, the principal and the agent attain economic efficiency.

We now exhibit an optimal payment scheme such that the efficient outcome can be achieved even though x is not directly observed. Suppose the principal (landlord) pays the agent (manager) the value of output, retaining only a fixed rent t:

$$r_i = y_i - t, \quad i = 1, 2$$

From (8.1.2), a risk-neutral agent's expected utility becomes:

$$U^A = (1 - \pi(x))y_1(x) + \pi(x)y_2(x) - t - K(x)$$
$$= E[\tilde{y}(x)] - K(x) - t$$

In maximizing this U^A the agent will also be maximizing $E[\tilde{y}(x)] - K(x)$, and thus choosing the efficient action. The economic interpretation is that, on the margin, the agent receives the full expected social benefit of her

---

[4] In an optimal contract, the agent's expected utility is equated to his reservation utility – the utility the agent can obtain from his next best alternative to working for the principal. For the most part, we do not explicitly state this additional constraint.

action. The principal will choose t so that the agent obtains his reservation utility in expectation.

This solution is no longer optimal for the principal nor is it efficient, however, if the agent is risk averse. For then even if the agent is induced to take the action that maximizes expected net output, there is an efficiency loss due to the absence of risk sharing.

Suppose there are just two possible actions $x \in \{L, H\}$, where L indicates that the agent chooses to be lazy and H indicates that she works hard. If she is lazy, her cost is lower, that is:

$$K(L) \equiv K(H) - \Delta K$$

where ΔK is the reduction in her cost of effort. We continue to assume that the agent's $v^A(r, x)$ is still separable so it can be written as:

$$v^A(r, x) \equiv V(r) - K(x) \qquad (8.1.4)$$

where $V(r)$ is the elementary utility associated with the separable income alone. But note here that $V(r) \neq r$, which means also that while $K(x)$ is commensurate with utility it need not be commensurate with the income payment r.

The agent's expected utility can be written:

$$U_x^A = (1 - \pi(x))V(r_1) + \pi(x) V(r_2) - K(x) \qquad (8.1.5)$$

Indifference curves for the two effort levels are depicted in Figure 8.1. For any payment schedule (r_1, r_2), the agent's Marginal Rate of Substitution is:

$$-\left.\frac{dr_2}{dr_1}\right|_{U_x} = \frac{1 - \pi(x)}{\pi(x)} \frac{V'(r_1)}{V'(r_2)}$$

Since effort raises $\pi(x)$, the indifference curve for a hard-working agent is flatter at each (r_1, r_2) point. Moreover, along the 45° certainty line the utility of working hard is lower than the utility of being lazy, since cost is higher and the same fixed payment is received. Thus, for example at D, utility is $\hat{U}$ if the agent works hard and $\hat{U} + \Delta K$ if she is lazy. It follows that the steeper $x = L$ indifference curve with utility equal to $\hat{U}$ must meet the $x = H$ indifference curve with utility equal to $\hat{U}$ to the left of the 45° line, or specifically, in the figure, at C. (At first glance, it might appear that, at any given point like C in the diagram, utility would surely be greater along the low-effort indifference curve $x = L$ – since the vector of payments received is the same. This is incorrect; what the diagram does not show is that greater effort raises the probability π of the more favorable outcome.)

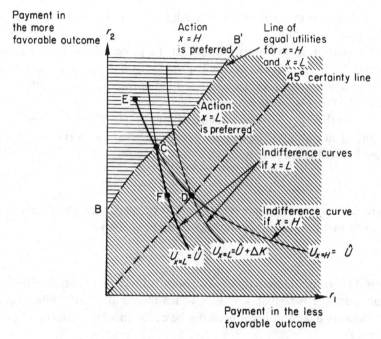

Figure 8.1. Agent's preference map.

The set of intersection points like C, for different levels of utility, is the "boundary curve" labeled **BB'** in the figure. Consider a point E to the left of **BB'**. If the agent works hard, her utility is $\hat{U}$. If she is lazy, her utility is lower since E lies below the indifference curve $U_{x=L} = \hat{U}$. As a utility maximizer, the agent therefore chooses to work hard. Conversely, at a point like F to the right of **BB'** her utility is lower if she works hard, and so the agent chooses to be lazy. Thus the agent will choose to work hard if and only if the contract is to the left of **BB'**, that is, if the differential between the payments r_2 and r_1 is sufficiently great.

The kinked curve ECF represents payment schemes that, given optimizing behavior on the part of the agent, yield her a utility of $\hat{U}$. That is, the information-constrained indifference curve has a kink as it crosses the boundary curve **BB'**. Or, we could say, the *effective* indifference curves (allowing for the agent's optimal H or L action) are kinked as shown.

For a risk-neutral agent, as seen above, the efficient contract implies that $r_2 - r_1 = y_2 - y_1$, i.e., the agent receives the full output increment between the favorable and the unfavorable outcomes. For a risk-averse agent, the contingent payment scheme can be interpreted as follows. In the event of

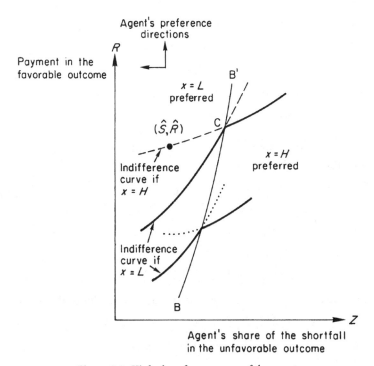

Figure 8.2. Kinked preference map of the agent.

a favorable outcome, the agent received a maximum payment R. For the unfavorable outcome, the payment is reduced by an amount Z. That is:

$$(r_1, r_2) = (R - Z, R)$$

The agent thus accepts a certain absolute share of the reduction in output, $y_2 - y_1$, associated with the less favorable outcome. From (8.1.5) the agent's expected utility at effort level x can be written as:

$$U_x^A(Z, R) = (1 - \pi(x)) V(R - Z) + \pi(x) V(R) - K(x) \qquad (8.1.6)$$

Figure 8.2 depicts the risk-averse agent's indifference curves once again, for $x = L$ and $x = H$, but now on Z, R axes. Note, first, that along the vertical axis (where $Z = 0$ so that the agent is not sharing in the reduction in output):

$$U_L^A(0, R) > U_H^A(0, R)$$

Second, since $\pi(H) > \pi(L)$, if the agent chooses to work hard she is more willing to give up income when the outcome is bad in return for a higher income when the outcome is good (since the bad outcome has become less likely). Formally:

$$\frac{dR}{dZ}\bigg|_{U^A} = \frac{-\partial U^A/\partial Z}{\partial U^A/\partial R} = \frac{(1-\pi(x)V'(R-Z)}{(1-\pi(x))V'(R-Z)+\pi(x)V'(R)}$$

$$= \frac{V'(R-Z)}{V'(R-Z)+\dfrac{\pi(x)}{1-\pi(x)}V'(R)} \tag{8.1.7}$$

For $x = H$ the denominator on the right-hand side is larger, and so the Marginal Rate of Substitution of R for Z is lower:

$$MRS_H(R,Z) < MRS_L(R,Z) \tag{8.1.8}$$

Third, rearranging (8.1.7):

$$\frac{dR}{dZ}\bigg|_{U^A} = \frac{1-\pi(x)}{1-\pi(x)+\pi(x)\frac{V'(R)}{V'(R-Z)}}$$

Given risk aversion, $V'(R) < V'(R-Z)$ for all $Z > 0$. Hence the denominator is less than unity and so:

$$MRS_x(R,Z) > 1-\pi(x) \tag{8.1.9}$$

In Figure 8.2 we see once again the boundary curve **BB′**, but now on Z, R axes. From Figure 8.1, when the agent's share in the shortfall is sufficiently great she prefers to work hard, and the reverse for a small shortfall. The *effective* branches of her indifference curves are shown as solid, so that again the preference map can be represented as set of kinked indifference curves, the kinks all occurring along **BB′**.

Continuing with the assumption that the principal is risk neutral, his expected payoff is:

$$U_x^P = (1-\pi(x))(y_1 - R + Z) + \pi(x)(y_2 - R)$$

Thus on (Z, R) axes his indifference curves are linear, as shown in Figure 8.3, with slope equal to the probability of the unfavorable outcome:

$$\frac{dR}{dZ}\bigg|_{U^P} = \frac{\partial U^P/\partial Z}{\partial U^P/\partial R} = 1-\pi(x)$$

The probability of the low outcome, $1-\pi(x)$, is larger when the agent takes action $x = L$ rather than action $x = H$. Therefore, along the principal's indifference line for $x = L$, the increment in R, the payment to the agent in the good state, is larger for a unit increase in the agent's share of the shortfall

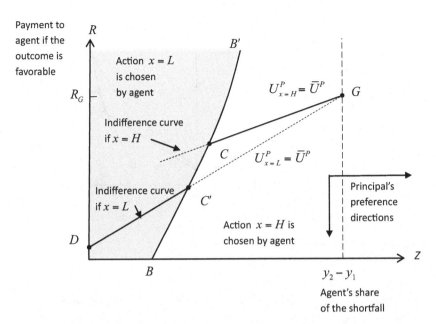

Figure 8.3. Discontinuous preference map of the principal.

Z. Thus, principal's indifference line is steeper when the agent takes action $x = L$.

Note that if the agent suffers the entire output reduction ($Z = y_2 - y_1$) the principal is indifferent as to the agent's action. That is, under the contract $(y_2 - y_1, R)$:

$$U_x^P(y_2 - y_1, R) = (1 - \pi(x))(y_1 - (R - (y_2 - y_1))) + \pi(x)(y_2 - R)$$
$$= y_2 - R, \quad \text{for } x = L, H$$

Therefore the principal's indifference lines for $x = H$ and $x = L$, for any given level of expected payoff, intersect along the vertical line $Z = y_2 - y_1$ in Figure 8.3. Moreover, the principal's indifference curves are discontinuous. To see this, consider the contract $(y_2 - y_1, R_G)$. In Figure 8.3, this is the point G. Because $U_L^P(y_2 - y_1, R_G) = U_H^P(y_2 - y_1, R_G) = y_2 - R_G$, an indifference line for $x = H$ and an indifference line for $x = L$ meet at the point G. Observe that the shaded area is the set of contracts for which the agent's preferred action is $x = L$. Thus, as the principal does not observe the agent's action, the relevant part of the indifference line with $x = L$ is the line segment $C'D$. By the same argument, the relevant part of the indifference line with $x = H$ is the line segment GC. Thus the complete

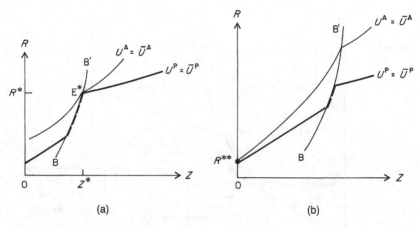

Figure 8.4. (a) Optimal contract with low cost of effort.
          (b) Optimal contract with high cost of effort.

indifference "curve" of principal is the pair of line segments GC and $C'D$. It follows that the principal's indifference curves have a *discontinuity* at **BB'**.

From (8.1.9) we know that the agent's indifference curve is everywhere steeper than the principal's indifference contour, except along the R axis where $Z = 0$. Then the optimal contract can take on one of two forms.

The first possibility is depicted in Figure 8.4a. The principal chooses the point $E^* = (Z^*, R^*)$ on the boundary curve **BB'** that maximizes his expected gain, subject to the constraint that the agent achieves some reservation level of expected utility. That is, the principal designs a contract which offers just enough of an incentive to induce hard work.[5] If, however, the utility cost of effort is sufficiently high, the optimal contract calls for a low work effort on the part of the agent – in which case she is paid a fixed wage. This is the point $(0, R^{**})$ depicted in Figure 8.4b.

In the exercises below you are asked to consider how the optimal contract varies under a variety of parametric changes. We conclude here by asking what happens as the wealth of the agent is increased. To answer this, we must determine the effect of higher wealth on the boundary of the set of contracts for which the agent prefers action H. Along **BB'** in Figure 8.2 the expected utility of the agent under the two actions is the same.

---

[5] Technically, at (Z^*, R^*), the agent is indifferent between the two actions. In such cases the standard convention is to assume that the agent selects the action preferred by the principal. Alternatively, one can view (Z^*, R^*) as the limit of a sequence of contracts in which the agent would strictly prefer $x = H$.

Substituting from (8.1.6):

$$U_H^A - U_L^A = (\pi(H) - \pi(L))[V(w+R) - V(w+R-Z)]$$
$$-K(H) + K(L) = 0$$

Differentiating by the wealth level w:

$$\frac{\partial}{\partial w} U_H^A - \frac{\partial}{\partial w} U_L^A = (\pi(H) - \pi(L))[V'(w+R) - V'(w+R-Z)]$$

Since the agent is risk averse, her marginal utility of income is diminishing, and so the right-hand side is negative for all positive Z. Therefore if $U_H^A - U_L^A = 0$ for some given wealth level, holding effort constant implies $U_H^A - U_L^A < 0$ for higher wealth levels. It follows that if for some contract (Z, R) the agent is indifferent between the two actions, then with an increase in endowed wealth she would strictly prefer action L. An increase in wealth thus shifts the boundary curve **BB'** in Figure 8.2 to the right.

The reason for this should be intuitively clear. The difference in utility associated with the agent's share Z of the total output reduction is smaller for an individual with higher wealth. She must therefore be penalized more to be willing to work hard.

We conclude by noting that the problem of insurance with "moral hazard" parallels the above analysis. Here the insurance company (assumed risk neutral) is in the position of the less well-informed "principal" while the potential insured corresponds to the "agent."

Let $\pi(x)$ be the probability of the favorable outcome, of *not* incurring a loss L, as a function of the insured's behavior x. Let F be the premium required under full coverage and let R be the reduction in the premium when the individual chooses to accept a "deductible" in the amount Z. For convenience we can assume that the premium is paid whether or not a loss occurs. Final wealths in the two possible outcomes are therefore:

$$c_{NL} = w - (F - R)$$
$$c_L = w - Z - (F - R)$$

The utility function for an individual with final wealth c who takes action x can be written as $v(c, x)$. Then if this individual has initial wealth w and chooses the insurance policy (Z, R), her expected utility is:

$$U_x(Z, R) = \pi(x) v(w - F + R, x) + (1 - \pi(x)) v(w - F + R - Z, x)$$

Comparing this expression with (8.1.6) it is clear that the insurance application is indeed a special case of our basic model. We shall consider insurance in more detail in the following section.

Exercises and Excursions 8.1

1 Effect of a Change in the Agent's Costs

In comparison with the agent whose circumstances are pictured in Figures 8.1 and 8.2, consider another agent identical in every respect except that $\hat{K}(H)$, her cost of taking action H, exceeds the first agent's $K(H)$.

(A) How will the optimal contract for this agent differ?
(B) What happens when $\hat{K}(H)$ becomes large?

[HINT: How is the curve **BB′** affected by the increase in cost?]

2 Competition among Principals and Agents

(A) Characterize the optimal incentive contract when principals compete for the services of an agent and so drive expected profit to zero.
(B) Contrast this with the outcome when there is a single principal and a perfectly elastic supply of agents at some reservation utility level $\bar{V}$.
(C) Modify the model, if necessary, to describe the outcome when there are many principals and many agents.

[HINT: In each case, one party or the other is on his or her reservation indifference curve.]

3 Costless Incentive Schemes

Suppose output is $\tilde{y} = \tilde{\varepsilon}\phi(x)$, where x is the agent's effort level and $\tilde{\varepsilon}$ is a random variable taking on the values $\tilde{\varepsilon}_1$ and $\varepsilon_2(\varepsilon_2 > \varepsilon_1)$ with equal probabilities. Suppose that the principal is risk neutral. The agent is risk averse, and her utility is unbounded from below as her income declines to zero. While output is observable, the principal cannot observe either x or ε.

(A) Let x^* be the optimal action under full information. Suppose that the principal offers to pay a fixed wage h as long as y does not fall below $\varepsilon_1\phi(x^*)$. If y is below this level, the agent must pay a penalty β. Show that, with the appropriate choice of h and β, the full-information optimum is achievable.
(B) Will the same conclusion hold if $\tilde{\varepsilon}$ is continuously distributed on the interval $[\varepsilon_1, \varepsilon_2]$?
(C) Explain why the incentive scheme breaks down if ε_1 is zero.
(D) If ε_1 is strictly positive, it appears as though the problem of hidden actions is readily solvable in practice. Do you agree? Explain.

4 Optimal Linear Contracting between Principal and Agent

The owner of a firm (the principal) hires a manager (the agent). If the agent chooses effort level x, the profit of the firm is:

$$\tilde{y} = y(x) + \tilde{\varepsilon}$$

The principal offers to pay the agent a percent share s of profit and a wage h. That is, the owner offers a payment schedule $h + s\tilde{y}$ which is a linear function of profit. The owner would like to choose the pair of parameters $\langle s, h \rangle$ that maximizes his expected utility, subject to the constraint that the manager's expected utility is at least equal to her reservation utility level $\bar{U}^A$. The owner's income is:

$$\tilde{y}_P = (1 - s)(y(x) + \tilde{\varepsilon}) - h$$

Finally, suppose $\tilde{\varepsilon}$ is normally distributed with zero mean and variance σ^2 and that both individuals exhibit constant absolute risk aversion (CARA). The expected utility of each individual can be written as:

$$U_i = E[y_i] - \frac{1}{2}\alpha_i \, \text{Var}[y_i], \quad i = A, P$$

where α_i is the coefficient of absolute risk aversion.

(A) Obtain an expression for the owner's expected utility in terms of s, x, and $\bar{U}_A$. Assume the opportunity cost of effort is $K(x)$.

(B) Explain why it is that s^* and x^*, the optimal levels of s and x, are independent of $\bar{U}_A$. What does vary as $\bar{U}_A$ varies?

(C) If the manager's effort level is observable, show that x^* and s^* satisfy the following conditions:

(i) $\bar{y}'(x^*) = K'(x^*)$

(ii) $s^* = \dfrac{\alpha_P}{\alpha_A + \alpha_P}$

(D) Suppose next that the principal is unable to observe the effort level. Explain why the agent will respond to a linear contract $\langle s, h \rangle$ by choosing $x(s)$ satisfying:

(iii) $s\bar{y}'(x(s)) - K'(x(s)) = 0$

(E) What conditions guarantee that $x(s)$ is an increasing function?

(F) Assuming that the above conditions are satisfied, prove that for $s \leq s^*$:

$$\left.\frac{dU_P}{ds}\right|_{U_A = \bar{U}_A} > 0$$

Show also that this inequality is reversed at $s = 1$.

(G) Draw a conclusion about the new optimal sharing rate relative to s^* and provide an intuitive explanation.

8.2 Hidden Knowledge

The preceding section explored the implications of the informational asymmetry associated with difficulty of monitoring *actions* of other parties. We now turn to the issues that arise when the private *knowledge* of one individual is hidden from another.[6]

Consider the case where a less well-informed monopolist or monopsonist on one side of the market faces a number of heterogeneous transactors on the other side, each of whom is well-informed about his own situation. Examples include: (i) a company offering life insurance to individuals who know more about their own health prospects than the insurance company does; (ii) an auto dealer purchasing used cars from sellers with better knowledge of their own cars' condition.

Taking up the insurance market as an example, in Section 8.2.1 we focus on "adverse selection." There are two central points. First, if the price associated with some contract reflects the *average* quality of the potential applicants for insurance, there will typically be a tendency for the highest quality applicants to self-select out of the market. Second, while the adverse selection may be severe, it is only in special cases that the market breaks down completely so that only the lowest-quality applicants (the "lemons") are present in equilibrium.

In Section 8.2.2. we show that the insurance company has an incentive to offer a schedule of contracts that at least partially separates the different types of insured. That is, the insurer designs contracts to act as a *screening* device.

---

[6] In Chapter 5 we explored ways in which an "expert" can be provided an incentive to truthfully reveal hidden knowledge. There, however, the expert's knowledge did not directly affect his utility. (Therefore, it is only because the expert is unable to provide verifiable information that the efficient contract is not a lump-sum payment.) In this chapter, the hidden knowledge is typically some characteristic of the informed individual and is therefore directly payoff-relevant.

Finally, Section 8.2.3 shows that monopolistic price discrimination is logically quite similar to the insurance problem considered previously.

8.2.1 Adverse Selection

In a simple insurance example, consider risk-averse individuals each of whom faces a possible loss L, the losses being equal in amount but independently distributed. While preferences and endowments are identical, the individuals differ in probability of suffering loss L. But we here assume that these loss-probabilities are not subject to influence by the individuals' actions. In insurance parlance, we are dealing with "adverse selection" rather than "moral hazard."

Someone whose probability of *avoiding* a loss is π may be termed a type-π individual. Let α be the lowest level of π and β be the highest. That is, type α are the worst risks (the "lemons" of the insurance industry) and type β are the best (the "peaches"). It is helpful also to define $A(\pi)$ as the average non-loss probability over the interval $[\alpha, \pi]$. Assume that, within these limits, the risk types are distributed continuously with density function $f(\pi)$. So the average is:

$$A(\pi) \equiv \int_{\alpha}^{\pi} if(i)di \bigg/ \int_{\alpha}^{\pi} f(i)di$$

Indifference curves through an endowment position E are depicted in Figure 8.5 for three types of individuals: α, β, and an intermediate type π. For any individual, the Marginal Rate of Substitution between income c_1 in his private loss state and income c_2 in his private non-loss state is:

$$-\frac{dc_2}{dc_1}\bigg|_{\bar{U}} = \frac{\partial U/\partial c_1}{\partial U/\partial c_2} = \frac{(1-\pi)v'(c_1)}{\pi\ v'(c_2)}$$

Since this *MRS* is decreasing in π, the higher the non-loss probability (the better the risk), the flatter is this indifference curve.

Consider a risk-neutral monopolist insurance company[7] offering *full coverage* insurance policies at a price P, where the premium (to be paid

---

[7] As pointed out in Chapter 4, ultimately all insurance is mutual. Despite the working of the Law of Large Numbers, the risk-averse individuals who make up a mutual insurance pool cannot ordinarily insure one another on a risk-neutral basis – even ruling out transaction costs. The main reason is that the Law of Large Numbers cannot fully cancel out variance of losses from the positively correlated risks ("social risks") that typically characterize actual insurance pools. However, since we are assuming independently distributed risks, the assumption of a risk-neutral insurer is acceptable here.

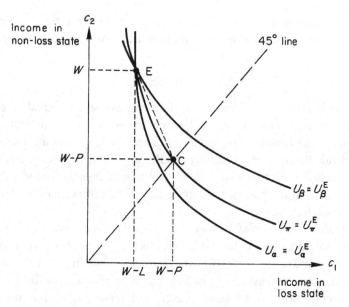

Figure 8.5. Indifference curves for different risk classes.

regardless of whether or not a loss occurs) is the same for everyone partici-pating. If an individual of type π purchases the policy, his state-contingent consumption bundle becomes $(w - P, w - P)$ at point C in the diagram. Note that, as depicted, type π is just indifferent between purchasing insur-ance and remaining out of the market. (Of course, for this to be the case the insurance has to be an adverse gamble; at fair odds, any risk-averse individual will want to fully insure.) Moreover, at the state-claim price ratio represented by the slope of EC all those individuals who represent more favorable risks are strictly better off out of the market, while all individuals who represent worse risks are strictly better off purchasing insurance. Thus the insurance company faces adverse selection: at any premium it offers, the poorer risks will be disproportionately represented among the customers who actually choose to insure.

Let $\hat{P}(\pi)$ be the maximum premium that an individual of type π is willing to pay for full coverage. In Figure 8.6, this is depicted by the curve $\hat{P}(\pi)$ over the range of individuals $\alpha \leq \pi \leq \beta$. The curve $(1 - \pi)L$ similarly shows the expected loss for each type. Note that $\hat{P}(\pi)$ is everywhere greater than $(1 - \pi)L$, meaning that each potential insured, being risk averse, is willing to pay more than his expected total loss. The third curve, $(1 - A(\pi))L$, is the expected loss averaged over the risks between α and π.

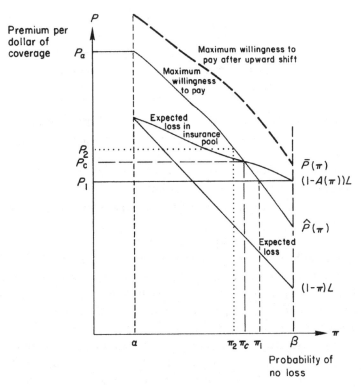

Figure 8.6. Adverse selection – yes and no.

Now consider the insurance pool. If anyone purchases insurance at all, the pool would always contain the worst risks α up through some borderline participant π, where π is a function of the premium. Then, on the assumption that in equilibrium there must be a non-negative expected profit for the insurance company, the premium P associated with participation from α up to π would have to at least equal the height of the curve $(1 - A(\pi))L$ that shows the average loss for that participation level.

There are two possible cases.

(i) Suppose that the insurance company, in the hope of inducing 100% participation, sets the premium for total coverage $P_1 = (1 - A(\beta))L$. As drawn in Figure 8.6, however, this premium exceeds the maximum willingness to pay of the favorable risks between π_1 and β – that is, the $\hat{P}(\pi)$ curve falls below P_1 in this range. But if only customers in the range from α through π_1 participate, $(1 - A(\pi_1))L$ will exceed P_1, so the insurance company will incur losses. At the other extreme, if the insurance company sets the premium above $\hat{P}(\alpha)$, the reservation price of the worst risks, there will be no takers. However, by setting an intermediate premium such as P_2, the insurance company would attract customers in the range from α through π_2. Since $(1 - A(\pi_2))L$ is less than P_2, such a contract is profitable.

At the premium P_c the expected loss of all those accepting the offer, $(1 - A(\pi_c))L$, is exactly equal to the premium. Therefore, unless the insurance company is willing to incur losses, the premium must lie between P_c and P_α. Given the $\hat{P}(\pi)$ curve as depicted here (the distribution of insureds' willingness to pay), even in the most favorable case, where the insurance company sets a premium just high enough to cover the average loss[8] there is adverse selection. Those in the best risk classes (those with sufficiently low probabilities of loss) have dropped out of the market.

On the other hand, a monopolist insurer will never charge so high a price as to eliminate all but the worst risks from the market. Given risk aversion, the willingness to pay $\hat{P}(\pi)$ strictly exceeds the lemons' expected loss $(1 - \alpha)L$ over some interval $[\alpha, \pi]$. Therefore the expected profit of the insurer increases as it lowers the price below P_α.

(ii) Thus far we have considered a case in which the curve $\hat{P}(\pi)$ intersects $(1 - A(\pi))L$ in the range between α and β. Alternatively, if the population were much more risk averse, maximum willingness to pay for insurance might be considerably higher at all levels of participation. The $\hat{P}(\pi)$ curve would then shift upward, as illustrated by the heavy dashed $\bar{P}(\pi)$ curve in the diagram. Since $\bar{P}(\beta)$ now exceeds $(1 - A(\beta))L$ over the entire population range between α and β, it is possible to avoid adverse selection. In this situation, P_1 would be the zero-profit premium, and there would be 100% participation in the insurance pool unless the insurer were to choose a sufficiently higher premium.[9]

Thus, adverse selection tends to come about when (a) the insurance pool contains a relatively wide range of risks (all of whom must be charged the same premium per unit of coverage, owing to the insurer's inability to distinguish among them) and (b) risk aversion is relatively mild. Conversely, a narrow range of risks and a high degree of risk aversion tend to retain the better risks in the insurance pool and therefore to prevent adverse selection.

---

[8] This may be reinterpreted as the "competitive" case in which premiums are bid down until expected profit is zero.

[9] Whether or not it pays to do so would depend upon the elasticity of demand for insurance, which would reflect (among other things) the distribution of risk classes in the population.

Exercises and Excursions 8.2.1

1 Adverse Selection in a Used-Car Market (Akerlof, 1970)
Suppose cars last for two periods. Cars have different qualities, such that the dollar value of a car per period is uniformly distributed on the interval $[\alpha, \beta]$. After one period of ownership, a consumer knows the quality of his car.

(A) Suppose the price of used cars is p. Which owners will wish to sell? Show that the average value of cars on the market will be $\frac{1}{2}(\alpha + p)$.
(B) Assuming free entry into the used-car market, what will be the equilibrium price of used cars and how many cars will be traded?
(C) How does this second-period price affect the price of new cars? (You may ignore time-discounting.)
(D) Are there any efficiency losses associated with the adverse selection in the example?
(E) How would your answer change if old cars can be polished up and sold as new?

2 Adverse Selection in a Labor Market
A worker with a marginal value product of θ can earn $w_r = (1 - d)\theta$ in self-employment. Marginal value products vary across the population according to the uniform distribution:

$$F(\theta) = \begin{cases} 0, & \theta < \alpha \\ \theta - \alpha & \theta \in [\alpha, 1 + \alpha] \\ 1, & \theta > 1 + \alpha \end{cases}$$

Firms cannot measure individual productivity, so all workers are paid a wage equal to the average of the marginal value products of those employed.

(A) Show that for any $d < 1/2(1 + \alpha)$, those with the highest marginal value products choose self-employment.
(B) Obtain an expression for the proportion of those self-employed as a function of d and α.
(C) Hence show that, as d becomes small, adverse selection becomes severe. In this limiting case is adverse selection economically important?
(D) More generally, let $w_r = (1 - \mu)\lambda + \mu\theta$. Show that, for w_r to be less than θ over $[\alpha, 1 + \alpha]$, λ must be no greater than α. Show also that adverse selection will never occur unless $\mu > \frac{1}{2}$. Under these assumptions, show that adverse selection will be complete in one limiting case. That is, only the "lemons" are actually traded.

3   Adverse Selection in Credit Markets (Stiglitz and Weiss, 1981)

By borrowing an amount D, an entrepreneur (with no other source of funds) can undertake a risky project. The gross return $\tilde{y}$ is a non-negative random variable with cumulative distribution function $F(y)$. If the project's return y is sufficiently large to permit this, the entrepreneur must repay his loan at the interest rate r; otherwise, the bank takes *all* the return y.

(A) Depict the return $\tilde{y}_B$ to the bank and the return $\tilde{y}_E$ to the entrepreneur for all non-negative values of y. Hence confirm that the former is a concave and the latter a convex function of y.

Suppose that both bank and entrepreneur are risk neutral. Projects A, B, and C have the same expected return but B is more risky than A and C is more risky than B. Suppose also that, at the interest rate r, project B just breaks even.

(B) If banks cannot distinguish among the three projects, and all three are offered, which will they end up funding? Which would they prefer to fund?

(C) Would your answer change if all borrowers were required to put up collateral y, where $y < D$?

4   Gambling at the Golden Kiwi

For a small entry fee, visitors arriving in Kiwiland have an opportunity to compete with a Maori at the airport casino. The Maori randomly selects a ball from an urn containing balls numbered from 0 to 99. The number N on the ball is observed by the Maori only.

The visitor may make some bid B in dollars. The Maori observes the ball drawn from the urn and then decides whether to compete by matching this bid. If the Maori does not match, then she pays nothing and receives nothing; the visitor pays B and receives N dollars. If the Maori matches, then she receives $(\frac{2}{3})N$ from the casino and pays B dollars; the visitor pays and receives nothing.

(A) What is the visitor's optimal bid, given that he has decided to play?

(B) What is the expected payoff to visitor and Maori?

(C) Extend your analysis to the case in which the Maori's payout is a fraction k of the number N on the ball, where $0 < k < \frac{2}{3}$.

[HINT: If the visitor bids B, the Maori will match when $B < (\frac{2}{3})N$, that is, when $N > (\frac{3}{2})B$. Use this to compute the expected payoff to the visitor for all B.]

8.2.2 Screening

When hidden knowledge results in adverse selection, those sellers with a product or service of above-average quality suffer from inability to secure a suitable price. In the insurance context, better-quality insureds may remain out of the market, which means they are unable to spread their risks. As a result they have an incentive to seek alternative, indirect ways of *signaling* product quality. On the other side of the market, buyers seek some way of *screening* products of differing qualities. Intuitively, an action taken or an offer made by a seller of a higher-quality product can be a signal only if it is sufficiently more costly for sellers of lower-quality products to do the same. In this section we show that, for the insurance case, such opportunities may exist and that, as a result, risk classes can sometimes be sorted *ex post.*

At the end of Section 8.2.1 we showed that, if insurers offer only full coverage, in a wide range of circumstances adverse selection will occur. However, the set of feasible insurance policies is much richer. In particular, an insurance company or mutual insurance pool can exploit the fact that high-quality risk-classes are more willing to buy partial coverage (insurance with a "deductible").

Consider the willingness of different risk-classes to accept partial insurance in exchange for a reduction R in the insurance premium. As before, all individuals face the same possible loss L, where π is the non-loss probability. A higher π thus represents a higher-quality risk. Rather that work directly with the insurance premium we define G to be some arbitrary premium and let R be the discount or "reduction in premium" offered by the insurance company. Then the insurance policy (R, Z) is a policy in which the actual (discounted) premium is $G - R$ and the coinsurance is Z. Note that the policy $(R, Z) = (G, L)$ is a policy in which the premium is $G - G = 0$ and the coinsurance is $Z = L$. That is, the insuree pays nothing and gets no coverage. This is the no insurance point N depicted in Figure 8.7.

In the nonloss and loss states, the final wealths are:

$$c_{NL} = w - (G - R) = (w - G) + R$$
$$c_L = w - (G - R) - Z = (w - G) + R - Z$$

Expected utility of an individual is therefore:

$$U_\pi(Z, R) = \pi v(w - G + R) + (1 - \pi) v(w - G + R - Z) \qquad (8.2.1)$$

Indifference curves in (Z, R) space are depicted in Figure 8.7. From (8.2.1), the individual's marginal willingness to accept further reductions in the

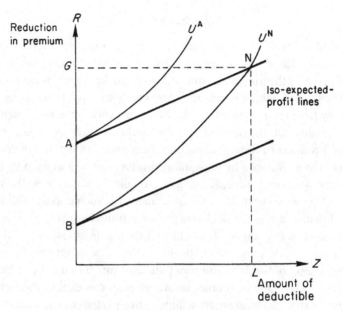

Figure 8.7. Optimal insurance contract.

premium, in return for accepting a larger deductible, is:

$$\frac{dR}{dZ}\bigg|_U = -\frac{\partial U}{\partial Z}\bigg/\frac{\partial U}{\partial R} = \frac{(1-\pi)\,v'(w-G+R-Z)}{(1-\pi)\,v'(w-G+R-Z)+\pi v'(w-G+R)}$$

$$(8.2.2)$$

The right-hand side is equal to $1-\pi$, the loss probability, when Z is zero; for all positive Z, it will be greater than $1-\pi$. Thus the slope of the indifference curves exceeds the loss probability except along the vertical axis.

For simplicity, assume that the insurer is risk neutral and thus interested only in expected profit on the contract (Z, R):

$$H_\pi(Z, R) = \text{premium} - \left\{\begin{array}{c}\text{loss}\\\text{probability}\end{array}\right\}\left\{\begin{array}{c}\text{payout in}\\\text{event of loss}\end{array}\right\}$$
$$= G - R - (1-\pi)(L-Z)$$
$$= (1-\pi)Z - R + (G-(1-\pi)L)$$

Iso-expected profit contours are therefore lines of slope $1-\pi$. These are also depicted in Figure 8.7.

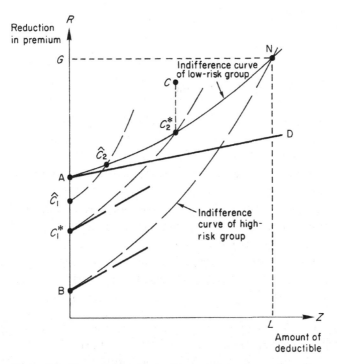

Figure 8.8. Characterizing the profit-maximizing insurance policy.

In Figure 8.7, point $N = (L, G)$ corresponds to absence of insurance (a deductible equal to the loss). The indifference curve through this point is the individual's reservation indifference curve, and the iso-profit line through this point is the zero-profit line, which also goes through point A, the actuarialy fair full-insurance point.

As the indifference curves, away from the vertical axis where $Z = 0$, are always steeper than the iso-expected profit lines, the profit-maximizing policy is to offer full coverage. A perfectly discriminating monopoly insurer would choose a premium such that the insured is just indifferent between purchasing the policy and going without insurance. This is the policy shown at point B in Figure 8.7.

We now introduce asymmetry of information. For simplicity, suppose there are just two risk-classes. If the insurance company can distinguish these risk classes *ex ante*, it maximizes expected profit by offering each risk class full coverage at a cost that extracts all consumer surplus. The two profit-maximizing insurance policies are represented in Figure 8.8 by point A for the low-risk and point B for the high-risk group. But suppose the insurer is unable to distinguish the two groups. If it continues to offer policy A, both risk-classes would purchase full coverage under that contract.

We now show that the insurance company can always do better. Specifically, to maximize expected profits it can offer two insurance policies (Z_i^*, R_i^*), $i = 1, 2$, with the following characteristics:

Characterization of the Profit-Maximizing Insurance Policies
  (i) The policy accepted by each individual in the good risk-class extracts his entire surplus.
  (ii) The policy accepted by each individual in the poor risk-class involves full coverage.
  (iii) The deductible level accepted by the good risk-class is strictly positive. The higher the proportion of poor risks in the market, the greater is the deductible.
  (iv) When there is a sufficiently high proportion of poor risks in the pool, there is no insurance coverage for the good risks. That is, adverse selection occurs.

To explain these results, suppose the insurer offers the single policy C depicted in Figure 8.8. As point C lies to the northwest of both the reservation indifference curves through the no-insurance point N, both risk-classes will find contract C preferable to no insurance. But C is not profit-maximizing for the insurer, since it can raise the premium (reduce R) by shifting the offered contract down to point C_2^* along the reservation indifference curve of the good risk-class.

Next, consider the indifference curve of the poor risk-class through C_2^*. As this has a slope exceeding the slope of the iso-profit lines for this risk-class, the insurance company increases its profits by offering the second policy C_1^*.

(C_1^*, C_2^*) is just one of an entire family of policy pairs that satisfy parts (i) and (ii) of the proposition. Another such pair is $(\hat{C}_1, \hat{C}_2)$. If the insurance company changes its offered pair of policies from $(\hat{C}_1, \hat{C}_2)$ to (C_1^*, C_2^*), its profit on poor risks will be greater and on good risks will be less. Therefore the higher the proportion of poor risks in the population, the more profitable such a move becomes. This is point (iii) above. When essentially all individuals in the population are poor risks, it is optimal to extract the entire surplus from this class and offer the pair of policies (N, B). That is, when the proportion of poor risks gets sufficiently high, the good risks are no longer offered insurance on favorable enough terms to be accepted by them.

When the proportion of poor risks is sufficiently low, the pair of policies $(\hat{C}_1, \hat{C}_2)$ dominates (C_1^*, C_2^*). It is tempting to conclude that, when the proportion gets very small, the optimal pair of policies will collapse to the single "pooling" policy A in Figure 8.8. However, this is not the case. Note that the indifference curve NA and the iso-profit line AD are tangential at A. Therefore, the marginal gain in profit from the good risks in moving around the indifference curve toward A declines to zero as $\hat{C}_2$ approaches A. On the other hand, the marginal loss in profit from the bad risks is positive and bounded away from zero. Because of this it is always optimal for the insurer to separate the two risk-classes.

More generally, with n risk-classes, it will always be optimal to offer full coverage to the lemons and less than full coverage to all other risk classes. However, as the next section makes clear, it is not necessarily the case that the insurer's profit is maximized by separating out each of the types. Instead, subsets of types may, in general, be pooled.

Also omitted from the analysis here are the effects of competition among insurance companies. We address these issues further in Chapter 9.

Exercises and Excursions 8.2.2

1 *Insurance with Three Risk-Classes*
  (A) Extend the analysis of Section 8.2.2 to the case of three risk-classes. Depict the insurance contracts C_1^*, C_2^*, C_3^* in a diagram.
  (B) Suppose the proportion of the intermediate risk-class is small relative to the other two classes. Explain why the profit-maximizing strategy is to offer only two policies. Which risk-classes are pooled?
  (C) To what extent can the proposition of Section 8.2.2 be generalized to the case of three risk-classes?

2 *Insurance with Different Levels of Loss*
Suppose that an individual of type t incurs a loss of L_s with probability π_s^t, for $s = 1, \ldots, S$ and $t = 1, 2$. An insurance policy is an offer to pay the entire loss, less some deductible Z, to any individual who pays a premium $\phi(Z)$.
  (A) Suppose that $\pi_s^1 < \pi_s^2$ for all s. Show that the analysis above can be readily extended to this case.
  (B) Does it really matter that $\pi_s^1 < \pi_s^2$ for all s or is it only the overall probability of a claim that is critical?
  (C) Discuss what the insurer might do if $\sum_{s=1}^{S} \pi_s^1 = \sum_{s=1}^{S} \pi_s^2$ but the first type has higher probabilities of large losses.

8.2.3 Monopoly Price Discrimination with Hidden Knowledge*

In this section we examine the selling strategy of a monopolist seller who cannot distinguish among different types of buyers. From past experience, he does, however, have information about the distribution of buyers' demand curves. We also assume that the product cannot be readily resold. Then, rather than sell all units at a single price, the monopolist might offer bundles of different numbers of items at various quantity discounts (one for $50, two for $95, etc.). We shall show that this problem of monopolistic price discrimination is essentially equivalent to the insurance problem analyzed above. In particular, the optimal schedule of quantity discounts is analogous to the schedule offering insureds a lower premium for accepting a bigger deductible.

We assume here that each buyer-type t has a demand curve $p_t(q)$ that is independent of income. Then, if q units are purchased for total outlay of R dollars, the type-t "buyer's surplus" is:

$$U_t(q, R) = \int_0^q p_t(x)dx - R \qquad (8.2.3)$$

where the first term on the right-hand side is the area under the demand curve. What makes this pricing problem simple is that buyers' preferences are linear in income.

For concreteness, suppose that there are T different types of buyers, where $p_1(q) < p_2(q) < \cdots < p_T(q)$. Suppose also that the proportion of type-t buyers is f_t, where $\sum_{t=1}^{T} f_t = 1$. Finally, to keep the analysis as simple as possible, we assume that the monopolist has an unlimited supply of the commodity available without cost.[10]

In Figure 8.9 the upper diagram depicts the demand curve of a type-t buyer while the lower diagram shows the corresponding preference map in (q, R) space. Differentiating (8.2.3):

$$\left.\frac{dR}{dq}\right|_{U_t} = \frac{-\partial U}{\partial q} \bigg/ \frac{\partial U}{\partial R} = p_t(q) \qquad (8.2.4)$$

That is, the steepness of the indifference curve is the buyer's demand price (marginal willingness to pay). Note also that, because of the linearity of $U_t(q, R)$ in R, the indifference curves are vertically parallel.

---

* Starred sections represent more difficult or specialized materials that can be omitted without substantial loss of continuity.

[10] In an exercise below, you are asked to show that the analysis holds for general cost functions.

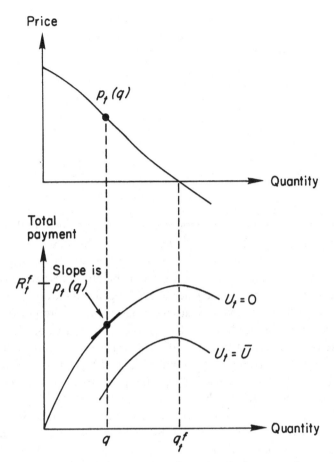

Figure 8.9. Demand curve and indifference curve for a type-*t* buyer.

If the monopolist has full information and can engage in perfect discrimination, the solution is straightforward. Each buyer is forced onto her reservation indifference curve, where she is indifferent between the transaction (q_t^f, R_t^f) and purchasing nothing at all. Since the seller wants to maximize the buyer's outlay, in Figure 8.9, (q_t^f, R_t^f) is at the peak of the indifference curve through the origin. Thus:

$$U_t\left(q_t^f, R_t^f\right) = \int_0^{q_t^f} p_t(x)dx - R_t^f = U_t(0, 0) = 0$$

In terms of Figure 8.9, the monopolist makes a take-it-or-leave-it offer of q_t^f units for a total payment of R_t^f, equal to the integrated area under the demand curve between $q = 0$ and $q = q_t^f$.

Table 8.1. *Direct revelation*

Buyer type	Best responses
0	$(q_0, R_0) = (0, 0)$
1	(q_1, R_1)
2	(q_2, R_2)
...	...
...	...
T	(q_T, R_T)

With complete information about types, the monopolist can then make T different offers $(q_1^f, R_1^f), \ldots, (q_T^f, R_T^f)$, each of which extracts all of the surplus from a buyer. However, if the monopolist cannot distinguish the different types, he cannot do this well. It is helpful, in what follows, to introduce a fictional buyer who places a large negative value on the product. This fictional "type 0" buyer will always choose to make zero purchases, so her presence or absence has no effect on the monopolist's opportunities. Suppose the monopolist makes T offers. (Certainly, he gains nothing by making more than T offers when there are only T types.) For any such set of offers, let $\{(q_0, R_0), (q_1, R_1), \ldots, (q_T, R_T)\}$ signify the best responses by each type, including type 0 who chooses $(q_0, R_0) = (0, 0)$. These need not be distinct. For example, if the monopolist makes just a single offer $(\bar{q}, \bar{R})$ each best response is either to accept this offer or to stay out of the market (equivalently, to choose (q_0, R_0)).

While each buyer's type is private information, the monopolist is assumed to know the demand curve for each type. He can therefore compute the best response to his initial set of offers. Therefore, instead of announcing the initial set, the monopolist could equivalently provide a list of types and the optimal choice for each, as shown in Table 8.1. The monopolist could then ask each buyer to announce her type. As long as the right-hand column is a set of best responses, each buyer has an incentive to announce her actual type.

The key point is that the original "game" between the monopolist and buyers has been converted into an equivalent game of *direct revelation* in which each informed party is asked to reveal her private information. As long as the monopolist has correctly analyzed the incentive constraints so that the schedule of offers is *incentive compatible*, no individual can do any better than reveal her true type.

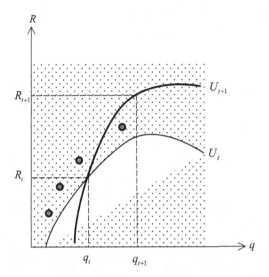

Figure 8.10. Incentive compatibility.

It should now be apparent why we introduced the fictional type 0 who always chooses $(q_0, R_0) = (0, 0)$. Each agent always retains the option of a zero purchase as well as the T offers made by the monopolist. Adding type 0 is thus equivalent to introducing a *participation* constraint for each type of buyer.

Converting a game into the equivalent *direct revelation game* often makes analysis considerably easier,[11] as is indeed the case here. The monopolist can be viewed as designing a table or schedule such that each buyer will choose the row corresponding to her true type.

Figure 8.10 displays an indifference curve for a type t individual and for a type $t + 1$ individual. If (q_t, R_t) *is* t's best response, all the other feasible contracts for her must be in the shaded region, on or above the indifference curve:

$$U_t(q, R) = U_t(q_t, R_t)$$

By assumption, type $t + 1$ has a higher demand curve, and hence, from Equation (8.2.4), her indifference curve through (q_t, R_t) is strictly steeper. Then, from the figure, type $t + 1$ will prefer (q_t, R_t) to any other offer

---

[11] When authors appeal to the *revelation principle* they are simply referring to the point made here that any game can be rephrased as an equivalent direct revelation game. See Section 10.2.3 for a statement of the revelation principle.

(q_i, R_i) such that $q_i < q_t$. It follows that, for the offer (q_{t+1}, R_{t+1}) to be incentive compatible, it is necessary that:

$$q_t \leq q_{t+1} \quad t = 1, \ldots, T \tag{8.2.5}$$

Consider any vector of quantities $(q_1, q_2, \ldots, q_T)$ satisfying (8.2.5). We shall now show that the corresponding revenue-maximizing incentive-compatible vector of payments $(R_1, R_2, \ldots, R_T)$ satisfies:

$$U_t(q_t, R_t) = U_t(q_{t-1}, R_{t-1}), \quad t = 2, \ldots, T \tag{8.2.6}$$

$$U_1(q_1, R_1) = U_1(q_0, R_0) = U_1(0, 0) = 0 \tag{8.2.7}$$

That is, each buyer type is just indifferent between his or her best response (q_t, R_t) and the best response of buyers with the most similar demand among those with lower demands. Moreover, the type with the smallest demand is just indifferent between her allocation and staying out of the market.

It should be noted that this last condition ensures that all types are willing to participate. For, the higher an individual's demand curve, the greater the willingness to pay for a given quantity. Hence:

$$U_t(q_1, R_1) > U_1(q_1, R_1) = 0, \quad t = 2, \ldots, T$$

Ignoring all types but the first, it is clear that revenue from type 1 buyers is maximized by choosing R_1 to satisfy (8.2.7). Suppose next that $\{(q_1, R_1), \ldots, (q_t, R_t)\}$ are incentive compatible for types $1, 2, \ldots, t$. Just taking into account the local constraint depicted in Figure 8.10, the best that the seller can do is to choose (q_{t+1}, R_{t+1}) so that (8.2.6) holds. But all buyers with lower demands have flatter indifference curves than type t. Therefore, since $q_{t+1} \geq q_t$:

$$U_{t+1}(q_{t+1}, R_{t+1}) = U_{t+1}(q_t, R_t)$$
$$\Rightarrow U_i(q_{t+1}, R_{t+1}) < U_i(q_t, R_t), \quad i \leq t$$

The inequality follows because the indifference curve through (q_t, R_t) for type $i \leq t$ is less steep than the indifference curve through (q_t, R_t) for type $t + 1$ (see Figure 8.10 for type $i = t$). Therefore the set of offers $\{(q_1, R_1), \ldots, (q_{t+1}, R_{t+1})\}$ satisfy (8.2.6) and (8.2.7) and so is incentive compatible for types $1, 2, \ldots, t + 1$. Since this argument can be repeated for each t, it follows that conditions (8.2.5)–(8.2.7) are together sufficient for incentive compatibility.

These offers are also revenue-maximizing for the given set of quantities. The final step is to choose the profit-maximizing quantities. Define:

$$B_t(q) = \int_0^q p_t(x)\,dx$$

Then (8.2.6) and (8.2.7) can be rewritten as:

$$R_t - R_{t-1} = B_t(q_t) - B_t(q_{t-1}), \quad t = 1, \ldots, T, \quad \text{with } (q_0, R_0) = 0$$

$$(8.2.8)$$

The monopolist's total revenue $R_M = \sum_{t=1}^T f_t R_t$ can be expressed as a function of the quantity vector $(q_1, \ldots, q_T)$.

If there are just two buyer types we have, from (8.2.8):

$$\begin{aligned}
R_M &= f_1 R_1 + f_2 R_2 \\
&= (f_1 + f_2)R_1 + f_2[R_2 - R_1] \\
&= (f_1 + f_2)B_1(q_1) + f_2[B_2(q_2) - B_2(q1)] \\
&= f_1 B_1(q_1) - f_2[B_2(q_1) - B_1(q_1)] + f_2 B_2(q_2)
\end{aligned} \qquad (8.2.9)$$

Revenue is therefore maximized by choosing q_1 and q_2 to maximize R_M subject to the constraint that $q_1 \leq q_2$. Actually, with just two types, this constraint is never binding. Differentiating (8.2.9):

$$\begin{aligned}
\frac{\partial R_M}{\partial q_1} &= f_1 B_1'(q_1) - f_2\left[B_2'(q_1) - B_1'(q_1)\right] \\
&= f_1 p_1(q_1) - f_2[p_2(q_1) - p_1(q_1)] \\
\frac{\partial R_M}{\partial q_2} &= f_2 B_2'(q_2) = f_2 p_2(q_2)
\end{aligned}$$

The optimum is therefore to choose q_2^* where a type-2 buyer's marginal willingness to pay is zero. On the other hand, q_1^* is chosen where a type-2 buyer's marginal willingness to pay is strictly positive.

This is illustrated in Figure 8.11. Suppose A and D are the optimal offers. Consider increasing the quantity supplied to type-1 buyers by Δq_1. Revenue from these buyers rises by an amount $B_1'(q_1)\Delta q_1$ as the offer moves from A to A'. This reduces revenue from type-2 buyers, however, by an amount DD'. Since the indifference curves are vertically parallel, this revenue loss is equal to the distance $A'C$. But $A'C$ is readily computed. It is just the difference in the slopes of the indifference curves of the two types times the change in quantity. Since these slopes are demand prices, it is profitable to increase q_1 if and only if:

$$f_1 p_1(q_1) - f_2[p_2(q_1) - p_1(q_1)] > 0 \qquad (8.2.10)$$

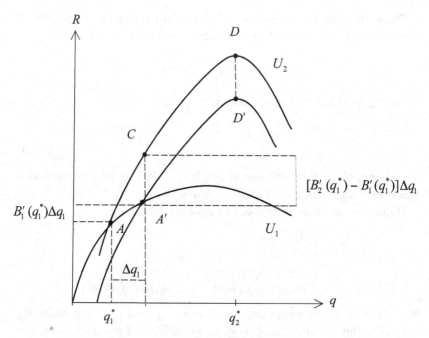

Figure 8.11. Benefit and cost of increasing q_1.

Note that, if either the proportion of type-1 buyers is sufficiently small, or the type-1 demand price is sufficiently low relative to type-2, this inequality is never satisfied and so $q_1^* = 0$.

This result holds quite generally. When the demand prices of some types are sufficiently small relative to others, the monopolist will make offers that exclude these types completely.

Finally, the analysis above can readily be extended to consider more than two types. Suppose there are three. The additional issue is then whether it pays the monopolist to separate all three types. With three types, it is profitable to increase q_1 if and only if the additional revenue from type-1 buyers is not offset by the loss in revenue from both of the higher types. Condition (8.2.10) therefore becomes:

$$f_1 p_1(q_1) - (f_2 + f_3)[p_2(q_1) - p_1(q_1)] > 0$$

Similarly, it is profitable to increase q_2 if and only if:

$$f_2 p_2(q_2) - f_3[p_3(q_2) - p_2(q_2)] > 0$$

It is left as an exercise to confirm that, as long as f_2 is sufficiently large, then $0 \le q_1^* < q_2^* < q_3^*$. Conversely, if f_2 is sufficiently small, then $q_1^* = q_2^*$. That is, it is more profitable for the monopolist to pool types 1 and 2 and make only two offers rather than three.

Exercises and Excursions 8.2.3

1 *Monopoly Pricing with Costly Production*
   (A) Suppose that the aggregate supply of the commodity is fixed and equal to Q. Starting with the two-type case, show that the first-order conditions need only be modified by the introduction of a shadow price λ.
   (B) What is the interpretation of this shadow price?
   (C) Hence, or otherwise, explain why, with a cost function $C(Q)$, the aggregate quantity supplied will be chosen so that $\lambda = C'(Q)$.

2 *Monopoly and Product Quality (Mussa and Rosen, 1978)*
There are two types of buyers. Type-2 buyers' value increases in quality more highly than type-1 buyers'. That is, for each quality level z, a type-2 buyer's marginal willingness to pay $B_2'(Z)$ exceeds $B_1'(Z)$, where $B_1(0) = B_2(0) = 0$.

Each buyer wishes to purchase a single unit. The unit cost of production of a unit of quality level z is $C(z)$. The price p that the monopolist charges can then be separated into two parts, the unit cost and profit II, that is:

$$p = C(z) + \Pi$$

We can therefore write the net gain to a buyer from type i as:

$$U_i(z, \pi) = B_i(z) - C(z) - \Pi$$

   (A) Assuming $B_i(z) - C(z)$ is concave with a maximum at z_i^*, depict the indifference curves of the two buyer types.
   (B) In particular, show the reservation indifferences curves, below which each buyer type would choose not to purchase.
   (C) If the two types are distinguishable, characterize the profit-maximizing quality levels and prices.
   (D) If the two types are not distinguishable, explain why:
      a. buyers who value quality less will not gain any consumer surplus
      b. it is always profitable to separate out the two types.
   (E) Explain also why one (and only one) of the two types will be offered a lower quality level when the two types are not distinguishable *ex ante* than when the seller has full information.

(F) From a mathematical perspective, does this model differ from the insurance model of Section 8.2.2? What are the essential common characteristics of the two models?

3 Non-Linear Pricing and Quantity Discounts

There are two types of buyers. Type 2 have a demand price $p_2(q)$ exceeding that of type 1. The marginal cost of production is constant and equal to c.

(A) If a buyer of type i accepts quantity q and pays a total of $\$T$ her gain is:

$$U_i = \int_0^q p_i(x)dx - T$$

By separating the total payment into cost and profit, show that the buyer's gain can also be expressed as:

$$U_i(q, \Pi) = \int_0^q (p_i(x) - c)\,dx - \Pi$$

(B) Using your answer to Exercise 2 as a guide, or otherwise, characterize the optimal selling scheme if it is not possible to distinguish the two types *ex ante*.

(C) Suppose that $p_i(x) = a - x/b_i$, so that individuals with a higher parameter b_i have larger demands. If $a = 10$, $b_1 = 1$, $b_2 = 2$, $c = 2$ and one half of the population are of type 1, solve explicitly for the optimal selling scheme.

[HINT: Show that $\Pi_1 = 8q_1 - \frac{1}{2}q_1^2$ and $q_2 = 16$. Then use the latter to establish that $\Pi_2 = 64 + \Pi_1 - (8q_1 - \frac{1}{4}q_1^2)$]

(D) Does the optimal selling scheme involve quantity discounting, that is, a lower price per unit for those buying more units?

(E) Is there quantity discounting for all possible proportions of type 1 in the population?

(F) For what market is this model most applicable?

4 Partial Separating and Partial Pooling

There are three types of demand curves:

$$p_t(q) = t + 10 - q, \quad t = 1, 2, 3$$

Output can be supplied at zero cost.

(A) Show that q_1^* is strictly positive if and only if the proportion of type 1 satisfies a constraint of the form $f_1 > \alpha$.

(B) Assuming this constraint is satisfied, obtain a necessary and sufficient condition for the monopolist to offer three separating contracts.**

SUGGESTIONS FOR FURTHER READING: Arrow (1971) is one of the first modern discussions of moral hazard. While the presentation in Section 8.1 is based on Grossman and Hart (1983), the principal-agent model was first analyzed in Holmstrom (1979). Mirrlees (1999) points out a problem with using the "first-order" approach in the principal-agent problem. See Shavell (1979) and Spence and Zeckhauser (1971) for moral hazard in an insurance setting. Akerlof (1970) illustrates the dramatic effect of adverse selection on equilibrium trades. Mirrlees (1971) is the earliest formal model of screening. Stiglitz and Weiss (1981) is an influential paper that shows that adverse selection in credit markets leads to credit rationing. See Riley (1987) and Arnold and Riley (2009) for more on this topic. In the model in Section 8.2.3, which is based on Maskin and Riley (1984, preferences are defined over quality and quantity. See Mussa and Rosen (1978) for a model of monopoly price discrimination where preferences are defined over quality alone.

References

Akerlof, George A., "The Market for 'Lemons': Qualitative Uncertainty and the Market Mechanism," *Quarterly Journal of Economics*, 84 (1970), 488–500.

Arnold, Lutz G. and Riley, John G., "On the Possibility of Credit Rationing in the Stiglitz-Weiss Model," *American Economic Review*, 99 (2009), 2012–2021.

Arrow, Kenneth J., "Insurance Risk, and Resource Allocation," *Essays in the Theory of Risk Bearing*, Chicago: Markham, 1971.

Grossman, Sanford and Hart, Oliver, "An Analysis of the Principal Agent Problem," *Econometrica*, 51 (1983), 1–45.

Holmstrom, Bengt, "Moral Hazard and Observability," *Bell Journal of Economics*, 10 (1979), 74–91.

Maskin, Eric S. and Riley, John G., "Monopoly with Incomplete Information," *RAND Journal of Economics*, 15 (1984), 171–196.

Mirrlees, James A., "An Exploration in the Theory of Optimum Income Taxation," *Review of Economic Studies*, 38 (1971), 175–208.

———, "The Theory of Moral Hazard and Unobservable Behavior – Part I," *Review of Economic Studies*, 66 (1999), 3–21.

Mussa, Michael and Rosen, Sherwin, "Monopoly and Indirect Quality," *Journal of Economic Theory*, 18 (1978), 301–317.

** End of starred section.

Riley, John G., "Credit Rationing: A Further Remark," *American Economic Review*, 77 (1987), 224–227.

Shavell, Steven, "On Moral Hazard and Insurance," *Quarterly Journal of Economics*, 93 (1979), 541–562.

Spence, A. Michael and Zeckhauser, Richard, "Insurance, Information and Individual Actions," *American Economic Review*, 61 (1971), 380–387.

Stiglitz, Joseph E. and Weiss, Andrew, "Credit Rationing in Markets with Imperfect Information," *American Economic Review*, 71 (1981), 393–410.

Competition and Hidden Knowledge

In the previous chapter we modeled situations with a large number of *informed* individuals on one side of the market, for example, potential purchasers of insurance who are aware of their individual likelihoods of suffering loss, or potential buyers who are aware of their own reservation prices. On the other side of the market we assumed a relatively *uninformed* individual possessing some degree of monopoly power – the insurance company, or the monopoly seller. The main issue addressed was contract design: an insurance deductible option to separate the better from poorer risks, or a schedule of options whereby the monopolist might induce the different types of buyers on the other side of the market to reveal themselves.

This chapter relaxes the assumption that the uninformed transactor has no close competitors. Instead, in each market a number of decision makers compete with one another in the design of contracts intended to separate the different types of trading partners they might be dealing with.

In Section 9.1 we consider situations where the traders on the uninformed side of the market move first, offering contracts aimed at *screening* their possible trading partners. Later, Section 9.3 takes up the opposite case in which the parties on the informed side of the market take the initiative, *signaling* their respective types by some choice of action. Interpolated between these two analyses is a discussion in Section 9.2 of "reactive equilibrium" in information-revealing situations.

9.1 Screening

Consider an industry in which workers have productivities of either θ_0 or θ_1, where $\theta_0 < \theta_1$. The proportions of type-0 and type-1 workers are f_0 and f_1. Firms hire workers without knowing which type they are. In the absence of outside opportunities, and assuming risk neutrality, competition among firms pushes the wage offer up to the average productivity:

$$w = \bar{\theta}_{01} \equiv f_0\theta_0 + f_1\theta_1$$

Suppose, however, that workers also have available an outside opportunity which, without requiring any educational credential, pays a wage w_0 that exceeds the average productivity $\bar{\theta}_{01}$. Since all workers will take up this offer rather than accept a wage of $\bar{\theta}_{01}$, the industry cannot operate without some screening mechanism. What is going on here is akin to adverse selection in the insurance market studied in Chapter 8. Just as adverse selection may rule out the possible social gains that risk-averse insureds could achieve from risk sharing, here the impossibility of screening makes it unfeasible for firms to achieve the potential social gains from employing high-productivity workers.

9.1.1 Screening by Means of a Non-Productive Action

Following the argument in Spence (1974), suppose there is some available action that is not productive of itself but (i) is observable and (ii) can be engaged in at lower marginal cost by higher-productivity workers. Specifically, consider educational credentials. Let $C(z, \theta)$ be the total cost of an education level z to a worker of type θ. Then, if paid a wage of w, the payoff of type θ (assuming risk neutrality) is:

$$U(z, w, \theta) = w - C(z, \theta)$$

In Figure 9.1, indifference curves of the two types are depicted. The type-1 workers' (dashed) indifference curves are flatter than the type-0 (solid) curve, reflecting the lower marginal opportunity cost of the credential for type-1 workers: $MC(z, \theta_1) < MC(z, \theta_0)$, where $MC(z, \theta) \equiv \partial C/\partial z$. Or, equivalently, $dw/dz|_U$ is a declining function of θ.[1]

Firms compete by associating a wage offer with a particular level of education. Consider the two indifference curves through the point $\langle 0, w_0 \rangle$. These are the reservation indifference curves of the two types of workers. Since the dashed curve for type 1 is flatter, any offer acceptable to the inferior type 0 will also be acceptable to the superior type 1. However, the converse is certainly not true. The shaded region in the diagram represents the offers

---

[1] The indifference curves of both types of workers are drawn as straight lines, i.e., $C(z, \theta) = zC(\theta)$ is being assumed. However, this is merely so that the diagram is not cluttered. The analysis would remain the same if the indifference curves were indeed curved lines.

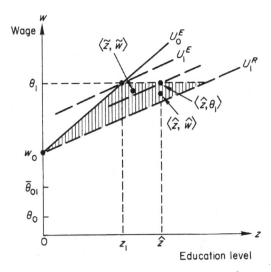

Figure 9.1. Screening out low-productivity workers.

that (i) only type-1 workers strictly prefer over the outside opportunity and (ii) are profitable to the firm ($w < \theta_1$).

One such offer is $\langle \hat{z}, \hat{w} \rangle$. This offer does separate the two types and therefore overcomes the adverse-selection problem. But, being strictly profitable, it is not viable in equilibrium. Another firm has an incentive to offer a higher wage for workers of education level $\hat{z}$ and thereby bid away the high-quality workers. In fact, competition will then bid the wage up to the zero-profit level $w = \theta_1$ at the point $\langle \hat{z}, \theta_1 \rangle$.

But this is still not the end of the story. If all other firms are offering the contract $\langle \hat{z}, \theta_1 \rangle$, any single firm can make an alternative offer such as $\langle \tilde{z}, \tilde{w} \rangle$ that is strictly preferred by high-productivity workers and is also strictly profitable. Indeed, such an alternative exists for all points in the shaded region, except for the offer $\langle z_1, \theta_1 \rangle$ at the northwest corner. This last is therefore the unique Nash equilibrium: all firms offer a wage θ_1 equal to the marginal product of high-quality workers, while screening out low-productivity workers by an educational requirement z_1 just tough enough to deter the entry of these workers.

Low-productivity workers are deterred because the benefit of satisfying the educational screen, in terms of the wage differential $\theta_1 - w_0$, is just offset by the total cost of the education $C(z_1, \theta_0)$. High-productivity workers are paid their marginal product but incur the screening cost $C(z_1, \theta_1)$. The presence of the low-productivity workers thus imposes a *negative externality* of $C(z_1, \theta_1)$ upon the high-productivity workers.

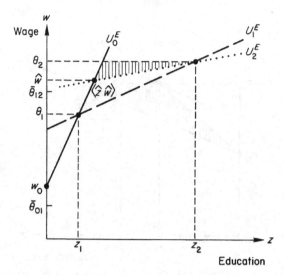

Figure 9.2. Separating zero-profit contracts.

Note that the size of this externality depends critically on the relative cost of education. As just argued, the cost of education level z_1 to the low-productivity workers is $C(z_1, \theta_0) = \theta_1 - w_0$. Then, if the difference in the cost of education is small, the negative externality has a cost almost equal to the wage differential. At the other extreme, if the cost of education for high-quality workers is very small, the negative externality has a negligible cost.

So far, the only issue has been sorting out those workers who should enter a particular industry from those who should work elsewhere. More generally, there will be more than one type of worker who is best employed in the industry. Suppose there were another type of worker with productivity level θ_2 in the industry, where $\theta_0 < w_0 < \theta_1 < \theta_2$. As before, let f_i be the proportion of type-i workers in the overall population.

Suppose that, if types 0 and 1 cannot be distinguished, their average productivity is $\bar{\theta}_{01} < w_0$. Finally, continue to assume that the marginal cost of education is lower for higher-quality workers, that is, $MC(z, \theta_0) > MC(z, \theta_1) > MC(z, \theta_2)$. Arguing exactly as above, the offer $\langle z_1, \theta_1 \rangle$ separates the type-0 and type-1 workers. This is depicted in Figure 9.2. Also depicted is the (dotted) type-2 indifference curve through point $\langle z_2, \theta_2 \rangle$. If type-2 workers are to be separated from type-1 and competition bids type-2 workers' wages up to θ_2, the only potentially viable contract is $\langle z_2, \theta_2 \rangle$.

But this is far from the end of the analysis. The shaded area in Figure 9.2 represents offers preferred by type-1 workers over $\langle z_1, \theta_1 \rangle$ and by type-2

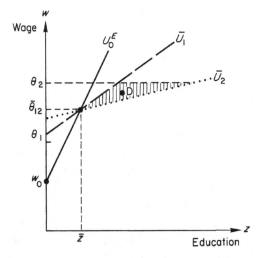

Figure 9.3. Skimming the cream.

workers over $\langle z_2, \theta_2 \rangle$. In particular, consider $\langle \hat{z}, \hat{w} \rangle$ at the southwest corner of the shaded region. For any wage in excess of $\hat{w}$, there are offers that are strictly preferred by types 1 and 2. Therefore if, contrary to the case depicted, the average productivity $\bar{\theta}_{12}$ of these workers exceeds $\hat{w}$, a firm can always enter with a contract close to $\langle \hat{z}, \hat{w} \rangle$ and make a strictly positive profit. So these separating contracts are not equilibrium contracts.

Thus, the $\langle z_2, \theta_2 \rangle$ contract is a separating equilibrium when $\bar{\theta}_{12} < \hat{w}$. But, if this is not the case, the alternative possible equilibrium involves pooling of different types as depicted in Figure 9.3. If types 1 and 2 are pooled, competition forces up the wage until it is equal to the average productivity:

$$\bar{\theta}_{12} = \left(\frac{f_1}{f_1 + f_2} \right) \theta_1 + \left(\frac{f_2}{f_1 + f_2} \right) \theta_2$$

As before, since a type-2 worker has a lower marginal cost of production, his (dotted) indifference curve through $(\bar{z}, \bar{\theta}_{12})$ is flatter than the corresponding (dashed) indifference curve for a type-1 worker.

Consider the offer represented by the point D inside the shaded region bounded by these indifference curves and the horizontal line $w = \theta_2$. Such an offer is strictly preferred by type-2 workers over $\langle \bar{z}, \bar{\theta}_{12} \rangle$. Also, it yields a strictly lower utility than $\langle \bar{z}, \bar{\theta}_{12} \rangle$ to type-1 workers. Since the wage is strictly lower than θ_2, the productivity of type-2 workers, the new offer is strictly profitable. Therefore the proposed pooling contract is not viable. To summarize, if a pooling contract were ever generally adopted, any individual firm could skim the cream from the pool by exploiting the fact that the highest-productivity workers have the lowest marginal cost of education.

It follows, therefore, that, in general, there may be no Nash equilibrium in pure strategies. Nevertheless, as will be shown shortly, it is possible to characterize those conditions under which a unique separating equilibrium does exist (Riley, 1985). (In Section 9.2 a modification of the game structure is described that always ensures a unique equilibrium.)

Consider Figure 9.2 once more. As has been seen, the separating contracts $\{\langle 0, w_0 \rangle, \langle z_1, \theta_1 \rangle, \langle z_2, \theta_2 \rangle\}$ are viable if and only if the wage $\hat{w}$ exceeds $\bar{\theta}_{12}$, the average productivity of types 1 and 2. It follows immediately that, if the proportion of type-1 workers in the population is large relative to type 2, equilibrium exists. For as the ratio f_2/f_1 declines, $\bar{\theta}_{12}$ declines toward θ_1. Following the same logic, whenever the critical wage $\hat{w}$ is sufficiently large, equilibrium again exists. Consider then a parametric change reducing the marginal cost of education for type 2. This flattens the (dotted) indifference curve through the contract $\langle z_2, \theta_2 \rangle$ and leaves the rest of Figure 9.2 unchanged. The lower edge of the shaded region therefore shifts up, and so $\hat{w}$ increases.

It is only slightly more difficult to show that a *ceteris paribus* increase in the marginal cost of education for type 1 also increases $\hat{w}$. The dashed indifference curve becomes steeper and so lowers z_2. This again results in an upward shift in the lower edge of the shaded region. Since the other two edges are unaffected, $\hat{w}$ must rise.

The conclusion, therefore, is that the relative marginal costs of signaling, for the different types, determine the viability of a separating equilibrium. An activity is potentially useful as a screening device if higher-quality workers can undertake it at lower marginal cost, but this is only a necessary condition for a Nash equilibrium. For sufficiency, marginal cost must decline rapidly enough as worker quality increases.

We will not extend the argument here, but it should be intuitively clear that additional types can be introduced without greatly complicating the analysis. As long as f_{i+1}/f_i or $MC(z, \theta_{i+1})/MC(z, \theta_i)$ is sufficiently small, for all i, the set of separating zero-profit contracts is the unique Nash equilibrium.

Exercises and Excursions 9.1.1

1 Screening by a Monopsonist

There are two types of workers. Type 0 has a marginal product of 1 and an outside opportunity of $w_0(\theta_0) = 2$. Type 1 has a marginal product of 4 and an outside opportunity $w_0(\theta_1) = 3$. The cost of education, z, is given by $C(z, \theta) = z/\theta$.

(A) In the absence of any educational screening, show that the monopsonist will face adverse selection unless the proportion of high-quality workers is at least 2/3.

(B) Assuming that this proportion is less than 2/3, establish that the monopsonist profits from screening. What contract will he offer?

(C) Contrast this with the competitive (Nash) equilibrium.

(D) Returning to the case of the monopsonist, for what range of outside opportunities $w_0(\theta_1)$ is it possible to screen for the high-productivity workers?

(E) Suppose the cost of education doubles to $C^*(z, \theta) = 2z/\theta$. Is anyone made worse off in either the monopsonistic or competitive allocations?

2 Screening and the Opportunity Cost of Time

Traditionally, labor economists have viewed time costs as the single most important part of the cost of education. Suppose that time costs are the only opportunity cost of education. To simplify matters, assume every individual works the same number of years, regardless of his time in school. The type-θ individual has a lifetime marginal product (discounted to his initial date of employment) of θ. Types are distributed continuously on the interval $[\beta, \gamma]$. To achieve an education level of z, a person must spend $T(z, \theta) = \alpha z/\theta$ years in school.

(A) Let $W(z)$ be the present value of lifetime earnings offered to an individual with education level z (discounted to the initial date of employment). Write down an expression for an individual's present value of lifetime income, discounted to birth. If $z = Z(\theta)$ is the choice of a type-θ worker, explain carefully why the following two conditions must hold in a separating equilibrium:

(i) $\dfrac{W'(Z(\theta))}{W(Z(\theta))} = \dfrac{r\alpha}{\theta}$ (ii) $W(Z(\theta)) = \theta$

(B) Hence obtain an expression for $W(z)$ in terms of z and the parameters r, α, and β.

(C) Substituting for z, show that the equilibrium mapping from time in school into discounted earnings is:

$$W^*(t) = \frac{\beta}{1 - rt}$$

9.1.2 Screening with Productive Actions

The analysis of Section 9.1.1 focused exclusively on the screening role of education and ignored its possible direct effect upon productivity. This section shows how the earlier model can be extended to allow for productivity effects. We will also see that the generalized model can be used to analyze competitive screening in quite different applications.

As before, assume that an individual of type θ has a utility function $U(z, w; \theta)$ over education-wage contracts $\langle z, w \rangle$. And, once again, an individual with higher θ requires a smaller increment in income to be willing to increase his education level. That is, the marginal opportunity cost of education, $MC(z, \theta)$, declines with θ.

In the earlier analysis, education did not actually contribute to the productivity of the worker, but only served to signal his quality to employers. In this section, in contrast, the value to a firm of a specific worker's contract $\langle z, w \rangle$ is a function not only of the individual's type but of his education level as well. To be precise, let the net value of the contract to the firm be:

$$U^f(z, w; \theta) = V(z; \theta) - w$$

Here V is increasing in both z and θ, where θ can be thought of as the individual's innate ability. $V(z; \theta)$ is then his marginal product after receiving an education level of z while $U^f(z, w; \theta)$ is the firm's profit after paying a wage w. Finally, assume that each worker can earn a wage w_0 in some other industry without accumulating any educational credentials.

Before analyzing the screening equilibrium, it is helpful to consider the outcome when θ is observable. Given competition among firms, the wage of type θ is bid up until profit is zero. The full-information contract, for an individual of some type θ, is then along the zero-profit curve $w = V(z; \theta)$ in Figure 9.4. The contract at point A satisfies the zero-profit condition. But it is not an equilibrium contract, since another firm can offer B instead. The latter is preferred by workers of type θ and is profitable since it lies strictly below the zero-profit curve. Evidently, the equilibrium contract for type θ is $\langle z^*(\theta), w^*(\theta) \rangle$ where the zero-profit curve and the indifference curve are tangential.

Mathematically, the equilibrium contract is that which maximizes the payoff of type θ subject to the zero-profit condition. That is, $\langle z^*(\theta), w^*(\theta) \rangle$ solves:

$$\underset{z, w}{\text{Max}} \{ U(z, w; \theta) | w = V(z; \theta) \}$$

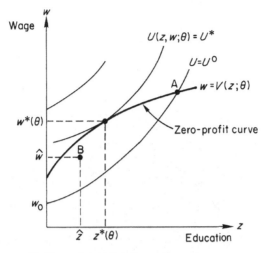

Figure 9.4. Full-information contract.

Substituting for w and then differentiating by z yields the first-order condition:

$$\frac{dU}{dz} = \frac{\partial U}{\partial z} + \frac{\partial U}{\partial w}\frac{\partial V}{\partial z} = 0$$

Rearranging, leads to the tangency condition:

$$\left.\frac{dw}{dz}\right|_U = -\frac{\partial U/\partial z}{\partial U/\partial w} = \frac{\partial V}{\partial z}(z;\theta)$$

That is, the opportunity cost of education is equal to its marginal product.

Figure 9.5 depicts the full-information equilibrium when there are two types, θ_1 and θ_2. If the types are observably distinct, their equilibrium contracts are $\langle z_1^*, w_1^* \rangle$ and $\langle z_2^*, w_2^* \rangle$. But, if the two types cannot be distinguished, workers of type 1 would strictly prefer the contract of type 2. Therefore, just as in the previous analysis, there is a further incentive for type-2 workers to accumulate education.

Consider the shaded region. It is bounded from above by the lower envelope of the zero-profit curve for type 2 and the indifference curve for type 1 through point $\langle z_1^*, w_1^* \rangle$. Therefore any new offer in the region will screen out the low-productivity workers and generate profits on high-productivity workers. Given competition among firms, the only potentially viable contract is $\langle z_2^s, w_2^s \rangle$ where the return to high-quality workers is maximized.

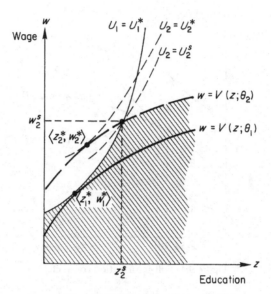

Figure 9.5. The two-type case.

   The analysis, therefore, proceeds exactly as in the previous section. Assuming an equilibrium is viable, it must separate out the different types in such a way that (i) there is zero profit on each contract, and (ii) workers of each type are just indifferent between their own contract and the contract of individuals of the immediately superior type.

   Given these conditions, once the contract of the lowest type is known the other contracts can, in principle, be computed.

   Since in equilibrium types are separated and yield zero profit, no individual can be better off than in the full-information equilibrium. It follows that any type θ choosing the reservation wage w_0 in the full-information equilibrium will also choose it in the screening equilibrium. Let θ^* signify the lowest-productivity worker type who would prefer to enter the industry under full information. In Figure 9.4, interpret θ as representing this θ^*. By hypothesis, if type θ^* is offered the full-information contract $\langle z^*(\theta), w^*(\theta) \rangle$, no lower-productivity type will wish to mimic. Therefore, if a firm offers this contract, there are only three possible outcomes. Either no one accepts, or only type θ^* accepts, or type θ^* and superior workers accept. Since none of these outcomes generate losses, competition will eliminate any inferior contract such as $\langle \hat{z}, \hat{w} \rangle$ in the figure.

   So individuals of the lowest type choosing to be screened will, in equilibrium, have the same contract as under conditions of full information. Higher types separated themselves by choosing education levels higher than what would be chosen under full information.[2] Intuitively, the lowest type to enter the industry gains nothing from being screened, in which case the private return to accumulating education equals the social return. However, for higher types, education has both a productivity and a screening effect. The net result is an equilibrium in which educational credentials are accumulated beyond the level dictated solely by productivity considerations.

Exactly the same analysis can be applied in contexts other than education. Returning to the insurance market of Chapter 8, recall that insurance companies might offer a reduction R from some maximum premium α in return for a deductible of Z. The net premium is then $\alpha - R$ and the payment on a loss L is $L - Z$. For an individual with non-loss probability π, the zero-expected-profit contract satisfies:

$$\alpha - R = (1 - \pi)(L - Z)$$

Premium = probability of loss × payout in the event of a loss

Rearranging:

$$R = \alpha + (1 - \pi)(Z - L)$$

In Figure 9.6, the zero-expected-profit contract therefore has slope $1 - \pi$ through the point $(Z, R) = (L, \alpha)$. At such a contract an individual's premium and coverage are both zero, i.e., this is the no-insurance point.

The zero-expected-profit lines are depicted in Figure 9.6 for two risk classes. The solid and dashed lines through (L, α) are the zero-expected-profit lines for the high-risk type π_1 and the low-risk type π_2, respectively.

As argued in Chapter 8, the better risks have flatter indifference curves. Because the probability of a loss is lower, they are willing to accept a smaller reduction in premium in exchange for taking on a larger deductible. Under full information (and ignoring moral hazard), all individuals receive full coverage. The full-information equilibrium contract for risk-class π_i is therefore the point $(0, R_i^*)$ on the vertical axis.

In the absence of information about type of risk, competitive screening in the insurance context operates exactly as in the educational example. The bad risks, type π_1, continue to receive full coverage. The good risks, type π_2, are offered a deductible just big enough to separate them from type π_1 while continuing to generate zero-expected profits. In Figure 9.6 this new contract is the point (Z_2^s, R_2^s).

---

[2] In the two-type case it is possible that the full-information equilibrium separates, in which case it is also the screening equilibrium. However, if differences between types are sufficiently small, this possibility is eliminated (as shown in an exercise at the end of this section).

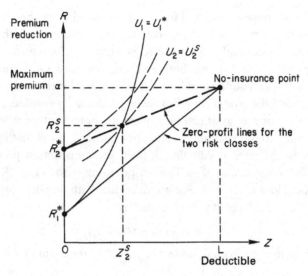

Figure 9.6. Screening out poor insurance risks.

Once again, however, the separating equilibrium may not be a Nash equilibrium. As explained earlier, the crucial condition for existence of a Nash equilibrium is the rate at which the marginal opportunity cost of the screening activity declines with improvement of "quality." In Riley (1985), it is argued that, when loss probabilities are numerically small (as is typical for insurance), this condition is likely to be met. However, for other applications, the existence issue is not so readily finessed. The next section describes an alternative approach to the problem of non-existence of a Nash equilibrium.

Exercises and Excursions 9.1.2

1 Equilibrium with Productive Screening
Suppose that a worker of type θ has marginal value product $V(z; \theta) = \theta(1 + z)/2$ and cost of education $C(z, \theta) = z^2/\theta$, where $\theta = 1, 2, 3$. All workers can earn a wage of 1 in some other industry that has no educational requirements.

(A) Confirm that, if θ were observable, a type-θ worker would choose educational level $z^*(\theta) = \theta^2/4$ if he were to enter the industry.
(B) Hence, or otherwise, confirm that, if marginal value product is observable, equilibrium levels of z are $(1/4, 1, 9/4)$.

(C) If θ were not observable which type(s) would be made worse off? Assuming that a Nash equilibrium exists, what are the education levels and wages in the screening equilibrium?

2 Screening and the Similarity of Types

An individual of type θ has marginal value product $V(z, \theta) = \theta + z$ and cost of education $C(z, \theta) = z^2/2\theta$.

(A) With full information show that type θ chooses an education level $Z^*(\theta) = \theta$ and earns a wage $W(Z^*(\theta)) = 2Z^*(\theta)$.

(B) Suppose that there are just two types, $\theta = 1$ and $\theta = \hat{\theta}$. If $\hat{\theta} = 3$ show that the full-information equilibrium is also a screening equilibrium. Show next that $\hat{\theta} = 3$ is a borderline case. That is, for all $\hat{\theta}$ between 1 and 3, the full-information equilibrium is not a screening equilibrium.

[HINT: In a diagram depict the full-information earnings function $W(Z)$ and also the indifference curve for type 1 through his equilibrium contract $(1, 1)$. Where do these two "curves" intersect?]

3 Screening in Financial Markets

By raising outside equity z, an entrepreneur with a product of quality θ can produce next period an output of value $f(z, \theta)\tilde{\varepsilon}$, where $\tilde{\varepsilon}$ is a random variable with a mean of unity. Suppose f is increasing in θ, concave in z, and that the elasticity of output with respect to equity input, $e \equiv (\partial f/\partial z)/(f/z)$, is higher for higher-quality projects.

Let P be the market price of the firm so that outsider shareholding is z/P. The remaining "promoter stock" held by the entrepreneur is non-tradable.

(A) Explain why the present value of entrepreneurial profit is:

$$U(z, P; \theta) = \left(1 - \frac{z}{P}\right) \frac{f(z, \theta)}{1 + r}$$

(B) If outside investors can observe z, and all individuals are risk neutral, show that the level of investment z^* will satisfy:

$$\frac{1}{1 + r} \frac{\partial f}{\partial z} = 1$$

(C) Confirm that the increase in share price that the entrepreneur is just willing to accept, in exchange for additional dilution of his ownership due to an increment of outside equity, can be expressed as:

$$\frac{dP}{dz}\bigg|_U = \frac{-\dfrac{\partial U}{\partial z}}{\dfrac{\partial U}{\partial P}} = \frac{P}{z} - \frac{P^2}{z^2}\left(1 - \frac{z}{P}\right)\frac{z}{f}\frac{\partial f}{\partial z}$$

(D) Hence confirm that the level of outside equity can be used by outsiders to screen out projects of lower quality. Illustrate graphically for the case of just two quality levels.

9.2 Reactive Equilibrium

Section 9.1 showed that, unless certain sufficient conditions hold, there is no Nash equilibrium in pure strategies that separates the different types. Moreover, there is no Nash equilibrium in which different types are pooled. (While there are always mixed-strategy Nash equilibria (Dasgupta and Maskin, 1986), these seem implausible empirically, at least for the applications considered here.) In this section, it is shown that if an additional stability property holds, the outcome will be a set of contracts that separates out the different types. Since this property is an assumption about the reactions of other agents to defection, the associated outcome is called a *reactive equilibrium*.

To illustrate, return to the pure screening model of Section 9.1.1. Let there be three types, where type 0 is better off accepting the outside reservation wage while types 1 and 2 are better off choosing $z > 0$ and being employed in the industry. The separate zero-profit contracts must, of course, involve wage rates of θ_1 and θ_2 for these two groups.

The efficient separating contracts are depicted in Figure 9.7. This is essentially the same as Figure 9.2 except that the point $\langle \hat{z}, \hat{w} \rangle$ now lies below the average productivity $\bar{\theta}_{12}$. All contracts in the interior of the shaded region are below the reservation indifference curve for type 0 and above the indifference curves for types 1 and 2 through the efficient separating contracts $\langle z_1, \theta_1 \rangle$ and $\langle z_1, \theta_2 \rangle$. Since any wage in the interior of the shaded region is less than $\bar{\theta}_{12}$, all such offers are strictly profitable. Therefore, starting with the separating contracts $\{\langle 0, w_0 \rangle, \langle z_1, \theta_1 \rangle, \langle z_2, \theta_2 \rangle\}$, any firm can enter and make a profit with a "pooled" contract such as $\langle z^*, w^* \rangle$. Thus, it appears, the separating equilibrium is not viable.

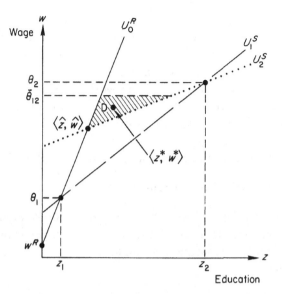

Figure 9.7. A profitable defection.

However, if a firm in fact exploits this opportunity, it exposes itself to risk. Figure 9.8 shows the indifference curves of the two types through the "defect" contract $\langle z^*, w^* \rangle$. Since the highest-quality workers have the flattest (dotted) indifference curve through $\langle z^*, w^* \rangle$, there is always a reaction $\langle z^{**}, w^{**} \rangle$ that can skim the cream from the defecting firm's pool.

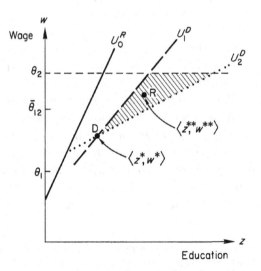

Figure 9.8. Skimming the cream from the pool.

Since $w^{**} < \theta_2$, such a reaction is profitable, and, since $w^* > \theta_1$, the reaction results in losses for the initial defector. Note, moreover (and this is crucial), that the reactor runs no risk from his reaction. That is, unlike the initial defector, he has no risk of being undercut and ending up with losses. The reason is that the reactor attracts only workers for whom $\theta_2 > w^{**}$, and employing them is strictly profitable. Therefore, the worst that can happen to a reactor is that other reactors outbid him, in which case he ends up with zero profit.

More generally, a reactive equilibrium is defined as follows:

Definition: Reactive Equilibrium

A set of offers (contracts) E is a Reactive equilibrium if, for any addition to this set D that one of the uninformed agents (the defector) prefers, there is a further addition R that another uninformed agent (the reactor) might offer such that:

  (i) When the informed agents can choose from E, D, and R, the defector is strictly worse off and the reactor is strictly better off than under the initial set of offers E.

  (ii) No further additions to the set of offers leave the reactor worse off than under E.[3]

In Engers and Fernandez (1987), it is shown that, under the assumptions of the screening model outlined in this chapter, there is a unique reactive equilibrium. This is the set of efficient, separating, zero-profit contracts. For finite sets of offers, the arguments are essentially those made above. That is, it is possible to show that, for any finite number of new offers made by a defector, there is a corresponding reaction that skims the cream and produces losses for the defector.

The key idea is that an offer announced and promoted by a firm cannot be quickly and costlessly withdrawn. Potential defectors cannot simply hit and run, announcing a new offer with the intent of withdrawing it as soon as other firms react. Instead, defectors must consider the possibility of incurring losses once these reactions occur. If the reaction time is short relative to the length of time over which a defector is committed to his new offering, all defectors from the efficient, separating, zero-profit set do suffer losses.

---

[3] Note that any Nash equilibrium is automatically a Reactive equilibrium since, for a Nash contract set, the set of strictly preferable defections is empty. See Wilson (1977) for the related concept of "anticipatory equilibrium."

Exercises and Excursions 9.2

1 Ice Cream Vendors

There are n vendors selling ice cream on a beach represented by the interval $[0, 1]$. Sunbathers are distributed uniformly along the beach. Vendor i must choose a location x_i, $i = 1, \ldots, n$ somewhere on $[0, 1]$. Without loss of generality, assume that $x_1 \leq x_2 \leq \cdots \leq x_n$. Sunbathers purchase exclusively from the nearest vendor (there is no price competition). If two vendors choose the same location, they share their market equally.

- (A) As Hotelling first noted, when $n = 2$ each ice cream vendor will locate at $x = \frac{1}{2}$ although the efficient location vector is $(x_1, x_2) = (\frac{1}{4}, \frac{3}{4})$. Is the latter a reactive equilibrium?
- (B) When $n = 3$, there is no Nash equilibrium. Explain why not. Show that there exists a reactive equilibrium with $x_1 = \frac{1}{4}$ and $x_3 = \frac{3}{4}$. Show also that x_2 may take on any value between x_1 and x_3. Are any of the reactive equilibria efficient?
- (C) What happens when $n = 4$?

9.3 Signaling

Up to now the analysis has had transactors on the uninformed side of the market designing contracts in an attempt to screen for quality. The informed individuals were supposed to respond in an essentially passive way, simply choosing among the offered contracts. This section asks what happens when it is the informed transactors who move first.

An individual trying to sell an item or service that he knows to be valuable may attempt to convince buyers by undertaking some *signaling* activity. Just as with screening, an activity is a potential signal if engaging in it is less costly for someone offering a higher-quality product. Returning to the basic model of Section 9.1.1, now suppose workers can first choose their level of education. The employer firms observe the distribution of educational achievements and only then make offers.

What makes the signaling game more complicated is the need to specify the beliefs of the uninformed transactors (firms). As will be seen, the hypotheses about how these beliefs are formed are critical for characterizing the equilibrium.

The key issues can be illustrated when workers are of two types. As before, let θ_i be the marginal value product of type i, for $i = 0, 1$. Let w_0 be the alternative reservation wage for both types, where $\theta_0 < w_0 < \theta_1$. Type i can achieve an education level z at a cost $C(z, \theta_i)$. As in Section 9.1.1, the cost of

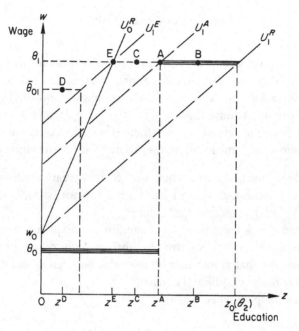

Figure 9.9. Educational signaling.

education is assumed linear in z and lower for the higher-quality workers (type 1).

In Figure 9.9, suppose the only two education levels observed are 0 and z^A. What wages should firms offer? One possible belief is indicated by the thick step function. That is, anyone choosing an education level less than z^A is believed to be of type 0, while anyone with an education level of z^A or more is believed to be of type 1. Given such beliefs, the most that any firm will offer an individual choosing $z = 0$ is θ_0. For those choosing $z = z^A$, competition among firms bids the wage up to θ_1 where expected profit is zero.

Now consider the educational choice of the two types of workers. Since competition bids the wage up to the expected marginal value product, each individual can attain any point on the thick step function. A type-0 worker is clearly better off remaining out of the industry and taking the reservation wage w_0. Type-1 workers, however, maximize their return by choosing the education level z^A. It follows that the assumed initial beliefs are consistent with optimal responses, and so the outcome is a Nash signaling equilibrium.

But these proposed beliefs are just one of a continuum of possibilities. Suppose instead that firms believe that only individuals with an education level of at least z^B are of type 1. Using exactly the same argument, it can be seen that the pair of education levels $(0, z^B)$ is also an equilibrium.

A rather different alternative belief is that education and productivity are uncorrelated. Expected marginal value product at each level of z is then the population average $\bar{\theta}_{01}$. With such beliefs, no one has an incentive to be educated. The resulting outcome is that both types are hired at the wage $w = \bar{\theta}_{01}$.

The Nash equilibrium concept therefore leads to a wide range of different possible outcomes, and so has little predictive power. It is natural to ask whether the predictions can be narrowed down by introducing some of the refinements of equilibrium concepts introduced in Chapter 7. As emphasized there, the problem of multiple Nash equilibria arises because beliefs are not fully tested via equilibrium behavior. Consider the beliefs depicted in Figure 9.9 that yield the education levels $(0, z^A)$. Beliefs are *defined* for all possible actions by the players. However, beliefs are only *tested* at the equilibrium education level $z = z^A$.

Since the signaling game has no subgames, all the Nash equilibria are also *subgame-perfect* equilibria. Turning to the requirement that a Nash equilibrium be *sequential*, it is necessary to consider what happens if each type pursues a completely mixed strategy. Since both types are better off choosing the reservation wage rather than obtaining education level greater than $z_0(\theta_2)$, only the completely mixed strategies over the interval $[0, z_0(\theta_2)]$ need be taken into account. Suppose type 0 chooses $z = 0$ with probability $1 - \alpha$ and a uniform mixed strategy over $[0, z_0(\theta_2)]$ with probability α. Suppose, also, that type 1 chooses $z = z^A$ with probability $1 - \alpha^2$ and a uniform mixed strategy over $[0, z_0(\theta_2)]$ with probability α^2.

Given these mixed strategies, the probability that an individual choosing $z \notin \{0, z^A\}$ will be of type 0 can be computed. Since a type-0 individual chooses $z \notin \{0, z^A\}$ with probability α while a type-1 individual does so with probability α^2, the probability that the individual is type 0 is:

$$\frac{\alpha}{\alpha + \alpha^2} = \frac{1}{1 + \alpha}$$

Taking the limit as $\alpha \to 0$, this probability approaches 1. Therefore it is *consistent* for firms to believe that an individual choosing $z \notin \{0, z^A\}$ is type 0 with probability 1. With such beliefs it is clear that the equilibrium offers by the firms $\langle 0, \theta_0 \rangle$, $\langle z^A, \theta_1 \rangle$ are best replies. That is, the Nash equilibrium is sequential.

Since exactly the same argument holds for any educational level between z^E and $z_0(\theta_2)$, it follows that the sequential refinement adds little or nothing in this context. Despite this, the educational level $z = z^A$ seems implausible. Why would firms believe that anyone with an educational level lower than z^A was of type 0? Consider Figure 9.9 once more. Suppose someone were to choose education level z^C. The most that a firm would pay is θ_1, the high marginal product. Even if offered this, a type-0 individual would be strictly better off choosing the reservation wage. So it is surely more plausible that the worker choosing z^C will be judged to be of high quality. The worker will then succeed in earning the high wage $w = \theta_1$. In the face of such logic, the sequential Nash equilibrium beliefs collapse.

In Chapter 7 the idea of logically testing a Nash equilibrium was made precise in two *communication tests*. The above argument is, in essence, a demonstration that the education level $z = z^A$ is not "weakly communication proof." Recall that an equilibrium is weakly communication proof if no message of the following class is credible:

I am sending you the message that my type is θ_i and you should believe me. For if you do and respond optimally, I will be better off while any other type who mimics me will be made worse off.

As has been seen, if a worker chooses $z = z^C$ and sends a message that he is of type 1, he should be believed. For, if he is and his wage is bid up to $w = \theta_1$, the reservation wage w_0 is still strictly preferred by type 0.

Such arguments rule out all separating Nash equilibria that are Pareto inferior to other Nash equilibria. In terms of Figure 9.9, any separating equilibrium with $z_1 > z^E$ is not weakly communication proof. As for the pooling equilibrium, the argument as to why it cannot be weakly communication proof proceeds almost exactly as in Section 9.2.

Figure 9.10 represents three types of workers. Once again, beliefs are represented by the thick step function. Suppose workers of type 0 choose the reservation wage while types 1 and 2 are pooled. For any such pooling contact, $\langle \bar{z}, \bar{\theta}_{12} \rangle$, there is always a level of education such as $\hat{z}_2$ that type-2 workers can choose as a credible signal. For, if an individual chooses $z = \hat{z}_2$ and is believed to be of type 2, he earns a wage $w = \theta_2$. While this makes him strictly better off, type 1 strictly prefers the Nash equilibrium pooling contract.

From all this the conclusion is that, of the family of Nash equilibria, only the efficient,[4] separating, zero-profit equilibrium is weakly communication proof. As seen in Section 9.1, this is the only potentially viable equilibrium when it is the uninformed (the employing firms) who move first by screening workers. Therefore, once a communication test is applied, the

---

[4] Efficient compared to other Nash equilibria.

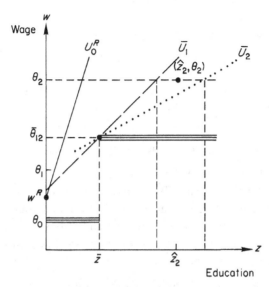

Figure 9.10. Non-credible pooling equilibria.

differences between signaling and screening turn out to be more apparent than real.

An even closer parallel can be drawn when the *strong* communication test is applied. Suppose, as in Figure 9.9, that type 1 strictly prefers to receive the average product $\bar{\theta}_{01}$ rather than the efficient separating contract $\langle z^E, \theta_1 \rangle$. Then a worker can choose $z = z^D$ and communicate to firms as follows:

Type 0 and type 1 are both strictly better off being paid the average product $\bar{\theta}_{01}$ with education level z^D rather than accept their Nash equilibrium contracts. Therefore you should use the population weights in estimating my value and so bid my wage up to $\bar{\theta}_{01}$.

The absence of such a credible message is precisely the requirement for an equilibrium to pass the strong communication test. Therefore, if this test is imposed there is, in general, no viable Nash equilibrium.

Evidently, the conditions under which no Nash signaling equilibrium satisfies the strong communication test are exactly the conditions under which there is no Nash screening equilibrium. This result is quite general. That is, the sufficient conditions for existence of a Nash screening equilibrium, described in Section 9.1.2, are sufficient for the existence of a signaling equilibrium that satisfies the strong communication test. On the other hand, the assumptions that lead to non-existence of a screening equilibrium also result in a signaling equilibrium that fails the strong communication test.

To conclude, when plausible restrictions are imposed upon beliefs, the question of existence and the nature of the equilibrium when it exists are essentially the same for screening and signaling models. Thus the order of the moves in the game does not matter. Very often, economic interactions are ongoing so that it is not clear who moves first. A theory in which the order of moves is immaterial is particularly applicable in such contexts.

Exercises and Excursions 9.3

1 Educational Signaling – A Discrete Example

There are two types of worker. Type 0 has marginal value product $\theta_0 = 2$. Type 1 has marginal value product $\theta_1 = 6$. The cost of educational level z for type θ is $C(z, \theta) = 4z^2/\theta$. Workers signal by choosing education levels from the set $Z = \{0, 1, 2\}$. Firms compete for workers by making a wage offer from the set $W = \{1, 3, 5\}$. For both types, the reservation wage is zero.

(A) If a worker of type i chooses an education level z and is offered a wage w, what are the expected payoffs to worker and firm?

(B) Compute the payoffs for worker and firm along each branch of the game tree. Depict this in a neat figure.

(C) If the proportion of type 0 is 0.8, show that there exists a Nash equilibrium. Are there multiple equilibria?

[HINT: Competition by firms bids wages up.]

(D) Does the Nash equilibrium satisfy both the weak and strong communication tests?

(E) Suppose the proportion of type 0 is 0.5. Confirm that there are at least two Nash equilibria in which the types are pooled, as well as a separating equilibrium.

(F) Which of these equilibria satisfy the weak communication test?

(G) Which satisfy the strong communication test?

2 Divine Equilibria*

Banks and Sobel (1987) have argued that the strong communication test is unreasonably strong. Essentially, their point is that an informed decision maker taking an out-of-equilibrium action will not be sure about the response to his action. Banks and Sobel describe an equilibrium as being "divine" if, whenever the set of responses that would benefit one type is contained in the set of responses that would benefit another type,

---

* Starred questions may be somewhat more difficult.

the uninformed party believes that the latter type is more likely to take an out-of-equilibrium action.

To illustrate, consider a simple signaling model with three types as in Figure 9.7.

(A) Confirm that, for all $z \in [z_1, z_2]$, the set of wages that would make type 1 better off contains the set of wages that would benefit type 2.

(B) Consider offers $\langle z, w \rangle$, with $z \in [z_1, z_2]$, such that only types 1 and 2 would be better off. Banks and Sobel then require that the wage offered, given such an out-of-equilibrium signal, should be based upon posterior beliefs in which the relative weight of type 2 is no greater than under the prior beliefs. That is, they would impose only the restriction that the firm's belief about expected productivity lies somewhere between θ_1 and the average productivity under the prior beliefs. Confirm that, for all prior beliefs, this implies that the best separating set of contracts is a "divine" equilibrium. (You must also apply the "divinity criterion" over the interval $(0, z_1)$.)

(C) If the proportions of the three types in the population are, respectively, 0.001, 0.010, and 0.989, does the line of reasoning by Banks and Sobel seem adequate?

SUGGESTIONS FOR FURTHER READING: The seminal work on signaling is by Spence (1973, 1974). Other important papers include Riley (1979), Rothschild and Stiglitz (1976), and Cho and Kreps (1987). Important papers on screening include the readings suggested at the end of the previous chapter and Riley (1985) for screening with competition. See Riley (2001) and Hörner (2008) for surveys on signaling and screening, and also Salanié (1997).

References

Banks, Jeffrey S. and Sobel, Joel, "Equilibrium Selection in Signaling Games," *Econometrica*, 55 (1987), 647–661.

Cho, In-Koo and Kreps, David M., "Signaling Games and Stable Equilibria," *Quarterly Journal of Economics*, 102 (1987), 179–222.

Dasgupta, Partha and Maskin, Eric S., "The Existence of Equilibrium in Discontinuous Economic Games: 1: Theory, 2: Applications," *Review of Economic Studies*, 53 (1986), 1–26, 27–41.

Engers, Maxim and Fernandez, Luis, "On the Existence and Uniqueness of Signalling Equilibria," *Econometrica*, 55 (1987), 425–440.

Hörner, Johannes, "Signalling and Screening," in *The New Palgrave Dictionary of Economics*, S.N. Durlauf and L.E. Blume (eds.), 2nd edition, vol. 7, pp. 479–484, New York, NY: Palgrave Macmillan, 2008.

Riley, John G., "Informational Equilibrium," *Econometrica*, 47 (1979), 331–359.

———, "Competition with Hidden Knowledge," *Journal of Political Economy*, 93 (1985), 958–976.

———, "Silver Signals: Twenty-five Years of Screening and Signaling," *Journal of Economic Literature*, 39 (2001), 432–478.

Rothschild, Michael and Stiglitz, Joseph E., "Equilibrium in Competitive Insurance Markets: An Essay in the Economics of Imperfect Information," *Quarterly Journal of Economics*, 90 (1976), 629–649.

Salanié, Bernard, *The Economics of Contracts*, Cambridge, MA: MIT Press, 1997.

Spence, A. Michael, "Job Market Signaling," *Quarterly Journal of Economics*, 87 (1973), 355–374.

———, *Market Signaling*, Cambridge, Cambridge, MA: Harvard University Press, 1974.

Wilson, Charles A., "A Model of Insurance Markets with Incomplete Information," *Journal of Economic Theory*, 16 (1977), 167–207.

10

Market Institutions

Market institutions come into place to solve extant problems. For example, with the advent of large corporations and multi-location merchandising in the early nineteenth century, posted prices replaced bargaining as the preferred method of retail.[1] More recently, prompted by advances in technology, which make it possible to serve geographically-dispersed bidders, auctions have increased in popularity. At the same time, in transactions involving real estate or cars, prices are determined through negotiations. In this chapter we explore some of the reasons underlying this variety of selling methods. In Sections 10.1 and 10.2 we assume that the seller has the ability to choose and commit to any selling method she likes. Under this assumption, the seller will find it optimal to either post a take-it-or-leave-it price or conduct an auction. When this assumption is relaxed (in Section 10.3), it leads to bargaining between the seller and the buyer.

10.1 Posted-Price Markets

A seller has one indivisible object to sell to a buyer. The seller's cost is normalized to zero. The buyer values the object at $V \geq 0$. The seller does not know V and believes that it is drawn from a probability distribution $F(V)$ with positive density $f(V)$. The seller has the power to decide how to sell the object and can choose any market institution that she likes. What should the seller do?

Suppose that the seller decides to make a take-it-or-leave-it price offer, p, to the buyer. The seller can pre-commit to this selling strategy. The buyer knows that he has only two choices: either he accepts the seller's offer to buy at price p, or he rejects the offer and does not consume the object which he

[1] See Arnold and Lippman (1998).

values at V. The best that the buyer can do is to accept the offer if the price p is less than or equal to his valuation V and walk away if $p > V$. Thus, the seller assesses probability $1 - F(p)$ that price p is accepted by the buyer.

What is the optimal take-it-or-leave-it price for the seller? If the seller sets a very low price then the buyer is very likely to buy but the seller's profit will be small. If, instead, the price is very high then there is a good chance that the buyer will not buy, but if he does then the seller's profit is large. Thus, the seller faces a trade-off between the profit when she makes a sale and the probability of making a sale. The seller's expected profit as a function price, $\Pi(p)$, is equal to p multiplied by the probability of making a sale: $\Pi(p) = p(1 - F(p))$. The derivative of expected profit with respect to price is:

$$\frac{d\Pi(p)}{dp} = 1 - F(p) - pf(p)$$

At p^*, the profit-maximizing price for the seller, the first-order condition $\frac{d\Pi(p)}{dp}\big|_{p=p*} = 0$ implies:

$$p^* = \frac{1 - F(p^*)}{f(p^*)}. \tag{10.1.1}$$

Starting at any price p if the seller increases price by a small amount Δp, her expected profit will (i) increase by about $(1 - F(p))\Delta p$ due to the higher price, and (ii) decrease by about $pf(p)\Delta p$ as the probability of making a sale decreases $f(p)\Delta p$. At the profit-maximizing price, p^*, the increase and the decrease must be equal. That is, $p^* f(p^*)\Delta p = [1 - F(p^*)]\Delta p$, which is implied by (10.1.1).

In order to ensure that any p^* satisfying (10.1.1) is indeed profit maximizing (i.e., p^* obtained from (10.1.1) satisfies the second-order condition for profit-maximization), we make the assumption that $p - \frac{1-F(p)}{f(p)}$ is an increasing function of p. This is called the *regular* case.[2] Then there is exactly one p^* that satisfies (10.1.1). For any price $p < p^*$ the seller can increase profit by raising price as $pf(p) < 1 - F(p)$ in this range, and for any $p > p^*$ the seller can increase profit by decreasing price as $pf(p) > 1 - F(p)$. Thus, p^* is the unique profit-maximizing price.

Is posting a take-it-or-leave-it price equal to p^* the best the seller can do? Observe that p^* is greater than the seller's cost, which is zero. Suppose she does not make a sale at this price. Rather than walk away, should not the

---

[2] Many common probability distributions, such as uniform, normal, and exponential, are regular. The hazard rate of a distribution is $f(V)/(1 - F(V))$. An increasing hazard rate is a sufficient condition for regularity.

seller offer to sell at a price lower than p^*? But if the buyer anticipates this, it is no longer optimal for him to buy whenever $p^* \leq V$. He would be better off waiting for a price reduction, and thus the seller's expected profit from the initial price offer would be less than $\Pi(p^*)$. As we shall see in Section 10.2.3, the seller is better off walking away from a deal whenever the buyer turns down the price p^* and no other selling scheme will give the seller greater expected profit.[3]

The story is essentially unchanged if the seller has m identical units of the indivisible object to sell to n identical buyers, $m \geq n$. Buyer i has value V_i for one unit of the object and value 0 for additional units. Buyers' values are drawn independently from the distribution F. We shall see in Section 10.2.3 that it is optimal for the seller to set the take-it-or-leave-it price p^* defined in (10.1.1). However, if $m < n$, then instead of posting price p^* the seller should conduct an auction.

Exercises and Excursions 10.1

1 Optimal Prices
For each of the following distributions of buyer reservation value, compute the seller's optimal posted price. Be sure to verify that the regularity condition is satisfied by these distributions.

(A) $F(V) = \sqrt{V}$
(B) $F(V) = V$
(C) $F(V) = V^2$

You should find that the optimal prices and seller's expected profit increase from (A) to (B) to (C). Explain this intuitively by comparing the value distributions in the three cases.

2 Declining Price Offers
Consider 1(B) above, where buyer values are distributed uniformly on $[0, 1]$. The seller announces to the buyer that she will make at most two price offers. Her first offer is the optimal price that you derived in 1(B). If there is no sale, then with probability 0.5 the seller will make a second offer equal to half of the first price, and with probability 0.5 she will not make any additional offers. The seller will not make a third offer, even if the first two offers are declined. Assume that the buyer believes that the seller will follow the announced pricing policy.

[3] See Riley and Zeckhauser (1983).

(A) What is the buyer's best response? That is, give the range of values in which it is optimal for the buyer to accept the first price offer, and the range of values for which it is optimal to decline the first price offer and accept the second price offer (if it is made).

(B) What is the seller's expected profit if she follows this strategy and the buyer plays his best response? Compare with the seller's expected profit in part 1(B).

10.2 Auctions

Auctions have become ubiquitous: witness the emergence of internet marketplaces such as eBay and the recent spectrum rights auctions in the United States and then in other countries. In a class-action price-fixing suit against auction houses Sotheby's and Christie's in the year 2000, the presiding judge auctioned the right to be the plaintiffs' lawyer! More prosaic uses of auctions include the sale of perishables such as fresh fish, tulips, durables such as used machinery, works of art, real estate, financial assets, mineral rights, and defense, construction, and other procurement contracts. Typically, the auctioneer is a seller who solicits bids from several buyers.[4] The seller's motive for using an auction is straightforward – to obtain the highest price that will clear the market. The seller depends on the auction to get the buyers to reveal what they are willing to pay. The amount a buyer bids depends on his preferences and on the competitive pressure from other bidders. When there is no collusion among the bidders, auctions are effective in obtaining favorable terms for the seller, and they have the practical advantage of being simple and quick.

Four common auctions for the sale of one indivisible object are described below. In each of these auctions, the highest bidder is the winner and pays for the object; the losing bidders pay nothing.

Second-price sealed-bid auction: Bidders submit sealed bids to the auctioneer. The highest bidder wins and pays an amount equal to the second-highest bid.

Open ascending-price or "English" auction: The auctioneer calls out ever increasing prices as long as at least two bidders are willing to buy at the asking price. When only one bidder remains in the bidding, this bidder is declared the winner and gets the object at the last asking price.

---

[4] Procurement auctions are an exception. Here the auctioneer is a buyer who solicits offers from several sellers. All the results from auction theory described here have counterparts for procurement auctions.

Auction houses such as Sotheby's and Christie's use this auction to sell art.

First-price sealed-bid auction: Bidders submit sealed bids to the auctioneer. The highest bidder wins and pays what he bid. The U.S. Department of the Interior uses a first-price auction to sell mineral rights.

Open descending-price or "Dutch" auction: The seller starts with a very high asking price, and calls out a descending sequence of prices until one bidder accepts the price. This bidder obtains the object at that price. The Dutch auction is equivalent to the first-price sealed-bid auction. A version of this auction is used to auction large quantities of flowers in Aalsmeer, the Netherlands.

We analyze bidder behavior in these four auctions, first, with the simplifying assumption that the bidders know each others' valuations. Throughout, we assume that there is no collusion between the bidders.

10.2.1 Bidders' Valuations Are Known

Buyer 1 (Alex) values the object at V_1 and buyer 2 (Bev) at V_2. These valuations are common knowledge among Alex and Bev.[5] As in Section 10.1, we assume that the seller does not know these valuations. The seller's cost is zero. Let x_i be individual i's expected spending and let q_i be the probability of winning. Then i's expected return is:

$$U_i = q_i V_i - x_i, i = 1, 2$$

Because no one is compelled to participate, in equilibrium both individuals have non-negative expected return.

How will the two buyers bid in these auctions? In the two sealed-bid auctions, bidders must decide how much to bid. In the open ascending-price auction, each bidder's strategy is a price level at which to exit the auction. The decision to be made by a bidder in the Dutch auction is when to stop the descending-price clock and claim the object. Despite differences in auction rules and bidder strategies, we will see that the Nash equilibrium outcome in each of the four auctions is the same: the bidder with the highest valuation wins and pays the same amount (equal to the valuation of the bidder with the second-highest valuation).

Consider a second-price auction. It is a (weakly) *dominant strategy*[6] for each buyer to submit a bid equal to his valuation. To see this, suppose that

---

[5] The results are easily generalized to more than two bidders.

[6] Recall from Chapter 7 that this is a strategy that does at least as well as any other strategy for the buyer no matter what the opponent's strategy.

Alex submits a bid $b_1 < V_1$. There are three cases to consider. First, if his opponent's (Bev's) bid b_2 is less than b_1 then Alex will win whether he bids b_1 or V_1; his payment for the object with either bid is the same, b_2. Second, if $b_2 > V_1$ then Alex will not win whether he bids b_1 or V_1. It remains to check the case $b_1 \leq b_2 \leq V_1$. Alex will win with a bid of V_1 and lose with a bid of b_1; as he pays b_2 upon winning, his profit with a bid of V_1 is $V_1 - b_2$, which is positive. Thus, in the first two cases, Alex is equally well off with a bid of b_1 or V_1. In the third case, expected profit is strictly higher from a bid equal to V_1. Alex does no worse and sometimes does strictly better with a bid equal to V_1 rather than a bid less than V_1. Therefore, a bid equal to V_1 *dominates* any bid $b_1 < V_1$.

A similar argument shows that a bid of V_1 dominates any bid $b_1 > V_1$. Observe that if $b_2 > b_1$ or $b_2 \leq V_1$ then there is no difference in the outcome for Alex whether he bids b_1 or V_1. However, if $V_1 < b_2 \leq b_1$ then Alex wins with bid b_1 but pays a price greater than his valuation ($b_2 > V_1$). He is better off losing the auction with a bid of V_1.

Likewise, Bev will also bid her valuation. Thus, the buyer with the higher valuation will win and pay the other buyer's valuation.

Next, we turn to an open ascending-price auction. Here, too, there is a dominant strategy for each bidder: stay in the auction till the asking price equals one's valuation and then exit. If, at any stage, the current asking price p is less than Alex's valuation V_1, then he should remain in the auction; if he were to drop out at p, Alex would forgo the possibility of winning the auction and making a positive profit if Bev drops out before the auction price reaches V_1. Suppose, instead, the current auction price p exceeds V_1. Then Alex should exit immediately because if Bev quits before him, Alex will win the auction and pay more than his valuation. Thus, in an open ascending price auction the bidder with the highest valuation will win and pay the second-highest valuation.

In both the auctions considered so far, it is a dominant strategy for each bidder to bid an amount equal to his or her value. The two auctions are strategically equivalent.[7] In the first-price auction and the Dutch auction, bidders do not possess a dominant strategy. However, when bidders know each other's valuations, the outcome is the same as in the second-price and English auctions.

For analytical convenience, suppose that there is a *discrete* set of feasible bids 0, β^1, β^2, ..., β^T where $0 < \beta^1 < \beta^2 < \cdots < \beta^T$. Further, assume that $V_1 < V_2$, and $\beta^r = V_1$, $\beta^s = V_2$ for some $r < s$.

---

[7] Vickrey (1961).

Suppose that Alex bids $b_1 = \beta^j < V_1$. If he wins, his gain is $V_1 - \beta^j$. The best reply for Bev is to bid a minimally higher amount, that is, $b_2 = \beta^{j+1}$. She then gains $V_2 - \beta^{j+1}$. (Recall that Bev has a higher value, $V_2 > V_1$.) But Alex can respond with a bid of $\beta^{j+2} < V_1$, and so on.[8] The only resting place is where the lower-valuing party, Alex, can no longer profitably raise his bid. In particular, when Alex's bid $b_1 = \beta^{r-1}$, Bev's best reply is the smallest higher bid $b_2 = \beta^r = V_1$. Since Alex cannot profitably bid more than V_1, an equilibrium of the first-price auction under full information is the pair of bids:

$$b_1 = \beta^{r-1}, \quad b_2 = \beta^r = V_1$$

Note that the equilibrium requires Alex to make a bid very close to his full value V_1, even knowing he will be outbid. This may seem somewhat implausible. As justification, suppose there is some chance that Bev will "underbid," that is, she "trembles" (as discussed in Chapter 7) and bids β^j with a small probability π^j for all $j = 0, 1, \ldots, r-1$ and $\beta^r = V_1$ with probability $1 - \sum_{j=0}^{r-1} \pi_j$. Of course, in the limit, as all the small probabilities approach zero, this mixed strategy approaches the Nash equilibrium strategy.

Consider Alex's best response to the mixed strategy. By bidding less than V_1 he has a strictly positive expected return. Which of the bids is optimal then depends upon the *relative* probability weights. Intuitively, if Bev's probability weight on β^r is large relative to the weight on lower bids, i.e., she is much more likely to make the smallest possible "tremble," Alex's best response will be to bid β^{r-1}. (You are asked to confirm this in an exercise at the end of this section.)

An almost identical argument holds for Bev. It is possible to choose arbitrarily small probability weights on out-of-equilibrium actions by Alex such that Bev's Nash equilibrium action remains a best reply. In the terminology of Chapter 7, the equilibrium is trembling-hand perfect.[9]

We now remove the limitation to discrete strategies and suppose instead that any non-negative real number is an acceptable bid. By analogy with the equilibrium strategy pair shown above for the discrete case, it might appear that the equilibrium for the continuous strategy space will be $b_1 = V_1 = b_2$. However, this is not correct. With these strategies Bev has a 50% chance of winning, whereas by raising her bid just slightly she wins for sure. But what

---

[8] We are not describing here a *dynamic process* of sequential response, which might not be feasible under the auction rules. We are only looking for an Nash equilibrium.

[9] There is a second Nash equilibrium with Alex bidding $\beta^r = V_1$ and Bev bidding $\beta^{r+1} = V_1$. However, this is not trembling-hand perfect.

bid will Bev make? Since in the continuum there is no minimum bid above V_1, there is no *best* reply by Bev.

Despite this difficulty, the intuition gleaned from the discrete case continues to be essentially correct. Even though the lower-valuing Alex does not bid V_1 in equilibrium, Bev will continue to do so as long as Alex's (random) bid $\tilde{b}_1$ is sufficiently aggressive. Define $G_1(b) \equiv$ Probability $[\tilde{b}_1 \leq b]$. Of course, Alex will never bid V_1 or more with positive probability. Therefore $G_1(V_1) = 1$. Alex bidding aggressively means that $G_1(b)$ is small for small b and rises rapidly for b close to V_1. That is, he almost always bids close to V_1.

We shall now show that any mixed strategy for Alex will be an equilibrium mixed strategy if it satisfies the following two conditions:

$$\lim_{b \uparrow V_1} G_1(b) = 1 \tag{10.2.1}$$

$$G_1(b) < \frac{V_2 - V_1}{V_2 - b}, \quad b < V_1 \tag{10.2.2}$$

If (10.2.1) holds then Alex bids V_1 or greater with zero probability. Therefore by bidding $b_2 = V_1$, Bev, the higher-valuing contender, wins with probability 1. Can Bev do still better by setting $b_2 < V_1$? For any such bid $b_2 = b$ she wins with probability $G_1(b)$. Then, from (10.2.2), her expected gain would be:

$$U_2(b) = G_1(b)(V_2 - b) < V_2 - V_1$$

Since Bev's payoff from bidding $b = V_1$ is $V_2 - V_1$, any lower bid $b < V_1$ is less profitable for her.

The "Dutch auction" is an open auction equivalent of the first-price sealed-bid auction. In the Dutch auction, a bid-value clock is started at some number known to be higher than any of the buyers' valuations. As the possible bid values tick down toward zero, the first player to bid wins the prize. As before, in equilibrium the higher-valuing buyer 2, Bev, will jump in at $b_2 = V_1$.

It is tempting to think that such an open auction conveys information not available in the first-price sealed-bid auction. However, the only information available to anyone is that no opponent has bid. Therefore, prior to the start of the auction, a buyer can ask himself whether he should raise his hand if the clock reaches any particular level. Having answered this question, he can then write on a piece of paper the price at which he will jump in. By looking at all these pieces of paper, the auctioneer can determine the outcome without actually introducing the clock at all. The paper bearing the highest stated price wins, exactly as in the first-price sealed-bid auction.

Thus, in each of the four auctions, the higher valuing individual wins and pays an amount equal to the second-highest valuation. In the next section we will see whether the outcomes are any different when each bidder's valuation is private information.

Exercises and Excursions 10.2.1

1 Trembling-Hand Perfect Equilibrium in First-Price Sealed-Bid Auction
In the first-price sealed-bid auction examined above, the strategy-pair $b_1 = \beta^{r-1} < V_1$ and $b_2 = \beta^r = V_1$ was a Nash equilibrium.

(A) Suppose individual 2 (Bev) bids β^j, $j = 0, \ldots, r - 2, r + 1, \ldots, T$, with probability λp and β^{r-1} with probability p, so that β^r is bid with probability $1 - p - \lambda(T - 1)p$, both λ and p being small. Explain why the expected return to individual 1 (Alex) is $((r - 1) p\lambda + p/2)(V_1 - \beta^{r-1})$ if he bids β^{r-1}.

(B) Obtain also an expression for his expected return if he bids $\beta^j < \beta^{r-1}$.

(C) Show that, if λ is sufficiently small, then bidding β^{r-1} is a best reply for Alex.

(D) Use a similar argument to establish that there is a completely mixed strategy for individual 1 such that bidding $\beta^r = V_1$ remains a best reply for individual 2. Hence confirm that the Nash equilibrium is trembling-hand perfect.

2 Auctions with Equal Valuations
(A) If there are n bidders, each with the same valuation V, show that, in both the first-price sealed-bid auction and open ascending-price auction, it is an equilibrium for each bidder to bid his full valuation.

(B) In the open ascending-price auction, another equilibrium is for one buyer to bid V and the others to bid zero. Is this a less plausible equilibrium?

(C) Are there other Nash equilibria in the first-price sealed-bid auction? If so, are all the equilibria equivalent from the seller's viewpoint?

3 Equilibrium Bidding in Open Ascending-Price Auction
Individual i has valuation $V_i = i$, $i = 1, 2$.

(A) Show that there are many Nash equilibria for the open ascending-price auction.
(B) Show that bidding one's reservation value is a trembling-hand perfect equilibrium strategy.
(C) Are other Nash equilibria trembling-hand perfect?

10.2.2 Bidders' Valuations Are Independent and Privately Known

In the previous section, there was one level of uncertainty: each individual had to make his or her choice without knowing the strategy or bid of the opponent. We now introduce a second level of uncertainty which arises when contenders are unsure about other players' valuations (preferences).

This new uncertainty does not change the optimal strategy of bidders in the second-price and English auctions. The analysis of these two auctions in the previous section did not use the fact that bidders' values are known to each other as each bidder has a dominant strategy, namely, to bid his or her own valuation. Thus, the bidder with the highest valuation wins and pays the second-highest valuation in each of these two auctions.

The analysis of the first-price sealed-bid auction is more complicated. Nevertheless, as we shall see, the expected price in the first-price auction is the same as in the second-price and English auctions.

We assume that the two bidders believe that their valuations are independent draws from the same probability distribution F, with probability density f. Each bidder knows his or her own valuation but not the other bidder's valuation. As valuations are independent knowing one's own valuation does not alter a bidder's beliefs about the distribution from which the opponent's valuation is drawn. All this is common knowledge among the bidders. These assumptions are referred to as the *independent, private-values model*.

An example illustrates the main ideas. Alex and Bev's valuations are distributed uniformly on the interval $[0, 1]$. That is, $F(V) = V$ and $f(V) = 1$ for values of V in $[0, 1]$. We show that $b^*(V) = V/2$ is a symmetric[10] Bayesian Nash equilibrium strategy. Suppose that Bev follows this equilibrium strategy and bids half her valuation, $V_2/2$. What is Alex's best response? Because Bev's bids are between 0 and 1/2 Alex should never bid more than ½ as he wins with probability one with a bid of ½. Similarly, he should not bid

---

[10] In the sense that each bidder uses the same equilibrium strategy b^*.

less than 0 as he will never win with a bid of 0 or less. If Alex, with valuation V_1, bids $b \in [0, 1/2]$ then he wins only if $\{\tilde{V}_2 < 2b\}$.[11],[12] His probability of winning is $F(2b) = 2b$ and expected profit is:

$$\Pi_1(V_1, b) = (\text{profit upon winning}) \times (\text{probability of winning})$$

$$= (V_1 - b) \times 2b = 2bV_1 - 2b^2$$

The first-order condition to maximize this expression with respect to Alex's bid b is:

$$\frac{\partial \Pi_1(V_1, b)}{\partial b} = 2V_1 - 4b = 0$$

The bid $V_1/2$ satisfies the first-order condition for a best reply. The second-order condition is also satisfied as $\partial \Pi_1/\partial b = -4 < 0$. Thus, we see that Alex's optimal bidding strategy is indeed $b^*(V_1) = V_1/2$.

In this example, the bidder with the highest valuation wins and pays his bid, which is equal to half his valuation. Are bidders better off in a first-price or second-price auction?[13] In both auctions, the bidder with a higher valuation wins. If Alex is the high valuation bidder (i.e., $V_1 > V_2$) in a second-price auction, then the price he pays is Bev's bid V_2. The expected value of the price paid by Alex, conditional on winning with a valuation (and bid) equal to V_1 in a second-price auction is:

$$E[\tilde{V}_2 | \tilde{V}_2 < V_1] = V_1/2$$

where we use a property of the uniform distribution in evaluating the conditional expectation. Thus, conditional on winning when his valuation is V_i, bidder i makes the same expected payment, $V_i/2$, in a first-price or a second-price auction. As the probability of winning is also identical, bidders are equally well off in either auction. Moreover, the auctioneer is also indifferent between the two auctions because in either auction her expected revenue is equal to the expected valuation of the losing (i.e., lower valuation) bidder. This is known as the *Revenue Equivalence Theorem*.[14]

---

[11] We follow the convention that $\tilde{R}$ represents a random variable and R a realized value of the random variable.

[12] Since Bev's bids are uniformly distributed between 0 and ½, the probability Alex and Bev bid the same amount is zero. Hence, unlike in the analysis of first-price auctions in the previous section, we ignore the possibility of ties.

[13] As the second-price and English auction lead to identical outcomes, we need only compare the first-price auction to one of the two.

[14] Revenue equivalence is true much more generally. See Riley and Samuelson (1981).

The Revenue Equivalence Theorem is true even when buyers' valuations have distributions other than uniform. Suppose that Alex's valuation is V_1 and he submits a bid $b = b^*(V')$, while Bev submits a Nash equilibrium bid $b^*(V_2)$, with V_2 being unknown to Alex. The probability that Alex wins is equal to the probability that Bev's valuation is less than V', which, because bidder valuations are independent, is equal to $F(V')$. Thus, Alex's expected profit under these circumstances is:

$$\Pi_1(V_1, V') = \text{(profit upon winning)} \times \text{(probability of winning)}$$

$$= [V_1 - b^*(V')] \times F(V')$$

$$= V_1 F(V') - b^*(V')F(V')$$

As $b^*(V_1)$ is an equilibrium bid for Alex when his valuation is V_1, $\Pi_1(V_1, V')$ as a function of V' must be maximized at $V' = V_1$. Thus, we have the following first-order condition:

$$\frac{\partial \Pi_1(V_1, V')}{\partial V'}\bigg|_{V'=V_1} = \left(V_1 f(V') - \frac{d}{dV'}[b^*(V')F(V')]\right)_{V'=V_1} = 0$$

or:

$$\frac{d}{dV_1}[b^*(V_1)F(V_1)] = V_1 f(V_1)$$

Integrating both sides of this differential equation and appealing to the boundary condition $b(0) = 0$:

$$b^*(V_1)F(V_1) = \int_0^{V_1} s f(s)\, ds$$

Hence:

$$b^*(V_1) = \int_0^{V_1} \frac{s f(s)}{F(V_1)}\, ds \qquad (10.2.3)$$

It turns out that b^* defined above satisfies sufficient conditions for maximizing Alex's profit as well (see Riley and Samuelson 1981). Thus b^* is an equilibrium strategy in a first-price sealed-bid auction.[15]

To facilitate comparison with a second-price or English auction, it is useful to write b^* in a slightly different form. Alex knows his own valuation is V_1, and he knows Bev's valuation $\tilde{V}_2$ is a random variable with distribution

---

[15] By the arguments outlined in Section 10.2.1, b^* is an equilibrium strategy in the Dutch auction as well.

function $F(V_2)$. In addition, the distribution function of $\tilde{V}_2$ conditional on the event that Bev's valuation is less than Alex's, (i.e., conditional on $[\tilde{V}_2 < V_1]$), is $F(V_2)/F(V_1)$ and the corresponding conditional density function is $f(V_2)/F(V_1)$. Thus, from (10.2.3) we see that $b^*(V_1)$ is the expected value of V_2 conditional on the event $[\tilde{V}_2 < V_1]$:

$$b^*(V_1) = \int_0^{V_1} s\frac{f(s)}{F(V_1)}\, ds = E[\tilde{V}_2|\tilde{V}_2 < V_1]$$

In other words, the optimal bid for Alex is equal to the expected value of Bev's valuation conditional on Alex's valuation being greater. Similarly, Bev's optimal bid is the expected value of Alex's valuation conditional on Bev's valuation being greater. Observe that b^* is an increasing function. Consequently, the bidder with the highest valuation is also the high bidder and wins the auction. The price paid is equal to the expected value of the second-highest valuation, conditional on the high bidder's valuation.

In the previous section, we established that when buyers' valuations are common knowledge among them, the higher valuing individual wins and pays an amount equal to the second-highest valuation in each of the four auctions. With private information, the outcome of the second-price auction and the English auction remains the same but the first-price auction (and the equivalent Dutch auction) changes. The bidder with the highest valuation continues to win in a first-price auction; however, instead of the second-highest valuation he now pays the expected value of the second-highest valuation conditional on his own valuation being the highest. Thus, the expected payoffs of the buyers and the seller remain the same in the four auctions. Moreover, because the highest valuation buyer wins, each of these four auctions is an efficient means of allocating the object.[16]

Exercises and Excursions 10.2.2

1 Linear Equilibrium Strategies in First-Price Sealed-Bid Auction with Uniformly Distributed Values

When buyer valuations are uniformly distributed on the interval $[0, 1]$, the equilibrium strategy in a first-price sealed-bid auction with two bidders takes a simple linear form with equilibrium bid equal to half the valuation when there are two bidders. Show that when each of the two buyers' values

---

[16] The equivalence between the four common auctions breaks down when buyers are asymmetric. In addition, the first-price auction need not be efficient when buyers are asymmetric. See Maskin and Riley (2000).

are distributed independently and uniformly on an interval $[a, b]$, where $a < b$, then it is a Nash equilibrium for each buyer to use the strategy $b(V) = \frac{a+V}{2}$.

2 More Linear Equilibrium Strategies in First-Price Sealed-Bid Auction with Uniformly Distributed Values

We saw that when buyer valuations are uniformly distributed on $[0, 1]$, the equilibrium strategy in a first-price sealed-bid auction takes a simple linear form with equilibrium bid equal to half the valuation when there are two bidders. Show that the equilibrium strategy is a linear function of the value when the buyer value distribution is $F(V) = V^\alpha$ for any $\alpha > 0$. Assume that two bidders participate in a first-price sealed-bid auction and their values are independently distributed.

Define the bid shading factor for strategy $b(V)$ to be $\frac{V-b(V)}{V}$. The bid shading factor for the equilibrium strategy you obtain should be a constant (which depends on α). Does the bid shading factor increase or decrease with α? Why?

3 Reserve Prices

Suppose that the auctioneer specifies a minimum reserve price $r > 0$. The winning bidder is the highest bidder whose bid equals or exceeds r; if every bidder bids less than r then there is no winning bidder and the object is not sold. In a second-price auction, the winning bidder (if there is one) pays the greater of the second highest bid and the reserve price. In a first-price auction, the winning bidder pays his bid.

(A) Show that in a second-price auction with n bidders it is a dominant strategy for a bidder to bid his value if it is greater than r and to not bid if his value is less than r.

(B) Suppose that buyer values are uniformly distributed on $[0, 1]$. Show that in a first-price auction with two bidders, the equilibrium bidding strategy is

$$b^r(V) = 0.5V \left(1 + \frac{r^2}{V^2}\right), \quad \text{if } V \geq r$$

$$= 0, \quad \text{if } V < r$$

What is the seller's expected revenue at this equilibrium?

(C) Compute the expected revenue in a second-price auction with $n = 2$ bidders, each with a uniform value distribution on $[0, 1]$. How does this expected revenue compare with the computation in part (B)?

4 Sealed Tendering

A firm solicits sealed offers from two potential contractors for the construction of a new plant. The contractor who submits the lowest successful offer will be awarded the contract. Each contractor i knows his own cost c_i and believes that others' costs are independently drawn from a distribution function $G(c)$. In a first-price auction, the successful contractor is paid his offer, whereas in a second-price auction, the successful contractor is paid the second-highest offer. Solve for the equilibrium bidding strategies in a first-price auction and in a second-price auction.

5 Risk Aversion in Auctions

(A) Explain why equilibrium bidding in the open ascending-bid auction is the same when buyers are risk averse or risk neutral.

(B) Explain why the first-price sealed-bid auction continues to be formally equivalent to the open descending-bid ("Dutch") auction if buyers are risk averse.

(C) In a Dutch auction, what effect will risk aversion have on a bidder's willingness to let the price drop below his valuation?

(D) From your answer to (C), or otherwise, explain why expected revenue will be higher in the first-price sealed-bid auction than in the open ascending-bid auction when buyers are risk averse.

[NOTE: The answer to this question does not require a single equation.]

10.2.3 Optimal Mechanisms*

A central conclusion of Section 10.2.2 is that, under the assumptions of risk neutrality and independent, symmetric beliefs, many seemingly different auctions elicit the same aggregate receipts from bidders, at least on average. From this, it is perhaps tempting to believe that a seller in such auctions would be indifferent as to the bidding rules. As we shall see, this is not quite correct. In particular, it is often in the interest of the seller to set a minimum reserve price that excludes individuals with low valuations. In fact, we shall see that it is optimal for the seller (in the sense that it maximizes the seller's expected revenue) to set a reserve price that exceeds her cost.

The key assumption underlying the analysis is that the seller knows as much about each buyer as the other buyers themselves do. That is, she knows

---

* Starred sections represent more difficult or specialized materials that can be omitted without significant loss of continuity.

the underlying distribution of all the buyers' valuations. The question is how to make use of this information.

We continue to assume that the seller has one indivisible object for sale to two risk-neutral buyers. Each buyer knows his own valuation and has independent and identical beliefs about the other buyer's valuation. That is, regardless of his own valuation V_i, buyer i believes buyer j's valuation V_j is drawn from distribution function $F(V_j)$. In addition, these beliefs are common knowledge. From Section 10.2.2, we know that the equilibria of the four auctions generate the same expected revenue. Therefore we need only compare any alternative selling scheme with the open ascending-price auction.

A selling scheme or mechanism is a set of rules that maps the bids submitted by buyers into a probability of winning the object and an expected payment for each buyer. A mechanism consists of two sets of functions $(q, x) = ((q_1, q_2), (x_1, x_2))$, where $q_i(b_i)$ is buyer i's probability of winning and $x_i(b_i)$ is the expected payment made by buyer i.[17] Note that $q_i(b_i)$ and $x_i(b_i)$ are functions of b_i, the bid submitted by buyer i. A mechanism is a game with private information in which each buyer's strategy is a function that maps his private information (his actual valuation or willingness-to-pay) into a bid (his report of his willingness-to-pay). The seller allocates the object and collects payments as specified by (q, x), the rules of the mechanism. In this game with private information, the buyers play a Bayesian Nash equilibrium.

A mechanism in which the equilibrium bids submitted by players are different from their valuations is known as an *indirect* mechanism. In Section 10.2.2 we saw that in a first-price sealed-bid auction buyers submit equilibrium bids that are strictly less than their valuations. A first-price auction is an example of an indirect mechanism. A mechanism in which the equilibrium bids submitted by players are always equal to their valuations is a *direct* mechanism. Second-price auctions and open-ascending price auctions are direct mechanisms.[18] A key result that simplifies the search for an optimal mechanism is the following:[19]

The Revelation Principle: Each Bayesian Nash equilibrium outcome in an indirect mechanism can be obtained as a Bayesian Nash equilibrium in a direct mechanism with truthful reporting of valuations.

---

[17] In a first-price auction, $q_i(b_i) = \text{Prob}[\tilde{b}_j < b_i]$ and $x_i(b_i) = b_i$.

[18] A second-price auction and an open-ascending price auction more than satisfy the requirement of a direct mechanism. Not only is it a Bayesian equilibrium to truthfully report one's value, it is a dominant strategy to do so; that is, submitting a bid equal to one's value is an optimal strategy even if other bidders deviate from this strategy.

[19] See Dasgupta, Hammond, and Maskin (1979) and Myerson (1979).

The basic idea underlying the revelation principle is the following. From a Bayesian Nash equilibrium of an indirect mechanism and (q^I, x^I), the allocation and payment functions of the indirect mechanism, construct a new mechanism as follows. In the new mechanism, treat the "bids" that buyers report as their true valuations. Compute the equilibrium bids that would have been submitted to the original (indirect) mechanism and apply (q^I, x^I) to these bids to compute allocation probabilities and expected payments under the new mechanism. Thus, (q^D, x^D), the rules of the new mechanism, are obtained by composing (q^I, x^I) and the Bayesian Nash equilibrium strategies of the original mechanism. The conditions for Bayesian Nash equilibrium in the original mechanism imply that truthful reporting of valuations is a Bayesian Nash equilibrium in the new mechanism.

In Section 10.2.2 we considered a first-price auction with two bidders, each with valuations distributed uniformly and independently on $[0, 1]$. It was shown that the strategy $b(V_i) = V_i/2$ was a Bayesian Nash equilibrium. The direct mechanism corresponding to this equilibrium is as follows. Bidders report their valuations; the mechanism computes each bidder's bid as one-half his submitted valuation and applies the rules of the first-price auction to the computed bids. It should be clear that truthful reporting is a Bayesian Nash equilibrium in this new mechanism.

The revelation principle makes our search for an optimal mechanism easier. We can restrict attention to direct mechanisms because if an indirect mechanism is optimal then so is the corresponding direct mechanism. In the rest of this section, we consider only direct mechanisms. From here onwards, $q_i(\cdot)$ and $x_i(\cdot)$, the probability of winning and the expected payment functions, are functions of bidders' (reported) valuations rather than their bids.

In the four auctions considered thus far, a bidder wins only if he has the highest value; his expected payment if he wins is the expected value of the losing buyer's value. Thus, equilibria in each of these four auctions translate into the same direct mechanism with:

$$q_i(V_i) = F(V_i), \quad x_i(V_i) = F(V_i) \times E[\tilde{V}_j | \tilde{V}_j < V_i]$$

Bidder i's expected payoff from a direct mechanism (q, x) when he truthfully reports his valuation V_i is:

$$U_i(V_i) = V_i q_i(V_i) - x_i(V_i)$$

If, instead, he reports V_i' when his valuation is V_i his expected payoff is $V_i q_i(V_i') - x_i(V_i')$. Note that the buyer's reported valuation V_i' affects only

$q_i(\cdot)$ and $x_i(\cdot)$. Because the mechanism is direct, truthful reporting of valuations constitutes a Bayesian Nash equilibrium. Another way of stating this is to say that the mechanism is *Bayesian incentive compatible*.

The payoff to buyer i from truthfully reporting his valuation V_i is $U_i(V_i)$. In a Bayesian incentive-compatible direct mechanism, this payoff is at least as large as buyer i's payoff from misreporting his valuation as $V_i' < V_i$. Thus:

$$U_i(V_i) \geq V_i q_i(V_i') - x_i(V_i') = U_i(V_i') + (V_i - V_i')q_i(V_i') \quad (10.2.4)$$

which implies that $[U_i(V_i) - U_i(V_i')]/[V_i - V_i'] \geq q_i(V_i')$. Similarly, when buyer i's valuation is V_i' and he misreports his valuation as V_i, Bayesian incentive compatibility implies that:

$$U_i(V_i') \geq V_i' \, q_i(V_i) - x_i(V_i) = U_i(V_i) + (V_i' - V_i)q_i(V_i)$$

or

$$q_i(V_i) \geq [U_i(V_i) - U_i(V_i')]/[V_i - V_i'].$$

Combining the two inequalities yields:

$$q_i(V_i) \geq [U_i(V_i) - U_i(V_i')]/[V_i - V_i'] \geq q_i(V_i')$$

Two conclusions follow from the above inequality. First, as $V_i > V_i'$ by assumption, we know that $q_i(\cdot)$ is non-decreasing in buyer i's valuation. In fact, this is the only restriction imposed on $q_i(\cdot)$ by Bayesian incentive compatibility.[20] Second, taking limits as $V_i' \to V_i$, we see that at points of differentiability of $U_i(\cdot)$, we have $\frac{dU_i}{dV_i} = q_i(V_i)$. From (10.2.4) we conclude that $U_i(\cdot)$ is non-decreasing. Therefore it is differentiable almost everywhere (see Royden, 1988, chapter 5). Hence, we have:

$$U_i(V_i) = U_i(0) + \int_0^{V_i} q_i(s)\,ds = -x_i(0) + \int_0^{V_i} q_i(s)\,ds$$

[20] We have established that a non-decreasing probability of winning function is a necessary condition for Bayesian incentive compatibility. This condition is also sufficient for Bayesian incentive compatibility. See Myerson (1981).

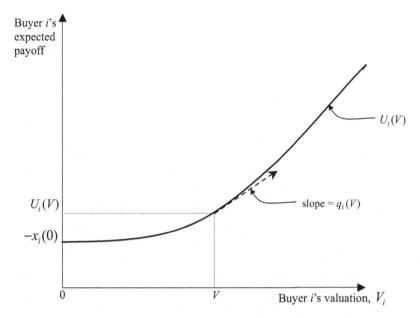

Figure 10.1. Buyer expected payoff from Bayesian incentive-compatible scheme.

where we use the fact that $U_i(0) = 0 \times q_i(0) - x_i(0) = -x_i(0)$. Thus:

$$x_i(V_i) = V_i q_i(V_i) - U_i(V_i) = V_i q_i(V_i) + x_i(0) - \int_0^{V_i} q_i(s) \, ds \quad (10.2.5)$$

The relationship between a buyer's expected payoff, $U_i(V_i)$, and his probability of winning, $q_i(V)$, in a Bayesian incentive-compatible mechanism is shown in Figure 10.1. The slope of the expected payoff function at any given valuation equals the probability of winning with that valuation. As the probability of winning is non-negative, the expected payoff is a non-decreasing function. Moreover, as incentive compatibility implies that the probability of winning is a non-decreasing function of the buyer's valuation, the slope of the expected value function is increasing. That is, $U_i(V_i)$ is a non-decreasing, convex function.

Equation (10.2.5) states that $x_i(V_i)$, the expected payment by buyer i when his valuation is V_i, is determined by the probability function $q_i(\cdot)$ and $x_i(0)$, the expected payment by this buyer when his valuation takes the lowest possible value, 0. As mentioned earlier, each of the four auctions in the previous section have the same probability of winning function

$q_i(V_i) = F(V_i)$. Moreover, $x_i(0) = 0$ in these auctions; this is because a buyer whose value for the object is 0 has no chance of winning the auction and therefore does not pay anything. Consequently, the expected payment functions and therefore also the seller's expected revenue are the same in these auctions. Thus, the *revenue equivalence theorem* of the previous section follows directly from (10.2.5).

Generally speaking, there is some freedom in selecting $x_i(0)$. However, as buyers are not forced to participate, it must be that $U_i(V_i) \geq 0$ for all V_i; and because U_i is a non-decreasing function, buyer participation is ensured by $U_i(0) = -x_i(0) \geq 0$ or $x_i(0) \leq 0$. Furthermore, in any revenue-maximizing mechanism, the seller will not give money away to a buyer of the lowest type (with $V_i = 0$). As we are interested in an optimal mechanism from the seller's viewpoint, we shall assume that $x_i(0) = 0$ and therefore $U_i(0) = 0$.

From (10.2.5), we see that the expected payment function $x_i(\cdot)$ is now determined entirely by the probability of winning function $q_i(\cdot)$. Any pair of non-decreasing probability functions (q_1, q_2) which feasibly allocate the object determines a Bayesian incentive-compatible mechanism. Thus, there are innumerable selling mechanisms. Which one of these is optimal? To answer this question, we analyze the expected payment by each buyer:

$$E[x_i(\tilde{V}_i)] = E[\tilde{V}_i q_i(\tilde{V}_i)] - E[U_i(\tilde{V}_i)] \qquad (10.2.6)$$

where the expectation is taken over the random variable $\tilde{V}_i$. Noting that $f(V_i) = \frac{d}{dV_i}[-(1 - F(V_i))]$ we can integrate the last term by parts to obtain:

$$E[U_i(\tilde{V}_i)] = \int_0^1 U_i(V_i) f(V_i) dV_i = \int_0^1 \frac{dU_i}{dV_i}(1 - F(V_i)) dV_i + U_i(0)$$

We have already argued that $\frac{dU_i}{dV_i} = q_i(V_i)$ and that $U_i(0) = 0$. Hence:

$$E[U_i(\tilde{V}_i)] = \int_0^1 q_i(V_i)(1 - F(V_i)) dV_i$$

Inserting this in (10.2.6), we obtain:

$$E[x_i(\tilde{V}_i)] = E[q_i(\tilde{V}_i)\tilde{V}_i] - \int_0^1 q_i(V_i)(1 - F(V_i))\,dV_i$$

$$= \int_0^1 \left[V_i - \frac{1 - F(V_i)}{f(V_i)} \right] q_i(V_i) f(V_i)\,dV_i$$

Let $Q_i(V_i, V_j)$ be the underlying allocation scheme from which the probability of winning $q_i(V_i)$ is obtained. That is, $q_i(V_i) = \int_0^1 Q_i(V_i, V_j) f(V_j)\,dV_j$. Thus, when buyer values are V_i and V_j, the probability that buyer i wins the auction is $Q_i(V_i, V_j)$. The expected revenue for the seller from the mechanism $[q_1(V_1), q_2(V_2)]$ is:

$$E[x_1(\tilde{V}_1) + x_2(\tilde{V}_2)] = \sum_{i=1,2} \int_0^1 \left[V_i - \frac{1 - F(V_i)}{f(V_i)} \right] q_i(V_i) f(V_i)\,dV_i$$

$$= \int_0^1 \int_0^1 \left(\sum_{i=1,2} \left[V_i - \frac{1 - F(V_i)}{f(V_i)} \right] Q_i(V_i, V_j) \right) f(V_1) f(V_2)\,dV_1\,dV_2$$

$$(10.2.7)$$

Let $J(V_i) \equiv V_i - \frac{1 - F(V_i)}{f(V_i)}$ be buyer i's *virtual utility* for the object. We restrict attention to the regular case defined in Section 10.1, where $J(V_i)$ is an increasing function of V_i. Define V^* such that $J(V^*) = 0$.[21] Since only one object is for sale, we must have $Q_1(V_1, V_2) + Q_2(V_2, V_1) \leq 1$. Therefore, the integrand in (10.2.7), and hence also the seller's expected revenue, is maximized by the following mechanism, denoted (q^*, x^*). Give the object to the buyer with the highest virtual valuation, provided that this is non-negative. In case of ties, randomly choose a winner. If $V_1, V_2 < V^*$, then the seller keeps the object. In this revenue maximizing mechanism:

$$q_i^*(V_i) = 0, \qquad \text{if } V_i < V^*$$
$$q_i^*(V_i) = F(V_i), \quad \text{if } V_i \geq V^* \qquad (10.2.8)$$

---

[21] Observe that V^* is identical to the optimal posted price p^* of Section 10.1. We return to this fact later.

Inserting these values in (10.2.5), together with $x_i(0) = 0$, we obtain the expected payments in this optimal scheme:

$$x_i^*(V_i) = V_i q_i^*(V_i) - \int_0^{V_i} q_i^*(s)\,ds = 0, \quad \text{if } V_i < V^*$$

$$x_i^*(V_i) = V_i q_i^*(V_i) - \int_0^{V_i} q_i^*(s)\,ds$$

$$= V_i F(V_i) - \int_{V^*}^{V_i} F(s)\,ds$$

$$= V_i F(V_i) - \left[V_i F(V_i) - V^* F(V^*) - \int_{V^*}^{V_i} s f(s)\,ds \right]$$

$$= V^* F(V^*) + \int_{V^*}^{V_i} s f(s)\,ds, \quad \text{if } V_i \geq V^*$$

where the second to last equality follows from integration by parts.

This optimal mechanism may be implemented by an open ascending-price (or a second-price) auction with a reserve price of V^*. To see this, observe that in an open ascending-price auction, the buyer with the highest valuation wins, provided his valuation is greater than the reserve price V^*. Thus, the probability of winning function is identical to $q_i^*(V_i)$ defined in Equation (10.2.8). If $V_i < V^*$ buyer i will not win the auction and his payment is 0. If $V_i \geq V^*$ then buyer i wins with probability $F(V_i)$; the price he pays if he wins is either the reserve price V^* (in the event that the other buyer's valuation V_j is less than V^*, which happens with probability $F(V^*)$) or it is the other buyer's valuation V_j (if $V_j \in [V^*, V_i]$). Consequently, the probability of winning and the expected payment in this ascending-price auction with reserve price V^* are (q^*, x^*) defined above.

Example 10.1: Bidders 1 and 2 compete for an indivisible object which is for sale. Each bidder's valuation is independently and uniformly distributed from 0 to 1. Thus, $f(V_i) = 1$ if $0 \leq V_i \leq 1$, $f(V_i) = 0$ otherwise and $F(V_i) = V_i$ if $0 \leq V_i \leq 1$. Buyer i's virtual utility function is:

$$J(V_i) = V_i - \frac{1 - V_i}{1} = 2V_i - 1.$$

$J(V^*) = 0$ implies that $V^* = 0.5$. The optimal mechanism for the seller is an open ascending-price auction with reserve price 0.5. Next, we compute the seller's expected revenue from this scheme.

There are three possible events, I, II, and III, defined below:

 I. Each buyer's valuation is less than the reserve price 0.5. There is no sale and the seller's revenue is 0. As valuations are independently distributed, the probability of this event is 0.25.

 II. Exactly one buyer's valuation is greater than the reserve price. The selling price is the reserve price, 0.5. The probability of this event is 0.5.

III. Each buyer's valuation is greater than the reserve price 0.5. This happens with probability 0.25. Conditional on event III, each buyer's valuation is independently and uniformly distributed between 0.5 and 1. The selling price is the smaller of these two uniform distributions. A direct computation shows that the expected selling price conditional on III is 2/3.

Combining these three cases implies that the expected selling price in the optimal auction is:

Expected revenue from optimal mechanism $= 0 \times 0 + 0.5 \times 0.5 + 0.25 \times \frac{2}{3} = \frac{5}{12}$.

How does this compare with revenue from the four auctions we analyzed in Section 10.2.2? Since these auctions yield identical expected revenues, we need compare the optimal expected revenue with expected revenue from an open ascending-price auction *without* a reserve price. The seller's revenue in an ascending-price auction without a reserve price is equal to the smaller of the two valuations. A direct computation reveals that the seller's expected revenue is $1/3$, which is 20% less than the expected revenue from the optimal scheme.

By setting a reserve price, the seller gets a higher price in case II. The cost of the reserve price (forgoing a sale in event I) is less than the gain.[22] □

---

[22] Empirical evidence that reserve prices increase revenues is provided in Ostrovsky and Schwartz (2009).

What does the optimal mechanism look like when there are more than two buyers? Myerson (1981) shows that it is identical to the one with two buyers: the seller maximizes his expected revenue by having an open ascending-price auction with reserve price V^* defined by:

$$J(V^*) = V^* - \frac{1 - F(V^*)}{f(V^*)} = 0$$

Further, suppose that the seller has $k \geq 1$ units of the object for sale to n buyers, $n > k$. Each buyer wants one unit of the object and has a valuation drawn independently from the distribution F. Then the seller cannot do better than to conduct an open ascending-price auction with reserve price V^*. The winning bidders pay the greater of V^* and the highest valuation among the losing bidders.

Optimality of Posted Prices

We now turn to the case where the seller is not supply constrained: there are at least as many units of the object as there are buyers and each buyer demands at most one unit. In other words, supply exceeds demand. Consider a setting with two buyers and two units for sale.[23] Each buyer knows his own valuation for the object and has independent and identical beliefs, summarized by the distribution function $F(\cdot)$, about the other buyer's valuation. Equation (10.2.7) is still valid; the number of units for sale affects the feasibility constraints $Q_i(V_i, V_j)$ but does not change the form of Equation (10.2.7). Now, we impose the feasibility constraint that at most two units may be sold: $Q_1(V_1, V_2) + Q_2(V_2, V_1) \leq 2$. With this relaxation in the supply constraint, we get an optimal mechanism different from that of the previous section. The integrand in (10.2.7) (and the seller expected revenue) is maximized when the seller allocates the object to buyer i if and only if his virtual utility is non-negative: $J(V_i) = V_i - \frac{1-F(V_i)}{f(V_i)} \geq 0$. Thus, in the optimal mechanism, a buyer gets the object only if his valuation is greater than or equal to V^*. Inserting $q_i(V_i) = 1$ if $V_i \geq V^*$, $q_i(V_i) = 0$ if $V_i < V^*$ in (10.2.5) we see that a buyer pays 0 if $V_i < V^*$ and he pays V^* if $V_i \geq V^*$ in this optimal mechanism. Thus, this optimal mechanism is implemented by offering each buyer a take-it-or-leave-it price of V^*.

When there are $n \geq 1$ buyers and at least n units of the object for sale, the optimal mechanism remains the same. In Section 10.1 we considered a

---

[23] If there are more than two units, the analysis is identical as each buyer wishes to consume only one unit.

situation where $n = 1$. Recall that $p^* = V^*$. Therefore, the mechanism of posting a take-it-or-leave-it price of p^* analyzed in Section 10.1 maximizes the seller's expected revenue among all possible mechanisms.

Exercises and Excursions 10.2.3

1 Bayesian Incentive Compatibility and Non-Decreasing Probability of Winning

Recall that in any Bayesian incentive-compatible direct mechanism the probability that a buyer wins cannot decrease with the buyer's (reported) valuation. Consider a mechanism in which buyer 1's probability of winning is not non-decreasing. In particular, $0 \le q_1(V_1) < q_1(V_1') \le 1$ where $V_1 > V_1'$. The expected payments under this mechanism at the two valuations are $x_1(V_1')$ and $x_1(V_1)$.

(A) Suppose that the expected payments are such that when his valuation is V_1 buyer 1 has no incentive to report his valuation as V_1' instead of V_1. Show that when his valuation is V_1' buyer 1's payoff increases if he reports his valuation as V_1 instead of V_1'.

(B) Suppose, instead, that the expected payments are such that when his valuation is V_1' buyer 1 has no incentive to report his valuation as V_1. Show that when his valuation is V_1 buyer 1's payoff increases if he reports his valuation as V_1'.

2 Optimal Auctions and Efficient Auctions

In Example 10.1, there are two bidders each with valuation uniformly distributed on $[0, 1]$. An optimal auction is a second-price auction with a minimum reserve price of 0.5. However, this auction is inefficient in that with probability 0.25 the buyers' valuations are less than the reserve price and thus the seller is left with the object even though her valuation is lower than each buyer's valuation. An efficient auction maximizes the gains from trade; the party with the highest valuation for the object leaves with the object. A second-price auction with a reserve price equal to the seller's valuation of 0 is an efficient auction.

(A) What is the total expected gains from trade in an efficient auction in this setting? What is the seller's expected revenue and each buyer's expected surplus in this auction?

(B) What is the total expected gains from trade in an optimal auction in this setting? What is the seller's expected revenue and each buyer's expected surplus in this auction?*

10.2.4 Bidders' Valuations Are Correlated**

One key simplifying assumption in the preceding analysis is that buyers' valuations are independent. A more realistic assumption is that buyers' values are positively correlated – often referred to as the *common values model*. If one buyer has a high valuation for the object for sale, it makes it more likely that other buyers have high valuations as well. One can think of the buyers' valuations as draws (with replacement) from an urn filled with numbered balls. If buyers know the distribution of balls in the urn, valuations are independent. But suppose instead that the buyers are unsure whether the urn is favorable (lots of high values) or unfavorable (lots of low values). Then if a buyer gets a very favorable draw, he will believe it likely that he drew from the good urn and so think it more likely that his opponents' valuation are also more likely to be high. In such a case, valuations are positively correlated.

Example 10.2: There are two buyers, 1 and 2, with identical value distributions. Buyers 1's and 2's values are V_1 and V_2, respectively. Let X_1, X_2, and C be uniformly and independently distributed on the interval $[0, 1]$. The two buyers' valuations are:

$$V_1 = X_1 + C$$
$$V_2 = X_2 + C$$

Thus, each buyer i's valuation is distributed on the interval $[0, 2]$ and consists of a common component C and an idiosyncratic component X_i. Buyer i's privately observes his own value V_i but does not observe the components X_i and C. The unobserved C leads to positive correlation between V_1 and V_2.

Let us analyze the problem from buyer 1's standpoint, the analysis from buyer 2's position being symmetric. The first task is to obtain the distribution of V_2 conditional on buyer 1's valuation being equal to some value V_1.

---

* End of starred section.
** Starred sections represent more difficult or specialized materials that can be omitted without significant loss of continuity.

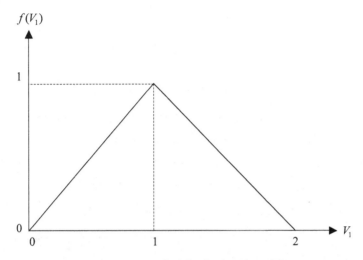

Figure 10.2. Marginal density function of V_1.

It turns out that the marginal density of buyer 1's values is:[24]

$$f(V_1) = V_1, \qquad \text{if } 0 \le V_1 \le 1$$
$$= 2 - V_1, \quad \text{if } 1 < V_1 \le 2$$

The density $f(V_1)$ is triangular as illustrated in Figure 10.2.

The density of V_2 conditional on V_1 depends on whether V_1 is less than or greater than 1. If $V_1 \le 1$, then (see Figure 10.3):

$$f(V_2|V_1) = \frac{V_2}{V_1}, \qquad \text{if } 0 \le V_2 \le V_1,$$
$$= 1, \qquad \text{if } V_1 \le V_2 \le 1$$
$$= \frac{1 + V_1 - V_2}{V_1}, \quad \text{if } 1 \le V_2 \le 1 + V_1$$

If, instead, $V_1 > 1$, then (see Figure 10.4):

$$f(V_2|V_1) = \frac{V_2 - (V_1 - 1)}{2 - V_1}, \quad \text{if } V_1 - 1 \le V_2 \le 1$$
$$= 1, \qquad \text{if } 1 \le V_2 \le V_1$$
$$= \frac{2 - V_2}{2 - V_1}, \qquad \text{if } V_1 \le V_2 \le 2$$

[24] See an exercise at the end of this section.

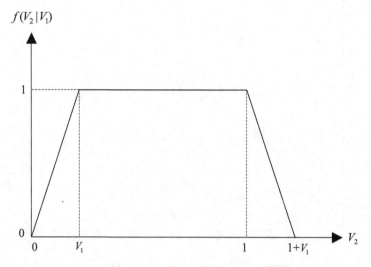

Figure 10.3. Density function of V_2 conditional on V_1 when $V_1 \leq 1$.

Suppose that the two buyers compete in a first-price auction. We first verify that $b^f(V) = 2V/3$ is a symmetric Nash equilibrium strategy. Suppose that buyer 2 uses the bidding strategy b^f and buyer 1 with valuation V_1 submits a (possibly non-equilibrium) bid $b = b^f(V')$. Recalling the analysis

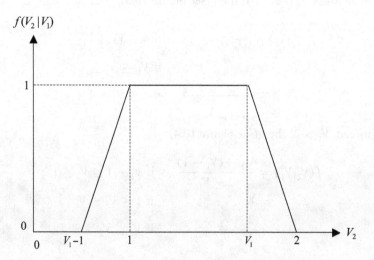

Figure 10.4. Density function of V_2 conditional on V_1 when $V_1 > 1$.

in Section 10.2.2, buyer 1's expected profit is:

$$\Pi(V_1, V') = (V_1 - \frac{2}{3}V')F(V'|V_1)$$

$$\left.\frac{\partial\Pi(V_1, V')}{\partial V'}\right|_{V'=V_1} = [V_1 - \frac{2}{3}V')]f(V'|V_1) - \frac{2}{3}F(V'|V_1)\bigg|_{V'=V_1}$$

$$= \frac{V_1}{3}f(V_1|V_1) - \frac{2}{3}F(V_1|V_1)$$

$$= 0$$

where we use the fact that $f(V_1|V_1) = 1$ and $F(V_1|V_1) = V_1/2$.[25] Differentiating $\partial\Pi(V_1, V')/\partial V'$ with respect to V' and setting $V' = V_1$ one sees that the second-order condition is also satisfied. Thus, the best response of buyer 1 with valuation V_1 is to submit bid $b^f(V) = 2V/3$, verifying that b^f is a symmetric equilibrium strategy. As buyer 1 pays his bid only if he wins, the expected payment by buyer 1 is:

$$b^f(V_1)F(V_1|V_1) = \frac{V_1^2}{3}$$

Suppose, instead, that the buyers participate in a second-price auction. It remains a dominant strategy for each bidder to bid his valuation even when valuations are correlated. Therefore, the expected payment by buyer 1 with valuation V_1 is the expected value of V_2 when it is less than V_1. This quantity is $\int_0^{V_1} V_2 f(V_2|V_1)dV_2$. A direct computation shows that the expected payment is:

$$\frac{V_1^2}{3}, \quad \text{if } V_1 \le 1,$$

$$\frac{V_1^2 - 1}{2} + \frac{V_1^3 - 3V_1^2 + 4}{6(2 - V_1)}, \quad \text{if } V_1 > 1$$

As $\frac{V_1^2-1}{2} + \frac{V_1^3-3V_1^2+4}{6(2-V_1)} > \frac{V_1^2}{3}$ provided $V_1 > 1$, the expected payment in a second-price auction is at least as large as in a first-price auction, it being strictly larger when $V_1 \in [1, 2]$. $\square$

An important conclusion reached in Section 10.2.2 was that when buyer values are independently distributed, there is revenue equivalence between common auction formats. Example 10.2 shows that this equivalence breaks

---

[25] To see that $F(V_1|V_1) = V_1/2$, compute the area under $f(V_2|V_1)$ to the left of $V_2 = V_1$ in Figures 10.3 and 10.4.

down when buyers' values are private known and correlated. Next, we generalize this example to show that the auctioneer can expect higher revenues in a second-price sealed-bid or an open ascending-price auction than in a first-price sealed-bid auction when buyer values satisfy a condition stronger than positive correlation.

To simplify the analysis, we consider only the two buyer case. Valuations are continuously and symmetrically distributed with joint density function $f(V_1, V_2)$. Each buyer's valuation has support $[0, 1]$. Buyers' marginal density functions are obtained in the usual way, with buyer 1's density function being $f(V_1) = \int_0^1 f(V_1, V_2)dV_2$.

As in Section 10.2.2, each buyer knows his own valuation and has beliefs about the other buyer's valuations; however, unlike in Section 10.2.2, a buyer's beliefs depend on his own valuation. Once again it will be convenient to represent buyer i's unknown valuation by the random variable $\tilde{V}_i$, and a specific realization of the valuation by V_i. Buyer 1's beliefs about $\tilde{V}_2$ depend on his realized valuation V_1. The conditional density of $\tilde{V}_2$ conditional on $\tilde{V}_1 = V_1$ is $f(V_2|V_1) = \frac{f(V_1,V_2)}{f(V_1)}$.

Therefore, buyer 1's conditional probability distribution function of $\tilde{V}_2$ conditional on $\tilde{V}_1 = V_1$ is:

$$F(V_2|V_1) = \Pr[\tilde{V}_2 \le V_2|\tilde{V}_1 = V_1] = \int_0^{V_2} f(x|V_1)dx$$

This is the probability assessment by buyer 1 that $\tilde{V}_2$ is less than or equal to a certain value (V_2) when $\tilde{V}_1 = V_1$. If valuations are independently distributed, this probability is independent of buyer 1's valuation, $F(V_2|V_1) = F(V_2|V_1')$, for all V_1, V_1', and V_2. If valuations are positively correlated it is natural to assume that this probability is a decreasing function of buyer 1's valuation. That is, whenever $V_1' < V_1$:

$$F(V_2|V_1) \le F(V_2|V_1')$$

We make a stronger assumption. The right-truncated conditional distribution of $\tilde{V}_2$ at V_2 is the distribution of $\tilde{V}_2$ conditional on the event $[\tilde{V}_2 \le V_2]$. The probability distribution of $\tilde{V}_2$ right-truncated at V_2 (i.e., the distribution of $\tilde{V}_2$ conditional on $\tilde{V}_1 = V_1$ and $[\tilde{V}_2 \le V_2]$) is:

$$\Pr[\tilde{V}_2 \le V_2'|\tilde{V}_2 \le V_2, \tilde{V}_1 = V_1] = \frac{F(V_2'|V_1)}{F(V_2|V_1)}$$

where $V_2' < V_2$. We make the assumption that conditional right-truncated distributions of $\tilde{V}_2$ are a decreasing function of buyer 1's valuation, that is:

$$\frac{F(V_2'|V_1)}{F(V_2|V_1)} \leq \frac{F(V_2'|V_1')}{F(V_2|V_1')} \quad \text{for all } V_1' < V_1 \text{ and } V_2' < V_2 \quad (10.2.9)$$

If (10.2.9) holds, then the joint distribution of $\tilde{V}_1$ and $\tilde{V}_2$ is said to satisfy *conditional stochastic dominance.*[26] As an immediate implication:

$$1 - \frac{F(V_2'|V_1)}{F(V_2|V_1)} \geq 1 - \frac{F(V_2'|V_1')}{F(V_2|V_1')}$$

Hence:

$$\frac{F(V_2|V_1) - F(V_2'|V_1)}{(V_2 - V_2')F(V_2|V_1)} \geq \frac{F(V_2|V_1') - F(V_2'|V_1')}{(V_2 - V_2')F(V_2|V_1')}$$

Taking the limit as V_2' increases to V_2:

$$\frac{f(V_2|V_1)}{F(V_2|V_1)} \geq \frac{f(V_2|V_1')}{F(V_2|V_1')} \quad (10.2.10)$$

This is also intuitive. The ratio $\frac{f(V_2|V_1)}{F(V_2|V_1)}\delta V_2$ is the probability that the truncated random variable $\tilde{V}_2$ is close to its maximum value V_2. Inequality (10.2.10) says that this probability is non-decreasing in buyer 1's valuation.

In the open ascending-price auction, or the second-price sealed-bid auction, it is a dominant strategy for each buyer to bid his valuation. The argument in Section 10.2.1 applies even when buyers' valuations are privately known, correlated, and satisfy conditional stochastic dominance. If buyer 1's valuation is V_1 then in a second-price sealed-bid auction, his expected payment conditional upon winning is:

$$b^s(V_1) = \int_0^{V_1} V_2 \frac{f(V_2|V_1)}{F(V_1|V_1)} dV_2 \quad (10.2.11)$$

Now consider a first-price sealed-bid auction. Let $b^f(\cdot)$ be the symmetric equilibrium bid function in a first-price auction. Suppose that the buyer 1's valuation is V_1. If buyer 2 uses his equilibrium bid function b^f and buyer 1 bids $b^f(V')$, buyer 1's expected payoff is:

$$\Pi^f(V_1, V') = [V_1 - b^f(V')] \times F(V'|V_1)$$

---

[26] Conditional stochastic dominance is implied if the joint density function has the following property:

$$f(V_1, V_2)f(V_1', V_2') \geq f(V_1, V_2')f(V_1', V_2) \text{ for all } V_1' < V_1 \text{ and } V_2' < V_2$$

Such a pair of random variables is said to be *affiliated*.

The first-order condition for a maximum must hold at $V_1' = V_1$:

$$\left.\frac{\partial \Pi^f(V_1, V')}{\partial V'}\right|_{V'=V_1} = [V_1 - b^f(V')]f(V'|V_1) - F(V'|V_1)\left.\frac{db^f(V')}{dV'}\right|_{V'=V_1} = 0$$

Rearranging this equation:

$$\frac{db^f(V_1)}{dV_1} = \frac{f(V_1|V_1)}{F(V_1|V_1)}(V_1 - b^f(V_1)) \qquad (10.2.12)$$

The solution to this differential equation is:

$$b^f(V_1) = V_1 - \int_0^{V_1} L(V_2; V_1)dV_2 = \int_0^{V_1} V_2 dL(V_2; V_1)$$

where $L(V_2; V_1) = \exp(-\int_{V_2}^{V_1} \frac{f(s|s)}{F(s|s)}ds)$ is defined for $V_2 \le V_1$.

The expected payment, conditional upon winning, of bidder 1 with valuation V_1 is $b^f(V_1)$ in a first-price auction, and it is $b^s(V_1)$ defined in (10.2.11) in a second-price auction. Along the equilibrium path, the probability of winning for bidder 1 with valuation V_1 is the same (equal to $F(V_1|V_1)$) in either auction. Therefore, if we can compare $b^f(V_1)$ with $b^s(V_1)$ then we can compare expected revenues in the two auctions. The key to this is to first consider equilibrium bidding if buyer 1, with a specific valuation $\hat{V}_1$ is naive and believes that buyer valuations are distributed independently with distribution function $F(V_2|\hat{V}_1)$. By revenue equivalence, his equilibrium bid is $\bar{b}(\hat{V}_1) = b^s(\hat{V}_1)$. Thus, the expected payment by buyer 1 with valuation $\hat{V}_1$ in a second-price sealed-bid auction is the same as the expected payment by this naive buyer 1 with valuation $\hat{V}_1$ in a first-price auction. Thus, we can compare the auctioneer's expected revenue in a first-price and a second-price auction by comparing two first-price sealed-bid auctions. In the first, buyers have correct beliefs, in the second, naive beliefs.

Consider bidding in a first-price auction by buyer 1 with naive beliefs $F(V_2|\hat{V}_1)$. In figuring out his optimal bid, buyer 1 believes that buyer 2 bids according to the naive equilibrium bid $\bar{b}(V_2)$. If, in response, buyer 1 bids $\bar{b}(V')$, buyer 1's expected payoff is:

$$\bar{\Pi}(V_1, V') = [V_1 - \bar{b}(V')] \times F(V'|\hat{V}_1)$$

The first-order condition at $V' = V_1$ implies:

$$\frac{d\bar{b}(V_1)}{dV_1} = \frac{f(V_1|\hat{V}_1)}{F(V_1|\hat{V}_1)}(V_1 - \bar{b}(V_1)) \qquad (10.2.13)$$

Suppose that $\bar{b}(\hat{V}_1) < b^f(\hat{V}_1)$. Because these functions are differentiable (therefore, continuous) and $\bar{b}(0) = b^f(0) = 0$ there is $V_1' \in [0, \hat{V}_1)$ such that $\bar{b}(V_1') = b^f(V_1')$ and $\bar{b}(V_1) < b^f(V_1)$ for all $V_1 \in (V_1', \hat{V}_1]$. Noting that (10.2.10) implies $\frac{f(V_1|\hat{V}_1)}{F(V_1|\hat{V}_1)} \geq \frac{f(V_1|V_1)}{F(V_1|V_1)}$, a comparison of (10.2.12) and (10.2.13) implies that:

$$
\begin{aligned}
\frac{d\bar{b}(V_1)}{dV_1} &= \frac{f(V_1|\hat{V}_1)}{F(V_1|\hat{V}_1)}(V_1 - \bar{b}(V_1)) \\
&\geq \frac{f(V_1|V_1)}{F(V_1|V_1)}(V_1 - \bar{b}(V_1)) \\
&> \frac{f(V_1|V_1)}{F(V_1|V_1)}(V_1 - b^f(V_1)) = \frac{db^f(V_1)}{dV_1}
\end{aligned}
$$

Therefore, $\bar{b}(V_1') = b^f(V_1')$ and $\bar{b}(V_1) < b^f(V_1)$ for all $V_1 \in (V_1', \hat{V}_1]$ implies that $\frac{d\bar{b}(V_1)}{dV_1} > \frac{db^f(V_1)}{dV_1}$ for all $V_1 \in (V_1', \hat{V}_1]$. But this implies $\bar{b}(V_1) > b^f(V_1)$ for all $V_1 \in (V_1', \hat{V}_1]$, and we have a contradiction. Consequently, we have $\bar{b}(\hat{V}_1) \geq b^f(\hat{V}_1)$. Because $\hat{V}_1$ was arbitrary we conclude that the auctioneer's expected revenue in a second-price sealed-bid auction is at least as large as his expected revenue in a first-price sealed-bid auction. If inequality (10.2.10) is strict, then the expected revenue in a second-price auction is strictly greater.

With two bidders, a second-price sealed-bid and an open ascending-price auction are revenue equivalent. When there are three or more bidders, an open ascending-price auction yields greater revenue. Revenue ranking results under more general conditions are obtained in Milgrom and Weber (1982). For an accessible exposition of revenue rankings of common auction forms, see Milgrom and Weber (1989) and Riley (1989).

Exercises and Excursions 10.2.4

1 Common Value Auction with 2 Bidders, Independent Private Information Buyer i's "type" t_i, $i = 1, 2$ is an independent realization of a random variable $\tilde{t}_i$ in the interval $[0, 1]$, with distribution function $F(\cdot)$ and density $f(\cdot)$. One object is auctioned in a first-price sealed-bid auction. Each bidder's valuation of the item is the average of the types, that is, $V(t_1, t_2) = \frac{1}{2}t_1 + \frac{1}{2}t_2$. Let $b^f(\cdot)$ be the symmetric equilibrium bid function from a buyer's type to bid.

(A) Show that if his opponent employs the equilibrium bid function and bidder i with type t_i bids $\hat{b} = b^f(x)$, his payoff is:

$$
\Pi(x, t_i) = \int_0^x \left(\tfrac{1}{2}t_i + \tfrac{1}{2}y\right) f(y)\,dy - F(x)b(x)
$$

(B) Establish the following necessary condition for equilibrium:

$$x f(x) = \frac{d}{dx}[F(x)b^f(x)]$$

(C) Solve for the equilibrium bid function.

(D) If, instead, a second-price sealed-bid auction is used, then show that equilibrium bid function is $b^s(t_i) = t_i$.

(E) Show that the auctioneer's expected revenue in a first-price auction (part C) is the same as the expected revenue in a second-price auction (part D).

[REMARK: Revenue equivalence obtains even though buyer values are common, i.e., perfectly correlated. The crucial difference is that in this question each buyer's private information is independent of the other buyer's private information whereas in the setting of Section 10.2.4 private information is correlated.]

2 *Common Value Auction with n Bidders, Independent Private Information*
Once again analyze the common value auction described in the previous exercise, this time with n bidders. Each buyer's value is $V(t_1, t_2, \ldots, t_n) = \sum_{i=1}^{n} \frac{1}{n} t_i$. Types are uniformly distributed on $[0, 1]$ so $F(t) = t$.

(A) Argue as in the previous exercise to establish that in a first-price auction:

$$\Pi(x, t_i) = \frac{1}{n} t_i F^{n-1}(x) + \frac{n-1}{n} F^{n-2}(x) \int_{\alpha}^{t_i} y \, dF(y) - F^{n-1}(x) b^f(x)$$

$$= \frac{1}{n} t_i x^{n-1} + \frac{n-1}{2n} x^n - x^{n-1} b^f(x)$$

[HINT: At a symmetric equilibrium in increasing bid functions, a buyer will win if his type is at least as large as any other buyer's type. The density function of the highest type among $n - 1$ independently distributed types is $(n-1) f(y) F^{n-2}(y)$.]

(B) Write the first-order condition and hence show that the equilibrium bid function is:

$$b(t_i) = \left(1 - \frac{1}{n}\right)\left(1 + \frac{2}{n}\right)\frac{t_i}{2}$$

(C) Confirm that for $n \geq 4$, the bid function declines as the number of bidders increases.

[REMARK: A buyer wins only if his type is the highest. He will overbid (a phenomenon known as the *winner's curse*) unless he takes this into account in computing his expected value of the item and accordingly reduces his bid. As the number of bidders increases, the winner's curse correction calls for a lower equilibrium bid, whereas the increased competition calls for a higher equilibrium bid. In this example, when there are four or more bidders, the winner's curse effect dominates.]

3 Bidding with Independent Finite Types

There are two bidders in a first-price sealed-bid auction. Each has an independent private valuation of 2 with probability 0.5 and 1 with probability 0.5.

(A) The equilibrium bid of the low valuation bidder is $b(1) = 1$. Sketch a proof that this must be the case.

(B) Explain why the bidding strategy of a high-valuation bidder must be a mixed strategy $\tilde{b}(2)$.

(C) Show that the equilibrium mixed strategy has support $(1, 1.5]$ and distribution function:

$$G(b) = \frac{b-1}{2-b}.$$

(D) Confirm that the equilibrium payoff of each buyer type is the same as in a second-price sealed-bid auction. Hence, or otherwise, establish revenue equivalence.

4 Bidding with Correlated Finite Types – Two Types

The only change from the previous question is that buyers' private valuations are now correlated rather than independent. The joint distribution of the values is summarized in the table below, with $\frac{1}{2} < p < 1$:

	$V_2 = 1$	$V_2 = 2$
$V_1 = 1$	$\dfrac{p}{2}$	$\dfrac{1-p}{2}$
$V_1 = 2$	$\dfrac{1-p}{2}$	$\dfrac{p}{2}$

Each buyer's value is still equally likely to be 1 or 2; however, buyer values are positively correlated.

(A) Show that the equilibrium bid strategy in a first-price sealed-bid auction is for a low valuation buyer to bid 1 and a high valuation buyer to use the mixed strategy $G(b) = \frac{1-p}{p}\frac{b-1}{2-b}$ with support $(1, 1+p]$.

(B) Confirm that the auctioneer's expected revenue in a second-price sealed-bid auction is the same as in a first-price sealed-bid auction.

5 Bidding with Correlated Finite Types – Three Types

In the previous exercise there is revenue equivalence between first-price and second-price auctions, even though (10.2.9) is satisfied as a strict inequality. That is because in a correlated finite values model, the lowest and the second lowest value buyers have the same expected surplus in these two auctions. As these auctions are efficient (in particular, have the same total surplus), with two correlated types they are revenue equivalent. We need at least three types of buyers to get a difference in revenues in these two auction forms. Therefore, consider the following exercise.

Urn T has an equal number of \$1 and \$2 balls. Urn H has an equal number of \$2 and \$3 balls. Either urn T or urn H is selected based on the toss of fair coin; the two buyers' values are drawn independently from the selected urn.

(A) Show that the equilibrium bid strategy in a first-price sealed-bid auction is for a buyer with valuation \$1 to bid 1, a buyer with valuation \$2 to mix on the interval $(1, 5/3]$, and for buyer with valuation \$3 to mix on the interval $(5/3, 7/3]$.

(B) Confirm that the auctioneer's expected revenue in a second-price sealed-bid auction is strictly greater than in a first-price sealed-bid auction.

6 Conditional Stochastic Dominance in Example 10.2

Show that conditional stochastic dominance is satisfied in Example 10.2 for all $V_2' < V_2 \le V_1' < V_1$.

7 Deriving the Densities in Example 10.2

Derivations of densities in this example require knowledge of distributions of sums of random variables. Let X and Y be independent random variables, where X is uniformly distributed on $[0, 1]$ and Y is uniformly distributed

$[a, b]$ with $0 \leq a < b \leq 1$. The density of random variable $Z \equiv X + Y$ is:[27]

$$f(Z) = \frac{Z - a}{b - a}, \qquad \text{if } Z \in [a, b]$$

$$= 1, \qquad \text{if } Z \in (b, 1 + a)$$

$$= \frac{(1 + b) - Z}{b - a}, \qquad \text{if } Z \in [1 + a, 1 + b]$$

$$= 0, \qquad \text{otherwise}$$

Use this fact to answer the following questions.

(A) Derive the marginal density $f(V_1)$ assumed in Example 10.2.

(B) Show that the joint density of C and V_1 is:

$$f(C, V_1) = 1, \text{ if } V_1 \in [0, 1], C \in [0, V_1] \text{ or if } V_1 \in (1, 2], C \in [V_1 - 1, 1]$$

$$= 0, \quad \text{otherwise}$$

(C) Show that the distribution of C conditional on V_1 is:

$$f(C|V_1) = \frac{1}{V_1}, \qquad \text{if } V_1 \in [0, 1], C \in [0, V_1],$$

$$= \frac{1}{2 - V_1} \quad \text{if } V_1 \in [1, 2], C \in [V_1 - 1, 1]$$

$$= 0, \qquad \text{otherwise}$$

(D) Derive the conditional density $f(V_2|V_1)$ assumed in Example 10.2.

[HINT: Show that conditional on the event $[\tilde{V}_1 = V_1]$, buyer 2's valuation may be viewed as the sum of two independent random variables X_2 and Y where Y has the same distribution as $C|V_1$.]**

---

[27] See Hoel, Port, and Stone (1971, chapter 6).
** End of starred section.

10.3 Bargaining

Previous sections have focused on market institutions a seller might choose to sell her goods under the assumption that she has the power to commit to a set of rules for the sale. This power may derive from the seller's need to establish credibility for future sales. If the highest bid in the auction of an oil lease by the U.S. Department of the Interior is below the reserve price, then the Department does not immediately re-auction the oil lease at a lower reserve price; to do so would call into question the seriousness of reserve prices in future oil lease auctions.

In this section, we consider more symmetric interactions between one seller and one buyer. Neither the seller nor the buyer has the power to lay down a set of rules governing trade. In particular, the seller does not have the power to make a take-it-or-leave-it offer to the buyer. The buyer can make a counter-offer to the seller if he turns down the price offered by the seller. The seller in turn may reject the buyer's counter-offer and make another price offer. This interaction is modeled as a bargaining game. To keep things simple, we assume that the seller's cost and the buyer's reservation value are common knowledge.

The bargaining game proceeds as follows. The reservation value V of the buyer is higher than the cost C of the seller. Moreover, V and C are common knowledge. Normalize units of value so that the seller's cost $C = 0$ and the buyer's reservation value $V = 1$. First, the seller proposes a transaction price P_S. If the buyer accepts this offer, trade takes place at this price; the seller and the buyer obtain payoffs P_S and $(1 - P_S)$, respectively. If the buyer rejects, then there is a delay of one period (one unit of time) during which the gains from trade shrink by discount factor $\delta < 1$. The period may be very short, in which case δ is close to 1. After this delay, the buyer proposes a transaction price P_B, which the seller may accept or reject. If the seller accepts, then trade occurs; the seller and the buyer obtain payoffs δP_B and $\delta(1 - P_B)$, respectively. If she rejects then there is another delay of one period during which the gains from trade shrink once again by discount factor δ and now it is the seller's turn to make an offer. Thus, starting with the seller the two individuals alternate in proposing a transaction price and once a proposal is accepted, trade takes place. After a rejection, there is a delay after which the rejecting individual makes the next proposal. This game continues indefinitely if each price proposal is rejected by the other player, i.e., it is an infinite-horizon game. Let t be the number of periods of delay, with the initial proposal at $t = 0$. If the players agree on a price P after a delay of t periods, then (the present value of) the seller's payoff is $\delta^t P$ and the buyer's payoff is $\delta^t(1 - P)$.

Consider possible Nash equilibria of this game. Let P be any price less than or equal to the buyer's reservation value 1 and greater than or equal to the seller's cost 0. The following strategies constitute a Nash equilibrium that leads to trade at time $t = 0$ at price P:

Seller's strategy: At times $t = 0, 2, 4, \ldots$ the seller offers P and at times $t = 1, 3, 5, \ldots$ she accepts any price offer greater than or equal to P.

Buyer's strategy: At times $t = 0, 2, 4, \ldots$ the buyer accepts any price offer less than or equal to P and at times $t = 1, 3, 5, \ldots$ he offers P.

To see that the seller's strategy is a best response to the buyer's strategy, suppose that no agreement has been reached after a delay of t periods. First, let us consider the case when t is even, so it is the seller's turn to make an offer. If she offers a price greater than P the buyer will reject it and offer price P in the next time period (in accordance with his Nash equilibrium strategy). Thus, if the seller offers a price strictly greater than P in period t, the offer is rejected and the best that player can hope for is an agreement at price P in a subsequent period. This results in a payoff to the seller of at most $\delta^{t+1}P$. The seller can obtain a higher payoff of $\delta^t P$ by following her Nash equilibrium strategy and offering the price P in period t. An offer of a price less than P will also be accepted by the buyer, but this gives the seller a lower payoff. Therefore, the best that the seller can do in period t is to offer P. Next, suppose that t is odd and the buyer offers a price P. The seller should accept it; if she rejects it then, along the Nash equilibrium path in the continuation game, she will get a price P in period $t + 1$. A symmetric argument shows that the buyer's strategy is a best response to the seller's strategy. No player can benefit from unilaterally deviating from these strategies, and therefore they constitute a Nash equilibrium. There is a continuum of Nash equilibria solutions, one at each and every price P between 0 and 1. Of course, some of these are highly asymmetrical in favoring one player over the other.

To most people,[28] the highly asymmetric Nash equilibria of this game seem implausible. Rubinstein (1982) was the first to provide dramatic theoretical support for this intuition. Consider a price P and the Nash equilibrium strategies that support this price. Suppose that at time $t = 0$ the seller deviates and instead of P offers a price $P + \varepsilon$, where $\varepsilon > 0$. The buyer's Nash strategy calls for rejection. If he rejects the offer $P + \varepsilon$, then along the Nash equilibrium path in the continuation game, agreement will be reached next period at price P. But for small enough ε we have $1 - (P + \varepsilon) > \delta(1 - P)$. Therefore, the buyer is better off accepting $P + \varepsilon$ at time $t = 0$. A similar argument implies that if at time $t = 1$ the buyer deviates and offers $P - \varepsilon$

---

[28] Economic theorists and everyone else.

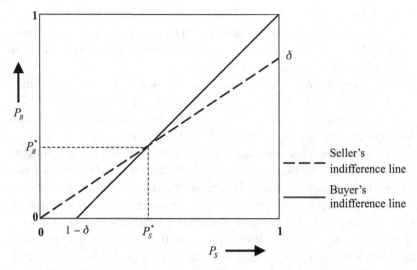

Figure 10.5. Solution to infinite-horizon bargaining game.

instead of P then the seller is better off accepting this price if ε is small enough. In other words, the Nash equilibrium is not subgame perfect as the Nash equilibrium strategy of each player is not a best response at some subgames that are not along the Nash equilibrium path.

There exists a unique subgame-perfect equilibrium in this game. The subgame-perfect equilibrium strategies are as follows:

Seller's strategy: At times $t = 0, 2, 4, \ldots$ the seller offers P_S^* and at times $t = 1, 3, 5, \ldots$ she accepts any price offer greater than or equal to P_B^*.

Buyer's strategy: At times $t = 0, 2, 4, \ldots$ the buyer accepts any price offer less than or equal to P_S^* and at times $t = 1, 3, 5, \ldots$ he offers P_B^*.

It remains to compute the subgame-perfect prices P_S^* and P_B^*. From the argument in the previous paragraph it is clear that at a subgame-perfect equilibrium, in even periods the buyer must be indifferent between accepting the seller's offer P_S^* or rejecting it and settling for P_B^* one period later. And in odd periods the seller must be indifferent between accepting the buyer's offer P_B^* or getting P_S^* one period later. This gives us two equations in two unknowns:

Buyer indifference line: $(1 - P_S^*) = \delta(1 - P_B^*)$ or $P_B^* = \dfrac{P_S^* - (1 - \delta)}{\delta}$

Seller indifference line: $P_B^* = \delta P_S^*$

These indifference lines are plotted in Figure 10.5. The intersection point yields equilibrium prices:

$$P_S^* = \frac{1}{1 + \delta}, \qquad P_B^* = \frac{\delta}{1 + \delta} \qquad (10.3.1)$$

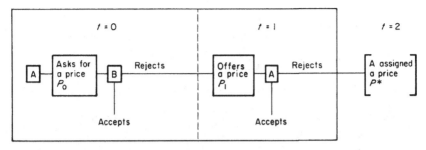

Figure 10.6. A two-round bargaining game.

Observe that $P_S^* > P_B^*$ and that the seller and the buyer end up by sharing the surplus in the ratio 1:δ. This, of course, is because the game assigned the first move to the seller. Allowing the buyer to make the first offer would give him the advantage.

While we considered an infinite-horizon game, these results can also be illustrated beginning with a simpler finite-horizon game and letting the number of rounds grow very large. Suppose initially there are just two rounds. Each individual then gets one chance to name the terms of exchange, with the seller making initial price proposal. If there is no agreement at the end of two periods, the seller gets an exogenously predetermined price P^*.[29] The extensive form of the game is depicted in Figure 10.6.

Consider the subgame that starts at B, the buyer's decision node. The buyer knows that, if his price proposal is rejected, the seller will end up with $\delta^2 P^*$. If the buyer offers a price P_1 in period 1, the seller gets a present value of δP_1 if she accepts. The seller will therefore have an incentive to reject only if $\delta P_1 < \delta^2 P^*$. The buyer's best strategy is then to ask for a price P_1 such that:

$$\delta P_1 = \delta^2 P^* \Rightarrow P_1 = \delta P^*$$

The present value of the subgame to the buyer is therefore:

$$\delta(1 - P_1) = \delta - \delta^2 P^*$$

A similar argument can now be applied at the initial node of the game. The seller reasons that any price P_0 such that buyer's payoff, $1 - P_0$, is less than $\delta - \delta^2 P^*$ will be rejected. The seller then maximizes by setting P_0 to equate these and so:

$$P_0 = 1 - \delta + \delta^2 P^* \tag{10.3.2}$$

This is the unique subgame-perfect equilibrium of the two-period game.

[29] In an exercise at the end of this section, you are asked to show that it does not matter whether the object is sold to the buyer after round 2 or to a third party (in which case the buyer gets nothing).

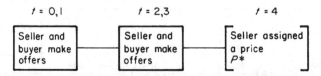

Figure 10.7. A four-round bargaining game.

Next, consider a four-period game in which the seller and buyer each make two price proposals. The extensive form of this new game is depicted in Figure 10.7. If P^* is the exogenously determined trading price when all offers are rejected, the final two rounds are exactly the same as in the two-round game. The seller will therefore ask for a price in period 2 of:

$$P_2 = 1 - \delta + \delta^2 P^* \qquad (10.3.3)$$

The extensive form of the four-period game is then reduced to the extensive form of the two-period game except that the end-price P^* is replaced by P_2. It follows from (10.3.2) that the seller's subgame-perfect equilibrium strategy calls for her to open with a price of:

$$P_0 = 1 - \delta + \delta^2 P_2$$

Substituting for P_2 from (10.3.3):

$$P_0 = 1 - \delta + \delta^2 - \delta^3 + \delta^4 P^* \qquad (10.3.4)$$

Comparing (10.3.2) and (10.3.4) it is easy to infer what the initial asking price will be if there are further rounds of bargaining. If $T - 1$ is the period in which the final offer is made (by the buyer), the unique subgame-perfect initial asking price is:

$$P_0 = 1 - \delta + \delta^2 \cdots - \delta^{T-1} + \delta^T P^*$$
$$= \frac{1 - \delta^T}{1 + \delta} + \delta^T P^* \qquad (10.3.5)$$

As $T \to \infty$ the equilibrium approaches that for the infinite game with discounting. From (10.3.5):

$$P_S^* = \lim_{T \to \infty} P_0 = \frac{1}{1 + \delta}, \text{ and } P_B^* = \lim_{T \to \infty} (1 - P_0) = \frac{\delta}{1 + \delta} \qquad (10.3.6)$$

Thus, we get the unique subgame-perfect equilibrium prices of the infinite-horizon game.

In the usual interpretation of this game it is then argued that, if the time between rounds is brief, the discount factor δ is approximately 1 and so total surplus is shared approximately in the ratio 1:1. Therefore, subgame perfection, typically regarded as the least controversial of all refinements, eliminates all but a very plausible Nash equilibrium in which the surplus is split almost equally.

However, this conclusion hinges critically upon the common knowledge assumptions of the game. Let us drop the assumption that the buyer's reservation value is common knowledge but continue to assume that seller's cost is common knowledge and equal to zero. The seller believes that the buyer's reservation value is either V_w (the weak type) or V_s (the strong type), where $V_w > V_s > 0$. The nomenclature for the buyer's type is due to the fact that greater the buyer's reservation value, the more he loses by delaying agreement, and this weakens his bargaining position.[30] Rubinstein (1985) shows that there exists a continuum of sequential (and subgame-perfect) equilbria in this model. These sequential equilibria are supported by the seller's (rather optimistic) off-the-equilibrium-path belief that if the buyer deviates from the equilibrium path in any way he must be of the weak type. This forces the strong type of the buyer not to deviate. Rubinstein imposes restrictions on off-the-equilibrium-path beliefs and shows that a unique sequential equilibrium survives this condition. While the restrictions imposed by Rubinstein are reasonable there are other reasonable restrictions that select different equilibria.[31] Many ways of refining the set of sequential equilibria have been proposed in the literature, but no single refinement leads to a sensible solution in various bargaining models with incomplete information. The bargaining literature based on game theoretic models has not provided satisfactory answers in models in which players have private information. Nevertheless, some general results are available. As shown in the next section, if both the buyer's value and seller's cost are private information and it is not common knowledge that there are gains from trade, then, no matter what mechanism is used by the buyer and seller, efficient trade is not feasible without a subsidy by an external party.

Exercises and Excursions 10.3

1 *The Finite Bargaining Game*
   (A) Consider the two-period bargaining game analyzed above. If neither offer is accepted, the seller gets P^*. Suppose the buyer gets $V^* \leq 1 - P^*$. That is, some or all of the surplus goes to a "mediator"

---

[30] If the type of the buyer were to become common knowledge before the start of the game then the preceding analysis implies that weak type would agree to a higher subgame perfect equilibrium price than the strong type: $P_w = \frac{V_w}{1+\delta} > \frac{V_s}{1+\delta} = P_s$.

[31] For instance, a different set of restrictions on beliefs in this model leads to a different selection from the set of sequential equilibria; see Bikhchandani (1992).

if bargaining fails. Show that the subgame-perfect equilibrium is independent of V^*.

(B) Suppose the buyer makes the first price proposal. Solve for the subgame-perfect equilibrium price in round 0 and show that it is independent of P^*.

(C) Extend your conclusion to T-period bargaining games.

2 Bargaining with a Disappearing Surplus

Suppose that, if agreement is reached in period t, the date-t value of the surplus is V_t where:

$$V_0 > V_1 > V_2 > \cdots > V_T = 0$$

For simplicity, assume that there is no discounting.

(A) Solve for the subgame-perfect equilibrium of the game assuming that the seller moves first and buyer moves last.

(B) What if T is odd so that it is the seller who moves both first and last?

(C) Compare your answers with the subgame-perfect equilibrium when:

$$V_0 = V_1 = \cdots = V_{T-1} > V_T = 0$$

3 Last-Mover Advantage in the Finite Bargaining Game

Two individuals take turns proposing how to share a pie. The pie shrinks with each period so that, after t periods, it is a fraction $f(t)$ of its original size, where $f(t) = \delta^t$, $t \leq T$ and $f(t) = 0$, for $t > T$.

(A) Explain why, if agreement is not reached prior to period T, the last mover has the bargaining advantage.

(B) Let α be the fraction of the original pie that the last mover will claim if agreement is not reached earlier. Suppose that δ is close to 1. Show that the subgame-perfect equilibrium is for the last mover to receive a fraction α of the pie plus an (approximately) equal share of the remaining $1 - \alpha$.

10.4 Efficient Allocation with Private Information*

In section 10.2 we explored the role of auctions as a market institution. The central result was the revenue equivalence theorem. An implication of

---

* Starred sections represent more difficult or specialized materials that can be omitted without significant loss of continuity.

the analysis is that any of the four common auctions allocates efficiently as long as the mechanism designer does not exclude some potential buyers by setting a reserve price above the minimum value.

In a standard auction, there is a net gain to the mechanism designer in that revenue is collected. One special feature of the auction environment is that, conditional upon knowing that a buyer has the highest value (or estimate of the item's value), a buyer knows the expected private and social value of the item. As we now show, if this is not the case, it is impossible to devise an efficient institution that is also self-financing. This arises naturally when a seller's cost and a buyer's value are privately known and it is not common knowledge that there are gains from trade; that is, the seller's cost might be greater or less than the buyer's value.

Consider the production and exchange of a single item. Agent 1 (the buyer) has a value V_1 known only to himself. The mechanism designer can produce the commodity at a cost k. However, agent 2 (the seller) can produce it at a cost of $C_2 = k - V_2$ where V_2 is also private information, known only to this second agent. The reduction in cost, V_2, is the value that agent 2 brings to the potential production and exchange, so we will refer to it as agent 2's value. We assume that values are independently distributed and that the support of V_i is an interval $[\alpha_i, \beta_i]$, where $\alpha_i \geq 0$.

Production of the commodity (and exchange) is efficient if buyer 1's value exceeds the cost, that is, if:

$$V_1 - C_1 = V_1 - (k - V_2) = V_1 + V_2 - k \geq 0$$

Reinterpretation as a Public-Goods Problem

Note that it is efficient to produce if and only if the sum of the private values exceeds the designer's cost k. This can be reinterpreted as a standard public-goods problem. Suppose that a public good can be produced at a cost of k. Consumption of a public good is non-rivalrous in that consumption by one agent has no effect on the benefit to the other agent. Let agent i have a value V_i, $i = 1, 2$, where $V_i \in [\alpha_i, \beta_i]$. The social value of the item is the sum of the private values less the designer's cost, that is:

$$S(V_1, V_2) = V_1 + V_2 - k$$

It is therefore efficient to produce the public good if and only if:

$$S(V_1, V_2) = V_1 + V_2 - k \geq 0$$

Given the symmetry of the public-goods model and the long history of public-goods analysis it is this interpretation of the model that we use here.

We then apply our results to the production of a private good when the cost and value are private information.

Associated with any mechanism selected by the mechanism designer is a probability $Q(V) = Q(V_1, V_2)$ that the public good is produced, given that agent i, $i = 1, 2$ has a value V_i. The (expected) social surplus when $V = (V_1, V_2)$ can then be written as follows:

$$S(V, Q(V)) = Q(V)(V_1 + V_2 - k)$$

For an efficient mechanism, the public good should be produced if and only if the sum of the values exceeds the cost. Thus the efficient allocation rule is:

$$Q^*(V) = \begin{cases} 0, & \text{if } \sum_{i=1}^{2} V_i < k \\ 1, & \text{if } \sum_{i=1}^{2} V_i \geq k \end{cases} \tag{10.4.1}$$

If $\sum_{i=1}^{2} \alpha_i > k$ it is always optimal to produce the public good. The designer can do so profitably by charging each agent his lowest valuation. If $\sum_{i=1}^{2} \beta_i < k$ it is never optimal to produce the public good. Therefore, the interesting case is when:

$$\sum_{i=1}^{2} \alpha_i < k < \sum_{i=1}^{2} \beta_i$$

so that it is optimal to produce the public good for some but not all values. Note that this condition is equivalent to assuming that it is not common knowledge that there are gains from trade in the single-seller single-buyer model. If $V_1 + V_2 < k$, then $V_1 < C_2$ and there are no gains from trade. If $V_1 + V_2 > k$, then $V_1 > C_2$ and there are gains from trade. Because each agent knows only his own value/cost it can never be common knowledge that there are gains from trade.

The goal is to design a mechanism that elicits the information about private values needed in order to maximize social surplus. The preferences of each agent are exactly the same as in the analysis of auctions. Thus, from that analysis, we know that higher types must receive a higher equilibrium payoff (informational rent). The issue that we examine here is whether it is possible to provide appropriate incentives for efficiency without either an expected loss for the mechanism designer or the coercion of any agent into participation. That is, is there an incentive-compatible mechanism that is efficient and also self-financed (at least in expectation)? As we shall see, this is not possible.

The Vickrey-Clarke-Groves (V-C-G) Mechanism

A V-C-G mechanism is a dominant strategy incentive compatible, efficient mechanism.[32] We focus on the revenue-maximizing V-C-G mechanism in this setting.

Given the efficient allocation rule (10.4.1), maximized social surplus can be expressed as follows:

$$S^*(V) \equiv S(V, Q^*(V)) = Q^*(V) \left(\sum_{i=1}^{2} V_i - k \right) \qquad (10.4.2)$$

As we will focus on agent i, it is helpful to write this as $S(V_i, V_{-i}, Q^*(V_i, V_{-i}))$. Then agent i's contribution to social surplus, over and above his minimum contribution, is

$$S(V_i, V_{-i}, Q^*(V_i, V_{-i})) - S(\alpha_i, V_{-i}, Q^*(\alpha_i, V_{-i}))$$

Suppose that each agent reveals his true value and is rewarded by the mechanism with a payment that makes his payoff equal to his contribution to social surplus, that is:[33]

$$\begin{aligned} U_i &= S(V_i, V_{-i}, Q^*(V_i, V_{-i})) - S(\alpha_i, V_{-i}, Q^*(\alpha_i, V_{-i})) \\ &= V_i Q^*(V_i, V_{-i}) + (V_{-i} - k)Q^*(V_i, V_{-i}) - S(\alpha_i, V_{-i}, Q^*(\alpha_i, V_{-i})) \\ &\equiv V_i Q^*(V_i, V_{-i}) + M_i(V_i, V_{-i}, \alpha_i) \\ &\qquad \text{private} \quad + \quad \text{payment by} \\ &\qquad \text{payoff} \qquad \text{mechanism} \end{aligned}$$

Suppose that agent i announces that his value is θ_i and agent $-i$ announces that his value is θ_{-i}. In the V-C-G mechanism, agent i is offered a payment:

$$M_i(\theta_i, \theta_{-i}, \alpha_i) = (\theta_{-i} - k)Q^*(\theta_i, \theta_{-i}) - S(\alpha_i, \theta_{-i}, Q^*(\alpha_i, \theta_{-i})) \quad (10.4.3)$$

based on the vector of announced values.[34] Agent i's payoff, when his value is V_i, is then:

$$\begin{aligned} U_i &= V_i Q^*(\theta_i, \theta_{-i}) + M_i(\theta_i, \theta_{-i}, \alpha_i) \\ &= V_i Q^*(\theta_i, \theta_{-i}) + (\theta_{-i} - k)Q^*(\theta_i, \theta_{-i}) - S(\alpha_i, \theta_{-i}, Q^*(\alpha_i, \theta_{-i})) \\ &= S(V_i, \theta_{-i}, Q^*(\theta_i, \theta_{-i})) - S(\alpha_i, \theta_{-i}, Q^*(\alpha_i, \theta_{-i})) \end{aligned}$$

[32] See Vickrey (1961), Clark (1971), and Groves (1973). The analysis of the V-C-G mechanism is essentially identical with more than two agents.

[33] The subscript $-i$ refers to the agent who is not i. Thus, if $i = 1$ then $V_{-i} = V_2$.

[34] An exercise at the end of this section asks you to show that the second-price auction discussed in Section 10.2.2 has a similar incentive payment.

Note that the second term is independent of θ_i. We now show that regardless of the responses of the other agent, the first expression $S(V_i, \theta_{-i}, Q^*(\theta_i, \theta_{-i}))$ takes on its maximum at $\theta_i = V_i$. That is, truth telling is a dominant strategy for agent i.

The efficient allocation rule $Q^*(V_i, V_{-i})$ maximizes social surplus, that is:

$$Q^*(V_i, V_{-i}) \text{ solves } \underset{q}{\text{Max}} \, [S(V_i, V_{-i}, q) = q(V_i + V_{-i} - k)].$$

Then for any V_{-i}:

$$V_i \text{ solves } \underset{\theta_i}{\text{Max}} \, [S(V_i, V_{-i}, Q^*(\theta_i, V_{-i})).$$

Simply by a change of notation it follows that for any θ_{-i}:

$$V_i \text{ solves } \underset{\theta_i}{\text{Max}} \, [S(V_i, \theta_{-i}, Q^*(\theta_i, \theta_{-i}))]$$

Exactly the same argument holds for the other agent and thus truth-telling is an equilibrium in dominant strategies.

Note also that if both agents report their true values, agent i's payoff is:

$$U_i^*(V) = S^*(V_i, V_{-i}) - S^*(\alpha_i, V_{-i}) \tag{10.4.4}$$

Thus the payoff of agent i if he has his lowest value is zero, and so the participation constraint is binding for such an agent. Hence, for each (V_1, V_2), the V-C-G mechanism with payment in (10.4.3) raises at least as much revenue for the designer as any other V-C-G mechanism.[35]

It will prove helpful to define $\bar{S}_i(V_i)$ to be the equilibrium expected social surplus and $\bar{U}_i(V_i)$ to be agent i's expected payoff, conditional on agent i's value V_i. Then, for the revenue-maximizing V-C-G mechanism, it follows from (10.4.2) and (10.4.4) that:

$$\bar{S}_i(V_i) = E[S(V_i, \tilde{V}_{-i}, Q^*(V_i, \tilde{V}_{-i}))]$$

$$= E[Q^*(V_i, \tilde{V}_{-i})(V_i + \tilde{V}_{-i} - k)] \tag{10.4.5}$$

$$\bar{U}_i(V_i) = E[U_i^*(V)] = \bar{S}_i(V_i) - \bar{S}_i(\alpha_i) \tag{10.4.6}$$

where we take the expectation over $\tilde{V}_{-i}$.

---

[35] We can obtain other V-C-G mechanisms by adding a lump-sum that does not depend on θ_i to the right-hand side of (10.4.3). If non-coercion is maintained, these V-C-G mechanisms must yield lower revenue.

Least Costly Efficient Provision of a Public Good

We now consider all possible efficient public goods allocation mechanisms. As we will see, there is a close parallel with the revenue-equivalence theorem of Section 10.2.2. Any efficient mechanism for which the participation constraint is binding, yields the same expected payoff to the agents and hence the same expected revenue to the mechanism designer. We weaken the requirement of incentive compatibility from dominant strategy to Bayesian incentive compatibility, thus increasing the class of mechanisms considered. We also assume that each agent's type is independently and continuously distributed.

Recall that V_i is the value of the public good to agent $i = 1, 2$ where $V_i \in [\alpha_i, \beta_i]$. Associated with any efficient mechanism $Q^*(V)$ is an expected payment schedule $X(V) = (X_1(V), X_2(V))$. As before, it proves convenient to rewrite this from the perspective of agent i as $Q^*(V_i, V_{-i})$ and as $X_i(V_i, V_{-i})$. Taking the expectation over $\tilde{V}_{-i}$, the unknown value of the other agent, we also define:

$$q_i^*(V_i) \equiv E[Q^*(V_i, \tilde{V}_{-i})] \quad \text{and} \quad x_i(V_i) \equiv E[X_i(V_i, \tilde{V}_{-i})]$$

Suppose that agent i deviates and announces a value of θ_i. Agent i's expected payoff is his private value times the (expected) probability of the public good provision less the expected cost, that is:

$$u_i(V_i, \theta_i) = E[Q^*(\theta_i, \tilde{V}_{-i})]V_i - E[X_i(\theta_i, \tilde{V}_{-i})] = q_i(\theta_i)V_i - x_i(\theta_i)$$

Let $U_i(V_i)$ be the equilibrium expected payoff. For the mechanism to be Bayesian incentive compatible, agent i cannot gain by announcing any other value, that is:

$$U_i(V_i) = u_i(V_i, V_i) = \underset{\theta_i}{\text{Max}} \, [u_i(V_i, \theta_i)]$$

$$= \underset{\theta_i}{\text{Max}} \, [q_i^*(\theta_i)V_i - x_i(\theta_i)], \quad \theta_i \in [\alpha_i, \beta_i]$$

Appealing to the Envelope Theorem, agent i's marginal expected payoff is:

$$\frac{dU_i(V_i)}{dV_i} = q_i^*(V_i) \tag{10.4.7}$$

There is a simple way to understand this result. Figure 10.8 depicts the graph of the equilibrium expected payoff $U_i(V_i) = q_i^*(V_i)V_i - x_i(V_i)$.[36] Suppose

---

[36] Note the similarity with Figure 10.1.

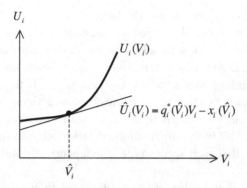

Figure 10.8. The Envelope Theorem.

that instead of choosing his best response, agent *i* always chooses the strategy that is a best response if his value is $\hat{V}_i$. Then his payoff function is $\hat{U}_i(V_i) = q_i^*(\hat{V}_i)V_i - x_i(\hat{V}_i)$. Note that this function is linear with slope $q_i^*(\hat{V}_i)$. As $U_i(V_i)$ is agent *i*'s expected payoff if he chooses his best response, agent *i* cannot be better off if he adopts this alternative strategy. That is, $U_i(V_i) \geq \hat{U}_i(V_i)$, with equality at $\hat{V}_i$. Therefore, as long as the function $U_i(\cdot)$ is differentiable, the two functions must have the same slope at $\hat{V}_i$. Hence, as shown in Figure 10.8:

$$\frac{dU_i}{dV_i}(\hat{V}_i) = \frac{d\hat{U}_i}{dV_i}(\hat{V}_i) = q_i^*(\hat{V}_i)$$

We now characterize the efficient mechanism that maximizes the designer's profit. Recall that $\bar{S}_i(V_i)$ is the expected social surplus when agent *i*'s value is V_i. As $Q^*(V_i, V_{-i})$ maximizes social surplus given the value vector (V_i, V_{-i}), it follows from (10.4.5) that:

$$\bar{S}_i(V_i) = E[Q^*(V_i, \tilde{V}_{-i})(V_i + \tilde{V}_{-i} - k)]$$
$$= E[\underset{\theta_i}{\text{Max}} \, [Q^*(\theta_i, \tilde{V}_{-i})(V_i + \tilde{V}_{-i} - k)]]$$

Appealing to the Envelope Theorem:

$$\frac{d\bar{S}_i(V_i)}{dV_i} = E[Q^*(V_i, \tilde{V}_{-i})] = q_i^*(V_i) \qquad (10.4.8)$$

If follows from (10.4.7) and (10.4.8) that:

$$\frac{d\bar{S}_i(V_i)}{dV_i} = \frac{dU_i(V_i)}{dV_i}$$

and hence that:

$$\bar{S}_i(V_i) - \bar{S}_i(\alpha_i) = U_i(V_i) - U_i(\alpha_i)$$

For the mechanism to be non-coercive, no agent can be worse off participating. As higher types have higher payoffs, the participation constraint is $U_i(\alpha_i) \geq 0$, $i = 1, 2$. Therefore a necessary condition for an efficient mechanism to be non-coercive and Bayesian incentive compatible is that:

$$\bar{S}_i(V_i) - \bar{S}_i(\alpha_i) \leq U_i(V_i)$$

But we have already seen that this constraint is binding for the V-C-G mechanism with agent payments defined in (10.4.3).[37] Therefore, this V-C-G mechanism is (expected) revenue-maximizing among all efficient Bayesian-incentive-compatible mechanisms.

We can now characterize the expected payoffs of the agents and mechanism designer. Given the above results, we need only consider the revenue-maximizing V-C-G mechanism. First, note that the mechanism designer's profit, as a function of agents' values, is equal to the social surplus less buyer utilities:

$$U_d(V_1, V_2) = S^*(V_1, V_2) - U_1^*(V_1, V_2) - U_2^*(V_1, V_2)$$

Let $\bar{S} = E[S^*(\tilde{V}_1, \tilde{V}_2)]$ be the *ex ante* expected social surplus under the V-C-G mechanism (i.e., under an efficient allocation rule), $\bar{U}_i = E[U_i(\tilde{V}_i)]$ the *ex ante* expected payoff of agent i and $\bar{U}_d = E[U_d(\tilde{V}_1, \tilde{V}_2)]$ the expected profit of the mechanism designer.

Appealing to (10.4.6):

$$\bar{U}_i = \bar{S} - \bar{S}_i(\alpha_i), \quad i = 1, 2$$

Therefore the expected profit of the mechanism designer is:

$$\bar{U}_d = \bar{S} - \sum_{i=1}^{2} \bar{U}_i = \bar{S} - \sum_{i=1}^{2} (\bar{S} - \bar{S}_i(\alpha_i)) = \sum_{i=1}^{2} \bar{S}_i(\alpha_i) - \bar{S} \quad (10.4.9)$$

As shown above, the incentive issue is easily solved unless $\sum_{i=1}^{2} \beta_i > k > \sum_{i=1}^{2} \alpha_i$. For then it is efficient to produce the public good for some but not all values. We will argue that expected designer profit must be negative in the revenue-maximizing V-C-G mechanism, and therefore in any efficient Bayesian-incentive-compatible mechanism.

---

[37] See Equation (10.4.6).

First, note that if $S^*(V_1, V_2) = 0$, then the public good is not provided, no cost is incurred, and no incentive payments made; mechanism designer's profit in this case is zero.

Suppose that $S^*(V_1, V_2) > 0$, that is, $V_1 + V_2 > k$. Thus

$$S^*(V_1, V_2) = \text{Max}[0, \sum_{i=1}^{2} V_i - k] = \sum_{i=1}^{2} V_i - k.$$

Case 1: $S^*(\alpha_i, V_{-i}) > 0$, $i = 1, 2$

Then, for $i = 1, 2$:

$$S^*(\alpha_i, V_{-i}) = \text{Max}[0, \alpha_i + V_{-i} - k] = \alpha_i + V_{-i} - k$$
$$= S^*(V_1, V_2) - (V_i - \alpha_i) \qquad (10.4.10)$$

Summing over agents:

$$\sum_{i=1}^{2} S^*(\alpha_i, V_{-i}) = 2S^*(V_1, V_2) - \left(\sum_{i=1}^{2} V_i - k \right) + \left(\sum_{i=1}^{2} \alpha_i - k \right)$$

$$= S^*(V_1, V_2) + \left(\sum_{i=1}^{2} \alpha_i - k \right)$$

$$< S^*(V_1, V_2), \quad \text{as } \sum_{i=1}^{2} \alpha_i > k.$$

Case 2: $S^*(\alpha_i, V_{-i}) = 0$, $i = 1, 2$.

It follows immediately that:

$$\sum_{i=1}^{2} S^*(\alpha_i, V_{-i}) - S^*(V_1, V_2) = -S^*(V_1, V_2) < 0.$$

Case 3: $S^*(\alpha_i, V_{-i}) = 0$, $S^*(\alpha_{-i}, V_i) > 0$.

Appealing to (10.4.10):

$$S^*(\alpha_i, V_{-i}) + S^*(\alpha_{-i}, V_i) = S^*(\alpha_{-i}, V_i) = S^*(V_i, V_{-i}) - (V_{-i} - \alpha_{-i})$$

$$\leq S^*(V_i, V_{-i})$$

Note also that the inequality is strict unless $V_{-i} = \alpha_{-i}$.

Thus, for each of three possible cases, we have:

$$S^*(\alpha_i, V_{-i}) + S^*(\alpha_{-i}, V_i) \leq S^*(V_i, V_{-i})$$

with strict inequality for almost all (V_i, V_{-i}). Finally, taking the expectation over $\tilde{V}_i, \tilde{V}_{-i}$:

$$\sum_{i=1}^{2} \bar{S}_i(\alpha_i) = E\left[\sum_{i=1}^{2} S^*(\alpha_i, \tilde{V}_{-i})\right] < E[S^*(\tilde{V}_i, \tilde{V}_{-i})] = \bar{S}$$

Thus, (10.4.9) implies that $\bar{U}_d < 0$.

Application to the Efficient Provision of Private Goods

As we have argued, the two-person public-goods model is identical to the single-seller single-buyer model with both buyer value and seller cost unknown. Hence, as an immediate application, suppose a single buyer's cost and a single seller's value are both private information. If the cost and value are distributed independently and continuously and it is not common knowledge that there are gains from trade, then for efficient exchange between the buyer and the seller the mechanism designer must incur an expected loss.[38]

Note, finally, that there is an immediate further generalization to the n buyer case. Simply reinterpret V_1 to be the maximum of the n buyers' values. Then efficiency can only be achieved at a loss to the mechanism designer.

Exercises and Excursions 10.4

1 Efficient Dominant Strategy Incentive-Compatible Mechanisms

In this section, we showed that if gains from trade are not common knowledge then any non-coercive, efficient, Bayesian-incentive-compatible mechanism for trading a single object must yield negative expected revenue to the mechanism designer.

Show that if the incentive compatibility requirement is strengthened to dominant strategy, then whenever there is trade (in particular, for (V_1, V_2) such that $S^*(V_1, V_2) > 0$)) the mechanism designer's revenue is negative.

[HINT: Use (10.4.4) to obtain the mechanism designer's revenue as a function of (V_1, V_2).]

2 Second-Price Auctions with Privately Known Values

Recall that when bidders' values are privately known (as in Section 10.2.2) truthful reporting is a dominant strategy in a second-price auction. This

---

[38] This is the Myerson-Satterthwaite (1983) Impossibility Theorem.

suggests that the payoff to a bidder in a second-price auction is equal to his contribution to the social surplus.

Consider a second-price auction with two bidders with values V_1 and V_2 in the interval $[0, 1]$. The seller's cost is 0.

(A) Show that in a second price auction bidder i's residual contribution to social surplus is $S_i(V_i, V_{-i}) = S^*(V_i, V_{-i}) - S^*(0, V_{-i})$, where $S^*(\cdot)$ is the maximum social surplus as a function of bidder values.

Suppose that $V_1 > V_2$. Thus, bidder 1 gets the object and pays V_2 whereas bidder 2 pays nothing.

(B) Compute $S_i(V)$ in this setting and show that bidder i's dominant strategy equilibrium payoff in a second-price auction is equal to $S_i(V)$.

SUGGESTIONS FOR FURTHER READING: In the auction models presented in this chapter, a single object is for sale. Krishna (2002) is an excellent and comprehensive book on such models. The analysis of multi-object auctions is an area of recent research, some of which is the subject of Cramton, Shoham, and Steinberg (2006). Osborne and Rubinstein (1990) is a review of non-cooperative and cooperative game theoretic analyses of bargaining.

References

Arnold, Michael and Lippman, Steven A., "Posted Prices versus Bargaining in Markets with Asymmetric Information," *Economic Inquiry*, 36 (1998), 450–457.

Bikhchandani, Sushil, "A Bargaining Model with Incomplete Information," *Review of Economic Studies*, 59 (1992), 187–203.

Clark, Edward H., "Multipart Pricing of Public Goods," *Public Choice*, 11 (1971), 19–33.

Cramton, Peter, Shoham, Yoav and Steinberg, Richard (eds.), *Combinatorial Auctions*, Cambridge, MA: MIT Press, 2006.

Dasgupta, Partha, Hammond, Peter and Maskin, Eric, "The Implementation of Social Choice Rules: Some General Results on Incentive Compatibility," *Review of Economic Studies*, 46 (1979), 185–216.

Groves, Theodore, "Incentives in Teams," *Econometrica*, 41 (1973), 617–631.

Hoel, Paul G., Port, Sidney C. and Stone, Charles J., *Introduction to Probability Theory*, Boston: Houghton Mifflin, 1971.

Krishna, Vijay, *Auction Theory*, San Diego: Academic Press, 2002.

Maskin, Eric and John G. Riley, "Asymmetric Auctions," *Review of Economic Studies*, 67 (2000), 413–438.

Milgrom, Paul and Weber, Robert J., "A Theory of Auctions and Competitive Bidding," *Econometrica*, 50 (1982), 1089–1122.

———, "Auctions and Bidding: A Primer," *Journal of Economic Perspectives*, 3 (1989), 3–22.

Myerson, Roger, "Incentive Compatibility and the Bargaining Problem," *Econometrica*, 47 (1979), 61–74.

————, "Optimal Auction Design," *Mathematics of Operations Research*, 5 (1981), 58–73.

Myerson, Roger and Satterthwaite, Mark, "Efficient Mechanisms for Bilateral Trading", *Journal of Economic Theory*, 29 (1983), 265–281.

Osborne, Martin J. and Ariel Rubinstein, *Bargaining and Markets*, San Diego: Academic Press, 1990.

Ostrovsky, Michael and Michael Schwartz, "Reserve Prices in Internet Advertising Auctions: A Field Experiment," working paper, Stanford University GSB, 2009.

Riley, John G., "Expected Revenue from Open and Sealed Bid Auctions," *Journal of Economic Perspectives*, 3 (1989), 41–50.

Riley, John G. and Samuelson, William F., "Optimal Auctions," *American Economic Review*, 71 (1981), 381–392.

Riley, John G. and Zeckhauser, Richard, "Optimal Selling Strategies: When to Haggle, When to Hold Firm," *Quarterly Journal of Economics*, 98 (1983), 267–289.

Royden, Halsey, *Real Analysis*, New York: Macmillan, 1988.

Rubinstein, Ariel, "Perfect Equilibrium in a Bargaining Model," *Econometrica*, 50 (1982), 97–109.

————, "A Bargaining Model with Incomplete Information about Time Preferences," *Econometrica*, 53 (1985), 1151–1172.

Vickrey, William, "Counterspeculation, Auctions and Competitive Sealed Tenders," *Journal of Finance*, 16 (1961), 8–37.

Long-Run Relationships and the Credibility
of Threats and Promises[1]

The last few chapters investigated strategic interaction between players in a variety of settings. However, the analysis presumed a one-time interaction among players. This chapter inquires into the further strategic opportunities that are introduced when individuals interact with one another *repeatedly*.

Long-run relationships lead to two types of phenomenon. First, the set of utility payoffs that can be supported as equilibrium outcomes expands. This may be achieved by threatening to punish opponents in later periods of play if they deviate from a sequence of actions that yields the desired utility payoffs. Second, an individual with private information should be able to make favorable information about himself (information that he is a high-quality or otherwise desirable trading partner) credible by actions taken in the early periods of a long-run relationship. That is, an individual should be able to develop a *reputation*.

11.1 The Multi-Period Prisoners' Dilemma

Let us begin by examining the Prisoners' Dilemma. In Table 11.1, each individual $i(i = 1, 2)$ may choose to play either "Defect" (strategy x_1) or "Cooperate" (strategy x_2). The Prisoners' Dilemma environment is *defined* by the ranked payoffs in Table 11.1 if $e > f > g > h$. Table 11.2 is a numerical example.

In Chapter 7 we saw that if the Prisoners' Dilemma is played just once, the Defect strategy x_1 is strictly dominant for each player. Therefore, the unique Nash equilibrium is for both individuals to choose x_1. In the illustrative example of Table 11.2, each player's payoff would be zero at the Nash

---

[1] This chapter relies heavily upon the discussions in Fudenberg, Levine, and Maskin (1986) and Fudenberg and Levine (1989).

Table 11.1. *Prisoners' Dilemma (e > f > g > h)*

		Defect	Cooperate
		x_1^2	x_2^2
Defect	x_1^1	g, g	e, h
Cooperate	x_2^1	h, e	f, f

equilibrium. We examine whether cooperative outcomes are possible if the same two players play the Prisoners' Dilemma more than once. We first look at fixed finite number of repeated interactions and then an infinite (or equivalently indefinite) number of repeated interactions.

11.1.1 The Finitely Repeated Prisoners' Dilemma

When the Prisoners' Dilemma (or any other game) is played repeatedly a finite number of times so that the parties will be interacting in an ongoing long-run relationship, the menu of possible strategies is widened. It would be possible, for example, for a player to choose Defect in each odd-numbered round and Cooperate in each even-numbered round. More interesting is the possibility of selecting a reactive or *contingent* strategy. That is, a player's choice of Cooperate or Defect in any particular round could be a function of the opponent's moves in previous rounds.

The issue here is whether, if the Prisoners' Dilemma game is repeated a large but finite number of times, a more cooperative strategy than playing Defect in every round might be attained as a Nash equilibrium outcome. One possible alternative is the contingent strategy known as Tit for Tat. A Tit for Tat player chooses Cooperate in the opening round and thereafter mirrors his opponent's previous move. Thus, a Tit for Tat player "punishes" an opponent who defects in any round, but in a measured way that leaves open the possibility of mutual return to a cooperative relationship.

Table 11.2. *Prisoners' Dilemma* (numerical example)

		Defect	Cooperate
		x_1^2	x_2^2
Defect	x_1^1	$0, 0$	$6, -4$
Cooperate	x_2^1	$-4, 6$	$2, 2$

We now ask whether Tit for Tat is a Nash equilibrium strategy – more precisely, whether the symmetrical strategy pair in which both players choose Tit for Tat is an Nash equilibrium. Recall that the game is played a finite number of times T. A player's actions in the last period T have no consequences beyond this period as there are no future games. Therefore, in period T each player does best by choosing action $x_1 =$ Defect, no matter what his opponent might do in this period or did in earlier periods. So in the final round it will always be more profitable to switch away from Tit for Tat. But then there is no way of rewarding cooperative play in round $T - 1$. Each player can foresee that no matter what happens in period $T - 1$, the period T dominant action for his opponent is to Defect. Therefore, as choices made in round T are not contingent on round $T - 1$ play, the players switch away from Tit for Tat in round $T - 1$ as well. Each player's dominant action in round $T - 1$ is also $x_1 =$ Defect. Moving one round back to $T - 2$, we see that choices made in round $T - 2$ have no impact on round $T - 1$ and round T play; each of the two players will play Defect in the last two rounds regardless of what happens in round $T - 2$. Therefore, it is a dominant action for each player to Defect in period $T - 2$. Arguing iteratively back through the periods, it follows that Tit for Tat is not an equilibrium strategy for any of the rounds.

In fact, we have proved more than this. The iterative argument against Tit for Tat applies to *any* alternative strategy that might be selected by either player. It follows that the unique Nash equilibrium strategy of the finitely repeated game is, after all, always to play Defect. Therefore, Nash equilibrium does not admit reputation building in the finitely repeated Prisoners' Dilemma game.[2]

11.1.2 The Infinitely Repeated Prisoners' Dilemma

The preceding argument depends critically on the existence of a final round of play. But what if the game is played for an infinite number of periods, i.e., if there is no final round? If so, in any period a Tit for Tat player should be able to reward an opponent's cooperation, or punish defection, in the next round. To see this, suppose that, while player 1 adopts Tit for Tat, player 2 has chosen another strategy in which he plays Cooperate until round t and then switches to Defect for one round only. Using the numbers of Table 11.2 we see that such a switch yields player 2 a net gain of 4 in period t (he receives

---

[2] In other games, it is possible to sustain outcomes other than the stage game Nash equilibria in finite repetitions of the stage game. See exercise 3 at the end of this section.

6 instead of 2) but a net loss of 6 in period $t + 1$ (he receives -4 instead of 2). Therefore, as long as the future is only mildly discounted, player 2 is worse off for his defection. And if he were to Defect for more than one period, while the very adverse payoff of -4 would be deferred, this would be at the cost of receiving payoffs of zero instead of 2 in the interim. Thus once again, so long as the future is only mildly discounted, player 2 does not gain by his defection.

In general, Tit for Tat is a Nash equilibrium for the payoffs of Table 11.1 if the future is only mildly discounted and

$$2f > e + h \qquad (11.1.1)$$

Inequality (11.1.1) ensures that the mutual cooperation achievable via Tit for Tat must exceed the average payoffs of alternately playing Defect against Cooperate and Cooperate against Defect.

How mild must the discount be? Let c_t^i be the round-t payoff to individual i. Let ρ be the per-period discount rate, and define the discount factor δ as:

$$\delta \equiv \frac{1}{1 + \rho}$$

Then, letting each player's utility U^i simply be the discounted sum of the payoffs:[3]

$$U_i = \sum_{t=1}^{\infty} \delta^{t-1} c_t^i \qquad (11.1.2)$$

Then the utility associated with mutual cooperation through Tit for Tat, in terms of the magnitudes in Table 11.1, is:

$$U_i = f + \delta f + \delta^2 f + \delta^3 f + \cdots = \frac{f}{1 - \delta}$$

We need only look at player 2's incentive to defect in the first round. Suppose he chooses x_1 (rather than x_2) in the first round, x_2 in the second and third rounds, and then reverts to Tit for Tat from the fourth round onwards. In response, player 1, who we assume sticks to Tit for Tat throughout, plays x_2 in round 1, and thereafter mimics in every round $t \geq 2$, player 2's choice

---

[3] The form of Equation (11.1.2) implies additive separability over time, and – since implicitly the utility function is $v_t(c_t) = c_t$ – risk neutrality at each moment of time as well. The second condition could be relaxed, however, simply by writing $v_t(c_t)$ in place of c_t on the right-hand side, so as to allow for the possibility of the individual being characterized by risk aversion or risk preference.

in round $t - 1$. Thus, player 1's action choices from round 2 onwards are $x_1, x_2, x_2, x_2, \ldots$ In terms of the magnitudes in Table 11.1, player 2's utility from this defection will be:

$$U_i = e + \delta h + \delta^2 f + \delta^3 f + \cdots = e + \delta h + \frac{\delta^2 f}{1 - \delta}$$

$$U_i = e + \delta h + \frac{\delta^2 f}{1 - \delta}$$

Thus the utility gain from defection is:

$$\Delta U_i = e + \delta h - \frac{f - \delta^2 f}{1 - \delta} = e + \delta h - (f + \delta f)$$

Evidently, ΔU_i will be negative if:

$$\delta > \frac{e - f}{f - h} \qquad (11.1.3)$$

Observe that the restriction, $2f > e + h$ of (11.1.1) is equivalent to $(e - f)/(f - h) < 1$, implying that there is a range of discount factors close to 1 for which ΔU_i is negative. For the payoffs in the example of Table 11.2, $(e - f)/(f - h)$ is $(6 - 2)/(2 + 4) = \frac{2}{3}$. A discount factor δ greater than $\frac{2}{3}$ corresponds to a discount rate ρ less than $\frac{1}{2}$. Thus, if the discount rate is no greater than 50%, Tit for Tat will be a Nash equilibrium for the infinitely repeated game with payoffs as in Table 11.2.

But one might well be hesitant about drawing practical conclusions from games that are (hypothetically) replayed an infinite number of rounds. A more believable situation, probably, is a game where in each round there is a fixed probability ω of continuation to another round of play. Then, evidently, all the results above will continue to hold allowing for both *time discount* and *probability discount*. The latter adjustment involves replacing δ everywhere above with $\delta\omega$. Thus:

$$\frac{1}{1 - \delta\omega} = 1 + \delta\omega + (\delta\omega)^2 + \cdots$$

Condition (11.1.3) for Tit for Tat to be a Nash equilibrium then becomes:

$$\delta\omega > \frac{e - f}{f - h}$$

In the numerical illustration, this means that the product of the discount and probability-discount factors would have to exceed $\frac{2}{3}$ for Tit for Tat to be a Nash equilibrium strategy.

Tit for Tat is just one of an infinity of possible schemes for penalizing an opponent who deviates from cooperative play. Another such, the "Grim" strategy, consists of initially playing Cooperate, but if any player defects, play Defect forever (Friedman, 1971).[4] Then the infinite stream of lower payoffs forevermore will outweigh any one-period gain from defection (from choosing x_1) if the discount factor is sufficiently close to unity. Moreover, once one individual is playing Grim, for the opponent Grim is a best response. So mutual choice of Grim is a Nash equilibrium. Along the equilibrium path, both players Cooperate. If, say, player 1 deviates, then player 2 is unforgiving and plays Defect forever. Thus, player 1's best response after a deviation to Defect is to Defect forever.

Of course, the Tit for Tat strategy is an equally good response to Grim, as is Grim to Tit for Tat. (In either case, the actual behavioral or payoff-relevant *moves* along the equilibrium path will be cooperation forever.) Thus not only are Tit for Tat and Grim both symmetrical Nash equilibria, but also there are asymmetrical Nash equilibria involving each of them played against the other. On the other hand, while the simple Cooperate strategy is also a best response to either Tit for Tat or Grim, it cannot form part of an asymmetrical Nash equilibrium when Defect is an available strategy. The reason is that Defect is strictly dominant against an opponent playing simple Cooperate.

The next section shows that cooperation can be sustained in the infinitely repeated Prisoners' Dilemma even if the equilibrium concept is strengthened to subgame perfection. However, Tit for Tat is not subgame perfect.

Exercises and Excursions 11.1

1 Talk Is Cheap

Suppose that, in the infinitely repeated 2×2 Prisoners' Dilemma, player 1 defaults and then finds that player 2 is responding with the Grim strategy. Player 1 pleads as follows: "We are both suffering from my brief moment of greed and your cussedness. I am now willing to demonstrate that I have reformed by playing Cooperate this period while you play Defect. After that

---

[4] The ancestral motto of one of the authors is "Never forget a friend, never forgive an enemy." No wonder the Grahams thrived! In contrast, Tit for Tat corresponds to the Old Testament "eye for an eye." Alas, there is little hope, on this earth, for those choosing the unconditional Cooperate strategy "turn the other cheek."

surely you should be willing to play Cooperate also?" If you were player 2, would you find this argument convincing?

2   *Grim versus Tit for Tat in Prisoners' Dilemma*
  (A) For the payoffs shown in Table 11.1, how high must the discount factor δ be for Grim to be a symmetric Nash equilibrium strategy yielding the cooperative-play outcome in the infinitely repeated game? Compare with the δ required for Tit for Tat to be a cooperative-play symmetric Nash equilibrium.
  (B) Suggest some other strategies that would yield a cooperative-play Nash equilibrium.

3   *Cooperation in a Finitely Repeated Game (Benoit and Krishna, 1985)*
Consider the following payoff matrix:

		Player 2		
		x_1^2	x_2^2	x_3^2
	x_1^1	5, 5	0, 0	0, 0
Player 1	x_2^1	10, 0	4, 4	0, 0
	x_3^1	0, 0	0, 0	2, 2

  (A) Confirm that there are two Nash equilibria of the one-shot game.
  (B) In the absence of any discounting, show that, if the game is played T times, where T is greater than 4, there is a Nash equilibrium of the repeated game in which cooperation takes place except during the last three rounds.

[HINT: Suppose players begin playing the Pareto-superior of the one-shot game. Player 2 has an incentive to propose "cooperation" with payoffs of (5, 5) even though player 1 has an incentive to cheat and play x_2^1. The reason is that player 2 can credibly threaten to switch forever to x_3^2 – leading, after player 1's best reply, to the Pareto-inferior Nash equilibrium with payoffs (2, 2). This will act as a disincentive as long as there are enough rounds of the game left to play.]

11.2 Subgame-Perfect Equilibria in Infinitely Repeated Games

It helps to make explicit what players know at each round of an infinitely repeated game. Restricting attention to two player games, we shall assume that at the end of each round, each player knows not only his own action choices in previous rounds but also the action choices by the other player in all previous rounds. (Think of the game in Table 11.1. If at the end of each round each player learns the utility he received in that round he can infer the action choice of his opponent in that round.) Now imagine the extensive form representation of an infinitely repeated simultaneous-move game. Because at each round players learn every action that was selected in the past, the end of round t (with a particular history h^t of actions choices) is a singleton node in this giant game tree. In other words, there is a subgame corresponding to each history of action choices. A subgame-perfect equilibrium requires that players' strategies be optimal at every subgame, including subgames that are not along the equilibrium path of play.

In Section 11.1.2 it was shown that Tit for Tat is a Nash equilibrium in the infinitely repeated Prisoners' Dilemma, provided the discount factor is close to one (see Equation 11.1.3). It turns out that it is not a subgame-perfect equilibrium for both players to play Tit for Tat. To show this, we need to find a subgame at which it is not optimal for at least one player to play Tit for Tat. Because, Tit for Tat is a Nash equilibrium, this subgame must lie off-the-equilibrium-path.

Suppose that both players are to play Tit for Tat, but player 2 departs from this strategy in round 1 and plays x_1 instead of x_2. If Tit for Tat is subgame perfect then it should be optimal for both payers to play Tit for Tat at the off-the-equilibrium-path subgame reached in round 2 after player 1 plays x_1 and player 2 plays x_2 in round 1. Tit for Tat calls for each player to mimic his opponent's choices in the preceding round. This generates outcomes (x_1, x_2) in round 2, (x_2, x_1) in round 3, (x_1, x_2) in round 4, (x_2, x_1) in round 5, etc. Player 1's utility from round 2 onwards is:

$$U_1 = \delta e + \delta^2 h + \delta^3 e + \delta^4 h + \cdots = \frac{\delta(e + \delta h)}{1 - \delta^2}$$

Consider the following deviation by player 1 at the off-the-equilibrium-path subgame starting in round 2 (after the deviation by player 2 in round 1). In round 2, instead of mimicking player 2's choice of x_1 in round 1, player 1 chooses x_2. Player 2 sticks to Tit for Tat from round 2 onwards, and player 1 sticks to Tit for Tat after round 3 onwards. That is, after player 2's initial deviation in round 1, player 1 deviates from Tit for Tat by not mimicking player 2's round 1 play in round 2. This deviation by player 1 in round 2 will generate outcome (x_2, x_2) in round 2 and in every round thereafter. Player 1's utility from round 2 onwards is:

$$U_1 = \delta f + \delta^2 f + \delta^3 f + \delta^4 f + \cdots = \frac{\delta f}{1 - \delta} = \frac{\delta(f + \delta f)}{1 - \delta^2}$$

The utility gain to player 1 from this defection (at the off-the-equilibrium-path subgame reached after player 2's defection in round 1) is:

$$\Delta U_1 = \delta(f + \delta f - e - \delta h)/(1 - \delta^2)$$

This utility gain is positive as long as $f - e > \delta(f - h)$. But condition (11.1.1) that $2f > e + h$ implies $f - e > f - h > \delta(f - h)$. Therefore, it is not optimal for player 1 to play Tit for Tat at the subgame reached after a defection by player 2 in round 1. In other words, it is not optimal for a player to follow through on the threat implicit in the Tit for Tat strategy. Thus, mutual play of Tit for Tat is not a subgame-perfect equilibrium.

Nevertheless, cooperation can be sustained as a subgame-perfect equilibrium. Both players playing the Grim strategy is a subgame-perfect equilibrium. Recall that the Grim strategy starts out with both players playing Cooperate. If at any round a player deviates and plays Defect, then both players play Defect forever thereafter. Thus, being the first to deviate from Cooperate is never optimal.

To verify that Grim is subgame perfect would appear to be an impossibly difficult task. There are innumerable subgames in an infinitely repeated Prisoners' Dilemma, and one would need to verify that at each subgame deviations are unprofitable. However, a result from dynamic programming greatly simplifies the task of checking the subgame perfection of a strategy. One need consider only those subgames that are reached after deviating at most once from the purported subgame-perfect strategy.

A strategy $\hat{\sigma}$ is a *one-shot deviation* from another strategy σ if $\hat{\sigma}$ differs from σ at exactly one history. Let $\sigma|_{h^t}$ be the continuation of σ after history h^t; $\hat{\sigma}|_{h^t}$ is similarly defined. Then $\hat{\sigma}$ is a one-shot deviation of σ if the two strategies differ after only one history, say, $\hat{h}^t$. That is, $\hat{\sigma}|_{h^t} = \sigma|_{h^t}$ for all $h^t \neq \hat{h}^t$.

If σ is a subgame-perfect best response to a strategy by the opponent, there should no one-shot deviations from σ that yield a higher utility. In verifying that mutual play of Tit for Tat is not subgame perfect, we showed a one-shot deviation from Tit for Tat that yielded greater utility for player 1. This one-shot deviation had player 1 Cooperate (rather than Defect) in round 2 after a Defect by player 2 in round one; in this deviation, player 1's strategy remained Tit for Tat at all other subgames. As this Tit for Tat example makes clear, because players' strategies depend on the history, a one-shot deviation at a particular history can lead to a different set of outcomes at each subsequent history.

The importance of the next result is that it is sufficient (and not just necessary) for subgame perfection that there be no one-shot deviations that improve utility:

The one-shot deviation principle:[5] Player i's strategy profile σ_i is a subgame perfect best response to strategy σ_j of the opponent if there are no one-shot deviations to σ_i that increase player i's utility against σ_j.

We use this principle to verify that mutual choice of Grim is a subgame-perfect equilibrium. There are no profitable deviations along the equilibrium path (that is, as long as both players have played Cooperate in every previous round) as (Grim, Grim) is a Nash equilibrium. Consider an off-the-equilibrium-path history h^t. As h^t is not along the equilibrium path, at least one player has played Defect at least once in the past. The Grim strategy calls for player 2 to play Defect forever at every subsequent history. The only best response for player 1 is to play Defect at h^t. The one-shot deviation principle implies that (Grim, Grim) is a subgame-perfect equilibrium.

While a restriction to subgame perfection eliminates some Nash equilibria in the infinitely repeated Prisoners' Dilemma, such as mutual choice of Tit for Tat, it does not reduce the set of utility outcomes that can be supported in equilibrium. Players can agree to any sequence of choices that yields them a payoff strictly greater than they would obtain from playing Defect forever. The agreement is sustained by switching to the Grim strategy if there is a deviation from the agreement. In the next section, we investigate this type of construction of subgame-perfect equilibria in the context of Cournot duopoly games.

Exercises and Excursions 11.2

1 Less than Grim Strategy
In the infinitely repeated Prisoners' Dilemma, the Grim strategy is unforgiving, and the Tit for Tat strategy is not subgame perfect. We will establish that the following strategy, which is more forgiving than Grim, is subgame perfect. While playing this strategy, the play can be in one of two states, COOP or PUNISH, as described below.

---

[5] See Mailath and Samuelson (2006) for a proof.

COOP   Player i plays Cooperate. Play starts in state COOP. In any subse-
          quent round the state is COOP if the state in the previous round was
          COOP, and both players played Cooperate in the previous round.
PUNISH In the event of any deviation from (Cooperate, Cooperate) while
          in COOP, the state in the next round becomes PUNISH and play
          remains PUNISH for τ periods. During PUNISH, both players play
          Defect. If there are any deviations from (Defect, Defect) while
          in state PUNISH, then begin state PUNISH again with τ periods
          (Defect, Defect) to follow. At the end of state PUNISH, return to
          state COOP.[6]

Answer the following for the payoffs in Table 11.2, with $\tau = 5$ and the
discount factor $\delta = 0.8$.

(A) Show that the above strategy is a Nash equilibrium in the infinitely
    repeated game.
(B) Show that the above strategy is a subgame-perfect equilibrium in the
    infinitely repeated game.
(C) Is this strategy subgame perfect if the discount factor is greater than
    0.8 (but less than 1)? What is smallest discount factor for which the
    above strategy is subgame perfect?
(D) If $\tau = 4$, how does the range of discount factors for which this
    strategy is subgame-perfect change?

[HINT: In answering parts (C) and (D), quintic and quartic equations in
δ have to solved. It may be best to program a spreadsheet and use trial
and error.]

(E) Are these strategies subgame perfect for any discount factor if $\tau = 1$
    or 2?

11.3 The Folk Theorem for Infinitely Repeated Games

We have established that in a Prisoners' Dilemma the set of payoffs that can
be sustained in a subgame-perfect equilibrium expands dramatically when
one goes from a single play of the game to infinite repetitions. We prove a
similar result – called a folk theorem – for a Cournot duopoly.[7]

---

[6] If $\tau = \infty$, then we have the Grim strategy with no possibility of a return to COOP once
    play reaches state PUNISH.
[7] The analysis here follows Fudenberg, Levine, and Maskin (1986). The expression "folk
    theorem" is used since it is not clear who proved what first.

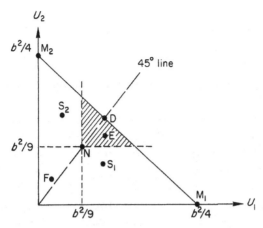

Figure 11.1. Payoffs in the one-shot duopoly game.

Consider a simple Cournot duopoly model. Two firms, each with constant marginal cost c, face a linear demand curve for their common product:

$$p = a - q_1 - q_2$$

Firm i's profit is therefore:

$$U_i = (b - q_1 - q_2)q_i \quad \text{where } b \equiv a - c$$

In the single-round game, the unique Nash equilibrium (the "Nash-Cournot solution") is for each player to choose $q_i = b/3$. The resulting profits are:

$$U_1^N = U_2^N = b^2/9$$

Firm i's profit is maximized when the opponent does not produce at all. The profit-maximizing output is $b/2$ and the resulting monopoly profit is $U_i^M = b^2/4$. Finally, if firm 1 is a Stackelberg leader and firm 2 chooses its best response given q_1, the profit levels are:

$$(U_1^S, U_2^S) = (b^2/8, b^2/16)$$

The per period profit levels of the two firms under monopoly (M_i), Nash-Cournot (N), and Stackelberg play (S_i) are depicted in Figure 11.1. The entire set of feasible profit levels is the region bounded by the axes and the line $M_1 M_2$. To see why this must be the case, note that joint profit can be written:

$$U_1 + U_2 = (b - q_1 - q_2)(q_1 + q_2)$$

Then joint profit is maximized with total output equal to the monopoly output $q^M = b/2$. Profit shares are then equal to output shares.

Consider point D on the 45° line. Output for each firm is $q^M/2 = b/4$ and profit is $b^2/8$. D is one possible outcome of "cooperative" play, to wit, where the firms split the monopoly output and profit equally. Arguing just as in the previous section, D can be attained under a number of different symmetrical or asymmetrical pairs of strategies – Nash equilibria of the infinitely repeated game when the discount factor is sufficiently close to unity. One such is again the Grim strategy: switching to non-cooperative play (e.g., producing an output larger than $b/4$) *forever*, if an opponent ever deviates from his cooperative output level.

Once again, it turns out that cooperative outcomes can be supported by readiness to engage in non-cooperative behavior. But this does not tell us what the outcome will be. First of all, the single-round Nash-Cournot solution is also a Nash equilibrium of the infinitely repeated game. But, more important, *any* outcome that is Pareto superior to the single-round Nash-Cournot solution can be supported by Nash equilibrium strategy pairs in the infinitely repeated game. Consider point E to the north-east of N in Figure 11.1, with associated output levels q_1^E and q_2^E Arguing just as above, if each player adopts the Grim strategy of responding to any deviation by switching to the Nash-Cournot strategy, then neither player will want to deviate.

All the points in the shaded region of Figure 11.1 are therefore Nash equilibria of the infinitely repeated game, as long as the discount factor is sufficiently close to unity. However, it will now be shown, the complete set of such equilibria will generally be much larger.

The intuition is fairly straightforward. Suppose that players 1 and 2 are currently playing q_1 and q_2. Suppose also that player 1 has available an alternative strategy q_1^* that would make his opponent strictly worse off, regardless of her response. Then player 1 can threaten to switch for a long time to q_1^* if player 2 deviates from q_2. As long as the future is discounted sufficiently mildly, carrying out such a threat would make agent 2 strictly worse off. Therefore, it effectively deters player 2 from any deviation. If player 2 also has an effective threat q_2^*, then q_1 and q_2 are equilibrium strategies of the infinitely repeated game.

The effective threats or alternative strategies q_1^* and q_2^* that are typically used in constructing equilibria in infinitely repeated games are the *minimax* strategies of the players. Let q_i^* be the minimax strategy of player i in the Cournot duopoly game. For player 1, this is the strategy that minimizes player 2's payoff, given that player 2 is choosing her payoff-maximizing response to player 1's strategy. Formally, q_1^* solves:

$$\underset{q_1}{\text{Min}} \, \underset{q_2}{\text{Max}} \, U_2(q_1, q_2)$$

Similarly, q_2^* solves:

$$\underset{q_2}{\text{Min}} \, \underset{q_1}{\text{Max}} \, U_1(q_1, q_2)$$

Let U_i^* be the payoff of player i, given that his opponent has adopted her minimax strategy. Intuitively, no matter what action player j chooses player i has a best response to it that guarantees him at least U_i^*; the smallest payoff that player j can hold player i to is U_i^*. It turns out that any payoff vector (U_1, U_2) that is strictly preferred over (U_1^*, U_2^*) is a subgame-perfect equilibrium when the discount factor is sufficiently large.[8]

For the duopoly example, firm 1's minimax strategy is to "saturate the market" – choosing an output q_1^* such that $p = a - q_1^* = c$. That is, price is driven down to marginal cost, even in the absence of sales by firm 2. Then firm 2's best response is to choose $q_2 = 0$, with resulting profit of zero for each of them. Since the same holds for firm 2, $(U_1^*, U_2^*) = (0, 0)$. So all the points in Figure 11.1 northeast of the origin and within the region bounded by $M_1 \, M_2$ can be equilibria of the infinitely repeated game. This therefore includes the Stackelberg outcomes as well as outcomes such as F that are Pareto-inferior to the single-round Nash-Cournot outcome N.

Consider some output pair (q_1, q_2) and associated profit levels $(U_1, U_2) > (U_1^*, U_2^*)$, that is, an output pair such that both U_1 and U_2 are strictly positive. Let U_i^0 be the profit to firm i if *both* firms choose their minimax strategies. Since price is equal to marginal cost when one firm produces $q_1^* = b$ units, the profit U_i^0 when both firms produce b units is strictly less than zero.

We now sketch a proof of the following result.

Folk Theorem

Let (U_1, U_2) be any feasible payoff vector strictly preferred over the minimax payoff vector (U_1^*, U_2^*). Let x^1 and x^2 be the strategies in the single-round game that generate the payoffs U_1 and U_2. Then, if discounting is sufficiently mild, there exists a number τ such that the following strategy, when played by both players, is a subgame-perfect equilibrium.

---

[8] In the Prisoners' Dilemma, each player's minimax strategy is to Defect, which is also the dominant strategy in that game.

(A) Player i plays x^i as long as (x^1, x^2) was played last period.
(B) In the event of any deviation from (A), both play the minimax strategy for τ periods and then start again with (A).
(C) If there are any deviations while in phase (B), player i begins phase (B) again.

To understand this result, first note that, with both firms playing their minimax strategies, payoffs are negative. Phase (B) therefore imposes a punishment upon any player who deviates. The basic idea is to design a scheme with a punishment phase sufficiently long to deter any deviations but not so long as to yield either player a negative present value. During phase (B), each firm gets U_i^0, the negative payoff obtained when both firms play their minimax strategies. Therefore, firm i's present value at the start of phase (B) is:

$$PV_i(B) = \sum_{t=0}^{\tau-1} \delta^t U_i^0 + \sum_{t=\tau}^{\infty} \delta^t U_i = \frac{1 - \delta^\tau}{1 - \delta} U_i^0 + \frac{\delta^\tau}{1 - \delta} U_i \qquad (11.2.1)$$

Now define:

$$\hat{U}_i \equiv (1 - \delta^\tau) U_i^0 + \delta^\tau U_i \qquad (11.2.2)$$

From (11.2.1) and (11.2.2):

$$PV_i(B) = \frac{\hat{U}_i}{1 - \delta} = \sum_{t=0}^{\infty} \delta^t \hat{U}_i$$

That is, $\hat{U}_i$ is the steady-state equivalent of the per-period payoff at the start of the punishment phase. From (11.2.2), for each δ sufficiently close to unity, τ can be chosen so that $\hat{U}_i$ satisfies $0 < \hat{U}_i < U_i/2$, $i = 1, 2$.

Suppose, then, that a player has deviated and the punishment phase is underway. For this phase of the strategy to be a Nash equilibrium of the associated subgame, any deviation must make the deviator no better off. Since his opponent is playing her minimax strategy, the most that agent i can obtain immediately, if he deviates, is zero. But then his opponent begins phase (B) again and the best response to phase (B) yields $\hat{U}_i/(1-\delta)$. The net present value of any further deviation is therefore at most $\delta \hat{U}_i/(1-\delta)$. But, by not deviating, agent i achieves a present value of $\hat{U}_i/(1-\delta)$. It follows that the punishment phase strategies are best responses to one another.

It remains to show that neither agent has an incentive to make an initial deviation. Let $\bar{U}_i$ be the maximum possible one-period payoff from a deviation by agent i. The present value of any deviation is therefore bounded from above by:

$$\bar{U}_i + \frac{\delta}{1-\delta}\hat{U}_i = \frac{1}{1-\delta}\left[(1-\delta)\,\bar{U}_i + \delta\hat{U}_i\right]$$

But, by construction $\hat{U}_i < U_i/2$. Therefore, for δ sufficiently large the expression in brackets is strictly less than U_i:

$$(1-\delta)\bar{U}_i + \delta\hat{U}_i < (1-\delta)\bar{U}_i + \frac{U_i}{2} < U_i$$

It follows that:

$$\bar{U}_i + \frac{\delta}{1-\delta}\hat{U}_i < \frac{U_i}{1-\delta}$$

The deviation therefore leaves agent i strictly worse off.

With more than two players, the strategies required to sustain outcomes other than the Cournot solution of the single-period game are slightly more complicated. But essentially the same conclusion continues to hold. As long as the discount factor is sufficiently close to unity, any payoff vector in the interior of the set of payoffs that Pareto dominates the minimax payoff vector can be achieved as a subgame-perfect equilibrium.

In this section we proved the folk theorem for infinitely repeated Cournot duopoly. This type of result applies to a variety of games, including the Prisoners' Dilemma. For general n player games, a folk theorem gives conditions on the payoffs of the game under which the following is true. Let $v = (v_1, v_2, \ldots, v_n)$ be a vector of payoffs such that player i's payoff v_i is strictly greater than i's minimax payoff. Then there is a $\delta(v) < 1$ such that if the players' discount factor δ exceeds $\delta(v)$, there exists a subgame-perfect equilibrium in the infinitely repeated game that yields the players payoffs $v/(1-\delta)$. The conditions under which a folk theorem holds are mild. Usually, there is a continuum subgame-perfect equilibria in an infinitely repeated game.

In the models we have considered, at the beginning of each stage each player knows the history of actions of all players. This is the assumption of *perfect monitoring*. More plausibly, each player is imperfectly informed about other players' action choices. For instance, it is more realistic that in the repeated duopoly model prices depend stochastically on total output, in which case player i cannot know player j's history of outputs after observing past prices. Repeated games with *imperfect monitoring* have been investigated over the last 20 years. In this literature, instead of observing others' actions, players observe a signal that depends stochastically on others' actions. If the signal is public – that is, observed by all players – and the set of possible signal realizations is large, then a version of folk theorem holds. If, instead, players observe private signals about others' actions the analysis is considerably more complicated and a subject of ongoing research. See Kandori (2008) for an overview.

Exercises and Excursions 11.3

1 Large Numbers in the Infinitely Repeated Game
In the formal theory, cooperative outcomes can be achieved via a Nash equilibrium no matter how many players participate. What assumptions, if any, make the model and such equilibria less plausible for large n?

2 Cournot Duopoly
(A) For the example discussed above, suppose $a = 14$ and $c = 2$. Each firm has a capacity of 12 units per period. For what discount factors δ is the symmetric outcome that maximizes total profits achievable as a Nash equilibrium?

(B) Suppose δ is the smallest discount factor for which the symmetric outcome that maximizes total profits is achievable. What other outcomes that maximize total profits are achievable?

(C) What does your answer to (B) suggest about the effect of a lower δ upon the set of achievable outcomes?

3 Cournot Oligopoly
Suppose there are N firms with constant marginal costs $c_1, c_2, \ldots, c_N$ such that $c_1 \le c_2 \le \cdots \le c_N$. They face a demand curve:

$$p = p\left(\sum_{i=1}^{N} q_i\right) = a - \sum_{i=1}^{N} q_i$$

(A) Show that, with $N = 2$, the strategies characterized in section 11.3 continue to be Nash equilibria.

(B) In the symmetric case with $c_1 = c_2 = \cdots = c_N$ the analysis of section 11.3 is easily generalized. Confirm that this is so.

(C) Can the analysis be extended to N firms whose costs are different?

Table 11.3. *Prisoners' Dilemma*
$(\alpha > \gamma > 0 > \beta)$

		Player 2	
		x_1^2	x_2^2
Player 1	x_1^1	0, 0	α, β
	x_2^1	β, α	γ, γ

11.4 The Role of Chivalry

The results of the previous sections suggest that cooperative outcomes are much more difficult to achieve for finitely as opposed to infinitely repeated games. However, up till now in this chapter it has been assumed that all players know the payoffs of their opponents and also know that all players adopt individually rational strategies.

It turns out that cooperation can be promoted if there is some uncertainty, to wit, a small possibility that an opponent is chivalrous and will always cooperate.[9]

Consider the Prisoners' Dilemma example once more, with payoffs as indicated in Table 11.3. (In this table, the payoffs for (Defect, Defect) are normalized to zero to economize on the notation.)

As before, the unique single-round Nash equilibrium is for each player to choose Defect, x_1. And, once again, the sole Nash equilibrium is where x_1 is played in each of finitely many rounds. Observe that if both players had a way to simultaneously commit to Cooperate, i.e., to play x_2, then each player would be better off. We show that a small amount of uncertainty about each player's payoff provides such a mechanism.

Suppose that a fraction ε of the underlying population are chivalrous (or perhaps, stupid) and will irrationally play the cooperative strategy x_2 up to and including the final round T, so long as the opponent also plays Cooperate. However, if a chivalrous individual finds that his opponent has deviated in some period, he responds as in Grim, playing x_1 thereafter.

There is, therefore, probability ε that an individual is matched with a chivalrous opponent for T rounds of Prisoners' Dilemma play. In these circumstances, it will be shown, for any ε there exists a τ such that it is an equilibrium for all players to cooperate as long as there are more than τ periods left to play.

---

[9] For our purposes, it does not matter whether "chivalry" is pursued through stupidity, or because it is believed to be morally superior, or because the chivalrous player has payoffs for which cooperation is a dominant strategy.

With imperfect information, it is necessary to take account of the players' beliefs about types if a deviation occurs in the game (that is, if an out-of-equilibrium strategy is played). Suppose that no individual believes that a chivalrous player would ever deviate, without provocation, from the cooperative equilibrium.

Assume first that player 1 is fully rational. Once he comes to believe that his opponent is not chivalrous, the argument of Section 11.1.1 applies. That is, his best reply is to play x_1 (Defect) thereafter. Moreover, by hypothesis, a chivalrous player responds to deviation from Cooperate in this way also. Suppose there has been cooperation for the first $T - \tau$ periods. If player 1 deviates with τ periods remaining, an upper bound to his payoff over the τ periods is just the immediate-period payoff α. In all future periods, his opponent plays x_1, and so the payoff is zero.

Next, suppose that player 1, although he is rational, in effect mimics the chivalrous strategy. That is, with τ periods remaining he plays x_2 and continues to do so until a deviation occurs, in which case he shifts irrevocably to x_1. With probability ε his opponent is chivalrous. In this case, if player 1 always plays x_2, then so does his chivalrous opponent.[10] The present value of player 1's payoff over the last τ periods would then be:

$$\gamma (1 + \delta + \cdots + \delta^{\tau-1})$$

But with probability $(1 - \varepsilon)$, player 1's opponent is not chivalrous. If so, for player 1 the worst possible situation is for his opponent to play x_1 in all future rounds. Then player 1 has an immediate payoff of $\beta < 0$ and zero thereafter. It follows that player 1's expected payoff from mimicking the chivalrous strategy is bounded from below by:

$$\varepsilon \gamma (1 + \delta + \delta^2 + \cdots + \delta^{\tau-1}) + (1 - \varepsilon)\beta$$

Since the payoff to deviating is α, cooperation is optimal as long as:

$$\varepsilon \gamma [1 + \delta + \cdots + \delta^{\tau-1}] + (1 - \varepsilon)\beta > \alpha$$

Rearranging, cooperation is optimal as long as:

$$1 + \delta + \delta^2 \cdots + \delta^{\tau-1} = \frac{1 - \delta^\tau}{1 - \delta} > \frac{\alpha - \beta}{\gamma \varepsilon} + \frac{\beta}{\gamma} \qquad (11.4.1)$$

---

[10] This is a feasible rather than an optimal strategy for player 1 since he can always do better by deviating in the final round.

As τ becomes large, the left-hand side approaches $1/(1-\delta)$. Therefore, inequality (11.4.1) necessarily holds, for sufficiently large τ, if:

$$\frac{1}{1-\delta} > \frac{\alpha - \beta}{\gamma \varepsilon} + \frac{\beta}{\gamma}$$

So cooperation is individually rational for non-chivalrous players during the early rounds of a game, as long as the future is discounted sufficiently mildly and the number of rounds is sufficiently great.

If the overall time period involved is short enough so that discounting can be ignored, then inserting $\delta = 1$ in the expression on the left of the equal sign in (11.4.1) we have:

$$\tau > \frac{\alpha - \beta}{\gamma \varepsilon} + \frac{\beta}{\gamma}$$

It then follows that, no matter how small the proportion of chivalrous players in the underlying population, cooperation is achievable as an equilibrium outcome in all but a fixed number of rounds at the end of the game. Therefore, as the total number of rounds T becomes large, the *proportion* of periods in which cooperation is achievable approaches unity.

While only a simple example has been examined, the point is quite general. That is, for any game in which there are outcomes that strictly Pareto-dominate single-period Nash equilibria, such outcomes are achievable except near the end of a finitely repeated game as long as there is a positive probability that players are chivalrous. A striking point is the potentially large social payoff for a small amount of chivalrous (altruistic) behavior. While we cannot pursue the idea further here, this raises intriguing questions about the evolution of altruism.

Exercises and Excursions 11.4

1 Cooperation with N Players
  (A) For the finitely repeated Prisoners' Dilemma, extend the analysis to the N-person case.
  (B) Holding other parameters fixed, does adding players lengthen or shorten the initial period of cooperation?

2 Cournot Duopoly in a Finitely Repeated Game
For the duopoly model of Section 11.3, assume there is no discounting and that the game will be played a finite number of times. Show that any payoff vector that Pareto dominates the payoffs in the single-period Nash

Table 11.4. *Chain store game*

		Potential entrant	
		Enter	Out
Chain store	Match	1, 2	4, 0
	Undercut	0, −1	3, 0

equilibrium is achievable except near the end of the game, if there is a positive probability that one of the participants is "chivalrous" in an appropriately defined sense.

11.5 Building a Reputation[11]

The previous sections considered long-term or repeated interactions among two or more decision makers. Here we examine situations in which one party is a long-run player while the identity of the opponent or opponents changes. An example might be a retail store (the long-run player) dealing with transient customers (short-run players). Another example, much analyzed in the literature, is the interaction between a firm operating in a large number of markets (the long-run player) and potential entrants, each in one specific market (short-run player).

In each case, the crucial distinction is that a short-run player makes a single decision while the long-run player makes a sequence of decisions. The issue addressed is how decisions by the long-run player influence the beliefs of short-run players in later rounds and thus affect the outcome of the game.

What follows is a variant of the "chain store" game (Selten, 1977), which is an extension of the entry game of Chapter 7. The chain store operates in n markets. In each of n periods there is an entry threat in one of these markets. The potential entrant must choose whether to enter or stay out. Simultaneously, the chain store prepares a pricing response in case entry occurs, the choices being to acquiesce, matching the entrant's price, or to fight by undercutting.

Suppose payoffs are as in Table 11.4.[12] The chain store's best response, if the potential entrant chooses Enter, is Match. Moreover, given that the

---

[11] The initial papers on this topic are Kreps and Wilson (1982) and Milgrom and Roberts (1982). Fudenberg and Levine (1989) have simplified and generalized the early results.

[12] While not numerically identical, these payoffs are qualitatively similar to those in Table 7.5 except in one respect. Where the earlier chapter had the incumbent's payoff remain the same as between (Match, Out) and (Undercut, Out), here the chain store is better off

chain store chooses Match the potential entrant's best response is Enter. The pair (Match, Enter) is therefore a Nash equilibrium when the game is played only once. Indeed, it is the unique Nash equilibrium.[13]

Now consider the game from the point of view of the chain store. At the (Match, Enter) Nash equilibrium, the chain store's payoff is 1. If it could establish a reputation for toughness by fighting early entrants, later ones might be discouraged. If so, a payoff higher than the Nash equilibrium payoff of 1 would be possible. However, just as in Section 11.1.1, the argument breaks down in the final stage. As there are no future entrants following her, the last entrant need not fear that the chain store will play tough to build a reputation. That is, the threat of choosing Undercut is no longer credible. As a result the last-stage equilibrium strategy pair is (Match, Enter).

But then the same argument can be applied to the penultimate stage and so on. This is the "chain store paradox." Despite a potentially large long-run payoff, the chain store is unable to build a reputation for toughness.

But this negative conclusion is not robust with respect to small changes in the model. In particular, dramatically different results can emerge if there is imperfect information about the payoffs of the long-run player. Specifically, suppose that with positive probability the long-run player has a payoff matrix for which Undercut is his weakly dominant strategy (in the stage game).[14] Given that entrants are uncertain about the long-run player's payoffs, the long-run player, regardless of his actual payoffs, should choose the strategy Undercut. For then, with each round of play, short-run players will apply Bayes' Theorem and revise upward their assessment of the probability that the long-run players does have Undercut as his dominant strategy. As will be seen, this probability rises at least geometrically each time there is an entry. From this it follows that the probability reaches unity after the number of entries has reached some bound $\bar{m}$, independent of the length of the game. For most of a sufficiently long game, therefore, the mimicking strategy deters entry.

Specifically, suppose there is a positive probability that the chain store's technology yields the payoff matrix of Table 11.5. For this "strong" chain store, Undercut is the dominant strategy of the n-period game. Clearly, if a

---

under (Match, Out) than (Undercut, Out). The explanation is that we are assuming here that *preparing* to fight a potential entrant is costly even if entry does not actually take place.

[13] Recall that in Chapter 7 the alternative Nash equilibrium (Undercut, Out) was not a sequential equilibrium. That alternative non-credible Nash equilibrium has been eliminated here by adjusting the payoffs (see previous footnote).

[14] Actually, all we require is that Undercut be the unique sequential equilibrium strategy of the repeated game.

Table 11.5. *Payoff matrix with a "strong"*
long-run player

		Potential entrant	
		Enter	Out
Chain store	Match	1, 2	4, 0
	Undercut	2, −1	4, 0

potential entrant knows for sure that she is up against a strong chain store, her best reply is to choose Out. Moreover, as long as the probability that the chain store is strong is sufficiently high, Out remains the best reply.

Let ε be the entrants' prior probability that the chain store is strong (with the payoffs of Table 11.5) and $1 - \varepsilon$ the probability that it is weak (with the payoffs of Table 11.4). For ε sufficiently close to 1, a potential entrant will always choose Out since she is almost sure to find the chain store playing Undercut. Let $\bar{\pi}$ be the borderline probability such that, for all $\varepsilon > \bar{\pi}$, a potential entrant will choose Out regardless of the strategy chosen by a "weak" chain store.

In terms of our numerical example, if a weak chain store also were to choose Undercut, a potential entrant will always choose Out. If the weak chain store chooses Match but the probability of a strong chain store is $\bar{\pi}$, the expected payoff to Enter is:

$$\bar{\pi}\,(-1) + (1 - \bar{\pi})\,(2) = 2 - 3\bar{\pi}$$

Since the payoff to Out is zero, in our example the potential entrant's best choice is Out for all $\varepsilon > \bar{\pi} = \frac{2}{3}$.

Now, if the first potential entrant's prior probability that the chain store is strong exceeds $\frac{2}{3}$, she will choose Out rather than Enter. If so, lacking information for updating his prior beliefs, the second potential entrant will choose Out also, and so on.

Alternatively, now suppose that the prior probability belief of potential entrants is that ε is less than $\frac{2}{3}$, so there could be at least one initial entrant. We know that a weak chain store's short-run equilibrium strategy is to choose Match. However, suppose that it chooses to disguise this fact and chooses Undercut over t initial periods. Then potential entrants will employ Bayes' Theorem to update their estimate of the probability that the chain store is strong.

Let x_{2t} be the action taken by the entrant in round t and let the vector x_{1t} be the chain store's planned responses to each of the entrant's possible actions. Then $x_t = (x_{1t}, x_{2t})$ completely describes the play of the game in round t. Also, let $X^{t-1} = (x_1, x_2, x_3, \ldots, x_{t-1})$ be the complete history of the play of the game prior to round t. To simplify the discussion, we assume that X^{t-1} is observable in round t. That is, the chain store's planned responses – even if not actually executed – are observable immediately after a round is played.[15] (Thus, even if entry did not occur, the chain store's *intention* to undercut in response to entry might have involved some visible preparation, for example, printing new price lists.)

As Fudenberg and Levine (1989) have observed, there is a simple rule for updating entrants' beliefs about the chain store's type. First, if the history X^{t-1} contains a match then because the strong chain store always chooses Undercut ($x_{1t} = U$ for all t) we can conclude that the chain store is weak. That is, the conditional probability that the chain store is strong is zero, $\Pr(S|X^{t-1}) = 0$, if the history X^{t-1} contains a Match. Consider then a history X^{t-1} that contains no matches, that is, $x_{1\tau} = U$, $\tau = 1, \ldots, t-1$. Applying Bayes' Theorem:

$$\Pr(S|x_{1t} = U, x_{2t}, X^{t-1}) = \frac{\Pr(S, x_{1t} = U|x_{2t}, X^{t-1})}{\Pr(x_{1t} = U|x_{2t}, X^{t-1})} \qquad (11.5.1)$$

Since $x_{1t} = U$ for a strong chain store:

$$\Pr(S, x_{1t} = U|x_{2t}, X^{t-1}) = \Pr(S|x_{2t}, X^{t-1}) \qquad (11.5.2)$$

Moreover, since the entrant knows the history of the game but not the chain store type, the entrant's strategy can be expressed as:

$$x_{2t} = f(X^{t-1}) \qquad (11.5.3)$$

Substituting (11.5.2) and (11.5.3) into (11.5.1):

$$\Pr(S|x_{1t} = U, x_{2t}, X^{t-1}) = \frac{\Pr(S|X^{t-1})}{\Pr(x_{1t} = U|X^{t-1})}$$

Therefore, for any history X^t that contains no matches:

$$\Pr(S|X^t) = \frac{\Pr(S|X^{t-1})}{\Pr(x_{1t} = U|X^{t-1})}$$

It is this relationship that drives the results. First of all, since the denominator is a probability:

$$\Pr(S|X^t) \geq \Pr(S|X^{t-1})$$

---

[15] An exercise at the end of this section extends the analysis to the case where the chain store's planned action is only observable if entry takes place. The analysis is essentially identical.

Second, as already argued, there is some $\bar{\pi} < 1$ such that entry will only take place if:

$$\Pr(x_{1t} = U|X^{t-1}) \leq \bar{\pi}$$

Therefore, for any round in which there is entry (along an equilibrium path):

$$\Pr(S|X^t) \geq \left(\frac{1}{\bar{\pi}}\right) \Pr(S|X^{t-1})$$

Since the initial probability of a strong chain store is ε, if there are m periods of entry then, in any subsequent round t:

$$\Pr(S|X^t) = \frac{\Pr(S|X^t)\,\Pr(S|X^{t-1})}{\Pr(S|X^{t-1})\,\Pr(S|X^{t-2})} \cdots \frac{\Pr(S|X^1)}{\Pr(S|X^0)}\varepsilon$$

$$\geq \left(\frac{1}{\bar{\pi}}\right)^m \varepsilon$$

Let $\bar{m}$ be the largest integer such that $(1/\bar{\pi})^{\bar{m}}\varepsilon \leq 1$, that is, $\bar{m}$ satisfies:

$$\frac{\ln \varepsilon}{\ln \bar{\pi}} - 1 < \bar{m} \leq \frac{\ln \varepsilon}{\ln \bar{\pi}} \tag{11.5.4}$$

Then, if there were more than $\bar{m}$ entries in the first t rounds:

$$\Pr(S|X^t) > 1$$

which is impossible. Therefore, there will be at most $\bar{m}$ rounds in which beliefs by the potential entrant will be such as to stimulate entry, along any equilibrium path.

What has been established is that a weak chain store prepared to fight over the early phase of the game will face at most $\bar{m}$ actual entrants. Such a chain store therefore has, in the numerical example, payoff 0 in at most $\bar{m}$ periods and payoff 3 in the remaining $n - \bar{m}$ periods. Taking the worst-case scenario in which entry occurs in the first $\bar{m}$ rounds, the present value for a weak chain store of mimicking a strong one is bounded from below by:

$$PV^0 = (1 + \delta + \cdots + \delta^{\bar{m}-1})(0) + (\delta^{\bar{m}} + \delta^{\bar{m}+1} + \cdots + \delta^{n-1})(3)$$

$$\equiv \hat{\alpha}\left(\frac{1 - \delta^n}{1 - \delta}\right)$$

where:

$$\hat{\alpha} \equiv 3\delta^{\bar{m}}\frac{1 - \delta^{n-\bar{m}}}{1 - \delta^n} \tag{11.5.5}$$

Table 11.6. *Lower bound to mimicking*

Number of periods, n	Single-period bound, $\hat{\alpha}_n$
48	0.9
54	1.0
60	1.1
120	1.6
∞	2.8

Note that a payoff of $\hat{\alpha}$ for n periods has a present value of:

$$\left(\frac{1-\delta^n}{1-\delta}\right)\hat{\alpha}$$

Therefore, $\hat{\alpha}$ is the steady-state equivalent single-period payoff.

It is plausible to assume that if a chain store chooses Match, all future potential entrants will be certain that they are up against a weak opponent. Then, if there is entry in the first round and the chain store chooses Match, there will be entry in every round. If so, the chain store would achieve a payoff of 1 per period, that is, a present value of:

$$(1 + \delta + \cdots + \delta^{n-1})(1) = \frac{1-\delta^n}{1-\delta}$$

Since $\bar{m}$ is independent of δ, $3\delta^{\bar{m}}$ exceeds 1 for all sufficiently large δ. Moreover, as n becomes large, $\delta^{n-\bar{m}}$ approaches zero.

Therefore, from (11.5.5), as long as the discount factor δ is sufficiently large and the number of time periods is sufficiently long, $\hat{\alpha}$ exceeds unity and the strategy of mimicking is indeed the equilibrium strategy.

To get an idea of the strength of this result, suppose that the chain store game is played monthly. An *annual* discount rate of 12% corresponds to a *monthly* discount rate of about 0.95%, so that the *monthly* discount factor is $\delta \approx 0.99$. From (11.5.4), if there is a 0.04 prior probability that the chain store is strong, the number of entries is bounded above by:

$$\bar{m} = \ln(0.04)/\ln\left(\frac{2}{3}\right) \approx 8$$

Under the mimicking strategy, the steady-state equivalent one-period payoff is bounded from below by $\hat{\alpha}$. From (11.5.5), $\hat{\alpha}$ is readily computed.

It follows from Table 11.6 that, as long as the number of periods (months) exceeds 54, mimicking is the equilibrium strategy for the weak chain store.

Of course, with a longer time horizon, the gain to mimicking is greater. In the limit, as n goes to infinity, the bound approaches 2.8. That is, the payoff to mimicking is close to the payoff of 3 that would ensue if the chain store were able to *commit* itself to always fight an entrant. It should also be noted that the actual payoff to mimicking is greater than the bound established above. The reason is that the "worst case" scenario used to compute the bound assumes that entry occurs in the first m rounds. In fact, however, there will be no entry until late in the game. Early in the game, when both a strong and a weak chain store play Undercut, the potential entrant's best choice is Out.[16]

While we have focused on an example in which the long-run player is one of only two possible types, the analysis is exactly the same with any number of types. The only factors affecting the bound are (i) the prior probability ε that one or more types will be strong (will always choose Undercut), and (ii) the critical probability $\bar{\pi}$ (that the long-run player is strong) above which short-run players will always choose Out. As one of the exercises shows, the analysis also extends to the case in which there are different types of short-run players as well. The key, once again, is that there is a long-run player who will always choose Undercut regardless of the type of opponent he faces.

The models of this section and the previous section imply that even in finitely repeated games, reputational concerns of a player drive the player toward actions that sustain the belief that he is strong (or "chivalrous" as in Section 11.4). Reputation building is achieved because it is in the self-interest of the concerned player to commit to a certain strategy: the non-chivalrous Prisoners' Dilemma player commits to cooperation and the weak chain store commits to match, at least until the last few stages of the game. However, Ely and Valimaki (2003) show, with a model that encapsulates the following example, that reputation effects can also undermine commitment power. Motorists are uncertain about the honesty of auto mechanics. Suppose that within a short period of time, an auto mechanic has an unusually large proportion of customers whose cars truly require costly repairs. If he recommends these necessary repairs then the mechanic will acquire a reputation for dishonesty and lose future clientele. Therefore, an auto mechanic may not commit to an honest strategy because of reputational concerns.

---

[16] Near the end of the game, the weak chain store switches to the matching strategy with probability 1. Moreover, as Kreps and Wilson (1982) show, it is quite possible for there to be a middle phase in which both players adopt mixed strategies.

Exercises and Excursions 11.5

1 Building a Reputation for Toughness with More than Two Strategies
Suppose that a chain store can choose mild fighting or hard fighting. The complete payoff matrix is as follows:

		Potential entrant	
		Enter	Out
	Match	1, 2	4, 0
Chain store	Mild fight	½, −½	3, 0
	Hard fight	0, −1	3, 0

Suppose that there are two other types of chain store. Type M, for which the prior probability is ε_M, has a dominant strategy of fighting mildly. Type H, for which the prior probability is ε_H, has a dominant strategy of fighting hard. The discount factor is $\delta < 1$ and the number of periods is $n = \infty$. You should assume that the chain store's strategy is observable, ex post, even if the entrant stays out.

(A) Let m^* be the maximum number of entries if the chain store chooses Mild Fight and let m^{**} be the maximum number of entries if the chain store chooses Hard Fight. Show that, if $\varepsilon_H = \varepsilon_m$:

$$m^* \approx 2m^{**}$$

(B) If the chain store matches, it earns a return per period of 1. Define $v^* = (1 - \delta) PV^*$ and $v^{**} = (1 - \delta) PV^{**}$ where PV^* is the present value of fighting mildly in the early rounds and PV^{**} is the present value of fighting hard. (You should assume the worst-case scenario so that all entry takes place in the initial rounds.) Depict v^* and v^{**} in a neat figure as functions of δ. By examining the derivatives at $\delta = 1$ confirm that, for all δ sufficiently close to 1:

$$v^{**}(\delta) > v^*(\delta) > 1$$

Mimicking the hard fighter is then the chain store's best strategy.

(C) Show also that, for the parameter values in the problem, the strategy of fighting mildly is never optimal.

(D) If the payoff to the chain store when it matches is $1 - \theta$, confirm that, for θ sufficiently close to $\frac{1}{2}$, there are values of δ for which fighting mildly is optimal. Is it still the case that the chain store will fight hard for δ sufficiently close to 1?

(E) How would your answer to (B) change if $\varepsilon_M > \varepsilon_H$?

2   *Building a Reputation with Two Types of Entrant*

For a type-1 entrant, payoffs are as in Table 11.4. For a type-2 entrant, the payoff matrix is as follows:

		Type-2 entrant	
		Enter	Out
Weak chain store	Match	$\frac{1}{2}$, 3	4, 0
	Undercut	0, 1	3, 0

With prior probability ε the chain store is strong and has a dominant strategy of choosing to fight. The number of rounds n is finite and the discount factor δ is strictly less than unity.

(A) Explain why the chain store will choose to acquiesce if the prior probability of a type-2 entrant is sufficiently high.

(B) Suppose instead that the prior probability of a type-2 entrant is low. Does it necessarily follow that a weak chain store's optimal strategy is to mimic and fight any entrant in the early rounds?

(C) Will it fight forever?

3   *Reputation-Building with Different Types of Long-Run Player*

With probability ε, the chain store is strong and always fights. With probability $\beta(1 - \varepsilon)$, the chain store is weak with payoffs given by Table 11.4. With probability $(1 - \beta)(1 - \varepsilon)$, the chain store is less weak with payoffs as follows:

		Enter	Out
Less weak	Match	2, 0	4, 0
chain store	Undercut	0, −1	3, 0

(A) Obtain conditions under which both the weak and less weak chain stores will choose to build a reputation by mimicking the strong chain store and undercutting any entrant.

(B) If these conditions do not hold, is it possible that one type of chain store would choose to mimic while the other would not? Explain.

4 Sequential versus Stackelberg Equilibrium Strategies

What is wrong with the following argument?

> Each entrant knows that there is a small probability that the chain store is tough. She knows also that a soft chain store has an incentive to mimic the tough chain store and fight any entrant. Given this, no potential entrant will ever wish to fight. Therefore, the bound discussed in the text greatly overstates the cost of establishing a reputation.

5* Building a Reputation When the Chain Store's Action Is Unobservable unless Entry Takes Place

Consider the chain store game summarized in Tables 11.4 and 11.5 but suppose that the chain store's action is observable only if entry takes place. Then after round t one of three possible outcomes will be observed: Out, In/Match, and In/Undercut. Symbolize this as: $h_t \in \{O, (U, I), (M, I)\}$.

(A) Explain why $\Pr(S|h_t = O, H^{t-1}) = \Pr(S|H^{t-1})$.

(B) Appeal to the argument of the section above to show that:

$$\Pr(S|x_{1t} = U, x_{2t} = I, H^{t-1}) = \frac{\Pr(S|H^{t-1})}{\Pr(x_{1t} = U|H^{t-1})}$$

(C) Hence show that, for any observable history H^t that contains no matches:

$$\Pr(S|H^\tau) \geq \Pr(S|H^{\tau-1}), \quad \tau = 1, \ldots, t$$

(D) Suppose the chain store always chooses $x_{1\tau} = U$ over the first t periods. Show that the maximum number of times that entry takes place is the same as if the chain store's actions were observable *ex post*.

(E) Explain why the equilibrium in this game will be for the weak chain store to adopt a mixed strategy except in the final rounds when it always chooses Match.

---

* Starred questions may be somewhat more difficult.

SUGGESTIONS FOR FURTHER READINGS: Friedman (1971), Aumann and Shapley (1976), and Rubinstein (1979) started a long literature on repeated games. Good entry points to this literature are Pearce (1995) and Kandori (2008). Cripps (2008) is an accessible overview of the reputations literature. For a comprehensive exposition, see Mailath and Samuelson (2006).

References

Aumann, Robert and Shapley, Lloyd, "Long Term Competition: A Game Theoretic Analysis," mimeo, Hebrew University of Jerusalem, 1976.

Benoit, Jean-Pierre and Krishna, Vijay, "Finitely Repeated Games," *Econometrica*, 53 (1985), 905–922.

Cripps, Martin W., "Reputation," in *The New Palgrave Dictionary of Economics*, Steven N. Durlauf and Lawrence E. Blume (eds.), 2nd edition, vol. 7, pp. 105–112, New York: Palgrave Macmillan, 2008.

Ely, Jeffery and Juuso Valimaki, "Bad Reputation," Quarterly Journal of Economics, 118 (2003), 785–814.

Friedman, James, "A Noncooperative Equilibrium for Supergames," *Econometrica*, 38 (1971), 1–12.

Fudenberg, Drew and Levine, David, "Reputation and Equilibrium Selection in Games with a Patient Player," *Econometrica*, 47 (1989), 759–778.

Fudenberg, Drew, Levine, David, and Maskin, Eric S., "The Folk Theorem in Repeated Games with Discounting or with Incomplete Information," *Econometrica*, 54 (1986), 533–554.

Kandori, Michiro, "Repeated Games," in *The New Palgrave Dictionary of Economics*, S.N. Durlauf and L.E. Blume (eds.), 2nd edition, vol. 7, pp. 98–105, New York: Palgrave Macmillan, 2008.

Kreps, David and Wilson, Robert, "Reputation and Imperfect Information," *Journal of Economic Theory*, 27 (1982), 253–279.

Mailath, George J. and Larry Samuelson, *Repeated Games and Reputations: Long-Run Relationships*, Oxford: Oxford University Press, 2006.

Milgrom, Paul and Roberts, John, "Limit Pricing and Entry under Incomplete Information," *Econometrica*, 50 (1982), 443–460.

Pearce, David G., "Repeated Games: Cooperation and Rationality," in *Advances in Economic Theory: Sixth World Congress*, Jean-Jacques Laffont (ed.), vol. 1, pp. 132–180, Cambridge, UK: Cambridge University Press, 1995.

Rubinstein, Ariel, "Equilibrium in Supergames with the Overtaking Criterion," *Journal of Economic Theory*, 21 (1979), 1–9.

Selten, Reinhard, "The Chain Store Paradox," *Theory and Decision*, 9 (1977), 127–159.

12

Information Transmission, Acquisition,
and Aggregation

We revisit a theme of the last few chapters – the interplay of private information and strategic behavior. Some of the questions addressed here were examined earlier, in Chapters 5 and 6, but not in a setting with explicit strategic behavior. In Section 12.1, the incentive of an expert to transmit his information to an uninformed decision maker is investigated. The expert controls the amount of information revealed in order to influence the action of the uninformed individual. We studied the problem of inducing an expert to reveal information truthfully in Section 5.3.1. What is different here is that the payment to the expert cannot depend on the reported information. The question of costly acquisition of information is re-examined in Section 12.2. As in Section 6.3, inefficient acquisition of information can be traced back to a divergence between the private and social value of information.

In the rest of the chapter, we ask how well private information dispersed among individuals can be aggregated when individuals communicate only through their actions. In Section 12.3 we investigate information aggregation when individuals take actions – whether or not to adopt a certain behavior – in sequence. Private information is conveyed only through actions. Individuals care only about the information content of actions of their predecessors. In this setting there is a tendency to herd on similar actions, which blocks information transmission and makes information aggregation very inefficient.

We end, in Section 12.4, with a political science application of information aggregation: the Condorcet Jury Theorem. Here the question is whether a majority is wiser than an individual voter. The setting differs from the herding model of Section 12.3 in that individuals act simultaneously and each intrinsically cares about the decisions (i.e., voting behavior) of others.

12.1 Strategic Information Transmission and Delegation

We consider information transmission in a two-person setting where there is direct communication between individuals. One of the two individuals is endowed with information. The payoff to each individual depends on the true state of nature (which is observed by the informed individual) and on the action taken. At each state of nature, the optimal actions from the point of view of the two individuals differ by a constant b. This constant will be referred to as the informed individual's "bias." Only one individual takes an action. In Section 12.1.1, we assume that the action is taken by the uninformed, after he receives a communication from the informed about the true state of nature. We will see that because of differences in their interests, the informed person does not perfectly reveal her information.[1] Indeed, if the bias is large enough then the informed person reveals nothing, forcing the uninformed individual to take an action without any information.

The setting considered here is similar to that in Section 5.3.1 in that there is a divergence of beliefs, and possibly also a conflict of interest, between the decision maker (the receiver) and the expert (the sender). It differs in that the payment to the expert cannot depend on the information that is transmitted by the sender. This might happen because the information is not directly verifiable by a third party such as a court of law. Therefore, scoring rules considered in Section 5.3.1 are not available.

In Section 12.1.2, the analysis is modified to allow the uninformed individual the option of delegating the choice of action to the informed. One may view this as a model of authority and delegation in an organization where a manager has an option of delegating decisions to a better-informed subordinate. Thus, in Section 12.1.1 we examine a model where decision making is centralized whereas in Section 12.1.2 we ask whether the manager (the uninformed individual) might benefit from delegation. The sender is always better off under delegation as she takes her optimal decision under this scenario. It turns out that when the bias is small, the receiver also prefers delegation to centralization; whenever centralization is better than delegation for the receiver, the bias is so large that there is no information revelation under centralization.

---

[1] For ease of exposition, the uninformed receiver of information is male and the informed sender of information is female.

12.1.1 Strategic Information Transmission[2]

We assume that the uninformed individual takes the decision. Applications of this model, apart from the manager-subordinate example above, include an entrepreneur seeking investment from a venture capitalist. The entrepreneur has information about his project's prospects which she sends to the venture capitalist. The entrepreneur knows the optimal investment in her project that maximizes the venture capitalist's return, but would like the venture capitalist to invest a little more than the optimal amount. In a lawyer-client relationship, the client has information relevant to her case and the lawyer's legal strategy depends on this information. To accommodate these examples, we refer to the two individuals in general terms: the informed individual is the sender (as she sends a communication), and the uninformed individual (the decision maker) is the receiver.

The receiver (i.e., the uninformed individual) takes an action x. His utility, $U(x, s)$, depends on the action and an unknown state of nature s:

$$U(x, s) = -(x - s)^2.$$

The receiver's prior is that s is uniformly distributed on the unit interval $[0, 1]$. If he does not get any further information, the receiver's optimal action is $x = 0.5$. To see this, observe that the receiver's expected payoff is:

$$\mathrm{E}[U(x, s)] \equiv \int_0^1 U(x, s) f(s) ds = -\int_0^1 (x - s)^2 ds = -x^2 + x - \frac{1}{3}$$

where $f(s)$ is the density of s. The expression $-x^2 + x - \frac{1}{3}$ is maximized at $x = 0.5$. More generally, if the receiver believes that s is uniformly distributed in an interval $[a_1, a_2]$ then the action $x = \frac{a_1 + a_2}{2}$ at the mid-point of this interval maximizes his expected utility.[3]

The sender knows the true state s. She sends a report about the true state to the receiver. After hearing the report, the receiver takes action x. Unlike Example 5.6 of Section 5.3.1, the sender (or expert) is not a disinterested party; her utility function depends on the action taken by the receiver and is:

$$V(x, s) = -[x - (s + b)]^2$$

where $b > 0$ is the sender's bias.

---

[2] This material is based on Crawford and Sobel (1982).
[3] See Exercise 12.1.1.2.

When the true state is s, the sender would like the receiver to take action $x = s + b$, as this action maximizes her utility $V(x, s) = -[x - (s + b)]^2$. However, if the receiver believes that the true state is s, then he will take action $x = s$ to maximize his utility $U(x, s) = -(x - s)^2$.

There is always a Nash equilibrium in which the sender conveys no information: she makes a random report which does not depend on s, and the receiver takes action $x = 0.5$ without regard to the sender's report. However, if the value of b is not too large, there exist other Nash equilibria in which the sender reveals some of her information. We investigate these (partially) informative equilibria.

Let $r(s)$ be the sender's report as a function of the observed true state s. The sender's initial reaction may be to (mis)report $r = s + b$ as the true state when the true state really is s.[4] But this cannot be a Nash equilibrium, because the receiver's best response to this reporting strategy is to subtract b from the report and take action $x = r - b$. By similar reasoning, if $r(s)$ is any equilibrium reporting strategy that is strictly increasing in s, then the receiver will correctly infer that the true state is $s = r^{-1}(r)$ by inverting the report r. Thus, a reporting function that is increasing in s reveals the state of nature perfectly to the receiver and will not bias the receiver's action toward a direction favored by the sender. We turn to sender's reporting strategies that are only weakly increasing (i.e., are step functions) in s.

Suppose that $b = 0.1$. Consider the reporting strategy of the sender where she sends one of two reports, r_1 if $0 \leq s < 0.3$ or r_2 if $0.3 \leq s \leq 1$, where $r_1 < r_2$. Upon receiving a report r_1, the receiver concludes that the sender observed $s \in [0, 0.3)$. The receiver updates his beliefs about s to a uniform distribution on the interval $[0, 0.3)$. With these beliefs, the action $x(r_1) = \frac{0+0.3}{2} = 0.15$ maximizes the receiver's expected utility. Similarly, upon hearing report r_2, the receiver believes that s is uniformly distributed on the interval $[0.3, 1]$. Therefore, his expected utility maximizing action is $x(r_2) = \frac{0.3+1}{2} = 0.65$. It can be verified that $V(x(r_1), s) > V(x(r_2), s)$ if $s < 0.3$, $V(x(r_1), s) < V(x(r_2), s)$ if $s > 0.3$, and that $V(x(r_1), 0.3) = V(x(r_2), 0.3)$. Therefore, the sender's reporting strategy is also optimal. To complete the construction of the sequential equilibrium, we need to specify the receiver's beliefs upon receiving a report other than r_1 or r_2. If the sender's report is less than r_1, the receiver believes that the true state s is uniformly distributed on the interval $[0, 0.3)$ and takes action $x = 0.15$,

---

[4] Recalling that s is distributed on the unit interval, the sender might consider such a report as long as $s + b \leq 1$.

and if the report is more than r_1, then the receiver believes that the true state is uniformly distributed on the interval $[0.3, 1]$ or greater and takes action $x = 0.65$.

In effect, the sender partitions the unit interval $[0,1]$ into two smaller intervals $[0, 0.3)$ and $[0.3, 1]$ and reports which one of these intervals the true state lies in. This partially revealing equilibrium and the uninformative equilibrium are the only equilibria when $b = 0.1$. These two equilibria can be Pareto ranked: both the sender and the receiver prefer the partially revealing equilibrium to the uninformative one.

Crawford and Sobel (1982) show that for each value of bias b, there exists a number $N(b)$ that represents the total number of equilibria in this information transmission game. For each $j \leq N(b)$, there exists a Nash equilibrium[5] in which the sender partitions the unit interval into j smaller intervals and reveals which of these j intervals s lies in.[6] In the most informative equilibrium, $j = N(b)$. Moreover $N(b)$ is decreasing in b and $N(b) \to \infty$ as $b \to 0$. As the bias of the sender goes to 0, not only does the number of intervals $N(b)$ in the most informative equilibrium (which is the equilibrium preferred by the two parties) become arbitrarily large, the width of each interval tends to zero. In other words, in the limit as $b \to 0$ this equilibrium becomes completely informative. At the other extreme, if $b \geq 0.25$, then the only equilibrium is uninformative.

Thus, the smaller the conflict of interest between the receiver and the sender, i.e., smaller the bias b, the greater the information transmission from the sender to the receiver.

Exercises and Excursions 12.1.1

1 Pareto Ranking of Nash Equilibria
Recall that when the bias $b = 0.1$ there exist two Nash equilibria: (i) an uninformative equilibrium in which the sender transmits the same signal regardless of the state s she observed and (ii) a partially informative equilibrium in which the sender informs the receiver whether $s \in [0, 0.3)$ or $s \in [0.3, 1]$. Show that the receiver and the sender both obtain a higher expected utility in the partially revealing equilibrium than in the uninformative equilibrium.

---

[5] Each of these Nash equilibria is also sequential. For brevity, we omit specification of the receiver's beliefs after possible off-the-equilibrium-path reports.

[6] The values of the end points of these j intervals depend on the value of b.

2   The Receiver's Optimal Action

(A) Prove the claim in the text that if the receiver believes that s is uniformly distributed in an interval $[a_1, a_2]$ then the action $x = \frac{a_1+a_2}{2}$ maximizes his expected utility.

[HINT: Obtain an expression for $E[U(x, s)|a_1 \le s \le a_2]$ in a similar way as $E[U(x, s)]$ was obtained in the text. Then differentiate this expression with respect to x.]

(B) Show that the receiver's expected utility at this optimal action is $-\frac{(a_2-a_1)^2}{12}$.

3   Constructing Equilibria – I

In the text we saw that when the bias $b = 0.1$ there is a Nash equilibrium in which the sender reveals whether the signal is in interval $[0, 0.3)$ or in the interval $[0.3,1]$. For any value of bias $b \in (0, 0.25]$ there exists a similar Nash equilibrium in which the sender reveals which of two intervals, $[0, a)$ or $[a, 1]$, the state s is in. In this exercise, we construct this equilibrium.

From the previous exercise, we know that the receiver takes action $\frac{a}{2}$ if he believes that $s \in [0, a)$ and takes action $\frac{1+a}{2}$ if he believes that $s \in [a, 1]$.

(A) Therefore, the sender must be indifferent between the actions $\frac{a}{2}$ and $\frac{1+a}{2}$ when she observes that $s = a$. Use this observation to show that $a + 2b = 0.5$.

(B) Show that there exists a sequential equilibrium in which the sender transmits message r_1 when $s \in [0, 0.5 - 2b)$ and message r_2 when $s \in [0.5 - 2b, 1]$. Be sure to specify off-the-equilibrium-path beliefs of the receiver if he receives a message other than r_1 or r_2.

4   Constructing Equilibria – II

Suppose that the bias b between the sender and receiver is larger than 0.25. Follow the steps below to conclude there is no Nash equilibrium in which the sender reveals some information to the receiver.

(A) First, show that there is no two-interval equilibrium in this game. (Mimic the steps of the previous question to conclude that there cannot exist $a \in [0, 1]$ where the conditions of a two-interval Nash equilibrium are met.)

(B) Second, show that there is no three or more interval equilibrium in this game.

[HINT: Suppose to the contrary that there is a three or more interval equilibrium. Let the first two intervals be $[0, a_1)$ and $[a_1, a_2)$, $0 < a_1 < a_2 < 1$, with the sender issuing report r_1 if $s \in [0, a_1)$ and report r_2 if and $s \in [a_1, a_2)$. What are the receiver's optimal actions upon receiving r_1 and r_2? If $b > 0.25$, then show that there do not exist a_1, a_2 in the unit interval, $a_1 < a_2$, such that the sender will be indifferent between sending r_1 or r_2 when she observes that state is $s = a_1$ and the receiver takes the respective optimal actions in response to the messages r_1 or r_2.]

5 The Total Number of Nash Equilibria, $N(b)$
Consider an equilibrium with j intervals $[0, a_1)$, $[a_1, a_2)$, $\ldots$, $[a_{i-1}, a_i)$, $[a_i, a_{i+1})$, $\ldots$, $[a_{j-1}, 1]$. In equilibrium the sender transmits one of j messages, $r_1, r_2, \ldots, r_j$, where signal r_i is sent if the true state lies in the ith interval $[a_{i-1}, a_i)$. From the definition of $N(b)$ we have $j \leq N(b)$.

  (A) What action will the receiver take if the sender transmits r_i? Transmits r_{i+1}?
  (B) Show that the difference equation $a_{i+1} = 2a_i - a_{i-1} + 4b$ must be satisfied.

[HINT: When the true state is a_i, the sender must be indifferent between sending r_i or r_{i+1}. Write the equation representing this indifference condition by equating the utilities of the sender at the two receiver-optimal actions in part (A) who observes that the true state is a_i.]

  (C) Verify that solutions to this difference equation in (B) are $a_i = a_1 i + 2i(i-1)b$, parameterized by a_1.
  (D) Show that (i) $N(b)$ is finite for any b and (ii) $N(b)$ decreases in b.

12.1.2 Strategic Delegation

In the previous section, the sender's bias causes her not to reveal the true state of nature completely or, for large values of the bias ($b > 0.25$), not to reveal any information about the state of nature. We modify this model and allow the receiver the option of delegating the decision to the sender. On the one hand, the receiver should benefit from delegation because the sender takes a decision with knowledge of the true state of nature. On the other hand, because the receiver's and sender's interests differ, the action taken by the sender will not be the one most preferred by the receiver. Therefore, it is not clear whether it is in the receiver's interest to delegate.

If the decision is delegated to the sender then she will choose action $x = s + b$ when the true state is s. Therefore, the receiver's expected utility, if he decides to delegate, is:

$$E[U(s + b, s)] = -b^2.$$

We compare this with the receiver's expected utility at the most informative equilibrium if he decides not to delegate. Suppose that the bias is $b = 0.1$. It can be shown that when $b = 0.1$, the most informative equilibrium has two intervals. The sender transmits message r_1 if $s \in [0, 0.3)$ or message r_2 if $s \in [0.3, 1]$. The receiver's best response to these messages is to takes action $x = 0.15$ or $x = 0.65$, respectively. The receiver's *ex ante* expected utility at this equilibrium is:

$$E[U(0.15, s)|0 \le s < 0.3] \Pr[0 \le s < 0.3]$$
$$+ E[U(0.65, s)|0.3 \le s \le 1] \Pr[0.3 \le s \le 1]$$
$$= -\int_0^{0.3} (0.15 - s)^2 ds - \int_{0.3}^1 (0.65 - s)^2 ds$$
$$= -\left[0.0225s - 0.15s^2 + \frac{1}{3}s^3\right]\Big|_0^{0.3} - \left[0.4225s - 0.65s^2 + \frac{1}{3}s^3\right]\Big|_{0.3}^1$$
$$= -[0.00225 - 0] - [0.10583 - 0.07725]$$
$$= -0.03083.$$

As $-b^2 = -0.01 > -0.03083$, the receiver is better off delegating the decision to the sender. The receiver's loss due to a sub-optimal (from his point of view) choice of action with delegation is less than the loss from lack of information revelation by the sender when decision making rests with the receiver. Moreover, the sender is always better off with delegation as she takes her optimal action at every state of nature. Thus, we have shown that delegation is a Pareto improvement over centralization when the bias $b = 0.1$.

Delegation dominates centralization not only when the bias $b = 0.1$ but for any bias level at which some information is revealed under centralization by the sender, i.e., when $b \le 0.25$. We show this is the case when, under centralization, the two-interval equilibrium constructed in Exercise 12.1.1.3 is played. In this equilibrium, the receiver takes action $0.25 - b$ if the sender reveals that $s \in [0, 0.5 - 2b)$ and takes action $0.75 - b$ if the sender reveals that $s \in [0.5 - 2b, 1]$. The calculation below shows that the receiver's *ex ante* expected utility from centralization is less than his *ex ante* expected utility from delegation:

$$
\begin{aligned}
E[U(x, s)] &\equiv -\int_0^{0.5-2b} (0.25 - b - s)^2 ds - \int_{0.5-2b}^1 (0.75 - b - s)^2 ds \\
&= -\left(\frac{1}{48} + b^2\right) \\
&< -b^2 = E[U(s + b, s)]
\end{aligned}
$$

For values of b close to 0 there exist other Nash equilibria in the centralized scenario in which the sender reveals more than two intervals. However, it turns out that even with this greater amount of information revelation under centralization when the bias is small, the receiver is better off delegating.[7]

In fact, as long as $b \leq 0.2887$, delegation is better than centralization for the receiver. We have already noted this for $b \leq 0.25$. To verify the superiority of delegation when $b \in (0.25, 0.2887]$, first note that under centralization there is no information transmission (see Exercise 12.1.1.4). The sender makes a completely random report regardless of the true state of nature and the receiver selects $x = 0.5$. The receiver's expected utility at this equilibrium is:

$$
E[U(0.5, s)] = -\int_0^1 (0.5 - s)^2 ds = -\left[0.25s - 0.5s^2 + \frac{1}{3}s^3\right]\Big|_0^1 = \frac{1}{12}
$$

His expected utility under delegation is $-b^2$. As $b^2 \leq \frac{1}{12}$ whenever $b \leq \frac{1}{2\sqrt{3}} = 0.2887$, the receiver prefers to delegate in this range. Only when the difference in interests of the receiver and sender is large enough (bias greater than 0.2887) should the receiver centralize.

12.2 Strategic Information Acquisition[8]

We depart from our usual assumption that individuals are costlessly endowed with private information. Instead, information is costly and how much information to acquire is a choice made by one (or more) individual(s). We return to questions about over- and under-investment in information that were raised in Sections 5.3.2 and 6.3. Recall that an individual acquires a socially efficient amount of information ("inventive activity" was the term we used) if and only if private and social benefits to information acquisition are identical. We investigate conditions under which there is an alignment between private incentives and social benefits in a model in

---

[7] See Dessein (2002).
[8] This section is based on Bergemann and Valimaki (2002).

Table 12.1. *Prior probabilities of states and corresponding buyer values*

	States (s)			
	$L_1 L_2$	$L_1 H_2$	$H_1 L_2$	$H_1 H_2$
Prior probability	0.25	0.25	0.25	0.25
Buyer 1's reservation value for object	0	0	10	10
Buyer 2's reservation value for object	0	10	0	10

which, unlike in Section 6.3, each individual is strategic and can influence the terms of trade through his decisions.

In the example we consider, information is useful in allocating an object efficiently. Two risk-neutral buyers, 1 and 2, are interested in buying an object from a seller. The seller's cost of the object is 0. Initially, each buyer believes that the object is worth either $10 or 0 to him, both possibilities being equally likely. The buyers' initial beliefs are independent. We represent this with four equally probable states of nature denoted $s = L_1 L_2, L_1 H_2, H_1 L_2$, and $H_1 H_2$. Thus buyer 1's valuation is $10 in the event $H_1 = \{H_1 L_2, H_1 H_2\}$, and it is $0 in the event $L_1 = \{L_1 L_2, L_1 H_2\}$. Similarly, buyer 2's valuation is $10 in the event $H_2 = \{L_1 H_2, H_1 H_2\}$, and it is $0 in the event $L_2 = \{L_1 L_2, H_1 L_2\}$. This is summarized in Table 12.1.

We assume (for simplicity) that only buyer 1 has the option to acquire additional information.[9] Information is parameterized by p, $0 \leq p \leq 0.5$, where $p = 0$ represents no additional information. The cost incurred by buyer 1 to acquire information p is $10p^2$. The marginal cost of information, $20p$, increases from 0 at $p = 0$ to 10 at $p = 0.5$.

After buyer 1 makes his information acquisition decision and observes his message, the seller conducts a second-price auction to sell the object. Buyer 1's information acquisition decision and the message that he observes are privately known to him; buyer 2 and the seller are not privy to this information. We shall see that buyer 1 acquires the socially optimal level of information only if the information signal and buyer 2's valuation are statistically independent.

12.2.1 Efficient Information Acquisition

Buyer 1's message takes one of two values, l or h. The likelihood of the signal depends only on whether buyer 1's valuation is low or high, as indicated in Table 12.2.

---

[9] Exercise 12.2.1.2 extends the analysis to allow both buyers to acquire information.

Table 12.2. *Likelihood matrix*

		Pr[l	State]	Pr[l	State]
	L_1L_2	$0.5 + p$	$0.5 - p$
States (s)	L_1H_2	$0.5 + p$	$0.5 - p$
	H_1L_2	$0.5 - p$	$0.5 + p$
	H_1H_2	$0.5 - p$	$0.5 + p$

Buyer 1's possible posterior beliefs about the events H_1 and H_2, computed using Bayes' Theorem (see Section 5.2.1), are shown in Table 12.3. Observe that if buyer 1 does not purchase any information ($p = 0$) then the signal is uninformative and his prior beliefs about H_1 and L_1 are unchanged. On the other hand, if he purchases the most informative signal ($p = 0.5$) then he knows with certainty whether the event is H_1 or L_1. For intermediate values of p, a message (i.e. signal realization) l decreases the probability of H_1 whereas message h increases the probability of H_1. Because the information signal and buyer 2's valuation are independent, the messages leave the prior probability of H_2 unchanged. This will turn out to be essential for socially optimal information acquisition by buyer 1.

In a second-price auction, it is a Nash equilibrium for each buyer to bid his expected value conditional on his information. Thus, buyer 1 submits either $5 - 10p$ or $5 + 10p$, depending on whether he observes l or h, and buyer 2 always submits a bid of 5. It can be verified that messages l and h are equally likely. Buyers' bids and surpluses as a function of p are computed in Table 12.4. Buyer 1's expected surplus is $\Pi_1(p) = 0.5 \times 0 + 0.5 \times 10p = 5p$, and buyer 2's expected surplus is $\Pi_2(p) = 0.5 \times 10p + 0.5 \times 0 = 5p$. Buyer 1's surplus does not take into account his information acquisition costs. The marginal cost of gathering information is $20p$. Consequently, the (privately) optimal amount of information collected by buyer 1 is obtained by equating buyer 1's private marginal benefit (i.e., the rate at which his surplus increases with p) to his marginal cost: $\frac{\partial \Pi_1(p)}{\partial p} = 5 = 20p$. Thus, it is optimal for buyer to purchase information $p^* = 0.25$.

Table 12.3. *Posterior probabilities*

		Pr[H_1	m]	Pr[H_2	m]
Messages (m)	l	$0.5 - p$	0.5
	h	$0.5 + p$	0.5

Table 12.4. *Outcome in auction*

		Buyer 1's bid	Buyer 2's bid	Buyer 1's surplus	Buyer 2's surplus	Social surplus
Messages (*m*)	*l*	$5 - 10p$	5	0	$10p$	5
	h	$5 + 10p$	5	$10p$	0	$5 + 10p$

The social surplus (excluding the cost of information acquisition) is the sum of the two buyers' surpluses and the seller's revenue. The seller's revenue is $R(p) = 0.5 \times (5 - 10p) + 0.5 \times 5 = 5 - 5p$. Therefore, the social surplus is[10]

$$S(p) = \Pi_1(p) + \Pi_2(p) + R(p) = 5p + 5p + 5 - 5p = 5 + 5p$$

More accurate information leads to greater allocative efficiency, thereby increasing social surplus. The social marginal benefit (i.e. the rate at which $S(p)$ increases with p) is 5, which is the same as buyer 1's private marginal benefit. Thus, the socially optimal information acquisition is $p^s = 0.25$, which is equal to p^*, the privately optimal information acquisition level for buyer 1.

In Chapter 10 we saw that a second-price auction is *ex post* efficient. This remains true here, as the second-price auction allocates the object to the buyer who values it the most – buyer 1 if *h* is observed and buyer 2 if *l* is observed. This auction is also *ex ante* efficient in that it induces the efficient amount of information acquisition.

To understand this, let us examine the private and social benefits from better information. In the absence of information acquisition ($p = 0$), the social surplus is 5 and buyer 1's surplus is 0 (achieved by allocating the object to either one of the two buyers at a price of 5). Social surplus increases with p because the object is allocated to buyer 1 if and only if he sees *h*. If *l* is observed, then the social surplus remains 5 (obtained by allocating the object to buyer 2) and buyer 1's surplus remains 0; thus, there is no increase in either buyer 1's surplus or the social surplus compared to the no information acquisition benchmark. Next, suppose that *h* is observed. Buyer 1 gets the object and the social surplus is $5 + 10p$; the next best thing

---

[10] An alternative calculation of $S(p)$ is based on "following" the object. The maximum social surplus is attained by allocating the object to the buyer who values it the most. Any price paid by a buyer to the seller can be ignored as this is a side payment. When message *l* is observed (by buyer 1) then surplus of 5 is created by allocating to buyer 2, and when *h* is observed surplus of $5 + 10p$ is created by allocating to buyer 1, which gives us $S(p) = 0.5 \times 5 + 0.5 \times (5 + 10p) = 5 + 5p$.

to allocating the object to buyer 1 is to give it to buyer 2, which would yield a social surplus of 5. Because buyer 1 pays 5 for the object, the increase in his surplus due to information acquisition (from 0 to $10p$) is equal to the increase in social surplus (from 5 to $5 + 10p$). Thus, as buyer 1 appropriates all the social gains from his investment in more accurate information, the level of information that maximizes his surplus also maximizes his social surplus – hence, the *ex ante* efficiency of the second-price auction.

Exercises and Excursions 12.2.1

1 *Computing Posterior Probabilities*
   (A) Use Bayes' Theorem to verify the posterior probabilities in Table 12.3.
   (B) Show that $\Pr[h] = \Pr[l] = 0.5$.

2 *Two-Sided Information Acquisition*
Let us generalize the analysis in this section by allowing buyer 2 to purchase information on the same terms as buyer 1. Let buyer i's information be p_i, purchased at a cost of $10p_i^2$. The likelihood matrix for buyer i's signal is:

		$\Pr[l_i \mid \text{State}]$	$\Pr[h_i \mid \text{State}]$
	$L_i L_j$	$0.5 + p_i$	$0.5 - p_i$
States (s)	$L_i H_j$	$0.5 + p_i$	$0.5 - p_i$
	$H_i L_j$	$0.5 - p_i$	$0.5 + p_i$
	$H_i H_j$	$0.5 - p_i$	$0.5 + p_i$

The information acquisition decisions of the two buyers are private, as are the messages that they observe. The valuations for the buyers depend on the states and are as specified in Section 12.2.1. After observing their messages, the two buyers bid in a second-price auction for the object.

   (A) Show that it is a Nash equilibrium in the second-price auction for the two buyers to bid their respective expected values conditional on their private messages.
   (B) Show that there exist two pure strategy Nash equilibria at the information acquisition stage: in one equilibrium, the information acquired is $p_1 = 0.25$, $p_2 = 0$ and in the other, it is $p_1 = 0$, $p_2 = 0.25$.
   (C) Show that each of these Nash equilibria is Pareto optimal. Thus, the second-price auction remains *ex ante* and *ex post* efficient even when buyer 2 can also acquire information.

Table 12.5. *Likelihood matrix*

		$\Pr[l \mid \text{State}]$	$\Pr[l \mid \text{State}]$
	$L_1 L_2$	$0.5 + p$	$0.5 - p$
	$L_1 H_2$	$0.5 + kp$	$0.5 - kp$
States (s)			
	$H_1 L_2$	$0.5 - kp$	$0.5 + kp$
	$H_1 H_2$	$0.5 - p$	$0.5 + p$

12.2.2 Overinvestment in Information

In the previous section, the social surplus and buyer 1's surplus increase at the same rate with better information. Buyer 1 appropriates the entire increase in social surplus due to better information, which leads to efficient information acquisition. It is essential that the information acquired by buyer 1 is independent of buyer 2's valuation.

Next, we allow for positive correlation between buyer 1's information and buyer 2's valuation. With better information, buyer 1's surplus increases faster than social surplus, leading to overinvestment in information by buyer 1.

The likelihood matrix for buyer 1's signal in Table 12.2 is modified to that in Table 12.5, where $0 \leq p \leq 0.5$, and $0 \leq k < 1$.[11] Once again, message h is more likely than message l in states $H_1 H_2$ and $H_1 L_2$, i.e., when buyer 1 has a high valuation. However, the probability of h in state $H_1 L_2$ is less than the probability of h in state $H_1 H_2$. Similarly, the probability of l in state $L_1 L_2$ is greater than the probability of l in state $L_1 H_2$, which in turn is greater than 0.50. Thus, the posterior probabilities of each of the events H_1 and H_2 increase after a message h, and decrease after a message l. The posterior probabilities are in Table 12.6.

Once again, it is a Nash equilibrium in the second-price auction for each buyer to bid his expected value conditional on his information. Therefore, buyer 1 will bid $5 - 5(1 + k)p$ if he observes message l and $5 + 5(1 + k)p$ if he observes message h. Buyer 2's (expected) valuations are $5 - 5(1 - k)p$ if buyer 1 observes l and $5 + 5(1 - k)p$ if buyer 1 sees h. However, buyer 2 does not know whether message l or h was observed by his opponent (nor does he observe the level p of information acquired). Therefore, he continues to

---

[11] If $k = 1$, then we get back to the case analyzed in Section 12.2.1, where buyer 1's information is uncorrelated with buyer 2's valuation. If $k > 1$, then it can be shown that the second-price auction is not *ex post* efficient.

Table 12.6. *Posterior probabilities*

		$\Pr[H_1 \mid m]$	$\Pr[H_2 \mid m]$
Messages (m)	l	$0.5 - 0.5(1 + k)p$	$0.5 - 0.5(1 - k)p$
	h	$0.5 + 0.5(1 + k)p$	$0.5 + 0.5(1 - k)p$

bid his *ex ante* expected value of 5 in the auction.[12] Table 12.7 summarizes buyers' bids and surpluses in this equilibrium. The expected buyer surpluses as a function of p are $\Pi_1(p) = 2.5(1 + k)p$, $\Pi_2(p) = 5kp$. At information level p, the marginal benefit of information (i.e., $\frac{d\Pi_1(p)}{dp}$) is $2.5(1 + k)$, whereas the marginal cost of information is $20p$. Equating the two, we obtain the information collected by buyer 1 is $p^* = (1 + k)/8$.

The last column in Table 12.7 lists the social surplus, which is equal to the expected value of the buyer who wins the auction – buyer 2 under message l and buyer 1 under message h. The expected social surplus is, therefore, $S(p) = 5kp + 5$, and the socially optimal level of information is $p^s = 0.25k$. As $0 < k < 1$, we conclude that $p^* = (1 + k)/8 > 0.25k = p_s$. Buyer 1 overinvests in information.

The second-price auction remains *ex post* efficient in that conditional on buyer 1's information, the object is allocated to the buyer with the greatest expected value – to buyer 1 if and only if h is observed. However, the second-price auction fails to be *ex ante* efficient as buyer 1 overinvests in information. Recall the intuition at the end of Section 12.2.1. In order to achieve *ex ante* efficiency, the increase in buyer 1's surplus (with better information) should equal the increase in social surplus. In other words, when buyer 1 is allocated the object under message h, he should pay the next best use for the object, which is $5 + 5(1 - k)p$, buyer 2's valuation for the object. However, this cannot be achieved in a second-price auction (or, as it turns out, in any other Bayesian incentive compatible mechanism). As buyer 1 pays only 5 when he wins the object, the increase in his surplus is more than the increase in social surplus. Thus, he overinvests in information. In fact, if $k = 0$, then information is socially useless as it does not matter whom the object is allocated to, both buyers having identical expected valuations conditional on the message. As k increases from 0 to 1, the

---

[12] A sophisticated buyer 2 could figure out how much information buyer 1 will acquire in equilibrium. As buyer 2 wins only when buyer 1 observers message l, a sophisticated buyer 2 might bid $5-5(1-k)p$, his expected value given message l. The conclusion of overinvestment in information acquisition remains unchanged with a sophisticated buyer 2. See Exercise 12.2.2.2.

Table 12.7. *Outcome in auction*

		Buyer 1's bid	Buyer 2's bid	Buyer 1's surplus	Buyer 2's surplus	Social surplus
Messages (m)	l	$5 - 5(1 + k)p$	5	0	$10kp$	$5 - 5(1 - k)p$
	h	$5 + 5(1 + k)p$	5	$5(1 + k)p$	0	$5 + 5(1 + k)p$

socially optimal level of information increases from $p^s = 0$ to $p^s = 0.25$. Recall that buyer 1 chooses accuracy level $p^* = (1 + k)/8$. Therefore, the amount of overinvestment decreases to 0 as k increases from 0 to 1.

Exercises and Excursions 12.2.2

1 Computing Posterior Probabilities

(A) Use Bayes' Theorem to verify the posterior probabilities in Table 12.6.

(B) Show that $\Pr[h] = \Pr[l] = 0.5$.

2 A Sophisticated Buyer 2

In this section, we were able to derive the amount of information that buyer 1 would choose to acquire. Therefore, a sophisticated buyer 2 should be able to make this calculation as well, even though he does not observe buyer 1's information acquisition decision. Suppose that buyer 2 infers that buyer 1 has acquired information level p. Then, knowing that he will win only when buyer 1 observes l, buyer 2 will bid his expected value conditional on buyer 1 observing l.

(A) Modify Table 12.7 to take into account the bids submitted by a sophisticated buyer 2.

(B) Write buyer 1's expected surplus function. What is his optimal information acquisition?

(C) Does social surplus change as a result of the change in buyer 2's bids? Does buyer 1 still overinvest in information acquisition?

3 Cost of Information Acquisition

Let us change the cost of acquiring information of quality p from $10p$ to a convex function $C(p)$, where $C(0) = 0$ and $C(0.5) = c$. That is, the cost of not acquiring information is 0 and the cost of perfect information is c. Everything else remains as in Section 12.2.2.

Suppose that the expected social surplus is maximized when buyer 1 acquires information of quality $p_s \in (0, 0.5)$. Show that buyer 1's surplus is maximized when he acquires information of quality greater than p_s.

4 Failure of ex ante *Efficiency in First-Price Auction*

In the model considered in this section, an *ex ante* efficient mechanism must give buyer 1 incentives to acquire the socially optimal level of information $p^s = 0.25k$, truthfully report his signal, and allocate the object to buyer 1 if and only if buyer 1 reports h. We saw that a second-price auction is not *ex ante* efficient as buyer 1 acquires more than p^s. Suppose that a first-price auction was used instead with buyers submitting bids in dollars and cents.

(A) Show that in any pure strategy Nash equilibrium, the informed buyer 1 gathers information.

(B) Suppose that buyer 1 gathers information of accuracy p. Show that in the first-price auction, if $k \in (1 - \varepsilon, 1)$ for sufficiently small ε, then it is a pure strategy Nash equilibrium for buyer 2 to bid $b_2^* = 0.5 - 0.5(1 - k)p$ and for buyer 1 to bid a penny more than b_2^* if his signal is h and a penny less than b_2^* if his signal is l.

(C) How does the equilibrium outcome compare with that in Exercise 2 above? What is the optimal amount of information gathered by buyer 1?

12.3 Information Cascades

Why do people tend to "herd" on similar actions? Why is mass behavior prone to error and fads? A model of information cascades helps explain some otherwise puzzling phenomena about human behavior and offers a vantage point for issues in economics and business strategy.

Consider a setting where individuals choose an irreversible action in a sequence.[13] The action consists of adopting or rejecting a behavior (e.g., adopting or rejecting a new technology). The order in which individuals take actions is exogenously specified and is known to all. The value from adopting is the same for all individuals but is unknown. Each individual has some private information about the value of adopting. An individual uses his private information, together with any inference drawn from observing the decisions of all those ahead of him, to take an action: adopt or reject.

An individual's payoff does not depend on the number of others who adopted or rejected. Hence, he does not care about the actions of later individuals; he cares about actions of predecessors only because their actions

[13] See Banerjee (1992), Bikhchandani, Hirshleifer, and Welch (1992), and Welch (1992).

Table 12.8 *Likelihood matrix*

	$\Pr[h_i \mid V]$	$\Pr[l_i \mid V]$
$V = +1$	$0.5 + p$	$0.5 - p$
$V = -1$	$0.5 - p$	$0.5 + p$

might convey information about predecessors' private information.[14] Private information is credibly communicated only through individuals' actions.

It turns out that often the information gleaned from predecessors' choices overwhelms the private information of an individual. When this happens, it is optimal for this individual to choose the same action regardless of his private information. Succeeding individuals find themselves in the same situation and they too take the same action regardless of their private information. This situation is an example of an *information cascade*.[15]

The essential ideas are seen in the following simple setting. The value to rejecting is 0 and is known to everyone. The value to adopting, V, is either -1 or $+1$, with equal prior probability. Thus, the prior expected value to adoption is 0, the same as the value to rejecting. Individual i's private information signal X_i either takes the value h_i or l_i.[16] The signal value h_i is more likely when the value to adopting is $+1$ and is less likely when the value to adopting is -1. As a tie-breaking convention, we assume that an individual who is indifferent adopts or rejects with equal probability. Individuals' signals are identically distributed and are independent conditional on V. The likelihood matrix for X_i is in Table 12.8, where $0 < p \leq 0.5$. Note that the distribution of X_i is symmetric: $\Pr[h_i|V = +1] = \Pr[l_i|V = -1]$. Thus, as $V = +1$ and $V = -1$ are equally likely, it is follows that either message is equally likely: $\Pr[h_i] = \Pr[l_i] = 0.50$. A simple application of Bayes' Theorem allows one to update individual i's posterior beliefs about the value to adopting after observing his own message (but not the messages or choices of preceding individuals). These posterior beliefs are in the first two columns Table 12.9.

[14] Actions of later individuals may also reveal something about their private information. But this information is of no use to the individual taking a decision today, as this decision is irreversible.

[15] An information cascade occurs when an individual, based on observations of previous decision makers, makes the same choice regardless of his signal. This can occur in more general settings than considered here. See Bikhchandani, Hirshleifer, and Welch (1998).

[16] In the language of Chapter 5, h and l as messages. The "message service" or information signal is X_i.

Table 12.9. *Posterior probabilities*

		$\Pr[V = +1 \mid m]$	$\Pr[V = -1 \mid m]$	$E[V \mid m]$
Messages (m)	h_i	$0.5 + p$	$0.5 - p$	$2p$
	l_i	$0.5 - p$	$0.5 + p$	$-2p$

The calculation for the last column of Table 12.9 is:

$$E[V|h_i] = (+1) \times \Pr[V = +1|h_i] + (-1) \times \Pr[V = -1|h_i]$$
$$= (+1)(0.5 + p) + (-1)(0.5 - p) = 2p$$

A similar calculation shows that $E[V|l_i] = -2p$.

For ease of exposition, we will refer to the individuals as Alex, Bev, Cade, Dolores, Esteban, etc. The first individual, Alex, adopts if his message is h_1, as the expected value to adopting is $E[V|h_1] = 2p$, which exceeds 0, the value to rejecting. Similarly, Alex rejects if his message is l_1 as the expected value to adopting, $E[V|l_1] = -2p$, is less than the value to rejecting. Bev, the second in the sequence, can infer Alex's message from his decision. If Alex adopted, then Bev infers that Alex's message was h_1. Therefore, she adopts if her message is h_2.[17] However, if Bev's message is l_2, then she computes the expected value of adoption to be $E[V|h_1 l_2] = 0$. Being indifferent between adopt and reject, she adopts with probability 0.50. Similarly, if Alex rejected, Bev rejects if her message is also l_2, and rejects with probability 0.50 if her message is h_2. The next individual in this sequence, Cade, is faced with one of three situations:

(1) *Adopt cascade:* Alex and Bev have adopted. Cade reasons that Alex must have observed h_1 and that more likely than not Bev observed h_2 (although she may have seen l_2 and flipped a coin). Suppose that Cade observed l_3. Then conditioning only on his own message l_3 and Alex's inferred message h_1, Cade computes the value to adopting to be $E[V|h_1 l_3] = 0$. When Cade also takes into account that Bev's message was more likely to have been h_2 rather than l_2, the expected value of adopting becomes strictly positive. Thus, after observing that Alex and Bev both adopted, Cade too will adopt even if his message is l_3. If, instead, Cade observed h_3 then he will also adopt. Thus, if Alex and Bev both adopt then Cade will adopt regardless of his signal. Cade is in an *information cascade* of adoption.

---

[17] Bayes' Theorem shows that $E[V \mid h_1 h_2] > E[V \mid h_1] = 2p > 0$.

(2) *Reject cascade:* Alex and Bev have rejected. By similar reasoning, even if he gets message h_3 Cade will reject, thus starting a reject cascade.

(3) *No cascade:* Alex has adopted and Bev has rejected (or vice versa). Cade knows that Alex observed h_1 and Bev l_2 (or Alex observed l_1 and Bev h_2). Because $E[V|h_1 l_2] = E[V|l_1 h_2] = 0$, Cade finds himself in exactly the same position as Alex, in that before observing his own message Cade believes that $V = +1$ and $V = -1$ are equally likely. Cade's actions are determined by his message: he adopts if h_3 and rejects if l_3.

In cases (1) and (2), Cade's actions are uninformative about his message: in one case Cade adopts whether he observes h_3 or l_3 and in the other case he rejects whether he observes h_3 or l_3. Therefore, if Alex and Bev take the same action, Cade will imitate them regardless of his own message, and Dolores's decision problem is identical to Cade's. Dolores's decision is based on her inferences about Alex and Bev's messages and her own private message. Cade's action (of imitating Alex and Bev's identical actions) is uninformative about his signal as it is optimal for Cade to imitate Alex and Bev whether he observers l_3 or h_3. Dolores too will be part of the cascade that starts with Cade and choose the same action as Alex, Bev, and Cade. By similar reasoning, Esteban follows the cascade. Hence, if Alex and Bev select the same action then a cascade starts and the actions of all subsequent individuals' are uninformative.

In case (3), Cade is in the same situation as Alex: his expected value of adoption, based only on Alex and Bev's predecessors' actions, is 0 and therefore his message determines his choice. Hence, Dolores's decision problem is the same as Bev's, Esteban's is the same as the Cade's, and so on.

Individual i's optimal decision rule may be summarized as follows. Let d_i be the difference between the number (of predecessors of individual i) who adopted and the number who rejected. If $d_i \geq 2$, then the individual should adopt regardless of his private message. If $d_i = 1$, then adopt if the private message is h_i and toss a coin if it is l_i. If $d_i = 0$, then he should ignore predecessors actions' and follow his private information: adopt if the message is h_i and reject if it is l_i. The decisions for $d_i = -1$ and $d_i \leq -2$ are symmetric. The difference between adoptions and rejections, d_i, evolves randomly and sooner or later must bump into the upper barrier of $+2$ and trigger an adopt cascade or the lower barrier of -2 and trigger a reject cascade. All but the first few individuals end up doing the same thing.

With the above decision rule, a cascade can arise very quickly, even if individuals' private information is very noisy. To see this, let us first calculate the probability that a cascade does not start after the first two individuals, Alex and Bev. This occurs if and only if Alex and Bev take different actions. One scenario in which this happens is when Alex observes h_1 and adopts, Bev observes l_2 and, being indifferent, tosses a coin and rejects. Observe that:

$$
\begin{aligned}
\Pr[h_1 l_2] &= \Pr[h_1 l_2 | V = +1] \Pr[V = +1] + \Pr[h_1 l_2 | V = -1] \Pr[V = -1] \\
&= \Pr[h_1 | V = +1] \Pr[l_2 | V = +1] \Pr[V = +1] \\
&\quad + \Pr[h_1 | V = -1] \Pr[l_2 | V = -1] \Pr[V = -1] \\
&= (0.5 + p)(0.5 - p)(0.5) + (0.5 - p)(0.5 + p)(0.5) \\
&= (0.5 + p)(0.5 - p)
\end{aligned}
$$

where we make use of the fact that h_1 and l_2 are independent conditional on the value of V. Thus, as Bev adopts with probability 0.5 after observing l_2 and after seeing Alex adopt, the probability that Alex adopted and Bev rejected is $0.5 \Pr[h_1 l_2] = 0.5(0.5 + p)(0.5 - p)$.

The only other scenario in which different actions are taken by Alex and Bev is when Alex rejects and Bev adopts. The probability of this is $0.5 \Pr[l_1 h_2] = 0.5(0.5 + p)(0.5 - p)$. Thus, the probability that there is no cascade after Alex and Bev, i.e., the probability that Alex and Bev take different actions, is $(0.5 + p)(0.5 - p) = \frac{1 - 4p^2}{4}$. The probability of a cascade after two individuals is, therefore, $1 - \frac{1 - 4p^2}{4} = \frac{3 + 4p^2}{4}$. By symmetry, an adopt cascade and a reject cascade are equally likely. Hence, the probabilities of an adopt cascade, no cascade or a reject cascade after two individuals are:

$$
\frac{3 + 4p^2}{8}, \frac{1 - 4p^2}{4}, \frac{3 + 4p^2}{8}
$$

Proceeding in this manner, it can be shown that the probability of an adopt cascade, no cascade, or a reject cascade after $2n$ individuals is:

$$
\frac{1}{2} - \frac{(1 - 4p^2)^n}{2^{2n+1}}, \frac{(1 - 4p^2)^n}{2^{2n}}, \frac{1}{2} - \frac{(1 - 4p^2)^n}{2^{2n+1}} \tag{12.3.1}
$$

From (12.3.1) we see that the closer p is to 0, the later a cascade is likely to start. However, even for a very noisy signal, such as when $p = \varepsilon > 0$ with ε arbitrarily small, the probability that a cascade has *not* started after 10 individuals is less than 0.001.[18] Cascades can arise even though predecessors' actions convey very little information. All that is required for a cascade is that the public information (that is, information gleaned from individuals'

---

[18] Insert $p = 0$, $n = 5$ in the middle term in (12.3.1) to obtain this upper bound.

publicly observed actions) swamp the private information of individuals. Consequently, even if private information is very noisy (p is very close to 0) a cascade forms once the public information is only slightly less noisy than an individual's private information.

The calculation in the preceding paragraph suggests that individuals may cascade on an incorrect action. To investigate this further, we derive the probability of a correct cascade. A correct cascade starts with Cade only if either both Alex and Bev adopted conditional on $V = +1$ or both Alex and Bev rejected conditional on $V = -1$. The probability that a *correct* adopt cascade starts with Cade (that is, the conditional probability of case (1) given that $V = +1$) is

$$\Pr(h_1 h_2 | V = +1) + 0.5 \Pr(h_1 l_2 | V = +1)$$
$$= (0.5 + p)^2 + 0.5(0.5 + p)(0.5 - p) = \frac{(1 + 2p)(3 + 2p)}{8}$$

The probability that an *incorrect* adopt cascade starts with Cade, which is the same as the conditional probability of case (1) when $V = -1$, is

$$\Pr(h_1 h_2 | V = -1) + 0.5 \Pr(l_1 h_2 | V = -1)$$
$$= (0.5 - p)^2 + 0.5(0.5 - p)(0.5 + p) = \frac{(1 - 2p)(3 - 2p)}{8}$$

However, a cascade may not start with Cade if Alex and Bev take different actions. A cascade can start next with Esteban, or with Giovanni, etc. (after an even number of individuals). The probabilities that eventually a correct cascade, no cascade, and incorrect cascade form are:[19]

$$\frac{1}{2} + \frac{4p}{3 + 4p^2}, 0, \frac{1}{2} - \frac{4p}{3 + 4p^2} \qquad (12.3.2)$$

respectively. The first expression is the probability of a correct cascade. This probability is increasing in p. The probability of an incorrect cascade (the third expression above) is decreasing in p. The probabilities of correct and incorrect cascades are plotted in Figure 12.1. Even for moderately informative signals the probability of an incorrect cascade is significant. For instance, if $p = 0.3$ then the probability of formation of a wrong cascade is 0.14. Compare this with 0.20, the probability of a wrong action taken by an individual who does not observe the actions of anyone else.

To obtain an idea of the inefficient information aggregation in a cascade setting (that is, when only actions and not the private information of predecessors are observable) we compare it to a setting where private

---

[19] See Bikhchandani, Hirshleifer, and Welch (1992) for calculations leading to (12.3.1) and (12.3.2).

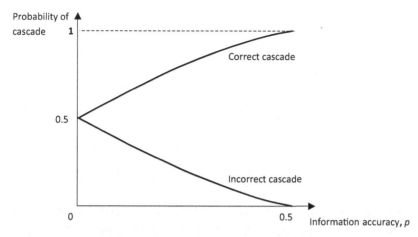

Figure 12.1. Probabilities of correct and incorrect cascades as a function of *p*.

information is observable but only a few individuals receive private information. To be specific, suppose that only the first four individuals – Alex, Bev, Cade, and Dolores – receive private information about the correct action and that they can directly communicate their private information to Esteban, Frank, Giovanni, etc. These later individuals take an action after observing the information messages of Alex, Bev, Cade, and Dolores. If these first four individuals' information has accuracy $p = 0.3$ then the probability that subsequent individuals take an incorrect action is 0.10.[20] This is smaller than 0.14, the probability of an incorrect cascade when $p = 0.3$. The probability that individuals from Esteban onward take a wrong action in the Four Signals scenario and the probability of a wrong cascade are listed in Table 12.10. For values of $p \in (0, 0.5)$, on average later individuals do better under the Four Signals scenario. In this example, cascades aggregate less than four pieces of private information, even though there are as many pieces of private information as there are individuals – an arbitrary large number.

If the private information of many previous individuals were somehow made public, later individuals would likely take the correct action. For instance, if in a cascade setting the first few individuals were to select a (sub-optimal) action that depends only on their privately observed messages (adopt if h_i and reject if it is l_i), their actions would provide useful information to later decision makers. However, because individuals care only about their own payoff, which depends on their own action but not on the actions of later individuals, it is in their self-interest to ignore their

---

[20] See Exercise 12.3.2 at the end of this section.

Table 12.10. *Probabilities of incorrect actions*

p	Wrong after four signals	Wrong cascade
0	0.50	0.50
0.1	0.35	0.37
0.2	0.22	0.25
0.3	0.10	0.14
0.4	0.03	0.06
0.5	0	0

private information once a cascade starts. Therefore, later individuals do not get the benefit of earlier individuals' private information after a cascade starts. This failure of individuals to take into account the welfare of later decision makers leads to inefficient information aggregation. Once a cascade has started, actions convey no information about private information. The social outcome is inefficient and error-prone.

In addition, the type of cascade is path dependent and sensitive to the actions of the first few individuals. It depends not just on how many h and l messages arrive, but the order in which they arrive. For example, if messages arrive in the order $h_1 h_2 l_3 l_4 \ldots$, then all individuals adopt, because Cade begins an adoption cascade. If, instead, messages arrive in the order $l_1 l_2 h_3 h_4 \ldots$ (which is as likely as $h_1 h_2 l_3 l_4 \ldots$) all individuals reject.

Exercises and Excursions 12.3

1 Information Acquisition

We modify the model of this section to allow the possibility that each individual's private information is costly. After observing the actions of predecessors and before taking an action each individual may acquire private information with likelihood matrix in Table 12.8 at cost $c \geq 0$. (In contrast, $c = 0$ in the example in Section 12.3.) Whether or not an individual acquires private information, he observes the actions and information acquisition decisions of their predecessors. Show the following:

(A) Alex will acquire private information only if $c \in [0, p]$.
(B) If Alex acquires information then Bev, Cade, and all subsequent individuals will acquire information only if it is costless $(c = 0)$.
(C) Is uniformity of actions selected by the individuals more likely or less likely if private information is slightly costly with $c \in (0, p]$?

2 Four Signals Scenario

Obtain the probability that the fifth individual (and any subsequent individual) takes a wrong action in the Four Signals column of Table 12.10.

[HINT: Start by assuming that the correct action is adopt ($V = +1$). If at least three of the four messages is H then this individual will accept. If exactly two of the four messages is H then the individual is indifferent and with probability 0.5 he will accept. Therefore, conditional on $V = +1$, the probability of taking the correct action is the probability that a binomial random variable with four trials and probability of success p has at least three successes plus 0.5 times the probability of exactly two successes. A symmetric argument applies when the correct action is reject ($V = -1$).]

12.4 The Condorcet Jury Theorem*

We end with an information aggregation application from political science. While information aggregation is also an issue in the cascades model of the previous section, the voting model considered here differs in two important respects. First, individuals care about the decisions taken by others, and, second, individuals take actions simultaneously rather than sequentially.

A group of individuals is to choose between two alternatives. All individuals in the group have the same objective in that if there were no uncertainty about the state of nature, then they would unanimously agree on which alternative is best. However, because the state of nature is unknown, the correct decision is unclear. For instance, all members of a jury would like to convict the defendant if he is guilty and to acquit him if he is innocent. Or, to consider another example, all members of a school board would like to improve academic achievement at the school; however, there is uncertainty as to whether a proposed policy change would lead to improvements. A third example is an election for public office in a small, homogenous community, there being uncertainty about the abilities of the two candidates.

Condorcet (1785) claimed that in this setting the majority decision (i.e., majority vote) is more likely to be correct than any individual's decision. Each individual, although more likely to be right than wrong, can make mistakes in judgment because of uncertainty about the state. But, according to Condorcet, the judgment of a majority of voters is less likely to be

---

* Starred sections represent more difficult or specialized materials that can be omitted without significant loss of continuity.

mistaken than the judgment of an individual voter. Political scientists refer to this assertion as the Condorcet Jury Theorem.[21]

A careful modeling of this setting is necessary before one can make a precise statement of the Condorcet Jury Theorem and investigate conditions under which this theorem is or is not true.[22] Let A and B be two alternatives that a group of n individuals will vote on. Individuals have identical preferences over A and B. However, their preferred alternative depends on the state, s, which is either s_a or s_b. If the state is s_a then each individual prefers alternative A to alternative B. If, instead, the state is s_b then B is preferred to A by each individual.

There is uncertainty about the state of nature. Each individual assesses probability $\Pr[s = s_a] = p \geq 0.5$ that the state is s_a. Individual i sees a private information signal (or message service) X_i that takes value 0 or 1. The signal X_i is informative about the state, and the conditional probability distribution of the signal is:

$$\Pr[X_i = 0 | s = s_a] = \Pr[X_i = 1 | s = s_b] = q \qquad (12.4.1)$$

where $q \in (0.5, 1)$. Individual i's posterior probability assessment that the state is s_a increases (from its prior value p) after observing $X_i = 0$ and decreases after observing $X_i = 1$. The posterior probabilities of $s = s_a$ after $X_i = 0$ and of $s = s_b$ after observing $X_i = 1$ are obtained by Bayes' Theorem:

$$\Pr[s = s_a | X_i = 0] = \frac{pq}{pq + (1 - p)(1 - q)} > p = \Pr[s = s_a]$$

$$\Pr[s = s_b | X_i = 1] = \frac{(1 - p)q}{(1 - p)q + p(1 - q)} > 1 - p = \Pr[s = s_b] \quad (12.4.2)$$

Conditional on the state s, individual i's signal, X_i, is independent of individual j's signal, X_j.

Each individual wants the best alternative – A in state s_a, B in state s_b – to be picked. This preference is conveniently represented by a utility function over alternatives and states:

$$u(A, s_a) = u(B, s_b) = u > 0 \quad \text{and} \quad u(A, s_b) = u(B, s_a) = 0 \quad (12.4.3)$$

Each individual's utility of choosing the right alternative is a positive amount $u > 0$, and the utility of choosing the wrong alternative is 0.

---

[21] Marquis de Condorcet's Voting Paradox, which shows that collective preferences can be cyclic even when individual preferences are not, is better known than his Jury Theorem. See Black (1958).

[22] The analysis here follows Austen-Smith and Banks (1996).

A *majority voting rule* selects the alternative with the most number of votes. For simplicity, assume that n, the number of individuals, is odd and that each individual will vote for either A or B. Therefore, the alternative with $k = (n + 1)/2$ or more votes wins. As there are only two alternatives, one alternative always wins. Voting is by secret ballot.

Individual i's vote is *informative* if he votes for alternative A after observing $X_i = 0$ and for alternative B after observing $X_i = 1$. If individuals vote completely uninformatively, i.e., each voter disregards his signal when taking his voting decision, then the majority vote does not reflect any of the information in the signals that individuals observed. Therefore, implicit in the Condorcet Jury Theorem is the assumption that individuals vote informatively. However, Example 12.1 shows that it need not be in the interest of all individuals to vote informatively.

Example 12.1: Three individuals, i, j, and k, select between two alternatives A and B. The underlying preferences and information structure are as specified above with $p > q > 0.5$. Suppose that individuals j and k vote informatively. It turns out that it is not in any of the three individuals' interest that individual i vote informatively!

With these parameters, A is the preferred alternative even if two of the three individuals observe signal 1. To see this, let $\Sigma X = X_i + X_j + X_k$. We need to compute the posterior probability of $s = s_a$ after $\Sigma X = 2$, i.e., after exactly two of the three individuals observed signals more likely to arise if $s = s_b$. Bayes' Theorem implies that[23]

$$
\Pr[s = s_a | \Sigma X = 2] = \frac{3q(1 - q)^2 p}{3q(1 - q)^2 p + 3q^2(1 - q)(1 - p)}
$$
$$
= \frac{p(1 - q)}{p(1 - q) + q(1 - p)}
$$

As $p > q$ we have $p(1 - q) = p - pq > q - pq = q(1 - p)$, and consequently $\Pr[s = s_a | \Sigma X = 2] > 0.5$.

Consider individual i's voting decision. If individuals j and k vote for the same alternative then i's vote has no impact on the alternative that is selected. The only time that i's vote makes a difference is when j and k vote for different alternatives. Individual i is said to *pivotal* in this case. Because voting is by secret ballot, i does not know at the time he votes whether or not he is pivotal; however, it is optimal for him to vote as if he were pivotal

---

[23] This calculation uses the fact that $\Pr[\Sigma X = 2 | s = s_a] = 3q(1 - q)^2$ and $\Pr[\Sigma X = 2 | s = s_b] = 3q^2(1 - q)$.

because that is the only case in which his vote determines which alternative is selected.

If i were to vote informatively then he would vote for B whenever $X_i = 1$ and vote for A whenever $X_i = 0$. If i is pivotal (i.e., j and k voted for different alternatives) and $X_i = 1$ then, under the assumption that j and k vote informatively, we can conclude that $\Sigma X = X_i + X_j + X_k = 2$; but if individual i votes informatively then B is selected even though A is the alternative preferred by each of the three individuals (because $\Pr[s = s_a | \Sigma X = 2] > 0.5$). Therefore, if j and k vote informatively then individual i should vote for A regardless of his signal X_i. In other words, if $q < p$ then it is not a Nash equilibrium for all three individuals to vote informatively. It is worth noting that j and k are better off when i best responds to their informative voting strategies by voting uninformatively for A.

In this example, it is a Nash equilibrium for i, j, and k to each vote for alternative A regardless of the signal they observe. A unanimous vote for A is the outcome at this Nash equilibrium. However, as each voter as well as the majority (indeed a unanimity) selects the right alternative with probability p, the majority is no more likely to be correct than the individual. The Condorcet Jury Theorem does not hold at this equilibrium.   □

Individual i votes *sincerely* if he votes for the alternative that he thinks is best based on his posterior belief, which is his prior belief updated by his private information. In a sincere voting strategy, the individual votes for A if $E[u(A, s)|X_i] > E[u(B, s)|X_i]$, votes for B if $E[u(B, s)|X_i] > E[u(A, s)|X_i]$, and votes for either A or B if $E[u(A, s)|X_i] = E[u(B, s)|X_i]$. Because individuals may observe different signal realizations, they may vote for different alternatives even when each follows a sincere strategy.

If an individual alone were to select between alternatives then this individual would vote sincerely. At first, this seems reasonable as all individuals have identical preferences. But, as we saw in Example 12.1, in determining his vote an individual should operate under the assumption that he is pivotal. Because an individual's belief (about the state of nature) upon being pivotal may differ from his prior belief, it is unclear whether it is a Nash equilibrium for all individuals to vote sincerely.

We are now in a position to give a precise statement of the Condorcet Jury Theorem. Implicit in the Condorcet Jury Theorem is the assumption that individuals vote sincerely. Moreover, as already mentioned, voting strategies must be informative and constitute a Nash equilibrium.

The **Condorcet Jury Theorem** states that:

(i) It is a Nash equilibrium for each voter to vote sincerely and informatively.
(ii) At this Nash equilibrium, the outcome selected by a majority is more likely to be correct than any individual's choice.

There exist several Nash equilibria in completely uninformative strategies. For example, it is a Nash equilibrium for every individual to always vote for B. An individual is never pivotal and therefore he may as well vote for B no matter what his private information. Therefore, (i) and (ii) do not hold at every Nash equilibrium.

It should be noted that the above statement of the Condorcet Jury Theorem is a modern reinterpretation. The idea of Nash equilibrium, or related game-theoretic concepts, was unknown during Condorcet's time. If one assumes that individuals vote informatively, then indeed the majority is more likely to be correct than the individual, provided $q > 0.5$. However, sincere and informative voting need not be consistent with a game theoretic view of behavior.

A sincere strategy is informative if $E[u(A, s)|X_i = 0] \geq E[u(B, s)|X_i = 0]$ and $E[u(B, s)|X_i = 1] \geq E[u(A, s)|X_i = 1]$. Each individual observes his private signal and then votes without knowledge of other individuals' private signals or votes. Therefore, using the utility specification in (12.4.3), the expected utility for an individual who observes signal 0 and considers the possibility that alternative A is chosen is:

$$
\begin{aligned}
E[u(A, s)|X_i = 0] &= u(A, s_a)\Pr[s = s_a|X_i = 0] + u(A, s_b)\Pr[s = s_b|X_i = 0] \\
&= u\Pr[s = s_a|X_i = 0] \\
&= u\frac{pq}{pq + (1 - p)(1 - q)}
\end{aligned}
$$

where we obtain the posterior beliefs from (12.4.2). Similarly:

$$
\begin{aligned}
E[u(B, s)|X_i = 0] &= u(B, s_a)\Pr[s = s_a|X_i = 0] + u(B, s_b)\Pr[s = s_b|X_i = 0] \\
&= u\Pr[s = s_b|X_i = 0] \\
&= u\frac{(1 - p)(1 - q)}{pq + (1 - p)(1 - q)}
\end{aligned}
$$

Therefore, after observing signal $X_i = 0$ individual i believes that A is the best alternative if $E[u(A, s)|X_i = 0] > E[u(B, s)|X_i = 0]$ if and only if $pq > (1 - p)(1 - q)$. This last inequality is always satisfied because we assumed that $p \geq 0.5$ and $q > 0.5$. Intuitively, individual i, who initially believes that

A is the better option ($p \geq 0.5$), should continue to prefer A after observing signal $X_i = 0$, which reinforces his belief that A is the better alternative.

By a similar argument, after observing signal $X_i = 1$ individual i believes that B is the best alternative if $E[u(B, s)|X_i = 1] > E[u(A, s)|X_i = 1]$ if and only if:

$$E[u(B, s)|X_i = 1] = u\frac{q(1 - p)}{q(1 - p) + p(1 - q)} > u\frac{p(1 - q)}{q(1 - p) + p(1 - q)}$$
$$= E[u(A, s)|X_i = 1]$$

if and only if $q(1 - p) > p(1 - q)$ if and only if $q > p$.

Therefore, if $q > p$ then the sincere strategy is informative. If $q = p > 0.5$ then $E[u(B, s)|X_i = 1] = E[u(A, s)|X_i = 1]$ and there are two sincere pure strategies: (a) always vote for A and (b) vote for A if $X_i = 0$ and B if $X_i = 1$. Strategy (b) is informative whereas (a) is not. Assume that sincere and informative strategy (b) is played by each individual if $q = p > 0.5$. Next, we check whether it is a Nash equilibrium for each individual to play a sincere and informative strategy whenever $q \geq p$.

As we saw in Example 12.1, in figuring out a best response to others' strategies, each individual i cares only about the scenario where he is pivotal. That is, when exactly $(n - 1)/2$ of the others vote for A and the remaining $(n - 1)/2$ of the others vote for B.[24] In every other scenario, i's vote is inconsequential. Therefore, for informative strategies to constitute a Nash equilibrium, we must examine the inference drawn by individual i under the assumption that he is pivotal. If i is pivotal then, as the others are presumed to vote informatively, individual i knows that between them the other individuals observed a total of exactly $(n - 1)/2$ realizations of signal 1 (and exactly $(n - 1)/2$ realizations of signal 0). Therefore, if $X_i = 0$ then $\Sigma X \equiv X_1 + X_2 + \cdots + X_n = \frac{n-1}{2}$ and if $X_i = 1$ then $\Sigma X = \frac{n+1}{2}$. By Bayes' Theorem:

$$\Pr\left[s = s_a | \Sigma X = \frac{n - 1}{2}\right] = \frac{q^{\frac{n+1}{2}}(1 - q)^{\frac{n-1}{2}}p}{q^{\frac{n+1}{2}}(1 - q)^{\frac{n-1}{2}}p + q^{\frac{n-1}{2}}(1 - q)^{\frac{n+1}{2}}(1 - p)}$$
$$= \frac{pq}{pq + (1 - q)(1 - p)} \tag{12.4.4}$$

$$\Pr\left[s = s_b | \Sigma X = \frac{n + 1}{2}\right] = \frac{q^{\frac{n+1}{2}}(1 - q)^{\frac{n-1}{2}}(1 - p)}{q^{\frac{n+1}{2}}(1 - q)^{\frac{n-1}{2}}(1 - p) + q^{\frac{n-1}{2}}(1 - q)^{\frac{n+1}{2}}p}$$
$$= \frac{q(1 - p)}{q(1 - p) + (1 - q)p} \tag{12.4.5}$$

---

[24] As n is odd, $(n - 1)/2$ and $(n + 1)/2$ are integers.

The informative voting strategy is individual i's best response to informative voting by all other voters if and only if $\Pr[s = s_a | \Sigma X = \frac{n-1}{2}] \geq 0.5$ and $\Pr[s = s_b | \Sigma X = \frac{n+1}{2}] \geq 0.5$. Because $p \geq 0.5$ and $q > 0.5$, we conclude that $pq > 0.25 > (1 - q)(1 - p)$ and therefore (12.4.4) implies that $\Pr[s = s_a | \Sigma X = \frac{n-1}{2}] > 0.5$. As Example 12.1 illustrates, $\Pr[s = s_b | \Sigma X = \frac{n+1}{2}] \geq 0.5$ need not always be true. From (12.4.5) we see that $\Pr[s = s_b | \Sigma X = \frac{n+1}{2}] \geq 0.5$ if and only if $q(1 - p) \geq p(1 - q)$ if and only if $q \geq p$. Thus, informative voting constitutes a Nash equilibrium provided that $q \geq p$. This is precisely the condition under which sincere voting is informative.

Consequently, part (i) of the Condorcet Jury Theorem holds in our simple symmetric signals model if $q \geq p$. That is, when the signal is informative enough that each individual, although initially predisposed to one alternative ($\Pr[s = s_a] = p \geq 0.5$), will prefer, based only on his own signal, the other alternative if his signal points to it (i.e., $q \geq p$ implies $\Pr[s = s_b | X_i = 1] \geq 0.5$).

We now establish a strong form of part (ii) of the Condorcet Jury Theorem at the Nash equilibrium of part (i). A sufficient statistic for the individuals' private signals is ΣX, the total number of 1 signals observed by the n individuals. The posterior belief based on ΣX is:

$$\Pr[s = s_a | \Sigma X = k] = \frac{q^{n-k}(1 - q)^k p}{q^{n-k}(1 - q)^k p + q^k(1 - q)^{n-k}(1 - p)}$$

$$\Pr[s = s_b | \Sigma X = k] = \frac{q^k(1 - q)^{n-k}(1 - p)}{q^{n-k}(1 - q)^k p + q^k(1 - q)^{n-k}(1 - p)}$$

$\Pr[s = s_a | \Sigma X = k] \geq 0.5$ if and only if $q^{n-k}(1 - q)^k p \geq q^k(1 - q)^{n-k}(1 - p)$ if and only if $(\frac{1-q}{q})^{2k-n} \geq \frac{1-p}{p}$. Similarly, $\Pr[s = s_b | \Sigma X = k] \geq 0.5$ (i.e., $\Pr[s = s_a | \Sigma X = k] \leq 0.5$) if and only if $q^k(1 - q)^{n-k}(1 - p) \geq q^{n-k}(1 - q)^k p$ if and only if $\frac{1-p}{p} \geq (\frac{1-q}{q})^{2k-n}$.

Suppose that there is an integer k^*, $n > k^* > 0$, such that:

$$\Pr[s = s_a | \Sigma X = k^*] \geq 0.5 \geq \Pr[S = s_a | \Sigma X = k^* + 1]$$

From the calculations in the preceding paragraph, this is equivalent to:

$$\left(\frac{1 - q}{q}\right)^{2k^* - n} \geq \frac{1 - p}{p} \geq \left(\frac{1 - q}{q}\right)^{2(k^* + 1) - n} \tag{12.4.6}$$

Because $\Pr[s = s_a | \Sigma X = k]$ strictly decreases with k, if such a k^* exists then it is unique (and at least one of the inequalities in (12.4.6) is strict). If all the individuals truthfully revealed their private information to each other, the decision rule that maximizes their utility is to select alternative A if $\Sigma X \leq k^*$ and select alternative B if $\Sigma X > k^*$. This is exactly the decision rule implemented at the Nash equilibrium in which each player uses a sincere, informative strategy. To see this, note that $q \geq p \geq 0.5$ implies

$$\frac{q}{1-q} = \left(\frac{1-q}{q}\right)^{-1} \geq \frac{1-p}{p} \geq \frac{1-q}{q}$$

Comparing this with (12.4.6), and noting that if k^* exists then it is unique, we have $2k^* - n = -1$ or $k^* = (n-1)/2$. In other words, the optimal decision rule is to select A if $(n-1)/2$ or fewer signal realizations are 1 and to select B if $(n+1)/2$ or more signal realizations are 1. This is exactly the decision rule that is implemented when all voters use sincere and informative strategies. These strategies constitute a Nash equilibrium provided $q \geq p$.

To summarize, if strategic individuals are sufficiently well-informed ($q \geq p$) then the majority is indeed more likely to be wiser than a randomly selected individual. Moreover, the majority decision cannot be improved even if the voters decide to communicate their signals to each other.

This may appear to be a strong justification for the optimality of majority rule and, more broadly, for democracy. But our model is a gross simplification of reality in two important ways. First, in our model differences in voters arise from signal realizations which give rise to differing beliefs rather than from inherently heterogeneous preferences and interests. Second, even if we modify our simple model by introducing slightly asymmetric signals (that is, if $\Pr[X_i = 0|s = s_a] \neq \Pr[X_i = 1|s = s_b]$) then the Condorcet Jury Theorem does not hold. This is the subject of exercises at the end of this section.

Exercises and Excursions 12.4

1 Asymmetric Signals

In this exercise we relax the assumption in Equation (12.4.1) that the information signals are symmetric. Instead, we have:

$$q_a = \Pr[X_i = 0|s = s_a], \quad q_b = \Pr[X_i = 1|s = s_b]$$

with $q_a \neq q_b$. We investigate whether the Condorcet Jury Theorem holds in this setting. For concreteness, let $q_a = 0.9$, $q_b = 0.6$, and $n = 3$. The initial belief is that $\Pr[s = s_a] = \Pr[s = s_b] = 0.5$.

(A) Find the sincere voting strategy for an individual in this setting.

(B) Is the sincere voting strategy informative?

(C) Show that it is not a Nash equilibrium for all three individuals to vote informatively.

2 More on Asymmetric Signals

We just saw that the strategy underpinning the Condorcet Jury Theorem need not be a Nash equilibrium when signals are asymmetric. This exercise is about finding Nash equilibria when the parameters q_a and q_b are as in the previous exercise.

(A) Show that it is Nash equilibrium for two of the three individuals to vote informatively and for the third individual to always vote for B.

There also exists a mixed strategy equilibrium. Let r_0 be the probability with which an individual votes for alternative A when he observes signal 0 and let r_1 be the probability with which an individual votes for alternative A when he observes signal 1. The probability of voting for alternative B is $1 - r_0$ when the signal is 0 and the probability is $1 - r_1$ when the signal is 1. Suppose that each of the three individuals uses the strategy r_0^* and r_1^*.

(B) Compute $\Pr[A|s = s_a]$, the probability that an individual using this strategy votes for alternative A conditional on $s = s_a$. Compute $\Pr[B|s = s_b]$, the probability that an individual using this strategy votes for alternative B conditional on $s = s_b$.

(C) Show that the mixed strategy (r_0^*, r_1^*) is a symmetric Nash equilibrium where $0 < r_0^* < 1$ and $r_1^* = 0$.

[HINT: Once again, an individual needs to think only about the case where he is pivotal. If the other two individuals have voted for A and B, respectively, what inference can this individual draw about the state of nature s? Think of the votes A and B as information signals correlated with s.][**]

SUGGESTIONS FOR FURTHER READINGS: See Farrell and Rabin (1996 and Krishna and Morgan (2008) for an introduction to the literature on cheap talk that started with Crawford and Sobel's influential paper. The decision to acquire information is not explicitly modeled in most papers, but nevertheless this is an important feature of any real market. Early papers that explicitly investigate information acquisition include Milgrom (1981) and Matthews (1984. Chamley (2003) is a comprehensive treatment of information cascades and social learning. For applications of game theory and economics in political science, see Ordeshook (1992).

[**] End of starred section.

References

Austen-Smith, David and Banks, Jeff, "Information Aggregation, Rationality, and the Condorcet Jury Theorem," *American Political Science Review*, 90 (1996), 34–45.

Banerjee, Abhijit, "A Simple Model of Herd Behavior," *Quarterly Journal of Economics*, 107 (1992), 797–818.

Bergemann, Dirk and Valimaki, Juuso, "Information Acquisition and Efficient Mechanism Design," *Econometrica*, 70 (2002), 1007–1033.

Bikhchandani, Sushil, Hirshleifer David, and Welch, Ivo, "A Theory of Fads, Fashion, Custom, and Cultural Change as Informational Cascades," *Journal of Political Economy*, 100 (1992), 992–1026.

——, "Learning from the Behavior of Others: Conformity, Fads, and Informational Cascades," *Journal of Economic Perspectives*, 12 (1998), 151–170.

Black, Duncan, *The Theory of Committees and Elections*, Cambridge: Cambridge University Press, 1958.

Chamley, Christophe P., *Rational Herds: Economic Models of Social Learning*, Cambridge: Cambridge University Press, 2003.

Condorcet, Marquis de [1785], *Essai sur application de l'analyse a la probabilité des décisions rendues a la pluralité des voix*, trans. in *Condorcet: Foundations of Social Choice and Political Theory*, ed. Iain McLean and Fiona Hewitt, Brookfield, VT: Edward Elgar, 1994.

Crawford, Vincent and Sobel, Joel, "Strategic Information Transmission," *Econometrica*, 50 (1982), 1431–1451.

Dessein, Wouter, "Authority and Communication in Organizations," *Review of Economic Studies*, 69 (2002), 811–838.

Farrell, Joseph and Rabin, Matthew, "Cheap Talk," *Journal of Economic Perspectives*, 10 (1996), 103–118.

Krishna, Vijay and Morgan, John, "Cheap Talk," in *The New Palgrave Dictionary of Economics*, S. N. Durlauf and L. E. Blume (eds.), 2nd edition, vol. 1, pp. 751–756, New York: Palgrave Macmillan, 2008.

Matthews, Steven, "Information Acquisition in Competitive Bidding Process," in Marcel Boyer and Richard Kihlstrom (eds.), pp. 181–207 *Bayesian Models in Economic Theory*, New York: North-Holland, 1984.

Milgrom, Paul, "Rational Expectations, Information Acquisition, and Competitive Bidding," *Econometrica*, 49 (1981), 921–943.

Ordeshook, Peter C., *A Political Theory Primer*, New York: Routledge, 1992.

Welch, Ivo, "Sequential Sales, Learning and Cascades," *Journal of Finance*, 47 (1992), 695–732.

Index

Printed in the United States
By Bookmasters